HISTORICAL VIEWS OF DEVONSHIRE • RICHARD POLWHELE

Publisher's Note

The book descriptions we ask booksellers to display prominently warn that this is an historic book with numerous typos or missing text; it is not indexed or illustrated.

The book was created using optical character recognition software. The software is 99 percent accurate if the book is in good condition. However, we do understand that even one percent can be an annoying number of typos! And sometimes all or part of a page may be missing from our copy of the book. Or the paper may be so discolored from age that it is difficult to read. We apologize and gratefully acknowledge Google's assistance.

After we re-typeset and design a book, the page numbers change so the old index and table of contents no longer work. Therefore, we often remove them; otherwise, please ignore them.

Our books sell so few copies that you would have to pay hundreds of dollars to cover the cost of our proof reading and fixing the typos, missing text and index. Instead we let most customers download a free copy of the original typo-free scanned book. Simply enter the barcode number from the back cover of the paperback in the Free Book form at www.RareBooksClub.com. You may also qualify for a free trial membership in our book club to download up to four books for free. Simply enter the barcode number from the back cover onto the membership form on our home page. The book club entitles you to select from more than a million books at no additional charge. Simply enter the title or subject onto the search form to find the books.

If you have any questions, could you please be so kind as to consult our Frequently Asked Questions page at www. RareBooksClub.com/faqs.cfm? You are also welcome to contact us there.
General Books LLC™, Memphis, USA, 2012.

⭒⭒ ⭒⭒ ⭒⭒ ⭒⭒ ⭒⭒ ⭒⭒ ⭒⭒ ⭒⭒

weft parts of Britain cane a *tons; voyage by sea."* We cannot conceive why the interesting part of these five volumes was not incorporated into-the larger work, I of being dealt out to subscribers *fix* shillings each, in a type and on a paper calculated to deter them from re ad'tng them , and unworthy the promised execution of the larger volumes. M r. P. seeompanies the first period with a prospectus, from which we learn that th e first volume of tha History will confist of the Introduction and Natural History, in *f tea* type.

Antiquities, from the British to the Si son period—type *English.*

General History, from thc-Saxon period to the present times—type *Grtat f rimer.*

Into this volume, we conceive, the fir e quartos might fairlyhave been in co ispnriaHaiaiiiis ia iniini I *T* 1 -SfoiiMfllsncjjjsl » Ww —«" *JrxStfn7oTKi:* firS part of the cliorogr a phial survey of the county, containing the diocese and archdeaconry of Exeter, in Graf *Primer,* is completely p rinted. But, "as all the views as yet e ngraved for the three volumes are to be i n sir ted in the second volume, now printe d," and, Mr. P. is urgent to have as m any places *given* to the,work as he can, the engravings may retard publication. It (i. e. the second volume) *viill be deli* w *red to the subscribers as soon as the t ngraver produces the slates.* We might o bject, that the delivering *all* the plates t ogethcr, is not for the author's interest; for too many of his readers, when they h a ve gratified their curiosity with pretty p icturcs, may think no more about the remainder of a dry county-history. This, however, will, in great measure, depend on the *execution* of the plates; the *choice* of which, from the iist given in the prospectus dated Exeter, July, »7»3, appears to have been well made, as far as we can judge without having seen the original subjects. The whole number

is '14.1, of which near 90 weTT *drawn aud retuis for the engraver,* 20 actually engraved, two in the engraver's hands, 11 engaged to be done, and near 20 of which nothing is said. Considering the unavoidable delay of engraving, the expectations of Mr. P's subscribers (and of // W«/eviewers, with the largest candle award, have almost pot our eyes out l the present extracts, and are really

Urge), though he has never to raise the price at *four guineat* for two the publick at pledged himself

(which was fixed at j volumes), even though enlarged, and repeats at the end of prospectus, *"the-whole subscription ft*

the HiJltrjf of Devon, in three volumes, 0

1 J—*four guineas,"* have yet a long terras *J* lvtc/

which ft will be kept in suspence. After'-*t f j*

the long train of difficulties he has had *'t4 j*

to encounter, they" may be sufficiently *' /*

assumed, that, for *tat future,* no comma *fJ'"J*

disappointments, no difficulties, no distresses, though they may suspend the work, can ever,induce him to abandon, it. The toil of collecting, and the irksomenest of arranging papers, are nearly over. What remains to be performed «s chiefly in the line of composition; and,

if the publick be not *soon* in polseflion' of the whole History, the delay, I ttust, will"

not be attributed, to its author, after ttiigv diffuse explanation of his views."

164. *Ah Essay towards a Hijhry / Bttesord, in the County of* Devon. Exeter, 179a. 8tw» MR. John Watkins", the author, ot this modest performance, tells us, that it " originated ia the intention of giving; some small assistance to the present ingenious historian of Devonshire. After he had collected a few materials for an account of this parish, some re-

spectable friends, to whom nothing could, with propriety, be denied, intimated a wish that the account should appear in a separate form. With their desires he chcarfully complied, and therefore began, to give the work filch a degree of body as would be necessary, to render it an independent publication Many particulars are, in consequence, added to the account, and a variep-of digressive observations and reflections made, which, though proper enowh in its present state, would not harr been so if ic were thrown together inl/o the general history of the county. Meither the town, nor its neighbourhoods, afford much matter for the exercisers a learned topographer. The characteraof a tew noted men. ia this day aseJttated with such historic plainness anay, perhaps, give a momentary oHjfnce to some who may consider themselves concerned in what is said of thenvf Let it then be duly observed here, Jejfore the work it read, that the publiihed, 1789, three sermons of James Hervey, with an account of bin; curate at Bideford, 1738—174a.

1 ,&3-*Historical Firm tf* Devonshire. i fn»

.*rjwmi. ft!. L Bj Mr.* Polwhele, *os* Polwhele, *Jt* Cornwall. Exeter, lyst. aar

IN the proposals circulated for a History of Devonshire, by Mr. Polwhele, without a date, but really 1789, he offers the work in one. volume folio, *or* two in lievers to faith in Christ; if it be a system which irreligious men are the first, .and.serious Christians the last, to emtbrace j-if-it be found-to relax the obligations to virtuous affection and bchaiviour, Jiy relaxing the great standard of (virtue itself j if it promote neither love .to God in his true character, nor bene-; volonce to men as it is exemplified in the spirit of Christ and his Apod les; if it lead those who embrace it to be wise rin their own eyes, and,.instead of;liberally deprecating God's righteous displeasure, even in their dying moments, arrogantly to challenge his justice; if the charity it inculcates be founded in indifFertnce to divine truth; if it be inconsistent with in ardent love to Christ, .or veneration for the Holy Scriptures; iif-the happiness which it promotes be

at variance with the joy of the Gospel j finaUy, if it diminish the motives to gratitude, obedience, and heavenlymindedness, and have a natural tendency to infidelity, then it is an immoral system,

.and, consequently, is not of God. It it not the Gospel of Christ, but *another Gospel.* Tlnse who preach ic preach .*another Jesui,* whom the Apostles did not preach; and those who receive it, receive.

.*another.Spirit,* which they never imbibed. It is not a light which cdrneth from above, but a cloud of darkness that has arisen from beneath, tending to eclipse it. It is not the highway of itruth, which is a way of holiness, but a byepath of error, which misleads the unwary traveller, and of which, as we value our inmost interests, it.behoves us rbeware. We need not be afraid of evidence or free enquiry, if irreligious men .be the first, and serious Christians the last, who embraced the Socinian system.

It is,easy to perceive that the avenues which lead to it are not, as its abettors -would persuade you to think, an openness to conviction, or a free and impartial enquiry, but a *heart Jeer it If disaffeS-*

.*ed to the character and government of* v*God. and diffatisjud vrttb the gospel* n*/uay*

joj salvation" (pp. aaa, aad).

tonea books

sions of the county; appendix, containing a list of parishes, sheriffs, geoealogiil tables, family papers, notes, c *Sec.*

In a circular letter in our Magazine for May, 1 789. p. 4". it was judged expedient to extend the work to two volume t *soli; taeb tvto gttimeae,* to which he the a had soo subscribers. It was natural to conclude that the *tux/e* of the plan would be comprised in these two volumes, or that Mr. Pulwhetc's subscribers would have received from hi m, some way or other, an intimation that they could not be comprclsed into them. But he had already informed them, that *compression* was not so easy *is a 1 tat often* ;

and, in proof of his observation, he proceeds to take of them *thirty fihllmgs* more, at five several tnstalmeatv fp

' Historical views of the inhabitant of *Danmonium,* in the *British, toman Brittib, Saxt-Danijh, fformam-Saxom,* and *Saxo-Laneastrian-Yerkisb* periods, and those of the *Rebellion* and

These," he observes, " do 1

tin the least with the main uodcrtakisia;, yet will probably be deemed a repository of curious notices. Here may be inrroduced at large a multiplicity of papers,

to which references only can be made in the *Hi, 1try,* and here he may be at liberty to throw., out conjectures on subjests of antiquity, and submit to confideration a variety of points that seem anabiguous, but which when elucidated,

may be worthy attention for the Urge r work."

Accordingly, the tuft periol open with a discussion, by a correspondent, of the very passage of the Saxon Chr ratclc which was ditfaded in our vol. L.XI. pp. stao, 1107, *l,XVll-*xjS, bat aot to Mr. P's satisfaction, who persists in has opinion, that th; first inhabitants of Britain came from Armenia, instead of Artnarua; and then, on the authority of this *variant rcaJimg of that stmglt MS,* contcoJs, titit the Saxon Ciirootcte *plainly iommatet* that the inhabitants who icaled ficst in the Sou th ot

CONTENTS.

VOLUME I.

From Vortigern to William The Conqueror.

CHAPTER III. SECTION I. *HEW os the CIVIL ami MILITARY HISTORY of DEVONSHIRE, during the SAXO. DANISH PERIOD.*

I. *Distress of Britain abandoned by Rome—Vortigern, Earl ofDanmonium—The Saxons in Devon/hire—Heroic Atchievements of Arthur—Wejsex—Various contests between the Cornubritons and Saxons—the Succession of Ina—Exeter entered by the Saxons—a Danish Elect at the western Coasts—Egbert, the West-Saxon Monarch, King of England—Junction of the Cornubritijh and Danish Forces—Battles between the Saxons and Cornubritons and Danes—Alfred—Danes wintering at Exeter, under the protection of the Cornubritons—a. Dani/h fleet sailing for Exeter, dispersed in a storm—Landarmy of the Danes marching towards Exeter—routed by Alfred—Danes obliged to abandon the City of Exeter—Frequent descent of the Danes, on the coasts of Devon and Cornwall—Danes besieging ExeterSeven Danijh Princes landing at the mouth of tb« Axe—Opposed by Athelstan—Great flaughter on both fides—Allied armies of the Cornubritons, Irijh, Scots, Welsh, and Danes —Athelfian victorious—Cornubritons abandoning Exeter—pasting the Tamar—the Tamar a boundary between Devon and Cornwall—Depredations of the Danes in the West—Exeter besieged by Sweno—taken by storm, and burnt to the ground—Exeter recovered from the Danes.* SECTION II.

VIEW of the CIVIL and MILITARY CONSTITUTION of DEVONSHIRE, during the SAXO-DANISH PERIOD.

I. *Saxon Heptarchy—Kingdom of'Wejsex—Devon/hire and Cornwall included in it—the Heptarchy united under Egbert—Alfred—His Survey of the whole Kingdom—Athelfian—Devon and Cornwall divided into two Counties—*II. *Dukes and Earls of Devon and Cornwall—Civil and Military Government—Stannary Regulations- -*III. *Government of Towns—Exeter—the Portgreeve. '* SECTION III. *VIEW of RELIGION in DEVONSHIRE, during the SAXO-DANISH PERIOD.*

I. *Religious Persuasions in Devon and Cornwall—Theodoric, the Pagan Prince—Arthur, the Christian Hero* II. *Bi/hopric of Dorchester near Oxford—Devon and Cornwall a part of it—-Birinus, the first Bi/hop—-Bi/hopric of Winchester—Devon and Cornwall a part of it.--Bishopric of Sherborne—Devon and Cornwall a part of it—Bi/hopric of Devon-—Episcopal Sees at Bijhop's-Tawton and Crediton—-Bi/hopric of Cornwall—Sees at Bodmin and St. Germains—-Devon and Cornwall united under one Bi/hopric—See removed from Crediton to Exeter—-*III. *Religious Foundations—The Cathedral Church at Exeter—-Religious Houses,—*IV. *Synods,* SECTION SECTION IV.

VIEW osCIVIL, MILITARY, and RELIGIOUS ARCHITECTURE in DEVONSHIRE, during the SAXO-DANISH PERIOD.

I. *Buildings in general, as scattered over the County—Roads.—*II. *Civil Archite&ure—Exeter —Barnstaple—in the time of Athelftan.—*III. *Military Architecture—Saxon and Danish Cajlles—Rouaemont-Castle.—*-IV. *Religious Architecture—at Tanxtton—at Crediton—at Exetei—Cathedral Church at Exeter—Progress of the Building—Abbey at Tavistoci.* SECTION V.

VIEW of AGRICULTURE, PLANTATIONS, and GARDENS in DEVONSHIRE, during the SAXO-DANISH PERIOD.

I. *Agriculture on the decline at the beginning of this Period—Villanage established by the Saxons—-King Ina—bit encouragement of Agriculture—bis Laivs relating to it.—*II. *Vineyards.* SECTION VI.

VIEW of MINING in DEVONSHIRE, during the SAXO-DANISH PERIOD. 1. *Tin-mines greatly neglected during this Period.* SECTION1 VII. *VIefV of MANUFACTURE in DEVONSHIRE, during the SAXO-DANISH PERIOD.*

I. *Exeter-—State of its Manufactures—7amervjorth or Plymouth.*

SECTION VIII. *VIEW of COMMERCE in DEVONSHIRE, during the SAXO-DANISH PERIOD.* I. *Navigation encouraged by the lavos of King Atheist an—Fairs and Markets regulated by the Saxon Kings—-Mints at Exeter, Lidford, and Totnes.*

SECTION IX. *VIEW of the LANGUAGE, LITERATURE, and LEARNED MEN in DEVONSHIRE, during the SAXO-DANISH PERIOD.*

I. *Cornubritijb Language in Devon and Cornivall—the Saxon Tongue—Names of Places greatly altered by the Saxons.—*II. *Seminaries of Educaum.—*III. *St. Winifred—St. Burchard—Frederic de Crediton—Alfred—Garland—among the literary Characters of this Period.* SECTION X.

VIEW of the INHABITANTS of DEVONSHIRE, during the SAXO-DANISH PERIOD. The Cornubritons—the Saxon Race—State of Population. , SECTION XI., *HEW of the MANNERS and USAGES of DEVONSHIRE, during the SAXO-DANISH PERIOD. flwt &er of the Saxons—Festivals,*

J. The NORMAN-SAXON PERIOD:

From William The Conqueror to Edward The First. CHAPTER IV.

SECTION I. *VIEW os the CIVIL and MILITARY HISTORY es DEVONSHIRE, during the NORMANSAXON PERIOD. William the Conqueror—ConduB ps the City os Exeter—Siege os Exeter—Capitulation os the City os Exeter—Oath os allegiance taken by the Exonians—Baldwin Rivers, Earl of Devon, fiding with the Empress Mawd against King Stephen—Siege ofRougemont-Castle by King Stephen —long and desperate—Exonians surrendering themselves prisoners at discretion —William de Tracey one os the murderers of Becket—Dartmouth burnt by the French in the reign of Richard the First—Exeter besieged by the Barons—Cotam'istion from King John to Robert de Courtenay and other Gentlemen of Devonshire—Henry de Brewer—l 's rank and influence in Devonshire—Conspiracy os William Morisco—his flight to the Isle of Lundy.* SECTION II. *VIEW of the CIVIL and MILITARY CONSTITUTION of DEVONSHIRE, during the NORMAN-SAXON PERIOD. A very curious Paper (never yet printed) entitled Modus tenendi Parliarnentum, fej posed t» have been drawn up by William the Conqueror.* SECTION III. *VIEW os RELIGION in DEVONSHIRE, during the NORMAN-SAXON PERIOD. The Normans—Bishops of Exeter during the Norman Period—Leofricus, OJbertus, Warlev-jast —Chichefter—Warlewast—*

Barthol. Iscanus — John the Chantor — Marshall—Simon de Apulia—Brewer—JBbndy—Bronscombe—Religious Foundations and Endowments during the Government of each Bishop—Archdeaconries—Deanries—PariJb-Cburches—Foundations of Monasteries, &c. &c.—History of these religious Houses—Synods—Ecclesiastical Courts— Conduit of the Bishops and other eminent Persons in Devonshire, as influenced by the religious spirit of the times. SECTION IV. *VIEW of ARCHITECTURE, CIVIL, MILITARY, and RELIGIOUS, during the NOR. MAN-SAXON PERIOD.*

I. *General Observations on the mode of Building amon% the Peasantry—on Gentlemen's Seats or Villas—on the military Works of the Normans—on Castles—on the religious Structures of this Period.—*II. *The City of Exeter—Rougemont-Castle—the Cathedral—the principal Towns in Devonshire, and the Buildings in the neighbourhood of each Town, surveyed in the same manner—Moreleigb-Church, built at this Period.* SECTION V.

VIEW of AGRICULTURE, PLANTATIONS, and GARDENS, during the NORMAN. SAXON PERIOD. Little attention paid to Agriculture—Continual fluctuation between Plenty and Famine. SECTION SECTION VI. *VIEW ts MINING in DEVONSHIRE, during the NORMAN-SAXON PERIOD. Working of the Mines encouraged by the Normans—Devon/hire producing great quantities of Tin—she Dartmoor 'Tinivorks in the reign of King John.* SECTION "VII. *VIEW of the MANUFACTURES of DEVONSHIRE, during the NORMAN-SAXON PERIOD.* SECTION VIII. *VIEW of the COMMERCE of DEVONSHIRE, during the NORMAN-SAXON PERIOD. Trade of Devon/hire, at the time of the Conquest—Exeter—its foreign Connexions extensive— Isabella de Fortibus—Tin trade very considerable—Markets at Exeter, Axminster, Honiton, Teignmouib, Moreton, &c.—Mints—at Exeter—&c. &c.* SECTION IX.

VIEW of the LANGUAGE, LITERATURE, and LEARNED MEN of DEVONSHIRE, during the NORMAN-SAXON PERIOD. Normans attempting to substitute the Norman- French for the Anglo-Saxon—the English attached to the Saxon Language—the Cornubritijh in Devon and Corniuall, the vulgar Tongue— spoken also by the higher ranks of people in Cornwall, and a great part of Devon/hire—Attention to the Sciences—to the polite Arts—Latin Poetry—Schools—Men of literary eminence in Devonshire—such as Johannes Devonius—Richard Fijbacre—Henry de BatheHenry de Bratlon—Simon Fraxinus—Jofepbus Ifcanus—Alexander Necham. SECTION X. *VIEW of the INHABIT ANTS of DEVONSHIRE, during the NORM AN-SAXON PERIOD. Ihe Normans—their bodily Strength—ASivity—the Plague in Devonshire—its Ravages in the West, particularly in the City of Exeter, in the Reign of Henry the Third—The Leprosy at Exeter—Dearth—Inundations.* SECTION XI. *VIEW of the MANNERS, &c. and USAGES in DEVONSHIRE, during the NORMAN SAXON PERIOD. Intemperate disputes among the County-Gentlemen—Tyranny of the Lords of Manors—Instances of such Disputes and Tyranny in Devon/hire—Manners of the Clergy—Cockstghting.* VOLUME VOLUME IV.

The SAXO-LANCASTRIAN-YORKISH PERIOD: CHAPTER V.

SECTION I.

VIEW os the CWll and MILITARY HISTORY os DEVONSHIRE, during-the SAXO-LANCASTRIAN-YORKISH PERIOD.

French landing at Plymouth—repulsed by Courtenay—James Lord Audley, Sir J. Carets), Brian Lord Guy, distinguifacd as warlike characters—Dartmouth, enriched hy the Spoils of France—a great part of Plymouth burnt by the French—Descent os the French at Dartmouth—Bravery os the Inhabitants—Contest bet-ween the bouses of Lancaster and York—Conduct of Devon/hire—principal Families in Devonshire at this Crisis—Richard Edgcumbe, knighted by the Duke of Richmond, after the Battle of Bofworth—Perkin Warbeck—Sieges of Exeter. SECTION II.

VIEW of the.CIVIL and MILITARY CONSTITUTION of DEVONSHIRE, during the SAXO-LANCASTRIAN-YORKISH PERIOD. SECTION III. *VIEW of RELIGION in DEVONSHIRE,* during the SAXO-LANCASTRIAN-YORKISH PERIOD. Synod held at Exeter, in 1187. SECTION IV.

VIEW of ARCHITECTURE, CIVIL, MILITARY, and RELIGIOUS, during the SAXOLANCASTRIAN-YORKISH PERIOD. Grandeur of the Buildings in the time of Edward the First—The Palace in the Reign of Edward the Third—Cathedrals—Parijb-Churches—Marks by which the Churches of this Period may be distinguished—St. Budeaux-Church, built about the Year 14.00—*Bulkworthy, in* 14.20.—II. *Public Roads—drchitetlural Survey of Exeter—Streets newly paved— the Guildhall—the Cathedral—Ottery St. Mary—its collegiate Church—other 7owns and Buildings in Devon/hire.* SECTION V. *VIEW of AGRICULTURE, PLANTATIONS, and GARDENS, during the SAXO-LANCASTRIAN-YORKISH PERIOD. Sea-Ore and Sand used as Manures—Istt of Lundy not " abounding with Vineyards," as Mr. Pegge supposes.* SECTION IV. *VIEW of MINING in DEVONSHIRE, during the SAXO-LANCASTRIAN-YORKISH PERIOD. Mines at Combmartin—at Bereferrtri* SECTION SECTION VIL. *VIEW of the MANUFACTURES of DEVONSHIRE, during the SAXO-LANCASTRIAN YORKISH PERIOD. The King's agents inviting the Dutch Apprentices into England—great Privileges granted t» the Clotb-Workers—State of Manufactures at Exeter—at Tiverton.* SECTION VIII. *VIEW of tie COMMERCE of DEVONSHIRE, during the SAXO-LANCASTRIAN TORKISH PERIOD. Exeter, considered in a commercial light—Plymouth—Dartmouth—the principal Harbours in the county of Devon—Fairs and Markets—Commodities—Coinage.* SECTION IX.

VIEW of the LANGUAGE, LITERATURE, and LEARNED MEN of DEVONSHIRE, during the SAXO-LANCASTRIAN-YORK1SH PERIOD. The French Language very generally adopted in England—the Anglo-Saxon fill the vernacular tongue—the Cornubritijb almost loft in Exeter—retained in a great part of the Southams—Seminaries of Learning, particularly Grammar-Schools, in Devon/hire—Divines— John de Bampton—Fitz-Ralph—J. Cutcliffe—Walter Britt—

&c. &c.—*Works of living Authors*— History—Topography—*Topograhical Writers—Prince, Izacke, Cleaveland, Milles, Chappie, &c.*—Miscellaneous Writers—*Kennel, &c*— Poetry *WEW of the INHABITANTS of DEVONSHIRE, during the PERIOD of the REVOLUTION and the UNITED KINGDOMS. Populousness of Devon/hire—of Exeter—of the principal Toivns in Devon—Discriminating features oj the people of Devon/hire — Family-resemblances — Instances of extraordinary Parturition—of Longevity—Epidemical Diseases—Chronic—Fires—Miscellaneous occur VIEW of the MANNERS and USAGES of DEVONSHIRE, during the PERIOD of the REVOLUTION and the UNITED KINGDOMS. Character of the different ranks of people in Devonshire—of the Inhabitants of Exeter—of the Inhabitants of Plymouth—of the Inhabitants of several other Towns in this CountyRelics of Supers ition in Devonshire—different articles of Luxury—Feasts—Diversions. rences.* SECTION XI. HISTORICAL VIEWS

O F DEVONSHIRE, CHAPTER The FIRST.

THE BRITISH PERIOD:

From the First Settlements in Danmonium, to the Arrival of Jvuus CÆSAR, FIFTY-FIVE YEARS BEFORE CHRIST.

HISTORICAL VIEWS Of DEVONSHIRE. CHAPTER *t*

Action L *VIEW of the INHABITANTS-of DANMONIUM, during the BRITISH PERIOD.*

I. *Emigrators from the East, settling in Demon—Said by the Saxon Chronicle to be Armenian! —Passage from the Saxon Chronicle—First Settlements in the Southams—Opposite opinion! as Carte, Borlafe, and Whitaker—Extracl from Ceesar—Period of the Eastern Emigration! —*II. *A second Colony—Phenicians.—Yll, A third Colony—Greeks.—*IV. *Other settler! from the continent of Europe—the Xelga—the Cimbri-the Carnabii.* TUB original settlements of countries, and particularly of those which lie at the most remote distances from the spot whence all the generations of mankind issued, are commonly enveloped in a cloud that the keenest eye cannot penetrate. But this obscurity naturally awakens curiosity; and conjecture will, of course, step in to

relieve it. Here opens a spacious field for the wanderings of the imagination, especially if it descry some glimmering light of history to direct its researches. By whom this island was first peopled, and at what period, and where and in what manner the subsequent colonist of Britain formed their settlements, till the invasion of Julius Cæsar, are point's, whichj though they have long exercised the ingenuity of historians, are, after every discussion, still ambiguous. That a writer, therefore, who seems to be confined by his subject within the limits of a particular province, should enter into the general question of the original peopling of the island, dark and involved as it confessedly is, might be attri buted, at first sight, to a daring spirit fond of encountering difficulties, which to avoid would incur no censure, but which to meet, would be impertinent and hazardous. Yet it will appear, in the course of the present chapter, that not to notice those early antiquities in a History of Devonshire, would be an unpardonable omission; since they are chiefly applicable to this very spot. And not only iri Devonshire, but in the South os' Devonshire, we may discover, perhaps, some traces of the original colonization of the island. That the Aborigines of Britain came from the neighbouring continent of Gaul, is the commonly-received opinion: But it has likewise been maintained, on no improbable grounds, that our primitive Colonists emigrated from the East before the existence of the European or Continental settlers.

And this is the Hypothesis, which, from its connexion with Devonshire, seems to claim, at least, a cursory attention.

That the original inhabitants of Danmonium were of eastern origin, and, in particular, were Armenians, is a position which may, doubtless, be supported by some sliew of authority. But, whilst I assort, that our first Colonists were ot eastern origin, I do not intend to deny what I conceive cannot be denied, that all Europe was peopled by emigrations from the east: I mean only to draw a line of distinction between the Aborigines of

this country, who came from the east by sea, and settled at once in Britain, and those tribes who came from the east by land, and gradually spread over the continent.

That thi distinction is not fanciful, may possibly appear, hereafter, from the religiorl of our first colonists, as well as their language, their manners, and usages, and several other particulars, in which they bore not the least resemblance to the Celtic rate that peopled Europe: With the Celtic race, indeed, they had no communication; and to the Celtic race they were not known.

In the mean time, let us consider the testimony of one of our chronicles, which speaks to the point of the Armenian emigration. The Saxon Chronicle positively asserts, that ' the original inhabitants of Britain came from Armenia, and that they seated themselves in the south-west part of the island:" (a) The same Chronicle next records " the arrival of («) " *In bac insular-Britannia—sunt quinque nathnes; Anglica, Britannica feu IvalUca, Scot'tca, Pic-'tic a et Latina. Primi bujus terra incila fuere Britanni, qui ex Armenia profelti, in Aujirali parti Britannia? primum fedem posuerunt. Postea contigit, PiEtos ex Aujirali parte Scytiiœ, hngit navibus, baud ita multis, adveblos, ad Bibernia? scptentrionales parses primum appulisse, ac a Scotis petijje, ut ibi babitare Jibi liceret. Ceterutn Us veniam dare nolebant; respondent autem Scoti: Possumus nibilo secius, constlio vos juvare. /Mam novimut insulam bine ad orienttnt, ubi (st visutit fMerit) babitare pojsuis; et st quifpiant A a ami! pf the Southt Scythians, by sea, in long (hips, whom the Scoti in Ireland declined receiving, but adviied their settling in Scotland—which they did: And afterwards the Scoti of Ireland intermarried, and were variously connected with this people."*

The Saxon Chronicle is said to have been written by a mpnk, at Lincoln: And similar chronicles were kept by the most learned monks in ieveral monasteries throughout the kingdom. The monk of Lincoln seems to hafre been well informed: And there is no more reason to diipute the authority of the passage before us, than that of any other part of the book. For it is not a conjecture: It is not hazarded as an opinion: It is a politive assertion and relation of an event, as a thing generally known and understood to be true The only doubt that can be thrown upon this passage, must arise from a note in Bishop Gibson's edition of the Chronicle, in which a different reading is suggested, and the word *4rtyorica* substituted for *Armenia:* And Bede is quoted a; authorizing the conjecture.(a)

I have *armit reJHteri', nos vobis fulven'umus, quo earn expugnare valejtis. Turn folvebant Piffit et bane terrain a parte boreali ingrejji Junt ; Australia cnim Britones cccupavcrant, uti tintca diximus. Turn Picli Jibi uxores a Scotis inipetrabant, ea conditioner ut suam regalem prosapiam semper a parte seminea eligertnt; quern morem longe poslea ervarunt. Contiglt deir.de, annorum decursti, Scutorum aliquos ex Hibernia profeclos in Britannia/n, bujus terras parlem aliqutm expugraJJ'e. Dux autem eorum Rcoda vocabatur—a quo hfi diili Junt Darheodi."* Saxon Chron. (Gibson's Edit. Oxford, 1692.) p. 1, 2.

(a) " It appears to me (fays a correspondent) that Armenia has here been substituted for Armorica. Bishop Gibson seems to have been well apprized of this blunder; for he refers the reader to Ven. Bede Hist. Eccles. 1. 1. c. 1. where I find these words, which agree both in Wheloc's and Smith's edition. ' *In primis autem beec ir.jula Brittones f lum a quibus nomen accepit, incolas babuitj qui de traElu* Armoricano, *ut fertur, Brittaniam adve&i, aujirales Jtbi partes illius vindicarunt.*' King Alfred's translation likewise has *Armorica,* The beginning of the Saxon Chronicle seems to be almost the same with the passage from bjch the foregoing is extracted, though the former is rather more concise. It is yet an unsettled point, whether the first part of the Chronicle was written (1) before Bede's time or not: Bishop Gibson and Bisliop Nicolson hold contrary opinions; but, if it were necessaiy, I think I could bring forward some substantial arguments to prove that the former part of the Chronicle is actually taken from Bede. Tacitus and Cæsar confirm what Bede relates, by the inference which they draw from the.similitude of language and manners in the respective inhabitants of Armorica and Britain. In the mean time, Bishop Gibson himself in his note. on this passage (which may be found in *Nominum Locorum Explications,* p. 12. subjoined to the Chronicle) observes: 1 *Armenia (legt Armorica) Gallia pan ab Occidents, ora maritima? proximo, et a jitu nomev for tit a 1 Armorica enim efi quaji ad-ihare. Cum Anglorum viribus opprejji erant Britanni, eorum sari hue Je salutis causa contulit, unde Britanni Armoricani. Hcdie Bretagnc."* To my doubts whether the passage in Bede similar to that in the Saxon Chronicle, was an interpolation or not, thp fame ingenious correspondent replies: " The question you now propose, is not, whether *Armenia* or *Armorica* ? but, whether the sentences in Bede, referred to as parallel with the passage in the Saxon Chronicle that notices Armenia, are really Bede's?—in other words—is the paragraph an interpolation? I do not scruple to declare that it is not: and, that you may rest satisfied of the truth of this assurance, I shall state such proofs as must, I think, produce conviction. Bede's ecclesiastical history with King Alfred's Anglo-saxon versjon was first printed, in this country, at Cambridge, in 1644, by Abraham Wheloe, who had the use of several MSS. A splendid edition was afterwards printed at Cambridge, in 1644, by Dr. Smith, who had the use of other MSS. Of these MSS. the most ancient is that which is deposited in the Royal Library at Cambiidge, and was written in 737, only two years after Bede's death. Neither Smith nor Wheloe have said that the passage is not in this MS. On the contrary, all the MSS. seem to agree in all points, as to this passage, for there is not the most minute variation noticed in the readings. Bede died in 735: King Alfred died in got. Alfred's Saxon translation closely follows Bede's Latin. Is it likely that at the short distance of a century and half, the king, whose extensive learning and sound judgment are so highly extolled, should have male use of a corrupted or interpolated manuscript, and should even have adopted and sanctioned an errour, and that in a most material point? Our passage forms the fourth paragraph of the first chapter of thi-first book. The title of the chapter is, ' *De situ Br'tttaniæ vel Hibernia,* & prifeis earum incolis." The first paragraph treats of the situation of the island; the second, of its fertility and natural productions; the third,'of the climate; the fourth, *of tbe languages and inhabitants*; the fifth, of the Picts and of Ireland; and the sixth and last, of the Scots. Now the fourth paragraph could not, at any rate, be a mere interpolation;. for supposing, for the sake of argurfient, that our passage was not part of the original work, this chapter would then have been defective, and not correspondent with its general title; for nothing was then left concerning the original inhabitants, of whom it professed to treat: And that the original paragraph should have been expunged, and a dissimilar one foisted in, is altogether incredible. Let ns now consider the fourth paragraph. The words are these, ' *Hate* jn præscnti, *juxta numerum librorum quibus lex divina Jcripta ejl, quinque gentium singuis, mam eam dtmque* (1) That it was written before Bede's time, might be easily proved.

I have to add, that the context of the passage does not seem to warrant the word *Armorica.* The Saxon Chronicle, speaking of the original inhabitants, plainly intimates, that " they who settled first in the South or South-western parts, came a long voyage by sea And next, says the Chronicle, " came also by sea, the Southern Scythians." About the Southern Scythians there seems to be no dispute. In the mean time, it is abiurd to describe a colony from the opposite coast of Gaul, as coming a long sea-voyage. If, indeed, the original inhabitants settled in the western parts of the ifland, before the Southern Scythians came, they formed their colony in Britain, when the coasts of Gaul were uninhabited; when on the coasts of Gaul, there were no settlers of any description, and of course noArmoricans: The Armoricans, indeed, are comparatively of a modern date.

Our first settlers not coming overland by way of Europe, the conclusion is, that they came by sea: Nor does there seem to be any difficulty in this supposition, if we allow that the Phenician merchants came hither, afterwards, by the fame channel. Fixm the passage I have quoted, it further appears, that a colony of South-Scythians touched at Ireland, and passed thence to North Britain. This is abundantly confirmed in the Iristi records, which never appeared ib advantageously as in Vallancey s ingenious Vindication of the Antiquity of the Irish. If the Picti, then, came from South Scythia, why not the Oanmonii from Armenia? Whilst the one was able to come from the east, was there any charm to prevent the other?

With respect to the part of the island where our Eastern emigrators settled, I have already observed that it was, probably in the South of Devon. This is intimated, as we have seen, by the Sazon Chronicle. And, that the Southams were inhabited in very early times, may be fairly inferred, I think, from the story of Brutus; though, with regard to facts$ we reject it as legendary.

According to Geossry of Monmouth, Brutus, son of Silvius, having vanquished the giants of this island, called it Britain, after his own name, in 1108 before Christ. In the mean time, those well known lines from the Architrenius of Havillan— *lnde dato cursu, Brutus comitatus Achate, Gallorum sf-oliis cumulatus, na-vibut aquor,* S?c. &c. tend to shew that this settlement was made in the *South-we&.*

In the fame Poem is described the conflict between Corinæus and the Giant: Arid the rock which the Poet mentions, is reported to be the Haw, a hill between the town of Plymouth and the sea. Thus sings Havillan: *Hoi, avidum belli robur, Corinaui Averno Pracipites mijit, cubitis ter quatuor altum Gogmagog Herculea suspendit in acre litclu, &e. fs?c.* Nor is popular tradition silent on the subject. Our first heroes and our first towns are placed in the

Southams by the voice of the people, that echoes, at this moment, to the Saxon Chronicle and the Britisli Annals.

The inhabitants of Totnes describe Brutus as landing at their town, and point out the very stone on which he first set foot, when descending from his vessel: And, though the sea be' now retired from Totnes,. yet the records of former ages instruct us, that it actually flowed up to the very walls of the town. These are remarkable coincidencies: I had almost laid, that they are such as must carry conviction of the fact I have been asserting, to every unprejudiced mind.

We have here the express declaration of the Saxon Chronicle; the tale of the British Annalist; and the song of the poet Havillan; the traditional notions of the people of Totnes, transmitted from the remotest ages to the present race; and a fact in natural history j distinct in themselves—independent 011 each other—yet all meeting in the fame point. *demqucsumma veritatis et wcra sublimitatis fcientiam serutatur et cottfitetur, Anghrum videlicet, Brittinum, Scottorum, PiClorum et Latinorum, qua med'itatione fcripturarum cateris omnibus eft fafta communb, In primis autem bac injula Brittones Jolum a quibus nomen accepit, incolas babuit, qui de traclu Armorieano, ut jertur, Brittaniam advtSli, Australes Jibi panes illius vindicarunt.'* Then proceeds the fifth: ' *Et cum plurmam injula partem, incipientts ab Austro,* possedissent, *contigit gentem Piclorum, &c. Hibernian, pervinijje, Sec'* Had the sentence *inprimis, Sec.* been wanting, the sense were incomplete; and we must have considered the subsequent paragraph as another interpolation. Had the latter been allowed to stand, where should we have found the nominative case to possedissent? The *libri quibus lex d'rvina feripta est f* or the *lingua quinque gentium?* Upon the whole, we must come to these determinations. 1. That there is no *interpolation* considered merely as such, namely, the *introdutlion* of extrinsic matter. 2. That there is not a shadow of reason for supposing that the passage is *corrupted,* or that

it does not stand, in the printed books, precisely as it came originally from Bede's pen."
Though

Though the Saxon Chronicle, singly taken, might not be admitted as decisive, yet', as strengthened by these collateral proofs, I cannot dispute its authority. Though the tradition of Totnes might, in itself, be allowed no great weight, yet, as supported by the' Saxon Chronicle, we consider it with respect. The monk ot Lincoln was a stranger to Totnes: He was ignorant of her traditions, and their enlivening relic. The inhabitants of Totnes were equally unacquainted with the Saxon Chronicle: They were unconsciousof its existence: Nor hath its fame, perhaps, yet reached the traditionists of this ancient town. Not less remote, I conceive, was the connexion between Geoffry of Monmouth,and the Totonefi3ns. Surely, no collusion between the parties can be suspected. I will not insist any further on this striking concurrence; though I cannot but remind the reader of the fact in natural history, which proves the tradition to be partly true. The tradition, therefore, claims some credit: And, thus acquiring force, it communicates its insluence to the axon Chronicle and to the firitilh Annals: And they all, mutually, corroborate each other.

Let us proceed to examine a few opinions, that apparently militate against this hypothesis. That Britain was peopled by the *Brigantes,* who were called also *Brigtones* and *Britanni,* is the positive assertion of Carte; though he owns that he differs front most other writers on the subject. But he alledges, that " most authors take things upon trust; whilst be fees and examines every thing with his own eyes." How far he really examined every thing with his own eyes, may admit of some doubt; since he expressly quotes Cæsar for his authority, in saying that the Aborigines of Britain were the Brigantes. I mention this to stiew, at the fame instant, both the ignorance and the boldness of Carte. Where doth Cæsar inform us that the Aborigines were the Brigantes? I defy all the admirers of Carte to point out such an intimation in any of Cæsar's writings *i* Vainly would they search for it even with Mr. Carte's " own eyes." Cæsar would have rejoiced at discovering who the Aborigines were, or whence they came.

The name of *Brigantes* was conferred upon the tribes who pasted from the Continent into Britain, and was the signature of their separation from their brethren in Gaul, (a)

The Belgic Trivonantes are particularly mentioned as Brigantes, by Galgacus, a na-tive of Britain: " *Brigantes famina duce, eiturere cohniam, expugnare castra." (b)*

Dr. Borlafe, a much more respectable author than Carte, does not venture to oppose the rulgar notion that this island was originally peopled frQm Gaul. But (not to notice in this place his ideas relating to the religions and manners of the Britons and the oriental nations) he evidently fees some ob ections, to prevent his implicit assent to the common opinion.

Among other topics, the sentiments which the Britons themselves entertained of their Origin, is the subject of his consideration. The Aborigines thought (fays Borlafe) that they were sprung from Dis, Or from the earth; whilst the colonists of the coasts acknowledged, with more judgment, that they were sprung from the Gauls. And Dis was imagined to be the fame person as the Egyptian Mercury or (7) Thoth, who was one of the leaders of the migration from Babel.

This is a very singular and striking circumstance. And this tradition of the British origin was *(d)* actually preserved by the Druids: And, we may well presume, it was founded on truth. There was something of mysteriousness in the tradition: And the communication of it to the people was, perhaps, very imperfect. It was probably reposited among those *secret* things of the Druids, which Cæsar mentions with reverence.

Bonduica, the queen of the Britons, affirmed, with some degree of triumph, that the wisest of the Romans were unacquainted with the true name of the Indigenæ. *(e)* This1 has, doubtless, an air of mystery. For simply to know the name of a colony, or the first founder of it, would be as much within the scope of the vulgar, as the more informed mind. To be acquainted with the name of the Indigenæ, would imply no great degree' of wisdom. It must have been some recondite knowledge, therefore, of which Bonduica says, the wisest of the Romans were ignorant.

This much, at present, for Carte and Borlafe. To introduce the Historian of Manchester, irf this place, with a view of controverting his opinions, might be deemed an insult both to his genius and his learning. That I intend, however, the slightest disrespect to Mr. Whitaker, can never be conceived; whilst I have uniformly professed my («) See Whitaker's Genuine History, p. *i* 73, and his History of Manchester, p. 9, to. *(b)* Agric. Vit. c. 31. (c) See Bochart, p. 463.

(d) Ab Due patre prognatos pradkant; idque ab Druidibus proditum dkunt. Caesar, L. 6. *(e) Sitejiimomo DionisCaJJii fides babenda est, Britannsrum Regina Bonduica ejjirmet) Romamrum fasten iiffmat verum nomen indigenarum ignorajse.* Not. in Ricard. p. 153, high high veneration of his antiquarian abilities, in a strain which could only be prompted by ideas of uncommon merit. The authority of Mr. Whitaker, must, doubtless, be allowed great weight. That Mr. Whitaker has derived the Britons from the Gauls, and placed the first inhabitation of this island, about one thousand years before Christ, appears from his Manchester and from his *(a)* Genuine History of the Britons. And, in a corresoondence with which he has lately favoured me on this subject, he thus expresses his sentiments. " When the Phenicians, fays he, first traded here, the Belgæ were the inhabitants, who came hither from Gaul, about three hundred and fifty years before Christ, and the Aborigines, who came hither from the fame country about one thousand years before Christ. As to the Saxon Chronicle, it is wholly incompetent to decide upon the point. The writer of it knows nothing of those early times but what was transmitted to him from the Romans and Greeks. To these, therefore, we must appeal. Cæsar is our earliest author, and in himself, also, our best. " *Britannia pars interior ab Us ineotitur, yuos natos in insula ipsa memoria proditum dicunt: Maritime pars ab Us, qui prada ac belli inserendi causa, ex Belgis tranjierant; et, bello illato, ibi remanferunt, at que agros colere eaperunt."* These lines form the grand distinction of our Island Fathers. When the Aborigines and the Belgæ came, successively, Cæsar does not inform us. He only fays, in another place, " *Plerofque Belgas,* of Gaul, *eje ortos a Germanis, Rhenumque antiquitus transduilos, prapter loci fertilitatem ibi confedijfe, Gallosque qui ea loca incolerent, expulijse.'* This incident is too evidently connected with that above, not to be allowed to be nearly contemporary with it. The Belgæ of Germany invaded Gaul, seized all the north-east to the Meme and the Seine, and then progressively pasted into Britain. As posterior colonists, they inhabited the line of the coast, having dislodged the prior colony from it, and confined them to the interior of the island. And *ivhen* either of these colonies came hither, is pointed out very happily, and with a full conformity to collateral history, by that little commentary drawn up by Richard of Cirencester, in the fourteenth century, which had been strangely smuggled out of Britain into Denmark, and which returned back to its native country about thirty years ago. " *Anno mundi M. M. M. Circa bac tempora cultam et babitatam primum Britanniam arbitrantur nonnulli*where we observe his actual reference to some ancient author or authors, and their dubiousness concerning the precise year of so remote an event. But for the second colony as coming in a period much nearer to the line of Roman history, he speaks from his authors thus positively s A. M. M. M. M. D. c. L. *Has terras intrarunt Belgæ."* On the whole, it appears, that Mr. Whitaker is disposed, not only to derive the original Britons from Gaul, but to fix the first colonization of the island about one thousand years before Christ; and that, in determinnig this point, he chiefly re-

poses on the authority of Richard of Cirencester. But, with all deference to Mr. Whitaker's judgment, I cannot but think, that the very passage which he cites from Richard, to corroborate his argument, has, in itself, a strong tendency to overturn it. Let us review his extract, with what immediately follows it, in the original: The whole passage will wear a very different aspect and lead to a very different conclusion. " *(b)* A. M. M. M. M. *circa bac tempora cultam & babitatam primum Britaniam arbitrantur nonnulli."* So far Mr. Whitaker— but Richard proceeds—" *cum illant Jalutarent Graci Pbanicesque mercatores.* " The obvious meaning of this passage, doubtless, is, that about the year of the world three thousand, (and about one thousand years before Christ,) this island was, in general, cultivated and peopled in every part of it—insomuch that the Phenician and Greek merchants were beginning to trade with the natives." Mr. Whitaker must certainly allow, that if this passage be cited to fix the date of the peopling of the island, it may be brought, at the fame time, to fix the date of the Phenician and Grecian commerce with the islanders. But, if we admit its authority with this double view, we must understand that the peopling of Britain and the Phenician trade commenced at the fame instant. This, however, is a manifest absurdity. Who can imagine that a race of adventurers, just landed on a defart island, could find themselves immediately in a situation to establish a mercantile connexion of any kind—much less, such an intercourse as the Phenician trade implies? By what (Y)divination were they instantaneously directed to the minerals of Danmonium—whether those treasures were deep buried in the bowels of the earth, or whether they lay not far below the surface of it? By what wonderful process could they so rapidly prepare their tin for exportation? Surely we (a) See Genuine History of the Britons asserted, p. 29, 30, 31, 31, *1) Rkard, Man, Dt Situ Britan,* Lib. 2, Cap. I. (/) I might fay « by what *Virgula Dhinatoria*!" might might allow some time for the settling of emigrants on an un-

known island—for clearing away part of its woods to make room for human habitations—for the culture of its foil', to supply the necessities of life—before we looked to the discovery of its subterranean riches. Such a discovery is generally prompted by motives of avarice, of curiosity, or of luxury.—motives which do not operate till the immediate wants of life are satisfied. But, after those productions of the earth were brought to light, could the natives (as I have already asked) have suddenly converted them into articles of commerce? And, when the Danmonian tin was become a marketable commodity, was it not by a strange concurrence of circumstances, that a regular trade began that very moment, with 16 remote a people as the Phenician merchants?—The conclusion, therefore, to be drawn from this passage in Richard, is, that so far from being now first colonized, the island, about a thousand years before Christ, was well cultured and peopled; and that foreign merchants had begun to trade with its inhabitants. So that the passage in question, whilst it memorizes the fertility and populousness of the island, refers to the first establishment of the Britisti commerce, *(a)* It is wonderful,- however, that Mr. Whitaker, whilst he lays some stress on the passage, as corroborating his opinion relative to the peopling of the island, not only rejects its more natural import, with regard to the Britisti commerce, but asserts in direct contradiction to Richard, that the Phenicians *first* traded with the Britisti *Belgee;* since, Richard plainly intimates, that the Phenicians and Greeks began to trade with the natives, full six hundred and fifty years before the Belgæ arrived in Britain from the Continent. ```

As to the inhabitation of the island, it must necessarily have taken place, many centuries before. r.

That the evidence may be summed up as satisfactorily as possible in so doubtful a cafe, Mr. Whitaker hath referred us to a higher tribunal than that of Richard. He hath referred us to Cæsar. All parties, indeed, seem " to appeal unto Cæsar:" let Cæsar, then, decide the

question. The principal particulars concerning Britain, in Cæsar's commentaries, are as follows. (A) In the 4th book, Cæsar gives his reason for invading Britain—the assistance afforded by the islanders to the enemy. The island (fays he) its inhabitants, harbours, coasts, and places of descent, were almost unknown to the Gauls. Some merchants frequented Britain, for the fake of trade: but they knew only the coasts opposite to Gaul. In every other respect, even they were strangers to the country and to the extent of the island, and ignqrant who were the inhabitants, or what their customs were, or art of war, or military force, or most commodious harbours. In the 4th book also, *(c)* Cæsar lands in Britain, and describes the war-chariots of theBritons armed with scythes, and adds (in the strongest language) that the Romans were *astonished xnA terrified* at this *netu* mode of fighting. He retreats into Gaul. In the jth book, Cæsar prepares for a second invasion of the island. He passes over into Britain: and he thus describes the inhabitants. The sea-coast or maritime parts are inhabited by different tribes from Belgium, who came from the Continent, allured by_ the love of war and plunder. And these different people,.settling in the country, retain the names of the tribes and states from whence they are descended. But the interior parts are inhabited by those, who, according to general fame, are reputed to be the original natives of the soil. In the 15th section, the enemy, supported by their chariots, vigorously charged the Roman cavalry and advanced guard—a (harp conflict ensued—Cæsar sent two cohorts to support his men—but they were *d) so terrified by the neiu manner oj fighting,* that they were broken through and routed. By this action it appeared, *(e)* that the legions were by no means a fit match for such an enemy: nor could even the cavalry engage without great (a) Had Richard intended to point out merely the original inhabitation of Britain, he would not have placed *cuham* before *babitatam.* That the island was cultivated *first,* and peopled *afterwards* seems rather odd. It is a *usterm-prot-*

cron of which so accurate a writer as Richard could not havv been guilty.

(b) Quod omnibus fere gatlkU bellis, hoftibus nosiris inde subministrata atucilia inttlligebat. See Delphin. Edit, of Cæsar's Comment. Lond. printed 1719. P. 79, 80, &c. *S/tetomus* assigns a very different eason for this invasion—intelligence of the wealth of the island: Cæsar had heard of the tin of Danmonium and of the pearl-fishery. (c) Section 23d, 33d, 34th. *Nostri ptrtcrriti—atque hu'vts omnino generis ptignee perterriti—ptrturbati mstris novitate pugnar—* In the 2d book of the Pharialia, Pompey says, that Cæsar: *Terr.ita quafitis ostendit terga Britasnis, ' ' (d):tlooo genere fugneeperterritit mjiriu* P. 95. («) Section ifth. danger— danger—the enemy sometimes fighting in their chariots, then suddenly quitting their chariots and fighting on foot, in detached parties. In the 6th book, Cæsar says—" Over all Gaul there are only two orders of men, who have in any degree honor or power—all thev rest are slaves. These are, the Nobles and the Druids. The Druids preside over matters of religion and of law: the whole study and occupation of the Nobles, is war. The institution of the Druids, is said to have come originally from (a) Britain. From Britain it passed into Gaul: and still, those who wiih to be perfect in this religion, travel into Britain for instruction. What the Druids committed to writing, is written in *Greek* letters."(A) The studies and religion of the Druids are in the fame book, described to be as follows —" An exact observation and knowledge of the motions of the Heavenly Bodies— enquiries into the origin and nature of All Things—and the power of the Immortal Gods; with a belief that the ever-living foul passes from one body into another. In the lame book, the Gauls esteem themselves to be descended from Father Dis.—So the Druids, who have the secret in their hands, instruct them. They reckon time by nights and not by days. The Germans differ widely from the Gauls. They know nothing of the Druids or of sacrifices." These notices of Julius Cæiar are faithfully reported. And they will elucidate several points of discus-

sion in the following sections. Our chief point, at present, is the first colonization of the ifland. I shall only observe on the whole extract, that in the first part— book the 4th—Cæsar is not so clear in his account as in the subsequent part— gathering his information only from merchants, previously to his landing, and not being able to procure intelligence of the Britons from any other description of people on the Continent, though after his landing, indeed, he speaks with more certainty as from his own knowledge. But in the 5th book, after his second descent, he talks no longer of obtaining intelligence from merchants: he speaks positively and clearly, as from his own knowledge and opinion, grounded upon a more intimate view of the people. And his distinction between the parts of Britain, which had been settled from the Continent, and the parts which were inhabited by those who did not come from the Continent, is strongly and decisively marked. And, in his account of the war-chariots of the Britons and their manner of fighting, utterly new and unknown to the Romans, and of their other customs as well as their religion, there are a clearness and a discrimination that speak a thorough acquaintance with his subject. With respect to the first settlers, Cæsar's account directly implies, that they did not come from the C6ntinent—for he speaks of those who did j and whom he well knew; and with whom, as knowing them, he negociated in private to facilitate the success of his invasion. Though the Belgæ, then, and various continental tribes of the Celtic race had passed over and settled in the maritime parts, with whom he had some acquaintance; yet none of these tribes were the Aborigines of the island: nor could any of these continental invaders give him the least satisfactory information relative to the Aborigines. We should remark, also, that the continental settlers carried their original names with them into the island: and the tribes from whom they were descended, retained those names on the continent. The Belgæ of Gaul had still their name re-echoed by the Belgæ of Britain. But where on the con-

tinent of Europe shall we find the name of the Aboriginal Britons? Yet they had a name; and their name was *Danmonii.* When, in a subsequent age, some of the Danmonii passed over from Britain into Ireland, they carried thither their hereditary name, though it was still retained in Britain. Such would have been precisely the case with a colony from Gaul. And the Danmonii, if derived from thence, would have been recognized on the Continent, as bearing the name of their progenitors. Their traditional (-) ideas of their own origin, indeed, ssiould render us, at least, cautious in deriving the Britons from Gaul; and still more cautious in deriving them from Gaul so late as about a thousand years before Cæsar. For if they had emigrated at so late a period from the Continent, they would probably have preserved some *(a)* In a note to Bishop Gibson's edition of Camden, it is observed: " that the Britons and Gauls having the fame religion, does plainly argue an alliance, as Mr. Camden urges. B,ut, if the discipline of the Druids, so considerable both for religion and government, Vvere, as Cæsar observes, first found in Britain, and thence conveyed into Gaul, does it not seem to intimate, *that Britain must ba-ve been peopled before Gaul,* as.having by longer experience arrived at a mere complete scheme of religion and government? Besides, if our island had been peopled from Gaul, would it not look probable to fay, they must bring along with them the religion and discipline of the place?" See Gibson's Camden. Britan. p. 14. () If *crajsis* be not the true reading—a point which will hereafter be discussed. *c)* Noticed above.

Vol. I. B account account os their original, in Cæsar's time: they would have retained at least an indistinct idea of their real descent. The Belgæ leaving Gaul 650 years afterwards, preserved the history of their emigration, and corresponded with their continental fathers. This emigration was about 350 years before Cæsar. They preserved, therefore, their history and their connexion with their fathers, for 350 years. Let us allow the Aboriginal Britons the fame space of time, for the same history and the same correspondence. If this be the cafe, they were in possession of their colonial history, and they were corresponding with their fathers on the Continent, 300 years before the arrival of the Belgæ. During the space of these 300 years, we may conceive that the clearness of their history was somewhat obscured, and that their correspondence with their fathers had ceased to be regularly maintained: but we cannot suppose, that, during this time, their colonial memoirs and their continental connexions were utterly annihilated. If, then, the traces of their alliance remained, however faint, at the arrival of the Belgæ, about 3 50 years before Cæsar, nothing is more probable than that those fading traces were refressied by the Belgæ, who came from Gaul and must have known their connexions on the Continent. The Belgæ, it is true, were their enemies. But the language of the Belgæ, the fame as their own, must have awakened every dormant idea of their former friends. For the last 350 years, therefore, before Cæsar, the native Britons would have been in no danger of losing the memorials of their origin. Even by a hostile communication with the Belgæ, they must have renewed the vestiges of their primitive alliance: and these vestiges, when once restored, could not have perished before the time of Cæsar. Their second tendency to decay, was surely not so rapid as their first. But history informs us, that the Aborigines actually kept up a correspondence with the Continent by means of the Druids of Britain and Gaul. Itis impossible, then, that they could have been ignorant of their true origin, if derived from Gaul—much less, could they have maintained a tradition of their immediate descent from one of the leaders of the migration from Babel. It is ridiculous to suppose that in so short a space of time such an idea could have been introduced and have Universally prevailed.among the Aboriginal Britons, if merely a Gaulissi colony.

If it be aslced, at what period are we to fix the emigration from the east or from Armenia to the British isles? I an-

swer, that, probably, it was nos long after the dispersion from Babel—at the destruction of the great monarchy of empire of Nimrod. Polydore Virgil recites the various traditions and accounts of the first peopling of Britain, and inclines to the opinion, that it was originally colonized not long after the, dispersion. Humphry Llhuyd quotes Aristotle *de Mundo* addressed to Alexander the Great; where it is asserted, that Britain, which he calls Albion, was settled A.M. 2210, and was so named by the ancient inhabitants long before the Roman name was ever known in Britain. We find Theophilus, Bisliop of Antioch, writing thus 160 years after Christ—" *cum, priscis temporibus pauci forent homines in Arabia et Cbalda-a, post linguarum divifonem auSii et multiplicati paulatim funt. Tune quidam abierunt-versus orientem ; quidam concejsere ad partes majoris continentis, alii porro prose £li funt ad feptentrionem, sedes quafituri; nec prius defierunt terram ubique occupare, quam etiam* Britannos *in Arctois climatibus accejferint."* Here it is to be observed, that Theophilus considers this *island as already peopled,* and inhabited by *Britons,* even before these emigrators, some time after the dispersion at the Tower of Babel, begun to colonize the different parts of the world. Nothing, in truth, is more credible, than that the south-west part of our Island was peopled by sea; whilst the western parts of Europe were absolutely uninhabited; since it was long before mankind could have migrated so far westward by land. In the nature of things, emigrations by land must go on much slower than by sea. In the mean time, the most ancient historians agree that the sea, now called the *Mediterranean,* was formerly an inland lake, as also the *Ponttts Euxinus;* but that in process of time, by a great deluge, the latter forced its way into the former, and the former into the ocean by the straits of Hercules or Gibraltar—Before that time, therefore, there could be no navigation from the coasts of Asia to the western ocean; and the communication, if any, must have been in part, by a journey overland from Marseilles, or

from Cadiz, and from thence by taking (hipping on the coasts of Spain. To fix the æra, therefore, of the deluge I mention, would probably fix the date of the peopling of Britain and Ireland.

But, without entering into conjectures on a period so remote, it seems unquestionable that Britain, as well as Ireland, was peopled in very early times, from the eastern countries. The Danmonii, in sliort, are entitled, beyond dispute, to rank among the *post ancient Nations* in the, world—as the Romans termed them *Aborigines*—that is, *among the first race of mankind.* The Romans never employed this expression in any other fense.

This much for the first peopling of the ifland, or rather the south-west parts of it: For' I consider the south of Devonshire as actually colonized, whilst the rest of the island was yet a desert, and even the opposite continent of Gaul and the greater part of Europe were uninhabited.

That there were other emigrations from very distant countries into Britain, before the invasion of Julius Cæsar, is extremely probable. The Indigenæ of the *Land of Promise,* the Canaanites, afterwards called the Phenicians, having been dispossessed by Jostiua, about one thousand four hundred years before Christ, made vast emigrations into the islands of the Mediterranean sea. And, perhaps, there was no great interval of time be fore they reached the British isles.

The voyages of the Phenicians to Danmonium were not mercantile only, (a) " It is so certain as to be universally allowed among the learned, (says (A) Wells) that the *Carthaginians* were a colony of the Tyrians or *Phenicians,* and so descendents of *Canaam* It is also generally believed, and that not without grounds, that this colony came from the *Land of Canaan* at the time when *Joshua invaded it."* Meantime it is worthy of re- mark, that the Phenicians, wherever they wished to six their trade, *planted colonies* and built cities. All along the coasts of the Mediterranean, they established themselves in this manner; and, hen they palled the Straits, they pursued the same plan. When they became acquainted, therefore, with the south-west coasts of our island, it is very unlikely that they should drop their original uniform plan, and not attempt to gain al permanent footing in so distant a country; the trade with which was certainly more precarious in

Iiroportion to its remoteness, and with which they were interested in preserving a reguar intercourse for ages. »

A *Phenician* colony must easily have united with the aboriginal Islanders, as they derived their religion from the lame source, and differed very little from the Armenian Britons, in their language, manners, or customs.

After the Phenicians, came the *Greeks,* to trade in the western parts for tin and lead) and other articles, and called the British isles the Casliterides.

And that a Grecian colony actually settled here, may appear from the number of Greek words introduced into the language of Danmonium.,

We now come to the common and popular notion—the peopling of some parts of our Island, by the nations from the neighbouring continent: For this we by no means intend to deny, though we maintain the probability of a prior colonization from the east.

Mr. Carte, who is totally mistaken in all his positions, and whole antiquities are replete with error, is even Ib negligent as to mistate the time, when the Belgæ made their incursion into this island. And he positively tells us, that " Devonshire and. Cornwall were all, in a manner, wild forest, at the coming of the Belgæ, as they continued to be in a great degree, till within one hundred and fifty years after the conquest." This false assertion, manifestly against the truth of *all* history, (r) while it militates against com-; mon fense, is too ridiculous to merit one moment's attention. The Belgæ, we find from Richard, made their expedition into this island, from. Gaul, three-centuries and half before Christ. And, in the course of two hundred and fifty years, as Mr. Whitaker thinks, they extended their conquests in this island, over Kent and a small part of Middlesex, over Sussex and the greatest part of Hampshire and Wiltshire, over Dorsetshire, Devonshire, and a part of Cornwall.

Driven out by these invaders, Mr. Whitaker tells us, many of the Britons, (aboriginal Britons, as I conceive) pasted over into Ireland.

When the Belgæ. fays he, first landed upon the southern shore of Britain, about three hundred and fifty years before-the christian æra, and took possession of Kent, Sussex, Hampshire, Dorsetshire, and Devonshire, the Britons, dislodged from their ancient settlements, tranlported themselves into the neighbouring isle ot Ireland.

(a) Dr. Stukely intimates in his Memoirs to Soc. Antiq. (Dec. jd, 1761) that the Britons, from their first plantation here, under the *Tynan Hercules,* by the *Phenicians,* from the Red Sea and Arabia, had been secluded many ages from the rest of the world; and that This Plantation Took PLACE P.EFOP.E GAUL WAS PEOPLED. (i) See his Geog. of the Old and New Ted. vol. 1. p. 149. *c)* Hume, in his short notice of the Antiquities of the Island, is almost as mistaken as Carte. Vol. I. B Th«

The Belgae, continues Mr. Whitaker, had been thus settled two hundred and fifty years in the island, when Divitiacus came over from Gaul, into it. He had acquired the sovereignty of the continental and island Belgæ. And, bringing over a large reinforcement of the former, he enabled the latter to extend their possessions into the interior parts of the country. And he subdued the rest of Middlesex and all Essex, all Surrey, the rest of Hamplhire, and the adjoining parts of Berkshire, the rest of Wiltshire, the remainder of Cornwall, all Somersetshire, and the south-west of Gloucestershire.

Hence a second emigration of the Britons into Ireland.

But it by no means appears from Richard, Mr. Whitaker's principal authority, that the Belgæ had conquered so great a part of the island, before the arrival of Divitiacus. Richard simply informs us, *Has terras intrarunt Belgæ.* That they at that time reduced f Devonshire, or obliged so great a number of its inhabitants (the *aboriginal* Danmonii) to.take refuge across the leas, and possess themselves of Ireland, is surely an assertion without proof. Not long after (says Richard) Divitiacus arrived and subdued a great part of this kingdom of the Britons.

" *Son din pojiea cum exercitu in hoe regnum tranjiit Rex Æduorum Divitiacus, magnamque ejus partem fubegit.*

But, according to Mr. Whitaker, a great part of the British kingdom was already subdued to his hands. Mr. Whitaker, however, assigns him his task with great precision, gives him several provinces to conquer, and represents a *second* party of aboriginal Emigrants flying before his arms into Ireland. Yet, from Richard's account, I should conceive that only one emigration had taken place, in consequence of the Belgic invasions.

A. M. M. M. M. D. c. L. *Circa bac tempora in Hiberniam commigrarunt ejecli a Bclgis* Britones, *ibique sedes pojuerunt, ex Mo tempore Scoti nppellati.*

That the Belgæ made such inroads into Devonflihe, as to force great numbers of the Danmonii, or Aborigines of the West, from their ancient feats, and occasion their emigration into Ireland, is evident beyond a doubt: But so complete a reduction of Devonshire, by the Belgæ, even before Divitiacus, is, surely, not to be admitted as an historical fact. I can scarcely imagine, indeed, that the Belgæ, thus reinforced by Divitiacus, made an entire conquest of Devon and Cornwall. But, whatever was the success of the Belgæ, it is certain, that the Britons of the coasts very soon combined together to oppose the common enemy. Before the cominj of the Romans, we find from Richard, that *gestum est Caffibelini cum civitatibus maritimis bellum.* Under CassibelinuS the Britons prosecuted the war against the Belgæ: And, if Britissi Exeter were ever occupied by the Belgæ, it was recovered by Cassibelinus before the arrival of Cæsar..

In the mean time, the Cimbri and the Carnabii (from the neighbouring Continent also) had formed settlements in the west of the island.

The Cimbri (fays Mr. Whitaker) occupied the south-west of Somerset, and the northeast of Cornwall, as far as the river Cambala.

But it is plain, from Richard, that the north of Devon, as well as part of Somerset and Cornwall, was inhabited by the Cimbri, from Bridgewater quite to Hartland Point; and that the Cimbri were a distinct people from the Danmonii, though they were afterwards considered as the fame people. This author, speaking of the first peopling of Britain, says, that although various nations seated themselves in various parts of Britain, yet it was not well known who first peopled the island, and that it was uncertain, whether the Cimbri were the Welch, or of a more ancient origin.

The Carnabii spread over the remainder of the north of Cornwall, and over all the south-west, as far as Falmouth Haven.

Such, then, were the different establishments of the tribes from the Continent. In fixing these settlements Mr. Whitaker is doubtless right. But when he endeavours to reduce *(a)* The Irish colony (says Mr. Whit2ker) was afterwards augmented by the addition of other Britons, equally dislodged from their native regions by the Belgæ, and equally repairing to the wilds of Ireland. This second embarkition was made about two hundred and fifty years after the first; when the Britons fled from Divitiacus.

' h) Yet Mr.Whitaker himself fays (fee his Appendix to the History of Manchester, No. 1.) that the Belgæ could not have settled in the more western counties at first. Passing, assuredly, across the narrowest part of the sea, and confining themselves, as Cæsar informs us, to the southern shore; they must *gradually* have extended their dominions from Kent to the Land's End. And their first possessions would be Kent, Sussex, and Hampshire j and Dorsetshire,, *Dcwnjhire,* Somersetshire, and Cornwall their last.

tire the Danmonii, or original Britons, upon the fame footing with the wandering tribes of Gaul; when he describes the Danmonii of Devonfliire as one of the five Belgic colonies, we cannot but consider him as involuntarily steering against the current of historical truth. And this will, I trust, appear hereafter, whether the name of the Danmonii, their persons, or their character, be the subjects of investigation.

On the whole, it mould seem, that whilst the common idea of a colony from Gaul, must be admitted as true, the less popular notion of prior colonizations from the east, may at least be speciously defended. He, who in addition to the extracts before us, would bring together the various passages in point, which occur in Herodotus, Strabo, Polybius, or Plmy, (not to notice obscurer authors,) would be induced, perhaps, to think, that if Devonihire and Cornwall were not the first inhabited of the island, yet that the Aboriginal Britons were Asiatic; and that, after several emigrations from the east, the Belgæ and other nations from the Continent possessed themselves (generally speaking) of the maritime parts of Britain, driving a great number of the Aborigines into Ireland, or into the heart of the island.

SECTION II. *VIEWof the DANMONIAN SETTLEMENTS, DIVISIONS of LANDS, and GOVERNMENT, in the BRITISH PERIOD.*
I. *Geography of Danmonium from Ptolemy—from Richard—Settlements of the Aborigines or Danmonii on the south-fide of thejugum Ocrinum—of the Phenicians on the north-fide of the Jugum Ocrinum—of the Greeks to the south-weft—of the Cimbri to the northeast—of the Carnabii to the northwest—The whole of Devonshire and Cornwall reduced by the Danmonii.—* II. *Division of Danmonium into diftricls or clanships—a number of clanships forming a cantred—a number of cantreds, supposed to bavc been fix in Danmonium, forming a kingdom—Landed Property—Tenures of Lands—Services of the Chiefs—of the Villains—* III. *Danmonian Government—Seats of Judicature in the clanships, cantreds and kingdom of Danmonium—Probable Vestiges of Courts or Judgment-feats in each of the six cantreds— PrefidingOsjicers in the Courts—Princes*

of Danmonium, as reported in the British chronicles. IN the former section, I enumerated the different emigrators from the east, from Greece, and from the continent of Gaul, by whom Danmonium was, successively, peopled. To draw the line of their respective settlements in Danmonium, to mark the divisions of their landed property, and to ascertain their government, before the Roman arrival, must be the business of the present section. In order to determine these points with some degree of precision, I (hall first endeavour to fix the geography of Danmonium; adverting to the descriptions of Ptolemy and of Richard, as far as they relate to the western part of the island. Ptolemy of Alexandria, who flourished in the former part of the second century, under the Emperors Trajan, Hadrian, and Antoninus Pius, is one of the most ancient geographers, whose works are now extant. It may be proper to premise, that there are two general errors in Ptolemy which affect the whole geography of the island. This writer has made all England decline from the true position as to the length of it, and entirely changed the position of Scotland, representing its length from east to west, instead of from south to north. And he hath placed the whole of South Britain too far north, by two or three degrees. I must observe, also, that Ptolemy computes the longitude from Alexandria in Ægypt, the place of his residence.

In the description of the western side of the isle which lies along the Iriih andVergivian seas, after the Estuary *OviaXa,* we have

Hfirx?,sB asitfov—iS—vy. Promontory of Hercules 14.00 53.00 *AtlioviTt""* To *text* $o?,£fio—*ice—y&* A Promontory Antivestæum, sometimes called Bolerium 11.00 52.30.

Aa/xov/o» To xoti Oxiyov axfo» *ifi va X.* Promontory Danmonium, called also Ocrinum 12.00 51.30.

In the description of the next side, lying towards the south, and bounded by the British ocean, after the promontory Oci inum, come *Kttmtos nso.* rxCoAjci X « .S. Mouth of the river Cenion 4.0.

00 51.45

Ta.uaft *iroi. txGtf.x' it* yo » r. Mouth of the river Tamarus 15.40 52,10

Ia-asxat *vol.* txfoAai; v/3 y. Mouth of the river Isaca 17.00 51.20 AA.«/»8 *vol. ixSoXat 1% ya tQ yo.* Mouth of the river Alænus 17.40 52.40

The Danmonii are placed next to the Durotriges. Mefl *us Svo-iaixuiixioi* Aoovov/S;, tv *01s mXeis*—Next to the Durotriges, in the most western part, are the Danmonii, among whom are these towns— *OvoXifix* Js AS *y@ y.* Voluba 14.45 5.20 *Ovt-tXœ is* K/3 Xs. Uxela 15. 00 52.45

Ta/icefij *11 yfi* S. Tamare 15.00 52.15 *io-xx* / A v/3 xS. Isca 17.30 52.45

In this geographical description, the Promontory of Hercules ii, confessedly, HartlandPoint, in the west corner of Devonshire.

The Promontory *Antivestaum,* or *Bolerium,* is the Land's-End—perhaps called *Antivejlerium,* from the British words *An diuez Tir,* which signify the Land's-End; and *Bolerium* from *Bel e rhin,* the head of a Promontory, (a)

The Promontory *Ocrinum* is the Lizard-Point in Cornwall; probably called *Ocrinum,* from *Ocb rhin,* a high Promontory: And, the *Lizard* is, probably, of Britisti derivation, from *Lif-ard,* a lofty projection, *(b)* Here ends Ptolemy's Description of the Western _Coast of Britain. 1

In his description of the next side, lying towards the south, and bounded by the British ocean, Ptolemy mentions— the mouth of the river *Cenion,* which is supposed to be Falmouth Haven, so called from the Britisti word *Genau,* a mouth; of which there is still some vestige in the name of a neighbouring town, *Tregony. (c)*

The river Tamarus retains its ancient name, being called Tamar, from *Tamar-wv, gentle river:* And its mouth is Plymouth-Haven, *(d)*

The river Isaca, or Isca, is the Exe, which, passing Exeter, falls into the sea at Exmduth.

The river Alaenus is supposed to be the Axe, and its mouth Axmouth. It was, perhaps, called Alaenus, from *Alaun iu,* the full river, *(e)*

The towns of the Danmonii were *Voluba,* according to *(f)* Camden and *(g)* Baxter, Grampound, but in *(h)* Horfley's opinion, Lostwithiel— *Uxela,* supposed by Mr. (i) Camden to be Lostwithiel—by Mr. (£) Baxter, Saltafh— by (7) Horsley, Exeter.

Tamare was certainly a town upon the Tamar. *(m)* Horstey thinks it was Saltafh— hut *(n)* Camden and (0) Baxter suppose it to be *Tamarton,* retaining its ancient name. *Isca,* or *Isca Danmoniorum,* was Exeter, the capital of the Danmonii.

So much for the geography of Ptolemy, as far as it relates to Danmonium. To Antoninus, the imperial Notitia, the Anonymous chorography, and the Itinerary of Richard, I shall have recourse hereafter.

In the mean time, however, Richard's descriptions must not be neglected in fixing the Geography of the island.

Mr. Whitaker was the first person who duly appreciated the value of Richard's work. (/) Richard's authorities, fays Mr. Whitaker, were Ptolemy and his contemporary writers, the tradition of the Druids, ancient monuments, documents and histories. And in Richard is a Map of Britain, (y) drawn up by himself, " *secundum fidum monumentorum perveterum.*" This Mr. Bertram thinks far superior to all the rest of Richard's commentary, for the curiousness and antiquity of it. And, as the oldest map of the island that is now extant, and the only old one of Roman Britain, Mr. Whitaker admits it to be a great curiosity. Maps of the island, however, were not uncommon in Richard's time. He himself speaks of some, as *recentiore a-vo descriptas,* and generally known, (r) And this is but of little value: It is frequently inaccurate: It frequently contradicts its own itinerary.

The following is Richard's description of the West of Britain, (s) " *Infra Heduorum terras fiti erunt* Durotriges, *qui et* Morini *alias nocantur. Metropolin habebant* Durinum *et promontorium* Vindeliam.

(a) Baxter, p. 19, 36. (£) Baxter, p. 186. (c) Baxter, p. 77. Camd. Brit. p. 16. *(d)* Baxter, p. 212. () Baxter, p. 10. *(f)* p.

17. *(g)* p. 54-() P-378. (i) p. 18. () p. 257. (/) p. 378. "(m) p. 376. (n) p. 25. (0) p. 221. (/) See History of Manchester, vol. 1. p. 83, 84, 85, 86, 87, 88, 89, 90. Cctavo edition. (?) In the 14th century. (-) p. 3. (s) p. 19, 20. is *In borutn finibus senfim coarctatur Britannia, et immensum efformare vidctur bracbiitm, quod irruptionem minitantem commode repellit oceanum. In boc bracbio, qua intermiffione* Uxellæ *amnis,* Heduorum *regioni protenditur, fita erat regio* Cimbrorum. *Utrumne vero modernum* Walliæ *nomen dederint, an vero antiquior Jit* Cimbrorum *origo—non aque conflat. Urbcs Mis pracipua* Termolus *et* Artavia. *Vifuntur hie, antiquis fie dicta,* Herculis columnæ, *et non procul bine infula* Herculea. *Sed a fiuminis* Uxellæ *finibus continuum procurrit montium jugum, cui nomen* Ocrinum, *extremumque ejui ad promontorium ejusdem neminis extenditur. Ultra* Cimbros *extremum infula angulum incolebant* Carnabii; *unde, forfitan, quod bodieque retinet nomen, obtinuit* Carnubia. *Urbet babebant* Musidum *et* Halangium. *Cum vero has olim dr.ft.rtas propemodum et incultas Britannia partes Romani numquam falutauerint, minoris omnino momenti urbes eorum fuijfe-videntur, et Hifloricis propterea neglecta, Geograpbit tamen memorantur promuntoria* Bolenum *et* Antivestæum. *Memoratis modo populis in littore oceani austrum versus affines ad Belgas-Allobroges, sedem babebant* Danmonii, Gens Omnium Validissima; *qua ratio moviffe videtur* Ptolemaum, *ut totum bunc terra tractum qui in mare brachii inftar pratenditur, illis adferipferit. Urbei habebant* Uxellam, Tamarara, Volubam, Ceniam, *omniumque matrem* Iscam, *flwvio cognomini imminentem. Flwvii apud ipfos pracipui memorati modo* Isca, Durius, Tamarus *atque* Cenius. *Ora. eorum maritima promuntoria exhibet tria, de quibus mox paulo dicemus. Hanc regionem, utpote Metallis Abundantem Phanicibus Gracis et Gallis mercatoribus probe not am fuijfe conjiat. Hi enim ob magnam, quam terra fertbat, ft ami copiam eo fua frequenter extendeb'ant negotia; cujus rei pracipua funt documenta supra nomi-*

nata tria promuntoria— Helenis*scilicet,* Ocrinum *et m* eWon, *ut et nomina civitatum,* Gkæcam PheniciamQue Originem *redolentia. (a) Ultra braebium in oceano fita funt infula* Sygdiles, *qua etiam* Oestrominides *et* Cassiterides *'vocabantur, dicta." (b)*

Such are our best documents relating to the Geography of Danmonium. And I mould dispose of our successive colonists in the following manner.

The Aboriginal colony from the east, occupied perhaps, at first, little more than the south coasts of Devonshire. And they afterwards extended their settlements along the *(n) Herculis frem.* Hartland Point.

jintiiieftaum prom. Land's End. „

Ocrinum prom. Lizard Point.

Ceniort.Jiuv. ofiia. Val!e River. i *Tamari fiu-u. oflia.* Tamar River. *Jfacafiuv. eftia.* Exe River. Rich. not. p. 175. *(b)* With respect to the west of the island, Mr. Whitaker says: " The *Durotriges* or *Mor'mi,* lived in Dorsetshire, and had *Durinitm, Durnwaria* or Dorchester for their capital. And the *Hædui* Ailed all Somersetshire to the *Æftuary Uxel/a,* Bridgewater Bay, or the river of Ivel, on the south; the southwest of Gloucestershire, to the hills of Wotton-Under-Edge, or its vicinity; and the northwest of Wiltshire, to the Avon and Cricklade. (1) These, however, appear from Ptolemy, to have been subdued by the Belgæ; their country being expressly ascribed by him to that people. (2) The Cimbri extended over the rest of Somersetshire, except a small part to the east of the Thone, (j) and along the north of Cornwall, as far as the river Cambala, the Camel, or Padstow Harbour. (4) The Carnabii spread over the remainder of the north of Cornwall, and over all the south-west, as far as Falmouth Haven. (5) And the Danmonii possessed, originally, the rest of Somersetshire, (6) the rest of Cornwall, and all Devonshire. But, before the coming of the Romans, the Danmonii had subdued both the Carnabii and Cimbri, and usurped their dominions. (7)" (1) Richard, p. 20 and 24. (2) lschalis & Aquas Calidje. So also Ptolemy places the Durotriges, not south-west as he is

generally translated but to the south and well of the.Belgar, *oclTO overscan ICLt .l?-riyi&yixs* ; the Durotriges being to the south of the Somersetshire Belgæ, and to the west of the Hampshire. (3) Uxella urbs is given to the Danmonii by Richard, and yet is given to the Hedui by the Map, in express contradiction to to the account. (4) Richard's Map. (,5) Cerria Urbs 8c Cenius Fluvius, given to the Danioonii by Richard. (6) Uxella Urbs. Richard. (7) Ptolemy and Richard, p. so. Djrwipnjam Promonlgrium. Aud the Dinmonii are *Svsfjuxulctloi,* or the mo westerly tribe, in the sormrr. line line of the Totonesian Shore, and occupied the country both to the south-east and southwest, whilst they had the *Jugum Ocrinum,* or that mountainous tract which runs through Devonshire and Cornwall, for their northern boundary.

That these Aboriginal settlers were the *Dartmonii,* I have little doubt. There is no evidence to the contrary. And there are several considerations, which, as they occur in their proper places, will gradually confirm our minds on this subject. Mr. Whitaker, however, has decided it otherwise: and he has degraded the Danmonii into a tribe of the Belgæ. But it is very plain from Richard, that the Danmonii were a distinct people from the Belgæ. Richard mentions the Danmonii as the most respectable of all the British nations. He calls them, in one place, *gens omnium 'validistima:* and, describihg the different settlements on the island, he mentions the kingdom of the Danmonii as *a most powerful state. Fiat vero ab extrema Prim provinciæ ora initium cujus littora Gallix objiciuntur. Tres vcro* laudatissimos validissimosque *status* Cantianum *nempe,* Belgium, *et* Danmonium *comflectitur hac Prcvinda. (a)*

And he notices thirty battles fought with the combined forces of the Danmonii and the Belgæ. (A) The Danmonii are not only introduced, in Richard's commentary, as a separate nation, but as a nation of much greater consequence than the Belgæ of the neighbouring continent.

Not many ages, probably, elapsed,

from the establisliment of the Danmonii, in the south of Devon, before the Phenicians, not content with trading voyages, fixed a colony on the north side of the *Jugum Ocrinum,* a country as yet uninhabited, and to which they might have been directed by the southern colonists: And their first town, perhaps, near Hartland or Hertland Point, was the *Town of Hercules,* their God of navigation; whilst the Promontory itself was called *Herculis Fromontorium,* and Lundy, at no great distance, *Heraclea* or the *Island of Hercules.*

In the mean time, the Greeks, perhaps, were planting a colony at the Ramhead, a promontory on the southern coast of Danmonium, beyond which the first oriental tribes had not, as yet, extended their habitations. This Promontory they called *xpiu* pcWon: And from this point they might have stretched their settlements as far west as they pleased, over a wild unpeopled country.

But, in process of time, these settlements (to the south at least of the *Jugum Ocrinum* were thrown into great disorder by the Belgæ from Gaul, who finally seated themselves as a people beyond the eastern limits, and, who, at the arrival of the Romans, were on a friendly footing with the Danmonii, or were induced at least to unite their forces with the Aboriginal Britons, in opposition to a common enemy.

Nor were the Phenician colonies to the north of *the Jugum Ocrinum,* undisturbed: The.Cimbri invaded Danmonium on the north-east, and established themselves there: And the Carnabii settled on the north-west.

After all these agitations, it appears, that the whole of Devon and Cornwall, both the south and north side of the *Jugum Ocrinum,* were reduced under the subjection of the Danmonii, before the arrival of the Romans.

After thus determining the Danmonian settlements, it is natural to enquire into the different ranks of the settlers, and to mark the distribution of property according to those ranks.

The first business of the leader of a colony, must have been to assign estates to his chiefs: And the assignment (c) of estates to each of the chiefs, would occasion the country to be divided into *tester* or *greater* districts; and *Devonshire* to be parcelled into districts co-evally with the first plantation of it.

These *lester districls* were similar to our present *townships,* and the actual origin of them. And the mansion of the chief and his tenants, and the neighbouring cotes and adjacent lands, would form *one division* or *township.* The mansion of another chief (with its appendages) formed a *second* townsliip. And these little divisions must have commenced with the first colony.

And, perhaps, the adjoining downs and extensiye woods, were assigned in common, to a determinate number of *townships. (a)* Richard, p. *ij. (i) p.* 21. (f) It is evident that the *Britons* had fixed property; since the Druids, we are toH, decided all disputes about the limits of lands,

For

For the more regular administration of justice, a number of these townships were soon combined into one *cantred.* Such divisions we actually find in ancient Ireland, whither the Danmonii had emigrated; and in Wales also, where, among the earliest institutes of that country, they are referred to the primitive Britons. («) Formed some time before the towns were constructed, the cantred9 would borrow their appellation from the most remarkable objects of nature within them.

(A) The south of Danmonium, including all that tract of land, that lies south of the *Jugum Ocrinum,* from the borders of Dorset to the Land's-End or the *Ocrinum Promontorium,* was, probably, divided into four cantreds; the *first* cantred extending from Dorset to the river Isca—the *second,* from Isca to the river Durius—the *third,* from Durius to the river Tamara—the *fourth,* from Tamara to the Ocrinum Promontorium. The north of Danmonium, including all that tract of land which lies north of the *Jugum Ocrinum,* from the Uxella to the east, to the *Anti-vestaum Promontorium* to the west, naturally divides itself into two cantreds—the north-east cantred, from Uxella to Cambala, in-

habited by the Cimbri; and the western cantred from Cambala to the *Anti'vestaum Promontorium,* inhabited by the Carnabii.

Danmonium, then, was divided into six cantreds. But what communication originally subsisted between the two cantreds north of the *Jugum Ocrinum,* and the four cantreds south of this mountainous chain, or in what manner or in what period the cantreds, on either fide of the hills, were so formed as to coalesce into one kingdom, it may be difficult to conjecture. That they were all united under one kingdom, before the arrival of the Romans, is an undoubted fact. Mr. Whitaker informs us, that when the Romans invaded the island, the Danmonii had conquered the Cimbri and Carnabii, and usurped their dominions. Certain it is, that, at this crisis, the names of Cimbri and Carnabii were funk in the name of Danmonii, and that all Devonsliire and Cornwall, in fact, was denominated Danmonium.

As a certain number of *clanjhips,* therefore, were united to form a *cantred;* so several *cantreds (fix* in Danmonium) were united to form a kingdom. Perhaps, the principal clanship in the cantred of Isca, was situated on the banks of the Exe; and the mansion of the *(c) Chief,* was that fastness or fortress in the woods, which gave rise to the city of Exeter. In the cantred of Durius, Totnes, possibly, had its origin—in that of Tamara, Tamerton or Plymouth—in that of Cenius, Tregony. And, whilst, among the Cimbri, we may observe the clanship of Herton or the town of Hercules, we may trace, perhaps, Redruth, or the town of the Druids, in the country of the Carnabii. Thus was property distributed in Danmonium. And it was, conditionally, distributed by the Sovereign amongst his subjects.

After the Sovereign, ranked the Chiefs, holding their lands immediately from the crown: And, as the immediate tenants of the crown, they were obliged, by their tenures, to certain services to it. They were obliged to wait on the King at dinner, for instance; or to follow him to the war. They were bound to con-

struct or repair the royal castles. They were assessed with rent either in money or kind. Under the reserve of these services and payments, the chiefs had a full property in their lands; and could transmit them to their heirs.

Inferior to the chiefs, the great body of the people were divided into two classes— the *free,* and the *complete-villains.* The former might relinquish their lands, or remain upon them, at their own discretion: The latter were the property of their lord, and saleable as a part of the estate. They were both subject, like the chiefs, to attendance in war, and to payments, in money or returns in kind.

The tenures of lands were anciently the fame in Wales. The discovery of the same holdings even so early as the tenth century and in the laws of Howel Dha— holdings, not formed by that legislator of Wales, but referred by Howel himself to prior institutes, and ascribed to the earliest Britons—very strikingly proves their great antiquity. And the general resemblance of the tenures among the natives of Wales, the Aborigines of Ireland and the Highlanders of Scotland, as well as the original tribes of the Britons, demonstrates the whole system of polity to have been derived from their common and *a)* The *cantred,* though including a larger district, gave rise to the *hundred. (b)* See Richard's Map.

(c) This *Chief,* probably, was the Danmonian Sovereign—his/orfre/j, a castle of great strength— and his *town,* very soon, a larg city.

Vot. I. ' C immediate immediate parents—the Emigrators from Asia. And it demonstrates this whole system, unknown to the neighbouring continental tribes, to have been introduced into the island by the primitive colonists of Danmonium.

Such (fays Mr. Whitaker) was the curious and original frame of the British tenures— tenures which seem to have been derived from a very ancient origin, and to have existed coeval with the first plantations of the island. And they were, plainly, I think, the joint result of a *colonizing* and a *military spirit.*

If we look to the eastern nations for such tenures, we shall find, in Genesis, a picture, of tribes or clans, and chiefs or petty princes: And we sliall discover the same holdings at the present day, on the plains of Arabia. From the difference of a continental er island-situation, as well as the climate and other circumstances, the nature of property was somewhat different in Arabia and Danmonium. The Patriarchs, in elder days, and the Arabian Princes, at the present hour, are described as traversing extensive tracts of country, and as removing with their dependents and their cattle, from one spot where the pasturage was exhausted, to another which had been hitherto unoccupied: And the Danmonii are commonly represented as a wandering people, and as feedings their flocks at one time in Devonshire and at another in Hampsliire. But this, from the nature of the island, and the populousness of it, was impracticable. Their origin, however, is iutficiently pointed out by their deposition to wander, which they discovered as far as their situation would permit them. Within the circle of his territories, the British chief was, undoubtedly, accustomed to shift the scene; sometimes attending his flocks on the cultivated hills—sometimes in the fertile vallies, and sometimes driving them to the downs, at a considerable distance. Even in the time of Cæsar, the Aborigines who had fled into the centre of the island, were discriminated by this roving genius from the tribes of Gaul: To Cæsar's own observation this formed a striking part of their character: Nor could the airiness of an Asiatic temper, so opposite to the European mind, that loves its accustomed habitation, be more clearly manifested than by their breaking up their establishments, as they repeatedly did, at the appearance of every invader. Though, *gent omnium 'validisjhna,* and well able to repel an enemy, yet so slight was their attachment to their native soil, that they abandoned it on the first attack, and either rushed from the sea-coasts into the central woods of Britain, and there began to build fresh fortresses and fix new clans, or rapidly embarked for other islands, and formed colonies on die Irish coast, or where-ever fortune might direct their

(hips. In the mean time, they resembled the Arabs, also, as nearly as their situation would allow, in die distinctions of rank or station.

But let us dismiss, for,the present, the idea of these resemblances; and pass to a consideration of the British government.

The institution of *toivnfiips* and of *cantreds* was particularly subservient to the administration of civil justice. Every *township* and *cantred* bad a distinct court of justice. The controvirsies which could not be decided in the court of the *town/hip,* was carried to the court of the *cantred:* and the controversies not determined in the *cantred,* was carried to *a court superior to all.* The government of a townsliip was that of a large family; where we might observe a species of patriarchal policy, originating from natural relationship and. necessary subordination. And from a combination of distinct families, clanlhips, or townslups, would result the government of a cantred.

In the same manner from a combination of cantreds would result the government of a kingdom. The regal government, however, of Danmonium, was not simply monarchical: The Druids, undoubtedly, participated with the Brititsi sovereign, both in the civil and military government. The Druids were the principal directors of the state. They had the fame influence in war as in peace; whilst, attending the military expeditions, they animated the troops to victory by their displays of future glory, or interposed between armies ready to engage, and prevented the bloody conflict by the dignity of their persons, and sublimity of their doctrines, and by the terrors of enchantment and prophecy.

l he Kings had no power even to punilh their soldiers. " To inflict punisliment (fays Tacitus) belongs to the Druids: And this they affect to do, in obedience to their Deities, who are more peculiarly present, as they tell us, with their, armies in war.' The Britisti sovereigns had little power, either in framing or executing the laws. The laws among the ancient Britons were not considered as the decrees of their princes, bat as the

commands of their gods. And the Druids were supposed to be the only persons t to whom the gods communicated a knowledge of their will. It was consequently the part of the Druids, to enact the laws as well as to explain them to the people. This venerable order, then, decided by their own laws, all public and private controversies, and pronounced judgment in criminal cafes. He who refused to submit to their decision, was excluded from their sacrifices, and shunned as a polluted person.

With respect to the seats of judicature in the clanships, cantreds, or kingdom of Danmonium, it is very remarkable that we have many corresponding accounts proving the Britilh courts to have been generally held in the open air and on high places. The Britisli courts of judicature were sometimes called *Gorseddau* % And these Gorseddau were convened in the open air, on the summit or Hope ot a hill, near a pillar or pillars ofstone, or within some appointed circle of stones, or some appropriated amphitheatre of stones and turf. In the regions of Caledonia and Ireland, they were held for ages after this period, on the side of a hill; and the judges were seated on green banks of earth. And there is an ancient law in Wales, that respects this usage. The judge is there directed, with a view to his personal accommodation, to sit with his back to the fun or wind. It is not improbable, that many of these situations, which were fixed on for enacting or administering the laws, or for other solemn occasions of the1 legislature, had been previously consecrated to religion. Where could legal assemblies be held more properly than in places consecrated to religion, *(a)* already reverenced equally by the higher and inferior orders, and therefore likely to influence the governors as well as theoverned? When any place had been distinguished by the rites of worlhip, and was considered with a kind of sacred dread, as the habitation of the Deity, the laws enacted or enforced on the spot, would be tffought to partake of its lacrednels. The monument cf Gilgal was first dignified by religious rites: And it afterwards became the seat of justice and national councils, *(b)* There are numberless spots in Danmonium, still marked by stone pillars or circles, or amphitheatres, which, in those early days, were, probably, let apart for the purposes of government. The single stone pillar often occurs in sacred writ. Samuel made Bethel and Gilgal the *annual* feats of judgement, (r) At Gilgal, Saul was confirmed king, and the allegiance of his people renewed with sacrifices and great festal joy. (/) At Mizpah, Jephtha was solemnly invested with the government of Gilead. (?) And the general council against Benjamin feeras to have been held at this place, *(j)* At the stone of Shechem, erected by Joshua, Abimelech was made king—*(g)* Adonijah by the stone of Zoheleth. (A) Jehoasli *(i)* was crowned king standing by a pillar. And Jonah *(k)* stood by a pillar, when he was making a solemn covenant with God. From these instances, it fliould seem, that pillars of stone were set up to distinguish places' extraordinary convention: But it is impossible to speak with precision on this point. Dr. Borlafe is, perhaps, too fanciful in discriminating his courts of council and of judicature. His " stones to itand by," and " stones to stand upon," and " his stones to sit on," are erected, probably, on a very sandy foundation. (/) To attribute particular pillars, or stone circles, to particular uses, mult be a matter of the most hazardous conjecture. At the lame time I allow, that the custom of " sitting on stones in council," was very ancient among the eastern nations. And in one of the sculptures on the shield of Achilles, the elders are convened in council, sitting on stone feats, within the sacred circle: Oi £s vspAr («f) *F.iatl'tvi* Efo/a; *Xi9ois icpu tu Kvxt.w.* Borlafe proceeds to observe, " that circular monuments had still other uses, beside those of religion and law." Where these stone-benches are semicircular, and distinguished by seats and benches of like materials, there is no doubt but they were designed to ex (a) See Borlafe, p. 191, 192, 193. (£)' 1 Sam. ii. 14. XV. 31, 33. (r) 1 Sam. VII. 16. (/) 1 Sam. XI. 14. () Judges, XI. 11. *(f)* Judges, XX. 1.3. (g) Joshua, XXIV. 16. *(b)* I Kirigs, 1. 9. '/) 2

K-itijcs, XI. 14. *(i)* 2 Kings, XX11I. 3. (/) The name of Dr. Borlafe hath, frequently, occurred: And I have, sometimes, been under the necessity of dissenting from this pleasing antiquarian, though in matters of mere speculation. On the whole, I am greatly indebted to his Antiquities, for assistance in my present research: They are replete with original investigation. If I have, any where, dropped a word that may appear disrespectful to Dr. Borlafe, it should be referred to the particular point in difcussien. I revere his mejnory! well assured, that he may justly be ranked among those few, whose learning was unaffected, whofe manners were ingenuous, and whose religion was sincere. (m) Homer's Iliad, p. 18, v. 504. ypL. I. Ci kibit hibit plays. There is a theatre of this kind in Anglesca, resembling a horse-shoe, including an area of twenty paces diameter, with its opening to the west, called *Bryn-givyn*, or *Supreme Court*. It lies in a place called *Trer-Dremv*, or *Druid's Tonon*; whence it nay be reasonably conjectured that this kind of structure was used by the Druids. It is somewhat singular that Borlase lhould have almost appropriated this theatre to plays and sports; when the name itself points out a place of judicature. He chose to call it a theatre; and he was afterwards misted by the found. But the people usually assembled (says he) to hear plays acted, and to lee the sports and games, in amphitheatres of stone, not broken as the cirques of stone-erect. The Doctor, then, notices an amphiteatre of the sort, " the most remarkable monument of the kind which he had yet seen"—the amphitheatre of St. Just, in Cornwall, which, if not appropriated to judicial matters, was chiefly designed, perhaps, for this purpose. And so, likewise, was the amphitheatre of Piran; both which (hall be described in their proper places. We have great reason, therefore, to conclude, that many of the more striking monuments inDanmonium, which we have at this day an opportunity of observing, were, generally speaking, erected as judicial seats; though we have not sufficient data to determine what kinds of pillars, circles,

or amphitheatres, were intended for ordinary meetings, or more solemn assemblies— or for the courts of a clan, of a cantred, or of a kingdom. In each of the *fix cantreds* which I have enumerated, we may possibly find such vestiges of the British government.

In the cantred of Isca there are several stone pillars and circles of stone, which are evidently druidical. Perhaps, in this cantred, there are few druidical stones more remafkable than two rocks in the parish of Widworthy, or that point more clearly to the judicial assemblies of the Britons. One of these stones is a large flint rock, situated at the northern extremity of the parish of Widworthy. It is known by the name of the Greystone. It is five feet in height, and four in width and depth. And, at the southern extremity of the parish, is another stone of nearly the fame dimensions. In the cantred of Durius, there seem to be a much greater number of druidical remains, than in the eastern part of Danmoninm. On Hameldown in particular, in the parish of Manaton, is a large circle of stone, which is called Grimspound. This circular line of stone incloses an area of near three acres. And, on the area, are many small circles, consisting of (ingle stones erect. That Grimspound was the seat of judicature for the cantred of Durius, is no improbable supposition. For the cantred of Tamara, we may fix, I think, the seat of judicature at Crockemtorr, on Dartmoor: here, indeed, it seems already fixed at our hands. And I have scarce doubt but the stannary parliaments at this place were a continuation even to our own times of the old British courts, before the times of Julius Cæsar. Those stannary parliaments were similar in every point of resemblance to the old British courts. Crockern-torr, from its situation in the middle of Dartmoor Forest, is undoubtedly a very strange place for holding a meeting of any kind. Exposed as it is toall the severities of the weather, and distant as it always hath been within our times, or within the memory of man, from every human habitation, we might well be surprised that it soould have been chosen, for the spot on which our laws were to be framed; Unless some peculiar sanctity had been attached to it in consequence of its appropriation to legal or judicial purposes, from the earliest antiquity. Besides, there is no other instance that I recollect, within our own times, of such a court, in so exposed and so remote a place, *(a)* On this Torr, not long since, was the warden's or president's chair, seats for the jurors, a high corner stone for the cryer,of the court, and a table, all rudely hewn out of the rough moorstone of the Torr, together with a cavern, which for the convenience of our modem courts, was used in these latter ages as a repository for wine. Notwithstanding this provision, indeed, Crockern-torr was too wild and dreaiy a place, for our legislators of the last generations; who, after opening their commission, and swearing the jurors on this spot, merely to keep up the old formalities, usually adjourned the court to one of the stannary towns. From the nature of this spot, open, wild, and remote, from the rocks that were the benches, and from the modes of proceeding, all so like the ancient courts, and so unlike the modern j I judge Crockern-torr to have been the court of a cantred, or its place of convention, for the purposes of the legislature. And this cantred, according to my division of Danmonium, must have been Tamara. For the Cantred of Cenius, the British courts might possibly have been held, near *a)* Crockem-torre was just such a seat of judicature as the Psalmist alludes to—" Let their *judge!* be overthrown in *stony places."* Psalm 141.

that tliat astonishing stone monument which Borlase describes in the parish of Constantine. *(a)* From its vast magnitude and position, and from the scenery around it, I mould conceive it to be well calculated to impress awe upon the multitude: and its extensive shadow might have diffused a more solemn air over chiefs assembled in council, or druids dispensing justice. In the cantred of the Cimbri, we may fix the judgment seat, amidst that wild recess, *the Valley of stones*; where those learned antiquarians, Lyttelton and Milles, had imagined a variety or druidicaj monuments, *(b)* "

I was pleased, (says Lyttelton in a letter to Milles) with the rude romantic scenes between Comb-martin and Linton, and particularly with what you apprehend to be a druid *gorseddau."* This *gorseddau* lie opposite to a karn of rocks, which is called the *Cheese-iuring*. In the cantred of the Carnabii, Karnbre-hill, will, doubtless, exhibit a *gorseddau-*. for, on this hill, we find almost every species of druid monuments, rocks, basons, circles, stones-erect, remains of cromlechs, karns, a grove of oaks, a cave, and a religious enclosure. On Karnbre-hill, Borlase has described a rock, which he supposed to be " one of the *gorseddau,* or placet of elevation, whence the Druids pronounced their decrees. In some places, indeed, these gorseddau were made of earth: but it was plainly unnecessary to raise hillocks of earth, where so many stately rocks might contribute full as well to give proper dignity to the scat of judgment." () " The town about half-a-mile across the brook which runs at the bottom of Karnbre-hill, was anciently called *Red-dreiv,* or more properly *Ryddreiv,* the *Druid's-Ford,* or *Crossing os the Brook1 "*—fays Borlase: and the Doctor refers for his authority, to a grant of the fairs there, to the Bassets of Tehidy, in the time of Henry VII. *(d)* In the mean time, Pryce asserts, (?) that " *Redruth—Dredruith—* signifies *the Druid's Tmvn."* And of this he is assured, " from its vicinity to *Karn-brea,* that celebrated station of Druidical superstition; where are to be seen a multifarious collection of monumental druidisin. *Redruth—Ryd-drytb,* is, also, *the Red Ford.* But that cannot be the name of the town, as there are deeds in the possession of Sir Francis Basset, Bart, where it is denominated *Dredruith.* This name is so very ancient, as to be given to the situation of the town, before this kingdom was divided into parishes; as old writings express thus: *In the parish osUny juxta Dredruith.* In fine, though the parish is now, and has been immemorially called *Redruth,* its real dedicatory name is *St. Uny:* and, therefore, if I mistake not, the town claims an evident antiquity, prior to any other in the county." At all

events, there is no doubt but *Redruth,* in the vicinity of Karnbre, was one of the chief towns of the Druids of Danmonium. And at *Plan-an-guare,* in *Redruth,* there were very lately the remains of an amphitheatre, *(f)* But the amphitheatres of St. Just and St. Piran, bear the most evident marks of the judicial court, in this cantred of the Carnabii. The amphitheatre of St. Just (in the hundred of Penwith) situated near the church, is somewhat disfigured by the injudicious repairs of late years; but, by the remains, it seems to have been a work of more than usual labour and correctness. It was an exact circle of one hundred and twenty-six feet diameter. The perpendicular height of the bank, from the area within, is now seven feet; But the height from the bottom of the ditch without, at present ten feet, was formerly more. The seats consist of six steps, fourteen inches wide, and one foot high, with one on the top of all, where the rampart is about seven feet wide. There is a larger circular work, of higher mound, fossed on the outside, and veiy regular in the amphitheatre, in the parish of Piran-sand. The area of the amphitheatre, perfectly level, is about one hundred and thirty feet diameter. The benches, seven in number, of turf, rise eight feet from the *(g)* area. That plays were acted in these amphitheatres, I have not a doubt. But I concur with Mr. Whitaker in thinking, that these circles were originally designed for British courts of judicature. As we find that the Druids bore a conlpicuous part in the legislature, perhaps we may place a Druid in each cantred, as the supreme judge; whilst the chiefs of the clanships

(a) See Borlase's Antiquities, page 166. *(b)* 1 have a. few scraps in the handwriting both of Lyttelton and Milles, relating to the Valley of Stones; but nothing satisfactory can be collected from them. *(c)* Borlase's Antiquities, p. 114.. (*(d)* Antiquities of Cornwall, p. 116. (e) Pryce's Vocabulary.

ffj See Pryce's Vocabulary.

(f) For a more particular description of this curious work, I refer my readers to Borlase's Natural History, p. 398, exercised exercised a subordinate jurisdiction and presided in their inferior courts. But since there was an appeal from these inferior courts to the druidical, so, probably, there was an appeal from the cantreds to one court in Danmonium superior to all: And this must have been the regal or archidruidical court. " As there was an *Archdruid* in Gaul (fays Borlase) to preside in all cases of difficulty, importance, and solemnity; Ib, doubtless, in Britain—*whence the Gauls had their plan*—there was lodged the lame or the like authority, in one, or more superior Druids." But I am inclined to think that there was one supreme Druid.in every kingdom—since in most instances, the different kingdoms or states of Britain, were independent on each other; and, since the Druids had the principal management in every state, both as legislators and judges. According to Cæsar, and other ancient authors, there was an Archdruid—to whom appeals were made from the tribunals of the inferior judges, and who always "held an annual court at a fixed time, in some central situation. The chief residence of the Archdruid of Gaul, was at *Dreux,* in the *Pais Char-train,* in the very centre of Gaul. Here, on a consecrated spot, he held his court. Of the Britiso Archdruid's residence, Mr. Rowland thinks he has discovered some vestiges in the isle of Anglesea. But if we confine ourselves within the limits of Devonshire and Cornwall, and fix an archidruidical seat in the west, I lhould imagine that Drewsteington would be the most eligible spot. The very name of *Drewsteington* instantly determines its original appropriation to the Druids. Aud that this (a) " *town of the Druids upon the ri'ver Teign,'''* was the fevourite resort of the Druids, is evident from a great variety of druidical remains which the most incurious spectator must necessarily observe, in the neighbourhood of the town, and which will hereafter be described. The only remaining Cromlech in Devonlhire, marks thii spot as more peculiarly the scat of the Druids: And the Archdruid, perhaps, could not have chosen a more convenient place for his annual assembly. (A) "

Such, then, are my conjectures on the subject of our Danmonian government. Who our governors were, it would be vain to enquire. It would be fruitless to search for the names of the subordinate Chieftains, or of the cantred Druids; when the chronicled names of our Kings are, I conceive, for the most part, fabricated. Who our Kings were, the British chronicles pretend to tell us: yet if we look into remote antiquity, with a view of discovering the succession of our western Princes, we lhall find, perhaps, not a single record that merits our notice, in the light of an historical document.

That Brute, commencing his reign over the Britons in the year of the world two thousand eight Hundred and fifty-nine, assigned these western territories to his valorous companion Corinæus, as the reward of an astonishing victory over the giant Gogmagog, whom the latter precipitated down the Plymouth cliff, is not literally the language of truth. But the founder of the western Kingdom had numerous successors to share his honors: and, if, when facts are wanting, we are willing to seize on fable to supply the deficiency, we may contemplate for more than a thousand years, the imaginary Princes of Danmo *a) Dru-Jlcn-ton,* fays Borlase, *Druid-Jianes-ttrjin:* But if our author mean *Drcivjieignton* ill Devonshire, he is certainly mistaken in his etymology. In his observations, however, on the druidical traces to be found in the names of towns, houses, hills, and brooks, he is, unquestionably, right." All names that have *Drudau Dru, Druivydd, Diudicn, Dcrivyddon, Der-w,* and *Dar,* may be reckoned of Druid original: Thus *Bod-dr. den, Druid's-bmtfe, Rbied-druhb, nobilumDruidarum vadutn*—DrusTenton, Druid's-stones-town—*Gaon-deriu, tht Druid's-doivns—Tin-deriv. Druid's-bill." b)* " From the central situation of the Cromlech, (says Chappie) we might infer the fitness of the place for a druidical assizes; supposing that the present limits of this county were, then also, nearly the boundaries of a distinct province of druidical government in this western part gf Britain. For we learn

from Cæsar, (r) that the Druids of Gaul met annually in a place consecrated and appropriated to that purpose, on the confines of *Carnutum* (now *Cbartra)* then taken to be the middle of all Gaul; where people at variance resorted from all quarters to have their controversies and law-suits finally decided by those absolute judges, from whose sentence lay no appeal. From this, and Caesar's further testimony, concerning the origin of this discipline, which he tells us was supposed to have been first instituted in Britain, and from thence transferred to Gaul—whence, even then, persons desirous of being more perfectly instructed in it, took a voyage hither to be better informed concerning it-we may reasonably conclude, that the Druids, in their distribution of justice, as well here as in Gaul, took all-possible care to shorten the journies of the people obliged to attend their courts of judicature." Chappie's Description and Exegesis of the Drewsteington Cromlech i) Be Bello Callico. Lib. 6.

nium. nium. Yet the eye wanders with dissatisfaction and disgust over a long and dreary tract of time, which seems diversified only by chimeras. Contenting myself, therefore, with a few observations, on the reputed Rulers of the west, before the time of Csesar, I (hall quickly hasten to more interesting enquiries. The annalist informs us, with all the gravity of truth, that about the time of the prophet Samuel, Guendolen the daughter of our hero, enjoyed Danmonium as her paternal inheritance. The most remarkable of her successors were Heninus, who married a daughter of King Lear, and his son Cunedagius, who filled the throne at the time of the building of Rome; and the two brothers, Belinus and Brennus, to the first of whom were allotted Loegria, Cambria or Danmonium—to the second, all from the river Humber to Cathness in Scotland. To Belinus and Brennus is ascribed the demolition of Rome j and, what is rather remarkable with respect to the sacking that great city, there is only the difference of twenty years between the British Chronology and the Roman Fasti. But to memorize the fictitious actions of these Princes would be tedious. It was in the year three thousand nine hundred and forty-six, *(a)* that Britain, invaded by Julius Cæsar, began to experience the stiock of the Roman arms: and Theomantius, the second son of the famous British King Cassibelan, was, at this moment, Duke of Danmonium. SECTION III. *VIEW of the RELIGION of DANMONIUM in the BRITISH PERIOD.*

I. *Druidism the Religion of Danmonium—Its great Antiquity in this Iſland— evidently derived from the East, mt the Continent of Europe.—*II. *Its Doctrines—secret—popular.—*III. *Its Rites and Ceremonies.—*IV. *Its Temples.—*V. *Parallel between the Danmonians and the Persians—proving the Eastern Origin of the Danmonians—Contrary Opinions examined.—* VI. *The corrupt Religion of the Pbenicians—of the Creeks—of the Tribes from the neighbouring Continent.* THE earlier inhabitants of the island, in proportion as they were known to the nations around them, became, more and more, the objects of curiosity. The various singularities, that Ib strongly marked the Danmonians, must have stood forth prominent and bold, in contrast with the general European feature. Among these national peculiarities, the religion of Danmonium was also new: And so striking was its character of sanctity and wisdom, that it attracted the attention of the more learned and inquisitive among the Gauls, who were before unacquainted with the aboriginal islanders. The Celtic tribes from the Continent of Europe, could give Cæsar very little information respecting the Britons, except what related to their religion, which had been recently introduced into Gaul from Britain; but which was totally unknown in Germany, and other parts of the Continent. This religion, therefore, differed widely from the religion of Europe: We shall find that it bore a strong resemblance to the religion of Afia. It was Drnidilm: Aud, whether we consider its antiquity in Britain, its secret or popular doctrines, its rites and ceremonies, or its temples, we shall, on every view of the subject, perceive its eastern origin.

Mr. Carte (6) asserts, it seems, from Cæsar, " that the Druidical religion was from the most ancient times, the common religion of Britain, Gaul, and Germany; though Britain was most skilled in it:" Cæsar, however, says-the very reverse. Cæsar informs us, that the Druid religion was but very lately introduced into Gaul, from Britain; and, that in his time, the Gauls still went to Britain for instruction. He expressly fays, that the Germans had no Druids. So that Cæsar's report amounts to this—that Druidisin was the religion of Britain long before it was known in Gaul, and was established in (a) Richard, p. co. / (i) In justice to Mr. Carte, I should observe, that setting aside the *Pens afimnus* of antiquities, hi history is well written. The antiquarian part of his work, is, doubtless, full of error. But his mistakes and inconsistencies on so obscure a subject, would have merited a very slight censure, had ingenuity thrown over his Hypothesis an air of speciousnefs. I do not blame his decisive manner: For, amidst the darkest ambiguities, a writer, who is animated by hit subject, cannot always avoid deci *a. .`*

Gaul long before it was known in Germany. It seems to have been communicated *to* Germany about the time of Tiberius. We fee, then, contrary to Carte's opinion, that Britain did not receive its religion from the Continent of Europe': Whence we may infer, that it was not originally peopled from hence; but that, probably, it was peopled long before the western parts of Europe were inhabited. Dr. Borlase himself admits the evidence of Caesar, *(a)* to prove the seniority of druidisin in Britain. " I must observe (says our author, with great propriety and good fense) that none of the ancient authors deny what Cæsar advances: Strabo and Ponponius Mela, in their observations on the Druids, copy Cæsar as their best guide: Tacitus does not contradict him in any one point: *(b)* and, to silence our wonder how the Britons mould give an order of priesthood to their nearest neighbours the Gauls, Pliny, who is more circumstantial in descri. bing the rites of Druidisin than any other writer, asserts, that the Britons were so excessively devoted to all the mysteries of magic, that they might seem to have taught even the Persians themselves this art. *(c)* There is another circumstance worthy of notice in what Cæsar says—which is, that the institution of the Druids was maintained in greater purity and strictness in Britain than in Gaul; and that, when the Gauls were at a loss in any point relating to this discipline, their custom was to go over to Britain for their better information. " Does not this (fays Borlase, cautious as he is in advancing any thing new or unpopular) in a great measure confirm our ideas that the Gauls were taught this discipline by the Britons; and that the Britons, whenever any difficulty occurred, had recourse to the first fountain for instruction? The *Druid Priesthood,* then, was more ancient in Britain than either in Gaul or in Germany. Though we might vainly labour to ascertain the exact time of its appearance, yet we are assured that it had been established in Britain many centuries before the arrival of Cæsar. There were Druids in this island, remarkable for their antiquity, long before the times of Pythagoras, who lived six hundred years before Christ. It is asserted by an ancient writer, that the ' Druids were venerated for their philosophy more than a thousand years before Pythagoras had promulged his doctrines in Italy, *(d)* And Aristotle and Clemens Alexandrinus concur in asserting the high antiquity of the British priesthood. But, setting these authorities aside, that single passage in Cæsar, where a popular idea is said to have been founded on a tradition from the Druids, (?) sufficiently speaks to their antiquity. It is a reference, in Cæsar's time, to the Druids of the earlier ages. In the mean time, the great resemblance which the Druids bore to the Persian Magi, Gymnosophists, and Brachmans, isa strong argument in favor of their antiquity. And Borlase Is near the point of asserting, that such a conformity between islanders in the west, and the most remote nations in the east, " who do not appear (fays he) to have had the least communication since the dispersion," can only be accounted for by supposing the Britons to be a colony from the east, at the very time of the dispersion. But enough on this topic.

Let us consider the Druid religion. And first for its doctrines. It appears, that the British Druids, like the.Indian Gymnosophists, or the Persian Magi, had two sets of doctrines—the first, for the initiated—the second, for the people. That there is *one* GOD, the creator of heaven and earth, was a secret doctrine of the Brachmans. And the *nature* and *ferfeclion* of the Deity were among the Druidical Arcana, *(f)* Pomponius Mela confirms *a) Disciplina in Britannia reperta al que in Galliam tranjlata ejse, exisiimajur.* Druidisin was found in Britain and from thence translated into Gaul.

(b) The author of *La Relig. de Gaulois,* ingenuously confesses, that the Gauls had their religion from Britain. Vol. I. p. 13. (f) *Druidarum disciplina in nostra Britannia reperta, atqae inde in Galliam tranjlata ejse existimatur. Vnde Plinius cleganter declamat lib,* 30. *bis verbis: u Sed quid ego bac commemorem in arte oceanum quoque tranjgrejja, et ad natures inane pervecta f Brittania bodieque earn attonite celebrat tantis ceremoniis, ut ded'ijje Per/is mideri pojjit." Idem Julius Ca Jar affirmat in Epbemeridis: " Et nunc, qui di/igentius earn rem cognofcere volunt, plerumque Mo, difcendi causa, proficiscuntur."* Richard Mon. p. 12. *(d) Pberecydes, Pythagora preceptor, primus fublicavit Druidarum argumenta, pro anima immortalitate.* Hoffman's Dict. in verb.— *Cceterum cuilibet vel modke perjpicaci patebit, Druidas pbilo fopbatos plus mille annos antequam eruditio Pythagora; innotuijset in Italia.* Steph. Forcatulus de Gall. Imp. et Philof. p. 41. (?) Cæsar L. 6. p. 127. *(f)* Selden (on Drayton's Polyolbion) observes: " Although you may truly fay with Origen, that kefore our Saviour's time, *Britain* acknowledged not one true God; yet it comes as near to what they should confirms this account of Cæsar: *Druidas terra mundtque magnitudinem et sormam, motus cali et Jidcrum,* et quid Dii velint *scirc se profiteri.* And Lucan: *Solis nojfe Deos, et call numina*

vobis. That these ideas were derived from (a) Noah, I have scarcely a doubt: Xhey were brought into this island by the immediate descendants of those holy men, to whom only the secrets of Noah were communicated, and who, as consecrated to religion, were thus entrusted with the secrets of heaven. The imperishable nature of the foul was another doctrine of the Druids, which in its genuine purity, perhaps, was incommunicable to the vulgar. But the souVs immortality connected with many sensitive ideas, was generally preached to the people. It was with unvarying firmness that the Druids asserted.the immortality of the soul. And the universal influence of this doctrine on the conduct, excited the surprize of the Greeks and Romans. It was this, which inspired the soldier with courage in the day of battle; which animated the slave to die with his master, and the wife to (hare the fates of her husoand; which urged the old and the feeble to precipitate themselves from rocks, and the victim to become a willing sacrifice. And hence, the creditor postponed his debts till the next life; and the merchant threw letters for his correspondents into the funeral fires, to be thence remitted into the world of spirits! (A) The Druids believed also, that the soul, having left one earthly habitation, entered into another—that from one body decayed and turned to clay, it passed into another fresli and lively, and fit to perform all the functions of animal life. This was the doctrine of transmigration, maintained in common by the Druids and the Brachmans. (r) Sir William Jones describes a great empire—the empire of Iran; the religion of which was *Sabian; £0* called from the word *Saba,* that signifies a host, or more properly *the baft of heaven,* in the worlhip of which the Sabian ritual consisted. *Mahabeli* was the first monarch of Iran. His religion he was said to have received from the Creator, as yell as the orders established throughout his monarchy—religious, military, mercantile, and servile. These regulations were laid to be written in the language of the Gods, *(d)* The tenets of this religion were, that there was but

one God, pure and good—that the soul was immortal, and an emanation from the Deity—that it was for a season separated from the supreme Being, and confined to the earth to inhabit human bodies, but would return to the Divine Essence again. The purer sectaries of this religion maintained, that the worship of sire was merely popular; and that they appeal ed only to venerate that fun upon whose exalted orb they fixed their eyes, whilst they really humbled themselves before the supreme God. They were assiduous observers of the motions of the heavenly luminaries, and establislied artificial cycles, with distinct names, to indicate the periods, in which the should have done, or rather nearer than most of others, either Greek or Reman—as Caesar, Strabo, Lucan, and other authors might convince us. For, although Apollo, Mars, and Mercury, were worshipped among the *vulgar Cauls* j yet it appears that the Druids invocation was to one all healing and all saving Power! *a) A Chaldean* inscription was discovered some centuries ago, in Sicily, on a block of white marble. A Bishop of Lucera, who wrote on the subject, asserts: That the city of Palermo was founded by the Chaldeans, in the earliest ages of the world. The literal translation of this inscription is as follows: " During the time that Isaac, the son of Abraham, reigned in the valley of Damascus, and Esau, the son of Isaac, in Iduinea, a great multitude of Hebrews, accompanied by many of the people of Damascus, and many Phenicians, coming into this triangular island, took up their habitation in this most beautiful place, to which they gave the name of Panormus." The Bishop translates another Chaldean inscription, which is over one of the old gates of the city. This is extremely curious—u *There is no other God but one God. There is no other power but this fame God. There is no other conqueror but this lame God whom we adore.* The commander of this tower is Saphu, the son of Eliphas, the son of Esau, brother of Jacob, son of Isaac, son of Abraham. The name of the tower is Beyeh; and the name of the neighbouring tower is

Pharat." (A) See Borlasc's Antiquities, p. 98. (c) That the Druids believed in the immortality of the soul, and in its transmigration from one body to another, is not only affirmed by Cæsar, as we have seen, but by many ancient writers, Apflajiaj *rxs-vXeos Xtyua-i—hys* Strabo. And Lucan: Vobis sutorjbus, *umbra Non tacitas erebi feetes, ditijque prefandi*

Pallida regna petur.t—regit idem fpiritus artus

Qrbe alio lorga, canitis Ji cognita, vita. See also Val. Maximus and Diodorus.

(d) All the sculptures of Perscpolis are purely Sibian.

Vol. I. D feed fixed stars appeared to revolve. They are also said to have known the *secret sowers of fiature,* and thence to have acquired the reputation of magicians. Sects of these still remain in India, called Sufi, clad in woollen garments or mantles. In ancient times, every priesthood among the eastern nations had several species of sacred characters, which they used in their hierogrammatic writings, to render their religion more mysterious; whilst they preserved its written doctrines and precepts in such characters as none but their own order could understand. These sacred characters have been often noticed by Antiquarians, under the denomination of *Ogham, (a)* The Ogham characters were used by the priests of India and Persia, the Ægyptians and Phenicians, and the Druids of the British isles. Sir William Jones tells us, that the writings at Persepolis bear a strong resemblance to the Ogham—that the unknown inscriptions in the palace of Jemschid are in the same characters, and are, probably, sacerdotal and secret, or a sacerdotal cypher; and that the word *Ogham* is Sanscrit, and means " *mysterious knowledge."* That similar inscriptions are to be found in Ireland, is abundantly proved by Colonel Vallancey. But, the most extraordinary circumstance is, that the word *Ogham* still continues among the people of Indostan, Persia, and Ireland, with the fame lacred meaning annexed to it! The Druids not only concealed, in this manner, their secret tenets from the knowledge of the peo-

ple, but they often instructed their pupils by symbolical representations, with the fame view of involving their doctrines in mystery, and rendering them too dark for the vulgar apprehension. This mode of instruction was truly oriental. And to prove that the Druids were even refined in their allegories, the picture of Hercules Ogmius, as described by Lucian, need only be produced. (A) There is another evidence ot the symbolical learning of the Druids in *Basso Relievo;* discovered, some time since, over the door of the temple of Montmorillon, in Poictou. It is a lively representation of the several stages of life, at which the Druid disciples were gradually admitted into the mysteries of tlie Druid system, *(c)*

From these mysteries of the Druids, let us pass to their *popular* doctrines. Amidst the sublimer tenets of this priesthood, we have every where apparent proofs of their polytheism. And the groflhess of their religious ideas, as represented by lbme writers, is very inconsistent with that divine philosophy, which we have considered as a part of their character. These, however, were popular divinities, which the Druids ostensibly worshipped, and popular notions which they ostensibly adopted, in conformity with the prejudices of the vulgar mind. TheDruids well knew, that the common people were no philosophers. There is reason, also, to think that a great part of the idolatries I am about to mention, were not originally sandtioned by the Druids, but afterwards introduced by the Phenician colony. But it would be impossible to fay, how far the primitive Druids accommodated themselves to vulgar superstition, or to separate their exterior doctrines and ceremonies from the fables and absurd rites of subsequent times. Cæsar thus recounts the popular divinities. " *Deum maxime Mercurium colunt. Hujus sunt flurimasimulacra. Hunc omnium artium innjentorem serunt;-hunc niarum atque itinerum ducem ; hunc ad qiiastus pecunut mercatifrasque habere njim maximam arbitrantur. Post hunc, Apollinem, et Martem, et Jo"jem et Minervam. De his eandem fere quam reliquæ gentes*

habent opinionem—Apollinem (a) In ancient Punic Hogham signifies wisdom.

(b) Hercules, as there exhibited, and known by his usual ornaments; but instead of the gigantic body and fierce countenance given him by others, the Druids painted him, toLucian's great surprize, aged, bald, decrepid: and to his tongue were fastened chains of gold and amber, which drew along a multitude of persons,-hose ears appeared to be fixed to the other end of those chains. And one of the Druid philosophers thus explains the picture to Lucian. " We do not agree with the Greeks in making Mercury the God of eloquence. According to our system, this honor is due only to Hercules, because he so far surpasses Mercury in power. We paint him advanced in age, because eloquence exerts not all her most animated powers but in the mouths of the aged. The link there is, between the tongue of the eloquent and the ears of the aged, justifies the rest of the representation. By understanding his history in this fense, we neither dishonour Hercules, nor depart from the truth: For we hold it indisputably true, that he succeeded in all his noble enterprizes, captivated every heart, and subdued every brutal passion, not by the strength of his arms (for that was impossible) but by the powers of wisdom, and by the sweetness of his persuasion." See Boilase's Antiquities, p. 100. (r) There is a plate of it in Montfaucon's Supplement, torn. 2, p. *221.* and in the Religion de Gaules, vol. 1, p. 144, And Borlase has very satisfactorily explained it— See his Antiquities, p.101, *toi,* 103. *morbas taorbos depeHere—Minervam operum at que artificiorum initia transdere—Jovem imperium tæiestium tenere—Martem bella regere."* (a) The origin of the British Gods, has been generally attributed to the Phœnicians or Canaanites. The God whom the Romans compared to *Jupiter,* was worshipped by the name of *Taram* or *Taramis,* and of *Tbor—* both which names signify *the Thunderer,* in Phenician. The God whom the Romans compared to *Mercury,* was worshipped by the name of *Teutates* or *Tbeutates,* or

Taautos or *Thoth*—the Phenician name for the *son of Misor.* The God whom the Romans compared to *Mars,* was worshipped under the name of *Hizzus* or *He/us,* and also by the name or *Cham* or *Camu* or *Camo*—called by the Romans *Camulus.* He was, also, called *Hues*—which is another name for *Bacchus* or *Bar-chus*—that is, the *son of Chus.* The Greeks adopted the *Hues* in the rites or orgies of Bacchus. It is of Phenician origin, and signifies *Fire I* And, as such, *Bacchus* was worshipped! The God whom' the Romans compared to *Apollo* was worshipped by the name of *Bel-ain,* or, as the Romans called him, *Belinus.* He was, also, called *Bel-atre-cadrus,* from the Phenician, *Bel-atur-cares,* signifying, *Sol AJj'yrite Deus.* The God whom the Romans compared to Diana, was *Belisama:* It is aPhenician word, signifying, the *Slueen ofbea'ven.* The God whom the Romans compared to Minerva, was worshipped by the name of *Onca, Onma,* or *Onvana*; the Phenician word for that Goddess. Tlie God whom the Romans compared to Venus, was worshipped by the name of *Andraste*—the *Assart e* of the Phenicians. The other Gods of the Britons were the *Pluto, Proserpine, Ceres,* and *Hercules* of the Romans,. Of these divinities the Druids had symbolical representations: A cube was the symbol of Mercury, and the (6) oak of Jupiter. But it would be a vain attempt to enumerate their Gods. In the eye of the vulgar they deified every object around them. They worshipped the spirits of the mountains, the vallies, and the rivers. Every rock and every spring were either the instruments or the objects of adoration. The moonlight vallies of Danmonium were filled with the faery people: And its numerous rivers were the resort of Genii. The fiction of Faeries is supposed to have been brought, with other fantastic extravagancies of a like nature, from the eastern nations, whilst the European christians were engaged in the holy war: Such, at least, is the notion of an ingenious writer, who thus expresses himself: " Nor were the monstrous embellishments of enchantments, the invention of romancers; but formed upon eastern

tales, brought thence by travellers from their crusades and pilgrimages, which, indeed, have a cast peculiar to the wild imagination of the eastern people." *(c)* That Faeries, in particular, came from the east, we *are* assured by that learned orientalist, M. Herbelot, who tells us, that the Persians called the Faeries *Peri,* and the Arabs *Genies;* that, according to the eastern fiction, there is a certain country inhabited by Faeries called *Ginniftian,* which answers to our *Faeryland* and that the ancient romances of Persia are full ot *Peri* or Faeries, *(d)* Mr.Warton,() in his observations on Spenser's Faery-queen, is decided in his opinion, that the Faeries came from the east: But he justly remarks, that they were introduced into this country long before the period of the Crusades. The race of Faeries, he informs us, were established in Europe, in very early times. But " *not universally,"* soys Mr. Warton. The Faeries were confined to the *north* of Europe—to the *ultima Thule*—to the *British isles*—to the *di-vifis orbeBritannis.* They were unknown, at this remote æra, to the Gauls or the Germans. And they were probably familiar to the vallies of Scotland and Danmonium, when Gaul and Germany were yet unpeopled either by real or imaginary beings. The belief, indeed, of such invisible agents assigned to different parts of nature, prevails, at this very day, in Scotland and in Devonshire and Cornwall—regularly transmitted from the remotest antiquity to the present times, and totally unconnected with the spurious romance, of the Crusader or the Pilgrim. Hence thole superstitious notions, now existing in our western villages, where *(f)* the *Spriggian* are still believed to delude benighted *(a)* Lib. 6.. *(/)* Their affected veneration for the oak, and even the oak-misletoe, is well known. *(c)* Supplement to the Trans. Pref. to Jarvis's Don Quixotte. *(d)* Herbelot tells us, that there is'an Arabian book, entitled *" Pieces de corail amaffecs fur ce qui regarde le* Ginnes, c» Genies." But, above all, lee the Arabian Night's Entertainments. (e) See vWarton's Obfervat. on Spenser, vol. i. p. 64. *(f)* " That the Druids..orfliipped rocks, stones, and

fountains, and imagined them inhabited, and actuated by *divine intelligences oj a loiuer rank,* may be plainly inferred from their stone-monuments. These inferior deities, the Cornish call *Spriggian,* or Spirits; which answer to *Genii* or *Faeries:* And the vulgar in Cornwall still discourse of their *Spriggian,* as of real beings; and pay them a kind fif.veneration." Borlafs's Antiquities, p. 1C7. Vol. I. Di-travellers, travellers, to discover hidden treasures, to influence the weather, and to rule the winds. —" This, then, fays our excellent critic, in the most decisive manlier—This, fays WARTON, STRENGTHENS THE HYPOTHESIS OF THE»NOTHERN PARTS OF EUROPE

Seino Peopled By Colonies From The East! " The inhabitants of Shetland *(a)* and the isles, pour libations of milk or beer through a holed stone, in honor to the spirit *Brvwny*—and I doubt not but the Danmonii were accustomed to sacrifice to the same spirit; since the Cornish and the Devonians on the borders of Cornwall, invoke, to this day, the spirit Browny, on the swarming of their bees, *(b)* With respect to rivers, it is a certain fact that the primitive Britons paid them divine honors. Even now, in many parts of Devonshire and Cornwall, the vulgar may be said to worship brooks and wells, to which they resort at stated periods, performing various ceremonies in honor of those consecrated waters. And the Highlanders, to this day, talk with great respect of the genius of the sea; never bathe in a fountain, lest the elegant spirit that resides in it should be olfended and remove; and mention not the water of rivers without prefixing to it the name of *excellent, (c)* And in one of the western islands, the inhabitants retained the custom to the close of the last century, of making an annual sacrifice to the genius of the ocean, *(d)* That at this day, the inhabitants of India deify their principal rivers, is a well-known fact: the waters of the Ganges possess an uncommon sanctity. And the modern Arabians (like the Islimaelites of old) concur with the Danmonii, in their reverence of springs and fountains. Even the names of the Arabian and Danmonian.tvells have a striking correspondence. We have *the e) singing-well, Ot the white fountain:* and there are springs with similar names in the deserts of Arabia, *(s)* Perhaps, the veneration of the Danmonii for fountains and rivers, may be accepted as no trivial proof to be thrown into the mass of circumstantial evidence, in favor of their eastern original. That the Arabs, in their thirsty deserts, mould even adore their " wells of springing water," need not excite our surprize. But we may justly wonder at the inhabitants of Devonshire and Cornwall thus worshipping the Gods of numerous rivers, and never-failing brooks, familiar to every part of Danmonium.

The Druid rites come next to be considered. The principal times of devotion among the Druids, were either midday or midnight. The officiating Druid was cloathed in a white garment that swept the ground. On his head he wore the tiara. He had the anguinum or serpents egg, as the ensign of his order: his temples were encircled with a wreath of oak-leaves; and he waved in his hand the magic rod.(g) As to the Druid sacrifice we have various *(a)* See-Martin,,p. 391.

() The Cornifli cry, *Browny! Brawny!* from a belief, that this invocation will prevent the return of the bees into tlieir former hive, and make them pitch, and form a new colony. (c) See Macpherson's Introduction to the History of Great-Britain and Ireland, p. 163, 164. *(d)* See Harris's Western Islands, Edit. 2. p. 28, 29. (*e) Fen-tergan, the fountain of the singers, thesinging-well,* or *the white fountain.* Dr. Pryce. *(f)* See Arabian Nights Entertainment — a *genuine* work. g) Among the Druid ceremonies, the cutting of the *mifietoe* should be noticed. One of Mr. Urban's correspondents mentions " a gentleman in the neighbourhood of Penzance, in the western part of Cornwall, who has been curious in making such a collection of antiquities, as chance or his endeavours could furnish him with. Among other things in this cabinet (fays the correspondent) I particularly distinguilhetl a piece of gold in the form of a crescent, supposed, I think upon suf-

ficient authority, to have been worn always by the Druid when he performed the ceremony of cutting the misletoe. Although the religious worship of the Druids was polluted with human sacrifices, yet it appears that these extreme propitiations of the Deity were resorted to only upon very extraordinary occasions, such, for instance, as when an invasion, or their darling liberty, was threatened. For we learn that many of the rites, which the crafty policy of that order of priesthood had imposed upon the ignorance and credulity of the people, were yet innocent in their nature, and well enough adapted to the rude notions of uncultivated life. The power of healing, which was found to reside in herbs, could not fail to attract the notice of the Druids, and to promote their interests by an obvious delusion. The natural effects, which resulted from their application to the human body, were by them ascribed to celestial influences and supernatural interpositions: but, when the herb was cut or gathered, the presence and consecration of a Druid were necessary, without which every hope of relief was vain; nor did any impious patient ever dare to provoke the anger of the gods by an unauthorized appeal to their interference. Among other" herbs or plants, the misletoe, from its near affinity to the oak, that principal object of the British worship, was held in peculiar veneration. No profane hand could presume to cut the sacred misletoe j nor were all times and seasons proper for the per
J formance various and contradictory representations. It is certain, however, that the Druids offered human victims to their gods. And there was an awful mysteriousness in the original Druid sacrifice. Having descanted on the human sacrifices of various countries, Mr. Bryant informs us, that among the nations of Canaan, *the viBims 'were chosen in a peculiar manner.* Their own children and whatsoever was nearest and dearest to them, were thought the most worthy offerings to their god! The *Carthaginians,* who were a colony from Tyre, carried with them the religion of their mother country, and instituted the

fame worship in the parts where they settled. It consisted in the adoration of several deities, but particularly of *Kronus,* to whom they offered human sacrifices, the most beautiful victims they could select. Parents offered up their own children as dearest to themselves, and therefore the more acceptable to the deity: They sacrificed " the fruit of their body for the sin of their soul." *Kronus* was an oriental divinity—thf *god of light and fire;* and, therefore, always worshipped with some reference to that element. He was the *Moloch* of the Tyrians and Canaanites, and the *Melecb* of the east. *Philo Byblius* tells us, that in some of these sacrifices there was *a particular mystery,* in consequence of an example which had been set these people by the god Kfov©-, who, in a time of distress, *offered up his only fin to his father ©Df«»of.* When a person of distinction brought an only son to the altar and slaughtered him by way of atonement, to avert any evil from the people—his was properly the *mystical sacrifice,* imitated from Kfo©-; or from Abraham offering up his only Ion Isaac. Mr. Bryant is of opinion, that this mystical sacrifice was a typical representation of the great vicarial sacrifice that was to come. At first, there is no doubt but the Druids offered up their human victims, witli the fame sublime views. The Druids maintained, *quod pro vita hominis nisi uita hominis rcddatur, non posse aliter dcorum imntortalium numen placari.* («) This mysterious doctrine is not of men, but of God I It evidently points out The One Great Sacrifice For The Sins Of The Wholk World! But after the Phenician colonies had mixed with the primeval Britons, this degenerated priesthood seem to have delighted in human blood: and their victims, though sometimes beasts, were oftener men. And not only criminals and captives, but their very disciples were inhumanly sacrificed on their altars; whilst some transfixed by arrows, others crucified in their temples, some instantly stabbed to the heart, and others impaled in honor of the gods, bespoke, amidst variety of death, the most horrid proficiency in the science of murder.

But the druid holo-caust, that monstrous image of straw, connected and sliaped by wicker-work, and promiscuously crouded with wild beasts and human victims, was, doubtless, the most infernal sacrifice, that was ever invented by the human imagination. *(b)* These cruelties were certainly not attached to primitive druidisms they formance of this rite: for so did the superstition of the people receive it. But *-when the moon bad. passed herstrj! quarter,* a Druid, specially appointed, arrayed in white, a golden hook in his hand, *a. golden crescent fastened upon kit garment,* approached the plant, and performed the ceremony of cutting, amidst the concourse and acclamations of the surrounding multitude. The hook or knife was of gold, that the misletoe might escape the pollution of every baser metal; and the crescent of gold represented, by a single image, thaf time of the moon before which it was not lawful to cut the mystic plant. This very Angular piece of antiquity was discovered by a common labourer in turning up the ground near Penzance; and saved from rustic ignorance, which would have sold it for old gold, by the good fortune and virtu of John l'rice, csq. of Chuane, in the neighbourhood of that town, in whose cabinet it remains for the inspection of the curious. The plate of gold from whence it is fashioned is extremely thin, much too thin for the superficial dimensions, probably on account of the great scarcity of metal in those days, whicli by the bye, if any doubt could be entertained, would be an additional proof of its original designation. With respect to ifs figure, the best description I can propose to the reader is, by referring him to the moon, its prototype, at that period of its increase when, as I before stated, the ceremony of cutting the misletoe was performed; its size and weight (Its weight very trifling) being such as to make it an ornament, and not an incumberancei Upon the garment. Gentleman's Magazine, vol. 61, p. 34. (a) Cæsar, p. 124.

(6) In an ode written on the isle of Mann, to the memory os biihopWilson, at the request of Dr. Wilson his fen, and Mrs. Macaulay Graham, the author thus describes the Druids and their (acrinces: 1 "

" Ye fleeting (hapes, I cried,
Amidst these glooms in pity glide,
Fpr, here he joy'd to rove
they are to be ascribed to the Phenician colonists, of a subsequent period. Among the Druid ceremonies, may be reckoned also the *turnings* of the body, during the times of worship. The numerous *round monuments* in Danmonium, (a few of which will be described in the next section) were formed for the purpose of this mysterious rite. In several of the Scottish isles, at this day, the vulgar never approach " the fire hallowing karne," without walking three times round it from east to west, according to the course of the sun. The Druids probably turned sunways, in order to bless and worship their gods; and the contrary way, when they intended to curse and destroy their enemies. The first kind of turning has been called the *deifol*: the second the *tuaphol.* Tacitus alludes to the latter in a very remarkable passage: *Druidatjue circum preces diras, fublatis ad cælum manibus, fundtntes, ncvitate ajpeflus peratlere milites.* The Roman soldiers, we fee, were terrified by the novelty of this rite—a plain proof that it was unknown to those countries which had been subjected to the Roman yoke. The holy fires of the Druids may also deserve our notice. We have, at this day, traces of the fire-worship of the Druids, in several customs both of the Devonians and the Cornish: But, in Ireland, we may still see the holy fires, in all their solemnity. The Irish call the month of May, *bel-tine,* or fire of Belus; and the first of May, *la-bel-tine,* or the day of Belus's fire. In an old Irisli glossary, it is mentioned, that the Druids of Ireland used to light two solemn fires every year; through which all four-footed beasts were driven, as a preservative against contagious distempers. The Irish have this custom at the present moment: they kindle the fire in their milking-yards—men, women, and children, pass through, or leap over it; and their cattle are driven through the flames of the burning straw, on *the first of May.* And,

in the month of November, they have also, their fire-feasts; when, according to the custom of the Danmonian as well as the Irish Druids, the hills were enveloped in flame. Previously to this solemnity, (on the eve of November) the fire in every private house was extinguished: Hither, then, the people were obliged to resort, in order to rekindle it. The ancient Persians named the

In elder times, when mystic strains
Echoed through consecrated fanes,
And rites of magic charm'd the reverential grove.
Who now, while memory views in tears
The curtain'd scene of former years,
Shall guard these dimwood rocks;
Where Genii, oft, on sounding wings,
Flutter'd, at evening, o'er the springs
, That lav'd the wreathing roots of yon fantastic oaks?
Who now shall join the minstrel's lay,
While glitter to the full moon's ray
Their high-strung harps of gold;
Or, who survey the sweeping pall
Of bards, amid the festal hall,
The Druid's floating pomp and hoary seers of old?
Who now, where, stain'd with sacred blood,
The central oak o'ertops the wood,
Shall see the victim laid
Shivering—on the dark slirine—and pale,
As midnight stills the spectred vale,
And, lifted for the stroke, the lightning of the fclade?
What! dost thou mourn the vanisli'd rite
That gave to horror the pale night,
And shook the blasted wood;
While, as the victim's dying cries »
Announc'd the *human sacrifice,*
Scar'd at the infernal scene, the moon went down In blood? " Sec bishop Wilson's works, quarto edition, vol. i, p. 137, appendix. The author well remembers, that after passing a truly philosophic hour, with Mrs. Macaulay antl Dr. Wilson, at Alfred House" in Bath, he proceeded to Oxford, where, at Ch. .Ch. he wrote the ode in question, on the evening of his arrival, and immediately dispatched it to the Bath printer j as Wilson's works, he understood, were

almost ready for publication..' month month of *November, Adur,* or *fire. Adur,* according to Richardson, was the angel presiding over that element: in consequence of which, on the ninth, his name-day, the country blazed all around with flaming piles; whilst the magi, by the injunction of Zoroaster, visited, with great solemnity, all the temples of fire throughout the empire; which, on this occasion,, were adorned and illuminated in a most splendid manner. Hence our British illuminations in November had probably their origin. It was at this season, ' that *Baal Sambam* called the souls to judgment, which, according to their deserts, were assigned to re-enter the bodies of men or brutes, and to be happy or miserable during their next abode on the earth. But the punishment of the wicked, the Druids taught, might be obliterated by sacrifices to Baal. The sacrifice of the black sheep, therefore, was offered up for the fouls of the departed, and various species of charms (a) exhibited.

Baal. (a) The primitive christians, attached to their pagan ceremonies, placed the feast of All-fouls on the La Samon, or the second day of November. Even now, the peasants in Ireland assemble on the vigil of La Samon, with flicks and clubs, going from house to house, collecting money, breadcake, butter, cheese, eggs, &c. for the feast; repeating verses in honor of the solemnity, and calling for the War *Jheep.* Candles are sent from house to house, and lighted up on the Samon, (the next day). Every house abounds in the best viands the master can afford: apples and nuts are eaten in great plenty; the nutshells are burnt; and from the ashes many strange things are foretold. Hempfeedis sown by the maidens, who believe that, if they look back, they (hall fee the apparition of their intended husbands. The girls make various efforts to read their destiny: they hang a smock before the fire at the close of the feast, and sit up all night concealed in a corner of the room, expecting the apparition of the lover to come down the chimney and turn the sinpck: they throw a ball of yarn out of the window, and wind

it on the reel within, convinced that if they repeat the pater-noster backwards, and look at the ball of yarn without, they shall then also see his apparition. Those who celebiate this feast, have numerous other rites derived from the Pagans. They dip for apples in a tub of water, and endeavour to bring one up in their mouths: they catch at an apple when stuck on at one end of a kind of hanging beam, at the other extremity of which is fixed a lighted candle; and that with their moutiis only, whilst it is in a circular motion; having their hands tied behind their backs. A learned correspondent, (whose name it would ill become me to mention in this place, but whose patronage I shall be proud to acknowledge hereafter) thus writes from Ireland: " There is no sort of doubt but that Baal and fire was a principal object of the ceremonies and adoration of the Druids. The principal seasons of these, and of their feasts in honor of Baal, were new-year's day, when the fun began visibly to return towards us: this custom is not yet at an end, the country people still burning out the old year and welcoming the new, by fires lighted on the tops of hills, and other high places. The next season was the month of May, when the fruits of the earth begun is the eastern countries to be gathered, and the first fruits of them consecrated to Baal, or to the *fun,* whose benign influence had ripened them; and I am almost persuaded that the dance round the may-pole in that month, is a faint image of the rites observed on such occasions. The next great festival was on the twenty-first of June, when the fun, being in Cancer, first appears to go backwards and leave us. On this occasion, the *Baalim* used to call the people together, and to light fires on high places, and to cause their sons and their daughters, and their cattle, to pass through the fire, calling upon Baal to bless them, and not to forsake them. This is still the general practice in Ireland; nor, indeed, in any country are there more Cromlechs, or proofs of the worship of Baal or the sun, than in that kingdom; concerning which, I can give you a tolerable account, having been, myself, an eye-wit-

ness to this great festival in June. But 1 must first bring to your recollection the various places in Ireland, which still derive their names from Baal, such as Baly-shannon, Bal-ting-las, Bal-carras, Belfast, and many more. Next I must premise, that there are in Ireland a great number of towers, which are called Fire-towers, of the most remote antiquity, concerning which there js no certain history, their construction being of a date prior to any account of the country. Being at a gentleman's house, about tRirty miles west of Dublin, to pass a day or two, he told us, on the 21st of June, we sliould fee an odd sight, at midnight. Accordingly, at that hour, he conducted us out upon the top of his house, where, in a few minutes, to our great astonishment, we saw fires lighted on all the high places round, some nearer and some more distant: We had a pretty extensive view, and I should suppose, might see near fifteen miles each way. There were many heights in this extent, and on every height was a sire: I counted not less than forty. We amused ourselves with watching them, and with betting which hill would be lighted first. Not long after, on a more attentive view, I discovered shadows of people near the fire, and round it: and every now and then, they quite darken'd it. I enquired the reason of this, and what they were about? and was immediately told, they were not only *dancing round,* but *passing through the fire* ; for that it was the. custom of the country, on that day, to make their families, their sons and their daughters, and ihtir cattle, *pas: through the fire,* without which they could expect no fugeess in their dairies, nor in the crops, that year.

I bowed, *Baal-fambaim,* a Phenician appellation of the god of Baal, in Irish signifies the *planet of the fun. Meni* is an appellation of the fame deity. " Ye are they that forget my holy mountain (fays Isaiah) that prepare a table for Gad, and furnisti the drink-offering unto Meni.'v According to Jerom and several others, Gad signifies *fortune,* or good-fortune, and, in this fense, is used in the nth verse of the 30th chapter of Genesis. Those passages in Jeremiah, where the prophet marks the superstition of the Jews, in *making cakes for the Slueen of heaven,* are very similar to this of Isaiah. At this very day we discover vestiges of the festival of the fun, on the *eve of All-fouls.* As, at this festival, the Pagans " ate the sacrifices of the dead"— so our villagers, on the eve of All-fouls, bum nuts and shells, to *fortune,* and pour out libations of ale to *Meni.* The Druids, who were the Magi of the Britons, had an infinite number of rites in common with the Persians. One of the chief functions of the eastern magi, was divination: And Pomponius Mela tells us, that'our Druids possessed the fame art. There was a solemn rite of divination among the Druids, from the fall of the victim and convulsion of his limbs, or the nature and position of his entrails. But the British priests had various kinds of divination. By the number of criminal causes, and by the increase or diminution of their own order, they predicted fertility or scarceness. From the neighing or prancing of white horses, harnessed to a consecrated chariot— from the turnings or windings of a hare let loose from the bosom of the diviner (with a variety of other ominous appearances or exhibitions) they pretended to determine the events of futurity. Of all creatures, however, the serpent exercised, in the most curious manner, the invention of the Druids. To the famous *Anguinum* they attributed high virtues. The *Anguinum* or Serpent'segg, was a congeries of small shakes rolled together, and incrusted with a (hell, formed by the saliva or viscous gum or troth of the mother-serpent. This egg, it seems, was tossed into the air by the hissings of its dam; and, before it fell again to the earth (where it would be defiled) it was to be received in the fagus, or sacred vestment. The person who caught the egg, was to make his escape on horseback; since the serpent pursued the ravifher of its young, even to the brink of the next river, (a) Pliny, from whom this account is taken, proceeds with an enumeration of other absurdities relating to the Anguinum. This *Anguinum* is, in Britilh, called *Glain-neider,* or the Serpent of Glass: And the fame superstitious reverence which the Danmonii universally paid to the *Anguinum,* is still discoverable in some parts of Cornwall. (4) Mr. Lhuyd informs us, that the Cornish retain variety of charms, and have still, towards the Land's-end, the amulets of *Maen Magal* and *Glatn-neidr*—which latter they call a *Melprev,* and have a charm for the snake to make it, when they have found one asleep, and stuck a hazel wand in the centre of her spiræ." Camden fells us, that " in most part of Wales, and throughout all Scotland, and Cornwall, it is an opinion of the vulgar, that about Midsummer-eve, (though in the time they do not all agree) the snakes meet in companies; and that by joining heads together and hissing, a kind of bubble is formed, which the rest, by continual hissing, blow on till it passes quite through the body; when it immediately hardens and resembles a glass ring, which, whoever finds, sliall prosper in all his undertakings. The rings, thus generated, are called *Gle'mu Nadroeth,* or Snake-stones. They are small glass amulets, commonly about half as wide as our finger-rings, but much thicker, of a green color usually, though sometimes blue, and waved 'with red and white." Carew lays, that " the country-people, in Cornwall, have a persuasion, that the snakes breathing upon a hazel-wand, produce a stone-ring of blue color, in which there appears the yellow figure of a snake, and that beasts bit and envenomed, being given some water to drink, wherein this stone has been infused, will perfectly recover of the poison." *(c)* From the animal the Druids passed to the vegetable world; and there, also, displayed their powers, whilst, by the charms of the miiletoe, the selago and the samolus, they

I bowed, and recognized the god *Baal.* This custom is chiefly preserved among the Roman Catholics, whose bigotry, credulity, and ignorance, has made them adopt It from the ancient Irish, as a tenet of the christian religion. The Protestants do not observe it: But it was the universal custom in Ireland, before Christianity, (a) Lib. 29, c. 3.
b) In his Letter, dated March 10, 1701, to Rowland, p. 342. *c)* See Carew's Survey, p. 22. Mr. drew had a stone-ring, of this kind, in his possession: And the person who gave it him avowed, that " he himself saw apaitof the stick sticking in it"— but " *ptnei wtborcmJit/*jet"— says Mr. Carew. prevented .prevented or repelled disease, and every species of misfortune. They made all nature, indeed, subservient to their magical art; and rendered even the rivers and the rocks prophetic. From the undulation or bubbling of water, stirred by an oak branch or magic wand, they foretold events that were to come. This superstition of the Druids, js even now retained in the western counties. To this day, the Cornish have been accustomed to consult their famous well, at *Modern,* or rather the *spirit* of the well, respecting their futur/e destiny. " Hither (says Borlase) come the unealy, impatient, and superstitious j and by dropping pins or pebbles into the water, and by shaking the ground round the Ipring, so as to raise bubbles from the bottom, at a certain time of the year, moon, and day, endeavour to remove their uneasiness: Yet the supposed responses serve equally to encreafe. the gloom of the melancholy, the suspicions of the jealous, and the passion of the enamoured. The Castalian Fountain, and many others among the Grecians, was supposes to be of a prophetic nature. By dipping a fair mirror into a well, the Patræans of Greece received, as they supposed, some notice os ensuing sickness or health, from the: various figures portrayed upon the surface. The people of Laconia cast into a pool, sacred to Juno, cakes of breadcorn: If the cakes funk, good was portended: If they swam, something dreadful was to eusue. Sometimes, tlie superstitious threw three stones into the water; and formed their conclusions from the several turns they made in sinking." The Druids were, likewise, able to communicate, by consecration, the most portentous virtues to rocks and stones, which could determine the succession of princes or the fate 9s empires. To the Rocking or (c)Logan-stone, in particular, they had recourse to confirm their authority, either as prophets or judges, pretending that its motion was miracu-

lous.

In what consecrated places or temples tiesc religious rites were celebrated, seems to V)e the next enquiry: And, it appears, that they were, for the most part, celebrated in the midst of groves. The mysterious silence of an ancient w &od, diffuses even a shade of horror over minds that are yet superior to superstitious credulity. The majestic gloom, therefore, of their consecrated oaks, must have imprest the less informed multitude with every sensation of awe that might be necessary to the support of their religion, and the dignity of the priesthood. The religious wood was generally situated on the top of a hill or a mountain; where the Druids erected their fanes and their altars. The Temple was seldom any other than a rude circle of rock, perpendicularly raised. An artificial pile of large flat stone, in general, composed the altar: And the whole religious mountain was usually enclosed by a low mound, to prevent the intrusion of the profane. Among the primæval people os the east, altars were inclosed by groves of trees; and these groves consisted of plantations of *oat*. Abram passed through the land unto the place of bichem —unto the *oat* of Moreh: And the Lord appeared unto Abram; and there he builded an altar unto the Lord, who appeared-unto him beside the oak of Moreh. *(b)* That particular places and temples in Danmonium, were appropriated to particular deities, is an unquestionable fact. Borlase tells us, that the old British appellation of the Cassiterides or Scilly Iilands, was *Sulieh* or *SyUeh*—which signifies *rocks consecrated to the sun.* (r) This answers to the temples of Iran, which were dedicated to the iiin and the planets: And the sacred ceremonies pf Iran are represented by sculptures, in the ruined city of Jemschid.(rf) *(a)* Of these Logan-stones, we have several yet remaining in Devonstiire, which I mail notice hereafter. *(t)* In Babylon, the oak was sacred to Baal.

(c) Of these islands, the British name was Sullih, signifying Jfar *nets dedicated to the fun.* Thus *St. Michael's Mount* was originally called Diksul, *ot the hill*

dedicated to the fun. And the vast flat rocks, common in the Scilly Isles, particularly *atPcninis, Kam Ich, Penlch, Karn-ivaveJ*; but, above all, the enormous rock on *Salakee* Downs, formerly the floor of a great temple, are no improbable arguments that they might have had the fame dedication, and so have given name to these islands. Nor is it an unprecedented thing to find an island, in this climate, dedicated to the fun. Diodorus Siculus, B. 3. speaking of a Northern Island, over against the Celtæ, says: " It was dedicated to Apolio, who frequently conversed with the inhabitants: And they had a hrge grove and temple of a round form, to which the priests resorted, to sing the praises of Apollo." And there can be no doubt but this was one of the British Islands, and the Priests, Druids. See Bodafe's Ancient and present State of the Isles of Scilly, p. 59, 60. See, also, his Antiquities of Cornwa.ll, B. 2. C. 17. *(d)* Cooke, in his enquiry into the Patriarchal and Druidital religion, fays: " Not to lay any greater stress than needs, upon the evidence of the affinity of words with the Hebrew arid Phcnician; the multitude of *altars* and *pillars,* or *terns les,* set up in the ancient patriarchal way of worship throughout England, Ireland, Scotland, and the islands, form a conclusive argument, that an oricnjal colony must have been very early introduced."

Vol. I. E And And a number of places in Danmonium still preserve in their names, the lasting memorials of the British deities. In *Tresadarn*, we have the *town* or *house of Saturn*—in *Nansadarn*, the *Valley* of *Saturn*. And many of the enormous rocks, which rife with peculiar grandeur in those wild places, were undoubtedly appropriated to the fire-worship of the God. We have, also, places in Danmonium, which retain the names of Mars and of Mercury, as *Tremer*, the *town of Mars,* and *Gun-Mar'r,* and *Kelli-Mar'r,* the *Downs* and the *Grove of Mercury.* It was in thePhenician age, the cormpted age of Druidifm, that temples were erected to *Belifama,* or *the 2(uecn of heaven,* both in the metropolis of the island, («) and in the chief city of Danmonium (A); that

a temple was consecrated to *Onca,* at Bath(s); and that sacred buildings were probably frequented at the *Start-point,* by the votaries of *Aftarte,* and at the promontory of *Hertland,* by the worshippers of *Hercules.*

From all those views of the Druid religion, I have no doubt but it derived its origin immediately from *Asia.* Dr. Borlase has drawn a long and elaborate parallel between the Druids and Persians; where he has plainly proved, that they resembled each other, as strictly as possible, in every particular of religion. It was the sublime doctrine of the primitive Druids of Danmonium, that the Deity was not to be imaged by any human figure: And the Magi of Persia, before and long after Zoroaster, admitted no statues into their temples. The Druids worsiiipped, indeed, the whole expanse of heaven; which they represented by their circular temples: And the Persians held, that the whole round of heaven was their Jupiter. From all their monuments that remain, it appears, that the Druids never admitted of covered temples for the worship of their Gods: And the ancient Persians performed all the offices of their religion in the open air. Both the Druids and the Persians worshipped, their God on the tops of the mountains. The Persians worssiipped the serpent, as the symbol of their god Mithras, or the fun: And from their veneration for the Anguinum, and other circumstances, we may conclude, that the Druids paid divine honors to the serpent. The Persians maintained, that their god Mkhras was born of a rock; beside other absurdities of this nature: And the rock-worsliip of the Druids is sufficiently known. The Druids maintained the transmigration of the soul; and the Persians held the fame doctrine. As to the priesthood, and the ceremonials of religion, the Druids, and the Persian Magi, were of the noblest order in the state: The Druids were ranked with the British Kings; and the Magi with the Kings of Persia. The Druid Priest was clcathed in white; the holy vesture, called the Sagus, was white; the sacrificial bull was white; the oracular horses were white. In like manner the Persian

Magus was cloathed in white; the horses of the Magi were white; the King's robes were white; and so were the trappings of his horses. The Druids wore sandals: so also did the Persians. The Druids sacrificed human victims: so did the Persians. Ritual washings and purifications were alike common to the Druids and Persians. The Druids had their festal fires, of which we have still instances in these western parts of the island: and the Persians had also their festal fires, at the winter solstice, and on the 9th of March. The holy fires were alike familiar to the Druids and the Persians. The Druids used the holy fire as an antidote against the plague or the murrain in cattle: and the Persians placed their sick before the holy fire, as of great and healing virtue. In Britain, the people were obliged to rekindle the fires in their own houses, from the holy sires of the Druids. And the fame custom actually exists, at this day, in Persia. The day after their feast, which is kept on the 14th of April, the Persians extinguish all their domestic fires, aud to rekindle them, go to the houses of their priests, and there light their tapers. To divination, the Druids and Persians were both equally attached; and they had both the fame modes of divining. Pliny tells us, that our Druids so far exceeded the Persians in magic, that he should conceive the latter to have learnt the art in Britain. The Druids foretold future events, from the neighing of their white oracular horses. Cyrus, King of Persia, had also his white and sacred horses: And, not long after Cyrus, the succession to the imperial throne was determined by the neighing of a horse. The Druids regarded their misletoe as a general antidote against all poisons: and they preserved their selago as a charm against all misfortunes. And the Persians had the fame confidence in (0 The Temple of Diana, where St. Paul's now stands.

(A) At Exeter was found, a few years since, a lamps which, evidently, belonged to a temple of
   Diana.
(c) Batb-onta—Badenka. the the efficacy of several herbs, and used them in

a similar manner. The Druids cut their *Mljletoe* with a golden hook: And the Persians cut the twigs of *Ghez* or *Haulm,* called *Bursam,* with a peculiar fort of consecrated knife. The candidates for the vacant British throne had recourse to the *fatal stone,* to determine their pretensions: And, on similar occasions, the Persians recurred to their *Artizoe.* Dr. Borlase has pointed out other resemblances: But I have enumerated only the most striking. It is of consequence to observe, that Dr. Borlase has formed this curious parallel without any view to an hypothesis. Every particular is related with caution and serupuloumess: No forced resemblances are attempted; but plain facts are brought together, sometimes, indeed, reluctantly; though the Doctor seldom struggled against the truth. His mind was too candid and ingenuous for such a resistance. In the mean time, a systematical collector of facts is always animated by his subject. Every circumstance that seems to strengthen his theory, imparts a brilkness to his circulation. From the ardor of his spirits, his ex preslions acquire new energy—his portraits a high colouring. But we cannot congratulate the Doctor on luch an enlivening glow: His narrative is tame; his manner is frigid. And, what is truly unfortunate, after he has presented us with all these accumulated facts, he is at a lols in what manner to dispose of them. He sees, indeed—he is startled at the discovery that they make against his own and the common opinion: He perceives, that they might be brought in evidence against himself. A faint glimmering of *the secret history is the ivorld* seems to moot across his mind; but he is lost again in darkness. Such is his diilresling situation. Observe how he labours to get clear from the difficulties in which he has involved himself. The Druids, he had maintained, were a sect which had its rise among the Britons. Here, we see, he owned the independency of our Druids on the Druids of the Continent; though his supposition that Druidism absolutely originated in Britain, is evidently absurd. At this juncture, it is a supposition that involves him in greater

perplexity. It evidently cuts off all resources in the Continent of Europe: However puzzled the Doctor may be, he cannot look to the Gauls or the Germans for the solution of the difficulties he has started. He cannot fay, that we received Druidism from the east (as is commonly said) through the medium of Germany and Gaul; and hence account for those various similarities—since he traces the birth of Druidism on this island itself! He has, undoubtedly, simplified the question: and he points our views through a very narrow vista to the east, or rather to Persia alone. He seems, indeed, to have insulated himself, and to have rejected the common succours. To account for these resemblances he might have recurred, had he not fixed the origin of Druidism in Britain, to the continental tribes, whom he might have represented as bringing Druidism, pure and uncorrupted, from Asia over Europe, into this remote island. He would, in this case, have followed the beaten track. Dr. Borlase, indeed, seems to be sensible, that this beaten track ought to be abandoned. If he had followed it, he would have wandered far from the truth: In the present case, he is as near the truth as he possibly could have been, without reaching it. But see his poor, his wretched conclusion—after such a noble accumulation of facts—such a weight of circumstantial evidence, as seems irresistible—See his miserable subterfuge: " It has been hinted before, that the Druids were, probably, obliged to Pythagoras, for the doctrine of the transmigration, and other particulars: And, there is no doubt, but he was learned in all the magian religion: It was with this magian religion that the Druids maintained so great a uniformity. Tis not improbable, then, that the Druids might have drawn by his hands, out of the Persian fountains." What can be more improbable than this? That a single man, who by travelling through a foreign country, had acquired some knowledge of its religion, should have been able, on his return from travel, to persuade a whole priesthood, whose tenets were fixed, to embrace the doctrines and adopt the rites he recommended, is surely a most ridiculous position. Besides, were this admitted, would it account for the strength and exactness of these resemblances? If Pythagoras introduced any of the Druidical secrets into Britain, it was, I suppose, through his friend Abaris—for it does not appear that this sage ever travelled into Britain, himself. " Abaris, the Doctor slyly hints, was very intimate with Pythagoras—so intimate, indeed, that he did not scruple to communicate to him, freely, the real sentiments of his heart." And Abaris, it seems, paid a visit to the Danmonians. Here, then, all is ligh. Pythagoras was fortunate enough in a remote country, to dive into the hidden things of its.inhabitants—to expiscate the prosoundest of all secrets, the mysteries of religion. These Arcana, it seems, he imparted to Abaris, his bosom frien4; And Abaris very civilly Vol. I. E» communicated communicated the whole to our Devonshire and Cornish priests. And our Devonshire atid Cornish priests, with a versatility that shewed their sense of his politeness, new-modelled their religion, on his plan. Hence the resemblance of the Druids and the Persians in a thousand different points '—Doctor Borlase, however, is by no means satisfied with this argument. But, too timid to divest himself of the opinions which he had long taken tipon trust, he mikes still another effort to account for a likeness so embarrassing. " Whence (fays'he) this *surprising conformity* in their priests, doctrines, worship, and temples, between two such distant nations as the *Persians* and *Britons,* proceeded, it is difficult to fay. *There npver appears to have been the leaf migration*—any accidental 5r meditated intercourse betWixt them, after the one people was settled in Persia, a"nd the other in Britain." This strict agreement was too obvious to escape the notice of the judicious Pelouti-er. Dr. Borlase attempts a solution of the difficulty, in the following manner. " The Phenicians were very conversant with the Persians for the" *fake* of eastern trade: And nothing is more likely than that the Phenicians, and after them the Greeks, findifig the Druids devoted be-

yond all others to superstition, should snake their court to that powerful order, by bringing them continual notices of oriental superstitions, in order to promote and engross the lucrative trade-which they carried on jn Britain for so many ages. And the fame channel that imported the Persian, might also introduce some Jewish and Ægyptiah rites. The Phenicians traded with./Egypt, and had Judæa at their own doors: And, from the Phenicians, the Druids might learn some few Ægyptian and Jewish rites, and interweave them among their own." That thePhenician merchants should have taught our Druids, the Persian, Jewish, and Ægyptian religion, is too absurd a supposition to require a formal refutation. Admitting that these merchants were in the habit cf retailing religion, and bartering it with the Britons for tin; can we think, that these religious tenets and ceremonies could be imported in such excellent preservation as we find them in this island; or, is so imported, would be, at once, honoured by our Druids, with a distinguished place among their old religious possessions? It is singular that Dr. Borlase, who was so near the truth, soould have wandered from it, immediately on the point of approaching it. Dr. Borlase, however, is remarkable for his fairness in stating eveiy question; though the conclusions he draws from his premises are not always the most obvious. Others have attempted to get rid of the question in a more general way. To account for this similarity in the opinions and institutions of our Druids, and all the oriental priests, it is said that they were derived from one common fountain—from *Noah* himself, who set apart an order of men for the purpose of preserving those doctrines, through successive ages, and in various countries, wherever this, order might be dispersed. But the descendants of those who travelled west of Mount Ararat, are not supposed to have reached Britain by travelling overland, till after many generations. Their progress must have been necessarily stow; ana discontinuous and variously interrupted. In this cafe, they must have lost the character of their original coun-

try, before they could have settled in Britain. And the spirit of their religion must have evaporated in the same proportion: We sliould expect, therefore, to find fainter traces of it, the further 'J/e pursued it from its fountain-head. We have observed, however, the contrary in this island. If the Druids had been Celtic priests, they would have spread with the several divisions of the Celts. They would have been eminent among the Germans: they would have been conspicuous, though less visible, among the Gauls. But, in Germany, there were no Druids: And Gaul had none, till slie imported them from Britain. In short, we need not hesitate to declare, that the Druidisin of Britain was Asiatic. The Danmonii, transplanted into the British isles, retained those eastern modes, which seemed little accordant with their new situation. And was not their worsli-ip of the fun so unnatural in the dreary climates of the north, their doctrine as to the stars, so little regarded for scientific purposes by the European nations, their*fiiblime tenets* concerning the *origin of nature* and of the *hea-vens*—were not all these strongly contrasted with the religion of the continent? Were not all these absolutely unknown to the Europeans; and deemed, as soon as discovered, the objects of curiosity and veneration? Were not all these new to Cæsar? In fact, the Britisli Druids knew more cf the true origin of the mythology adopted by the Greeks and Romans, than the Greeks and Romans probably did themselves: And I cannot but observe, that every part of Cæsar's account of their religious tenets, merits a dissertation; for they refer to the first ages of mankind. Does Cæsar, any where, speak thus of the *Belgæ*—those fugitive Germans, driven-by their stronger neighbours over the Rhine into Gaul, and afterwards, perhaps, driven from Gaul Gaul to take Ihelter on the sea-coast of Britain? Does he any where speak thus of one tribe or state on the Continent?—I believe no where. The doctrines of the British Druids were peculiar to themselves in Europe—full of deep knowledge and high antiquity. Mr. Whitaker himself exclaims in a style truly oriental: " There was something m the Druidical species of heathenism, that was peculiarly calculated to arrest the attention and impress the mind. The rudely majestic circle of stones in their temples, the enormous Cromlech, the massy Logan, the huge Carnedde, and the magnificent amphitheatres of Woods, would all very strongly lay hold upon that religious thoughtfulness of foul, which has been ever so natural to man, amid all the wrecks of humanity— the monument of his former perfec- tion!" That Druidism then, as originally existing in Devonshire and Cornwall, was immediately transported, in all its purity and perfection, from the east, seems to me extremely probable.

But we have seen that this religion is not entirely consistent with itself—that though wisdom and benevolence are sometimes exhibited as its commanding features, yet the grossest folly and in- humanity are no less prominent, on oth- er representations of it. The Phenicians, however, introducing their corrupt doc- trines, and degenerated rites, will ac- count at once for these incongruities. And we have already observed the inter- mixture of the Phenician with the Abo- riginal doctrines and ceremonies. If a Phenician colony, subsequent to the first peopling of the island, fettled here (as I have stated in the second section) about the time of Joshua, there is no doubt but they disseminated in Danmo- nium a. vast variety of superstitious no- tions. At this juncture, their religion was stained with manifold impurities.(a) But, as I have hinted above, it would be impossible to separate all the superstitions which were countenanced as pop- ular tenets by the Druids before the ar- rival of the Phenician colony, from the superstitions which this colony intro- duced. I shall not, therefore, in this place, attempt to discriminate the Pheni- cian from the primitive Danmonian reli- gion. For the Grecian colony, they were ftrely not inactive in spreading their re- ligious tenets where they settled; though there is more of fancy than of real truth in the accounts which are pretended to have been transmitted through the line of history, respecting their *deities or*

tbeir temples, in this country. The au- thorities, on which such traditions rest, are very doubtful, if not palpably spuri- ous: And yet our chronicles had a cer- tain Ts *snaai;* though, when they got footing on a simple fact, they so embell- ished it by poetical fictions, that many are led to suspect Hie whole to be false, because they are convinced that the greatest part is so. That the Grecian colony built a temple at the Kpia *pAami,* or incorporating with the Danmonii, erected a temple at Exeter, I will not presume to assert. But if the existence of the colony Be granted, we need not doubt but they had buildings appropri- ated to religious orsliip. The Belgæ, in- vading our coasts, drove the Britons of Danmonium into the central farts, and thus contributed to spread the Druid re- ligion" over' the rest of the island. With respect, however, to the religion of the Belgae, and of the" other continental tribes, I (hall not attempt to characterize it. Certain it is, that before the time of Cæsar, the Gauls were in possession of Druidism, though in a very imperfect state. Their religion could have ill-re- sembled the Druidism of Danmonium, whilst they blindly adopted those cor- rupt notions and impure ceremonies which prevailed in the greater part of Europe. But, amidst these tokens of de- generacy, they still displayed some proof both of wisdom and of diffidence, whilst, conscious of their religious in- feriority, and not ashamed to avow it, they frequently recurred, for instruction, to the Aborigines of Britain!

(a) In conformity to this idea, we find, that the Persian religion was first Ma- gian entirely: Then esme in Sabianism, with all the additions of image-worship: Then came Zoroaster, and his reforma- tion of magianism. The Phenicians an- ciently worshipped only the fun and moon, under the names 6f Baal or Belus, and Astarte—*frortpentt auterrt U(hirg, Hrrcittu Pheenix eliie/ue Deo- rum mimerum puxerur.t.* (i) (i) Wife, Bodlr. Med. p. 218. SECTION SECTION IV. longed to a second clan, and in thus spreading such intelligence from town to town; fi» that all the cantreds, and in short the whole kingdom of Danmo-

nium, might be almost instantaneously apprized of a hostile attack. A beacon then, it sliould seem, belonged to every clanship or town in Danmonium; some- times placed on the natural hill, and sometimes on an artificial mount of earth or stone, where the brow of the hill was not sufficiently commanding. Not only the high antiquity of beacons, in various countries, but the frequent ves- tiges of ruinous beacons in Danmoni- um, in situations exactly adapted to the purposes I have mentioned, may asture us of this fact. But artificial mounts were at first, perhaps, thrown up by the Aborigines with a different view: They were, probably, raised as marks of the progress of colonization. An ingenious correspondent (a) has observed, " that the great marks of an Asiatic crossing the Euxine sea, are to be traced out in our modern maps, through Moldavia and Germany, into Britain, by the landwears or divisions, such as that at Lexden-heath, in Essex; and that anoth- er vestige is in the mounts, or *tumuli,* such as Silbury in Wiltsliire, and the Grange Barrow in Ireland." Thus the Asiatic emigrants into this island, prob- ably, erected mounts in the vicinity of every new habitation, as they proceeded in colonizing Danmonium. But these mounts, becoming useless as colonial landmarks, must have been soon es- tranged from their original destination, and adopted for military purposes, orig- inally, I conceive, for fire-beacons. In the mean time, to finish the whole, a road from one town to another, was ab- solutely requisite. It would be vain to diffuse alarms over Danmonium, by the beacon-fires, if there were no roads from fortress to fortress—if the whole of the intervening spaces were still overhung with thick-branching trees, and overgrown with briars or coppice. In thisl case, every town would have been in a manner insulated; and, though with difficulty approached by an ene- my, yet, when invaded, must have long trusted to itself, before any succours could arrive. A road, therefore, was soon struck out from one town to an- other, for the convenient intercourse of the different clans. If we imagine, then, a strong *mansion-bouse* built on the side of a hill, and a cluster of *inferior habitations* rising on the bank of a river, immediately under the eye of the fortress, and a *road* winding through the valley, and sloping away till it gains the higher grounds, and a *beacon* on the natural or artificial eminence overlooking the whole, and commanding the circumjacent country, we may conceive a tolerable idea of a Britisli town as represented in its primæval rudeness. Thus have I exhibited a rough draught of an *infant Britijh town,* both in a *civil* and *military* light, according to the vulgar idea of the towns of the Britons. That there are, at this day, relics of such habitations and military.works as I have delineated, on the hills or amidst the combes and cliffs of Danmonium, would appear without much labor of investigation. Of the round houses of the Britons which I first noticed, Dartmoor, perhaps, might furnish us with some remains. There are a great number of round structures scattered over this extensive moor. They are built with stone, and, in general, resemble the British house in their dimensions, as well as the rotundity of their form. But, unfortunately, they are all roofless: The bare walls only remain; and these walls are, for the most part, in a very ruinous condition. Towards Whiston's wood, these houies seem to be in a less dilapidated state. And here, as in several other places on the moor, they lie contiguous to each other; so as to suggest the idea of a village or town. The common notion is, that they were erected to secure the flocks and herds of the Danmonians, against wolves and other wild beasts which infested the country. But a great part of Dartmoor, was probably peopled in ancient times: And tradition concurs with probability, in settling this opinion. All the inhabitants of the skirts of the forest, relate, as a certain fact, which their fathers had told them, that " the hill-country was(A) peopled, whilst the vallies were full of serpents and ravenous beasts." The forest, undoubtedly, abounded with trees: And, as the Britons invariably preferred the woods to the plains, there is no doubt but they erected many fortresses

on the sylvan heights of Darti.'jor. Indeed, the round walls I have just noticed, admitting that tljey were mere pens for flocks, would tend to prove the inhabitation of Dartmoor; since the Britons, like the Arabs, had always apartments for their cattle near their own. In Whiston's wood, then, and in the ruinous cabins around it, we may contemplate the *VIEW of the CIVIL, MILITARY, and RELIGIOUS ARCHITECTURE ofDANMONIUM.*

I. *The Danmonian Houses—their form and Materials—their Situation—The Danmonian Caverns—The Danmonian Tovjn, consisting of a Mansion-House, and a number of inferior Houses—a Beacon overlooking it—a Road from one Town to another—Vestiges of the British Houses on Dartmoor—British Caverns in Devonshire and Cornwall—Line of Beacons Oh each Side of the Jttgum Ocrinum—and on the Jugum Ocrinum itself.*—II. *Architecture of the Britons more respectable than it is usually considered—City of Exeter—Plan of a Briti/b City on a Gold Coin of the Britons, probably Exeter—Exmouth—Okehampton—Drevosteingtoit— —Totnes—Armenton—Plympton—Tamara— Viluba—Uxella— Cenia— Termolus—Artavia —Musidum—Halangium—Redrutb— Military Structures—Karnbre-Castle— Castles vjith Keeps—Rougemont-Castle— Okehampton-Cajlle— Totnes-Castle—Plymton-Castle— Trematon-Castlc—Reflormel-Caftle—Launceston-Castle—British Roads in Danmonium*—III. *Religious Architecture—the Rock Idol—the Logan-Stone—the Rock-Bason—the single Stone' Pillar—tivo, three, or more Stone-Pillars—Circular Stone-Pillars—the Cromlech—Affem blage of Druidical Monuments at Drevjsteignton—the Stonehenge of the Druids, or the complete Druid Temple.* —IV. *Phenician,-Grecian, and Belgic Temples—the Barrovj— Ctnctufion.* THIS period might be rendered, perhaps, peculiarly interesting, from an extensive survey of the British Architecture: But the nature of the work obliges me to contract my yiews within a very narrow circle. For the present subject, I pro-

pose, first, to consider the houses and towns of the Danmon:ans, cursorily inspecting both their *civil* and *military* buildings; and secondly, to notice their religious structures.

With respect to the architecture of the Danrnonians, nothing can be advanced with certainty. The Greek and Roman writers observed the arts and manners of the ancient Britons so superficially, or received such vague and false accounts of the British islanders from others, that I cannot recur to those authors with any degree of confidence. Diodo rits Siculus informs us, that the Britons dwelt in houses constructed with wood, and covered with straw. And, in regard to their form, Dio calls the British houses *axmai;* and Zomaras *(a)* makes Caractacus call them *o-nmiix.* Mr. Whitaker describes the bouses of the Britons as great round cabins, built principally of timber, on foundations of stone, and roofed with a sloping covering of skins or reeds. But the British houses were sometimes constructed in a different form—not rounded, but nearly squared, and containing about sixteen yards by twelve within. Such, at least, as Mr. Whitaker informs us, was the groundwork of a building which was discovered within Castlefield, in 1766, and laid in a manner that bespoke it to be British. About half a yard below the surface of the ground, was a line of large irregular blocks; and under it were three layers of common paving stones, not compacted together with mortar, but with the rude and primitive cement of clay. (4) Thus the houses in the western isles of Scotland, to this day, are built of stone and cemented with earth. And the fame fort of foundation has been discovered about thole huge obelisks of the Britons, near Aldborough in Yorksliire, which are so similar to the stones erected frequently without their circular temples. As to their materials, the Britisli dwellings must have somewhat varied, according to their situations. In the neighbourhood of Dartmoor, for instance, their walls, probably, consisted of granite; and near the Denyball quarry, they were roofed, perhaps, if not entirely built with state, (s) Such is the case at the present day. Though cob-walls are generally preferred in Devon and Cornwall, yet in the vicinity of the Denyball-quarry, and along the north coast of Cornwall, the cottages of the meanest peasants are chiefly constructed with slate. The Danmqnians dwelt, also, in caverns. In the mean time, we are not to imagine, that the Danrnonians could boast no structures superior to the habitations I have described. The houses I have noticed were those only of the people in general: And, there *a)* Basil. p. i?;.

(b) Mr. Whitaker thinks, that this *square house,* at Manchester, was rather for the cattle of the Britons; since " the Britisli houses were roomy buildings, of a round form, and covered with a convex roof." *lc)* In Bjitish, *Sglattt,* wa.s, was, doubtless, a great distinction between the dwellings of the chiefs and the villains. The Lord's mansion was, as our superior houses remained in the last century, all constructed of wood, on a foundation of stone; was one ground story; and composed a large oblong and squarish court. A considerable part of it was taken up by the apartments of such as were retained more immediately in the service of the seignior. And the rest, which was more particularly his own habitation, consisted of one great and several little rooms: In the great room was his armoury; the weapons of his fathers, the gifts of friends, and spoils of enemies, being disposed in order along the walls. Such is the dwelling of the chieftain in the Scottish isles. And as the first class of the nobility, the Druids were surely provided with more commodious habitations than are generally assigned them. It is commonly imagined that the houses ot the Druids were mere excavations in the rocks, or little stone cabins, such as are to be seen, at this moment, in the Scottish isles, and which, tradition has consecrated to the Druids. The structures to which I allude, are called, *Tig-the-nan-Druidh.* They consist of a few large unwrought stones, piled up in the simplest manner, without lime or mortar *j* and they are capable only of holding a single person. I speak not of accommodation—even the peas-

ants on the skirts of Dartmoor, would disdain these Druid houses. In stiort, whilst I aflent to the opinion, that the little buildings in question were-Druidical, supposing them to be *Sacella,* to which the common people resorted for various religious purposes, I conceive that the family-seats of the Druids were edifices as large and as convenient as any in the British period. Yet, the common people resided in meaner houses or in caves. And the dwellings of the vulgar, numerous ia comparison to those of the chiefs, met the eye in every direction: Hence the descriptions of British houses in ancient writers are, for the most part, taken from these rude habitations. For the situation of the Danmonian houses, we have to remark, that the seat of the Chieftain was lbmetimes fixed on the summit of a hill, but more commonly in the hollow of a valky, either on the margin of one stream, or at the confluence of two. This latter mode of building, for security from winds and conveniency of water, continued almost to the present day. The falhion of this moment has a particular regard to prospect, erecting houses on eminences that overlook the surrounding plantations, and command all the neighbouring country. In the vicinity of the Chieftain's seat, were built the different cottages of his tenants, either on the slope of the hill, or along the margin of a river that pursued the course of the winding combe. From this collection of houses, all subordinate to the great house, originated the British town: and the inferior houses were so placed as reciprocally, to guard each other, whilst they stood under the immediate command of the chief mansion: So that, on a military view, the clanstiip was a fortified town, with a castle to defend it. And, indeed, the first towns of the Britons have generally been described as mere fortresses or strong holds. They were not scenes, we am told(«), of regular and general residence. They were only places of refuge amidst the dangers of war, where the Britons might occasionally lodge their wives, children, and cattle; and the weaker resist the stronger till succours could arrive. This was more particularly

the case with the caves of the Daninonii, which are certainly to be regarded ia a military light. Of such caverns we have many instances in DanmOnium, partly, perhaps, natural, and partly artificial. That these caverns were places of temporary residence in the time of war, whither the Danmonii retired, for the security of their persons, their domestic furniture, and their warlike stores, I mould judge not only from the dilpositioa of the Aborigines so congenial with the oriental turn of mind, but from the resemblance, also, of our Danmonian excavations to thole in Scotland and Ireland, which are allowed to be military retreats. But, whatever was their use, they were very similar to the caves of the eastern nations, and especially of Armenia. Before, however, we enter into particulars, it may be necessary to complete our sketch of the British fortified town. The fortress in which the chief resided, was the principal military work in every clanstiip: It was a fastness strengthened by Considerable outworks. Yet, from '» scite on the side of a hill (and sometimes in *&* valley) it was by no means equal to the command of the neighbouring country, andtonsequently subject to surprize from an enemy, if it stood independent and unconnected with any other work. We may naturally place, therefore, some work on the brow of the hill; such as a watch-tower or beacon, whence the approach of an enemy might be observed, and an alarm might be given to the clanship. Such a structure might also be-uscful in communicating with;inotLer of a like nature, which be *(a)* Colonel Simcoe, now Governor of Quebec. (A) Peopled " by *christians"* (an old man informed me) meaning *human beings,* " The bottoms (or the low-ground) he said, were all slime;" And he had a strange notionof winged serpents. fading fading features of a Danmonian clanship, (a) But, as the Danmonians sometimes resided in caves, let us look, also, to their rock recesses, in Devon and Cornwall. The cave in the rock near Chudleigh, has been already described as a natural hollow. Yet it seems to be as well formed for the purpose of concealment in time of war, as several of the Danmonian excavations, which are evidently artificial. Kent's Hole, which has also been described, would furnish a safe asylmn in time of war. About two miles to the S. W. of Berryhead, there is a remarkable hole in the rock under Dark point: And the remains of a mound, or old wall, are to be seen on that promontory, about a mile S. E. of Brixham. Just within the Bolt-head, at the west end of Salcombe-bar, is a subterraneous passage, called Bull-hole, which, the common people have an idea, runs quite under the earth to another such place in a creek of the sea, called Sewer-mill, at three miles distance. The tradition is, that a bull should enter it at one end, and come out at the other. How far these two caverns are really the fame, has never been determined; none of those who have entered them having had the resolution to proceed sufficiently far to ascertain the fact. On the east side of the parish of South Huish, is an entrenchment on the declivity of a hill, but very near the summit, facing the north. About twenty yards in the rear of this entrenchment (which will be described in its proper place) a walled cave was discovered a few years since: The farmer who made this discovery, dug up the foundation of it. It was about twenty feet long, seven or eight feet broad, and ten or twelve feet deep: but nothing was found in the cavern. On the weft side of the village of Lower Torr, and near the river Yalm, is a cavern in a marble rock. The entrance is by a long narrow cleft; but, as we advance, it becomes mare spacious, and goes near two hundred feet under the rock. The country-people have a tradition, also, relating to this cavern. And they believe, as they were taught by their fathers, diat from this cavern a way passed under the river to the church of Yalmton, which stands about two or three hundred yards distant, on high ground, to the north. The cavern discovered about twenty years ago, on the west side of the Haw, at Plymouth, and looking into Mill-Bay, was partly, perhaps, an artificial work of the ancient Britons. As I have but slightly men-

tioned it in my (ketch of the natural history, I shall here give a particular description of this subterraneous abode. This cave was accidentally laid open by some miners, in blowing up a contiguous rock of marble. The aperture disclosed by the explosion, was ibout four feet in diameter, and looked not unlike a hole bored with an auger. It was covered with a broad flat stone, cemented with lime and sand; and, twelve feet above it, the ground seemed to have been made with rubbish brought thither, perhaps for the purpose of concealment. Here was, doubtless, some appearance of art, and vestige of malonry. The hill itself, at the northern side of which this vault was found, consists, for the most part, of marble. From the mouth of this cave (through which we descend by a ladder) to the first base, or landingplace, are twenty-six feet. At this base is an opening, bearing N. W. by W. which resembles a tent, stretching upwards somewhat pyramidically, to an invisible point. Hence it was called *Tent-Cave.* It is about ten feet high, seven broad, and twentytwo long; though there is an opening which, on account of its narrowness, could not well be examined, and which, probably, hath a dangerous flexure. In each side of this Tent-Cave is a cleft: the right runs horizontally inwards ten feet; the left measures six by four. The sides of the cave are, every where, deeply and uncouthly indented, and here and there strengthened with ribs naturally formed, which, placed at a due distance from each other, give some idea of fluted pillars as in old churches. In a direct line from this cave, to the opposite point, is a road thirty feet long. The descent is deep and rugged—the road is strongly but rudely arched over; and many holes on both sides are to be ieen; but being very narrow do not admit of minute examination. Having scrambled down this deep descent, we arrive at a natural arch of gotliic-like structure, which is four feet from side to side, and six feet high. Here some petrifactions are seen depending. On the right of this arch, is an opening like a funnel, into which a slender person might creep: On the left is another cor-

relpondent funnel, the course of which is oblique, and the end unknown. Beyond this gothic pile, is a large (pace, to which the arch is an entrance. This space, or inner-room, is eleven feet long, ten broad, *a)* Not but a part of Dartmoor might have been waste, where the lords of the neighbouring clans had a right of common, and where flocks and herds were pastured, at particular seasons, under the «are of Ihepherds and herdsmen.

Vol. I. F twentytwenty-five high: Its sides have many large excavations: And here two columns, which seem to be a mass of petrifaction, project considerably. On the surfaces of those pillars below, are seen some fantastic protuberances, and on the hanging roofs above, some chrystal drops that have been petrified in their progress. Between the columns, is a chasm Capable of containing three or four men. Returning from this room, we perceiye, on the left hand, an avenue thirty feet long, naturally floored with clay, and vaulted with stone. It bears S. S. W. and, before we have crept through it, we fee a passage of very difficult access. It runs forward twenty-five feet, and opens over the vault thirty feet high, near a very large well. Oppolite to this passage are two caverns, both on the right hand. The first bears N. W. by vv. and running forward in a straight line, about twenty feet, forms a cave that verges somewhat to the N. E. Here we walk and creep in a winding course, from cell to cell, till we are stopped by a well of water, the breadth and depth of which are not fully known. This winding cavern is three feet wide, ih some parts, five feet high, in some, eight. On our return to the avenue, we find adjoiriing to this cavern, but separated by a massy partition of stone, the second cavern, in a western direction: And, by descending some small piles of lime-stone, or rather broken rocks, the bottom here being slielving slate (or, more properly, a combination of slate and lime-stone) we discover another well of water. This is the largest. The depth of it is, in one place, twenty-three feet, the width uncertain. Opposite to this well, on. the left hand, by mounting over a small ridge of rocks, covered with wet and slippery clay, we enter a vault eight feet broad, eighteen long, thirty high. Here, towards the S. E. a road, not easy of ascent, runs upwards of seventy-two feet towards the surface of the earth, and so near to it, that the sound of the voice, or of a mallet within, might be distinctly heard without—in consequence of which a very large opening has been made into it. At the bottom of-this vault, in a place not readily observed, is another well of water j the depth of which, on account of its situation, cannot be easily fathomed, nor the breadth of it ascertained. Each cavern has its arch; and each arch'is strong. The way to the largest well is, in 6ne part, roofed with solid and smooth stone, not unlike the arch of an oven. It is very likely that the hill itself is hollow—Some of the caverns have reciprocal communications; but the clefts are often too narrow for accurate inspection'. The water, here and there, is still dripping; and incrustations, usual in such grottos, in some places coat the surface of the walls. There are some whimsical likenesses, which it would be difficult to delineate. —In the parish of Shepstor, rises that steep high hill, full of moorstone (with which the whole country abounds, lying on the edge of Dartmoor) called *Sheffior-Torr*. Among the rocks, towards the top, is a small cleft, opening within to a wider room. From this place, the inhabitants of the cavern might command the whole country. The country-people have many superstitious notions of this hole. " In the tenement of Bolleit,'in the parish of St. Berian, at the end of a little inclosure, is a Cave, called the Foou: Its entrance is about four feet, high and wide. The cave goes straight forward, nearly of the fame width as the entrance, seven feet high, and thirty-six from end to end. About five feet from the entrance, there is on the left hand, a hole two feet wide, and one foot fix inches high, within which there is a cave four fe,et wide, and four seet six inches high. It goes nearly east about thirteen feet, then to the south five feet more; the sides and end faced with

stone, and the roof covered with large flat stones. At the end fronting the entrance, is another square hole, within which there was also a further vault, now stopt up with stones, through which we perceive the light. And here, must have been a passage for light and air, if not a back way of conveying things into and out of these cells. This cave is about a furlong distant from the village of Bolleit: And, indeed, the ground is so level above and each side of it, that no one would suspect there was a cave below, but for the entrance. There is a cave of the fame name, in the parish of St. Eval, near Padstow. In the tenement of Bodinar, in the parish of Sancred, somewhat higher than the present village, is a spot of ground, amounting to no more than half an acre of land (formerly much larger) full of irregular heaps of stones, overgrown with heath and brambles. It is of no regular stiape; neither has it any vestiges of fortification. In the southern part of this plot, we may, with some difficulty, enter mto a hole, faced on each side with a stone wall, and covered with flat stones. Great part of the walls, as well as covering, are fallen into the cave, which does not run in a straight line, but turns to the left hand, at a small distance from the place where I entered (says Borlase) and seems to have branched itself out much farther than I could then trace it, which did not exceed twenty feet. It is about five feet high, and as much in widths *a. -» `; -'- caljed* called the Giant's Holt, and has no other use, at present, than to frighten and appease froward children. As the hedges round are veiy thick, and near one another, and the inclosures extremely small, I imagine thele ruins were, formerly, of much greater extent, and have been removed into the hedges; the stones of which appearing sizeable, and as if they had been used in masonry, seem to confirm the conjecture. Possibly, here might. be a *large Britijh town* (as'I have been informed Mr. Tonkin thought) and this cave might be a private way, to enter or sally out of it: But the walls are every where crushed down, and nothing regular is to be seen. I will only add, that this cave or *under-*

ground passage, was fb well *concealed,* that though I had visited it in the year 1738, yet, when I came again to fee it, in 1751, I was a long while before I could find it. Of all the artificial caves I have seen in Cornwall, Pendeen *Vau* (by the Welsh pronounced *Fau)* is the most entire and curious. It consists of three caves or galleries: The entrance is four feet six inches wide, and as many high, walled on each side with large stones, with a rude arch on the top. From the entrance we *descend six steps,* and advance to the N. N. E. the floor dipping all the way.. This first cave is twenty-eight feet long. The sides and roof of the second cave, are formed in the fame manner as those of the first—the sides, the fame distance, but the roof only five feet six inches high. Through a square hole, two feet wide, and two feet six inches high, we creep into a third cave, six feet wide and six feet high—neither sides nor roof faced with stone, but the whole dug out of the natural ground; the sides formed regularly and straight, and the arch of the roof a semicircle *We fee nothing of this cave, either in the field or garden, till ive come to the mouth of it*; as much privacy as possible being consulted."(«) In the. isles of Scotland, and in Ireland (to which I resort, as originally peopled like Danmonium, by Asiatic colonies) there are a great number of artificial caverns. In the isle of Skie, are several little stone houses, built *under-ground,* called earth-houses, " which serve to hide a few people, and their goods, in the time of war."(A) In the isle of Ila, there is a large cave, called VagVearnag, or Man's-Cave, which will hold two hundred men. And there are many such, caves in Ireland; not only under mounts, fort?, and castles, but under plain fields; some winding into little hills and risings, like a volute, or ram's horn; others running zig-zag; others again right forward, connecting cell with cell. That the Asiatics, from whose country the Danmonians are uipposed to have emigrated, " made them the dens which are in the mountains, and caves, and strong holds,"(c) is evident, both from sacred and profane history. There is a remarkable passage in Xenophon, (/) describing the caves of the Armenians. Xenophon informs us, " that the houses of the Armenians were *under-ground*—that the mouth or entrance to these subterraneous habitations was like that of a *well,* but that underneath, they were *wide and spreading*—that there were ways for the cattle to enter, but that the men *went down by stairs."* In Armenia, at this day, the people dwell in caverns. " In a narrow valley (fays Leonhaut Rauwolf) lying at the bottom of an ascent, we found a great stable, wherein we went. This was quite cut into the hill: And so was that wherein we lodged the night before. So that ou could *fee nothing of it, but only the entrance.* For they are commonly so in these hilly countries, *under-ground,* that the caravans may safely rest there, and defend themselves from the cold in the winter. This stable, twenty-five paces long, and twenty broad, was cut 'out of a rock." These descriptions of the Armenian caves agree, in several points, with that of the cave near Plymouth, as well as the Oornisli caverns. Xenophon's cave is subterraneous: So is that near Plymouth: The apertures of both are narrow: And both caverns are, afterwards, sufficiently capacious, prom such resemblances, however, I would by no means draw any conclusion. Nor, when I observe that the caves in Devon (so like the under-ground habitations of *Armenia)* are mostly in the Southams, at no great distance from the river *Arme,* or the town of *Armenton,* on the bank of the *Arme,* where the emigrators from *Armenia* are supposed to have first lettled, would I be understood to reft my theory of the Asiatic colonization on this circumstance; though, I confess, it strikes me as singularly curious.—Of the Beacons in Danmonium, we' have numerous ruins: And there arc a few entire, both to the south and the north of the Jugum Ocrinum. In some of these beacons (particularly in the north *(a)* Borlasc's Antiquities, p. 273, 274, (A) Martin of the Isles, p. 154. (f) Judges, vi. 2. *d)* De Exped. Cytii Lib. 4. Voi. I., Fa of of Devon) there are large excavations, not unlike the caverns I have just noticed. Oft the south side of the

Jugum Ocrinum, there was, probably, a line of beacons that ran from the eastern limits of Danmonium (the country of the Durotriges or Morini) along to the Ocrinum Promontorium, its western extremity. Membury-beacon, near the eastern limits, would look far into Devonshire: And a beacon would not be useless at Axbridge; the bearings from which (to notice present objects) are Colyton-church, one mileN.N.W. Shute-hill, three miles N. Musbury-camp, two miles E. N. E. Axmouthchurch, one mile S. Hogsdown-hill, one mile S. by E. The bearings from Hogldownhill, over Axmouth, are—Colyford, one mile due N. Colyton, a point to the W. Axminster, six miles, N. E. From the hill, two miles S. E. of Colyton, where, possibly, was a beacon—Axmouth-head, three miles S. S.E. Axmouth-town, two miles S. E. CombePyne, four miles E. by S. Musoury-church, three miles due E. Axminster-church, six miles between N. E. by N. and E. N. N. Shute-hill, four miles N. E. Membury-beacon, between N.E. by N. and N.E. two little hills by Beer, two miles S. The bearings from Shute-hill by the beacon, are Axminster, three miles E. Membury-church, four miles N.E. by N. Musbury-church, two miles S. by E. Old Shute-house, half-a-mile W. *by* N. Watton-Pen, three miles W. S.W. Widworthy, two miles N.W. by W. On Sidmouth-hill, in the road to Salcombe, a beacon might have been erected in former times. The bearings from this eminence are, Sidbury-castle N. Bulverton-hill, N.W. by N. Harpford-beacon, N. N.W. North end of Sidmouth-hill N. W. Sidmouthchurch and Peak-hill W. by S. the greatest headland between W. S. W. and S.W. by S. Harpford-beacon N.N.W. might correspond with the beacon on Sidmouth-hill. On. Beacon-hill, a part of Blackdown, stands a beacon perfectly round. Hembury ford commands a large tract of country. The bearings from Hembury are Broad-hembury church, one mile and half, N. by W. Samford-Peverell church. sixteen miles N. N.W. Willand-church, six miles between N. W. by N. and N.N.W. Halberton-

church, nine miles, between N.W. and N.W. by N. Cblumbton, six miles and three-quarters N. W. Bradninch, seven miles W. N. W. Cadbury-castle and Silverton, twelve miles W. by N. Rewe, a little to the left. Plymtree, three miles between W. and W. by N. Thorverton, twelve miles W. Clist-hydon, four miles W. Broad-clist, ten miles W.

head S.W. Ottery, six miles S.W. by S. Otterton-Pool, the fame. Bokerel, one mile S. S. E. Gittistiam, half-a-point more to the S. Aulescombe, a mile and half S. E. Honiton, three miles, half-a-point more to the E. Heytorr-rocks, thirty-five miles W.S.W. The Obelisk at Mamhead, between S.W. and S.W. by W. There was formerly a beacon on Warborough-hill, in the parissi of Kenton, where a fire being kindled, would instantly communicate with Woodbury-hill, on the other side of the river Exe. On Haldon-hill, there were, doubtless, several beacons in the British Period. The following are the bearings from the point of the Ronian road, on Haldon, overlooking Exeter. Exeter, six miles, twenty degrees to the E. of N. Whitston-church, due N. Alphington-church, ten degrees E. of N. Ken-ford, a little to the east of Exeter. Kenchurch, N. E. Exminster, fifty odd degrees from N. Topfham, sixty degrees. Powderham, E. Beyond it, Peakhill in the fame line. Sidmouth-gap, eighty degrees from N. And Woodbury-castle in a line with it. Exmouth-point, and ope of the river; twenty degrees S. of E. On a hill on Radway estate, in Bifhop's-teignton, are the remains of a beacon. A lane, called Beacon-lane, leads W. from Hennock-village, to an eminence that bears the name of Halsewood-hill. Here stood a beacon, the traces of which were visible a short time since. In the Southams, also, beacons may be traced; the link between those already noticed, and the beacons on the southern coasts of Cornwall. The bearings taken from Fire-beacon-hill, on Bozumseale, in the parish of Ditsham, are as follows: The summit of the hill by Ivy-bridge W. N. W. Brent-hill, N.W. by W. Ashprington-church, four miles N.W. Holn-church, N.W. by N. Broadhempston-church, eight miles N. N. W. Totnes, a little more to the north, six miles. Dartington, a little more to the north of Totnes. Hey-torr-rock N. Torr and Mary-church, eight miles, N.E. Ditsham-church, one mile N.N.E. East-point of Torbay N.E. by N. Opening of the harbour of Dartmouth S. S. E. Tunstal-church, two miles S. On the skirts of Dartmoor, in the parish of Ugborough, are four vast heaps of stones, oval and concavated. One of these is called *Sharpitorre,* from the sliape, I suppose, of the eminence on which it is placed. The largest and two least lie on the opposite side of a vale, and are by the moor-m;n *culledVree-kr-riej,* doubtless a corruption of *three barrows.* On enter ing ing from the waste into the inclosed lands of Ugborough, we pass to the south, between tJbber East, and West beacons, two steep and lofty hills, or rather rocks, seen far and wide, and each commanding prospects surprizingly extensive. From the one may be surveyed a considerable part of East Devon, with the western coast of Dorset. The other (twelve miles distant) looks down on Plymouth-sound, and over the S. W. of Devon, deep into the S.E. of Cornwall: And, from both, we have numberless and grand views of the British channel. Thus was the chain of beacons extended to the moil westerly extremity of the island. In the fame manner, on the north side of the Jugum Ocrinum, there were, probably, communications through the whole country of theCimbri and the Carnabii, from the river Uxella to the Antivestæum promontorium. In the parish of Stoodley, there is a noble eminence, which the Danmonians must soon have occupied. From the centre, where Stoodley-beacon was fixed, tht ground rises gradually, til it comes to the inner bank; between which and the outer bank, there is a fill or ditch. This work is nearly circular, and contains about half an acre, including the entrenchments. It is on the summit of a high hill, and affords a very extensive prospect, especially towards the N. and N. W. so that the Severn sea may thence be plainly seen. It also commands Dartmoor, to the W. and S. W But the prospect to tlve E. and S. E. is

not Ib extensive; nor the hill so steep, on the E. and S. as *on* the N. and W. It is situated to the N. W. of Stoodley-town. About a furlong N. of North-Molton, is a large hill, called Beacon-hill, from the beacon or light-house, which was standing not long since. On the E. adjacent to this, is an open tract of ground, called Old-Park, which was a deer-park. The wall that inclosed it, is still standing in some places; ia others it is to be traced. In this plot of ground, on the summit of an high hill (above the level of the town) was a fortification. Part of the rampart and ditch are still visible— and through this park runs the *Mole,* in a line almost N. and S. Bratton-down, the turf of which is as smooth as a bowling-green, and nearly as level, commands an extensive view of the country round; in which circular survey lies Youlston on the N.W. and jlearer at hand, Arlington; the tower of Bratton; Hertland-Point; and towards the east, Exmoor. On all the circumjacent eminences, beacons are discoverable; in some places several together. And these beacons are in the form of barrows, except that they are not conical: indeed, they have the cone, as it were, inverted, and are hollowed out in the middle. Some of them are of considerable magnitude, being, in diameter, no less than sixty feet. With respect to the use of these hollows, there may be some reason in the conjecture, that, as intelligence was conveyed from beacon to beacon, during the darkness of the night, by means of fires, such excavations may have been formed to prevent the extinction of those fires through the violence of the winds—since, in the hollow, the fuel would be undisturbed, and the flame would ascend above the summit of the beacon, sufficient to answer the purpose. On Berry-down, are several tumuli, and a beaconAnd at *High-Eiciington* were ancient *beacons*—whence, indeed, its name: And this is.one of the highest spots in the whole county of Devon. The mount of Torrington-castle was, probably, a British beacon. And a beacon on the hills above Stratton, would communicate with all the heights along the northern coast of Cornwall. To connect the

southern and the northern hills of Devon and Cornwall, there would be a line of beacons, also, along the Jugum Ocrinum. *Canvfon,* one of the principal heights of Dartmoor, seems to have been formerly a *beacon.* That it was used as such, indeed, is confirmed by the tradition of the country. But it would be tedious to enumerate the beacons oa the Dartmoor hills. It is already sufficiently clear, that the intelligence of any invasion of Danmonium from the east, or on the south or north coasts, might be communicated through Devonshire and Cornwall, by a rapid succession of beacon-fires. And we find beacons familiarly in use among the primitive Britons, and the Highlanders. The besieged capital of one of our northern isles, in the third century, actually lighted up a fire upon a tower; and Fingal instantly knew " the green flame edged with smoke," to be a token of attack and distress. And there are, to this day, several kames or heaps of stones, upon the heights, along the coast of the Harries, on which ths inhabitants used to bura heath, as a signal of an approaching enemy.(a) *(a)* Offian, vol. 1, p. 198, and Martin's Western Islands, p. 35, edit. 2. Signals, by means cf lighted torches, called pftixiw, or by smoak, on the approach of friends or enemies, were in use among the Greek';: Rut their use is more particularly described in the Agamennonof Æschyius; where, by means of these beacons, communicating from Mount Ida, to the Promontory in Lemnes, thence to Mount Athos, and so on, Clytenestra receives immediate notice of tlie taking of Troy.
Here,

Here, according to the common ideas of the towns of the Britons, at the invasion of Cæsar, we fliould close our views of the civil and military structures of Damnonium. Yet there are some, who maintaining a higher opinion of the ancient Britons, would represent them in possession of towns and cities, laid out with architectural skill on a far more extensive scale.. And this opinion merits our consideration.

The idea of the British forrtess in the woods is, undoubtedly, just: But, amidst the numerous clanships, there were, probably, a few superior towns. And, from the (kill of the Britons, in various arts, we may presume that they were not unacquainted with architecture. That the Britons were excellent sculptors, several figures in their coins and their war-chariots unquestionably prove. Can we hesitate, then, in allowing them some credit, as architects? Architecture is surely more obvious than sculpture. In the pro gress of the arts, a convenient house must be anterior to an elegant en-graving: In many countries, the former is frequent, where the latter is unknown. And, indeed, the useful arts invariably precede the ornamental. The British chariot was, doubtless, of Asiatic inven-tion: It was introduced into this island by its first colonists, theDanmonians. Here, therefore, we stiould naturally look for architecture of a higher descrip-tion; though we leave the Gaulish colonies in quiet possession of their vil-lages embosomed in the woods. As our first colony is supposed to have come from the east, not long after the disper-sion, the sacred volume may, perhaps, suggest to us some hints of the British architecture. Those who journeyed from the east, " found a plain in the land of Shinar, and they dwelt there. And they said, one to another, go to—let us make *brick*, and burn them thoroughly. And they had brick for stone, and slime had they for mortar. And they said, go to— let us build us a *city* and a *tower*, whose top may reach unto heaven." We may naturally suppose, then, that the art of making *(a)* bricks, so well known to the builders of Babel, was carried away at the dispersion by the first colonists of Danmonium. And Devonshire would readily supply them with brick-clay. But, whatever were the materials of their edifices, it is certain that the dis-persed Asiatics had conceived the most magnificent ideas of architecture. They had planned a city, and a tower that might reach the heavens. And the east-ern nations have always displayed a greatness of style in their buildings. *t* is very improbable, therefore, that the first inhabitants of Danmonium, abandoning all fheir«notions of former grandeur,

should have been satisfied with a little fortress in the woods. That they dis-played, indeed, this taste in their reli-gious structures, will soon appear: The monuments of Druidisin, though rude, are yet magnificent. With these impres-sions, let us visit a few British towns in the several cantreds. First, for the city of Exeter, in the cantred of Isca. What time the city of Exeter was built, or who was ita founder, it is impossible to deter-mine; since,probability is all we have to expect in these obscure discussions. Iza-cke, therefore, very ignorantly fays, that " Exeter, he finds, was built before Lon-donx even at Brute's first landing here, by his nephew Corinæus, on whom Brute bestowed this western county, A. M. 2855— the fame being before Christ's incarnation one thousand one hundred years and upwards— and presently, thereafter, Brute built Lon-don, calling it Troynovant." There was, assuredly, a British town, of very high antiquity, on the banks of the Exe; if not exactly on the scite of the present Ex-eter, yet at no great distance from it. In attempting to fix the scite of the Bri-tissi Exeter, there are many difficulties. Some name, or some record, or both, ssiould ascertain the point; and tradition ssiould, also, come in: But we have nei-ther records nor tradition to assist our enquiries.*(b)* We are left to the uncer-tain guidance of mere names. Exeter had various British appellations. That it was situated in the midst of woods, is evident from its Britissi name *Penhul-goile*, or *the prosperous chief town in the 'wood*. Not that these woods imme-diately overshadowed the town. They must have covered the hills at distance; where nature pursued " her horizontal march, with sweeping train of forest. " But the appellation of *Penhulgoile* is vague: Nothing can be deduced from it. One of the names of the Britissi Exeter, however, points-out the (a) The name it-self is British—*Brite*—plur. *Brh'un* in Irish. *Whitaker.* (b) The people of Hol-combe-Burnell, indeed, have an idle tale on this subject. On a common in Holcombe-Burnell, is an old military work, which the village-historians as-cribe to the ancientBritons. They have a

tradition, handed down from generation to generation, that the Britons had fixed on this spot for the scite of their capital, and that in this ditch we trace the foun-dations of the , original Exeter; which, however, for the convenience of water, was shortly removed to its present situ-ation.

nature nature of the soil on which it stood: And the word is *Caeratb*, which signifies, *the city of the red soil*. This the Britons applied to Exeter. And *Rouge-mont*, or the *Red-Mount*, corresponding with this name, would lend us to fix the original Exeter at RougemontCastle, where the color of the whole mound is *Jeep red*. In the mean time, the name ot *Isca*, derived from its river, and *Caerijk*, the *water-city*, or the *city on the river*, would bring the original town, perhaps, more to the west. Mr. Whitaker was in-clined, on a very cursory view of Ex-eter, some years since, to place the Bri-tish town upon the old ford. " The old ford (fays Mr. Whitaker) («) was and is, I think, slanting over the river below the old bridge. The high ground, then, at the city-end of this ford, or the island it-self there, is not too much overflowed in winter, must be the scite." But I suspect, that the island was overflowed in win-ter, and even under water in the sum-mer season.' The island, indeed, could scarcely have existed at this early pe-riod, when the river, probably, strayed at liberty over the adjacent valley, con-fined by no artificial barriers. There is reason to suppose, that the Exe over-flowed all the low grounds from the town to the fields under Cowick. It seems, then, that the British names of Exeter, tend to embarrass the subject, rather than to clear it from its difficul-ties, whilst *Caeratb* directs us to the north, and *Caerijk* to the south-west of the city. But, perhaps, these appellations may be brought to reflect light on each other, if we conceive the Britisli city to have occupied the whole intermediate space between Rougemont and the Is-land. And indeed, all the Britisli names of Exeter, ambiguous as they are with regard to its situation, very plainly mark its superiority over the Danmonian towns; a distinction, doubtless, owing to the extent of its buildings. In *Penhulgoile (the prosperous chief town in the wood)* in *Caeratb (the city of the red foil)* and *Caerijk (the city on the waters)* we cannot but fee its eminence. And *Pe/icaa;* or *the chief city* (another name of Exeter) more peculiarly points out its greatness. The ground-plot of the Britisli Exeter, was certainly not so contracted as is generally imagined. Among the *British* gold coins found at (Cambrels) in 1749, there is one remarkable coin, on which is engraved *the plan of a city.* Borlase has given us a view of thole coins;(r) and he thus describes the coin in question. No. XII. has, on the head, several parallel lines, fasnioned into squares, looking like the *plan of a town* ; of which the streets cross nearly at right angles, and the whole is cut by one straight and wider street than the rest." The Doctor afterwards adds: " The figure in the head of number XII. has been before observed to resemble the ichnography of a pity, and was, probably, inserted in the coin by the founder, to record the erection of some city; for that the Britons had such cities is very plain from the noble ruins (a circuit about three or four miles) near Wrottesley, in the county of Stafford, where the parallel partitions, within the outwall, whose foundations are still visible, and represent streets running different ways, put it out of doubt that it must have been a city, and that of the Britons." I am rather surprised, that Dr. Borlase mould have thus remarked upon the ground-plot of his city, without venturing to conjecture what city it was. The gold-coin, on which this plan is exhibited, is evidently a coin of the Britons. It represents a Britisli city: And it was found in Danmonium. Is it not natural to suppose then, that this was a city of Danmonium—and, probably, the metropolis? This plan of the Danmcnian city must immediately suggest the idea of the *original* Exeter, even to those who have never seen the *modern.* But, whoever has visited the modern Exeter, must instantly recognize it in the Karnbre coin. It exhibits a very good groundplot of Exeter. We have here the fore-street, from east to west, running

through the city in straight lines. And there is a wonderful accuracy in the plan. The fore-street does not pass through the centre of it; but the larger part of the plot lies to the south, and the smaller segment to the north; which is precisely true of the city of ExeteK Surely this was not a random plot of some British town. Though, possibly, the other streets that intersect it may not bear examination, as compared with the present Exeter, yet it sufficiently resembles the modern city, to be received as an engraving of the ancient. What should rather excite our admiration is, that this engraving should be so similar to the present Exeter, allowing for the alterations in the streets and buildings, in (a) In a letter to the author. Had this excellent Antiquary leisure to inspect the city, I doubt not' but he would soon fix the scite of the or iginal town, to the satisfaction of the learned. (i) See Antiquities of Cornwall, p, (0 Plate J 9. siirfi a course of time, (a) That this is the ichnography of the British Exeter, is certainty a new discovery, and, on account of its novelty, will be regarded at least with a suspicious eye. But if the coin on which it is found be British, which Borlase has clearly proved, it is, assuredly, the ichnography of a British city. And, if it represent a British city, has not Exeter, for the realbns I have stated, the best claim to be considered as its archetype? At all events, it corroborates our argument in favor of the British architecture. It not only corroborates our argument, but it decides upon the point with the most happy precision. It dissipates from our minds every doubt of the British slcill *in* building; whilst it exhibits a large city, with one grand street stretching through the length of it, and a variety of inferior streets passing in different directions through the whole. After all this dilquisition, we may safely, I think, 'conclude, that the *Isca Danmoniorum* was no mean fortress in the woods, but a metropolis of the western kingdom, well worthy the oriental genius. But, though the metropolis was thus magnificent, we are not to look for an extensive display of architecture in the other Danmonian

towns. *Isca* had become the royal residence: Here, therefore, the most numerous as well as the molt stately buildings, would naturally be erected. The Danmonian genius, however, was versatile and capricious: Its exertions were not long confined to any single spot. la the mean time, I think it highly probable, that there were towns,, in each of the cantreds, more respectable than are generally attributed to the Britons. Richard mentioni the *ostium Isca! flwvii:* And, from the mercantile charadler of the Danmonians, I should conceive a town of some consequence to have been built at the mouth of the Exe. Ia this commercial light, *Okehampton,* also, rises to view; situated on the*Ocrinumjugum,* by the rivers *Ocktnent,* and preserving the communication between the metropolis of Dantnonkrm, and the country to the north of this chain of mountains: And Okehampton, in a line with Exeter, might have been included in the cantred of Isca. But Drewsteinton, the town of *the Druids upon the Teign,* was exceeded, perhaps, only by the metropolis in extent or magnificence of building. Its name announces it to have been *the chief to-xvn of the Druids, upon the Teign.* (A) As Exeter was probably supported by its manufacturers and merchants, so Drewsteington might have been supported by its priests. That it was their favourite residence, is clearly proved by the many Druidical vestiges around it. It has not flourished, indeed, as a town for ages: But this is no objection to my supposition. As Druidism declined, its chief mansion funk: And with its Druids, Drewsteington perished. Nor is it likely, that the Romans would attempt to prop the mouldering ruin. The Romans would rather have razed it to the ground. They were the inveterate enemies of Druidism: And its chief scat was, probably, the first object of their vengeance. And Totnes, from its high antiquity, has, doubtless, some claim to distinction among the British towns. Totnes is situated on the ascent of a (r)rocky hill. It may be described, at present, as one good street about a mile in length, from s» The 6th coin in the 19th plate, in Borlase, seems to be a duplicate of. the 11th coin, though freatly defaced. *b) Drewflon* in the parish of Drewsteignton, and *Dreivjlcv* in Chagford, were also Druid towns. *c)* Letand thipks its original name was *DodrnicjJ'e*, signifying " *a rocky toiun."* *Ntjse* is a promontory. Westcote, speaking of Totnes, fays: " It prescribes»for antiquitie before any great Bryttanie yeildes; I speak vpon the good warrant of Geffry of Monmouth, who resolutely affirmeth, that the famoui lloman Trojan landed in this country, first at this place, when hee conquered this land: which it confirmed alsoe by the strength of the l'oet Havillan (if hee presume not a little too boldly) when bee savth. *yd dato Cursu Brutus Comitalus Acbate Gallorum fprtlis cvmulatui navibus aquor Exarat, et fuperii, auraque faventibus vfus Littora fælkes ititrat Totonefia portus.* This granted (for who will question the long belieued history of Brutus) wee may boldly *tt* clearly prescribe before all the townes and cityes in Great Bryttaine, for if there were any in Albion before jjis arrivall wee finde noe mention of them. Now let vs make a brife computation (to aver our tenet and to pass the time withall while wee are in this good towne) Brute aniued here in the time (as Grafton faith) that Hely was high Priest of Israel Anno mundi 2856: before our redemption 1108 yeares, who astir hee had conquered many famous Gyants, and his Cofen Corineus had in fayr play at a pull of wrestling thrown their Chiefe Leader Gogmagog over the Haw of Plymouth (though the ᴊᴄentish-men will haue it to bee at Dover) hee tooke a Survey of all this island, and coming by the ivvef T»ines for «he great pleasure hee tooke in the fayr meadowes, pleasant pastures, amenitie of ' " »! from east to west. It was once walled, and had four gates. Nor ought we to forget Armenton. Baxter in his glossary maintains, that Armenton or Arminton, was the *Ardua* of' Anonymous Ravennas, and that this was an erroneous transcript of Armina— *Ar-min-au, ad labiurn unda*—so called by the Britons. According to this writer, therefore, it was an ancient British town. And

where could the first Britons(a) have more conimodiously fixed their habitations, than on the banks of the river *Arme?* The town of Plymton seems to be marked as British by its conspicuous mound. The *Tamara* of Ptolemy and of Richard, which is still echoed by *Tamerton,* was, assuredly, a town of the Danmonians; and placed on the banks of such a fine river as the Tamar, it was, probably, a town of high commercial character. And the Voluba and Uxella of Ptolemy and Richard, as well as the Cenia of Richard, in the more western parts of Danmonium, must be placed among the ancient towns of the Britons. In the mean time, *Termolusb)* and *Artavia,(_c)* which Richard attributes to the Cimbri, and *(d)Mufidum* and *e)Halangium,* which the fame writer places among the Carnabii, are to be considered as flourishing towns before tiie Roman arrival: And, though not noticed by the ancient geographers, *Redruth* or *the Druid"s-totvn,* is peculiarly distinguished by the castle of Karnbre in its vicinity. Thus, then, have I placed the *civil* architecture of Danmonium in a more respectable light than it is generally considered. And, according to this theory, the *military* architecture of the Britons must proportionally rife in our esteem. Cæsar informs us, that the whole study of the nobles was war. That they should have made, therefore, a very great proficiency in the science of fortification might naturally be expected. The notion of the simple fortress in the woods, seems to be chiefly taken from Cæsar's description of a British town. But this description has not been sufficiently regarded. It is a picture of Britons skilled in war: It conveys to us an exalted idea of their military architecture. The fortress of Caffivellaunus, was *oppidum Jilvis paludibusque munitum.* And the Britons, fays Cæsar, *silvas impeditas valla atque jojj'a mttnierant.* the ayre, and bucksorne soyle, bordering her bankes (I doe but exemplifie the history) bee there began to build a citye, which in remembrance of the ancient razed Troy hee called Troye-novant which some 1041 yeares after by King Lndd named Luddstowne, now

bieifly London: Soe suppose Brute posted through the country, yet could hee not make such hast with his armye, in a strange countrye, in mountainous woodye, untraded wayes, nnmanured land, but it would require time; and hee could hardly conquer the whole Island which had such strong inhabitants, and especially build such a citye in less then 20 yeares, foe beeing 20 years before London it must bee 376 yeaies antienter then Rome, which was after London 356. and Chayr Ebrauck (now called Yorke) as built by Ebrauck king Mcmpricius sonn, 140 yeares after Anno mundi 2972. soe wee are clear for antiquitie. Now let vs fee what other matter it yieldes worthy our observation, we finde that Aurelius Ambros with his brother Vter Pendragon, sonnes to Constantius (of the mixed blood of the Bryttaines and Romanes) who fled very young from hence into Little Bryttaine (vpon the death of their elder brother king Constantius the younger ttaytetoufly slain by Vortigern termed the scourge of the countrye and king-killer) returned hither in their riper yeares, and besieged the Traytor in his Castle in Wales and consumed him with fire, about the yeare of our Lord 450. yet whence it should tike name, or of the Etymologie not a word is spoken: some take it from tlie french word Tout alesle which by interpretation is *all at ease;* as if Brute at his arrivall! in such a pleasant and fruitfull soyle, & healthy ayre, after soe painful! a navigation should assure himselfe & his fellowe trauellers of ease and rest, and soe fay vnto them, *tent alcjse* & the L in foe long time changed into N. (which is noe great alteration) we call it *Toutan.jJ'c;* this I could easily and willingly applaud, could I think of Brute being a Roman Trojan spake soe good french, or that the french tongue was then spoken at all; therefore I shall rather joyne in opinion with those which will haue it called Dodonesse which signifyeth the rockie towne, or towne on stones, which is very probable (and agreeable to the mind of Leland that ancient Antiquarie) for it standeson the declining of a hill verie stonie and rockie: others shall have leave to m ke conjectures & hunt further for the derivation of the name; I have done." Westcote's View of Devonshire (Portledge M.S.) p. 205, 206.

(a) " It was with these Armenians (fays Vallancey, on the authority of Sir George Yonge) that the Phenicians traded for tin: And we have, at this day, many places of Phenician origin in their names, both in Devon and Cornwall. And in the S.W. of Devonshire, there is stil! a river, called *Arm'me* ; and the town and hundred are called *Armne-ton* to this day. So, likewise, there was the *Scotium Mom* in Armenia." This is an odd coincidence! (A) Molland. (r) Camden speaks of " two towns, called *Hertcn* and *Hertland,* on the *promontory of Hercules* called, at this day, *Herty-pointl.*" (d) St. Maiva—qu. (e) *Helftont*—qu.

Vol. I. G And And the fort in question was *locum egregie natura atque of ere munitum.(a)t* The British fortress, we fee, was planted in the centre of the woods, defended by the advantages of its position, and secured by a regular rampart and fosse. And Cæsar speaks in the highest terras of its strength and contrivance. But this fastness in the woods, was no other than such a clanship as I at first described, agreeably to the vulgar idea of the British town. It was here, that the chief resided at intervals, together with his vassals and his cattle. Fond of changing the scene, he frequently removed from one fortress to another: And the number of his fortresses must have been determined by the extent of his property. If, then, the Britons could display such admirable workmanship in these occasional habitations, they must have exerted their ingenuity much more conspicuously in fortifying those cities or towns, where commerce or other causes had fixed their residence. Here, the fortress of the chief would be built on a more enlarged plan: And a castle would rife, in the bosom of the wood, perhaps in a turret-like form, and fortified wilh more extensive outworks. Of this sort of structure, perhaps the castle of Karnbre is the only one remaining, which we should venture to ascribe to the Britons. Karn-

brecastle(i) stands on a rocky knoll at the eastern end of Karnbre-hill. " The building is footed on an irregular ledge of vast rocks, whose surfaces are very uneven, some high, some low; and, consequently, the floors of the rooms on the ground-floor must be so too. The rocks were not contiguous; for which reason the architect has contrived so many arches from rock to rock, as would carry the wall above. The ledge of rocks was narrow; and the rooms purchased by so much labor, neither capacious nor handsome." There were some buildings, at the N. W. end, which were the outworks to this castle: But its greatest security was the difficult approach to it; the hill being strewed with large rocks on every side. But in the more improved clanslip, the fortress where the chief resided, was by no means sufficient for its defence. Some building must have been necessary, perhaps, on a more elevated scite, capacious enough for a large garrison, and for the residence, also, of the chief and his domestics. I have already observed, that a mount was, probably, erected on the highest grounds, in the neighbourhood of every clansliip—that it was, at first, the mark of a new settlement, agreeably to the Asiatic custom, but that, very sliortly, it was used as a beacon. In process of time, however, these mounts presented themselves to the Britons, as the most convenient situations for their castellated structures: And, for the defence of the more populous and flourishing clanships, which had been enlarged into considerable towns, and in which the inhabitants, at length, were stationary, the *beacon* became the *(c)ieep* of a castle. Thus, in Ireland, are a great number of round hills, for the most part artificial, on which turrets or castles are erected, *(d)* The castle of Rougemont stands on the highest part of the hill on which Exeter is built, and on the N. E. extremity. The mount, was, probably, volcanic j and the masonry on the top of it, raised by the labor of the ancient Britons: But the outworks must be attributed to subsequent times. Okehampton-castle, which stands a little west of the centre of the county, and near the town of Okehamp-

ton, is said to have been built by Baldwin *de Brioniis,* who, as it appears from Domesday-book, was in possession of it, when that survey w as taken. But, I think, this castle has the appearance of much higher antiquity. Its scite near *Ockinton* (the town on the *Ock)* and just on the *Ocrinum Jugum,* which carries with it the name of the river, suggests to us the idea of a British fortress; whilst its artificial mount, thrown up on so commanding a spot, seems equally calculated for the purposes of a colonial landmark, a beacon, or a keep. At present, Okehampton-castle is in ruins; though there remains a part of the keep, and some fragments of high walls, the solidity of which, together with their advantageous situation, and the space they occupy, clearly evince, that when entire, this castle was both strong and extensive. The castle of Totnes stands on the N.W. side of the town, not far from the ruins of the north-gate. Its keep, of great acclivity, rises to a towering height, and commands the circumjacent country to a vast extent. The mount of earth at Plymton, was, doubtless, thrown up by the Britons. This mount of a pyramidical form, is about twp hundred feet in circumference, and seventy in height: On the top, *(a)* Cæsar, lib. v. sect. xx.

(/) Eorlase's Antiquities, p. 319, 320.
(f) A Keep is a building elevated above the rest, by a mount or tumulus, for the most part artificially raised. Eorlase's Antiquities, p. 318. (/) See Wright's Louthiana. it it has a circular wall. Trematon-castle, near Saltasli, from its keep and other particulars, I conceive to have been Britilh. That it existed before the Norman Conquest, will be proved hereafter. And it was certainly neither Danish, Saxon, nor Roman. But whether it was raised by the Britons in this or a subsequent period, we cannot determine. Restormel-castle was, likewise, anterior to the conquest; But when it was built by the Britons, is uncertain. It stands about a mile north of the town of Lostwithiel, not on a factitious hill, but on a rocky knoll on the edge of a hill, overlooking a deep valley. The rock is planed into a'level, and ihaped round by a ditch: And the keep erected

upon the rock, has sufficient elevation. At Trematon, the keep is raised on an artificial hill. As Launceston, or Dunheved-castle was, undoubtedly, the strongest and the moll spacious of all the Danmonian castles, I (hall give a more particular description of it. Leland, who had seen the most remarkable buildings in England, observes: " The(a) hill, on which the keep stands, is large, and of a very terrible height, and the arx of it— the keep—having three several wards, is the strongest, but not the biggest that ever I saw in any ancient work in England." 1 The principal entrance (lays Borla(e) (b) it on the N. E. the gateway, one hundred and twenty feet long. The whole keep is ninetythree feet diameter. It consisted of three wards. The wall of the first ward was not quite three feet thick, and therefore, I think, could only be a parapet to defend the brow of the hill. The wall of the second ward is twelve feet thick, and has a stair-cafe three feet wide, at the left hand of the entrance, running up to the top of the rampart: The entrance of this stair-caie has a round arch of stone over it. On the left of the entrance into tire third ward, a stair-cafe leads to the top of the innermost rampart, the wall of which 13 ten feet thick, and thirty-two feet high from the floor. The room is eighteen feet six inches diameter. The lofty taper hill on which this strong keep is built, is partly natural and partly artificial. It spread farther into the town anciently than it does at present; and by the *radius* of it was three hundred and twenty feet diameter, and very nigh. Norden gives us a wall at the bottom of this hill: And, though there is no stress to be laid on his drawings, yet it is not unlikely that it had a wall or parapet, round the bottom of it, towards the town; as the principal rampart of the bass-court breaks otf very abruprly, fronting the town. More than half the bass-court is now covered with houses. " Mr. King's remarks on this castle aie ingenious. " *Launceston-castle(c)* (fays Mr. King) must be placed among castles of very great antiquity; both on account of the manner in which the stair-cales are constructed, and on account of the

small dimensions of the area of the inner tower. Perhaps, it was erected in the first ages, by the Danmonii, who had acquired a degree of art beyond the rest of the Britons, from their commercial intercourse with the eastern nations." But my conjectures relating to the eastern origin of the Danmonii, will best answer to the subsequent description. " We cannot but remark (continues Mr. King) the similarity between this Castle of Launceston, and that ofEcbatana, the capital of Media, as described by Herodotus. The keep of our magnificent fortress, which was built in the first ages of the world, greatly resembles the keep of Ecbatana. At Launceston we find three great and elevated circular walls, towering *ever* and *behind* each other; namely, the wall of the first ward; that of the second ward; and that of the innermost ward or central tower. Besides which, there is, on one part, the outward wall of the bass-ceurt of the castle— which would appear in many directions at a distance, as a fourth wall beneath the rest. Herodotus(?) tells us, that Dejoces compelled the Medes to come under one polity, and to build a city, surrounded with fortifications; and that seven strong and magnificent walls (known by the name of Ecbatana) were then built. They were, he fays, of a circular form, one within the other; and each gradually raised just so much above the other as the battlements are high; the situation of the ground, which rose by an easy ascent, being favourable to the design. The *king's palace and treasury* were built within the *innermost circle* of the seven which composed the city. The first: and most spacious of those walls, was equal, in circumference, to the city of Athens; and white from the foot of the battlements; the second black; the third of a purple color; the fourth blue; and the fifth of a deep orange—all being coloured with different compositions. And of the two innermost walls, one was (a) Vol. 2, p. 79. (i) Antiquities, p. 326. (c) Arch. vol. 6. p. 291. ' (/) Book 1st.
Vol. I. 6 » painted painted on the battlements, of a silver color; and the other gilded with gold. Having thus provided

for his own security, he ordered the people to fix their habitations without the walls of this city. This is very nearly a description of Launceston-castle, and the adjacent town—almost the only difference being, that the scale in one instance, is larger than in the other, and that the battlements of the walls of the one were painted with different colors, and those of the other left plain. As to the affinity of these buildings, or the derivation of the plan of Dunheved, from the east, every one must be left to form his own conclusions: But when I read in the 9th chapter of the *zd* book, of Kings, that on Jehu's being anointed King over Israel, at Ramoth-Gilead, the captains of the host, who were then fitting in council, as soon as they heard thereof, took every man his garment, and put it under him, *on the top os the stairs* ; and blew with trumpets, proclaiming— " Jehu is King!" and when I consider the historian's account of Ecbatana, which was at no great distance from Syria, and in a country much connected with it, and reflect also, upon the appearance of the top of the staircase, at Launceston, I am apt to conclude, that at Launceston, is still to be beheld nearly the fame kind of architectural scenery, as was exhibited on the inauguration of Jehu at Ramoth-Gilead."

Thu3 I have described two sorts of British castles; the first fort turretwile; the second with a keep. And I have described the British architecture, both *civil* and *military,* in a more advanced state than is generally conceived. In the mean time, there were roads, which not only passed from town to town, but formed extensive communications through Danmdnium and the neighbouring kingdoms. That Belinus made a high road through the whole length of the island, is asserted by our chronicles: But this, sorely, is apocryphal.*(a)* The existence of British roads rflay be maintained on better authority. The trading spirit of the Danmonians could not have rested for a moment without fitch communications. Before the Romans (fays Mr. Whitaker) there were, probably, several ways in the southern parts of the island; which had been previously laid out, though rudely, for the public u!e, and adapted, though indifferently, to the conveyance of its natural commodities to the ports, and to the introduction of foreign from them.(A) Mr. Whitaker plainly proves, that the two great roads of the *Wailing* and *Ikening* streets (the first leading to the *Guethcli* or *Gatheli* of Ireland—the second, to the *Iceni* of the eastern coast) were originally undertaken and executed before the invasion of the Romans. *a* Both must have been begun, he fays, by the Belgæ of the south countries: Aud, what is very extraordinary, both plainly appear to *hiwe* commenced from the south." According to my theory, the first British roads would have been framed by the Danmonii, in whose country the British trade originated: And, in the progress of commerce from the weft, these roads would have been gradually extended, and new communications opened through the island.

Such

' (3) Sammes tells us, In his *Britannia Antiqua Illustrata,* that " *Be'yn* set himself to the finishing of that great work begun by his father *Duirzvallo,* the making and paving of four great high-waves through his kingdom of *Loegria,* now called *England.* The first is named *Fofs,* and beginneth at the corner of *Totnejs* in *Cornwall,* and passeth through *Devon/hire* and *Somtrfetjhirt,* and so to *Coventry, Leicester,* and from thence (as *Ranulph,* a monk of *Chester,* recordeth) through the -.*castes* to *Newark,* and ended at *Lincoln."* P. 173. " Att this town held the most south or south most part of this kingdo.Tie began the Ffosta-street which with Watling-street & Ikmeld-street & Exming-street were the 4 high-wayes that trauerfed over England, first began by that sapient Lawguier Mulmutius kinge of this Realme, and finished *ic* paued by his martial fonne Belynus vpon the credit of the Bryttyfh storye 500 yeares before the jncarnation of Christ, thes 4 wayes crossed over the whole Land, being very needmll& necessary both in warrsas peace, and previledged as well by Mulmutius his own edicts, as the Roman Lawes, and should bee in like re-

spect with vs, the name intimating as much j the Kings High way. and Bracton faith they are *Res sacra, et qui aliquid occupaverit, excedendam stnei et terminus terra jua, dicitur fecijfe preepresturam super ipsupi regem:* They are priviledged places, and hee that makes trespass there committs preprasture vpon the King himfelfe. This ftbssestreet tooke beginning here (1)at this town & runneth through the whole (hire & Somerset (& in some places to bee perceived) and foe (as an Author faith) toTutburye & by Chesterton, by Coventry, vnto Leycester, and foe from thence by wildes and playnes to Newark and thence to Lyncoln." Westcote's View (Portledge M.S.) p. 206.

(b) Col. Simcoe is of opinion, that the British commerce must have required public roads before the Roman arrival. In a letter to the author, the Colonel fays: " The mountainous region of (1) Totntt.

Dartmoor

Such are the two different representations of the *civil* and *military* architecture of the Britons; which, I think, may be brought to harmonize, by considering the little towns in the woods or the caverns in the rocks, as the immediate resource of the settlers, and the larger towns or cities as the product of an advanced colonization. Nor is it at all improbable, that a great number of such fastnesses in the woods, which were by no means contemptible, lhould have remained in their original state, the temporary residence of their respective chiefs; whilst a few from their advantageous scite, or other circumstances, might have been surrounded with buildings to a great extent, the sents of manufacture and the marts of commerce. If, however, these different representations cannot be reconciled, I do not scruple to attribute the meaner architecture to the Belgic tribes; whilst the more splendid and magnificent, undoubtedly, belongs to our colonists from Asia.

From the *dvH* and *military* buildings of the Danmonii, let us pass to the *religious.* The »estiges of Druidilm that are to be traced in Danmonium, must be our chief guide, on the present subject. I

(hall describe our Druidical monuments in the following order-, the Rock-Idol—the Logan-Stone—the Rock-Bason—the single Stone-Pillar—tiuo, three, ar more Stone-Pillars—Circular Stone-Pillars—Inscribed Stone-Pillars—and the Cromlech.

In the Druid ages, stones of various shapes were consecrated to religion. The Arabians, the Syrians, and the Phenicians worshipped conical or quadrangular stones, the images of their Gods. But the eastern people confined not their homage to rocks of a particular shape: They prostrated themselves before the rudest. In Danmonium, the Druids, as I have already observed, professed to believe, that rocky places were the favourite abodes of their divinities. And, wherever we find stones, which are at the fame time massy and mistiapen, there we look for the druidical gods. Vastness, in short, and rudeness, were the characteristics of the Druid *Rock-Idols.* In Cornwall, Borlale has noticed a great number of these stone deities; though he seems to have indulged his fancy in attempting to give exact and discriminating delineations of idols that mock description. In Devonshire, we have an ample field for such investigation. But, the misfortune is, that nature has exhibited her wild scenery in so many places, that we know not whither to direct our first attention. She has scattered the rocks around us so profusely, that we are afraid to fix on a Druid-Idol, lest the neighbouring mass should have the fame pretensions to adoration; and all the stones upon the hills and in the vallies, should start up into divinities. If Bowerman's-Nose, for instance, in the vicinity of Dartmoor, be considered as a rock-idol of the Druids, there is scarcely a torr on the forest, or its environs, but may claim the fame distinction. Yet this enormous mass of stone upon Heighendown, in Manaton, has been marked as druidical. Placed on a most elevated spot, it rises to the height of more than fifty feet. Viewed at a distance, it has the appearance of a human figure: and its gigantic form has given rife to a variety of fables. On approach, ing it, we find that it consists of several ledges of granite, piled one upon another, in the rudest manner. If, however, we bow down to this gramtical god, we ihall meet deities at every step; whilst (a)Heytorr, a hundred feet in height, the tons of Believer and of Heslkry—whilst Mistorr, and the torr of Ham,(A) Steeperton-torr, and Mil torr and Rowtorr, frown on us with new majesty. Thus Dartmoor wouid be one wide Druid(r temple;

Dartmoor (part of the Ocrinum Jugnm of the ancients) separates Devonshire into two districts, each of which must have had its *disiinfl road;* while a third must have penetrated the mountains, to afford a ready conveyance for the tin, which abounded in those regions. These roads, from the nature of the country, mult have passed the F.xe at the fame ford, in their progress towards the isle of Wight: and this ford I take to have been that above Cowley Bridge, between Pynes and the camp on the heights of Stoke, above *Duryard, the ancient-wood,* as its name signifies. This road, upon the fame principles, may be traced over the Clyst, the Otter, and the Axe, till it leaves Devonshire; and must have been prior to Vespasian. Sir R. Worsley, in his History of the Isle of Wight, to the best of my recollection, mentions the ford, and where it is probable (according to Diodorus) that it passed to that ifland." This far Colonel Simcoe. That passage of Diodorus Siculus, which relates to the Danmonian commerce, will be examined in the eighth section of this chapter.
(a) Certainly a rock-idol: Its *bajon,* added to its *enormity* and *unshapelines,* determines the point, *(b)* Hamstorr on Dartmoor. (-) Figuratively speaking. The principal rocks on Dartmoor, however, might have been British idols. And in the vicinity of each idol, was, probably, a British town. Blackstone and Whitstone, we may conclude, were rock-idols, from the terms of wonder with which they are noticed both by Rifdon temple; and its dark waste, now consecrated ground, would breathe a browner horror. In the parish of Drewsteignton, which seems to have been

singled out by the Druids, as the peculiar feat of their religion, there is, at the end of a down, at no great distance from the Cromlech, an awful precipice; where the rocks are divull'ed into gloomy chasms, and terminate abruptly in a perpendicular manner. Than this spot, none could be more adapted to religious worship *sub dio,* or to the accommodation of a numerous assembly. One rock in particular, about sixteen feet high, detached from other masses and plane on the superficies, the quoit of which hanging over the stratum below projects three or four feet, appeared well suited for an orator to address the multitude. Adjoining to this spot is another detached body, most singular in its appearance—having two ledges approaching towards each other, yet not touching, being separated by a perpendicular hollow about a foot wide, through which may be discerned other rocks lying behind. Over these, in the manner of a Cromlech, a transverse enormous impost superintends, decorated with old fantastic ivy, and tufted with a moss peculiar to the moorstone. At a s little distance from Grimlpound, on Hameidown, in Manaton, is *Grimstorr* ; to the south of which, on Withecombecommon, is Broad-burrow, and still further south, Threeburrows, About four miles from Ashburton, in the parish of Dean-Prior, the vale of Dean-Burn unites the terrible and the graceful in so striking a manner, that to enter this recess hath the effect of enchantment; whilst enormous rocks seem to close around us, amidst the deep foliage of venerable trees, and the roar of torrents. And Dean-Burn would yield a noble machinery for working on superstitious minds under the direction of the Druids. In the mean time, sliapelef's piles of stone, on Exmoor or the adjacent country, might be approached as rock-idols of the Britons. The Valley of Stones, indeed, in the vicinity of Exmoor, is so awfully magnificent, that we need not hesitate in pronouncing it to have been the favourite residence of Druidism. And the country around it, Is peculiarly wild and romantic, *(a)* This valley is about half a mile in length, and, in gen

eral, about three hundred feet in breadth, situated between two hills, covered with an immense quantity of stones, and terminated by rocks which rife to a great height, and present a prospect uncommonly grotesque. At an opening between the rocks, towards the close of the valley, there is a noble view of the British channel and the Welsh coast. The scenery of the whole country in the neighbourhood of this curious valley is wonderfully striking, (i) The Valley of Stones has a close resemblance

Risdon and Westcote. The latter thus expresses himself: " T recall myself to Moreton, vpon fight of those two workes which shew themselues so great and huge, they are distant one from the other three miles, and are distinguished by severall names of White; one and Blackstone. the last scemeth somewhat strange to all beholders, to other some a fearefull wonder, for it is a very great woike set vpon another of much lesse quantity, which it overlayeth ffar on each syde. And embossed with so great a bellye that many men and beasts may be sheltered vnder the coverture thereof yet so equally peazed that there is noe ffeare of ffalling though it sceme at first doubtfull." Westcote's View (Portledge M.S.) p. 2ao., (a) The Valley of Stones is, in some measure, indebted, for the distinction to which it hath lately been raised, to Dr. Fococke, Bishop of Upper-Ossory, who visited it some years since, with Dr. Milles, Dean of Exeter. (i) A Gentleman, who lately visited this valley, was so kind as to communicate the following description of!t to the Author: " At the lower end, where the valley of stones was the widest, about four hundred feet, in the middle (as it were stopping up the valley) arose a vast bulwark of rocks, tier upon tier, like some gigantic building in part demolished; and the stones that composed it flung across each other in the wildest confusion—a mass more rude and enormous than any I had yet observed. More than half of the valley was shut from the sea by its bread base, which tapering by degrees, closed at its apex in a conical form. The imagination would be at a loss to figure a ruder congeries than was here beheld. Rocks piled upon rocks at one time in unequal and rough layers; at another, transrerse, and diagonally inclined against-each other; in short, in every form possible to be conceived; threatening, however, every moment to be released fronr their contiguity to one another, and to precipitate themselves into the valley or the depth of waters. On the left fide, one only rock attracted my notice. This projected boldly from the inclining steep, and thrusting itself forward, braved the cold blasts of the Severn sea with its7 broad perpendicular front chequered with creeping ivy, and teinted with variegated moss. The valley lost itself rapidly, on either side the conical mountain in the sea. Beyond it, the cliffs rose higher and higher, upright from the waters—towards the interior country cloathed with wood, which (though at a distance) formed a pleasing and striking contrast with the scenery on this side, which had nothing of the picturesque in it, but comprized every thing that was wild, grand, and terrific.' to to several of those spots in Cornwall, which tradition has sanctified with the venerable names of rock-idols, Loganstones, or rock-basons: And the north of Devon, though it may furnish us with no tradition of the Druids, must yet be examined with an eye to druidical antiquities. If the hills or the vallies which have been long consecrated to the genius of the Druids of Cornwall, deserve so high an honor, I have fittle doubt but that the fame distinction is due to those romantic scenes in Devonshire, which hitherto we have been led to view with an incurious eye; or to admire, perhaps, for their rude magnificence, whilst we carried our ideas no farther than the objects themselves. Not that the Druids formed these scenes: No—they only availed themselves of such recesses; to which they annexed sanctity, by commemorating there, the rites of religion. The rock idols are *surely natural*—as natural as the groves of Mona: But as they suited the superstition of the times, and served to add a solemnity to the druidical institutions, the policy of those who governed the devotions of the multitude,

turned this fantastic scenery to the best account; and secured the public reverence by impressing every imagination with the wild and the terrible. But this was not all. Whilst the fancy was awed with such rude grandeur, an attempt was made to attract admiration by something that bore the appearance of art: And the Druids endeavoured to gain credit among the vulgar, for the extent of their mechanical powers, by pointing to objects which to a careless eye might appear an artificial structure more than a natural mass, the effect of design and not of chance. But those rocks are, undoubtedly, natural; though some labor was employed, in a few instances, to make them look artificial. Nature, or some great convulsion in nature, left those rocks in their present fantastic state: Or, if any art were applied to rock-idols, it was only to remove some earth, or some surrounding stones from the larger or more curious mass: And, then, the whole would put on the tremendous appearance which it now bears. The whole army of Xerxes could not have raised, by force or skill, such ledges of rock, piled up in the Valley of Stones, as if by human industry. The most remarkable rock-idol in this valley is the Cheesewring. Lyttelton(a) oblerves, that it greatly resembles the cheesewring near Alternon. Between Combmartin and Linton (fays the Dean) (4) and opposite to what you apprehend to be a Druid gorseddau, is a karn of rocks, which they call the Cheesewring. It is much like that at Alternon." Dr. Borlasc has taken no notice of the cheesewring at Alternon; but he describes a wringcheese in the parish of St. Clere—" a groupe of rocks that attracts the admiration of all travellers. " The whole heap of stone (he fays) is thirty-two feet high: and the great weight of the stones above, and the flenderness of those below, makes every one wonder how so ill-grounded a pile could resist for so many ages the storms of such an exposed situation. It may seem to some, that this is an artificial building of flat stones laid carefully on one another, and raised to this height by human skill and labor: But, as there are

several heaps of stones on the fame hill, and also on a hill about a mile distant, called *Hell-man;* of like sabrick to this, though not near so high, I should think it a natural cragg, and that what stones surrounded it and hid its grandeur, were removed by the Druids. From the well-poised structure, and the great elevation of the groupe (as well as other circumstances) I think we may truly reckon it among the rock-deities; and that its tallness and nice ballance might probably be intended to express the statelinefs and justice of the supreme Being. (r) Borlafe discovers the traces of Saturn, Mars, and Mercury, in the names of several places, where his rock-idols are situated. Thus in *Bellever-Torr* upon Dartmoor, we have the rock of *Bel* or *Belus*—in *Belfton,* at its northern extremity, *the ton:n of Belus*—in *Mi/lorr* the rock of *Mi/or*—in *Hejsary-torr* the *(a)* Afterwards, Bishop of Carlisle. *(b)* In a letter to Milles. *(c)* Borlase's Antiquities, p. 165. Perhaps the most curious stone-deity in Cornwall, Is that *f* vail oval pebble in the parish of Constantine, which is placed on the points of two natural rocks. The longest diameter of this stone is thirty-three feet, pointing due north and south: And it is fourteen feet six inches deep. See Borlase's Antiquities, (i)plate XI. p. 166. A very ingenious , friend lately informed me, that he had long considered this *To/men* as " *Cutbite,* and as a representation of the ARK resting on Mount *Ararat."* He once suggested this idea to Mr. Bryant, who, pn looking at the plate in Borlafe, was struck at the conjecture, and thought it extremely probable. The *Icimeu* is, undoubtedly, an exact figure of the *Ark.* rock of *Hesus.* Thus *Hamftorr,* also, was the rock of *Ham* or *Ammon:* And the numerous *(a)Hams* in Devonshire, all carry us to the lame original. This much for the Rock-Idol.

The *Logan* or *Rocking-Stone* must, also, be noticed among the rude stone-monuments of the Druids. Pliny hath, evidently, the Logan-stone in view, when he tells us, that at Harpasa, a town of Asia, was a rock of a wonderful nature. " Lay one ringer on it and it will stir; but thrust at it with your whole body, and it will not move."(A) There is another passage in Pliny's Natural History, extremely apposite to the present subject: Yet I have never seen it quoted in any account of these natural or artificial wonders. " *Talis* (Colossus) *et Tarenti faSus a Lyfippo* XL *cubitorum. Mirum in eo, quod manu, ut ferunt, mobilis, ea ratione libramenti efi, ut nullis con-vellatur frocellis: Id quod pro-vidi-jj'e et artifex dicitur, modico intervallo, unde maxime flatum opus erat frangi, oppofita columna. Itaque propter magnitudinem dijficultatemque movendi non attigit eum Fabius Verrucofus, cum Herculem qui eft in capitolio hide transferret."* (r) In Wales, this stone is called *Y Maen Sigt,* that is, *the Shaking-ftone.* But, " in Cornwall, we call this stone *Logan* (fays Borlase) the meaning of which I do not understand." This is singular. In the language of the vulgar, to *logg* is *to move to and fro:d)* It is a frequent word both in Cornwall and Devon, at the present day: And it always implies this kind of vibratory motion, *(e)* Toland seems to be of opinion, that the Logan-stone was placed in its present position by human art. But, in general, it is thus nicely balanced by the hand of nature. In the parish of Drewsteignton, under Piddledown, and in the channel of the Teign, is a druidical monument of this description. The *Moving-rock* is thus poised upon another mass of ftone, which is deep-grounded in the bed of the river: It is unequally sided, of great fee, at some parts six, at others seven feet in height, and at the west end, ten. From its west to east points, it may be in length about eighteen feet. It is flattisli on the top. It seems to touch the stone below in no less than three or four places; but, probably, it is the gravel which the floods have' left between, that causes this appearance. I easily rock'd it with one hand; but its quantity of motion did not exeeed one inch, if so much. The equipoise, however, was more perceptible a few years since: And it was, probably, balanced with such nicety in former times, as to meve with the slightest touch. It is remarkable, that the surface of the lower stone is somewhat sloping,

so that it should seem easy to shove off the upper ftone; but the united efforts of a number of men, who endeavoured to displace it, had not the smallest effect. Both the stones are granite, which is thick strewn in the channel of the river, and over all the adjacent country. It seems to have been the work of nature. Shall we suppose that it has subsisted from the beginning; or that the upper stone fell from the rocks of the adjoining steep; or was left here by the deluge? On the brow of a hill, near the fame river, at Holy-street, in the parish of Chagford, is another Logan-stone. It is not so large as that at Drewsteignton is more easily moved, and rocks more. I thought I discovered a cavity in the centre os the surface of the lower ftone, seeming to receive a corresponding part of the upper. That this Logan-stone is the work of art, copied by the Druids from similar ones in nature, would not admit of a doubt, if the circumstance of the mortice *weve(f)* ascertained. The scenery around the

Drewsteignton *(a)* Places consecrated to the *god Ham,* or colonized by *Ham the fin of Noah,* afterwards worshipped as a god under various forms.
() Pliny—Lib. II. c. 69. (s) L. 34, c. 7. *(d)* So a Cornish tinner explained the word to me: And, on Ashburton-Downs, a common labourer, on my mentioning a rocking-stone, instantly called it a *Iigan-rotk.* On my asleing him the meaning of *hgan,* he said: *-l Why, he lc£gs* (moves) *to and fro."* (e) Hist. Druid. p. 103. *(f)* Before I had paid a visit to the Logan-stones, I received the following remarks on the druidical scenery of Drewsteignton and the neighbourhood, from a gentleman, whose keen insight into antiquities excites my admiration, whilst his good-nature and unaffected manner of communicating his discoveries, no less awaken my gratitude. " On the very edge of the river Teign, is a most enormous stone, or piece of rock, supported on the sharp points of two others, in such a manner that this stone which hangs over them, may be set in motion by a man, and will vibrate backwards and forwards with an appearance as if it would fall into the

river: Yet no power or force can displace it. This hanging-stone is nearly the size of that which covers the three pillars at Drewsteignton. On each fide of the banks of the Teign, and throughout the parish of Chagford, the fields and roads were covered with huge stones, not quite so large as those at Drewsteignton or at Sticklepath, but which have, also, the appearance of *ruins.* Large clusters of them are seen in some grounds Drewsteignton Logan-stone has an uncommon grandeur. The path that leads to it by the margin of the river Teign, winds along, beneath the precipitous hill of Piddle-down. This hill rises majestically high, to the north: And, at the greatest distance, is seen a channel, like a streamwork, evidently formed by the floods, which have washed down, in many places, me natural foil into the river, and left it bare and rocky, or sandy. On the other fide of the Teign, and opposite to this hill, the richness of Whiddon-park forms a beautiful contrast with these craggy declivities. Such is this druidical scenery, which inspires even the cultivated mind with a fort of religious terror. We need not wonder, then, that the ignorant multitude were struck with astonishment at the fearful magnificence of every object, whether they turned their eyes up the steep where the rocks frowned over them, or whether they looked onward through the valley, where foamed the waters of the Teign; since, to the vulgar, every rock was a god, or the residence of some spiritual intelligence, and even the gloom it slied was sacred—since the river was the habitation of genii, by whose agency its waters were restrained within its banks, or burst forth to deTuge the country. Amidst such a scene, therefore, the Logan stone, Which, doubtless, acquired a more than common degree of sanctity from its position in the very channel of the river, must have been an admirable engine of priestcraft, and have operated on the multitude precisely as the Druids wislied. In the parish of WitheCombe, between Withecombe-church and Rippen Torr, there is a Logan-stone, of a roundish form, measuring eleven feet in diameter. It is called the Nutcrackers; having been the resort of the common people, during the nut season, for the purpose of cracking their nuts. But in consequence of its being thus frequented, the owner of the estate where it stood (if I was rightly informed) got it removed from its ancient position: So that it is, at present, motionless; though, before it was displaced, it was made to vibrate by a very little force. On East-down, in the parish of Manaton, is a Logan-stone, called in the neighbourhood the *(a) rVbooping-rock,* from the noise which it used to make, when set in motion by the winds. In stormy weather, it might be heard at the distance Of at least three miles, with the wind. A few years ago, several persons moved it by main force, off its balance t So that it *loggs no* more. It is evidently a druidical Loganstone—and has been venerated by the superstitious neighbourhood as an enchanted rock, from the time of the Druids to the present day: And the hands that wantonly displaced it from its primitive position, are execrated by the villagers around, as having profanely violated the spirit of the rock. Two ledges of stone run parallel to each other, with a considerable opening between them; or rather one large rock, disparted by some violent convulsion. A stone was placed at the west end of the south ledge, on one little point. This, then, was the Logan-stone, that moved at the slightest touch, whilst it preserved its equipoise. Near the Valley of Stones, there is a Logan-stone on the top of a very high cliff. The upper stone is of a different quality from that on which it rests. It is more solid and gritty: A large piece of rock is fallen on it. *(b)*—The use of the Loganstone is uncertain. According to Toland, " the Druids made the people believe, that grounds adjoining to Whiddon-park: And on a high hill, just above the house of a Mr. Sonthmead, there is a huge mass, supported at one end by an enormous pillar, and the other end leaning against the hill." I can only add, that in consequence of these remarks, I have narrowly inspected all this scenery—with a strong prepossession on my mind, that it was, in

a great measure, *artificial,* i was almost determined to convert every cluster of stones into a *ruin:* But I was much disappointed on viewing these phenomena. They are certainly *natural.* If they are *ruins,* they are the *fuins* only of nature, deluged by torrents or convulsed by earthquakes. *(a)* Giraldus Cambrensis mentions a large flat stone, ten feet long, fix wide, and one foot thick, which in his time served as a bridge over the river Alun, in Pembrokeshire. It was called in British, *Lecb Lavar,* that is, the *Speaking-fane:* And the vulgar tradition was, that when a dead body happened to be carried over, this stone spoke, and with the struggle of the voice cracked in the middle; and the chink, from which the voice issued, was then to be seen. Possibly, this tradition might be owing to its having been once in a situation to make a *whooping* sound; like the *Wboopivgrock* or slogan-stone of Manaton. (i) Mr. Badcock says, " that he cannot be certain that it ever moved." But his correspondent informs him, that " some years ago, there was a rock in the Valley of Stones that was balanced and moved, but that one of the fragments near it having fallen through decay, the end rested and still rests on this stone, so that it can no longer be moved. From the whole of what I have heard of it, says this gentleman, I have no doubt but these rocky fragments are the ruins of a Druid temple."
Vol. *X,* H they they alone could move these stones, and by a miracle only; by which pretended miracle, they condemned or acquitted the accused, and often brought criminals to confess, what could in no other way be extorted from them."(«) And, surely, it is not improbable, that the Druids discovering this uncommon property in the natural Logan-stones, loon learned to make use of it as an occasional miracle, and that they consecrated artificial Logan-rocks, where nature had not already prepared them. Spirits were then reported to inhabit these rocks; the vibratory morion I have described, was adduced in proof of this; and, to complete the whole, the Logan-stone became an idol.

The two Druidical monuments which

I have now represented, are both so rude, and of such different sizes, that to convey a just notion of their form, is impossible. They are, indeed, in a great measure, natural. But it is their enormity, the singularity of their position, the#curiousness of their combination, and the grotesque appearance of surrounding objects, that suggest the idea of their druidical ianctity. Yet the Rock-idol and the Logan-ftone have frequently less dubious marks of Druidism. The *Rock-bason,* which is often found on both, is a vestige of the Druids, less equivocal. The *hollows* or *artificial basons,* funk into the surface of the rocks, are monuments of a very singular kind. They are generally found on the highest hills, and on the tops of the most conspicuous karns. They are never seen on the side of rocks, but always on the top; their openings horizontally facing the heavens. These basons are not uniform in their (hape: some are quite irregular, some oval, and some are exactly circular. Their size is from fix feet to a few inches in diameter. Some have lips or outlets: Others have none. The (mailer basons have often little falls into a larger balbn, which receives their tribute, and detains it, having no outlet. Other large basons, intermixed with little ones, have passages from one to another, and by successive falls uniting, transmit what they receive into one common bason, which has a drain, that serves itself, and all the basons above it. Dr. BorkuVs remarks on Rock-basons, are to this purpose: And my own observations have confirmed the truth of them. Of the basons on the Rock-idols, the following have fallen under my notice. On a rock, at no great disance from the cataract in Christow, is a bason of this description: And there are several Rock-basons on the top of that vast pile of stone, at the end of the Druidical down in Drewsteignton. On *Willingstom-rock,* in Moretonhampstead, are two *Rockbafins. Kefior-roci,* on the east side of Dartmoor, and *Heytorr* on the S. E. border of the forest, on Ashburton downs, are natural rocks, rising out of the earth: But they have *small basons* hollowed out on their tops; of whicli some will hold four or five gallons, being two feet or more in diameter, and from six to ten inches deep. There is a flight of steps, regularly cut out, in Heytorr-rock, by which the Druids might ascend to the bason on the top, and perform the accustomed ceremonies, whilst the multitudes were assembled below. In Withecombe parilh, *Miltorr* must have been a rock in high estimation with the Druid priesthood. On the top ledge of stone (which is twelve feet by eight) there are four *basons*. The largest baton is two feet three quarters; the second, one foot three quarters; the third, one foot and one quarter; the fourth, one foot. The first and fourth, are placed south; the second, due east; the third, north. These Rock-basons have, each of them, a lip: But they do not communicate as is the case in some monuments of this kind. To one of these basons there are little ducts, designed to lead the water from the inclined plane into the cavity. From this eminence of *Miltorr,* a wild collection of karns are seen, at various distances, consisting of different species of granite, unmixed with any other stone— such as Belt-torr—Beniietorr—Yarter-torr—Quarnell-torr—Sharper-torr.— On Bel-torr, are two very large Rock, basons, on one detached fragment of rock; and one Rock-bason on another fragment ot rock. They are»all without lips*;* and on the very verge of the rocks—which is always, indeed, the case. The fragment (for such I call it from its appearance) on which the two basons appear, is at some distance from the other enormous masses of stone. Benjie-torr is a bare stone hill—Yarter-torr consists of large ledges of rock, irregularly piled—Quarnell-torr will occur among the barrows—On Sharper-torr there is a bason, on the edge of the rock, with one lip. On Dartmoor, within the limits of the paristi of Holn, there are various grotesque rocks, with basons. On *Pentorr,* in Dartmoor, are *four basons,* cut on the top stone, each about two feet in diameter. On the Loganrock which I have described, in the-channel of the Teign, is a bason of an elliptical *(4)* Hist, *fl* the Druids, p. 203.

form. The above are the Rock-basons which I have had an opportunity of noticing-iu Devon. And they correspond with Borlase's description of the Rock-basons in Cornwall. Eat many of thele basons are mere natural hollows. And their formation is to be attributed to the water. The surface of the rocks was, at first, rugged: And rainwater, repeatedly falling, and naturally resting in the little hollows, would wear them into deep hollows. Yet there are, surely, Rock-basons that are not owing to such attrition; particularly those which have lips: Most of the lip-hollows are, confessedly, artificial. With respect to the use of these basons, I think we may easily conjecture, that they were contrived by the Druids, as receptacles of water, for the purpose of external purifications by warning and sprinkling. The rites of water-lustration and ablution, were too frequent among the Asiatics, not to be known to the Druids, who resembled the eastern nations in ail their religious ceremonies, fashions and customs. In the channelled basons, the lips are generally pointing to that part of the stone, whence the water collected, might be most conveniently discharged into some vessel placed below. Of those which have no lips, the larger cavity hath often a number of little basons in its circumference, to supply it with their tributary water. From such basons, the officiating Druid might sanctify the congregation with a more sacred lustration than usual. In this water he might mix his misletoe, or infuse his oak leaves, for a medicinal or incantatoi nl potion. But on the Logan-stone (whether channelled or otherwise) the motion of the stone might so agitate the water, as to delude the multitude by a pretended miracle; whilst it extorted confession of crimes from the guilty or accused, satisfied the credulous, and reconciled, in short, the minds of the people to the druidical decisions which it sanctified.

Hitherto, I have noticed only huge masses of mishapen rock. I shall now proceed tomark the monuments of Druidisin, which assume a less irregular appearance: Such are the stones of a columnar form, which, though suffi-

ciently rough, mew, in their position at least, the hand of man. First, for the *Single Stone cre£l.*—The Single Stone erect wasfrequent among the earliest inhabitants of the world. The patriarch Jacob raised several of these pillars, as religious monuments: And Joshua set up a great stone under an oak, that was by the sanctuary of the Lord. The Gentiles erected pillars of the fame kind, in every country, for the purposes of superstition. They worshipped, indeed, the pillar: And it hath been conjectured, not without reason, that the appearance of " God in a pillar of fire by night," might have given rise to this species of idolatry. That the Canaanites worshipped these pillars as gods, we learn from several texts in scripture. " Neither shalt thou rear up a standing pillar; nor set up any image of stone in your land to bow down unto it." Yet the Jews, though thus expressly forbidden to imitate the people of Canaan, set up pillars on every high hill, and beneath every green tree. To this we may add, that the Brachmans professed to worship the deity under the figure of a little column of stone. Those countries, which had any communication with Syria, Ægypt, or Greece, very soon adopted this idolatrous practice. In this country, there are a great number of high stones, still standing in many places. The *Single Stunt ere3,* was sometimes a sepulchral monument. To mark the spot where she was buried, Jacob set a pillar upon the grave of Rachel. Thus, also, the burial-place of Boban, the son of Reuben, was distinguished. Ilus was buried in this manner, on the plain before the city of Troy: And the barrow and the pillar are mentioned in Homer, as " the meed of the dead." The monuments of this kind, which Borlase hath described as druidical, are plain columns of stone, without the least inscription. Longstone, in the parish of East Worlington, is, perhaps, a druidical pillar. It is situated in a farm, called *Stone,* about a mile to the north of Dray ford, at a little distance on the lest hand from the turnpike road leading from Drayford to Southmolton. _ The farm, doubtless, derived its name from this monument. It is perfectly rough, as if cut out of the rock. Its elevation is about six feet; and it is thirteen inches square. Though it inclines, at present, a little to the south, yet at first it was erected perpendicularly. This inclination is skid to have been occasioned by a man's digging under it, in hopes of hidden treasure. But its depth below the surface of the ground, is nearly equal, we are told, to its elevation. Stanborough-Rock may be seen from the road between Morleigh and Harberton-Ford. It has been called a druidical pillar: But it appears more like a natural rock. In this manner were pillars erected, *singly*: And *Mvo, three,* or *more* columns, were, also, assembled for various purposes.— With respect to the *two* stone monuments, t is thought that they originated among the oriental nations, in honor of their two divi

V%t. I. H» nitkt / nities,, the *sun* and the *moon, (a)* And the graves of considerable persons were often distinguished by an erected stone at each end of the body interred. Of the /too *stone* monuments, the most famous were the pillars of Hercules, erected at the ancient Gades, as terminations of his western travels. They are called *afoaiai vrslpai.* In the fame manner, two pillars are said to have been erected in honor of *Hercules,* at *(b)Hertland-vomt,* or the Promontory of Hercules, in Devonshire: And at *Start-point,* there are still the remains of columns, it is supposed, in memory of the Phenician *Astarte.* Westcote has described *two* stone pillars near the village of Kenneford.(f) Of *three* stones v (a) In places of ancient sepulture, we sometimes find three stones, placed in such a manner as to constitute one monument; where three persons were, perhaps, interred. A number of stones were frequently erected, as memorials of particular circumstances or incidents. Elijah built an altar, Composed of t welve stones, according to the number of the twelve tribes of Israel.

(A) At *Herthnd,* according to Richard of Cirencester (than whom no better authority can be cited) were *pillars* commemorative of *Hercules.* At *Artavia* " *vijuntur* Hexculis Columnæ." Ricard. p.

10. (c) " Then this Ryveret nameth a village Ken-ford, throughe which yt fleeteth. And here is a fytt oppertunitie offred to tell you of a wonder, or old fable, or what you please to think yt. I could well forbear to relate yt, but I intend not to stem the tyde, but swymme with the stream and current of the world: for I think (let me well remember) I have seen fewe men in my tyme, which were free from speakinge som folish (at least ydle vayn commentitious fancye) at one tyme or other. But his fortune is worst that speakes them in earnest and with affectation; curiously and ambitiously scekinge to procure credyt and belief, when little or none is due. It shall not rightly be sayd pf me y f yt be, I reckon not.

Ne iste magno conatu magnas nugas dixerit. This fellow (sure) with much a-doe, Will tell strange tales and triffles too. It shall not byte me. You shall have yt srely at the same price it cost me, and in the same measure as near as I can.

Somwhat above this village as you discend from the great hill of Haldowne toward Exeter, at the foote whereof stood along tyme (I cannot say now stand) two stones, pitched on the ends, which to strang travellers seemed to be ther placed for passengers with the more ease (especially woemen, which then perchanc were not used to be lysted upp, and in that age went not in coaches) to take ther horse; for commonly all men walk down that steep dil'cent. But from the neighbours, Mid thoes that anciently dwelled neer yt, you have another and stranger relation.

They first name them the gyants stones. And they fay by an ancient tradition, that a gyant (so men of an extraordinary stature are called, and seme such men are seen in every agge,) was ther buried, who not only for his large bulke, and length, but for his strength and valour surpassed (by farr) all men of his tyme. And that I spinne not out the thread of this tale at a farder length, how he fell here sodenly down dead, and the cause of his death worth (I can tell you by a good fyre syde in a winters cold night,) the hearinge, that he was buried in this place. And thes two stones

were placed one at his head and the other at his feetc; which expressed him to be no pigmye, but of the longest size; yet not peradventure so large as he whom the noble poet (by a hyperbolical licence) defcribetli thus:

His Iegges two pillars, and to fee him goe
He seem'd some steeple reeyling to and fro.

But the wonder was, that albeit the placinge of thes two stones, shewed wher his head and feet lay, yet the true lengthe of his stature, could never be dyrectly knowen. For measure the distant betweene then) as often as you would, yet should you not take yt twice together alyke equall: but at every? severall tyme, ther would be som difference, longer or shorter. What fallacye ther was I cannot conceive, but that report was general!, yea and by such whoes credit was not to be questioned, that eyther themselves had found yt so by tryall, or heard yt by those affirmed, of the truth of whoes relation no doubt or mistrust was to be made. But to call them now to witnesse is needlesse. Yet would I not persuade you to believe more of this, then of other of lyke nature. As mayn Amber stone in Cornwall, yet to be perceived, a huge rock fencibly moving to and fro (as tis verified) by power of a finger: but not to be removed by the strength of many shoulders, as pies verses fay.

Be thou thy mother natures worke Or proof of gyants might,
Worthlesse and ragged, though thou shew,
Yet art thou worth the fight.

Thil stones so placed as to constitute one monument, I know no instances in Devonshire; though Wormius tells us, that Speed, in his description of Devon, hath mentioned some stones on Exmoor, triangularly disposed. " J. Speed *in descriptione Devon, ad Exmort* Saxa in Triangulum, *alia in orbem ereSa (trophaa certe vifioriarum quas Romani Saxones, vel Dani obtinuerunt) ac Danicis literis unum inscribi refers'.* "(a) All this is desultory. These stones erect are Roman, Saxon, or Danish: And why not British?—Of an *indefinite number of pillars,* not in a circular direction, the down in Drewsteignton, near the Cromlech, furnishes us with a striking specimen. Towards the west of the Cromlech, I remarked several conical pillars, about four feet high. On the south side, there are three, standing in a direct line from east to west. The distance from the more western to the middle, was two hundred and twelve paces—from the middle to that oa the east, one hundred and six—just one half of the former; by which it should seem, that an intermediate pillar, at least, had been removed. In a parallel line to the north, are two others remaining erect— the one from the other distant about fifty-two paces, nearly one-fourth of the greatest space on the opposite line. The area between, is ninetythree paces; in the midway of which, at the eastern extremity, stands the *Cromlech.* And I do not scruple to assert, that this *Druid ivay,* beginning on the environs of the Cromlech, was intended to inspire those who were approaching the monument, from Dartmoor, with greater awe and reverence; where, probably, on a solemn anniversary, the Druid priests might have met the attendant people, and commenced the procession.— With respect to *columns ereded on a circular plan,* the number of stones erect are various. The distance of the pillars from each other, is different in different circles, but is the fame, or nearly so, in one and the fame circle. The figure of these monuments, is either exactly circular, elliptical, or semicircular. The columnar circles which have occurred to observation in this county, are the following; which I have distinguished either by their situation, or their connexion with other druidical monuments—simple and detached circles on downs or plains—simple circles on artificial mounts—circles contiguous to each other—circles including kistvaens—circles enclosed by amphitheatrical heaps or walls of stone. On several parts both of Dartmoor and of Exmoor, there are small circles of stone erect; simple in their construction, and detached from each other: They are too trivial

This huger rock on fingers force Apparently will move,

Bu; to remove yt many strengths Shall all too feeble prove. Some years since, thes stones secretly in the night were undermyned and taken upp: but by whome, and for what cause is not vulgarly knowen, neither is it discovered what was/ound under them. Som suppose they made search for treasure conceived there to be hydden; others agayne imagine to seeke out the certeintye, whether ther were any bones ther to be seen as the remaynder of that large corps, yf so thereby to confirme the beliefe (of divers incredulous persons) that there were such tall men in forepassed agges. As Virgil in the first of his Georgickes fays touching the plowinge of Emonian and Emathyan fields.

Scilicet tempus veniet cum finibus illis

Agricola incurvo terram molitur aratro

Crandiaque effossis mirabitur ossa sepulcris.

The tyme will come one day, when in that bound

The paynfull husband plowing of the ground

Shall wonder at the huge bones therin found."(i)

la) Worm. p. 67.

(1) Thii extract is taken from Westcote'i M.S. in the British Museum. To enable my readers to judge of the great difference between the two M.S.S. 1 shall subjoin the passage that corresponds with the above, from the Portledge M.S. " Then this ryver nameth a Village Kenforde through which it passeth somewhat aboue this village as you descend front the great Hill called Halldowne, stood a long time 2 stones pitched vp at the ends, the neighbours name them Gyant, fiones, from an antient tradition that a Gyant was there buried, who nor only for largeness of body but for valour & strength surpassed (by far) all men living in that age. & how hee fell here suddainly down dead, & the cause os his death; that ne of the stones was placed at his jnterment at his head 8c the other at his feet, which declared him to' bee of a large size, but the thing to be wondered at was. That albeit the

placing of these 2 stones showed where his head & feet lay, yet bis true stature could never be directly known, for measure the distanoe betwixt them foe often as you would, yet should you ncuer take it twice alike equal, some yearet since these stones were secretly in a night digged vp and s« the wonder ceased," Westcote't View, p. 117. for for particular description. In the central part of the Valley of Stones, there are several plain circles, in diameter about forty feet. Risdon says, that on Maddoc's Down, in the parish of Eastdown, there " stand certain stones circularwise, of more than the height of a man." And Westcote notices the curious stones on Exmoor and Maddoc's Down.(«)

There («) " Now you expect & hope for more pleasing objects, & more comfort after these vneven, rockye, tyring, stumbling melancholy wayes: but I cannot promise you presently: I see a spacious course barren & wild object, yeilding little comfort by his rough complexion, haue but a little patience your stay shall not bee long, I will shorten the way by guiding you by a direct lyne without ambages, you shall not haue a bow of a tree to strike off your hatt, or drop in your neck. It is Exemoore we are come vnto: the greatest part whereof lyeth in Somersetshire Ic yeildeth noe metde, as yet known, onefy good summering for sheep & cattle, Sc that in good qualitye and quantity, and therefore wee should soon pass ic over, were I not to shew you certain stones, supposed as I am informed to bse there erected, some in tryanglewise, other in circle, as Trophes of victories, gotten of (or by) the Romanes, Saxons or Danes, on which are engraven certen Danish or Saxon characters, of some thought to bee there fixed in memory of the great slaughter, at the ouerthrow & death of Hubba the Dane, who hauing with Hungar his Associat huryed over all the country from Eglisdon (now St. Edmondsourye) to this Countrye, was here with many other slain Anno 879. And their Banner (which was wrought by the Daughters of King Lothbrook (in english Letherbreech) whereon they reposed noe little confidence for good soccesse, hauing been foe often displayed fortunately in the Danes partye) taken: And the place euer since called Hubblestow; but for that place wee shall firtde it perchance elsewhere neer the mouth of Towridge. Others again suppose them to bee set as markes and guides to direct Passengers: But let vs leaue the cause and find those stones, which I could neuer as yet, neither can they, that I haue purposely employed in quest of them find any such, either in the North-moore, between Horeoke-Rydge and Snabhill; nor southward, from Exa-borrough to Exridge, or in the Middle-Moore westward, bctweene the Long Chayne to Rexable and Settacomb, or in the south from Dryflade to Vermyball, neither from Wester Eramott to Lyddenmoore, & all the other noted Hills & Combes therein, to name all which, would bee I think somewhat wearisome to you as the Journey to myselfe. for I was vext with a jelous care, to a particular *Ic* serious inquisition of what occurs in reading, taken vp of the writers vpon credit of the Reporters, for I find only neare Porlock Commons a stone not pitched but lying, which they call Longdone, but that may breed auother question, why it should be foe named being not aboue 4 soote in length & less in crassitude. Alsoe in the west from Woodborrough towards Rodely-hedd vpon Choltocomb Commons is a plain stone erected, in heyth near 6 foote, and 2 in thicknefse, yet withorrt any antique engraving. But somewhat nearer to our purpose doe I find in the parish of EastDowne in the ffarm of Northcott (the seat sometime of a gentleman of that name John Northcott who-was Sheriff of this County the 29th yeare of Edw. 3d. and though it bee out now of the name, we shall finde one of his posteritie & of his name his equal in the 2d yeare of King Charles) in a large spacious field inclosed, by the name of Maddock or Maddocks-dovvne, 4 or 5 miles from the fforrest; certain stones erected in this manner: first there stand two great stones in nature or fashion (though not curiously cutt) of Pyramydes, distant the one from the other 147

foote: the greatest is in height aboue the ground nine foote and halfe. every square bearing fowr foote: The heighth of the other stone is fiue foote and a halfe, but in square well nigh equalU, the other being somewhat aboue three foote. These two stones or as may bee said Pillars, stand in a right lyne, one opposite to the other, fixtie fix foote on the fide of these, are layd a row or banck of 23 great vnformed £ones alsoe, but not equalling the other two by much, & reaching from one of these stones to the other in direct lyne and making a reciprocal figure as hauing the sides equally proportioned but double as long, or more then square (which as I am told is called a Parellelogram) but for your better vnderstanding I present them this to your view.
0QonaaDDO0aQanQQODD0D c c c j IA vo 47 foote
There Is a small columnai-circle, as I have.been informed, on *Auckland Beacon,* m the parish of Buckland in the Moor. Somewhat south of the Druid way or *via sacra,* at Drewsteignton, are two curious *circles,* contiguous to each other, on the descent of the hill. The first circle is marked by a vallum, which on the outer part declines, and ii about four feet high. Though the greater part of the stones which were erected on the top of the mound, are gone, and the stones that remain are deep funk in the ground;

But on neither of these are there any Characters to be perceiuefl neither are they capable of any sucli, being impossible (as I suppose) or very difficult to engraue in them; that these stones mould grow foe here by nature I cannot bee persuaded, neither can I as yet by any reading or reason or by any mans else vndersfend or by tradition ghesse, why they should be here erected, but for some victorie there gotten; and the monument os the interment of some famous or eminent performs: but to conjecture by the name of Maddock or Mattock I cannot allude to any authentical historic or person; to thinke vpon Madock who in the 23d yeare of Edv. 1st 1194, raised an Uproar or Rebellion in Wales, from whome the King won the Ifle of Angle-

sey, and after in the 15th yeare of the said King was taken, drawn and hanged, his rebellion being in Wales and his death in London, were without any congruitie. to fetch'it as farr as Madock the 4th sonne of Owen Guinerh Prince of Wales, who seeing his 3 Brothers contending for the Gouernment rigged certaine shipps & sought Adventures by sea and was the first (as is supposed with great likelyhood) that discovered the Weft Indies, & inhabitted itt, giuing Bryttish names to diuers things Anno 1170. of whom Meredith the sonne of Rhefi (als Ap-hes) who liued sometime aster him leaveth this remembrance Madoc wyf mwyeda wedd Madoc I am the sonne of Owen Guiuedd lawn genan, Owen Guenedd With stature tall, & comely grace adorned

Ni annum dir fyeoaid oedd Noe store of Landes at home or welth mee please

Na da Mawr ondy morodd My minde was whole to serch the Ocean Seas.

I finde noe likelyhood therein, *tc* therefore will leave itt to the scrutiny of him that is better read then my seise, and foe may leave Ex-moore." Westcote's View (Portledge M.S.) p. 45,46, 47,4.

On this down and its environs, are a great number of rocks and columnar stones, of various size and in various figures. They are thus noticed by a correspondent of Dean Milles: " On *Madduccommon,* one stone is of a remarkable size, and one only. It is of a conic figure, not so large at the base, as near its center, occasioned by the sheep rubbing against it. At the center, it measures fifteen feet sour inches. The height, about whicli I could not be so exact, I take to be eleven feet, if not more. In a line parallel to this great stone, from south to north, and at the distance of twentyfour paces, lies a trunk of stone, above a foot from the ground, whose diameter is two feet eight inches. About twelve paces distant from this, in a line from west to east, is a stone not a foot above the ground, and about a foot in diameter. Were there another to correspond to the large one, these four would include a space of ground, whose opposite fides would be equal. I counted more than an hundred clusters of stone in different parts. In some places, six, eight, or more are to be seen together, but not remarkable for their height. At one groupe of fix, the eye is particularly engaged. These stand circular-wife, and are the only ones in which the circular figure can be discovered. At the distance of four paces from this circle, is the trunk of a stone, nearby three feet above the surface, whose diameter measures about three feet. The opinion of the country is, that the first stone 1 have described being one entire solid stone, was erected by human hands. Concerning these stones, we have two traditions. One is, that there was a battle fought between Biry, or Berry, and Maddoc, two potent lords; and that Maddoc erected these monuments to perpetuate his victory. The other tradition is, that two Lords had a battle on this spot of ground, and that, though the conqueror is forgotten, the name of the vanquished was Maddoc, and that the stain were all buried in a common adjoining to this, hence called *Deadbury* common: Yet I could perceive no *tumuli* there." Thus writes a Gentleman from Barnstaple, in 1751. Mr. Badcock informs Sit George Yonge, that " of the stones that bear the name of Maddoc, the larger ones still remain and that the smaller ones may be traced out, though they are almost buried beneath the turf. They are (fays he) undoubtedly, sepulchral: And, I thilk, they are commemorative of a distinguished personage, who was killed on the spot, in some great battle. On the Welsh coast, opposite to that part of the country, where these stones are erected, there is a stone called *Maen Madock.* It is particularly mentioned in a paper written by Mr. Strange, in the *Arcbttolopa,* concerning some hitherto unnoticed curiosities in Brechnochfhire. Perhaps, on a careful examination, the one might throw light on the other." And a late correspondents 1) also, writes: " On the north-side of the parish of *Eaft-Dovirt,* is an estate which, though now inclosed, still bears the name of *Maddoc's-Dvan.* On this place stands a remarkably large stone of the

spar kind—in the midst of a plain, about twelve feet above ground, and of a size too large ever to have been fixed there by art. At the distance f some yards, are several other stones, lying flat—which they call the Gyants' Quoits." (1) Whose saiU&ictsr; csmmuinsayoM the «.uthot hop', ere long, ta hive «n opportunity of acknowledging, in the Jsrgcf wmk.

yes yet from these relics we can clearly trace out the whole round of the circle. The stones, composing its circumference, were placed at equal distances. The area is quite clear: And the diameter of this circle is ninety-three feet. Contiguous to this, is another circle, nearly of the fame size. One vallum, in the point of approximation, serves for both. On Quarnell Down (between Quarnell Torr and Sharper Torr) there are a number of druidical circles. One of these circles encloses a *kistnaen,* or a stone sepulchral chest. It originally consisted of eleven stones erect; nine os' which are standing, and two are fallen. It is of an elliptical figure: And the area of it measures ten feet by eight. In the centre of it, is this kistvaen; which is a cavity, enclosed by side-stones pitched on end, measuring in the clear four feet by three, and covered by a capstone. These sidestones are placed at right angles, and have plane surfaces: And the covering-stone is five feet long, four feet wide, and three feet deep.—Within that curious amphitheatre, in the parish of Manaton, called Grimspound, are no less than twenty circles; not one of which exceeds a land-yard in diameter. They all seem to have been formed by stones erect: But in each circle where the pillars are fallen or have disappeared, the circumfe-, rence is distinctly marked by heaps of small stones. Some of the pillars which lie on the ground, plainly point out their original station, and might easily be replaced. At present, there are only two perfect circles; one of which consists of thirty-five pillars—the other of twenty-seven. In both circles the pillars are placed at equal distances. And there are six circles (each about twelve feet in diameter) in contact with each other. The wall that

encloses these twenty circles, is ninety-six land-yards round. It was built with rough moorstone, without cement. In several places where it is entire, it is about fix feet in height, and of the fame thickness. But it is, in general, in ruins, and a mere heap of stones. From the east part of this circular mound, to the west, are twenty-two land-yards; and from the north to the south, twenty-eight. There is an entrance on the east side of this amphitheatre, and another on the southwest side of it: And at each entrance, there is an appearance of a flat pavement. The north side of this wall, which is washed by Grimstake, is the boundary between North-Bovey and Manaton. —As to the uses of the circle, there is no doubt but these monuments, in general, were of religious institution; and designed originally for the rites of worship. The Persians grasped the whole compass of the heavens in the idea of their Jupiter: The Druids worshipped the fame deity in the manner of the Persians: And what could be more expressive of his unconfined essence, than the circular figure? Where could they perform with so much propriety, their adoration to every region of the heavens, as in the midst of the circle (a) Though these circles are of different sizes, yet they might all have been places of worship: The larger circles might have been designed for general aslemblies; the smaller, for private uses; the large, for sacrifices and festal solemnities; the small, for particular intercessions and predictions. (4) And priests and worthies were often interred in the midst of the (acred circle. Bones have been frequently found in the kistvaen. The circles within the stone enclosure of Grimspound, are the most remarkable in Devonshire. It i& probable, that this spot was one ot the principal temples of the Druids.(c). I have, hitherto, noticed *plain* pillars only . But the Druids had also *inscribed* pillars. Dr. Borlase is of opinion, that all our inscribed pillars are posterior to the British Period; " because the Druids were averse from committing any thing to writing." But the Doctor is here mistaken: And the error originates in his misapprehension of the following passage in Cæsar: " Nonulli annos vicenos in disciplina permanent: neque fas esse existimant ea literis mandare; *quum in reliquis fere publicis pr'puatifque rationibus (e) (Gracis) literis utantur.* Csesar here plainly intimates, that though the Druids forbade their scholars to commit what they learnt to writing, yet that letters were used both on public and private occasions. Cæsar remarks, that this prohibition was, probably, for two reasons —*quod neque in vulgus disciplina efferri velint; neque eos qui difiunt, literis confisos, minus memoria jludere."* Borlase's inference, therefore, from the passage, is absurd. Many of *r (a)* The Phenician Hercules, or the Snn, was worshipped in an open temple. *(b)* It has appeared, indeed, that circles were often applied to other uses. (c) Of an amphitheatrical mound, similar to that at Piran or St. Just, in Cornwall (which I have described in the second section) Grimspound is the only specimen in Devonshire. Tradition says, that Grimspound was used to enfold cattle, " when the people lived upon the hills, before the vallies were cleansed, and when wild beasts infested the country," (/) Cæsar, Lib. 6. Sect-XIII. () *Crassii.* the the pillars, which the Druids erected, were, I doubt not, inscribed with their sacred characters. The monuments of the iTisli Druids are a sufficient evidence of this fact. In Danmonium, however, we have no inscribed pillars, which we can with any degred of confidence attribute to the Druids. The few Danmonian columns with inscriptions, are of a very doubtful nature. But there is a probability that they are very ancient. Several of these monuments, supposed to have been erected in the British Period, are ascribed to the Greeks. Badcock, in his notes on Chappie, mentions a *Jione* near *Holyiveil,* on the borders of *Exmoor,* on which some large characters were engraved. " I have searched for this stone, fays he, and employed others in the fame pursuit. At last I was informed, to my great mortification, that about ten or twelve years since, it was made the foundation of a little bridge, on the rivulet where it originally stood.

The man who erected this bridge, said, " there were nearly twenty letters on it—that they had aft indenting between them, and were not of the common figure; for many persons, who examined them, pronounced them to be *Greek."* A rough ntborstone in the parish of Colebrook, is inscribed with unknown characters. Prince tells us, " that this column, which is called *CopleJloue,* is about twelve feet high from the surface of the earth, and twenty inches broad, each square, and that it is an entire stone, roughly carved with various flourishes, which some have taken for old Saxon characters:" And a correspondent writes: " There seems to have been an inscription on this stone: But, at present, the characters are illegible." There is a threshold-stone at Lustleigh church, with an inscription boldly cut. And there is an upright stone, by a smith's shop, near the churchyard of Buckland Monachorum, which is, also, inscribed. It is a large unpolished granite. The inscription runs lengthways. From the top of the stone to the beginning of the inscription, are two feet. From the end of the inscription the stone is fixed in the ground, about fifteen inches broad where the inscription is, and eleven deep.(a) There is n,ow lying in the parish of Yalmton, in the churchyard, a long stone, which grows gradually less towards the upper part; and the bottom part, for near a foot, is left in a very rough state—as if it were intended to be set upright in the earth. This stone measures, in length, nine feet. It lies east and west; and, being somewhat sunk in the earth by its weight, its thickness does not appear; but it must be from eight inches to a foot thick. On the side that is uppermost, about the middle of the stone, and lengthways, are some letters strongly cut, which make the word Toreus. One of my correspondents lays: "I should guess the inscription on this stone to be Greek; and I take the word *Toreus* to be an epithet of Hercules the navigator, from whom is named Hertland Point, or Herculis Promon. near Hertland Abbey. Not that there ever was such a Hercules: But ancient navigators emigrated under the pa-

tronage or.sanction of that name, as a tutelary faint." There is certainly such a word as *"Ttsfivs* in the Greek; but I cannot discover its connexion with the navigator Hercules: Nor does it appear that the epithet of *Toreus* was ever applied to Hercules. Another gentleman fancies that this word has some connexion with *Torini*—a people of ancient Scythia. But these are mere conjectures. There is no doubt but the,word *Toreus* is on the stone: It is so boldly cut, that he who runs may read it. But I mould refer this monument to a later period;(A) as well as the stones, perhaps, at Lustleigh and Buckland-Monachorum. They have the fame kind of characters, and are placed in similar situations. With regard to the Exmoor and Colebrook pillars, we have no *iruTvrxi* for conjecture j since the inscription on the first is inaccessible, and that on the second illegible. pillars. Its situation is generally on the summit of a hill."(a) The Cromlech wcuhj often assume, perhaps, jts proper form, by the mare removal of earth and loose stones

Having concluded my account of the ruder and less shapely stones of the Druids, I proceed to a description of the *Cromlech,* which has something in its appearance more artificial than even the columnar circle; though consisting, indeed, of rough stones, and sufficiently simple in its construction. According to Borlase, " a Cromlech i» a large gibbous stone, nearly in an horizontal position, supported by other flat stones', fixed on their edges and fastened in the ground. The number of the supporters is seldom more than three. The supporters commonly mark out'an area about fix feet long and four feet wide, in the form of a stone-chest or cell. The Cromlech is either placed on the common level of the ground, or mounted on a barrow, or raised amidst a circle of (?) Dean MUles's M.S.S.

(4) The latter end of the *Romen-Btinjh* Period. from *a)* On Dr. Boihfe's definition of a Cromlech, Chappie comments as follows: " A'Cromlech, as the Doctor defines it,(i) is " a larje fiat stone, in a horizontal position (or near it) supported by other flat stones fix'd on their

edges, and fasten'd in the ground, on purpose to bear the weight of that stone, Which rests upon, and overshadows them, and by reason of its exte ded surface, and its elevation of fix or eight feet, or more, from the ground, makes the principal figure in this kind of monument." I have already taken notice of the Doctor's observation that the situation generally chosen for them is the very summit of a hill; which however true of those in *Cornwall,* and peihsps judg d most convenient in others, yet being not so in ours, (hut on a gentle descent fro:n the *north)* could not be always deem'd absolutely necessary. The Doctor further observes, that " sometimes this flat stone, and its supporters, stand upon the plain natural soil, and common level of the ground" (of which ours, at *Shilfiox* in *Drenvjieignton,* is an instance) j " but at other times it is mounted on a barrow, made either of stone or earth. It is sometimes placed in the middle of a circle of stoneserect, and when it has a place of that dignity" he thinks it " must be sopposed to te erected on some extraordinary occasion;" but that when a circle has a tall stone in the middle, it seems to have been unlawful to remove that middle stone, and therefore we find this' mom ment of which we are speaking sometimes placed in the edge of such a circle." Of this, in a note subjoin'd, the Doctor gives an istance in *Bofcatccn-un,* referring to an Icon of it, and thence deducing this consequence, " that the Cromlch was posterior in date to the circle, and the former erected there or the fake of the latter:" But we (hall hereafter suggest some reasons for supposing them coæval; and possibly such at may induce the reader to believe their real uses were very different from those the Doctor assigns for their erection. Not that 1 imagine *all Cromlechs* to have had such circles of stones, around them or join'd with them, as he there speaks of; for, as he proceeds to observe, some have been found " erected on such rocky situations, and so distant from liouses, (where r.o stones-erect do stand, or appear to have stood,) that we may conclude, they were often erected in places

where there are no such circles:" Of this he gives instances; and perhaps other reasons might be given for their being so, were this a proper place to enter upon the subject.

The Doctor next proceeds to some account of their construction and name; and fays, be finds the number of supporters in *all* the monuments of this kind whkh he has seen to be no more than Tmti: And yet in his plan of *Lanym Cromlech* (which seems the most carefully drawn of all the five he has given, and is the only one that has an arrow to indicate its position in respect to the points of the comp.ss), it is (hewn to have *four: A* peculiarity, of which he takes no notice in his verbal description of it, p. 117; where he however remarks its particular position, and informs us of its dimensions as to length, breadth, and girth; as also of his having caused a pit to be dug under its quoit, in search for a supposed grave there. To reconcile him to himself in reflect to its number of supporters, I should have imagin'd *that* which is most to the *i.onb icrst* (and which is hidden in the view of it engraved over the plan), did not rife quite so high as the under-surface of the tablestone, so as to give it any support; and indeed, if it be, as lie there fays, " so high that a man cn horseback can stand under it," this in respect to some part of it may not be quite improbable; for it may possibly appear hereafter, that the height ot its inner edge need not be above 5 feet 4 inches or a very trifle more, for the purpose for which I guess it was design d: But then, what follows in the Doctor's description, shews, that the outer edge at least must be at its full height; for this I take to be one of those two *principal Juppcriers* which he refers us to, as marked A and B in his plan, but these letters are omitted by the engraver in the edition of 1754 which I use. He thinks these two, because they " do not stand at right angles with the front lire," as he supposes them to be in other *Cromlechs* which I much, doubt; and am Ave they do not in *ail),* but in an oblique 'position, must therefore have been forced from its original one, and, as he imagines, by the weight of the

table stone, *ox-quoit,* as the *Cornijh* call it: But for some reasons, needless to be here assign'd, I rather think they still retain their original pesitien; and particularly that the western point of that nearest the center of the plan, is very accurately fix'd to answer the purposes for which it was principally design'd, but for which, a fourth *fulcrum* in ours at *Drcivs Teigntcn* would have obstructed its application to another use, for which it appears to have been also intended; and there is little reason to think otherwise of the other supporters in that of *Lanycn."*

" Dr. Borlase's reasons for having *generally* at least, for I at present take that of *Lanym* to be an exception) no more than *three* supporters to a *Cromlech,* as being on several accounts the most convenient; and for preferring unequal to equal ones in respect to their heights and level; tho' just in themselves, in cafe the general design admitted of an indifference in the choice of either, yet will not here appear to have induced the fabricators either to fix on that number exclusive of all others, or to have them of unequal heights. For though, as he s.ys, such supporters were easier to be found than those of one and the same height; and tho' it be indeed " much easier to place and fix *11)* Arui. of Cornw.

i sccuroly from the natural rocks. The supporting stones were found in their present position; or, is not, were moved into it, with very little exertion: And the top stone, supcrimpeuding from securely any incumbent weight on *three* supporters than on four or more," as not requiring the nicety of levelling and planning, which he mentions as requisite in the latter case; yet the difficulties attending such nicety, had it been necessary for their purposes, would not have deterr'd the fame persons from attempting and carrying it into execution, who, as we shall fee, were no less nice and exact in fixing those unequal heights, than in the other dimensions of this structure; the inequality of those heights being not the result of chance, nor wholly of choice; but found necessary to the due adjustment of the whole fabrick, and fitting it to answer its end and design.

The Doctor proceeds to take notice of the usual dimensions of *Cromlechs,* their firmness, and their permanency. " The supporters," lie fays, " mark out and inclose an area, generally, fix feet long, or somewhat more, and about lour feet wide," and adds, " *in the form of a fine chest or cell:"* But perhaps 'tis very rartly that they can be reduced to that form, even by the aid of fancy; and that they are not *always* so form'd, is undeniably evident, there being more than one instance of the contrary; notwithstanding what *Worm'ius,* whom he quotes, has said concerning them, and conjectured to have been their original use and design, viz.. to receive the blood of the victims there sacrificed; in which last he is certainly mistaken, and Dr. *Sorlafe* himself has afterwards shewn that it could not have been applied to that use. —" On these supporters rests a very large flat or gibbous stone;" and this ii deed is what chiefly distinguishes a *Cromlech* from other monuments of *druidkal* design. " Jn what manner they proceeded to erect these monuments, whether by heaping occasional mounds, or hillocks of earth round the supporters, in order to get the covering stone the easier into its place, or by what engines," the Doctor thinks it in vain to enquire; but what he looks upon as most surprizing is, " that tills rude monument of four or *f-ve* stones" (so he expresses it, and consequently here admits of some with *soar* supporters, the fifth being the covering stone,) " is so artfully made, and the huge incumbent stone, so geometrically placed, that though these monuments greatly exceed the christian æra (in all probability), yet 'tis very rare to find them give way to time, storm, or weight; nay, we find the covering stone often gone, that is, taken down for building, and yet the supporters still keeping their proper station."—But we cannot suppose those thrifty wise-acres, who sometimes capriciously choose rather to.demolish an old structure to supply material;, for a new one, than to be at perhaps a less expence in procuring them elsewhere; would —after having been at the labour and charges of removing so great a weight as the covering f'one of a *Cromlech,* generally is,— leave its supporters behind, if not more difficult to be got up than the roof to be taken down: Wherefore the preservation of these from such dilapidators, can only be accounted for, by the great depth to whish they were probably funk in the earth to prevent such removal. For "tis observable of some other stones erected by the ancients for unknown purposes, and attempted to be taken up to be applied by the moderns to their own uses, that they have frequently bten found funk so deep under-ground as their heights were rais'd above-ground; which has sometimes induced these underminers to desist from their enterprise, and leave them fix'd in their places. Of this divers Instances might be given where no pressure required so much firmness; and much more might be expected where the stability of an excessive iucumbent weight depended on the strength and immobility »f its supporters.

I woukl not be understood, by these, or any suture animadversions on Dr. *Bcrlase's* account of those dmidical monuments, to depreciate his work; or derogate from the veneration and respect due to the memory of an author, to whose researches we are indebted for many curious particulars concerning them, which have contributed more to elucidate the subject than those of any preceding writer. His learned observations and happy conjectures on these and other remains of remote antiquity, doubtless dcscrv'd the thanks of all persons conversant in such studies; and common candor will acquiesce in the apology he makes in his preface for such imperfections as might appear in his work. " Great perfection (as he there fays) cannot be expected, where the subject is so obscure, the age so remote, and the materials so difpers'd, few, and rude; where we must range into such distant countries for history and examples, and into so many languages for quotations." —And a little lower;—" In treating of the superstition, and *Rock-monuments* of the *Dr:i:ds,* 1 may seem too conjectural to thos:, who will make no allowances for the deficiencies of history, nor be satisfied with any thing but evident truths; but where there is no certainty to be obtain'd, probabilities must suffice, and conjectures are no faults, but when they are either advane'd as rca truths, or too copiously pursued, or peremptorily insisted upon as decisive.—In subjects of such distant ages, where history will so often withdraw her taper, conjecture may sometimes strike a new light, and the truths of antiquity be more effectually pursued, than where people will not venture to guess at all. One conjecture may move the veil, another partly remove it, and a third, happier still, borrowing light and strength from what went before, may wholly disclose what we want to know." From hence we may conclude, that were he now living, he would, on a nearer view of those truths, of which he was in quest but had only an obscure and distant prospect,

Vol. Ir . *1 z,* ie from the rocks, was brought down upon those supporters with as little labor or contrivance. There are large masses of rock near Sticklepath, and, indeed, in several parts of the county, which are so grouped as very easily to admit of their being formed into a Cromlech, without calling in the aid of the mechanical powers, (a) With respect to the . name be well pleased to have them duly distinguissi'd from those extraneous objects with which he had supposed them connected, hut to which they on further examination prove to have little or no relation;— to have his well-founded judgement in other matters confirm'd,—and his conjectures corroborated by new proofs, or perhaps fully establissi'd as indisputable certainties.—With such views he professedly writ; and accordingly he tells in p. 216, he has exhibited elevations and plans of *Cromlechs* in *Cornwall,* that, as there are some peculiarities in each, they might not only afford some light and confirmation to what he had before advane'd, but might also " possibly contribute, when in the hands of others, towards a much happier explanation of monuments of this fort, than had as yet appear'd." *Chaff le's Description and Exegesis of the Drewjieignton Cromlech,* p. 33 to 38, 39 to 46.

(æ) " By what contrivances (fays Mr. Chappie) such an enormous weight was raised to the above-mention'd height, and, what is more astonishing, so exactly fix'd, and so nicely accommodated to the purposes for which it was originally design'd, and moreover, with such firmness as to continue for ib many ages in the fame position, (for had it been but half an inch out of its proper place, we shall hereafter find, the error would be even now discoverable;) is, in Dr. *Bor/ase's* opinion, in vain to enquire, and indeed can now be only guesss'd at.— Monsieur *Mallet,* who, in his *Northern Ant';quitiesi),* plainly enough describes the monuments of this fort (tho' not by the British name of *Cromlechs)* stili to be met with in *Denmark,* &c; and who mistakes them to be altars for sacrifice; expresses his surprize at their stupendous magnitude, and the powers and strength required to erect them. His previous account of these, and the stone circles that sometimes surround them, as translated in the *English* edition, may not improperly be recited here, as it introduces his remarks on their bulk and difficulty of erecting them. " We find (fays he) at this day here and there in *Denmark, Sweden,* and *Norway,* in the middle of a plain, or upon some little hill, altars" (for such he will have them to be), " around which they assembled to offer sacrifices, and to assist at other religious ceremonies. The greatest part of these altars are raised upon a little hill, either natural or artificial. Three long pieces of rock set *upright"* (not strictly so, I presume, in these northern latitudes; nor is their perpendicularity, perhaps, more necessary, whatever equality of their heights might be expected, in such parts of *Germany* or *Hungary* as are in Lat. 45".) " serve for bases to a great flat stone, which forms the table of the altar. There is commonly a pretty large cavity under this altar, which might be intended to receive the blood of the victims." So fays this author, adopting the copjecture

of *Wormius,* and drawing inferences from thence relative to the *Danish* superstitions, as if *that* conjecture were to be regarded as an undeniable truth; and as if they could be design'd for no other use but that of altars. and therefore their appendages in all respects subservient to the purposes of sacrifice: An opinion, for good reasons rejected by Dr. *Bor/ase,* as has been befoM observ'd. And if the author is mistaken in this, he is probably so also in what follows (and which I take to be only a conjecture grounded on the sandy foundation of the former), viz. that as »' they never fail to find stenes for striking fire scatter'd around it," so he thinks no other fire but such as was struck out with a flint " was pure enough for so holy a purpose."—Sometimes (adds he) these rural altars are constructed in a more magnificent manner; a double range of enormous stones surround the altar and the little hill on which it is erected. In *Zealand* we fee one of this kind(i) which is formed of stones of a prodigious magnitude. Men would even now be afraid to imdertake such a work, notwithstanding all the assistance of the mechanic powers *which in these times they wanted."*—One may here ask, How does this author know they wanted such assistance? Bp. *Wilk'ms* indeed in his Mathematical Magic, chap. 11. is much of the fame opinion; but it may be question'd whether the other advantages lie tells us they then had over the moderns, will alone satisfactorily account for their stupendous works. For, as our author proceeds to remark, " What redoubles the astenissiment is, that stones of that size are rarely to be seen throughout the island *(viz.* of *Zealand),* and they mull have been brought from a very great distance. What labour, time, and sweat thep, must have been bestowed upon these vast rude monuments, which are unhappily more durable than the fine arts?" The author then suggests what he takes to have been the inducement to such great works, taking it for granted they must have been for religious purposes: " Men in all ages(3) (savs he) have been persuaded that they could not pay greater honour (i) Vol.

i, p. 8tc. (2) P. 126. For this he quotes 01. Worm. Monum. Danic. (;) It must he remember'd, that the Author is here speaking of past ages only, not of modern times; otherwise hc: or his Translator, should have excepted those of the present age, at least among Us, the descen.ients of hii northern religionists; of whom those who conceit themselves the wisest, are withal so frugally disposed, as to giudge every shilling bestow'fl on persons or places dedicated to the service, even of that God, whom alone they pretend lo acknowledge aS suchi—bu; this oily on condition that he claims n0 share of cheir gold. Chappie. to fiame of this monument, Dr. Borlase intimates, that *Cromlech* means " the *crooked stone;* the upper stone being generally of a convex or swelling surface, and resting in an inclined plane or crooked poiition."(a) Tsle Cromlech was not peculiar to the Druids. The

Cromlechs to the deity, than by making for him (if I may so express it) a kind of strong bulwarks; in executing prodigies of labour; in consecrating to him immense riches."—In another part of his woik,(i) M. *Mall/t,* who, as we have seen, supposes (but perhaps without sufficient grounds for such a fippofition) that the ancients were unacquainted with those mechanical engines by which the moderns are assisted in raising huge weights, and overcoming the greatest resistance by a very small force;—after speaking of the advantages in respect to their health and bodily force, which the northern nations derived from their hardy way of living, and inuring their children thereto, alledges their stupendous works as so many standing evidences of it.—" The greatest proof (fays he) of their prodigious strength, arises from the rude enormous monuments of architecture which were raised by these northern people. We have all heard of that monument on *Salisbury* Plain in *England,* where we see a multitude of vast stones set up endwise, and serving as bases to other stones, many of which are in length sixteen feet. Nor are the monuments of this kind less astonishing which we meet with in *Iceland,* in *West-*

phalia, and particularly in *East Friez-land, Brunswick, Mecklenburgb,* and many parts of.the north. The dark ignorance of succeeding ages, not being able to comprehend how such stuendous edifices could be constructed by common mortals, have attributed them to dæmons and giants." But altho' the founders of these had not, in our Author's opinion, all the assistance we derive from the mechanic powers, yet he tliinks " great things might be accomplish'd by men of such mighty force co-operating together. The *Americans* unaided by the engines we apply to these purposes, have railed up such vast stones in building their temples, as we do not undertake to rrnove(2). One may however conceive, that patience united with strength, might by taking time be able to move such vast bodies from one place to another, and afterwards to set them upan-end, *by meant of artificial banks, dtnvn the slope of-which they tvere made to slide;"*— and why might not a very ponderous body be as easily drawn *up* the slope of such an *artificial bank t* which would allow those ancient architects the knowledge of at least *one* of our mechanic powers, for as such, the *inclined plane* (tho' not one of the six) is not improperly esteem'd; and this seems to me, to be most probably the method taken to raise the table-stone of our *Cromlech* high enough to be properly fix'd on its supporters. These being first firmly fix'd, and the flat heavy stone to be suftain'd by them, being, by means of such bank or otherwise, rais'd so high as to be somewhat elevat?'l above them; and there by the help of some proper machine (for I cannot suppose, with this author, they were utterly destitute of any), suspended directly over them; might then,—by the previous suspension of a plumb-line to each of its angles, and observing where, or how near, those plummets drop on-oints before mark'd out on the ground for that purpose, agreeable to the general plan,—be easily so guided as to be let down to its proper position, and so exactly to cover that very spot of ground, and *that* only, for which it was intended. —Thus it seems we need not, with our

author, wholly ascribe it to the natural tho' united strength of numbers of those hardy northern-men; nor can we conclusively infer from such works of theirs, the superior size and strength of the first inhabitants of the earth, compared with that of our debilitated moderns; tho' he thinks it without dispute, that it is from such proofs of it " that ancient history has generally painted them as giants." There may be indeed some difference in these respects between the ancients and moderns; but how far this author's attempt to account for it, by the greater cold of the atmosphere in *Eumpe* formerly than now; the continual exercises of our manly ancestors; their avoiding a too early commerce with females, their simple diet, *&c.* may be deem'd satisfactory, it is not our business here to enquire; having already cited from him, perhaps more than sufficient, as to their management of enormous weights, in the erection of permanent monuments, whether of their skill or their strength, or both." Chappie's Descript. p. 54 to 63.

(a) *Name* of the *Cromlech.*—" Before we proceed to any disquisitions concerning its primary use, or more particularly recite the opinions of others concerning it, it was proposed to make some enquiry into the origin of its most usu.U name; tho' this perhaps will not, like the ancient *British* and *Saxon* names of most places, appear either to express any material circumstance relative to it, or afford any l'ght into its original design. For its *British* name, *Cromlech,*—which the Cornish somewhat vary in its spelling and pronunciation, by only accenting the latter syllable and adding the aspirate *h* instead of *cb;* but for which the *Irish,* perhaps more agreeably to the old *Celtic,* have *Cromtiacb,*—signifies (j) P. 337, &. of the fame Volume. (2) The Translator here quotes Acosta' History of the ladies, for an instance of a stone in a fortress of the Inca's at Cufco, 38 feet long, 18 feet broad, and 6 ftet tlml."— On which we may heie remark, that this stone, enormous as it is, little, if at all, exceeds the bulk of some stones in the. tgyptian Pyramids: And yet Heiodutus

informs us of a simple method, by which they wire railed to gr'at heights, " with machines conlttuctcd of short timbers;" a method well explained by Governot Pownall in the Podia ipt to his Desinption os a srpu'.chral Monument at New Grange in Ireland. Arcbjeologia, vol. e. p. fc7a— 27$. in Ll these languages, as well as in their *Armoric* dialect, nothing more than a *curved* or *creaked stone;* doubtless from the gibbosity of the upper surface of its table stone, unless we would derive it, with Mr. *o Ha/!oran,(i)* from the old *Irish* deity, *Crom,* by whom he fays was meant *Jupiter;* of which more farther on. This, fays Dr. *Borlase(z)* (but witli its *Cornish* orthography), is the general name by which these structures are commonly known among the learned; but observes, that " from its oblate and spreading form (resembling a *Discus J"* it is also, both in *Wales* and *Corn-wall,* called a quoit; and " in the Isle of *Jersey* (where there are many) they are call'd *Pouju-cleyi,"* perhaps rather *Ponts-levees* and so call'd as if they were *raised bridges,* but All these appellations being only expressive of their general form, and having no relation to their use, were probably not adopted till after the original purpose, for which those structures will hereafter appear to have been erected, was forgotten; when they were look'd upon, either as the ordinary productions of nature, tho' with a somewhat romantic appearance, or the rude efforts of ancient art, for purposes unknown, and not easily to be guess'd at. —It should here be further noted concerning this its modern *British* name, that the *cb* with which it terminates is to be pronoune'd like the Greek %; not like our *cb* in the word *such,* but as in the words *character, chronicle, Sec.* like an asperated *k,* as if it were written *Cromlekh;* for which reason Dr. *Borlase,* with the *Cornish,* omits the *c,* and, to denote the want of it, circumflexes the *e;* and so, having given directions how to pronounce it, every where spells it *Gromkb:* But with this previous caution concerning its pronunciation, it is he-re thought more eligible to retain the *British* orthography. Were we to suppose

Cromlech, or *Cromliacb* the most ancient name, and that, according to the opinion of some writers, it was meant for a temple of the *Druids,* or used for the purposes of that ancient idolatry which might be supposed to be introduced by the *Phœnicians* when they traded here for tin, we might indulge ourselves in conjectures, in fetching its etymology from the Hebrew, or its *Phœnician* dialect: In which case, I should have imagined it might be derived from *Chir rahbam lucb, the table of the tripod of thunders);* or rather from *C.hir ribbem meiech, the tripod of the thundering king.* For, that *Jupiter* was worshipped by the *Phœnicians,* and by them, as wtll as other nations, imagined to have the command and direction of the thunder-bolts, with which they supposed him arm'd, cannot be doubted. We find *Jupiter* the son of *Neptune* taken notice of by ancient writers as a god of the *Sidcnians;* (and if so, doubtless of their colonists the *Tyrians,* and the other *Phœnicians* connected with, or descended from them;) distinguished, indeed, by the adjunct or surname of *Maritimus,* because they were wholly addicted to navigation: And even their god *Bal, Belus,* or the sun, (who seems to have been their principal deity,) was, according to *Eusebius,* call'd *Jupiter* by the *Greeks;* as was also *Dagen* the god of *Axotus* or *AJhdod* by the husbandmtn. "(4)—But whatever worsliip the *Phœnicians* gave this thundering King of the Gods, we are assured by *Cæsar($)* that he was adored by the *Druids* of *Gaul,* and of course by those of *Britain,* and the people who in matters of religion were under their government and direction. Bat tho" these, like other nations, esteem'd him *(lmperum cathftium tenere)* to be the supreme or chief among the gods themselves, yet they paid the greatest honours to *Mercury.* To him, fays *Co-far,* they erected many images; esteem'd him the inventor of arts, the conductor of travellers, and the principal protector of merchants and mercantile acquisitions. But next *o Mercury* (whom they seem to have peculiarly regarded as their tutelar deity), they had a more particular veneration for

Afolh, or the *Sun,* the original object of idolatry; (perhaps because he was the principal deity of the *Phœnicians,* with whom they traded j) ascribing to him the cure of their diseases; and even preferring him to *Mars,* who otherwise, as the god of war, stood higher in their esteem than either *Jupiter* or *Minerva.* From this their veneration *(ot Apollo,* I had at first imagin'd, that the position os the *CromUch* we are here to examine, might have some respect to the sun rising; the worship of the rising sun having been by some of h'n votaries deem'd a mark of the highest reverence to him: And to be satisfied of this, I was very desirous to ascertain its bearing, with respect to the j»ints of the compass; which after I had carefully obscrv'd and determin'd, was soon convine'd that its position no otherwise respected either the rising or setting sun, than as subservient to gnomonical or astronomical purposes. And being, from this and other observations to be mention'd hereafter, well assured, that the-*Cromlech* itself at leal, could not have been defign'd as a temple either of the *fun,* or of *Jupiter;* or indeed of any other of the heathen gods; I presumed we might as well acquiesce in the *British* derivation beforementioned, which suppose? its name given it from its form and composition, not from its use; and that therefore little or no regard could be due to an etymology, which supposed it the original name, and to have been introduced by the *Phœnicians* or others who spoke a dialect of the *Hebrew;* and this too, expressive of a use, for which it was now manifest it could not have been primarily intended. It may however be alledg'd, that tho' the *Cromlech* itself were not intended either as a temple or an altar, yet if it were erected near a college of the *Druids,* or any Druidical Court of Judicature, as this at *Drenvs Teignton* has been (in p. 7 of (1) Intr. to Irish Antiq. p. 34. (') "ce his Antiq. of Cornw. p. 2 1 1, 2 12, anH the Note on the latter. *('j)* Cliir signifies a tripod or brandiron to let a pot or cauldron on, as well as that lor the laver or washing bason os *t.6* (atrisking priests:-And I-trch a smooth tible, whether a plank or slab

of Hone, scr any purpose, particularly to write; ©1 engrave on. (4) Vide Danet in Jujuter. (.5) De BeUo Gallico. Lib. tS. this this tract) corijectur'd to have been, which would occasion at least an annual concourse of people near this spot; it might then be customary to have altars, and to offer sacrifices, near to, or in view of the *Cromlctb:* And as the fun and planets were objects us their idolatrous worship, at least ac name-fakes or representatives of their gods, its astronomical use might induce them to choose such a place for it, father than another; and then the *Cromlechs* near which such religious worship was wont to be perform'd (tho' not used as altars or temples for that purpose) might take their denomination, amongst the vulj ir at least, from the god or gods there principally adored; in which cafe, the presumed etymology beforenuntion'd may not be wholly inadmissible 'Tis granted, this might possibly have been the cafe; but even then the etymology will require some farther explanation, to render it consistent with the notions of others on this subject, or to correct them where inconsistent therewith. On this supposition indeed (for it is only here to be regarded as such), we might partly admit of the conjecture of Mr. $ Halhrani); who, taking *Crom* to mean *Jupiter,* as derived from *Crum* the obsolete *Irish* for thunder, would have *Crom-lia* to mean the altar of *Jupiter.* However, tho' we should allow the pretensions of *Jupiter* to it, we can by no means admit of its being an *altar,* as he takes for granted it was, and *that,* without producing any reason for its being so j all he alledges, tending only to prove, that the stones, which he calls altars, and supposes the *Druids* to have sacrificed on them, had some relation to *Crom* who, he says, was the fame as *CeanCrcitbi,* the chief deity of the *Irijh.* But as to the signification of *Crom,* as he would have Druidifm to he an *Irijh* institution, and of course takes the word to be of *Irijh* derivation; and finding this *Cidn-Croitbi* by the *Irijh* writers sometimes call'd *Crom-Cruadh,* he from thence, and the *Irijh* word for *thunder* abovemention'd, forms the word *Crom-*

lia; by which name, he fays, the *Lia-fail* or stone of destiny, on which their ancient monarchs were crown'd, was also call'd j and which he interprets, the *altar of Crom,* but which seems only to imply *the stone of Crom,* or the *Thunder-ftene,* without indicating its use; and might as well be taken for a whetstone, for the use of the *Crumtbear* or *Flamen* ill sharpening the edge of his *Secejpita.* Had it occurr'd to Mr. *i Halloran,* that *Crom* might be, as above supposed, only an abbreviation of *Cbir rahhant,* the *Tripod of Thunder,* and consequently not *Irijh,* but *Htbreto* or *Phœnician,* he needed only to have added to it the *Irijh* word *Liu,* which was probably derived from *Luch,* a table or slab of stone, to compose the word *Crom-lia,* which might be render'd, the *Table Stone of the Tripod of Thunder,* or, by metonymy, *of the Thunderer:* And this supposition, that the word *Crom* is here » compound of two others, which have no relation to *curvature* or *bending dtzvn,* would not lave needed his deri¥atir.n of the Celtic word *Criv-m* or *Crom,* which has that signification, from any supposed custom of *halving* at the name of *Crom,* in the worship of the *Irijh Jupiter.(i)* — Perhaps also, he and *Harris,* against whom he alledges that the *fun* was not understood by that name as he had supposed, but was in *Ire/and,* worfhipp'd under another, *viz.* that of *Bial,*—might also be partly reconciled by examining into the origin of the latter; on which it would appear, that there is not always so.greit a difference between the significations of the names given to *Jupiter* and the *fun* as objects of heathen worship, as some may imagine. For, we can scarce doubt but that *Beal* came from *Bail* or *Ball,* a *lord* or *powerful ruler;* which the *Chaldeans* contracted to *Bel,* and the *Phœnicians* to *Bal:* And tho' the *Assyrians* are said to have worfhip'd the *fun* by the name of *Bel,* the fun being in their language so call'd, but was also probably meant to represent *Belus* the son of *Nimrod;* yet, that *Jupiter* was more generally worfhip'd by that name than the fun, is sufficiently evident from what *Sclden* and others have collected, from the sacred scrip-

tures and the writings of the antients, on that subject.) *That* learned author doubts not but that *Jupiter* originally meant the true God, and that the name was derived, not *a juvando,* as *Cicero, Aulus Gellius, Laflantiut* and others have supposed, but from the sacred *Tetragrammiton* whence the Greeks had their Iota *loxai ltvio, Jvva;* and thence (as the principal gods had the common title of *Pater* annex'd to their names, in the solemn prayers and sacrifices to tliem) *Jovis* became *Jovifpater, Jovifpiter,* (i) Introd. to the Antiq. of Ireland, p. 34 & 35. (n) On communicating this to an intelligent Jewish Rabbi (who happen'! to rail on mo whilst writing it), and mentioning to him, inter alia, the human sacrifices of the Druids, he imagined the word Cromliach might mean a place for the wot ship of Moloch, and might therefore he rather foini'dsrom Chorehh Molock (from the root Charahh, to bend, how or kneel down, and the word Makom Locus, understood), a place fur the bending to, or worship of Moloch: A god os the Ammonites, Sec. who, 'tis well known, was supposed to have requited such horrid offerings; aud to whom children wete sacrist! ed much in the fame manner as Cæsar describes the sacrifices of men by the Druids oi Gaul to their gods, viz. by putting them into large hollow images, and setting sire to ttiem: Jlut Tcrtullian (in his Apologetic, c. 9.) having mentron'd the sacrifices of children to Saturn, adds, Majot jetas apud Callos Mercurio prosecatur With the Gauls a grown man is cut to pieces as a sacrifice to Mercury. Cicero also (in Orat. pro M. Fonteio) takes notice of the cruel and barbarous human sacrifices of the Gauls, hut mentions not in what manner they were offes'd: yuis enim ignorat cos fcil. Gallosj usque ad hanc diem retinere illam immanent ac barbarim consuetudinem hominum immolaodorum? The Carthaginians also offer'J the like sacrifices to Saturn. See Selden de Diis Syris, Syntagma 1. c. 6 —Moloch signifies a king, (being only distinguish' from it by the points) and has been generally taken to mean the fun, as the prince or chief of the heavenly luminaries, ' but sometimes for

Jupiter, &c. If the Druids offer'd such sacrifices here, it was most probably to Mercury, but it may be queuion'd whether they ever gave him the name of Moloch, and if not., the last-mentioned etymology can have little probability. Chappie. (3) V. Selden de Diis Syria, Syntagma 2. c. 1, tft . -and and at length *Jupiter.* Hence in like manner, the *Marfpater* or *Marfpitcr* of Cato, for *Mars;* and so of the rest. That *Baal, Beet,* or *Bel,* tho' at first meant as one almighty ruler, whose perfections the heathens attributed to their *Jupiter,* yet these being afterwards transferr'd to a multiplicity of idols (however still regarding *Jupiter* as the principal and all-powerful God), the fame author tells us, became a collective name for them all. But this perhaps most properly in its plural *Baalim* And that this sometimes meant *all the host of heaven,* i. e. the fun, moon and stars, to which *Manajfes* is said to have built altars in the courts of the temple,(2) his worship of *Baalim* being just before mention'd, seems very probable; but it is sometimes taken for the heavens themselves, and *Selden* supposes it should be so understood here. The *Phœnicians* indeed appear to have worship'd the *fun* by this name in the singular, with the addition of *Samen,* calling him *Baal Samen,* the *lord, ex ruler of the heavens:* So St. *Augustine,* (who understood Paris) interprets it *Samen,* being the fame as the *Shamaim* of the Hebrews. And this is expressly asserted by *Sanchoniathon* (as translated by *Phi/o Biblius* and preserv'd by *Eufebius);* speaking of ("hx'm) the sun, " This god, fays he, they esteemed to be the only *lord of heaven,* calling him *Beel-famen,* which in the *Phœnician* language is *lord of heaven,* and to the fame purport with the Greek Zti-ffj." So also the *Bal, Bet,* or *Belus* of the *Tyrians* or *Phœnicians,* as render'd into Greek by *Menander* (in *Jcfephus)* from the *Phœnician* annals, is taken for Zew the well-known name of *Jupiter:* For speaking of a golden column pieserv'd in his temple at *Tyre,* he mentions it as «» *fott* Tb Sior.(4) But *Hefycbius* distinguishes them by their genders, and fays, *Belus* meant the *heavens,* or *Jupiter;* and that the *fun* was called *Be la* (a feminine name).(5) And we find in *Herodian,* that the people of *Aquiteia* gave *Apollo,* or the *fun,* the name of *Be/es.6)* In short, the name seems not to have been strictly confined to any one of the gods; for tho' the *Assyrians,* as above observ'd, meant the *fun* by their *Bel,* and tho' this name is thought to be first introduced by them, yet even *they* also worship'd *Mart,* the god of war, by the name of *Belus.* From all this, we learn, that both *Jupiter* and the *Sun* (and not only these, but other of the heathen gods,) have been worship'd under the name of *Baal* or *Beel, Bel* and *Belus*; and in like manner *Beal,* by which Mr. *0 Halloran* says(7) the old *Ir'fh* adored the fun, might have the like collective signification, and their *Cram* included with the rest; and tho' more propeily, perhaps, taken for *Jupiter,* to whom the superior power was ascribed, might be sometimes confounded with them. Or perhaps, both he and the fun, consider'd as distinct deities, might have sacrifices offer'd them, as well as *Mercury* or any of the rest, at or *near* the fame *Cromlech*; 1 will not fay *upon* it, as an *altar;* for, were we not otherwise assured it was not delign'd for such a purpose, its being manifestly inconvenient for the sacrificing either men or beasts upon it, would forbid us to suppose it. The general height of such *Cromlechs* (of which some will admit the tallest man to walk under them without rubbing his head against the ceiling, and others, a man on horseback to shelter himself from a shower under their coverture, of which an instance has been already mentioned) would not allow the priest to officiate at one of them standing by its fide, nor could any large beast Le easily listed up upon it without some machine for that purpose; so that we must rather suppose *men,* if any victims at all were offered upon it, and the whole business perform'd on the top of it. Among die wretches set apart for this immolation, thieves, robbers, and other offenders (according to *Cafar*)(8) were deem'd the most acceptable to the gods; but in cafe rogues were wanting, the innocent were obliged to supply their places: And being the offerings of the

public, and mostly in times of public danger, may be fuppos'd to have been offer'd in the molt public and conspicuous places, and 011 such an elevated altar as a *Cromlech* (if it were such) rather than another: That they were mounted on its table-stone like a condemn'd nobleman in our times on a scaffold; but ascending to it by a ladder, like common criminals to a gibbet, together with the flamen or priest, who was to do the double duty of confessor and executioner. But tho' the difficulty of getting upon it might be thus overcome, yet, as Dr. *Botlafe* obferves,(Q) it would be much less easy to kindle a fire there, sufficient to consume the victim. This, with the gibbosity and slope of the upper surfaces of most if not all *Cromlechs,* and the want of proper footing to stand easily and safely on them, or room to (1) See Jerem. 2. 83.28.—Hosea 2. 13. and 11. 2. *fScc.* (2) 2 Kings 21. 5.-2 Chron. 33. 3—5. (3) His words ate, " TgToy ©toy (yo/Aioy /xoyoy eosvtt *xvgioy BtiXorx/jLr;,* xaXavTEr, o ls *7?X£ot QolvlS-t xygl®️ tlgXlti,* Zfi/c TTAg Eh-*lert.*" Philo apud Eufeb. Prrp. Evang. Lib. 1. c. 10. Chappie. (4) Joseph, contra Apiooem Lib. 1. (5) See Danct on JSelus. (6) BiAly Ss *xaXacri* TBToy, *signer! Tc Intgfyvus, AttiXKuvx iitxi vSlXorns.* Belem vocant indigene:, magnaqne cum religione colunt, Apollineca interpretantes. Herodian, iab.8, p. 376, 377. Edit. Saftorii IngotHad. 1693. Chappie. (7) Mr. o Halloran (whose disquisitions on this subject I am far from being inclinable to censure, but would rather endeavour to elucidate) will excuse the freedom here taken, in pointing out, what now appear to be his mistakes, but to some os which I mould have readily subscribed, 'till 1 had the strongest conviction of their being such. Such mistakes are unavoidable, where the subject is *So* obscure; and as I cannot expect to keep wholly free trom them (tho' the construction of our Cromlech may prevent many to which 1 might be otherwise liable,) 1 should be glad to be set right u»'lny tbau aay be disco ver'd in what is here submitted to public censure. Chappie. *»)* Da Bello Gallice, Lib. 6. (9) Autiq, Cornw. p.

413. perform the requisite ceremonies, even supposing them quite plain, and also free from any hazard of that disruption to which some sorts of moor-stone (of which ours, and those in *Cornwall* consist) are? liable, from the force of an intense fire(i); and moreover the danger of the officiating stamen, in such a case, to be roasted himself, by the same sire he had prepared for the miserable victims, before he could compleat the horrid and diabolicar sacrifice j— are so many irrefragable proofs'of the absolute onfitness of a *Cromlech* for any such Use. But arguments, deduced from the unfitness of *Cromlechs* for altars, might be spared, as needless for the conviction of any who reflect on *Julius Casals* positive testimony, that these human sacrifices were perforn'Vd in a very different manner j *vix.* that the *Druids,* to whose care the persons devoted to this mactation were committed, put them alive into huge hollow images, bound about with osiers (or perhaps sometimes with twists of hay, as *Strabo* seems to hint), and then by setting fire to them, the men within were scorchd to death by the surrounding flames. He doth net add, that they were cut into steaks, or laid upon altars after being thus buccaneer'd, as an improvement in priestly cookery far a yet unsatisfied deity; nor is it likely they were so: For *Straboz)y* who describing the sacrifices in *Gaul,* at which the *Druids* were always present, who derived their customs and discipline from those in *Britain* after mentioning their auguries, and their divers methods of previously preparing and securing the victims to be immolated, (via. by thrusting darts through some, fastening others to crosses, others to Hocks of wood, and inclosing others in such a colossal fabrick as beforemention'd j) adds, that cattle and all sorts of. beasts, and men, were then all burnt together.(3) Before we dismiss this subject, it may be requisite to remark, that the etymology before given is liable to be objected to, as supposing all *Cromlechs* to be *Tripods,* whereas some have *four* supporters. But this objection (unstrengthened by others) is of no moment. Tis enough that the sup-

porters are *generally* but *three;* and as the word *Chir* in itself has no affinity to the number *three* more than to any other, we cannot (i) That the Moor-stone of which our Drews-Teignton Cromlech i3 composed, will not resist the force of a fervent, fire, I-had, since the above was written, the unexpected opportunity of an ocular and palpable demonstration. For the present tenant of Shilston having made it a receptacle for ferns and furze, intended to be burnt and the ashes to be applied in manuring the farm, had sometime before my last visit to it (16 Feb. 1779), burnt the whole under the table-stone of the Cromlech itself; and (as 1 was inforra'd) kept the hot ashes there for 2 or 3 days, till they could be conveniently carried off for his purposes. In consequence of this, so much us the under part of the stone as had been thus heated and smoak'd, and which was easily distinguish by its blackness, would admit of my pulling off large scales from it with my fingers only (of which scales 1 brooght home one, near a foot in length, 6 inches broad,, and about an inch thick): Whereas the ubarrrt parts of the Cromlech retain'd their usual firmness. The effect of the lire on it, some intelligent people there, attributed to the black Tin-Spar, with which this, and the other Moor-stone in that neighbouihood, abounds; and which, they said, had from the force of the fire been expanded, and suffcrM some degree of fusion. This seems not improbable, but must be submitted to the judgment of those who are more conversant in such matters. They however assured me, that some kinds of Moor-stone, which are free from this black spar, will stand the fiercest fire unhurt.—The farmer, who meant not any hurt to the Cromlech by burning his ferns there, has been prohibited by his landlord from doing the like for the future; and he being now aware how liable it is to be damaged by such sites, and no less inclinable to preserve it, 'tia hoped it is now free from all further danger from his good husbandry. Chappie. (2) Lib. -j. prope finem. (3) How happy! that the introduction of Christianity into this island, freed us and our children from

such horrible rites I and from all danger of their future re-establishment. For, at present, we have no cause to dread a relapse into ancienl superstition, but rather the rejection of real religion as such. We still indeed call ourselves christians, yet many among us contemn the memory of those from whom we receiv'd Christianity: Nay some, who will readily acknowledge the benefits derived to us from it, and the gratitude due to its divine author; and who are zealous in commemorating national deliver ances, (tho' perhaps on a wrong day) yet, on pretence of abuses and uncertain chronology, neglect or refuse to celebrate even the nativity of him, whose benefits extended to the world at large, and who came to destroy (Among others) those works of the devil above described: Who by the sacrifice of himself, superseded and rendeied all other bloody sacrifices superfluous; his most perfect law of true liberty (undepraved by licentiousness,) requiring none but that pure Mincha, or unbloody sacrifice which was offer'd by ti e primitive patrian hs; with an eucharistic commemoration of his dying love; a stedfast belief of his divine mission, and the truths he revealed; a renunciation of vice; and our best endeavours (with the assisting grace of the holy spirit) to perform the conditions on which he purchased our pardon. A dispensation, that regulates our selfish passions, improves oui morals, and extends our social connections, by making the love of ourselves the measure of our duty to others; and intitling even our enemies to our forgiveness, our prayers, our charity, and our pity: Binding us by a baptismal covenant, not to any slavish subjection to insupportable burdens, but to such a reasonable service, as conduces to augment our happiness here, and to insure it hereafter: Inviting us by' his own example, to a chearful obedience, firm trust, a reverential respect mix'd with filial love, and a ready resignation to the divine will: In short, engaging ns in, and inciting us to, a religious observation of the duties compt ized in the angelic hymn on his incarnation; via. to give £Jory and divine honour to the most-

high GOD, to whom alone it is due; to cultivate and promote private friendship and public peace; and, to the heft of our power, to enlarge our affections and extend our liberality, by a boundless benefit cence, and universal benevolence.—
—Such are the out-lines os the christian scheme; and snch the easy yoke and light burden which our Lord has imposed upon us, in lieu of the diabolical rites and abominable supeistitions of our pagan Ancestors. And as this occasional retrospect to their barbarous butcheries, and their shocking immolations, both of men nd beasts, by roasting them alive, after the augurs had tortur'd them by the requisite stabbings or stashes to inspect their blood and their entrails,—naturally and almost unavoidably prompts us to reflections like these, on so happy a change; the candid reader will therefore excuse a few biblical phrases, which some may ridicule as the cant of a lay-man torn'd lecturer. But however deem'd impertinent in a treatise of this fort, as digressive from its main design, and tho' the writer bereof has no better opinion of theological than medical empiricism, yet an exhibition of the contrast between paganism and Christianity, whenever either of them claims notice, whether professedly or incidentally! cannot be wholly unseasan »Me Chappie.
Vol. I. K

Cromlechs of Danmonium, however, from their situation at least, may be safely admitted as druidical. (a) Though in the western part of Danmonium, there occur severa? Cromlechs.

cannot be sure!t was never applied to denote any quadrupedal stand, as well as the tripedal one for which we find it used. Mr. *o Halhran* makes the like objection to the derivation of *Cromlech* from the crookedness of its table-stone; for we find, fays he, " many of these covering-stones quite flat, which destroys the very principles of this derivation:" He does not fay *where* such are to be met with:—Indeed *Kit's Cat-House* in *Kent* is so represented (how truly I know not) in the plate facing page 116 of the zi volume of the *Archeeologia*; otherwise I should have thought it very doubtful whether there were any such in *England, Ireland,* or any where else but in the latitude of 450. If such there really are in other latitudes, they must be, in one remarkable instance, of a different construction from ours at *Drews-Teignton,* and from that of *Lanytm* in *Cornwall.* But supposing there be some quite flat, either in *Ireland* or *Kent,* yet if they are *generally* otherwise, in their upper surface, this is enough to justify the derivation. After all, it seems unlikely that *Cromlech* was the original name; it being much more probable that the ancient *Druids* gave it some name expressive of its use and design: And tho' ti» possible this of *Cromlech* might also be afterwards given it, in reference to the deity or deities to whom public sacrifices were offer'd near it (for it is not denied that such religious worship might be there perform'd, for the reasons before given); yet it seems to me the most probable conjecture of the two, that it took this subsequent name (for such I imagine it to be) from the form of its covering stone, as was at first supposed; without any regard to such sacrifices, and possibly after they were discontinued—It may here be ask'd,—Why then this tedious comment on another etymology, which must be rejected at last, or at best represented as dubious *i* The answer is,—To prevent a more diffusive recital hereafter, of the opinions of others relative to the use of such monuments; which were proposed to be examin'd into, but which the foregoing references to them have partly precluded: And also to shew how little, etymologies are to be depended on, for the establishment of any hypothesis that wants other evidence to support it." Chappie's Description, p. 72 to 97. *(a)* Having particularly examin'd the weight of the covering stone of our *Drews-Teignton-Cromlech,* and perhaps been rather too tedious in our enquiries by what strength or contrivances such structures were probably rais'd, it may not be impertinent to our subject to add a few words concerning the people to whose industry and art they are to be ascribed (for whatever purpose erected), and the permanency and preservation of

such monuments in general; of which many yet remain, not only in the western parts of *England,* in *Ireland,* and the *Britijb* isles, but also (asobscrv'd by *V)r. BorIae(i* M. *Mallet* above quoted, and others) in *Denmark, Sweden, Norway, France, Germany,* and in the Isles of the Mediterranean sea adjacent to the coasts of *Spain* and *France;* as also in the Isle of *Jersey,* &c. Hence Dr. *Borlase* concludes, they were probably " *Celtic* monuments, and with that numerous people carried into all their settlements:" Not peculiar to the *Druids,* tho' there can be no doubt that the *Druids* among others erected monuments of this kind: And that ours were of their erection (for the christians never erected any such, and the *Danes* never had footing in places where some of them are still to be met with), the Doctor seems to have undeniably proved The roughness and apparent deformity of their unpolisli'd supporters; the gibbosity and seeming disproportion of their prominent unornamented chapiters; the general simplicity of their construction; yet the grandeur, the firmness and strength of the fabrick; tho' at first view ie may seem the production of a people just emerged from barbarity and beginning to cultivate the arts, yet on a closer inspection exhibits the strongest evidence, that they could design boldly, and execute effectually. Composed of few, but those the most solid and durable materials; sustain'd by strong pillars deeply and imtnoveably fix'd in their foundations; and the *Abacus* that crowns the whole, by its magnitude and weight little less secured from subversion, cither by accident or external force, than the *Fulcra* that support it;—these structures, like the pyramids of *Ægyft,* have out-lasted the memory of their founders; and still remain objects of the admiration of common spectators, subjects of speculation for the curious, and silent witnesses of the hitherto disputable claims of hypothetic antiquarians.(e) Chappie's Description, p. 63 to 66. (1) Antiq. of Cornw. p. aii. (2) Nothing is here meant with a view to censure or ridicule the laudable resets chea f those who have heretofore labour's? on

this subject; and endeavotir'd, tho' perhaps unsuccessfully, to account for the origin of such structures, from the best lights that ancient history could afford them, in a matter which time had inveloped in so much obscurity; as if we would wholly reprobate every ingenious hypothesis that might be framed to elucidate it, and were disposed (whilst we avail ourselves of their labours) to blame them for every deviation from the rectitude of a path, where there remain'd scarce any visible tract to direct their foot-steps. Even those hypotheses which have only mere fiction or surmise for their basis, may tend to the discovery of truth; if only by exciting some critical opponent to detect their errors, or point out their absurdities: much more so, those, which are partly sounded on facts, observations and experiments, but not on a sufficient number of them to ascertain every-thlng they are produced to prove, as is the cafe with some alluded to here. The great Roger Bacon (that blazing comet which, in a very dark age, affrighted the ignorant, and fiil'd them with the dread of his magic and inchantnent,) was certainly in the right, when bx affirm'd, thattiic moon's vicinity 19 the oarth gave her greater influence 09 *t* Cromlechs (for a description of which I refer my readers to the Antiquities of Cornwall) yet, on this side of the Tamar, in a far more extensive tract of country, we have only to exhibit one solitary Cromlech. It is true, there are other places in Devonshire that have laid claim to this distinction: But the claim has been allowed only by those who, having an indistinct idea of druidkal monuments, conceive *Cromlech* to be a general name for them all. On a down, in the parish of Shaugh, commonly called Shaugh. moor, there is, doubtless, some resemblance of a Cromlech. Many represented it at really a Cromlech: Others thought it nothing more than the rude natural rock. Curiosity, however, lately induced a gentleman to go to Shaugh-moor, purposely to look, at this rock-: And he returned, " perfectly convinced that it was a Cromlech; and of the most durable kind, the top-stone *being supported on natural rocks.* The coveringstone was about fifteen feet long, and twelve feet broad." And this monument,! it seems, was " *on the fide of the hill"* This account requires little ©r no comment. The gentleman who pronounces theie rocks to be a Cromlech, discovers nothing that has the leait appearance of art, excepting in the position of the top-stone. But the position of this stone, is surely accidental. It might easily have fallen from the hill above, on the rocks that support it. And, as to the situation of this imaginary Cromlech, *the fide of a bill* is not the usual place for erecting filch a monument, (a) The only *Cromlech* in this county (which is indisputably such) is situated in *(J)Drev/feignton (the town of the Druids upon the a)* In the neighbourhood of these rocks, however, there are several druidical circles.

b) " *Dreivfieignton* has been by *Rijdon, Westcot, Prince,* and others, imagined to derive the prefix to its name, by which it is distinguished from other *Teingtons* or towns on or near the river *Teign,* from *Drogo de Teign,* who flourished in the reigns of *Henry* II, and *Richard* I, and from whom the *Hre-.vcs,* a noted family in this county, have been supposed to be descended."

" But as we find it call'd *Ttign-Dru* or *Drues-Teignton* in some ancient records, it seems to me most probable it was thus distinguished, as having been, before the *Roman* conquest, the residence of a principal *Druid:* For, that some considerable one govern'd here, and had great numbers under his command, may fairly be inferr'd from the stupendous monument of their labour and skill, of which we are here to give an account; and which having for ages resisted the ravages of devouring time, still remains a standing testimony of the industry and consummate ingenuity of those who erected it. From a tradition of such residence of a chief *Druid,* or perhaps some college or community of them here, the *Britons* of those times might denominate it *Derzvyddon Caer-Tegn* or *eu Caer ar Tegn,* the town of the *Druids* on the *Teign.* That its present name was form'd from *Druids Teign-*

ton, with the omission of the-second *d,* has been the opinion of most persons who have seen its *Cromlech,* and j udged it to be a druidical structure, tho' uncertain for what purposes it was erected.—Hence also *Drcwston,* the name of a farm there, had probably its origin; having been perhaps once the feat of some *Druid* or *Druids.* And the like may be observ'd of another *Drcivston,* situated in the adjoining parish of *Cbagford,* but on the other side of the *Teign.* If it be objected against our supposed *British* name of *Drew's Teignton,* that the word *Caer* or *Cair* was by the *Britons* applied only to *fortified* places, and old camps and intrenchments; for which reason the *Saxons* generally turned it into *Coaster,* and whence our present terminations of *Cefier* and *Chester* in the names of many such places, but being not so here, it may well be deem'd doubtful whether the *Britons* prefix'd their *Caer* to this name any more than the *Saxons* added to it their suffix of *Chester:* It is acknowledg'd that the *Saxons* most commonly turn'd the *Britijh* Cair into *Cester* or *Chester,* but this not without some exceptions, and in the *Armoric* dialect it is used for any common town or village. But supposing it restricted to fortifications the tides, andoperated more strongly on the ocean, than the fun or stars, tho much exceeding her in magnitude, but withal at a much farther distance; and that her action on the sea was the greatest, when her rays most nearly approach'd to right angles with its surface. See his Opus majus, Distinct. 4, cap. 5. p. 85 and 86 of Jcbb's Edit. 1733. For which reason he elsewhere (as I remember, tho' I cannot now turn to the place) modestly queries, whether there might not be something in the nature of light, which, according as the rays fall more or less obliquely on the ocean, occasions the varieties observ'd in its flux and reflux7 But he was as certainly wrong, in the hypothesis by which he attempted to account for them; viz. tire power of the lunar rays to extract arid consume its vapors; as if they had the like force with the solar, or the heat of a fire on the broth in a pot (with which he compares

it), to cause the like ebullition and evaporation I It was reserv'd for a Newton, to clear up those then mysterious phenomena; to detect the mistakes of his great predecessor; and to consirm what he had, with fewer helps but no less sagacity, observ'd and rightly asserted; but this now more strongly fortified, by uiore cogent and conclusive arguments, and on more certain and indisputable principles. Such a detection of the fallacy of Bacon's theory, is no reflection on, nor any-wav tends to depreciate his judgment and penetration: We rather admire, that Jus lyncean eye c6uld fee so far into the Milstone, without farther improvements on those spectacles, of which he was most probably the first inventor In short, hypotheses founded partly on observation and partly on conjecture, only become

Jtdiculoiis and contemptible, when magisterially proposed as indubitable truths; and when, tho' they have only the feeble support of fallacious conclusions from insufficient evidence, the proponent claims an exclusive right to their admission, in preference to all others, as if they were infallible certainties. Chappie.

yoL.j. K *the feign)* on a farm called *Sbiljion:* And the word *Sbiljion,* in ancient deeds *Sbilsejian,* signifies the shelf-stone or slielving-stone.(ct) With respect to the original name of this Cromlech, fortifications and intrenchments, we are still justified in its supposed application here: For at *Preston* farm, within this parish, on the summit of a very steep rocky hill, now distinguilh'd by the name of *PrestonBerryi),* close'to that part of the *Teign,* where the road over *Fingle-Bridge* leads *KxomDrews leignton* to *Moretonhampstead* (to which parishes the *Teign* is a common boundary), are the remains of a *Roman* encampment; and that it was really such, and not a *Saxon* or *Danish* one, is evident from its form; of which a more particular account is intended to be given elsewhere. But if our *Der wyddon Caer-Teign* should after all be rejected as the result of an arbitrary and ill-grounded supposition, why might it not have been one of the 28 famous cities or towns of the ancient *Britons t* Among these the venerable *Bede* calls the 26th *Cair Droithan* or *Droitboi,(2)* which seems at least as likely, if not more so, to mean this place, as a then noted residence of the *Druids,* than *Draiton* in *Shropshire,* as some have imaginsd it to be, from the orthography of *Henry* of *Huntingdon,* who calls it *Ca'f Daritbou* vel *Diaiton.%'i)* Chappie's Descript. p. 1 and 2. 12 to 16. A correspondent commenting on Chappie's Description, observes, " I entirely agree with Mr. Chappie inopirion that it is called *Drue* or *Drews,* not from *Drogo,* or the family of the *Drews,* or any such trifling origin, but from the word *Drui,* of which I will fay more presently; but I will first confirm the author's opinion, by just mentioning, that it so happens that there is a similar structure between Bath and Bristol, of which Governor Pownall has given a memoir to the Society of Antiquarians; and th« name of the place is not, indeed, *Druisteignton,* but it is *Teignton-Druis,* which is the fame thing, and both are of the fame origin.(3) I must here make a remark on the name of the river, *Teing,* which word, as well as *Tein, Tin, Tanna,* signifies *fire:* and there seems some analogy between this and the structure itself: and I am assured there are ruins of similar structures in several places on the banks pf this river, before it reaches the sea. I have now to remark on the word *Drui,* that it comet not from *Drus,* neither does it mean the *oak,* or the - *wood* where the priest retired, but is of Pe.fian or rather oriental origin, and signifies a *Jage,* a -*wife-man,* a *prophet,* a *priest,* whose office it was to preserve the rites of the *Cuthite* religion, and to observe the motions of *the host of heaven,* which they worshipped. This word has still the fame signification in the ancient Erse, or Irish language; and a *Druid* temple, therefore, means a temple at which the *wife-men* presided: In this, then, the author and I pretty nearly agree.—I come next to his endeavours to explain the meaning of the word *Cromlech,* about which the author took a great deal of pains, but I think has left the matter very near where he found

it t I will endeavour to clear it up. He has got part of the way by deciding that it is derived from *Cromleach,* or *Cromleagh,* or *Cromliach,* all of which mean the fame thing— but I do not hesitate to say that it means the fame thing as *Stonehenge,* concerning which much learning has been exerted, not to much purpose. *Cromlech,* then, is derived from *Cromleagh,* which is composed of *Crom* a stone, and *leagh* lying or leaning, poised or hanging. I saw one of these structures in Ireland, with a flat *enclined stone* supported by three upright ones, which the Irish called *Cromlech,* and I was assured *that* was the *derivation* of it: And so, in like manner, is *Stonehenge* derived from *Stein* a stone, and *henge* to hang, or poise, or lean— Nothing could be more natural than these names; for stones thus placed were the characteristics of these structures." *a)* " What renders this farm more remarkable is its *Cromlech;* which is situated in a small field or inclosure belonging thereto, the measure whereof is not quite 2 acres and half; which field, tho' on the ascent of a hill, and not above a furlong or two below its summit, is nearly plain and level. Indeed we might rather have expected to find it on the summit itself, as Dr. *Borlaje* fays structures of this fort are generally so situated; from whence, and from the exactness with which some of them are placed, he concludes,(4) " that those who erected them were very solicitous to pUce 'em as conspicuously as possible." But the above situation of our *Cromlech* perhaps was rather chosen, as being less exposed to the bleak northern winds, and yet sufficiently commodious for the uses to which it was appropriated. For tho' its northerly prospect be obstructed by the higher part of the hill call'd *Church-Down,* which excludes almost every object within 2 or 3 points to the east or west from the north, yet the view from it every-way else is so extensive as to exhibit for the most part an open and fair horizon, from the fun-rising to fun-setting in the longest day; and gives the *Shilston* farmer, tho' he cannot from hence fee his own parish church (which is hidden by another little hill),

a distinct view of four others *viz.* those of *Moretonbampstead, Chagford, Gidley,* antj *Tbrowleigb.* (1) Doubtless so call'd from the Saxon Byrig, which, signifies not only Urbs, but also Arx, Propugnaculum, Castrum, Bee. And accordingly most old castles, fortifications, and encampments in Devonshire, still retain their Saxon appellation of Berry. Chappie. , (2) See Smith's Bede (Append.) p. 655 and 658; and Hen. Huntingd. Hist. Lib. 1. sol. 170 of Savile's Ed. of the Scriptores post Bedam.

(3) The remains of this monument near Bath, bear the name of the Wedding among the common people, from a tradition, that as a bride was going to be married, she and the lest of the company were changed into pillars of stone. (4) Anticj. of Cornw. Ch IX. p. aio. .« Cromlech, it would be absurd to conjecture. It is, at present, known in the neighbour, hood by the name of the *Spinster's-rock.a)* This Cromlech is of moor-stone i And

Mr.

Tbrowleigh. The *Cromlech* stands within a mile and a quarter nearly west of the church of *Drrwt Teignton,* and directly north from that of *Chagford,* at the distance of not quite 1 miles from it; which situation is nearly in the middle of the county of Devon, being within i miles and half of the center of its circumscribing circle: For this center, if Mr. *Donn* has accurately delineated the sea coasts of *Devon* in his map,— which, whatever other faults it may have, or be supposed to have (for it has been charged with some unjustly), I think has never been questioned,—is about a mile and quarter to the southwest of the church of *Hittcstcigb.*" Chappie's Description, p. 28 to 30. *(a)* " What name the *Druids* gave our *Drews-Tcignion Cromlech* at its first erection, cannot now be certainly known; and can only be guess'd at, either from its *present* name, or its original use. With respect to the former, the name, by which the learned have distinguish'd it from other *Druidical* monuments, fails us; for we may infer from the latter, if this can be determined with more certainty, as 'tis presumed it may, that *Cromlech* could not, with any propriety, be its *original* name. Let us try then, what light its modern *vulgar* name may afford us, on a supposition it was derived from some appellation originally expressive of its use. This *Cromlech* is vulgarly known to the inhabitants of *Drews Teignton* and its neighbourhood by no other name than that of *Spinster's or Spinner's Rock;* and their common saying is, that it was erected by three spinsters one morning before their breakfast. These *Spinsters,* tho' the appellation among lawyers is peculiar to maiden women, but seems to be originally derived from the common employment of young girls in former ages, the inhabitants represent as having been not only spinsters in the former fense, but also spinners'by occupation. For according to their account, they did it after finishing their usual work, and *going home-with their pad,* as the phrase here is; that is, carrying home their pad of yarn to the yarn-jobber, to be paid for spinning it: And on their return, observing such heavy materials unapplied to any use, and being strong wenches (giantesses we may presume, such as *Gulliver's G/umdahlitch,* or the blouzes of *Patagonia),* as an evidence of their strength and industry, and to shame the men, who either from weakness or laziness had desisted from the attempt, they jointly undertook this task, and rais'd the unwieldy (tones to the height and position in which they still remain. This is the tale, which they fay has been handed down from generation to generation; and thence the) tell you, this romantic structure had its name. It is usual with the vulgar, to ascribe almost everythitig that they think beyond the reach of human power, to the devil, or diabolical arts: In the present case, however, they have not thought it necessary to call in his devilfhip's assistance; but having a notion that the people of former ages were of a gigantic stature and *Herculean* strength, they imagin'd this sufficient to account for the erection of such structures as these; taking for granted they could lift up, and properly place, such huge blocks of moor-stone, as the pigmies of the present time are

unable to move. But granting their strength and their bulk were as supposed, still 'twas an odd undertaking for spinsters! Had a *Talmudic,* or a legendary romancer after the *Saxom* conversion, been author of the tale, he would rather have constituted them bed-makers to *Og* the king of *Basan,* the dimensions of whose Iron bedstead are recorded by *Moses(i);* it being in length nearly the same as our *Cromlech,* but this in its breadth would make room for his queen also (for the canopy would overshadow both) 1(2) And having this certain evidence of its dimensions, and *r'* the (1) Deoterony 3. M« (2) The Writer hereof is far from intending any ridicule on the sacred scripture!: Uninfatuated by the fashionable scepticism of the times, he would not even inGnuate anything derogatory to any part of the Mosaic history: A history, which those who deny iu inspiration must allow to be the molt ancient, and the best authenticated, os any that pretend to the highest antiquity. Nor would he charge every extraordinary incident there recorded, that might shock the belies of a BoKngbroke or a Voltaire, on a supposed corruption os the text. Such, 'tis acknowledg'd, theie certainly are, in some parts of those writings, but none can be pretended in that here quoted; it appearing from the accurate collations of our very learned and indefatigable countryman, the Rev. Dr. Kennicott, that not only all the ancient printed copies collated by him, but also all the manuscript ones to tlic lumber of 119, agree with the present reading in the dimensions of the bedstead abovemcnton'd, save only one MS, wherein the words expressive of its breadth are omitted. Indeed there seenia avo reason to doubt of the gigantic stature of Og, or of the other descendentl of Anak, as there attested; but tho' hia bedstead were six cubits long, it doth not follow that he himself was of that height. We may allow him however full five cubits, which I take to be somewhat less than the stature of Ordulph or Edulph the son of Ordgar Duke of Devonshire must liave been, even supposing the leg and thigh bones prefei v'd, and shewn for

his in Tavystoke Church, were really his, and taken out of his enormous sepulcher at the dissolution of the abbey there, where Malmfbury tells us it was to be seen; he being " gigantea: molis fk immania robori,:" But if these bones he admitted as evidences of his proportionable height, I imagine, (from what I remember of their size) it hardly exceeded 8 feet, or very little more than 5 cubits. Such a man anight find loom to stretch himself between two of the supporters of our Cromlech; but perhaps not to that length to which the fame Historian stretches the legs of this Ordulph, when, at a hunting in Dorsetshire, he makes him stride over a rivulet that was ten feet wide from bank to bank. He also represents him as having strength proportional to his statuie; and gives art' instance of his exertion of it when coming to Exeter with King Edward the Confessor (to whom he was related), and approaching that city he found the gate shut against them; the people within being then, it seems, careful to preserve their right to (bat the fates against all strangers, ac least 'till they give a satisla &ory account of themselves: Or perhaps, as our the gigantic stature of *Og,* a fanciful narrator, when geography and chronology, the two eyes of history, were both stiut, might as cleverly bring him hither, in a voyage with some *Sidoniati* trader, on a *temporary visit* to *Britain,* and perhaps with as much assurance ofa ready reception by credulous and uninquiſitive people, as *Jeffery* of *Monmouth* could introduce a *Trajan Brute to settle* here: And to make the story plausible, his *Bafannic* Majesty had only to appoint a regent in *Argob* during his absence—But leaving such fancies, to make room for others; which, tho' not so far fetch'd, but of home-fabrication, may possibly, for that very reason, be the less esteem'd by some, and contemptuously rejected, as little better authenticated than the childish and fabulous story itself on which they are founded. Indeed nothing to our purpose can be deduced from it as simply told; only from its texture, 'tis sufficiently evident, that the supposed erection of this *Cromlech* by 3 spinsters (except as to their number, which might be from that of its supporters), must have had its origin from its common name; not the name from them, as the *Drewsleigr. tomans* would persuade us. Yet, as the wildest and most ridiculous traditions, generally retain some shadow of their original, whether founded on fable or fact; so the most disguised and corrupted words xnd names may, after all, preserve so many of their radical letters as spelt, or so much resemblance of their original sounds as spoken, as, with the concurrence of other circumstances, may invite an etymologist to attempt an investigation of their meaning; tho' not always with the desired success. Permit me however, to offer a conjecture, after taking for granted that the original name of this *Cromlech* was expressive of the use for which it was design'd. And as it will hereafter appear, that its fabrication was not only for sciatherical purposes, but also for such geographical as well as astronomical observations and conclusions as might be generally deducible from thence; it being certain that the ancients were guided in such observations by the æquinoctial shadow of a perpendicular gnomon or style, and fitted their instruments to it: (1) Why then might not the astronomical *Druids* give it some *Celtic* appellation significant cf that use; such as *Lie Tfpiennior rhongea* (in the *British* dialect of the *Celtic*), ike *Place* of the *open* or *hollow Observatory f'z)* Or possibly *Tspienddyn Ser rongea,* the *open Star-gazing Flace.z)* This the *Britons* themselves, if we may suppose them to have discontinued its use and forgotten the meaning of its name, after the extirpation of the *Druids* by the *Romans,* might change for other words of a similar sound, but having regard only to the massive and ponderous stones that composed it, such as *Si›p pynnerog,* the *weighty Pile—Sivp* signifying a pile, a heap, a lump, a bunch, &c. and *pynverog* heavy; from *pynner,* an old *Britijh* word for a *load, burden,* or *-weight.* But whether they had thus corrupted it or not, at the time of the *Saxon* conquest, the *Saxons* not understanding the Britifll language, and mistaking their appellatives for proper

names, as has been elsewhere observ'd in respect to our rivers, might do the like here; and softening the rough and guttural pronunciation of the *Britons,* would naturally adopt instead of it some word or words, of a somewhat similar sound, in their own language; by which it became easily exchanged into *Spinners Rocc.* Where note, the word *Xcct* meant not the same with the modem *English* word Rock, answering to the Latin *Saxum* or *Perns;* but svas the old *Teutonic* word for *Colus,* a *Distaff;* which is still called by the *Germans,* UN Sh-nnrocken, in *Loiu-Dutch* Sunn-rock. *Rock* indeed, in the fame languages as well as in the *Anglo-Saxon,* also signifies a *Coat* or *Goivn;* whence perhaps the *French Roquet* and *Roqueleau:* And the *English Saxons* besides the word *Rocc* likewise used the same word for *Distaff (Distxs)* which we have author observes, the porter, not knowing of their coming, might be too far off to give them ready admission. Enraged: at this, Ordulph (or Edulph as he rails him) with both his hands, apparently without much difficulty, broke the bars and bolts, and using also the force of his sect, unhinged the valves of the gate, fhatter'd them to pieces, and threw down a part of the wall adjoining: As if he meant to shew the king how far he could match Sampson, who forced open and car. ried off the gates of Ga;a; but the other courtiers present it seems, to diminish his applause, ascribed the whole to diabolical assistance rather than to any human power. Vide Malmsb. de gestis Pontif. Angl. lib. 2. p. 146. £d. Savil. Script, post Bcdam. See also the Extracts from him in Leland's Collectanea, torn. 2. p. 256. (1) Claud. Salmasius in Solinum, pag. 64J. " Ad æquinoctialis diei partes duodenario numero æqualiter dividendaa, Babylonii Græciquc omnei Astrologi voteres et Gnomonici rationes suas accommodarunt. Nec fane aliter fieri potuit. Et boc ita siebat oondum puhlicato horarum nomine et ufu. Post eas repertas et Horologia inventa, quum horx ipsae variarent et pro dierum ratione modo breviores modo longiores ponerentur. Astronomi tanicn Astrologique oranes,

et Gnomonici, insuper habita horarum civili observatione, aequinoctiales solas ad ufum ac rationes suas observabant. Etenira cum horologia omnia turn ad cursum Solis facta, horas exhiberent omnium anni mensium ex umbrarum momentis crefccntesac deorescentes, folittS Gnomonis æquinoctialis umbras refpiciebant, gnomonici et rationes omnes Mathcmaticas ad cum dirigebant-"-p-He then refers to Vitruvius, lib 1. c.vi. and adds,—" Etiam diversi regionnm situs, quos varia facit inclinatio cceli, quique ex umbrarum incretnentis ac mutationibus dep ehenduntur, non aliter colligi sokbant, nisi per utnbrz alqumoctialis gnomonem." And after citing lib. ix. c.8. of Vitruvius, to which this is inserted as a note under p. 19/ of Laet's edition (Leyd. 1649, to shew that various places have various lengths of the equinoctial shadow (as indeed they must, if ef different latitudes, varying according to the elevation of the pole and consequent depression of the equator), he concludes, " Idea ciiihufcumque in locis horologia deferiberentur, eo loci fumtbant æquinoctialem umbram. Quinctiam ad dierum augments ac decrementa per Cngulos menses indicandanon aliis horis quam æquinoctialibus utuntur veteres Calendartorum auctores."— Annotat. in Vitruv. cdiL subtradict. p. 197. Vide & Strab. lib 2. sub finem, et alibi passim. (2) Being not sufficiently acquainted with the requisite changes of letters and other distinctions which the various inflections in the composition and construction of the British or other Celtic dialects frequently require, to be answerable for the strict propriety of these supposed appellations; I must desire the excuse of the Canibro British reader, for any deviation from orthographic nicety in them; since any little error of this kind cannot materially affect the general deduction from *its* m respect to their subsequent changes for words of similar sound. Chappie.

Mr. Chappie informs us, " that like most others, it has only three supporters; flat, and irregular in their shape; their surfaces rough and unpolish'd; and their position not directly upright but more or less leaning, (two to the northward, and the other to the south and east), and yet ib as firmly to sustain the very ponderous table-stone whiclt covers them: The whole forming a kind of large irregular tripod, and of such a height as if designed for the feat to the queen of *Brobdingnag*s dwarf, or the footstool of *GulEver's* nude; its *upper* surface being, where highest, near 9 feet and half from the ground, and the whole on an average at least 8 feet. The greatest length of its table-stone between its two most distant angles is about 15 feet, but taken parallel to its sides about 14, and at a medium not above 13 feet and half; its greatest breadth 10 feet, but this meafiir'd at right angles in that part where its two opposite sides are nearly parallel, is at a medium but 9 feet 10 inches. Its form, on a superficial view, has been commonly considered as that of an irregular *Trapezium,* two of whose 4 sides are partly curv'd, another wholly so, and only one appears to be in a right line; but even this is not strictly so. This, some would have to be the shape in which it happen'd to be form'd in its quarry, with little or no alteration by the hand of a workman; but on a nicer examination it appears to form an hexagonal figure, three of whose sides are straight lines (saving a very small curvature at the extremity of one of them), and the other three, curves; and these described with the utmost regularity and exactness: Wherefore, tho' we may sometime occasionally call it a T*rapezium,* it must not be Ib strictly understood as having that kind of figure to which geometers confine that name. The upper part of this trapezium or table-stone, is sis usual in other Cromlechs, bulging md. gibbous, or, as the countrypeople express it, *saddle-backed*; but its under surface, tho' not smoothly polistVd, is, or originally was, almost every-where a plane, and free from irregular knobs or bunches. This plane makes an angle with the plane of the horizon of about 3 degrees and 55 minutes: For it is to be observ'd, that its three supporters are of unequal heights, and consequently the plane they support cannot be horizontal, but inclines a little downward, as is the

cafe in most other *Cromlechs* we have any account of, at least of those in the *British* isles that have been with any degree of precision described. Among other seeming irregularities, the inequality of the heights of the supporters, which occasions this inclination or declivity, and gives ours a dip towards the south-west, was not accidental, but designedly chosen as most expedient to answer the purposes for which the *Cromlech* was erected. The thickness of the table-stone is different in different parts of it. In the part over the middle supporter, which most bulges or swells upward, it has been found, on a late careful mensuration of it, to be not less than 3 feet and seven inches: From thence this thickness have retain'd; but that they also (and perhaps more frequently) used the former in this fense is sufficiently evident. The *Saxon* name of our *Cromlech* being thus established, and the Spinners employment at their rock implied in it, however understood at first, this ambiguous word, *Recit* came at length to be taken in its most common fense, as referring to the rock from whence tho materials of this structure were supplied; Distaffs being little used in *Devonshire,* and scarce known in this part of it, where no flax or hemp is grown. Hence the story of the three spinsters, and their labour in erecting the fabrick fuppos'd to have its denomination from them, might easily have its rife; and, only changing the Distaff for a Spinning-wheel, and adding some embellishments, became the subject of a common tale among nurses, to please children, and amuse the ignorant. Let it however be remember'd, that this derivation of its vulgar name, (tho' perhaps not less probable than any hitherto given of the *British* word *Cromlech,)* is proposed as conjectural only; and its probability or improbability submitted to the discussion of the judicious reader. " Chappie's Description, p. 97 to 108.

My commentator on Chappie further observes: " I must make one remark on the *tradition* which the author gives relative to this structure, concerning the *three. 'adies*—with regard to which, my accounts differ and go rather farther.

My accounts fay that the tradition varies—some times it is *three young men,* and sometimes *three young ladies.* But the tradition goes farther, and fays, that not only the *three pillars* were erected in memory of the *three young ones,* but that the *fiat* one which covers them was placed there in memory of *their father,* or *mother,* according as you supposed the young ones to be male and female, and that each of these, both young and old, fetched these stones down from the highest parts of the mountain of Dartmoor, where, for some reason or other, they had thought fit to take up their residence. Perhaps the expression *Lie T Sfienmvr,* which the author seems to think implies a *spying* or *surveying* place, might give rife to the idea of *spinners,* and this turo them into *three ladies.* But you will perhaps guess why I encline to suppose these stones might be erected, among other reasons, in memory of an *old man* and his *tkret sons,* who descended from an exceeding high mountain, oi? a certain occasion." thickness diminishes more or less every way towards the sides of the trapezoid respectively, where the thicknesses also vary. For, towards the north-west, it is from 20 inches to feet thick: the arch'd part at the north-east is rounded off to a blunt edge, both above and below: the south-east side (where its thickness would otherwise be 17 inches) is undercut inward, so as to form a reclining plane 22 inches in the slope back, or 14. inches horizontally; and this reclining continues for 7 feet and 7 inches in length, to that point where the curvilinear boundary begins. Between this point and that part which projects over the eastern edge of the lower prop, there has been an excavation of its upper surface, and a seeming abruption of some part of it; whether originally so design'd, or the effect of violence since, we may hereafter have occasion to enquire. On the whole, the average thickness of this covering stone may be estimated at one foot and 9 inches, or near half the greatest thickness of its bulging part. But more of this, and of the nature and length of the curves which form three on its sides, when we come to specify its dimensions and properties more minutely. This may suffice at present, with regard to its general dimensions and form; of which latter however, the View of it prefix'd to this tract will give those who have not seen it a more perfect idea than any verbal description, (a) But as, among other dimensions, having repeatedly survey'd it, in order to have a perfect plan, I took care (by girthing and otherwise) to have sufficient to determine its *solidity* also; and from thence, and the known specific gravity of the moor stone of which it wholly consists, to be enabled to estimate its --*weight;* it may be more proper here to give the result of those measures, than to interrupt our intended enquiries into its geometrical construction by introducing it there. The areas of the leverai parts into which the plane of its under surface was to be divided, as the different thicknesses required, in order to obtain their respective solidities, being requisite to be first ascertain'd; I thence found the sum of those areas, or the whole superficial area of this undermost surface or plain part of the table-stone, to be 125 square feet; being not quits half of a square perch, tho' very little short as wanting not a 12th part of it. And this is the quantity of ground it covers, or rather overshadows, at about 6 feet and 3 or four inches, on an average, in height from the surface of the ground: which height is meant of the *under* part of the stone only; that of its *upper* (as may be gather'd from the above dimensions) being from 6 to at least 9 feet and half. The different thicknesses being carefully dilidnguiih'd as above, with the superficial areas under each, and the bulging upwards allow'd for; I thence found the whole solidity of the said stone (disregarding a very small fraction of a soot) to be 216 cubic feet very nearly. Now a cubic foot of water weighing 62 1b. *avoirdupois,* and the specific gravity of moorstone being found, by the experiments of Mr. *Labelye* the *Westminster* Bridge Engineer, to be to that of water, as 1.656 to 1; from the above solidity we have 216 x 62,5 x 2.656 = 35856. *avoirdupois, for* the neat weight of the covering stone of this

Cromlech: that is, in gross weight (reckoning as usual nzlb. to the hundred, and 20 such hundreds to make a tun), *sixteen* tun, with an addition of 16 pounds *avoirdupois.by* The use of the Cromlech has been a subject *(a)* Mr. Chappie is perfectly right in this observation. The *View* intended for his tract, might have precluded this tedious description.

V) A former computation made it not quite 12 tun; but on re-examining the dimensions, it ap. pear'd, that the greatest thickness had been therein reckon'd a whole foot less than it really is: And even the present correction of that mistake, makes it still less than a person, from a rough guess at it on a view only, would have taken it to be. Our *Cromlech* at *Drews Te'igntm* has, perhaps, suffered less, either from internal decay or external violence, than most others. This (like those in *Corn-wall)* Is of moor-stone, which is known to stand all weathers; and accordingly it has hitherto resisted the furious assaults of the most raging storms. No less firm in its fabrication than other structures of the like kind are said to be, it still continues free from all danger of removal by the utmost efforts of human force, unless assisted by artificial contrivances; and only obnoxious to be thrown down by the (hock of an earthquake, the accidental direction of a thunder-bolt,' or the modern imitation of thunder by the help of gunpowder. It is moreover secured, by the care of its present worthy owner, as it has hitherto been by the plenty of other stones at no great distance from it, from the avarice of such persons as have else-where blown up. other structures of the like kind, for building or other uses: And tho' by some deem'd a monument of ancient idolatry, yet this being unsuspected by the depredators of the last century at least, has also happily escaped the wantonness of military mischief, a subject of much' conjecture, *(a)* An ingenious writer fays, that the Cromlech is the *Bith he ram* of the Canaanites and that its name, declares it to have been a temple dedicated ,mischief(i) and the fury, of fanatic reformers. So that we still have its essential parts entire (tho' unattended by the

satellites which probably once surrounded it), and can the better examine into, and judge of its original design, and the uses for which it was erected. " Chappie's Description, (a) One would have the monument in question for the purposes of a heathen temple: For a regard for heathen templet is no less in the taste ot the times, thari prospects of the venerable ruins of dilapidated churches, desecrated chapels, and suppress'd religious houses: Nay, some (as if ashamed of the christian piety of their ancestors) choose rather to subvert and efface all remains of the latter, to make room or supply materials for the former.— Another demands it as an ancient altar for human sacrifices; and which, if restored to its original use, might make quicker dispatch in that business, than the modern mode of sending the victims on shipboard, or into the army, for the ease and benefit of the parish, (z)—A third lays claim to it as a family burying-place; and digs Up tho bones of his ancestors (who, to signify to posterity their own great importance, chose to take their long steep under so grand a canopy), to be produced as unquestionable evidences of uninterrupted possession.—A fourth, with more appearance of reason, insists on its havirg been the place of a driiidical court-leet; and pleads (unbribcd by a fee) in behalf of the lord of the manor, that he, having not only the chancellorship of the court-baron incident thereto, but also the view of frankpledge, has consequently a legal right to hold that court in the anciently accustomed place.(3)— Some, who are not so immediately concern'd, are content to wait the issue of the dispute j whilst others, observing, and desirous to avail themselves of, the flaws in the pleas and proceedings of the disputants, are inclined to protract it, and to postpone any final decision by demurs and delays; hoping in the mean while to set up some claim of their own, to some share at least, of the premises contended for. Thus stands the matter at present: How far any-thing here to be alledg'd may conduce to put an end to the contest, must be left to the determination of the judges." Chappie's Description, p.

67 to 70.

" The different opinions of antiquarians concerning their primary use and design, may be reducible to these: viz. That they were either temples, or altars, or courts of judicature, or places of legislation, where new laws were proclaim'd, or the old enforced; or for public orations to the people, on these or other subjects; or lafily, for sepulchral monuments.—That sacrifices might be offer'd, courts of judicature held, or laws promulgated, in convenient places at or near them, is not altogether improbable: And that some of them have been occasionally applied to the purposes of sepulture and memorials of the dead, is pretty certain; there being one or more in *Cornwall* that have cairns, or (as the *Devonians,* from the Saxon, most properly call them *(ftone-hurrows)* under their covering-stones: Some of the *Danijh* Cromlechs are also said to be placed on the top of a barrow(4), and an um is said to have been found under one of them in *Ireland.* But that they were originally design'd for neither of these purposes (at least that ours at *Drews Teignton* was not), 'tis presumed will sufficiently appear from what follows. Mean while, let it be heije observ'd, that as far as their uses have been guess'd at, from the stone circles by which some of them were surrounded, or to which they were annexed, so far the design of such circles has of course become the object of enquiry among the writers on this subject; as being deem'd prior to the *Cromlechs* with which they are frequently connected, and which have been supposed additional appendages to them: so that a discovery of the designs of the *Druids* in those, was thought the most likely to indicate the subservient uses of these. But it will perhaps appear, that the real uses of such C'rcles may, with greater probability, be discovered from the construction and design of the *Cromlechs,* if this can from other evidence be (1) The soldiers during thecivil wars, out of wantonness, and to try the conjunctive force of a number of men in removing1 the largest stones pois'd od each other in divers parts of Cornwall, arc said to have thrown some of them

down: And Ir. Borlase from Mr. Scaw-clVs MS informs us (Antiq. of Cornw. p. 171), that " in the time of Cromwell,' when all monumental things became despicable, one Shrubsall then Governor of Pendcnnis by much ado, caus'd" the Logging Stone call'd Men-amber in the parish of Sithney in that county, " to be undermined and thrown down, to the great grief of the country." (2) This practice is said to have been prevalent in Q. Anne's time: and some think it is, in some places, not yet wholly discontinued.—However rhis be, we know of no lock-up houses in Devonshire.

(3 It has been the opinion of some lawyers, that where a court-leet has been, time immemorial, held at one certain place within its precinct, it ought to be continued there and not elsewhere: And Jacob (in his Court keeper p. 3.) quotes Magna Charta as requiring it to be held in loco certo ac determinato: But that statute (cap. 35) only says, the Sheriff's Tom in the hundred shall be kept, non nisi in loco debito & consueto; and with respect to the leet (which indeed was derived from it), only limits the time when, but not the place where, it is to be annually held. So that the place for the leet seems to he left ad libitum, provided it be within the precinct; and accordingly Sir William Scroggs fays, a court-leet may be lield in any place within the hundred, parish, or manor, for which it is kept. See Scroggs of Courts Leet, p. lg. This (which in 3 serious view is foreign to our subject) is only noted here, to prevent any mistake of the allusion to it above. p. 70 to 72. more dedicated *to* their god, *the heavens,* under the attribute of the *projeSor,* or mover of things projected. Mr. Chappie was of opinion, that the Cromlech was designed for the apparatus more certainly known, as tis presumed it may: And therefore the examination of such circles will most regularly follow that of the *Cromlechs*; and only here require notice as commonly join'd with them in the disquisitions of the authors recited concerning the latter. They have been generally supposed open temples of the *Druids,* and the *Cromlechs* as so many altars for their sacrifices. We have al-

ready taken notice of this, as being the opinion of M. *Mallctt* and Mr. *o Ualloran;* and indeed in this they agree with the generality of the latest writers on the subject, who have evinc'd these. rock-monuments to be undoubtedly *Celtic,* and most of them, if not all, to be contrived by *the Druids j* who, besides their sacerdotal offices and pretend d prophetic character, were not only the arbiters of all controversies in respect either to the religion or the laws of the Celtic nation and colonies, but were also the only professors of philosophy and science amongst them: So, that such stone cirques and entablatures were really productions of their art and ingenuity (for whatever purposes desigr.'d) may be presumed on as indisputable, and now generally taken for granted. For the notions of their being erected by the *Romans* as some have supposed, or as trophies of victories obtained by them, or by the *Saxons or Danes,* as others would persuade us, have been deservedly reprobated, as utterly destitute of the least probability. But tho we must admit them to be undeniably druidical, yet that they were *all* originally intended for religious purposes, is not so unquestionable, however consonant to the united suffrages of the best writers concerning them, not excepting Dr. *Bor/ase;* rho" indeed he on good evidence differs from them all, in denying that the *Cromlechs,* with which they are frequendy connected, could possibly be intended for *altars;* of which, after what has been already said on that subject in the preceding pages, we need not here adduce his proofs. Were it to be granted that all such monuments were (as he thinks) originally of religious institution, or even tho' not so primarily design'd, yet if afterwards thought proper to be connected with any such, and had altars and fit places near them dedicated to the worship of the gods, the supposed subsequent uses of these, as places of council, treaties, elections, and dispensations of law and justice, would all very nanmlly follow. For " next to religion," (as the fame author observes)(i), " government must be supposed to have claim'd the attention, and employ'd the labour and arts of mankind; and in order to give weight to the most solemn acts of the society, where could assemblies be held more properly than in places consecrated to religion, already reverene'd equally by the nobles and the commonality, and therefore likely to influence those who were to make laws and govern, as well as awe those wh» were to follow them and obey?" Places distinguished by the rites of religious worsliip, and sanctified by the supposed presence of tlie Deity, would (as he further observes) be thought " most likely to inspire the rulers with justice and knowledge, and the people with submission," add a sanction to the laws there made, render oaths more obligatory, and double the impiety of any violations of compacts there made, or disturbance of friendships there contracted. — " Besides (adds he) the ancients took care that all civil treaties, laws and elections mould be attended by sacrifices; that place must therefore serve most commodiously for ratifyii g such acts of the community, where they could so easily have all the means of the most sacred attestations, as priests, altars, and victims to confirm them."—Places thus dignified by religious rites there perform'd fas he proceeds to observe,(i) still speaking of the stone circles), would afterwards be naturally chosen as most proper for assemblies on any emergent or extraordinary occasions, and be accordingly used both as places of worship and council; and having altars near them (tho' he admits not their *Cromlech* to be such) would of course become the *curia* and *fora* of the same community. But whether those circles of stones were originally intended for temples or not; or whether for the judges, counsellors, or nobles, to stand or" sit by or upon, according to their dignity and rarik, at their courts, treaties or elections, as the Doctor and many other writers have supposed; is (for the reason before given) not so properly the subject of our examination at present, tho' it has been commonly interwoven therewith, as a recital of the sentiments of those writers concerning the *Cromlechs* that have been erected in or near

them. With respect to these, Dr. *Borlasc-i),* after shewing their unfitness for altars (tho he thinks it not unlikely that the ancients might sacrifice *near them,* whence the great quantities of ashes found near those in *Jersey),* assigns his reason for supposing them *sepulchral monuments.* This lie not only infers from the *tumuli,* to be met with under some of them, but *inter alia* alledges, in support ot this opinion, their resemblance of the Cornilh *Kist-vaem,* which, he says, " certainly inclosed the bones of the dead;" and asks, " what else is a *Cromlih* but a *Kisi-vaen* consisting of larger side stones, cover'd with a still larger and flat one on the top?" Therefore the estimate he had just before given (in p. 114) of the dimensions of such a monument, to render this kind of evidence consistent, should mean those of a common *Kist-vaen;* not of a *Cromlech;* tho'it be there express'd as if spoken of the latter, and the supposed fitness of its size for a human body, but representing the area under its quoit as only about 6 feet and half long by 4 feet wide, which gives no more than 16 square feet, agreeable to the dimensions of the ancient *Sarcophagi;* whereas those those of the *Cromlech* at *Molsra,* and others which he himself describes, as weD as of oors at *Drecœt Teigrtrar,* give near 5 times that area (some perhaps more), and consequently room for as many dead bodies, instead of the single ones inclosed in the common *Kifl-vaens,* Accordingly *Wormius,* whom sir. *Borlaje* quotes in his next page, as mentioning a *Cryfta* and a *Cromlech* together in one barrow, from the many human bones taken out of the first, might well conclude it u to have been the burying place of some illustrious family j" but the Doctor's conclusions from these premises seem to limit even the *Cromlechs,* notwithstanding their superior magnitude, to the more confined contests of the *Kist-vacns,* and as appropriated to the sepulture of single persons only. For having before obferv'd, after inferring from the suppos'd similarity of *Cromlechs* to *Kstwaews,* that the former were for the fame purposes, only constructed on a

larger plan,—that " the supporters, as well as covering-stone, are ho more than the suggestion of the common universal sense of mankind, which was, first, on every side to fence and surround the dead-body from the violences of weather, and from the rage of enemies; and in the next place, by the grandeur of its construction to do honour to the memory of the dead;—he here concludes thus (p. 215): " It is very probable therefore, that the use and intent of the *CromL b* was *primarily* to distinguish, and to do honour to the dead, and also to inclose the dead body, by placing the supporters and covering-stone so as they should surround k on all sides." But then he thinks persons of eminence only were dignified with such a sepulchral monument; such as a Chief Priest or Druid, or some Prince, a favourite of that order; especially when it was erected in the middle of a sacred circus, or on the edge of such a circle, when its middle was already taken op by a single obelisk, which he supposes to have been always regarded as a symbol of something divine, and generally worship'd; and that the *Cromlech* so placed might perhaps respect a particular region of the heavens: And then adds (p. 216), " Princes and great commanders were not only interr'd in a barrow, but had their sepulchres farther dignified by a *Cnml.b* erected for them."

Having thus epitomiz'd the observations and sentiments of Dr. *Borlaje* in respect to the uses of *Cnmlecis,* which he too hastily concludes to have been *originally* designed for sepulchral monuments, 1 w. old only here recommend to the reader a suspension of his judgment thereon, as he may probably hereafter, be fully convine'd, that they could not have been originally intended by *xheDmids* as sepulchres for their Chiefs, or indeed for any-one else; at least that ours could not be so applied, 'till after its primary uses were probably forgotten. But that some of them were in aftertimes applied to such purposes, is sufficiently evident from the human bones found under one in *Ireland,* and from the cairns and barrows, or burrows, under some in *Cgrttxvall* and elsewhere t After which, we may grant that as places of burial they might become " scenes of the *farentalia,* or where divine honours were paid, and sacrifices perform'd to the *manes* of the dead *y* but we must agree with the Doctor in observing, that " these rites must have been transacted at some distance from the *Croml h,* which (as has been evidently proved) could never serve for sacrifices." Toiand's specimen of a proposed History of the Druids, in three letters to Lord Vi'count *Moleftvatbi')* contains many things relative to the remains of ancient Celtic and Druidical monuments, well worth notice, and on which, some of his conjectures seem not improbable: But his chief aim in this epitome of the history he promised to give more at large, of the *Druids,* or of their *priestcraft* as he thinks it might most properly be styled (fee his first letter, p. 8 and 9) being to parallelize it, with, and to vilify the christian priesthood, which he appears to have held in superlative contempt; he with this view labours to warp and distort it into the most frightful form, and to disfigure and disguise it in the most odious and disgustful dress; catching at every conjecture, however groundless, that might afford him the least handle to expose and ridicule, not only the delusive-objects of pagan superstition, but whatever had been at any time deservedly held sacred. Due allowance ought theiefore to be given for his prejudices, whilst we avail ourselves of that intelligence which his acquaintance with *Ireland* and its ancient language (the least corrupted dialect of the old *Celtic J,* and the many reliques of Druidical antiquity there to be met with, enabled him to give us. In this respect, as I can no more approve of his antichristianity than *he* could of that extreme superstition which he complains of (p. 112) in Mr. *Aubrey,* yet acknowledging him an honest man, and most accurate in his accounts of matters of fact; so I may here make the like use of tit, as he him-.

self (1 For the opportunity os inspecting this,—and a Latin tract on the fame subject, poblisti'd »» 1664, and entitled Syntagma de Druidum Moribus ac In-

stituti: Auctorc T, S. (i. e. T. Smith, S T. P.)—is well as for many former favours of the like kind, 1 am indebted to the kindness and friendship of the Hev. William Hole, Archdeacon os Barnstaple, in the Diocese os Exeter; whose judgment and erudition, which no less enable htm to distinguish, than his benevolence prompts him to communicate, such intelligence as the heft authors can afford, for the cultivation of useful literature, give him a higher claim than the private thanks only, of those on whom such favours, aie bestowed;—-and whose obliging condescension to furnish, from his curious collection, whatever tract might conduce to throw additional light on, or tend to the improvement of, even such uninteresting lucubrations as mine, cannot but merit my most grateful acknowledgments.—On perusing this of Dr. Smith, I had the satisfaction to find what has been herem before observ'd, concerning the human sacrifices of the Druids and the objects of their worship, more sully confirm'd; not only from tlie authorities already cited but alio from the additional testimonies of Diodorus SicuJus, Tacitus, Pliny, Solinus, &c. which need not here be enlarged on. Bot the letters of Toland on this subject, affording much information that may be subservient to our present purpose, may occaliosialy require larger extracts from, and remarks on them. Chappie.

Vol. I. *L %* self tells us he did of the numerous instances of Druidical monuments vit!i which *Aubrey* supplied him. " The facts he knew (fays he), not the reflections he made, were what I wanted:" So the facts Mr. *Toland* knew, or has on good authority given us accounts of, relative to the subject in hand, are all I want j without regarding those sneers at priests and their sacerdotal functions, for which he and *T'mdal* were so notorious.(i) Not that I would equal his authority in *other* respects to that of *Aubrey* his informant, whose meaning he might possibly sometimes mistake or misrepresent; and with respect to what he *(Inland)* asserts of his own knowledge, Dr. *Borlaj'e* (in his preface, p. vi.) doubts," whether ever he copied or mea-

sured one monument;" and adds, that " the authorities upon which he asserts many extraordinary particulars, have never yet been produced:" For the Pruidical iiistory at large, wherein he promised to produce those authorities, if ever really intended to be written (as the editor of this and some other tracts of his in 1726 supposes it was), was not so much as begun before his death, which happened in March 1721-2 (as we learn from the fame editor); and this is another reason for quoting him with caution. However, his accounts of the places in Ireland, *Sec.* where Druidical monuments are yet to be seen, and of what kind of construction they respectively are, doubtless deserve all that credit which is due to any man of common prudence; who would be cautious of giving a false account of any such monuments, when he could not but know that every-one on the spot might in such a case easily detect it. In this specimen of his Druidical history, describing the *K:Jiieu-uaen* (for this he fays is, in *British* or *Weljh,* the proper plural of *Kii-vacn,(z)* i.e. a stone chest), of which he tells us many are to be seen yet entire in *Wales,* &c.(3)—he asserts them to be so many Druid Altars j and that tho' denominated stone chests, " they are things quite different from those real stone-chests or coffins (commonly of one block and the lid) that are in many places found under-grotind. "(4) In *Ireland,* which by his account seems to have abounded with these supposed altars, the vulgar Irish call them *Dermot* and *Grama's,* bed, from a story, which he recites, of the elopement of the latter from her husband, with one *Dermot 0 Duwy;* who beipg every where pursued were said to have been secreted in those *Kiflieu--jaen.* One of these, he thinks, was originally in every circle of obelisks or stones erect, tho' now frequently wanting; as he observes, such " altars (for so he calls them) are found where the circular obelisks are mostly or all taken a way for other uses, or out of aversion to this superstition, or that time has consumed them." These stone circles he, with most other writers, takes to be undoubtedly Druidical temples, but disagrees with those " who from the bones which are often found near those altars and circles (tho' seldom within them) will needs infer that they were burying-places;" forgetting " what *Cæsar, Pliny, Tacitus,* and other authors write of the human sacrifices offer'd by the Druids; and, in mistaking the ashes found in the cams," he fays, " they shew themselves ignorant pf those several anniversary fires and sacrifices" for which he had before shewn they were rear'd. But of these and the stone-circles, more hereafter; let us now return to this author's further account of the *Kijli u--iaen.* He describes them as ordinarily consisting " of four stones; three being hard flags, or large tho' thin stones set up edgewise, two making the sides, and a shorter one the end, with a fourth stone of the same kind at the top: for the ether end (adds he) was commonly left open, and the altars were all oblong. Many of them are *not* entire. "(5) But in the next page he fays many of them *are* so, as quoted above; tho' he adds here, that, " besides the alterations that men have caused in all these kinds of monuments, time itself has chang'd 'em much more." But perhaps he here ascribes to time and weather some of those seeming irregularities in their form, which a nicer examination and more accurate measures of their several parts than appear to have been hitherto taken, might possibly demonstrate to be really regular, and consistent with their original design. Not but that some diminution of their then dimensions must, in a long tract of time, result from their age and exposure: To this purpose *To/and(6)* quotes Mr. *Brand,* who, speaking of the obelisks in *Orkney,* fays, " Many of them appear to be much worn, by the washing of the wind and rain;" from whence he infers they are of long standing: But perhaps *he* also mistakes their original form, and might think some parts worn away which were never included with them, nor otherwise existed than in his own imagination: Wherefore, we must not without due allowance for this, admit what *Toland* himself subjoins, viz. that " 'tis naturally impossible, but that in the course of

so many ages, several stones must have lost their figure" (or rather suffer'd a diminution in their magnitude; for their shape or figure might probably be not so much alter'd as he imagines; their proportions at least may be still prcscrv'd, tho' somewhat reduced in their size), " their angles being exposed to all weathers, aivl no care taken to repair any disorder, nor to prevent any abuse of them. "(7) Hence he supposes " some of them are become lower, or jagged, or otherwise irregular and diminiflied;" but I should rather imagine they were originally so, and that their supposed irregularities were, in these, as we shall find them to be in the ltructure we propose more particularly to examine, not the effects of accident, but of art and real regularity in their design " Many (he adds) are quite wasted" by which perhaps he means carried off or demolished j " and moss or scurf hides (1) See Pope's Dunciad, B. ii. 399.

(2) These names, he tells us, with a small variation, ate good Irish '(Mifl. of the Druids, p. 95); ami e-f this, being hi:utelf an Irishman, anil the ancient Irish his vernacular tongue, he must be allow'd to be a cenijiMcnt judge,

P-94. (4) P. 94-(5) *f-93-*(6) Ibid. (7) P. 94.

hides the inscriptions or sculptures of others; for such sculptures (he fays) there are, in several places, particularly in *Wales* and the Scottish Isle of *Aran"* He had before (p. 92) taken notice of characters and inscriptions observ'd on Druidical obelisks in *Scot/and* and *scales,* which, except the Roman and Christian inscriptions, were unintelligible to such as had hitherto seen them; but which as he justly observes, " ought to have been fairly represented for the use of such as might be able perhaps to explain them. They would at least exercise our antiquaries."—But his repeating this here in his account of tile *Kiftieu-vaen,* seems a digression from them to the obelisks; for if 1 rightly understand him, he meant not that any such inscriptions had been observ'd cn the former; concernifig which, perhaps more than enough has been cited from him to our purpose, but to which I was

induced by the supposed similarity os those *KiJlieu-vaens* to the *Cromlechs.* How far they were really similar, or design'd for similar purposes, can only be determin'd (as before-hinted) by more accurate examinations of their dimensions and proportions than appear to have been hitherto taken. Mean while. Dr. *Borlafc* is not alone in his inference from their likeness, that they were intended for, and applied to, the like uses, whatever they were; but in these, authors are no; yet agreed.— For *Toland* seems also to take a *Cromlech* to be only a larger sort of *Kist-vaen,* tho' he describes it,(t) not only as much bigger, but also as " consisting of a greater number of stones" (which I much question the truth of, in general, tho' there are some sew instances of it),(2) " some of them serving to support the others, by reason cf their enormous bulk." These structures, he fays, " tltc *Britons* term Ciomlech in the singular, *Cromlecbu* (rather *Cromlecbiau)* in the plural number; and the *Irijk* Cromleach, or *Cromleac"* (or, as others spell it, *Cromliacb)* with the addition of the letter *a* to make it plural. These *Cromlecbu,* as well as the *Kijiieu-vaen,* he will have to be (not burying-places but) Altars: For, as he takes the word *Cromleacb* to signify the Bowing-stone, he thence concludes they were all places of worship; and in short gives mnch the fame account of *Crumcruacb* " the chiefest in all *Inland"*— which he takes to be an idol, and fays it was overlaid with gold and silver, and that it stood in the midst of a circle of 12 obelisks (which had lesser figures on them, of brass only) on a hill in *Brefin,* a district of the county of *Caman,* formerly belonging to *Letrim;*()—and has recourse to the like conjectures concerning its original designation and supposed derivation from *Cruim,* signifying thunder, as Mr. *0 Halloran* has since adopted; whose sentiments having been already animadverted on, need not be here repeated.——Besides the *Cromlech* at *Poitiers,* mention'd in our note (d), this author tells us(4) of one in the parish of *Nevern* in *Pembroke/hire* "where the middle stone is still 18 feet high, and 9 broad towards the base, growing narrower upwards. There lyes by it a piece broken off 10 feet long, which seems more than 20 oxen can draw; and therefore (adds he) they were not void of all skill in the mechanics that could set up the whole."—He mentions also " a noble *Cromlech* at *Bodouyr* in *Anglesey*;" and adds concerning *Cromlechs* in general, " Manj of them, by a modest computation, are 30 tun weight; but they differ in bigness, as all pillars do" (meaning I suppose the supporters of such *Cromlechs*), « and their altars" (by which he seems here to mean the quoits or covering-stones only) " are ever bigger than the ordinary *Kifticu-naen*. In some places of *Wales* these stones are called *Meineuguyr*, which is of the fame import with *Cromlecbu*. In *Caithness* and other remote parts of *Scotland*, these *Cromleacs* are pretty numerous, some pretty entire; and others, not so much consumed by time or thrown down by llorms, as disorder'd and demolish'd by the hands of men."(5) He goes on to *(hew, that no such altars were ever found by *Olaus Wormius* or others in the temples of the Gothic nations, by which he means all those " who speak the several dialects of Gothic original, from *Iceland* to *Switzerland,* and from the *Briel* in *Holland* to *Prejburg* in *Hungary,* the *Bohemians* and *Polanders* excepted." The *Druids,* he fays, were only co-extended with the *Celtic* dialects; and then quotes *Ceesar* as faying expressly " there were no Druids among the *Germans,* " they only worshipping the sun, moon, and *fulcan* or fire, which they constantly saw, and by which they were manifestly benefited; rejecting all other deities, and sacrificing to none: Which of course, says our author, " made altars as useless there (tho' afterwards grown fashionable) as he thinks they were necessary in the Druids temples," meaning the stone circles; and that those altars (meaning the *Cromlechs, tec.* and taking for granted that they were design'd as such) shew them " more than probably to have been temples indeed;"(6) and so, he tells us, the Highlanders and their Irish Progenitors have always call'd and taken them to be.—But if by *altars* he

here means *Cromlechs,* as indeed he does, and supposes them every-where druidical; and if his assertion, that no such were ever found within the limits he prescribes, be found false in fact; this renders all this reasoning inconclusive, and militates against all his favourite notions relative to these supposed altars and temples. And that they (1) P. 96. (s) That Cromlechs have most commonly no more than three supporters, has been before observ'd; but some have sour, and this author (p. 97) quotes Chevrcau Mcniotres d'Angletcrre, p. 380, as mentioning one remaining at Poitiers ip France, supported by five lesser stones, and which (he thinks) exceeds all in the Biitisll iflands, its covering flone being 60 feet in circumference: La pierre levee dc Poitiers a soixante pieds de tour, & clle est posee sur cinq autres picnes. —But our author fancies this was a rocking-slone, tho' what induced him to that conjecture he doth not fay. Possibly there may be Cromlechs in Briiain as large as that at Poitiers, tho' u-.iknown to him. Ours at Drews Tcignton indeed wants somewhat more than one third of the same circumference, supposing the above measure of it meant in French feet: for 60 Paris feet arc nearly equal to 64 feet English. (3) P. too. («) P. 97. (i)P. 98. (6) P. 99. apparatus of an astronomical observatory, *(a)* So numerous were the scientific properties which he ascribed to the Drewsteignton Cromlech, that he could have written (m they are really thus founded on a mistaken negation of a known fact, may be collected1 from the testimony of M. *Mallet* and others, who, as before quoted in page 64, assure us such monuments are now to be found in Germany, as well as in other countries and places there mention'd: And then, if *Casar's* evidence be also admitted, that there were no Druids among the *Get mans,* and that the *Germans* offer's no sacrifices, and consequently had no altars till the *Romans* introduced theirs; it follows, that those more ancient monuments there, whether *Cromlechs* or *Kist-vaens,* could not have been intended for altars, but for some other, and possibly very different, purposes: Nor could they be the works

of rhe *Druids,* but of a people within that Gothic pale which this author has here mark'd out. And hence it also follows, that those *Celtic* monuments, as we have already observ'd from *Borlafe* in the above-mention'd page 64, were not peculiar to the *Druids*; tho' ours in the *British* iflands, which only were meant in what we said of them p. 112, must be admitted to be, as there observ'd, undeniably druidical . But some monuments of this kind having been erected by the ancient *Germans,* who differ'd so essentially from the *Druids* in their religious customs, as to reject all altars and sacrifices, we might hence also conclude, had we no other proofs, that those monuments were not originally des gri'd-for religious purposes. We have now only to add to these extracts from, and remarks cn the sentiments of *Toland,* that he, *inter alia,* (1)takes notice of the many altars (as he calls tliem) and *Cromlechs* in *Jerjey,* as well as in the other neighbouring islands, formerly part of the Duchy of *Normandy,* where we have already observed they are call'd *Pouqueleys;* and quotes p. 115 of Dr. *Fal/e's* account of *Jersey,* who there fays, *u* They are great flat stones of vast bigness and weight; some oval, some quadrangular, raised 3 or 4 foot from the ground, and supported by others of a less size;" and thinks them evidently altars, " both from their figure, and great quantities of ashes found in the ground thereabouts." He moreover insets, from their standing on eminences near the sea, that they might be " dedicated to the divinities of the ocean." This *To/and* disputes, and thinks " the culture of the inland parts is the reason why few of them are left, besides those on the barren rocks and hills on the sea-side:" But perhaps better reasons might be given for this their situation, than either he or the Doctor were aware of.—Dr. *Falle* adds, " At ten or twelve feet distance there is a smaller stone set up an end, in manner of a desk; where 'tis supposed the priest kneel'd, and perform'd some ceremonies, while the sacrifice was burning on the altar:" But the erection of such a stone, and at such a distance from the *Cromlech,* might be accounted for, without supposing them defign'd for sacerdotal devotions." Chappie's. Description, p. 109 to 137. *a)* " This Cromlech of Drews Teicnton was first recommended to my notice by a worthy and judicious lady, who to her other amiable accomplishments has added a general knowledge of the antiquities of her country; and tho' that modesty which always accompanies real merit, and is of itself a silent testimony of it, with-holds the additional honour this page might receive from her name, yet gratitude no less forbids me here to pass over, unacknowledg'd, the helps to facilitate another undertaking, which I owe to the beneficence of the fame patroness, by her procurement of of divers valuable manuscript copies of' *Rijdon's* and *ffejlcot's* surveys, mostly transcribed by Mr. *Pr'.nce* (author of *the Worthies* of Devon) with his own hand, and all under his direction; and were lately in the possession of the Rev. Mr. *Anthony Trifc*— Ignorant of any monument of the *Cromlech-kind* in *Devonshire,* till thus pointed out to me by my fair informant as well deserving the attention of the curious, it might otherwise have escaped that examination, whereof I am now to give the result: But I afterwards observ'd it to be noticed as such in Mr. Dora's map of this county; whose engraver however, has there given it the form of a Greek n, as if it had been a Druidical gallows for the execution of criminals.(2)—Being thus excited to a view of this *Cromlech,* and desirous of ascertaining its real form, some business in that neighbourhood soon after gave me an opportunity of seeing, and taking a rougli sketch of it; but being then straiten'd in time, and having no other instrument with me but a pocket rule, I contented myself with only taking the length and breadth of its covering stone, and such other dimensions as might limit the angles, and enable me to plan the ground it cover'd, and the position of its three supporters; in which all I then observ'd remarkable (besides the inequality of their heights, by which the covering-stone has such an inclination as we have elsewhere taken notice of) was, as mention'd in the preface to this tract, that their (1) Ibid (t) This is not meant as a reflection on my friend Mr. Donn himself; who, supposing it were indeed so mark'd by him in the engraver's copy, might in the course of his survey only have a sight of it from some distant point of view; where the middle fulcrum happening to be in a line with one os the others, was hidden by it, and so only two such mark'd in his field-book. But more probably this was one among many errors of the engraver, left uncorrected in the proof sheets of the plates j which Mr. Donn, to my knowledge, sent to his friends in divers parts of the county, desiring their examination of them, and correction of any mistakes they might observe in them: but this being overlook'd, among other minutia?, by such examiners of the plate it was in, (and which I also saw, but had not then seen the Cromlech,) 'tis Sio wonder, considering also the short time to which he is said to have been limited for *its* publication, that so minute a figure in ti-ie crowd of others escaped his correction. Chappie. their three edges were, at the surface of the ground, ui a right line with each other; from whence I then indeed concluded there might be somewhat more of geometrical exactness in its construction than was generally imagined; but had no idea of what now appears to have been the occasion of its erection, nor any the least doubt hut that *this,* and all other such Druidical monuments were some way or other subservient to religious purposes; and perhaps some of them moreover delign'd for the sepulture of the dead, which among the Druids as v. ell as other wor/ hippers of the Pagan deities, was always accompanied with some religious rites, sometimes with sacrifices, and other ceremonies, more or less solemn, as custom and the honour and dignity of the deceased demanded. For the burial of the dead, was, by all nations, anciently esteemed one os the principal duties of religion; which, according to the accounts transmitted to us by all historians, was denied neither to friends nor enerraes.(i) It has been before observed", that the covering or table-stone of this, is, like those of moit other *Cmmlccbs,* not truly horizontal, but, from the inequality of the heights of its supporters, appears as it were bent or bowed down at one end: but towards what point of the compass 1 had not observ'd when I took the rough plan abovemention'd, having then neither sun-shine net compass by which to ascertain its bearings or position with respect to the cardinal points or otherwise. Afterwards, considering with what views this its deviation from the horizontal level might possibly be design'd, if it were not wholly accidental; and recollecting that *C/cjar* and other ancient writers had assured us that the Druids in *Britain* and *Gaul,* among other pagan deities, next to *Mercury* who was by them thought to claim their highest honours, had a particular veneration for *Apollo* or the Sun; I imagin'd, that if the part so depress'd were meant to betoken any such veneration for, or respect to, that luminary, it would probably be directed towards that part of the horizon where he rises: And to be satisfied whether this were the cafe here, I determin'd on a more accurate survey of the premises with proper instruments, by which being also enabled to take more truly the several angles, as also those which the sides would respectively make either with a magnetical or a true meridian line, its exact position in respect thereto would thence be truly afeertain'd. Accordingly on the 20th of *August,* 1777, I went a second time to view and more strictly examine it, taking with me a plain-table for its more exact admeasurement; this, vith its needle and other usual apparatus, being the most proper instrument for such a purpose. But previous to this survey, I had to get removed a large quantity of dry ferns with which I found the whole area fill'd up, and closely stuff'd in, as high as the covering or table-stone would permit, with an intent to be burnt there by the then *Sbilstin* tenant, and their ashes to be used as manure: And altho' when freed from these, there still remain'd in the midst of the area a pretty large heap of ashes, the produce of some such former sacrifice to *Ceres,* which in some respects obstructed my proposed measures,—preventing my *then* taking as intended (but which has been also since done) the necessary dimensions for connecting the upper part of each *fulcrum* with a plan of the under surface of the table-stone, so as to ascertain their respective deviations from perpendicularity, and mark their bearing places;—and moreoverconceal'd from my then notice some remarkable stones fix'd into the ground,—yet the position of this ash-heap hinder'd not my taking the very true and exact ichnography not only of the table-stone itself, but also of the bases of its supporters, and what else was requisite to determine the area or ground-plot cover'd or overshadow'd by it, and at what heights respectively. And this I chose to do at a scale so large as would distinctly (hew any distance measured, within less than a quarter of an inch at most. This being done, and a true meridian deduced from the magnetic, by allowing the fame variation of the needle here at *Sbilston* as at Exxtir, where it was *at that time* nearly 230. 35' west,(2) this was presum'd sufficiently near the truth; it being not likely to have any sensible alteration in a distance of about ten miles, only: Nor does any error of this sort appear on re-examination; for tho' it then happen'd to be a cloudy (1) Vide Danet in Funo, and the authors he cites, (2) The variation (or as sometimes railed the declination) or deviation of the magnetic needle from the true north point, i. now well known to be itself continually varying, hoth with respect to time and place; being different in different place, at the same time, and at different tiuics in the fame place: And tho' it was formerly easterly, the needle has long since passed the noith, and in this part of the world now declines many degrees to the well of that point. At Exeter, on the 13th of March 17 17-18, (O. S.) a judicious observer found it to be 130. 20'. westerly: On the 20th of May 1762,1 found it by observation increased to 21 degrees: Iu Nov. 1772 (as noted occasionally at that time in another work) it was further increased to 22". and 3 quarters: On the 20th of August 1777 as above, it was

estimated at 230. 35'; and 18 months after (viz. in Feb. 1779), when it was become nearly 230. 50'. was found by an azimuth at Shilston to be the fame there, or very nearly so: And now, Aug. 17 th 1779, I find by another observation of it at Exeter, carefully taken, by the help of an exact meridian line and a well-touch'd nine-inch needle, placed at a due distance from any iron liable to disturb it, that it wants but a very little of 24 degrees; viz. such a trifle as was but barely discernible with so short a needle, and could not appear less by above one 12th of a degree at most, had it been more nicely meafur'd on a larger arch; but *I* had no opportunity of adjusting it by one of a longer radius. So I estimate the present variation here at Exeter to be 230. 55', agreeable to the uniform increase resulting from former observations here, where it seems to be continually increasing (perhaps more regularly than is generally supposed) at the rate of 10 minutes and about ao seconds annually, or 1 degree and a minutes in 6 years: And should it continue to increase thus regularly, the needle at and near Exeter, may be expected to f)oint directly west about the year of Christ 2164, and to make a whole revolution in and about 2090 years. I am sensible how. much this disagrees from the accounts we hav e of the needle's variations as observ'd at London; not only in respect to its cloudy day, and consequently no azimuth of the sun could be then and there taken to adjust It, it lias been since confirmed by one taken on the spot, which, allowing for the increase of variation in the mean time, shew'd it had been *tbin,* when the plan was taken,.. ithin a minute or two of the above-mention'd variation; or differing so little from it as to make no discernible difference in the geometrical projection at the scale above-mention'd. A meridian line being thus carefully adjusted to my field-map, this immediately evinc'd the futility of my conjecture besore-mention'd; for instead of any bending down on the table-stone towards the rising fun, its lowest part appear'd to be *south loefterly,* and so rather respecting the *setting* sun, and

this at the winter solstice, when his light and heat is generally the least perceptible (tho' the *Druid:* perhaps might deem this a fit season for gathering their idolized *Misletoe,* when, according to *Bradley,* its berries or feeds become ripe for propagation." Chappie's Description, p. 151 to 160.

" From all my observations, it is evident that the Drcwsteignton Cromlech could not be primarily intended either as a religious structure, or a sepulchral monument, but was partly designed for scia therical purposes, and in general as the apparatus of an Astronomical Observatory And of this, 'tis presumed, we (hall be enabled to produce such proofs, as will be abundantly satisfactory, not only to proficients, but to any who have but the slightest acquaintance with the first rudiments of geometry and astronomy. —But however plain this may be on a candid examination, I am aware how liable the most conclusive arguments are, to be oppugned by the sophistry of wrangling disputants; and how obnoxious the most unexceptionable, to the censure of some sceptical cavillers, who, inclined to doubt of every-thing, resolve to approve of nothing: whom even mathematical evidence will hardly convince; and who professing that Pyrrhonic Philosophy which may be acquired without learning or parts, and with little or no study, affect a Socratical negation of knowledge; complaining of the prevalence of error, the disguises of truth, the imperfection of arts, and the vanity and incertitude of the sciences; and yet perhaps-despising the only one that pretends and may justly lay claim to absolute certainty, lest it should happen to convict them of the absurdity of having substituted ignorance and scepticism for the perfection of wisdom, and oblige them unwillingly to acknowledge, that others enlightened by its lamp may fee farther and more clearly than themselves. Such as these, at first view of a geometrical plan so seemingly complex as one or more of those we are here to exhibit, may enter their caveat in the court of criticism against a too hasty determination in this matter: Their business being ever to demur, never to decide, we must not be surprized at any weak endeavours to support their plea for a suspension of judgment, by starting imaginary difficulties, and by the impertinence of cross questions and nugatory objections: Representing all attempts to reduce this rude monument of antiquity to regular form and geometrical exactness, as the mere effects of fancy; and alledging, that any other irregular production of bungling artifice, or even the spontaneous disposition of natural rocks, which, freed from their interstitial and surrounding earth, had been left there in the form of such a *Brcbdingnag* tripod as this, might by the like adjustment of lines, angles, and circles to it, be exhibited as a specimen of antient ingenuity and skilful contrivance; tho' it were in reality, either the mere fortuitous effect of chance, or the clumsy workmanship of some bungling fabricator—Others, who may readily grant this piece of stone-work to be artfully constructed, and well adapted to its intended uses, whatever they were, may however, at first view of our plan, be apt to suspect, that all this geometrical parade is wrested and forced into regularity, to support a favourite notion or preconceiv'd hypothesis t since we want not instances of ingenious triflers and fanciful projectors, who, by the aid of a pregnant imagination and ready invention, will undertake to make anything out of anything; like the ale-house cook, who being requited to dress the boots of an itinerant quack, hy order of his zany, and having, by fiiclng and mincing them *secundum artem,* with proper additions for seasoning and sauce, transform'd them to a *French fricassee,* scrv'd them up as a delicate dish for his Doctorship's supper. Nay, some venture yet farther, and assuming to themselves a creative power, boldly undertake to rival Omnipotence, by a practical refutation of the old maxim, *Ex nihilo nihil ft;* pretending, in virtue of a magic process peculiar to themselves, to deduce anything from nothing. There is, it must be confess'd, a kind of antiquarian knight-errantry, which amuses itself with its own dreams. These, strongly impressing a

prejudiced mind, the dreamer at length persuades himself mult be somewhat more than the sports of fancv; indulges the infatuation; catches at every shadow of an argument to confirm himself in it; considering the phantom he has rais'd, in every point of view; and then introduces others to support it, and convince himself of its reality. Thus fascinated with the charms of imaginary objects, no wonder if he mistakes, like Don *Siuixotte,* a windmill for a giant a baiber's bason far it, annual progress to the westward, but also a to the regularity of gradual increase. This is evident from comparing the successive observations of(Messrs. Burrows, Gunter, Gellibrand, Bond, Dr. Halley, Mr Graham, Dr. Bevis and others. They seem to have thought the variation to have incrcaVd or decreas'd more Uowly; and so contented themselves with regisl'ring the years of their observations, without mentioning at what time in each J whereas in order to determine accurately the law of such increase or decrease, and whether accelerated or retarded, the month at least, if not the day os observation, ought also to-be known, and should be duly register'd for the information of suture observers. However, enough appears from their dates to evince, that the variation at London has not varied uniformly; nor (if the accounts we have of it may he relied on) doth it seem to have always differ'd from that at Exeter by any certain, or constant quantity; tho that difference has generally been from a. 48 Ot 50'. to a9. 55'. Chappie.
for the morion or defensive skull-cap of a *Roman* foot-soldier; an *Irijh* baWrt, for the *quondam* assembly-room of Druidical bards; or a ponderous old rat-trap, for the model of an ancient *Catafulta.* Positive in his adopted opinions, and confident in his owivconjectures, a visionary of this fort starts not at common difficulties. Self-sufficiency supplies what ignorance denies; and a fanciful presumption, or happy guess, compensates for deficiency of evidence. Is persons thus qualified, the fragments of unintelligible inscriptions, obliterated manuscripts, Corroded coins, mutilattd

statues, broken columns, &c. &c. are easily explicable, and.as readily expiain'd. Hence new ani strange discoveries are sometimes suggested, or absurd hypotheses form'd, and no less stiffly maintain'd than prematurely adopted; however repugnant to the common fense and receiv'd notions of more sagacious inquisitors, relative to the laws, arts, policy, religion or learning of the ancients: And hence we are now-and-then amused with new models of their architecture; new codes of their laws; new rituals of their superstitions; new keys to their mythology, or new standards for regulating their history, and for stretching or curtailing their chronology. But in these,'as well as in matters of less importance, in which these fantastic scliemists are sometimes no less assiduous, when fancy and conjecture supply the want of authentic evidence, no wonder if their imperfect conceptions prove abortive, and their illogical conclusions from such disputable premises, frequently become subjects of ridicule and contempt.(i) Some of those dreaming *virtuosi,* for instance, have pretended to fix the exact chronology of a supposed antique shield, among other of its properties, by the colour of its rust 1(2) Others have busied themselves in bottling up air, for occasional supplies of it in ætherial voyages, to have an insight into *lunar* antiquities, and a prospect of undiscover'd countries here; extending their boundless curiosity far beyond the clouds, and those gross vapors which here inflate the lungs of sublunary mortals; impatient of confinement to their own, tho' most forcibly attractive, sphere; and no longer acquiescing in that humbler (but to mechanicks more interesting) enquiry, whether the artificial sphere of *Archimedes* were wholly composed of brass, as *Laliantiut* fupposes(3); or whether, as suggested in an epigram of *Claudian(),* its outside or casing at least, were not rather of transparent glass, like that of a modern globe-lanthorn.(5)— Suchare the reveries, not only of some assuming fmatterers in antiquity and pretended restorers of ancient arts, but sometimes even of more learned triflers on such subjects:

And as such, some may be disposed to ridicule the production of a (hort-fighted novice in such researches as the present subject demands, and which would more properly exercise the speculations, and require the more penetrating inspection of persons eminent for their erudition, long conversant in the works of the ancients, and well acquainted with the learning, the manners, and customs of different ages and nations. The attempt of any other, to account for the fabrication of such a relique of the remotest antiquity as we are now examining; and especially to discover an internal mark by which to judge of its age, v ith no less certainty than a huntsman can that of a hart by his antlers and croches; may possibly be deem'd a presumptuous encroachment on their prerogative, and not easily escape the like scouring with Dr. *Woodivard'i* rubiginous shield. But the cock in the fable, having chanced to find'a jewel where he only sought a barley-corn, left greater connoisieurs to judge of its worth, and avail themselves of£ his discovery. And in like manner the present and, 'tis prefum'd, first discoverer (for such he takes himself to be) of the real design and geometrical construction of the Cromlech in question, chearfully submits *bis* to their better judgment, and to their candid correction of his oversights and mistakes, (1) The reader who adverts to what has been inserted from Dr. Borl.isc, will not misunderstand anything here said, as meant to censure or ridicule the laudable researches, or acute sagacity of real antiquaries, cr their having recourse to probable conjectures where certainty cannot be obtain'd; since such conjectures frequently lead to more certain truths: But granting they may be sometimes too far indulg'd, or even conduce to multiply errors; yet such abuses of any branch of science, furnish no good argument against its generat utility; nor is any thing like this, here intended. I have been speaking the language of an objector, and endcavour'd to state in its full force every foreseen objection to the account I am now to give of the Drew's Teignton Cromlech sagainst which ac-

count, even whilst in embryo, some such have been already, however prematurely, started; and before 1 proceed to exculpate myself from any charge of prejudice, or bigotry to the dictates of fancy or Action, have here fairly admitted whatever may be plausibly pleaded, fiom the failings of others in attempts of this kind, against any hasty conclusions concerning it; which in short, only amount to this: viz. That if not only pretended connoisieurs in such matters have had strange dreams, but real ones have sometimes nodded, and both perhaps merited reproof by the publication of visionary schemes; much more may one, who has no pretensions to the abilities or judgment of the latter, nor to the prolific imagination of the former, be liable to, and ought therefore to be eautious of incurring the like censure.—. This must be readily granted. Rut the lowest pedljr in antiquity may chance to strike out lights, conducive to detest the mistakes, or to improve the discernment of the most learned: And we should blame the timidity of that pusillanimous farmer, who could be deterr'd from the cultivation and tillage of his own little spot, by observing the luxuriant crops' in richer and more fertile lands, to be here and there intermix'd with no less luxuriant weeds; or that the barretter foil of others was more productive of poppies than corn. The directions of reason and prudence in such cases would be, 1 Let not sloth or distrust prevent the proper culture of any; and let the weeders have, their due share of employment in all: but let them be cautious not to root up any part of the wheat, together with the tares and wild poppies.' Chappie (2) See Pope's Memoirs of SciiMerus. (3) Instit. 1. 2, c. 5. (4) Jupiter in parvo quum cerneret æthera vitro, Rifit (5) See Huygeas'a Cosraotheoros; Wilkins's World in the Moon; and his Mathematical Maglck, p. 164, 165.

Vol. I. M (as he often said) in describing them.(«) The first thing he mentioned was a most exact meridian line, made by the coincidence of the three supporters—that is, the outside edges of two, and the inside edge of the third, are lo truly fixed on the meridian

as could possibly be done by the most accurate astronomer. The next was the latitude of the place, which was shewn by some part of the Cromlech, even to the *nearest minute*; as were the fun's greatest meridian altitude in summer, the least in winter, and consequently the obliquity or the ecliptic—which last article afforded a most curious circumstance; for, by allowing the known diminution of the obliquity, he found that upwards of two thousand two hundred years had elapsed since the Cromlech was erected. After describing these, and many other astronomical properties, he said he had lastly discovered, that the cover-stone was inseribable in an ellipsis. And that the Cromlech served also for gnomonical purposes, he had the most positive proof. For by its construction, he found that there was a certain point under the Cromlech, whence reflections mould be cast; and, by removing the earth from that spot, he discovered a curious little triangular stone, which must have been placed there for that purpose. All this is wonderful indeed! But though I have the highest opinion of Mr. Chappie's diligence and integrity, yet I am apt to believe that his curious hypothesis, which might first be suggested by some fortuitous position of the stones, will not Dear the test of cool and impartial examination. Were there any regular planes cut on the surface of these stones, we might suppose them designed to point out different phenomena of the sun and planets: but, as there is no mark of a tool on any of them (which, indeed, would profane them in the opinion of a Druid) I would as soon believe that the earth was formed by a concourse of atoms, as that four rude and shapeless stones, to all appearance selected only for their magnitude, should exhibit an ex?ct correspondence with every circle in the heavens.(A)

After takes, if any; tho' he roust expect the most strict and critical examination from those, who, disinclined to approve of whatever tends to depreciate the merit of their own discoveries, may be Hnwilling to recall that temporary coin which originated from their mint;

and which having had the stampof public credit and approbation, has hitherto pafs'd current, but whose deficiency may be detected by the touchstone here offered for its trial.—For, among persons of found learning and acknowledged judgment, some who have been generally successful in their endeavours to brighten up the oLfcunty, and rub off the rust of antiquity, have yet condescended to form strange hypotheses, to account for the most difficult subjects that have puzzled preceding antiquaries; and fortifying them with all the plausibility of argument and elegance of language, with which such *literati* can attract the attention of the most discerning, and conceal all defects and absurdities from the superficial inspector (who charm'd with the gilding, examines not the weight or solidity of the apparently sterling gold) scruple not to obtrude their visionary systems on the publick, as infallible regulators of historical truth. And as such perhaps, they may be for some time accepted; and continue in vogue, 'till some other inventive and penetrating genius treads the like fairy maze, subverts the enchanted castle of his predecessor, and erects another of his own, in a different taste perhaps, but on a no less unstable foundation. And this *deceptio vijus* at length vanishes in its turn, vh;n possibly some transient spectator, or cursory reviewer of the premises, may happen accidentally to stumble on a demonstrate proof of tje fallacy of all their plausible schemes; throw a new and unexpected light on the subject; and free it froin those mists by which it had long been obscured, and which men of more extensive discernment had in vain attempted to dispel. Partiality in favour of a beloved hypothesis must indeed be expected, as unavoidable in him or them who first promnlgtd or adopted it, and who cannot be inclinable too hastily to abandon their own offspring, or fuel? as they have taken into their paternal care and protection." Chappie's Description, p. 13S to 150.

(«) At which no person will Wonder, who has seen the innumerable circles, lines, curves, *&t.* on the plates designed for his Book. (i) With respect to the Lanyon Cromlech, Mr. Chappie expresses a wish " that it were reviewed and re-examined by some judicious person, such as the Rev. Mr. *Hitcbins* of*Maraxhn* (a gentleman every way qualified for such an undertaking, and who, if I mistake not, resides within a very few miles of *MaJsrtie,* in which parish this and another *Cumltcb* are situated); and that he would take the trouble of making an accurate plan of it, at a 1-irger scale than that in Dr. *Berlaje-s* bonk; measuring also the exact height, not only of each supporter, but also of every part of the perimeter of the covering or table-stone; and taking such other dimensions, and making such requisite observations thereon, as may be suggested to him in the subsequent parts of this tract. Such a plan, and the observations of such a judge in geometrical and astronomical productions, with the inferences naturally deducible from thence, would doubtless be acceptable to the curious; and we might thereby be enabled to ascertain in what particulars its construction differs from ours, as in divers respects it certainly does; tho' similar in others, and both, very probably, design'd for the like purposes." — Chappie's

After all Mr. Chappie's curious disquisitions, I cannot but concur with Dr.. Borlase *m* thinking, that the Cromlech was originally designed for a *sepulchral monument.* Its general

Chappie's Description, p. 38, 39. This Mr. Hitchins has done: And he hath been so obliging as to favour me with his sentiments on the siibject(i): " Mr. Chappie (fays Mr. Hitchins) thought he had made a wonderful discovery of various astronomical and gnomonical properties in the Cromlech at Drewsteignton, and he was about to publish a description of it with plates, &c. I know not whether you design to say much on that subject in your History or not; but if you think it an object worthy of your attention, as Mr. Chappie in his intended publication called on me to inform the public, whether Lanyon Cromlech, near I'enzance, had the fame properties, I mall give you my senti-

ments on that subject. 1 have attentively examined the Cromlech at Lanyon, the most considerable one in Cornwall, but cannot discover the least astronomical or gnomonical use to which it can be applied, not excepting even the simple contrivance *at* a meridian line, the first property Mr. Chappie observed in his Cromlech." The correspondent, from whose letter I have already made extracts relating to Chappie's Description, has an eye to the use of the Cromlech in the following remarks: " Moses, in his history, which 1 take to be most faithful (since, exclusive of divine assistance, he drew his information from the Royal College of Ægyptian Priests, being educated as the royal offspring were) speiking of the descendants of Noah, mentions Nimrod, as being the first that began to be great—that is, founded a great kingdom, and who delighted in war and in hunting: He fays that this was before the Assyrian monarchy, which came out of it, and that the place, *at first,* of this monarchy, was *Babel:* and it was probably under his authority that the worship ot Baal, or of fire, was instituted; which, in fact, was an act of idolatry like that of the Roman emperor's since; for it was a deification of himself—he being the son of Chus, who was the son of Ham or Cham, which signifying heat or sure, the natural emblem of this was the fun— at once the type of his power and of his descent: no wonder therefore that they instituted this worship. '1 lie power of Babel had for its object the fame worship, and fuitjier, the counteracting of the designs of providence, that they might flee to it in cafe of a second deluge, and that they might never be dispersed, or lose their home or language. They were, however, dispersed and defeated in their purpose: And it is to this remarkable event that the passage probably alludes, which fays, that *Cod spared not tie angels of God,* that is, the holy race of Noah, which could not but be reverenced by their descendants as angels or gods, on account of their supposed divine origin, but *cast them tut.* 'she words are, *ctK'Koo ixTotfTotoucrst* eacraf—a very remarkable expression, which occurs but that once, and is generally understood to mean *dispersed them j* which words, added to the history of this empire, makes it probable that *Nimrod* founded his kingdom in *Tanery;* which, the learned admit, is derived from *Tatar,* which signifies *dispersion.* From hence this monarch and descendants made the molt extensive conquests, the memory of which is retained in the ancient, and supposed to be fabulous accounts of the conquests of *Bacchus,* which indeed was a proper deity to name and to ascribe it to, since *Nimrod* was the descendant of *Cbus,* and from hence his kingdom was called the kingdom of the *Scythian Tartan* ; for the *Scutbi* and the *Cutbi* are the fame race. The original dispersion, tiie confusion of languages, and probably the cruelty of his conquests, scattered men much further than this. Some probably fled to *America,* which, it is now well known, was peopled from *Tartary:* and it is remarkable, that on the arrival of the Spaniards, the worship of *Baal,* or of the *Sun,* was the great national religion of the people *oiCbujcoor Cufcoi* The Runic or Scandinavian annals also agree in declaring, that they were driven from the *east* by some great calamity: and the same people were probably spread, by degrees, to the more western parts of Europe Wherever they went, they continued their original love of war and hunting, and the worship of Baal, or of the son, pr of fire, and of the *best oj biaveir,* which, it is proboble, they made also their more particular study. Wherever they went to, they erected fire towers in honour of Baal, and those other most stupendous structures, partly that they might for ever preserve their name and nation, partly that they might baffle the effects of time, and perhaps, as they hoped, even the divine vengeance; and partly that the solidity of these structures, and the almost inaccessible heights and fastnesses where they were erected, might preserve them from the fury of their enemies, and always afford them a retreat where they might exercise their rites in security. Of this species of structure, I am of opinion, is this *Cromlech* at *Dretvsteigntox;* I mean that it is of *Cuthite,* or as it was called

by the Romans, *Druidisal* origin, which has been the name adopted ever since for them." I have thus, at the request of several of my subscribers, permitted Mr. Chappie to accompany me in the notes, tedious and desultory as he is. To proceed, however, any further with Mr. Chappie, is impossible. He is now entering, after all the dulnefs of his *generalities,* into a *particular* examination of his astronomical instrument. In this examination he refers continually to his plates. Several of these plates, however, are Iost.(2) Yet even by their assistance, it would be extremely difficult to unravel Mr. Chappie's meaning.

(1) In a letter dated.St. Hilary, 3d August 1790. (a) Mr. Chappie's daughter, Mrs. Buikley, of Surcrofs, his one or two of the plates. Toe other;, she fays, were ruitUtd: nor does she think it possible to recover them.

Voi,. I. M 2 general figure and the size of its area, seem to suggest this idea. Not that the covering, stone or the supporters were intended to secure the dead from violence. They are but ill-calculated meaning. His two learned friends, Mr. Hitchins and Mr. Hugo, have both repeatedly assured me, that they could never follow Mr. Chappie through the maze of his astronomical discoveries, ever, with the united aid of the written description, of the plates to which it referred, and of his own oral explanation. " The plates (Mr. Hitchins fays) were so extremely complex, that if they were now before us, to retrace Mr. Chappie's ideas, v/ould be impracticable." In all his writings, in short, Mr. Chappie is involved: and often, in the moments of perplexity, have I thus addressed his shade: *By thee,* we dim the eyes and stuff the head,

With all such reading as was never read: *By thee,* explain a thing till all men doubt it, k And write about it, *Chappie!* and about it:

So spins the Silk-worm small its slender store,

And labours till it clouds itself all o'er.(i) That Mr. Chappie's admirers, however, may not complain of my having suppress any part of his Cromlech MSS. I shall here present them with the

Preface Which he meant to prefix to the. curious treatise in question: " This tract owes its present publication more to accident than to any premeditated design: For, although some notice of the Driwsteignton Cromlech was intended in another work, and to that end I had, some years since, taken a transient view of it, and such of its dimensions as might the better enable me to give some general description of it, as the only *Druidical* monument of its kind in this county; my then intention was, to refer to Dr. *Borlase* and others for further particulars concerning such structures. Indeed I then observed, that three edges of its supporters were nearly in the fame right line; and therefore suspected there might be somewhat more of geometrical nicety in its construction than its rough and irregular appearance would induce an incurious observer to imagine; but had not the least idea of its being accommodated to the purposes mentioned in the following sheets, or to any other of a similar kind; taking for granted this apparently rude monument of remote antiquity was some structure subseivient to the Druidical worship of our British ancestors, and sacred to some or other of the pagan deities. What induced me afterwards (viz. in *August* 1777) to take a more exact plan of it, and ascertain its situation in respect to the points of the compass, will be noted'in its place, and need not be enlarged on, here: At which time, having with proper instruments, carefully observed and adjusted its dimensions, bearings, angles, and, in short, every-thing requisite to delineate the true ichnography of it, as also the exact heights of its supporters, &c. some avocations to other affairs, and an afflicting family event which happened soon/after, obliged me to desist, for the present, from any minute examination of its properties: So that my field-map, and other papers relative to it, were laid by, uninspected, for a whole year; till an occasional revisal of those papers, and a few days accidental interruption of my other work before-mentionedi and which I had for some time resumed, induced me to review and examine the whole. This led me gradually to the discovery of some properties in it, which left no room to doubt of the original use and design of this antiquated fabrick; and tho' the seeming irregularity of some of its parts, and the position and proportion of others, in some measure tended to entangle and perplex the subject, yet having once got the clue, this, with the unexpected help of a master-key which I chanced to meet with by the way (I mean the *Vitru-vian Analcmma),* facilitated the search; all difficulties vanish'd, and I was soon enabled to unravel the whole. For every step I took, open'd unexpected views, all tending to confirm and demonstrate the rectitude of the former; and every calculation, when compared with the actual measures of the *Cromlech* itself, bore witness to the accuracy of its plan, and the boldness and elegancy of its construction. My first discoveries of this sort, whilst yet unassisted by this key, being communicated to some respectable friends, they advised me to pursue my enquiries concerning it; as being, in their judgment, from what had hitherto appeared on the subject, a new and not unimportant discovery: And tho' it might for some little time interrupt my progress in the work I had before undertaken, yet instead of reserving it for a proper place in *that,* persuaded me not to delay publishing the result of my disquisitions concerning it, as a separate tract, (1) The following letter from the late Lord Courtenay to Mr. Chappie, plainly intimates his Lordship's apprehensions, that his steward would not easily distipute this cloud of science.

Chappie, Powderham Castle, 25th January, 1779

Si this afternoon received your letter with your further remarks on the Cromlech. I saw it last Saturday, in my way between Kerflake and Moreton, entirely ftee from all asties or rubbish whatever. I could not avoid viewing it with pleasure, when I considered that the structure was a-means of affording not only utility to those who raised it, but of informing us, they were less ignorant in many mathematical observations than they have-hitherto received credit for: I

must confess that what you mewed me carries with it both truth and conviction; I only hope it will make its appear. a.nce soon and very soon, being convinced that you will gain great credit fn m the discovery. I wish you would be expedi. tious, as 1 am rather apprehensive your scheme is lot so much concealed as 1 could wish.

I am, Stc, COURTENAy.

I iil-calculated for protecting the dead from the inclemencies of the weather, or any other injury. There is something of grandeur in the construction of the Cromlech; which was probably tract. And indeed, it soon appear'd, the subject would require a longer dissertation than could with any propriety be inserted in any review of the county at large: and 1 the more readily acquiesced in its more immediate submission to public inspection, as having a full assurance that, as it carried it own evidence with it, it would, like other truths, appear the more conspicuous, the more strictly it should be scrutinized. A separate tract being thus resolv'd on, it became requisite, however, to introduce it by some few particulars relative to the *farijh* and *farm* in which the CROMLECH is situated; since their names, and those *of* their supposed possessors in former ages, at least so far claim'd notice as obliquely reflecting some light on the subject: But no more of these, or the etymologies of such names, are here enlarged on, than appear to have either an immediate, or at least some remote tendency thereto; this principal object of my enquiry being still kept in view. This indeed had been hitherto much clouded in obscurity; but the accidental spark now struck out, I imagined, might, if duly improved, conduce to its further illustration: And tho' in abler hands it might doubtless be kindled into a brighter flame, such as would add much to its brilliancy, yet it scem'd to Invite even such feeble endeavours as mine, to make the best use I could of the favourable opportunity that offered, in some measure to dispel that gloom which had more or less bewilder'd former enquirers. This invitation 1 could not well resist; and having fortunately

met with an unerring guide to conduct me in my researches, and open a way to a clearer view of the object before me, I Co. Id not shut my eyes against that irresistible light that pour'd in upon me. Such accidental discoveries have little or no claim to-be consider'd as meritorious: If any thing in this tract can have pretensions of that fort, 'tis the care and diligence with which I have pursued the clue thus accidentally acquired; which has cost me some time and trouble indeed, but this mixt with pleasure and satisfaction to find, among the innumerable properties more or less remarkable that successively offer'd themselves to observation in this seemingly rough but really well executed piece of ancient workmanship, every newly-discovered one harmoniously conCorded with, and conduced more fully to confirm the former, and the consummate ingenuity of the artists who contrived it. Of this, many remarkable instances will appear, in the descriptive part of it, in the following sheets; to which, were it necessary, a far greater number might be added. Purity of style, and elegance of diction, must not here be expected s nor would the subject admit of it, were the author capable of superadding embellishments of that kind. Language rough and unpolislYd as the *Cromlech* itself, may be sufficiendy intelligible in a description of it, provided it be free from ambiguities and nonsensical phrases: These I have endeavoured to avoid, perhaps sometimes by too much circumlocution; my aim being to lender the whole as plain and intelligible as I could, to all sorts of readers, even to those who have been Iktle conversant with such subjects. The mathematical parts indeed, and some etymological enquiries, may not be so well rclistVd or understood by some: But these may see enough to satisfy them in general, that such a *Cromlech* as ours is a work of art and ingenuity, and not of chalice or caprice, as some have imagined it to be. Even a bare inspection of the plates will afford them some evidence of the contrary. And, for the sake of the *Engljh* reader; nothing is here cited in another language, but what is explain'd, or its substance and purport inserted in plain *English* either in the text or notes. The notes here and there interspersed, may serve to relieve the reader from a too close and constant attention to so dry a subject: Some of them indeed necessarily relate to it; and the rest, tho' digressive, yet not so wholly unconnected with it, or remote from it, as to lose fight of, or impede a seasonable recurrency to it. And tho' such *Cromlechs* as ours will here appear applicable to, and were doubtless originally design'd for, such uses as seem to have been hitherto unsuspected! at least by any writer I have seen on the subject; yet no fanciful hypotheses are here obtruded on the reader, or forcibly wrested into a conformity with any preconceiv'd opinion of the proposer relative to the *Cromlech* in general, or to that we have here undertaken to describe j since the nature of its construction, and the purposes for which it was contrived will, it is presumed, fully and clearly appear from its own internal evidence, and on due examination afford such full and satisfactory proofs of the care and skill of the artists by whom it was erected, and how nicely accommodated to the purposes lor which it was intended, as to preclude all cavils and disputes concerning it; except perhaps those, who, prejudiced in favour of some adopted hypothesis, are determined to oppose all evidence inconsistent therewith. Should we chance to meet with an old timepiece, that on diligent inspection, appear d to have every part fitted for the indication of hours and minutes, and duly proportionate to them, tho' the workmanship were antique, and perhaps deemed too clumsy to suit a modern taste, and in some respect awkwardly constructed j—or find some fragment of a collection of astronomical tables, in which every particular, when examin'd by strict calculation, appear'd truly to adjust the places of the planets, tho' perhaps its title and some introdujry pages were wanting; surely we should not hesitate to conclude them originally design'd for those purposes respectively: and Would be apt to laugh at the folly of that man who should pertinaciously

insist, that the one was no more than a paltry childish play-thing, and the other a mere promiscuous and random jumble of characters and figures, to amuse and deceive the ignorant, and answer the collusive purposes of a pretended probably meant to do honor to the deceased. And the size of its area very well agrees with the dimensions of the human body. In the mean time, we mould recollect that the Kistvaen is but a Cromlech in miniature: and the Kistvaen is a sepulchral chest. Besides, the relics of the interred have been frequently discovered in the area of the Cromlech. But the Cromlech was not a common burying-place: It was the sepulchre of a chief Druid, or of some prince, the favourite of the Druid order. Hence the Cromlech acquired a peculiar degree of holiness: And(a) sacrifices were performed, in view of it, to the manes of the dead.

From the usual situation of the Cromlech, we must doubtless perceive, that it is no ordinary monument of the Druids. At Drewsteignton, the Cromlech is placed on an elevated spot—overlooking a sacred way, and two rows of pillars that mark out this processional road of the Druids, and several columnar circles; whilst at the end of the down, there are rock-idols, that frown with more than usual majesty. Nor are the Loganstones and rock-basons of Drewsteignton and Chagford, at any considerable distance. Thus we hive, even now, an opportunity of surveying in assemblage, almost all the monuments of Druvdism, near the " *(b)town of the Druids upon the Teign.*" And this Druidical scenery seems to have been included jn a circuit of about twenty miles.

From these observations on the relics of Druidism in Danmonium, it appears that we can boast no structures like the temple of Stonehenge j though several, indeed, of the monuments before us are marked'by the fame style of wild magnificence. Rude grandeur, not graceful elegance; gigantic massiness, not beautiful proportion; was, every where, the character of she eastern architecture: And such traits of the Asiatic genius are as obvious in the Cromlech of Danmo-

nium, as m those ruins, which Oft-times amaze the wandering traveller, By the pale moon discern'd on Sarum's plain, *(c),* The most perfect temple of the Druids hath been represented by some writers, as a deep recess in the centre of an ancient wood. And this Druidical wood has been placed on an eminence. (/) Tacitus describes such a wood as enclosed by a fence of pallisadoes t And, sometimes, the whole mountainous wood was surrounded at the bottom by a vallum. The Druids had certainly no covered temples: But Stonehenge is a striking specimen of a Druidical temple, erected on a regular plan. And nothing is more probable, than that such a temple once existed at Drewsteignton. Not that I can trace at this moment, with an ingenious correspondent, " the ruins of a very great temple at Stickle path near Zeal-Monachorum, not far from Drewsteignton; the fragments of which (he lays) are scattered through the village and over the sides of the mountain on which it was probably erected." The fame gentleman declares, that " the Valley of Stones is filled with the stupendous ruins of some Cuthite or Druid temple—where there was a *banging, font* (so characteristic of these structures) till the wind blowing down a great mass of the ruins, tended fortunetellers conjuring-book. Yet some such bigots to their own crude notions may be expected: And it were in vain to use arguments with those, who will never acknowledge themselves convinc'd that their judgment has deceived them. Such bpinionists are best left, like madmen, in quiet possession of their own wild conceits and visionary systems. But having carefully scrutinized every inch of the *Cromlech* in question, to guard against all mistakes concerning it, I am fully persuaded that any rational and unprejudiced person, who will-take the pains and care to examine the whole, will be no less convinc'd of the general design of this ancient structure, and on what principles it was evidently constructed: Yet, however certain of these, I pretend not to be less liable than another to mistakes in the application of those principles to some particular parts of it: But whatever flips or mistakes may have escaped me in these or any other particulars, being not desirous of deceiving myself or others, I shall always be glad to fee rectified by more accurate observers, and ready to retract any error, which, in this or any other production of mine, may be fairly detected." *(a)* Rowlands, in his *Mona Annjua Restaurant* observes, that as our first colonists were probably *m more than fivt descents from Noab,* they certainly brought with them the *mode of worship by sacrifice*: And, as so awful an event as the destruction of the world was then recent, and their minds imprest with a deep fense of an invisible and irresistible power, it was natural for them to *ereil altars* where-ever they sojourr '-1 during their peregrinations, and to multiply them where they took up their abode. Of these .rs he supposes the Cromlech to be the remains: And he conjectures, that *Cromlech* is derived from the Hebrew *Caremluacb,* a *devoted stone or altar. (b) Drms-tcign-tcn.* It is remarkable, that there is a *Teignton-Drew* or *Steignton-Drui* near Bristol, where Governor Pownall discovered very strong vestiges of the Druids.

() See Dr. Stukeley's Description of Stonehenge. *(A)* See Section III. p. 33. ruins, the end of one piece of rock fell against this stone; and it is now quite immoveable."(a)

This much for the ages pf primitive Druidism. In subsequent times, the Phenicians, Greeks, and Belgic settlers erected, also, their sacred edifices: Of such, howevar, we have no vestiges in ijanmonium j unless the lamp which was found some years since, at Exeter, hath any connexion with a Phenician or Grecian temple. This lamp is of brass, and has the crescent or half-moon as represented in Montfaucon: And it is generally conceived to have belonged to a temple of Diana. " Upon the coast of *Cornwall* and *Devon/hire,* I find a Promontory, fays *Sammes,* called *Hercules* his Promontory by *PtoJemy,* and called to this day *Herlj-point,* containing in it two pretty towns, *Herton* and *Heriiand,* whereof *Herton* is the greater, and corruptly called *Harton.* Now as I

will not aver as ever *Hercules* was here and named it so, as *Franciscus Pbilelphus* and *Lileut Geraldus* aver, because Mr. *Cantden* says there were three and forty *Hercules's,* as *Varra* will have it, he cannot admit of one of them to arrive at this point. Well let it be so, though I think *Diodorus Siculus,* nor any of the *Greeks,* to be competent judges of the voyages of the Phœnicians, yet I do believe that the Phœnicians rather than the *Grecians* might give it the name, and build some temple in honour of their own *Hercules,* as he almost got the honour of the temple in the *Streigbts,* so has he almost robbed the *Phœnician Hercules* of this allb."() 1

There is one British monument in Danmonium, still remaining to be described, I mean the *Barrow* or *Burrow;* which I have reserved for this place, as it was equally common in this country, to all the settlers before the Roman Period, and afterwards, to the Romans themselves, to the Saxons, and to the Danes. But, on examining the Barrow, we may often judge by its contents to what people it belonged. *Barrows* are found in most counties, and were primarily intended for protecting the remains of the dead. Among the Assyrians, the Persians, the Greeks, and the Romans, we have various instances of this ancient monument. We read in Livy, that Claudius, Nero buried his own soldiers after this manner, in the second Punic war: And Cæsar Germanicus brought the first turf himself, to raise the Barrow over the fallen troops of Varius. This mode of interrment prevailed in all the northern kingdoms. But, no where, are Barrows found in greater number than in this island. These monuments are called *Kainis,* or *Karnes,* if consisting of stone materials; and *Crigs* (in British, *round heaps)* from their circular plan; and *Burrouus,* from their use, as *Burrow* signifies a *sepulchre-.* 'Barrows, however, is their more general name. It was commonly on the third day after the funeral-pile had been fired, that they, who were to construct the Barrows, proceeded to collect the bones and heap together the materials; which were either a quantity of stones, or earth

only, or stones and earth mixed together. The stones, in some of these monuments, are of an astonishing magnitude. In the construction of the plain Barrow, the original design was nothing more than to keep up the earth or stones as high as the base would bear. Hence was produced a conic figure—the most simple and the least subject to injury from time or violence. There were Borrows more artificial—some surrounded by a single row of stones that formed the bale-others with a ring of earth—some having a large flat stone on the top—others, a pillar—some encircled both at the top and bottom, with stone or earth and others planted with oak or beech. If these monuments were for private persons, they were generally placed near the public roads: If the sepulchres of soldiers, they were commonly thrown up on the field of battle, where the soldiers fell; and on those plains, that have been the scenes of military action, they are often found in straight lines, as regular as the front of an army. We sometimes meet with the Barrow in a valley; but more frequently on a hill or plain. The size of these sepulchral works was various: That of Ninus, near the city of Nineveh, was, according to Ctesias, nine furlongs in height, and ten in breadth. In this country, *Silbury-Hill* is one of the most extraordinary works of the ancient Britons; though but a mole-hill compared to the Assyrian monument. In most instances, (a) Mr. Badcock seems to have been of opinion, that " those ancient pillars at Combe-Martin, that were called the *Hanginr-stmei,i)* were some Druidical remains of a temple: And the *Hangingstone* is the *Stonebenge* or *Balancedflone,* which was.remarkable in all these edifices. It is said, that there is but one pillar left—which served as a boundary between Combe-Martin and the adjoining parish." () Sammes, p. 56.

(1) Not from a atMp-Aeakrt having been hanged there, according to the silly tradition of the neighbourhood. instances, the size of the Barrow was determined by the quality of the deceased. This mode of burial was so universal, that it will be almost impossible to say

to what nation any Barrow belonged; unless the interior parts of it mould furnisli criteria to assist our determinations. In some Barrows urns were reposited; in others were round or square pits, containing a black greasy mould, without urns; in others, skeletons, that (hewed no signs of having pasted through the fire. The contents of Britissi and Phenician Barrows were, probably, much alike: these were the assies of the dead, enclosed in urns more or less polished, or little repositories instead of them. In the Grecian and Roman Barrows, we may look not only for urns, but frequently for pavement underneath. The Saxons and Danes (we are told) had left off the custom of burning the bodies of the deceased, before their arrival at this ifland; though they continued to bury their dead under earthen hillocks. So that Barrows, containing unburnt bodies or skeletons (with neither urns nor cells) may be Saxon or Danish. After all,.however, these are very uncertain criteria. The urns designed to contain human bones, were of gold, silver, brass, marble, or glass; but, more frequently, of pottery ware. The urn was deposited in the middle of the Barrow; and, not unfrequently, another near the outward edge. The urn at the extremity was, I suppose, that of the person who had a desire to be entombed in the same Barrow with a deceased relation or friend. Two or more urns were sometimes placed round the central sepulchre. And, indeed, there have been instances of no less than fifty surrounding the principal urn. The urn was generally placed erect on its bottom, and covered with a flat ltone or tyle. The Druids applied these Barrows to various purposes. On the Stone-barrows, especially where there was a large flat stone on the top, they kindled their annual fires; and the enclosed Earthbarrows, they used as altars for sacrifice, or places of inauguration. Here too, they pronounced their decrees, and made the most important decisions, as from a sacred eminence, (a) In Danmonium, there are numerous Barrow s on the *Jugum Ocrinum*, and on each side of this chain of mountains. They told me

(fays Dr. Stukeley) of a great Karne or heap of stones, on *Black-Doivn*, called *Lapper-fiones*, probably a sepulchral monument. On the northern extremity of Hemyock, towards Wellington, there is a large Barrow, composed of flints: it is called *Sjmanjborough*, as is the estate on which it stands, and the next estate adjoining to it. The common people have a notion that a king called *Symon* was buried there. The tradition of the country plainly stiews, that it was the burial-place of some person or persons of eminence. On the right side of the turnpike-road leading from *Columbton* to *Honiton*, over *Kent/moor*, are two Barrows, contiguous to each other. There are Barrows also on East-hill, near the town of Ottery St. Mary. On Haldon there are a great number of Barrows, particularly on the Kenne side; formed, for the most part, of flinty stones; several of which are, at this time, the reputed boundaries between the Lords of the neighbouring lands: Thus they have generally been considered as *Termini*, and neglected as sepulchral monuments. On the 19th of May, 1773, some workmen upon Haldon discovered an urn in a large oblong stone heap, from the middle of which, they had taken a considerable quantity of flints, for repairing the road that leads over the down from Kenneford to Newton-Buslicl. This *Tumulus* is situated near the Kenneford road, about thirty perch to the eastward of the eighth milestone from Exeter. The urn was four feet deep from the crest of the *Tumulus*, and let into the solid earth beneath, to the depth of half a foot: It was covered with an irregular flat stone, about five inches tliick. It consisted of earthenware evidently baked. The workmen, fancying the urn to be a crock of money, instantly broke it with their ssiovels into several pieces: These pieces were in thickness about three-fourths of an inch. The interior diameter of the urn itself, taken in the most bulging part of its curvature, was at least ten inches: And its height was about fourteen inches, as well as Mr.Chappie could judge from the fragments. The workmen eagerly grasped its contents in handfulls; but

found themselves only in possession of a greasy kind of alhes, that lmelt like foot. Among the assies were some small fragments of bones. There was a yellowifli tinge on the urn, and the flints aboveit; which the workmen positively asserted to be gold, dissolved and evaporated through the vessel. This was afterwards found (by a microscope) to be a diminutive mass, bearing yellow flowers, with a few black and globular berries. On this large *Tumulus*, which measured twelve feet in length, and twenty-eight in breadth, a further search was made the fame (a) For curious Information on the subject of *sepulchral Tumuli*, see Pennant's Tour in Wales— p. 381 to 388. same year, on the 28th of June, when a second and third urn were discovered. The second urn was at the distance of fourteen feet from the spot where the first lay; and the third urn twelve feet distant from the second. These urns, also, contained a black and greasy kind of aflies; and in each of them about a handful of splintered bones. The interior diameter of the second urn, as it stood in the ground, was full thirteen inches j its depth below the surface of the ground being nearly the same, and the whole height of the urn about eighteen inches: But this could not be exactly ascertained; as its neck above the surface of the ground was so rotten, that it mouldered into dust, on the removal of the stones which surrounded and covered it. Of the third urn, no dimensions could be taken; for, on emptying it of the ashes, it quickly fell to pieces. These two urns seem not to have been so well manufactured as the first; which was so little decayed, that it might have been preserved entire, but for the accident I have mentioned. This vessel was. composed of a dark grayish clay, found in some parts of Haldon, and afterwards dipt in a brighter brown composition, by way of glaze; and then ornamented with several figures, before it was burnt or baked. The latter part of the process must have been done in some mould; the basket-work towards the bottom being regular and distinct: And the like regularity appears in the other decorations. At a small distance from this Tumulus, to the northward, is a large circular Tumulus; the diameter of which is sixty feet. A continuation of flinty stones under the mossy turf, shews that there was some connection between these Tumuli. This circular Tumulus might have been the burial-place of superior officers. We may observe, that the circular Tumuli on Haldon, are true circles, and the periphery of their bases regularly footed up with stone. Not long after this, Mr. Tripe, late surgeon at Astiburton (whose ingenuity and various learning entitle him to a place among the literary characters of Devon) undertook to examine several of the Haldon-Barrows; into the centre of which he made sections, and found them all to be uniform in their structure: His hopes were, however, not gratified in this pursuit: For, though in some of these Barrows he found pieces of urns wrapt up in mo(s, and particularly in one of them, a shoulder-bone of a child, met with nothing by which he might venture to decide upon their antiquity. A gentleman who accompanied Mr. Tripe on this expedition, thus proceeds with the narrative:" We resolved upon renewing our pursuits, merely for a single trial more: and the Barrow we pitched upon, was one ot the most apparent eminencies on the down; that which is the present reputed boundary between the parishes of Kenton and Kenne, not far from the head of *Holloivay-la.ne,* leading from the down towards Oxton. We called together a regiment of labourers, and made a bold attack upon this Barrow, through which we made a wide opening, home to the center; but meeting with nothing to reward our desires (except an exact uniformity of construction with all the others we had before opened) we then agreed to give up our searches, and were nearly upon departing: But, before we dismissed our labourers, I happened to clean away the base of the Barrow, near the center, and at last discerned a very large flat-headed stone, quite even with the ground upon which the Barrow was erected: I imparted this to my friend; and, on viewing it more nicely, we found ourselves once more quick-

ened in our hopes. Mr.-Tripe then undertook to keep off all the labourers, except a couple to assist me in starting and getting up this cap-stone: And under it I found an *urn,* compleat and uninjured, with its mouth downward, resting upon another large flat stone. I took it very carefully up, and delivered it to my friend: and under the urn we found the; bones and ashes of the deceased. Gratified as we were by this discovery, we had, however, the mortification still to remain ignorant as to its antiquity; for it happened to be an *unbaked* urn, without any inscription or other marks to assist us in deciding upon it. It was in shape, much like aBarnstaple or Bideford butter-pot: and I left it with my friend Mr. Tripe, in whose custody it probably still remains." This urn is, at present, in the! possession of the Rev. John Swete,(a) of Oxton-House, who is animated, and at the fame time exact in the following description: " Quitting the grounds of Oxton, we rode up Holloway-lane, and having mastered an ascent of a hill, emerging from a deep defile, we gained the level heights of Haldon. Turning short to the right, we inspected a large Barrow, known by the name of the *great stone-heap;* which, though originally of a conical form (as are all the Tumuli in these parts) yet, being now' intersected by an opening made some time before, afforded a very conspicuous object to the subjacent country. The form of this Barrow was nearly circular, being rather more than two hundred feet in circumference (a)' Son of the late Mr. Tripe, of Ashburton. Vol. I. N cumference, and about fifteen in height. By the aid of fourteen men, a passage into it was' effected, almost; due east, about eight feet wide: Nearly at the fame space from the margin', was discovered a dry wall, about two feet high, which was separated from without by very large stones, in the form of piers or buttrefles. On arriving near the center, were seen a great many large stones (all of them flint) placed over one another in a convex form; and, in the middle thereof, a large stone nearly round, two feet in diameter, six inchesthick, covering a cell on the ground about two

feet square, formed by four large stones placed on their edges. In this was an *urn* (inverted, which was rather remarkable) containing the ashes and burnt bones of probably a youth; as they were small, with little muscular impression. When the urn was removed, these appeared as *white as snoiu*— Aeux os-rea—though, soon after they were exposed to the air, they lost that whiteness. From the size of the Tumulus, and this circumstance, we may gather, that they were the remains of a person of dignity; whose surviving friends, in honor of his memory, had taken care to have them well burnt and blanched by the intenseness of the fire. The urn is thirteen inches high, ten in diameter at the top, five at the bottom, near half an inch thick, and holds about ten quarts. It is made of unbaked earth, smoked and discoloured by its exposure to the fire, and consequently without inscription or embellishments. " In a high field, called Castle-Park, in Hennock, I met with a small earth-work, which is evidently sepulchral. Its shape is elliptical: and its round is formed of small stones. The (clergyman of Hennock, a short time afterwards, sent me the following account of it. " We opened the hillock that you suspected might be a Tumulus. After the small acre-stones were taken away, we found earth and stones regularly laid on: the earth used was the vegetable foil. The stones were flat, and some of them of considerable size. We found the hillock thus formed, till we came four feet and half deep, when we perceived the stones to lie a contrary way; and we suspected some pavement; but upon removing all the top, we found only three stones placed on edge, and let down about half their depth into the fast. The two side stones were of the fame size; their ends in a straight line, and their upper surface level with the middle stone: they were placed, north and south. When we came thus far, we hesitated whether we should let them remain: we removed them, and funk into the fast, but could find nothing. The two side-stones were thirteen inches, the middle one three feet two inches." There are several circular stone-heaps in the neighbourhood of this earth-work. On the opposite hill to the east is the old Beacon, about half a mile distant from the Castle-field. On opening one of the sepulchral monuments a few years since, upon Mare-down, in the parissi of Moreton, were found *ajbes, burnt-wopd,* and *pieces of earthen vessels,* the fragments of urns. The greater number of the Barrows which I have noticed, consist chiefly of stone; which might have been collected, as convenience led, from the adjacent grounds, where the scantiness of earth would have rendered the operation more laborious. On the wild downs of Withecombe, and the surrounding parissies, the Tumuli invariably consist of moor-stone. There are several stone Barrows in the parissi of Ilsington. But on *Sfuarnell-Doixin,* there is a most magnificent Barrow; such as a numerous army might have been some time employed in raising. The circumference of the Barrow, is ninety-four paces. Here, probably, in the centre, were deposited the remains of some great personage—perhaps aBritissi Prince; for the discovery of which we need not dig deep, as in the central part there is very ssiallow earth. There is a large circle of high heaped stones, loosely thrown around this Barrow; under which were buried, perhaps, the bodies of the Prince's relations; or of those, possibly, who fell with him in battle. A vast deal of stone is scattered about the down, in the neighbourhood of this burial-place. There is another immense Barrow on Quarnelldown, consisting entirely of small loose stone. On Hazwell-down near Assiburton,' is a very large stone-heap. And on Dartmoor, and on Roborough-downs, near Plymouth, are a variety of karnes. On the north-side, also,, of the *Jugum Ocrinum,* we might investigate a great number of Barrows. There are large accumulations of stone, in various parts of the forest of Exmoor. The parissi of Northmolton is separated from Exmoor by stones set Jn the ground, along the summit of the hills. On these hills are a number of Barrows; seven of which are within or near the limits of Northmolton. They are confused heaps of earth and stone, over-

grown-with moss. The people in the neighbourhood fay, they were simply land-marks; but they were, doubtless, burying-places. Lyttelton discovered many Barrows in the north of Devon; though it does not appear, that (a) Mr. Hill; one of the best informed, and at the fame time, most communicative of my correspondents. that either himself or Milles, his brother antiquarian, made the slightest use of the discovery. " («)I met (says he) with two or three Barrows on *Bratto/i-dou/n,* near Arlington; and ib many large ones on *Berry-down,* that I suspect they gave name to the place. (A) The five hills, or rather the *billy ridge ivitb Jive swellings,* on the summit above the down of *Ilfardcombe,* is so singular a configuration of ground, that I would have given a good deal to have been able to draw it."(r) Mr. Badcock takes notice of " a fine

Barrow, *(a)* In a letter to Milles, dated July 17, 1756. As Lyttelton and Milles were both Deans of Ixeter, and as Lyttelton was Bishop of Carlisle, I have thought proper, in several places, to mention their *slain* names, lest, by giving them different titles at different times, 1 should occasion perplexity; or, by attempting to avoid perplexity, I should be guilty of circumlocution; or, by endeavouring to steer clear of both, I should fall into anachronisms.

(b) A gentleman, who lately visited the north of Devon, thus informs the author: " Proceeding to Parracombe, at the center ot' the village, 1 turned out of the *Ilfracombe* road, and by a rough ascent rising towards the south, I attained the high ground of *Rowleigb-Common* ; over which having rode for three miles, nearly on quitting it I perceived on the. west of the track, a large Burrow, which had been opened in several places, and was in diameter above one hundred feet. Its-situation was contiguous to the lonely farm of *Carbrocken* Burrow, deriving its name fromthe Tumulus in question."
(c) Westoote speaks of several Barrows in the north of Devon: " At the north end of the towne stalls in the ryveret called Yeo or North Yeow which springs at Challucomb, als Chaldecomb, sometyme the land of William de Rawleigh

now of Hatch. In this parish being bordering on the fforrest of Exmoore are dyvers round Hillocks of earth, and stones antiently cast vp, which they terme Burj-owes and'distinguisli them by names which 1 can imagine to be nothing else but monuments of some interments of persons of note slayne at some battayle or fkirmige. of some of them there are yet remembred old tales, how fierie dragons or meteors haue often been seen to light on them: bee pleased to heare this that happened within these 6 or 7 yeares verified by the partye and credited for his honestye. A dayly labouring man hauing gotten a 'little money, bellowed it for some acres cf land & thereon began to build an house, which was not farr from one of those Borrowes named *Broken Borrowe,* whence hee letcht his stones to build wkhall, and hauing digged into the bowels of this hillock, hec found a small place as if it had been an oven fayrely, strongly and closely walled vp, which put him in very ioyful hope, that some great good happ had befallen him, and that hee should sinde some treasure to maintayne him more liberally in his old age. and breaking an hole in the wall where in the concavitie hee espied an earthen pott (some Vine I thinke) and fastning his hand thereon, hee sodainly heard or seemed to heare the noyfe of the treading of many horses coming tovards the place, which caused him to withdraw his hand, fearing the comers would take the purchase from him (for hee doubted no'hing but that it was treasure) but turnii.g about to see what they were, there was neither man nor horse in veiw: to the pott againe hee goes, and heard the like noyse the ad time, yet looking about saw nothing, at the 3d time hee brought it forth, and the treasure was onely *a few bones as if they bad beene cf children or lambts er the lykc.* But the man (whyther with the fear which hee denyed or other cause I cannot ghelle at) in very short time after lost both hearing & fight, & in less than 3 monthes declyning dyed: hee was held very honest & constantly reported this, diuers times to men of good qualitie with protestations of the truth thereof, even to his death. Of another of the Borrowes the name I haue forgotten, but it is nere another that is named *Wood-Bcrrow* of which a gentleman worthy credit both for honestye & wealth told mee this tale, which happened some yeare or two before the other, two good fellowes that inhabited not far from it were informed by one that was held skilful in metaphysical studyes, that there was in that hillock a great brasse pann, and therein much treasure ossiluer & gold, which if they would dig for hee promised them (by his art) to secure them from all danger, foe hee might haue a part j they willingly consented, and made a 4th man acquainted therewith whome they knew to bee valiant and hardye; but hee, better qualified then to vndertake such coursfis to purchase wealth, absolutely refused to bee partaker therein, but promised secrecic. the other two with the conjurer fall to their work & ply it foe lustily that it was not long ere they found the pann covered with a large stone; with the fight whereof *tc* their protectors words encouraged, they earneltly follow their business, with their vtmost abilitie. for the conjurer told them, that if they fainted when it was in sight it would bee taken from them, and all their labour lost, and now the cover was to bee opened, & the younger of them at the work hee was sodainly taken with such a faintness, that hee could not lift his hand to doe any thing & therefore called to the other to supply his place, which hee did, & was instantly taken with the like numness which continued a very small time, yet tlieir protector told them tho birds were flown away & onely the nest left which they found true; for recovering tlieir strength they tooke out the pann, wherein they found nothing at all but the bottome thereof (where the treasure should seeme to have layn) very clean & the rest all cankered. Hee that told mee this protested hee saw the pann, & that the 2 labourers constantly avouched the other circumstances to bee true." Westcote's View (Porfjedge MS.) p. 1.53, 1.54.

Vol. I. Ni

Barrow, immediately beyond the out-

er row of stones on Maddoc's-down: And my curiosity (lays he) will lead me to open it." I do not find that he put his design into execution. *(d)*—-But to enumerate the Barrows in this county, would be endless.

And the present Section is already extended to too great a length; scanty as my materials were, For a history of the Danmonian Architecture. If, however, I have indulged a little in conjecture, it mould be considered, that such a subject requires illustration: And a few scattered facts, at so remote an æra, can neyer be rendered interesting, unless they are mingled with probabilities.

SECTION V., *VIEW os PASTURAGE and AGRICULTURE in DANM0N1UM, during the BRITISH PERIOD. . Danmonium, originally, a Wilderness—The Ground prepared for Pasturage—The Flocks and Herds of the Danmonians—Dartmoor and Exmoor.—,11. Agriculture—Cxfar quoted— The Danmonian Farm—Orchard or Garden.—III. Remarkable Fertility os the island, as reported by the Phenicians and Greeks; a plain Proof of its very early Inhabitation.* AS the Danmonians had made some progress in architecture before the arrival of the Romans, it is natural to expect, that they were not deficient in other arts which pontributed to the conveniencies and comforts of life. Even of a people just emerging from barbarism, the first picture is that of sherherds and herdsmen: And the view of husoandmeq follows in quick succession. With husbandmen we connect the idea of the farm, and all its obvious appendages: Nor from the neighbourhood of the farm-house, is it easy to detach the garden or the orchard. To the first people that landed in Danmonium, the face of the country was every where rough; the higher grounds were darkened by sorest trees, or covered with coppice, brakes, and heath; and the low-lands were overgrown with wood or with the rankest herbs; where the rivers which must have run lawlessly, obstructed not the progress of vegetation. Amidst (uch luxuriance, the beasts were furnished with coverts, the birds had built their nests securely, and the waters were replenished with fish.

To the Aborigines of Danmonium, therefore, the wild animals of the country must have afforded a ready sustenance; whilst the necessity of hunting, of fowling and of fishing, was instantly suggested. But these' exertions for the supply of their immediate wants, were flight, in comparison of the various labors imposed on the first colonists. To clear the grounds, to fell trees, and to destroy wild beasts, was a task preparatory to their settlement. And, among the animals which they hunted, for food or diversion, or in order to the security of their persons, they must have taken some, whose gentleness conciliated regard; and whose docility soon rendered the attempt successful to domesticate " the pensioners of nature", or confine the rovers within certain boundaries. To discuss the point, whether the Danmonians thus subdued, by gradual means, those animals which are so useful in subservience to man; or whether they imported with them their dogs and their cattle, would here be impertinent or unneceflary. Certain it is, that when Cæsar invaded the island, the riches of the Danmonians chiefly consisted in their cattle. It was their practice to keep large herds upon the uninhabited grounds that skirted *(d)* Long before his death, his literary pursuits had been often interrupted by a dreadful indisposition: Heaven knows, that, at this moment, I am but too sensible of what his sufferings must have been! The ill-health of my predecessor, I fear, was entailed on me, with the history! There seems to be a fatality in the attempt—Not to mention the imperfect works of Sir. W. Pole, of Westcote, or of Rifdon; Milles, and Chappie, and Badcock, have either fallen victims to the History of Devon, or died in the midst of. their labors! It was this idea, which chiefly induced me to print my *Collections* for the Ginjral History, in the present form, without loss of time. If I drop, before the completion of this work, the Dumic will, here, possess a variety of useful Notices; which, from the multiplicity of my p ipers, their disorder in numerous instances (to any other eye than mine) the endless diversity of the MS. ar.d the difficulty of decyphering a great part of it, snd from many other circumstances, no writer, succeeding me, could possibl) bring forward: They are Notices, which, in this cafe, would be inevitably lost. skirted the confines of their country. " Retaining, under their own care, as many as they could conveniently furnish with pastures, they detached the rest into the woods, or the borders, under the inspection os their servants. And these they sometimes called *Ceangon,* or foresters. "(a) According to Mr. Carte, the Danmonians had a wide scope, indeed, for their flocks. " Westmoreland and Somersetshire (says he) being moist and morassy countries, served the Brigantes and *Dumnonii* for their summer pastures, as Cumberland and Cornwall, having a dryer soil, did for their winter. " But, as Mr.Whitaker tells us, " all the change of pastures that was made by the Britons, was the lame as is made to this day by the Highlanders; driving the cattle to the valleys in summer, and redriving them to the hills in winter." The *Caffini* and *Ostidamnii,* as some conjecture, were keepers of the flocks and herds of the Danmonians. These flocks and herds were, probably, fed along the extensive tracts of Dartmoor; where the Caffini and Ostidamnii, had their temporary habitations; fixing their residence on a particular spot, as long as the pasturage around them was sufficient for the maintenance of their cattle. And (Exmoor must have afforded a noble range for the flocks and herds of the Britons. Not that the uplands of Danmonium were the resort of shepherds or of herdsmen only: The contrary has already appeared. (7) At this juncture, the care of cattle was a hazardous employment; since every night the peasants must have watched with their mastiffs, for the protection of the sheep and kine, from those ravenous beasts that inhabited the woods. The dangers of this occupation, however, daily decreased; since the Danmonians, still incroaching on the habitations of the wolf and the bear, soon thinned their numbers, and harrassed the beasts that escaped, or drove them into distant coverts. On those spots, which were thus rendered

compatibly secure, they would naturally turn their attention to the soil: And, barren in many places, in others rocky, in others overgrown with briars or with the rankest weeds, the soil could be made productive, only by unremitting labor and assiduity. On the point of the British pasturage and agriculture, we may gather, perhaps, a feiv hints from ancient authors. Cæsar's distinction between the interior Britons, and the Britons of the coasts, must easily recur to memory: What relates to the present topic is vague. Whilst the Belgæ were well acquainted with agriculture, it seems that most of the Aborigines depended for sustenance on their flocks and herds.— *f Interiores plerique* (the Aborigines) *frumenta nor. serunt, fed lacie et carne vivunt."* But *some* of the interior inhabitants of the island, were agriculturists. That the Aborigines should, even in Cæsar's time, notwithstanding the lapse of so many ages, in which numbers of them, difpossest of their original settlements in Danmonium, had been driven into the heart of the island, prefer the vagrant life of sliepherds to the steadier occupation of husoandmen, is surely probable from the Asiatic character. Yet I cannot conceive that so ingenious a people had been utterly inattentive to husbandry. Accordingly, we may infer from the very passage before us, that some of the interior Britons were tillers of the ground. The maritime Britons, however, were more generally employed in agriculture. Such were the Belgæ, who settled as a nation to the east of Devonsliire; though great numbers of these continental intruders had incorporated with the Danmonians. The Danmonians, in the mean time had, doubtless, adopted all those modes of cultivating the ground, which ingenuity would dictate, or the practice of their neighbours would present to observation; though they retained their original love of change, still shifting their habitations from place to place, as the pasturing of their cattle required. And the attention of this people, seems to have judiciously divided between pasturage and agriculture: Whilst the Danmonians saw the

neighbouring nations, some for the most part occupied by the former, and others by the latter; they reconciled both in themselves. Of a Danmonian farm, therefore, a certain portion of ground was, probably, allotted to the feeding of cattle, notwithstanding the extensive range of the neighbouring downs or *com*mons; though the greater part was tilled with corn, for the provision of the family. The farm-house of the Danmonians, seems not to have been deficient in articles of convenience. If the Britons, as Mr. Whitaker informs us, had bee-hives near the mansions of («) See Wliitakcr's Manchester. *(i)* " *Btlga: flerilcm et montosum ilium terra traBum*—Exmoor —*in accidents, invadere vel subigere volujffe, nuttam vcri fpeciem prase serf, fed tantum cigri Somersetenjis MlarH in occidente vallem, qua Us, citra mantes ad* Dunstar *usque pertinent, omni fere avo grata, salubris et jucunda suit, agricolaqueveto respondent."* Musgrave, from whom this passage is taken, judges of Exmoor, in the British Period, fiom its appearance at the present day: But this judgment js erroneous. *(c)* See the IVth Section. os their chiefs, and near their farm-houses, we can hardly avoid giving them credit for every comfortable accommodation. Whilst the house was guarded by the British mastiff, the wild boar of the Danmonian woods had become a peaceful inhabitant of the farmyard; the cow was ready with her supplies of milk; and the horse, had, also, passed intoservitude. The Danmonian horses, however, must have frequently run wild in the woods and mountains. They are expressly described by the Romans, as at once diminutive in their size, and swift in their motions: *a)* And the breed still subsists in the little horses of ExmooT and Dartmoor, as well as those of Wales and Cornwall. As to the Danmonian modes of cultivating the ground, we cannot expect much information. Pliny tells Tss, that the Britons manure their ground with marie, instead of dung: And what Pliny knew relating to this ifland, was, probably, collected from the Danmonian merchants. It seems, that a variety of marks was used by the Britons as well as Romans, in manures: And sea-sand was employed in the western counties, as at the present day.(A) With respect to the process of the Britilh husbandry, it would be fruitless to enquire. I cannot but remark, indeed, that Diodorus Siculus mentions tine Britons as *boufing* thencorn; which seems, at this moment, to be the custom in Devonshire, though not in. many other counties.(r) In the passage *(d)* to which I allude, the Britons are said to lay up their corn in caverns: And the people of Devonshire have, in many places, barns capacious enough for their corn. In the more eastern counties, however, the corn is chiefly preserved in mows in the open air. After the partition of lands, the woods and coppices were considered as another part of the estate: And they were a valuable part of it.' Though Danmonium abounded with woods, perhaps we had no great variety of forest trees. The number of our indigenous trees were few. Cæsar intimates, that the beech and the fir were strangers to our woods. But Mr. Whitaker thinks, from its British appellation, *Gius* in Scotland, *Giumhus* in Ireland, and *Fynniduydth* in Wales, that the fir was a native of Britain. The sirs of Scotland and Ireland are often noticed in the poems of Oslian. And the fir, though no longer growing wild in Devonshire or Cornwall, has been found among subterraneous substances in both counties; particularly on the BoveyHeathfield, where it lies imbedded in the £lay, and from its resinous quality and the nature of its grain, is evidently the fir-tree. In the mean time, the beech was certainly not a native of the isiand. And it is, at this moment, very scarce in Devonshire, *(e)*

Among *(a)* D 'w, p. T280. *(b) ffbitaker's* Manchester.

(c) The Belgæ of Devonshire were in possession of the Gallic instrument of threshing before the Romans: They were well acquainted with the use of our flail. *Whitaker. (d)* Diodorus (1) tells us, that, from their subterraneous granaries, they took as much as was necessary for the day, and having dried the ears; beat the grain from them, which

they bruised, and made into a sort of bread for present use. (2) (e) It has been a subject of dispute among naturalists, whether the *Tew* is an indigenous or exotic plant. That it was indigenous, I have scarcely a doubt. In several parts of Devonshire, yew-trees are now flouristiing, of the plantation of which we have no memorial. In Scotland, it was certainly indigenous. " Lift thy terrible sword! Bend thy crooked *Tew!* Throw thy lance through heaven! Lift your shields, like the darkened moon! Be your spears the meteors of death!" A correspondent, however, writes: " I have never seen the yew-tree growing in this country, except where planted: It has, in many instances, proved fatal to cattle: At a funeral, some years since, in a neighbouring parish, two or three horses were killed by eating it, being as is supposed, forced by hunger. The deleterious effects of this plant were well known to the ancients: Cæsar knew the power of yew. As I do not recollect having seen the passage quoted, it (hall find a place here. *Cativulcus, rex dimidiæ partis Fburonut/ty qui una cum Ambiorige con/ilium inierat, cetate jam onfeilus, quum labortm aut belli aut Juga; serre tion po/Jetj omnibus precibus detejlatus Ambiorigem qui ejus conjilii autlor fuijfet* taxo, *cujus tnagna in Gallia Germtuuaaut copia eft, fe exanimavit.* A yew-tree is still found in almost all our church-yards. (1) *te* Ksle *QvitTXVpiovTES9* &c. " In Brittannia, si valuit, quod in Cappadocia et Thracia usus introduxerat ut frumentum in spccubus adherent, proba vulgata est." Varro I. R. R.C. 57. " Quidam granaria habent subterrit, speluncas *Jbuas* vocant *aEffitsS9* ut in Cappadocia et Thracia. AHi, ut in-Hispania citeiiorc, putcos, ut in agro Carthaginiensi ct Ofrensi." Not. Diod. Wcs». T.I. p. 347. (2) Some vestiges of this ancient way of dressing corn, were discavered not long ago in several of the islands of Scotland. " This method is called Graddan, from the Irish word Grad, which signifies quick. A woman sitting down, takes a handful of corn, holding it by the stalks in the left hand, and then sets sire to the ears, which ave presently in a flame: she has a ick in

her right hand, which she manages very dexterously, beating out the grain at the instant the husk is quite burnt, for if she miss of that she must use the kiln; but experience has taught them this att to perfection. The corn may be so dressed, winnowed, ground, and baked within an hour." Martin's Descrip. of the western islands of Scotland, p. 204.

Among the fruit trees of Danmonium, the apple was, undoubtedly, British. In the Cornish, the Irish, the Welch and the Armorican, it is invariably denominated the *a vail* or *aball:* And it seems to have been brought into Devonshire by the first colonies. The *availonia,* or the *apple-orchard* of the *Hadui* (the present scite of Glastonbury) is mentioned by Richard. For(a) other fruit-trees, it is difficult to fay, whether they were indigenous or not. Though the British garden was chiefly composed of fruit-trees; yet the orchard, and the flower and kitchen garden, were all united in one. And gardens near the British houses, in the southern counties, are remarked by Strabo.(A)

Obscure and unsatisfactory as these accounts of the Danmonian pasturage and agricul ture are, we may be assured, that this island was remarkable for its fertility in very ancient times. In some of the earliest notices of Britain by the Greeks, tire island, or rather Danmonium, is celebrated as prolific of the fruits of the earth. Orpheus called this island *the royal court of Ceres.* In after times, Strabo(r) and (/)Diodorus Siculus, agreed in their reports of its fertility: And these authors drew their materials from Greek geographers and historians, who lived long before Caesar. That Danmonium could have produced fruits in such abundance, without human ingenuity and human labor, long and perseveringly exerted in the cultivation of it, is impossible to be conceived. Its uncommon fertility, therefore, leads us to think, that it must have been very early known to the oriental nations.(f)

The general principle of fertility in every country, is the application of man; by which the beneficial productions that naturally spring up, may be freed from every impediment to their growth, and removed into more genial situations, and by which the fruits of one country may be transplanted and cultivated with success in another. If this were not the cafe, mankind could not have spread over rjie face of the earth: and the far greater part of the world would have remained in a state of nature. The capacity of producing, when directed by skill and supported by labor, certainly extends the bounties of providence, and meliorates even the most ungrateful foils and climates. But these happy effects are produced, only in a course of time. Danmonium was, at first, a *wilderness.* Nor did it become *the court of Ceres,* till after the lapse of ages,*(f)* church-yards, *three* reasons may be assigned for their situation s The *first* is, that before the invention of gunpowder, the warrior might never be at a loss for a bow. The *second* is, its being an evergreen, and as such, an emblem of immortality. The *third* motive which may be supposed to have induced mankind to plant the yew in church-yards, is the idea of its being endued with a power to attract to itself the noxious particles that may arise from dead bodies: This last opinion has been of late much strengthened by the experiment of Dr. Priestley, who has discovered, that growing vegetables are wonderfully effectual in the purification of foul air." Mr. *Cornish,* of *Totnn,* in a letter to the author. A *fourth* reason has been given. The Yew, we are told, was there planted, to prevent the introduction of cattle into sacred ground: But this is improbable. The peculiar GloomIniss of the Yew, and the Beadliniss of its Poison, seems to suggest the propriety of its situation, more strongly than all.

(a) " The *Damson* (fays Mr. Whitaker) had been long taken from the vicinity of its native Damascus, and accustomed to the foil of Italy, when the Romans took possession of this island: And the *British* appellation of it, *Damshon* or *Damson,* remaining among the *Irish* and *ourselves,* denotes it to have been introduced into Britain by the Romans." But the *name* of this fruit remaining among the *Irish,* by no means proves its introduction into Britain by the Romans. I

should draw a different conclusion from this circumstance. The *peach* was, probably, transplanted from its own Persia into Britain. (i) p. 306. (c) Geor. lib. 3, p. 200. *(d)* lib. 5, p. 209. (e) The fertility of this island, in the British Period, as the ingenious and learned Dr. Campbell intimates, is a *certain proof* that it was inhabited long before our antiquarians have thought proper to colonize it.., *(f)* " Sir Walter Raleigh reports, that the Spaniards, in some parts of America, scarcely proceeded into the Continent *ten miles in ten years;* which if they (with aU necessary instruments) could not do, how can we expect, that in (we first ages after the deluge, colonies could go on so fast, when they were to encounter with no less difficulties, and had not the fame means to overcome them. And if by this measure we should calculate the progress of the first planters, we might not be far out of the way; but certainly as Europe extends in length Iqcccc German miles, so we might modestly assign so many years to the filling of it, which is four times the speed that the Spaniards made in America." *Sammts' Biitarn, Antiqu. Illuftr.* p. 9. SECTION SECTION VI. *VIEWof MINING in DANMONIUM, during the BRITISH PERIOD.*

I.   *Quarries—Tin-Jhoding—Streaming—Vestiges of Tin-Works in different parts of Devonshire —Lead—Iron—Cold—Silver.—*II. *Preparation of these Metals for Use.—*III. *Conclusion.* WE have seen the Danmonians pasturing their cattle and cultivating their grounds— the most natural employment of man. But there is reason to suppose, that their attention was not long confined to the vegetable productions of the earth. The Aborigines of this country poslest a spirit of research, which led to new pursuits and prompted new discoveries: And Danmonium was now to be explored for mineral treasures. The use, indeed, of several kinds of stone, which met their eye, either scattered on the surface os the ground, or imbedded in the soil, or in various other situations, was as obvious as that of the timber which their woodlands supplied. The slate and the moor-stone, particularly

the latter, were of this description. Thus the working of a quarry was soon an unavoidable labor: And there was an easy transition from the quarry to the mine. To conduct, however, the Danmonians, step by step, to the mines, is needless: For, though the use of stone seems more obvious than that of metals, the latter were procured, perhaps, with as little trouble in Danmonium. (a) This, at least, seems to have been the case with the

Danmonian (a) On the discovery of Mines, Dr. *Pryce* expatiates thus: " Lucretius, who ascribes the first discovery of Metals to the burning down of woods, fays, that the heat of the flames melted the Metals, which were dispersed here and there in the veins of the earth, and made them flow inta one mass:

Whatever 'twas that gave these flames their birth,

Which burnt the tow'ring trees, and scorch'd the earth;

Hot streams of Silver, Gold, and Lead, and Brass, ' As nature gave a hollow, proper place,

Descended down, and form'd a glitt'ring mass.

This when unhappy mortals chane'd to spy,

And the gay colour pleas'd their childish eye;

They dug the certain cause of misery. Cadmus, the Phenician, is, by fume, said to have been the first who discovered Gold; others fay, that Thoas first found it, in the mountain Pangæus in Thrace: the Chronicon Alexandrinum, ascribes it to Mercury, the son of Jupiter; or to Pisus, king of Italy, who quitting his own country went into Egypt; where, after the death of Misraim, the son of Cham, he was elected to succeed him in the royal dignity, and, for the invention of Gold, was called the Golden God. Æschylus attributes the invention of this, and all other Metals, to Prometheus: and there are others who write, that either Æaclis, whom Hyginus calls Cæcus the son of Jupiter, or Sol the son of Oceanus, first discovered Gold in Panchaia. Aristotle says, that some shepherds in Spain having set fire to certain woods, and heated the sub-stance of the earth, the silver that was near the surface of it, melted, and flowed together in a heap; and that a lit-tle while after there happened an earth-quake, which cleaved the earth, and dis-closed a vast profusion of silver. This is confirmed by Strabo, lib. iii. and Athenarus, lib. vi. who fay, that the Mines in Andalusia were discovered by this accident. Cinyra the son of Agry-opa, first found out the Brass (Copper) Mines in Cyprus; and the discovery of Iron Mines Hesiod ascribes to those in Crete who were called Dactyli ıHæi: and Midacritus was the first man that brought Lead (Tin) out of the island Casliteris. (Lucretius, Pliny, Polydore Virgil). We shall close this ancient ac-count of the first discovery of Metals, with the following lines from Dr. Garth's Dispens»y.

Now those profounder regions they explorej Where Metals ripen in vast cakes of Ore. Here, sullen to the fight, at large is spread, The dull unweildy mass of lumpish Lead; jThere, glimmering in their dawning beds, are seen The more aspiring seeds of sprightly tin; The Cop-per sparkles next in ruddy streaks, And in the gloom betrays its glowing cheeks. Mines have been often discovered by accident, as in the sea cliffs, among bro-ken craggy rocks, or by the washing of the tides or floods; likewise by irrup-tions and torrents of water issuing out of hills and mountains; and someumee by the wearing of high roads. Another way of finding veins, which

Danmonian tin and lead. The *Moina-Statue* or the Daumonian Tin-mines, were not deep mines, as at the present day. The greater part of the tin produced in Danmonimn, before we have heard from those whose veracity we are un-willing to question, 5s by igneous ap-pearances, or fiery coruscations. The Tinners generally compare these efflu-via to blazing stars, or other whimsical likenesses, as their fears or hopes sug-gest; and search, with uncommon ea-gerness, the ground which these jack o'lanthorns have appeared over and pointed out. We have heard hut little of these phenomena for many years:

whether it be, that the present age is less credulous than the foregoing; or that the ground being more perforated by innu-merable new pits funk every year, some of which by the Stannary laws are pro-hibited from being filled up, has given these vapours a more gradual vent; it is not necessary to enquire, as the fact it-self is not generally believed. The art of Mining, however does not wait for these favourable incidents, but directly goes upon the search and discovery of such Mineral Veins, Ores, Stones, &c. as may be worth the working for Metal. The principal investigation and discov-ery of Mines, depends upon a particular sagacity, or acquired habit of judging from particular signs, that metaHick matters are contained in certain parts of the earth, not far below its surface. But, as ignorance and credulity are the por-tions of the illiterate, we have people constantly in search for Tin, where our dreaming geniuses direct them to follow after the images of wild fancy; conse-quently, we have a *Hucl-drcam* in every Mining parish, which raises and disap-points by turns the sanguine hopes of the credulous adventurers.—Mines are also discovered. by the harsh disagree-able taste of the waters which issue from them, especially those os Copper: but this seems to be, only when the Ore is above the level at which the water breaks out; for, otherwise, it is unlikely that the water should participate of much impression or quality from the Ore that is underneath it, or untouched by it. A better expedient to find whether the water is impregnated with Copper, is to immerge a piece of bright Iron in it, for two or three days; in which time, the Iron will look of a Copper colour, pro-vided the water is of a cupreous qual-ity, or at least contains a certain (hare of vitriolick acid: further, if some Aqua Fortis be affuscd to aJittle of this water, in a clear phial, it will presently exhibit a bluish green colour, either fainter or fuller according as it is impregnated with the acid of vitriol. A candle or piece of tallow put into the fame water for a few days, may be taken out tinged of a green colour.—Hooson fays, that " the first inventor of the Virgula Divina-

toria, was hanged in Germany as a cheat and impostor:" on the other hand, Dr. Diederick Wessel Linden fays, in an-swer to him, that " Dr. Stahl, when he was president of a chemical society in his country, published a reward of twen-ty-five ducates for any one that could prove who was the inventor of the Vir-gula Divinatoria." It is impossible to as-certain the date or personality of this discovery, which appears to me of very little consequence to posterity: but per-haps we may not be far off from the truth, if we incline to the opinion of Ge-orgius Agricola, in his excellent latin treatise *De Re Metallica,* that " the ap-plication of the inchanted or divining rod to metallick matters, took its rife from magicians, and the impure foun-tains of inchantment." Now the ancients not only endeavoured to procure the necessaries of life by a divining or in-chanted rod, but also to change the forms of things by the fame instrument: for the magicians of Egypt, as we learn from the Hebrew writings, changed their rods into serpents*;* and, in Homer, Minerva turned Ulysses when old into the likeness of a young man, and again to his former appearance: Circe also changed the companions of Ulysses into beasts, and again restored them to the human shape; and Mercury, wi' h his rod called Caduceus, gave sleep to the wakeful, and awakened those that were asleep. *And* hence, in all probability, arose the application of the forked rod to the discovery of hidden treasure." p. 111 to i 4.

" Another way of discovering Lodes is by finking little pits through the loose ground, down to the fast or solid coun-try, from six to twelve feet deep, and driving from one to another across the direction of the Vein; so that they must necessarily meet with every Vein lying within the extent of these pits; for most of them come up as high as the superfi-cies of the firm rock, and sometimes a small matter above it. *1* his way of seek-ing, the Tinners call *Ctftethmg,* from *Cabas Slean;* that is, fallen or dropt tin. —Another and very ancient method of discovering Tin Lodes, is by what we call *Sbcdelng;* that is, tracing them home by loose stones, fragm ents, or Shodes (Irom the Teutonick *Sbutten* to pour forth) which have been separated, and carried off, perhaps, to a considerable distance from the Vein, and are found by chance in running waters, on the superficies of the ground, or a little under. When the Tinners meet with a loose single stone of Tin Ore, either' in a valley, or in plowing, or hedging, though at a-hundred fathoms distance from the Vein it came from; those who are accustomed to this work, will not fail to find it out. They consider, that a metallick stone must have originally appertained to some Vein, from which it was severed and cast at a distance by some violent means. The deluge, they suppose, moved most of the loose earthy coat of the globe; and, in many places, washed it off from the upper, towards the lower grounds, with such a force, that most of the backs of Lodes or Veins which protruded themselves above the fast, were hurried downwards with the common mass: whence the skill in this part of their business, lies much in directing their measures according to the situation of the surface—Upon the top of most Tin Lodes, in the shelf or stratum under the loose mould and rubbish of the earth, is that mineralized substance, which is called the *Broyle* or *Bryls* of the Lode. Though it is a part of the Lode, yet it is different

O in before the time of the Romans, was, probably, from *Shade* and *Stream.* " Tin (fays *Dr.* Borlase) is found disseminated on the sides of hills, in single stones, which we call *Shodes,* in situation and appearance from all other parts of it; forasmuch as It is not confined between two walls, the stratum so near the surface being of a more lax tender texture, than in the solid rock a fathom or two under it. The *Bryle,* therefore, is very loose, and in some places scarcely metallick, for want of depth, and of those lateral chinks and cracks, which feed and nourish the Lode, at deeper levels, with Mineral principles educed from the strata of the earth.—Such is the *Bryle* of a Lode i consequently, when the waters of the deluge retired into their reservoir, great part of the

Bryles of Lodes were carried off by the force of the waters to various distances, according to the gravity of Shode Stones, and the declination of the plane upon which they were dispersed. Tinners who describe this distribution of Shode, to make it more easily understood, compare it to a bucket of water discharged upon the declivity of a hill; near the bucket, it will take up but a small space; but as it descends, will spread wider, in the manner of a truncated cone. Hence it is manifest to reason and experience, that the more distant Shodes are from the *Bryle* of the Lode, the more diverged they are, and fewer in number; and, by parity of reasoning, they are more in quantity near to the *Bryle,* and are co-lectively in less space. Nevertheless, in some certain situations, they are in greater quantities in vallies, than on the tops or fides of hills; but such are smaller, and more easily carried down by water, and formed into strata, which furnishes our stream works. In level ground, they are found scarcely removed from the *Bryle;* but on a declivity, they are always found dispersed on the sides of the hill, at a greater or less distance, in proportion to the length or declivity thereof, and their own specific weight: consequently, the heaviest stones are nearest to the Lode, and the lighter are protruded to a greater distance (even to five miles distance, as it is said in *Phitofop. TranJaSions* No. 69) which are also nearer to the soil, by means of their levity and size; while the more gross and weighty lie deeper interred as they are nearer the Lode. It is almost needless to observe, that as the texture, gravity, and black or brown colours of Tin Shodes, are different from all others; so they are thereby known and distinguished, as well as by the smoothness of them a gr eat distance from the Lode, and the acuteness of their angles when near to it; which entirely depends upon the trituration they have undergone, rolling over rough surfaces, by the force of water, and the attrition of other bodies passing over them.—Henckell and Rosier fay, " That Mundick Shode is very common; and that Wolfram, Granate, and Iron Corns,

nay Quicksilver, are found in Shode and Stream." " All of which," Henckell further fays, " were washed and torn away from their Veins, by the violence of the Noachian deluge."—Copper and Lead Shodes are very seldom met with;.yet such there are. Their *Bryles* being chiefly composed os tender unmetallick *Goffhn,* are not so well disposed for bearing that force and attrition, as the more stony matter of Tin Lodes are; and the former generally is not mineralized into Copper Ore at the *Bryle* It is a mistake in those who deny the existence of any other Shode but Tin: So far from it, every hard stratum of the earth which is uppermost, will shew us numbers of their Shodes dispersed from them at a distance, and reclined upon strata of quite different natures, as hills and vallies are situated to help forward or retain those rocky fragments. I think our distinct loose Moorstone, or Granite rocks, upon the fides, and at the bottoms of our mountains, are the Shodes of their strata underneath; and many large Shodes of Irestone are to be seen, though in less plenty, dispersed upon *Kil/as* strata at a distance from their pat ent rock: all of which are inoontestible witnesses of those violent conquassations and convulsions of our country, at the time of the flood.—It is much to be lamented, that the science of Shoding is greatly lost in the present age. Among all our Miners, we have not fifty, who scientifically or experimentally understand any thing of the matter; and those that are intelligent therein, are become old and feeble; whereby it is much to be seared, that this useful, and I think improve-.ble science, is in danger of being practically lost, —Almost every Lode has a peculiar coloured earth or *grewt* (grit) about it; which is also sometimes found with the Shode, and that in greater quantity, the nearer the Shode lies to the Lode; beyond which that peculiar *greiut* is seldom found with the Shode. A valley may happen to lie at the feet of three several hills, and then they may find several *deads greivt* or earth moved by the waters of the deluge, but not contiguous to the Lode, with as many different Shodes in the middle of each.

This is also termed the *Run* of the country; and here the knowledge of the cast of the country, or each hill in respect of its *greivt,* will be very necessary, for the surer tracing them one after the other as they lie in order.—Likewise, when the Miners find a good Stone of Ore or Shode in the side or bottom of a hill, they first of all observe the situation of the neighbouring ground, and consider whence the deluge could most probably roll that Stone down from the hill; and at the same time they form a supposition, on what point of the compass the Lode takes its course: for if the Shode be Tin, or Copper Ore, or promising for either, tlrey conclude that the Lode runs nearly east and west; but if it is a Shode of Lead Ore, they have equal reason to conclude that the vein goes north and south. After finding the first Stone or Shode, they sink little pits as low as the fast rubble (which is the rubble or clay never moved since the flood) to find more such Stones; and if they meet with them, they go further up the hill in the fame line, or a little obliquely perhaps, and sink more pits still, while they find Shode Stones in them, but they seldom sink those pits deeper than *Shades,* sometimes a furlong pr more distant from their lodes: And, sometimes, these loose, stones are found together in great numbers, making one continued course from one to tea the rubble upon the Shelf, except they are near the Lode. Jf the Shode is found in the vegetable soil, the Lode is not hand; but if it lies deep, massy, and angular, it is a certain sign that the Lods is not far off, and that it is to be found opposite to the base or heaviest part of the Stones. The account which the learned Alvaro Alonzo Barba gives of discovering Silver Mines, by what I take to be Shoding, is very much like mine, and is as follows, p. 79. " The Veins of Metal are sometimes found by great Stones above ground; and if the Veins be covered, they hunt them out after this manner, viz. taking in their hands a fort of mattock (a pick) which hath a steel point at one end to dig with, and a blunt head at the other to break irones with, they go to the hollows of the mountains, where the downfall of

rain descends, or to some other part of the skirts of the mountains, and there observe what Stones they meet withal, and break In pieces those that seem to have any metal in them; whereof they find many times both middling sort of Stones, and small ones also of Metal. Then they consider the situation of that place, and whence these Stones can tumble, which of necessity must be from higher ground, and follow the tract of these Stones up the hill, as long as they can find any of them." But to return—As they advance thus nearer the Lode with their pits, they find their Shode more plentiful and deeper in the ground; but if they chance to go further from the Lode, 0. pass the yonder fide of it, there is a greater scarcity of the Shode, or perhaps none at all: in which cafe, they return to their last pit which produced Shode most plentifully, and work the intermediate ground, with more care and circumspection, by drifts from one pit to the next, until they cut the Lode. Sometimes they find two different Shodes in the fame pit at different depths; then they are sure, that there is another Lode further on; and in training up to the second, they may meet with the Shode of a third. However, when they are just come to the Vein they set out for, they find art uncommon quantity of Shode Stones answering to the description before given, and then they say, that they have the *Bryle* of the Lode; upon which they dig down into the solid hard rock, which Was never moved or loosened, until they open the Lode, and find its breadth by the walls in which it is enclosed Some Lodes, however, are so disposed, that they yield no Shode at all, nor are they to be discovered in a good depth; which may happen to be the case for several reasons. The situation of some places might have preserved their Veins from having their surfaces torn up and dispersed by the flood 5 or else being so much torn and disturbed, their loose *Bryle* might have been totally carried off to a vast diltance, towards which its poverty for Metal and consequential levity might contribute; in the place of which, a sediment or earthy part might

have settled, and buried the Lodes so deep, that they are not discoverable by shoding. Again, the backs of some Veins arc depressed, and so deep under the firm solid rock which lies over them, that they do make a rife or back immediately up to the loose stone or earth; that is to fay, some Lodes make no back at all, and therefore produce no Shode, so that it is impossible to discover them, except by some favourable accident, of which I have known several instances.—These different dispositions of the strata I have taken notice of, sometimes deceive the miners in shoding for Veins; for when they suppose that there is but one bed or layer of stones or earth over the firm ground, and there happens to be a double stratum of rock and rubble between, which is far from being uncommon, perhaps they dig no deeper than the first shelf; in other words, they dig no deeper than till they think they are come down almost to the fast or firm ground, where they expect to find cither the Shode or the *Bryle* of the Lode; but aa they are covered by the other shelf or stratum, which the Miners are not apprized of, they have their labour for their pairs, in sec-king in such uncertain ground, which perhaps contains a double or treble lhelf.—The Miners are of opinion, that the waters by their great emotion, did not only remove, and confuse the surface of the earth, but also broke the looser parts of Veias from off their superficies or backs; and thereby disordered and removed the face of the earth as deep as the fast and firm rock or stratum, as I have said before: and indeed our apprehension of the matter very much favours this supposition: whence, undoubtedly, those Shodes or fragments of Veins are the vestiges or remains of the deluge. Hence it is, that part of the Shode has been rolled down the declivities of hills from the Mines; moreover, that Shode which is found a great way distant from the Mines, is much more worn and smoother than that which is nearer to it, as it happens to stones on the sea shore, or on the fides of rapid river;, which are fretted and worn smooth by the agitation of the waters, and the friction of other bodies. If any person will but consider the sea cliffs, he may observe, in several places, that the upper coat or covering of the earth, has been greatly moved and agitated; and that the loose stones did preponderate and subside on the firm rocks, pursuant to their specifick gravities; next those, the rubble resided, and over all the pure light earth rested. Yet this order is net absolutely perfect and without exception; for loose stones are often found in the light earth, and on its superficies; which by the impetuosity of the waters, and situation of particular places, were molested in subsiding. For we are not to suppose our globe to resemble a trough, er the like excavated figure, wherein the variously mixed earths are to be regularly disposed, as in the operation of *huddling* or washing of Ores; butto be of a spherical arched figure, where the waters, as on a hanging bottom, powerfully rend, and pull it asunder: and this force of the waters

Oz we ten feet deep, which we call a *Stream*. And, when there is a good quantity of tin in it, the tinners call it, in the Cornish tongue, *Beubeyl,* or a *Living Stream*—that is, a course of stones impregnated with tin. In like manner, when the stone has a small appearance of tin, they say it is *just alive*; when no metal, it is said to be *dead*; and the rubble which contains no metal, is called *Deads.* These streams are of different breadths, seldom less than a fathom, oftentimes scattered, though in different quantities, ewer the whole width of the moor, bottom, or valley, in which they are found: And when several such streams meet they oftentimes make a very rich floor of tin, one stream proving as it were a magnet to the metal of the other."(«) Dr. Pryce explains *Shading,* to be " the method of finding veins of tin by digging small pits in order to trace out the lodes of tin, by the scattering loose Hones and fragments that were dispersed from them by the retiring waters of the deluge: The loose stones thus dispersed, are called *Shade-Hones. "*(Z) " If the *Shade* (says *Dr.* Borla.e) is found in the vegetable foil, it gives no evidence of any lode's being

nigh; but if in the *fast* (that is, the rubble or clay never moved since the flood) it is taken as a never failing proof that it came from a lode farther up in the hill. As soon as the mode is found impregnated with tin, to find the lode it came from, is the next care. The process consists in digging pits at a proper distance and depth, and in a proper direction, and judiciously regulating their advances to the lode, according as the properties of the modes direct."(0 With respect to the operation of *Streaming,* Dr. Pryee informs us, that the tinner, having fixed on a favourable situation, and settled the preliminaries, " sinks a *batch* or (haft, hree, five, or seven fathoms deep, to the rocky shelf or clay; on both of which in the same valley, the Tin is frequently stratified, without any difference in its being more abundant *in* one than the other. It is found in different places, at different depths, and sometimes stratified between what is called a first, second, or third shelf. The stratum of Stream Tin'may be from one to ten feet thickness or more; in we may suppose to be greatest at the beginning and end of the deluge So likewise, In some places, the loose earth and stone, which cover the firm rocks, lie in strata; for immediately on the rock, there may be, for instance, a layer of sand or clay, and ovef that, a bed of large stones, and so alternately stratum fupor stratum, for some depth. Now these variations might very well happen on the decrease of the deluge: for when the flood was high and more at rest, the slimy light earth was deposited downwards; but when the waters came lower, and bent their course to the beach, then it came to pass that there was a strong current from off the land to the sea, which rolled down the loose stones upon the mud or sediment that fell and setded beforehand; so this current might have been interrupted again by the situation of the place and interposition of high ground, till the water had let fall another sediment, and afterwards found or perhaps broke another passage for itself through the land. This might fcave happened several times in the deluge, till at last the remaining water partly evaporated and partly funk in-

to the ground, leaving the deepest earth or sediment where it continued longest; as it happens frequently in floods or overflowings of water, where we may observe the situation of high and low grounds do not a little contribute to the fame kind of effects that are here spoken of.—Another way of discovering Lodes, is by working drifts across the country as we call it, that is from north and south, and vice versa. I tried the experiment in an adventure under my'management, where I drove all open *at grafs* about two feet in the slielf, very much like a level to convyy water upon a mill wheel; by so doing I was sure of cutting all Lodes in my way, and did accordingly discover five courses, one of which has produced above one hundred and eighty tons of Copper Ore, but the others were never wrought upon. This method of discovering Lodes, is equally cheap and certain; for a hundred fathoms in a shallow surface may be driven at fifty shillings expence.— In feasible (tender standing) ground, a very effectual proving, and consequential way is, by driving an adit from the lowest ground, either north or south; whereby there is-a certainty to cut all Lodes at twenty, thirty, or forty fathoms deep, if the level admits thereof. Such depths are proving the Lodes discovered by them, and the adit will serve to drain all parts of the strata above it; and likewise be a discharge, for all water drawn from the Mine into it; so that it is effectual, for discovery, proving for trial, and consequential to the future working of a Mine. But in Granite, Elvan, and Irestone strata, this cannot be complied with, neither is it adviseable but under certain circumstances, where the ground is to be wrought for eighteen shillings per fathom, unless a *Crcfi-Gojsjn* lies ready at hand, when the method in use is to drive partly on one fide of the *Gossan,* breaking down the adjunct wall of it, whereby they drive the adit cheaply, expeditiously, and effectually for discovery. In driving adits or levels across, north or south, to unwater Mines already found, there are many fresh Veins discovered, which frequently prove better than those they were driving to. Witness the Pool adit in Illugan, where the late John Pendarvis Basset, Esq. cleared above one hundred and thirty thousand pounds." p. 124 to 132. *(a)* Natural Hist. p. 161, 162. *(6)* Pryce's Mineralog. p. 327. *(e)* Nat. Hist, p, 166. in breadth, from one fathom to almost the width of the valley; and in size, from a wallnut to the finest sand, the latter making the principal part ot' the Stream, which is intermixed with stones, gravel, and clay, as it was torn from the adjacent hills. When he finks,down to the Tin stratum, he takes a (hovel full of it, and washes off all the waste j and from the Tin which is left behind upon the shovel, he judges whether that ground is worth the working or not. If it is proving work, he then goes down to the lowest or deepest part of the valley, and digs an open trench, like the tail or low *Jlo-van* of an adit, which he calls a Level, taking the utmost care to lose no levels in bringing it home to the Stream. This level serves to drain and carry off all water and waste from the workings, in proportion as he hath a weak or powerful current of water to run through it. Some places are very poor and not worth the'expence for working; others again are very rich, and thence called *Beuheyle* or Living Stream, as is most commonly the cafe if it is of *a. Grouan* nature, which being more lax and sandy, is more easily sep. rated from its native place or Lode, and therefore more abundant and rich in quality according to the known excellence of *Grouan* Tin. In the latter cafe, the Streamer carries off what he calls the *O verburden,* the loose earth, rubble, or stone, which covers the Stream, io far and so large, as he can manage with conveniency to his employment. If in the progress of his working he, is hindred, he *teems* or Jades it out, with a scoop, or discharges it by a hand pump: but if those simple methods are insufficient, he erects a *rag and chain pump* ; or if a rivulet of water is to be rented cheaply at *grafs,* he erects a water wheel with ballance *kbs,* and thereby keeps his workings clear from superfluous water, by discharging it into his level: mean while his men are digging up the Stream

Tin, and washing it at the same time, by casting every (hovel full of it, as it riles, into a *tye,* which *it* an inclined plane of boards for the water to run off, about four feet wide, four high, and nine feet long, in which, with (hovels, they turn it over and over again under a cascade of water that washes through it, and separates the waste from the Tin, till it becomes one half Tin. Though there is little dexterity in this manœuvre, yet care is requisite to throw off the *Stent* or rubble from the *tye* to itself, whilst another picks out the stones of Tin from the *Garde* or smaller *pryany* part of it. During this operation, the best of the Tin, by its superior gravity, collects in the head of the *tye* directly under the cascade; and by degrees becomes more full of waste, as it descends from that place to the end or tail of the *tye,* where it is not worth the laving. If there is a copious stream of water near at hand, they cast this refuse into it, by which it is carried so far as to. make its exit inlo the sea; for which practice they certainly deserve our severest censure; at least, if the choaking of harbours and rivers, and the destruction of thousands of acres of improveable meadow land, are not more than an equivalent for the casual and temporary profits arising from Stream Tin."(«) It was nearly in this manner that the Danmonians procured their tin: And they were, doubtless, well acquainted with tin in its richest mineral state; since Shode and Stream Tin must have been found plentifully disseminated upon the surface of the vallies, and the sides of the hills and mountains. Those fragments and nodules, by their color, shape, and gravity, must have attracted the notice of the first natives. The Aborigines could not observe the singular shape and weight of Shode and Stream Tin, without considering the contents as a mineral, which by its superior gravity would afford some metallic substance; especially when by a comparison with the mineral ores of other metals, known long before the flood, they must have judged its consistence to be metalline. There are some who would confine our original Tm-works to the Casliterides, as including only the

iflands of Scilly. But, to wave all other considerations, the Shode and Stream Tin of the Scilly Ides, though abundant, was not sufficient for the wants of this adventurous and mercantile people.(A) Besides, we have the clearest vestiges *(a) Mineral. Comiib.* p. 132 to 134. (4) The vestigia of any Tin Lodes, Mines, or workings, In the Islands of. Scilly, are insufficient to convince us, that they only gave this beautiful Metal to the world: the remains of any such workings are scarcely discernible; ior there is but one place, that exhibits even an imperfect appearance of a Mine: And so necessity an appendage to a Mine as an adit to unwater the woi kings, is not to be seen in all the islands. If, in those days, the Metal was produced from stream or (node stones only, we must undoubtedly have discovered, in latter timesjvthose Lodes ot veins from whence they were dismembered by the deluge. They must have been wrought for Tin since the earlier ages; and some remains of such Lodes would now be visible on the sea coasts or cliffs, if many such had ever been: we are, therefore, strongly induced to believe, that the Mineral Ore of Tin was anciently procured vestiges of ancient Tin-mines in various parts of Danmonium. To fay nothing of Cornwall, there are numberless stream-works on Dartmoor, and in its vicinities, which have lain forsaken for ages. In the parishes of Manaton, Kingsteignton, and Teigngrace, are many old Tin-works of this kind, which the inhabitants attribute to that period, when wolves and winged serpents were no strangers to the hills or the vallies.(«) The BoveyHeathfield hath been worked in the fame manner: And, indeed, all the vallies from the Heathfield to Dartmoor, bear the traces of stioding and streaming, which, I doubt not, was either British or Phenician.(A) Lead was, also, familiar to the western Britons. " For lead, the mines of the Scilly isles (fays Mr. Whitaker) were worked by the Aborigines, and those of the Peak by the Belgæ."(s) In the Scilly Isles, the veins of lead lay 16 immediately below the surface of the ground, and branched out in so great an abundance, that the search for this metal was attended with little trouble or expence. Here again, there seems to be no warrant for the supposition, that the working of lead was circumscribed by the Scilly Isles. Mr. Whitaker fays, that " it was late before any mines of Iron were opened in this island. They appear to have been begun only a few years before the descent of Cæsar, and even then were earned on not by the Britons, but the Belgæ."(/) As Mr. Whitaker is of opinion, that the *Danmonians* were a tribe of the *Belga-*, he doubt less means to include the former under this general appellation. That the Danmonians had /r«-works, is plain from Cæsar, who mentions the *ex-igua copies' (e)* of our iron in the maritime parts. The Iron-pits on Blackdown, were, I conceive, originally Britisli; and were afterwards worked by the Romans. That gold and silver (particularly the former) were discovered in Danmonium, before the arrival os Caisar, is plain, I think, from f/JStrabo and Tacitus.*(g)* From the frequent discoveries of gold in particular, among the few stream-works of the present day, we should conclude, that this metal must have been inevitably found by the Danmonians, who had no other works than those of stream or shode, and who in the prosecution of their labors, had, probably, broken up half the surface of Danmonium, before the Roman Period. " It is suspected (lays Borlale) that there is gold, more or less, in all the stream-tin in Cornwall. What has been found, is always intermixed with grains of tin-ore, which, by their roundness and smoothness, lhew that they have been warned down from the neighbouring hills. That gold lies, sometimes, so intermixed with tin, was not unknown to the ancients." (i)Pliny gives us an accurate description of these metals found together, in the fame manner as they are now discovered in our stream-works— the tin in *calculi* (that is, smooth pebbly ore) of the same gravity as the ore of gold, and separated by scarfing. " *Separantur canijlris,* savs he (not *caminis,* as in some editions) that is, by baskets of the fame nature and use as our scarces.

In what manner the Danmonians prepared these metals for use, Polybius, perhaps, would have informed, us, had not that valuable work which Strabo mentions, been lost in the wreck of time. The Aborigines, probably, loon learnt the method of extracting metal procured within the four western hundreds of Cornwall, and there smelted into white Tin, by charcoal fires, as the want of a proper bitumen in those days, and the entire demolition of all the woods near the Tin Mines, very plainly evince. Besides, unless we make great allowances indeed for encroachments of the ocean since those early ages, the islands of Scilly are merely in their present state a cluster of barren rocks, the principal of tham measuring but three miles long and two wide. Whence should all this Tin arise? Likewise the state os population then could not admit of emigrations from the insular continent for digging, raising, and smelting a Metal, which tlie mother island produced in such vast profusion from her own bowels." *Pryee't Miner. Cm nub.* Introd. p. iv.

(a) The ancient Tin-works of Manaton, it seems, are at this day, haunted by the winged serpent! (A) A Phenician coin was found at Teignmouth, a fe.v years since. (c) Cæsar, p. 88, and Strabo, p. 265. *d)* Cæsar, p. 88. te M When Cæsar, speaking of Britain, says, ' *najctlur ibi plumbum album in mediterraneit regioniiu:, in maritimis ferrum; fed ejus exigua est copia* he elucidates our western history. To Cæsar it appeared that the tin came from the inner country. The original road by which this tin was conveyed, mould be an object of your investigation; and, probably, you will find it carried over fords and forming towns, in its progress between Dartmoor and where Sir R. Worsley now traces it to havt entered the Isle of Wight. On these fords too, you will probably find a Roman settlement, and not impossibly account for *Crockern-Torr, Chagfcrrl,* &c. having been formerly places of eminence. The roads on each fide of Dartmoor, were, probably, used for similar conveyances and centered at the first passage over the Exe, probably through

Exeter." *Ctl. Simcoe* to the author. *(f)* Lib. iv. *(g) Vit. jfgrif.* Cap. xii,—*Fert Britannia aurum et argentum, prtt'uan i-itleriee.* (.4) Lib. xxxv. Cap. xvi. metal from mineral substances: And it was easy to purify tin from its native dross. The richness of the metal, and its ready fluxility in the fire, must have confirmed their conjectures; whilst its beautiful color and innocent properties, rendered it, perhaps, as valuable in their estimation as silver and gold, until, by great abundance, which renders all things cheap, it funk in the Icale ot comparative excellence. Polybius is said to have described the ancient method of preparing tin for the furnace. And as Polybius was a very accurate writer, it is much to be regretted, that his account of the process hath not reached our times: All we can do, is to acquiesce in a few vague notices of Diodorus Siculus. The tinners, as (a)Diodorus intimates, manufacture their tin by working the grounds which produce it, with great art. For though the land is rocky, it hath soft veins of earth running through it, in which the tinners find the treasure, *extracl, melt,* and *purify* it; then shaping it by moulds into a kind of *cubical figure.* With respect to other ores, I have nothing to add; as nothing remains on record. I might conjecture, that as the Romans had iron forges in Danmonium, the Britons might have been furnished with the lame apparatus. And I might proceed in this manner, in regard to other metals. Here, however, I (hall stop. I have been, sometimes, hypothetical: And, to enliven a barren sub'ect, it was almost necelary to be so. But to Indulge often in theory, is to throw a romantic color over the truth of history. Let me, therefore, close the present view, whilst the spirit of conjecture slumbers. SECTION VII. *VIEW of the MANUFACTURES of DANMONIUM, in the BRITISH PERIOD.*

I. *Necessary and Secondary Arts— Among the necessary Arts, Cloathing— The Cloth-Manufacture and the Art of Dyeing Cloth, ino-zvn to the Aborigines.—*II. *Among the secondary Arts, the Danmonians skilled in the ivoriing of Wood—and in the ivorking of Metals—*

Tin, Lead, Brass, Iron, 'variously man-ufatlured—the War-Chariot, an ad-mirable Specimen of British Ingenu-ity—Gold and Silver Smiths—Pot-tery—Glass.—III. *Conclusion.* THE Manufactures of Devon may properly be classed under two heads—the *neces-sary* and *secondary* arts.

Among the *necessary* arts, that of Cloathing first presents itself to notice. The more prevailing opinion, is, that the first garments of the Britons were made of fleins; and that the art of dressing wool, of spinning it into yarn, and of weaving it into cloth, was communicat-ed to the Britons by the Belgic colonies. Accordingly, we are told, that our Bel-gic colonists manufactured several kinds of woollen-cloth—that one of these kinds consisted of a coarse sort of wool, woven very thick; and that of this, the Britons made their mantles or plaids which they used in winter. Another kind of cloth attributed to the Belgic Britons, consisted of fine wool dyed several dif-ferent colors. This being spun into yarn, was woven chequerwise; which made it fall into small squares, some of one col-or, and some of another. The art of man-ufacturing cloths from the filaments of flax and hemp, is ascribed, also, to the Belgic colonies. That the Belgæ manu-factured linen, and wore linen garments, is unquestionably true. And the Belgæ have all the credit for introducing into the island, the art of dyeing cloth; which, we lee, was not unknown to the Britons.

How these opinions can any way be reconciled with the history of the Druids, it is difficult to fay. The Druids are described, as wearing long white garments: And the inhabitants of Devon and Cornwall, and of the Scilly Isles, are said to have been cloathed in black—*Ia.i'kxvxxiixi* is Strabo's expres-sion. Ancient authors, indeed, repj-esent the Britons as variously habited: And this diversity was unavoidable. The aboriginal Danmonii would naturally wear one kind of habit; and the Belgic colonies, another. And from the distinc-tions of station, would ari e other vari-eties of dress. The Druids were arrayed in long white garments, that swept the

ground; whilst the nobles of Danmoni-um wore, perhaps, the loose black robe, and the common people the plaid or (kins of beasts. That the inhabitants of Danmonium, were unacquainted with the cloth-manufacture till the (#) Book IV. p. 301. Edit. Hanover, 1664. the arrival of the Belgic colonies, is an opinion to which I can never assent. Even if we wave the idea of an eastern colonization, our connexion with the Phenicians and the Greeks, would renier such ignorance improbable. The writers who entertain this notion of the western Britons in general, aftirm, that " if the Phenicians or Greeks imparted any knowledge of these arts to the Britons, *it ivas certainly fiery imperfect,* and com-municated only to a few of the inhab-itants of the Scilly Islands, with whom they chiefly traded."*(a)* Here is all the hesitation that marks an extorted truth: Nor is the passage free from abliirdity. That the knowledge of the cloth-man-ufacture was communicated by the Phenicians to the western Britons, is al-lowed from the pressing necessity of the cafe. Yet, as this concession plainly contradicts the notion of the Belgæ long after introducing the cloth-manufacture into the island, it is instantly qualified by terms that feem almost to annihilate it: It is fettered with unauthorized re-strictions. On what grounds do we pre-sume, that the knowledge which the Phenicians imparted, was *certainly uery imperfetl,* or that it was communicated to a few inhabitants of the Scilly Ides only, with whom they *chiefly* traded? The *chief* trade of trie Phenicians was not with the inhabitants of the Scilly Isles: Their commerce was with Devon-shire and Cornwall and the Scilly Isles. Why, then, ssiould we confine this com-munication within the narrow bound-aries of the latter? Who stiall prove, that it was not coextensive with the Pheni-ciar trade? *(b)*

In the mean time, I am disposed to think, that those British manufactures were even anterior to the Phenicians. The plaided drapery, I conceive, was an original British manufacture, intro-duced by our first colonists. The (c)Highlanders, who emigrated from the

east, manufactured (/)plaids. Of the cloth which was composed of hemp and of flax, the manufacture was_eastern, from the very earliest antiquity. The *Kannaib* of the Irilh, and the *Kanab* of the Armoricans, faintly echoed in the English *hems,* was called *Cannabis* by the Romans. And it is likely that *Kan-naib* was the original word, and that *hemp* was introduced into Britain by our first eastern colonists, and derived from thole Aborigines to the Romans.—That flax was cultivated in the land of Ægypt, the book of Exodus iuforms us: It was very common in Palestine and other eastern countries. And the robes cf the Druids are said to have been linen. ()That linen, indeed, was very generally used by the western Britons, we ssiould infer " from the spear-heads, axes for war, and swords of copper, that have been found in Danmonium, wrapt up in linen coverings."*(f)* That the art of dye-ing cloth was familiar to the ancient Bri-tons, before the Belgæ, we have every reason to infer, from the known fact of their painting and staining their fkin.(,g-) And with the, fame color which they used in staining their (kin, the Danmo-nians, probably, dyed their garments. The art of dyeing cloth was early in use among the people os the east. " Is-rael made Joseph a coat of many colors. " Among the Britons, the *glafirum* or vvoad was a favorite color: And the fa-mous *purpura* was surely not unknown to the nobles of Danmonium. Very pos-sibly, the purple dye of the Tyrians gained its high reputation, among the ancients, from the use of our tin in the composition of the dye-stuff; as the tin trade was solely in their own manage-ment. That its use as one of the »«z-col-oring retentive ingredients, was known to the Phenicians, will appear probable, when we consider the unfadingness of their purple; which was a leading char-acter (j) See Henry's History of Great Britain, vol. I, p. 326.

/) Sammes thinks, that " the black gar-ments (/jm""') of tne western Britons, were Phenirian. The habits of these western Britons were remarkable for their *length* and *colour* ; the former cf whicb, together with the staff they used to carry, argues that some eastern colonies, and especially the Phenicians, traded with them". Britan. Antiqu. p. 118. (c) See Offian, vol. 1, p. 140 — 156. d) To this day, the striped woollen mantles of the Highlanders, are denominated *Breacan:* And the coarse rough cloth of the Welch, was termed *Brychan.* In this county, a rent in a garment is called a *briac:* And, whatever they *tear,* the Devonshire people say, they *break. (e)* The Scutiiae of Colchis (soys the scholiast i:pon Pindar) are a colony from Egypt: they are of a dark complexion, and they deal jn flax, of which they make linen after the manner of the Egyptfans. The Irish have been ever famous for the manufacture of linen and woollen cloths. Vallancey has proved the names of every implement used in the weaving of linen, to be oriental. *(f)* Borlase's Antiqu. p. 217. (g) Which may be reconciled with their wearing cloaths. In war, they threw off their garments, and painted their bodies, to render their aspect more terrible. The Highlanders fought almost naked within the present age. raster in that celebrated color produced by the shell-fish purpura. It is not likely, that the simple *blood* of a shell-fish, however beautiful at first, would have proved a *lasting dye.* The addition of some retentive ingredient, must have been necessary to secure its brightness and preserve its beauty. Tin, dissolved in *aqua sortis,* is, at present, a necessary article in the new scarlet dye. And our fine cloths owe the permanence of their delicate colors to the retentivenels given by the finest grain tin i So that the English superfine-broad-cloths, dyed in grain by the help of this ingredient, are become famous in all markets of the known world.

After Cloathing, there are arts of an inferior degree, which may be called the *secondary* arts. Of this kind, are the arts of working wood and metals. That the Britons were not uninstructed in the business of the turner and carpenter, is evident from the formation of their shields either in circles or lozenges, from the tapering of the masts of their spears and arrows, and from the rounding of the axles of their chariots. The

arts of working wood, were more obvious than thole of refining and working metals. With respect to the tin of Danmonium, I have already intimated in my notices of the mines, that this metal, being collected in the sand or glebe, was cleared from the earth with water, fused in the furnaces, and beaten into squares *(a)* Lead was another metal which the Danmonians used for different purposes, and which was one of the Phenician exports. And brass was worked into various shapes by theDanmonians. The first formation of brass was prior to the stood—though not previous to the knowledge of iron. Without brass or iron weapons, the first colonists could neither have built their houses nor cleared away the woods about their settlements. And, as the nations in the east appear to have worked mines of iron or copper, in the remotest periods of their history, so the Danmonii were particularly acquainted with both, *(b)* The Danmonians had, certainly, brass-founderies: And they had one brass foundery, at least, in the cantred of Isca, in order to supply the armoury of the principality. The armouries of the Britons were furnished with spears, daggers, swords, battle-axes, and bows, and with helmets and coats of mail, shields and chariots. In Ireland, and in the Highlands of Scotland, we find many of these weapons at the present day." Swords, composed of copper, speltæ, and iron, of the same sliape, and of the lame mixture as to the quantity and quality of each metal, have been found on the plains of Cannse and in Ireland. Concerning the origin and use of celts, which were of brass or copper, many have ignorantly conjectured. Celts have generally been supposed to be purely Roman.. They seldom, however, occur in Italy; and when they do, they are regarded as transalpine antiquities. For this and other reasons, Dr. Borlase is inclined to believe, that the celt is not to be ascribed to the Romans in general, but that it was originally of Britilh invention, and afterwards improved and used by the provincial Romans. " Celts, fays Dr. Borlase, are of different sizes. The larger and heavier seem to have

been the heads of spears—the middle sort were designed, perhaps, for javelins, and the lighter and smaller for the heads or arming of arrows. Some celts, found in a stone-quarry in Yorkshire, were enclosed in cales; and, doubtless, they were thus cautiously stieathed, to preserve the keenness of their edges." What Borlase here calls the brass cafes of the celts, were actually the moulds in which they were call. Moulds have been found much burnt by the constant casting of the hot metal. A great number of celts have been dug up in Ireland—a country never visited by the Romans. I stiould judge them, indeed, to have been the manufacture of the original Iristi, before the Romans existed as a nation. Mr. Whitaker has given us a particular description of these instruments :(c) And he has proved, beyond all contradiction, that the celt was the head of a light battle-axe. " And it was a British one," adds our excellent histo- rian It was an aboriginal instrument: The Asiatics of Danmonium, of Ireland, and of Scotland, all uied it. With relpect to Devonsliire and Cornwall, celts have been frequently found in these counties. A small brass celt() was discovered some years ago, at Place, in Chudleigh—It is now in the possession of John Hale, Esq. in Chudleigh. And another brass celt was found at the fame time and place, which had a hole in it, probably for a handle, and was given to a gentleman in Dorsetshire. A celt was, aiso, dug up at

Ingldon, (a) Pliny,!. 34, c. 16. Dioclorus, p. 347. (I) See Deuteronomy, c. 3 & 8. Cæsar, p. 88.

(c) Ste his Manchester, vol. 1, p. 17 to 22. *(d)* Near this celt was found, at the farm; time, a small brass oval ring, now in the possession of Mr. John Pike, of Chudleigh.

Vol.. I. P

Ingsdon, in the parish of Ilsington, a few years since: There was nothing remarkable in it. And Dean Milles has left us a draught of a brass celt, which was found in the parish of Puckfastleigh, " under a wall (fays he) lately pulled down. They suppose by the situation of the place, that the ground has not been broken there, for at least a century back: Formerly mines were worked there" The working of the mines, however (though the Dean seems to lay some stress on this circumstance) has no connexion with the use of the celt. In several parts of the north of Devon, also, celts nave been dug up: Mr. Badcoclc mentions one in particular, which was submitted to his inspection as a curiosity. (#)—Iron utensils and weapons, were coeval, at least, with those of brass. And, before the Roman arrival, the Britons are thought to have established founderies for making iron, and forges for manufacturing arms, tools, and utensils of all kinds. Near Beaford-moorhead, and several other places in this county, cinders have been dug up in considerable quantities, that seem to point out the iron-works either of the Britons or the Romans. At the place J have mentioned, the cinders lay between two and three feet deep. From the remains of old intrenchments here, I rather suspect that these cinders are to be classed among Roman relics.—Jn the war-chariot, both wood and metals appear to have been combined with wonderful art. Of the mechanical abilities of the Britons, this vehicle is a sufficient evidence. Its ingenious construction was admired by the Romans. On one of the British coins, we have an elegant picture of the war-chariot. (A) There we fee the charioteer mounted on his carriage before us, a quiver of arrows peeping over his left shoulder, and a spear protended from his left hand; his feet resting upon the pole or a footboard annexed to it, and his body leaning over the horses, in the act of accelerating their motion. And we have the description of a military chariot in Ossian, similar in one or two particulars, and more circumstantial. It is the chariot of a British monarch. " The car, the car(s) of war comes on like the flame of death! The rapid car of Cuthullin, the noble son of Semo! It bonds behind like a wave near a rock; like the fun-streaked mist of the heath. Its sides are embossed with stones, and sparkle like the sea round the boat of night. Of polished yew is its beam; its feat of the

smoothest bone. The sides are replenished with spears; the bottom is the footstool of heroes 1" That the Britons had neither discovered gold nor silver besore the Romans, hath been asserted; though the contrary is an absolute fact. To the Romans, gold and silver were the reward of victory—*pretium victoria,* fays Tacitus: And a great number of gold chains were taken from Caractacus, and triumphantly carried to Rome. Hence it appears, that the Britons were furnished with po small quantity of gold; and that they were able to refine and work this metal in the time of Caractacus. Yet it is presumed, from the silence of Cæsar, that at his arrival, the Britons were unacquainted with gold. But to the Britons of Danmonium, gold was, probably, familiar long before Cæsar. The golden hook of the Druids, with which they cut their mistetoe, proves that they had artificers who worked this precious metal.—Vessels for containing and preserving liquids, was a very early invention in all countries. And the Danmonians, it is said, were supplied with earthen vessels by the Phenicians. But, as clay is found in various parts of Danmonium, and the formation of it into vessels is so obvious and so simple an art, I have no doubt but pottery was known to the Danmonians before the existence of the Phenician trade. Earthen vessels have been often discovered in the British sepulchres, both in Devonshire and Cornwall—some unbaked, and others burnt in the kilns. (/) Clay is easily moulded into form, and naturally hardens in the fun or by fire: But the vitrification of sand by the force of sire, was a discovery hot so obvious: It was known, however, to the Phenician settlers, if not to the aboriginal Eiritons. Indeed, the first glass-houses that history mentions, were erected at Tyre. In

Danmonium, *(a)* " This celt was discovered (fays Mr. Badcock) in the military road, which, branching off from the castle of Termolus, runs towards Bamstaple, not by the present turnpike but in the bottom; and which, avoiding the hills, pursues its course in the tract of the ancient road, and joins the present

road near Landkey; I examined the celt, which is a perfect ant'que: And the girl who found it, pointed out the spot where it was discovered—immediately affer some labourers had been digging for gravel cn the right side of the road, to repair the road itself." *Badcock* in a letter to *Sir Get. Yorge, (b)* See Borlase's Coins, No. 22. (c) Ossian-vol. 1, p. 231, 232.

(d) It appears from the kiln-burnt pottery that has been discovered in the British sepulchres, and from the British word *odyn,* or w«i, that furnaces for baking were generally known among the Aborigines. (1) See P-oman-Briusti Period.

Danmonium, glass annulets and beads of glass have been often discovered. And, if such ornaments were the production of our glass-makers, they, doubtless, applied their art to domestic uses. Dr. btukeley giving ah account of *a.glass urn* discovered in die ille of Ely in the year 17 57, observes, that *the Britons "Mere famous for glass-manuja£lorj,* which he looks upon as a strong presumptive proof that Britain wa» originally peopled from Tyre, *a)* On the whole, whether we adopt the Armenian, the Tynan, or the Gallic system of colonization, we may be assured, that the Britons in general, and the Danmonians in particiilir, were more civilized and ingenious than-.they are commonly considered. This character appears 011 every view of them: Nor is it obscurely marked in those few simple notices of the mechanical arts in Danmomtfm.

SECTION VIIL *VIEW of the COMMERCE of DANMOMUM, in the BRITISH PERIOD,*

L *Internal Commerce—Trade with the Phenicians—When first established—Where—Phenician Exports—Imports—Trade with the Greets—Greek Exports—Imports—Trade with the Romans—Greeks oj Marseilles—Passage from Diodorus Siculus discussed—Various Emporia on the coasts oj Danmonium—New channels qj Commerce opened in Gaul—TheBrittJh Irade no longer confined to Danmonium.—II. Land-carriages of the Danmonians—Ships—Ihe Danmonians not ignorant either of Ship-building or of Navigation.*

—III. *The Trade of Danmonium not carried on by way of Barter, according to the common opinion.—The Danmonians acquainted with the use of Money— Conclusion'.* IN treating of the commerce of this island, we naturally enquire, what intercourse waa maintained between the different Britisti states; before we look abroad to their foreign connexions. But on this subject, we have not a gleam of information that any way relate to Danmonium. Of our (A)internal commerce, therefore, I sliall lay nothing. 'Ihe first *foreign* people with whom the Britons had any commercial dealings, were the *Phenicians.* This is a remarkable circumitance. We should'naturally suppose, that the Danmonians would have formed the firlt connexions with their neighbours on the Continent. And this supposition is founded on the convenience of such a connexion. But if those Britons were no other than a colony from Gaul, we must necessarily imagine them ac-qtiainted with the product of their original country, and carrying on some species of trade with their progenitors.*(c)* The contrary, however, was the tale—which furnilhes a presumptive proof, that Danmonium was not peopled from the Continent. Various have been the con ectures respecting the *time* when the Phenicians traded with the British islanders. A little unprejudiced attention, however, to ancient history, both *sacred* and *profane,* would have long since settled our wandering ideas on this curious iubiect. Mr.

Whitaker (a) The people of Sidon (whom the prophet Zechariah calls *thewise Sidctiiaits)* were eminently skilled in the most useful arts and sciences; if we may regard the joint authorities of Diodorus Siculus, Dionyfius Perieg. and Pliny, as well as many other celebrated historians of ancient times. '. he Sidonians, and theif descendants the Tyrians, universally studied astronomy and navigation; they excelled in ship building; Hiey invented *glass;* they introduced dyeing; and they carried arehitedtur to great perfection. In the people of Sidon and of Tyre originated, in a great measure, the commercial inter-

course of the world. Wherever they came, they endeavoured to diffuse their own spirit of industry, and to propagate civility among mankind.
(A) Indeed, it is probable, that the Danmonians had some t arnck in cattle; since at first the riches of the Britons, like those of the *Patriarchs,* fays Mr. V hitaker, consisted almost entirely in their cattle." As the Britons were, *also,* famous fof the neatness of their basketwork, the *Bajcau,at* I conceive, must have been an article of internal commece, before their acquaintance with tie Romans. (c) And emigrators from the Continent, would probably have transplanted the island commodities thither, and carried them to the coasts of the Mediterranean: And it would have been well known, at least in Europe, who these people were, and whence this merchandize came. But it is a fact, that the Phenicians *alone* fetched these valuable goods *by sea,* from a people »nd a country long unknown even to Asia, and still longer unknown to Europe, Vol. I. 2 a

Whitaker hath placed the original peopling of this island, even after the probable date of the Phenician trade. " When mankind (lays he) («) were dispersed from the plains of

Shinar, (a) In a letter to the author; who considers Mr. Whitaker's correspondence as the greatest literary honor he ever received. Yet, from the nature of his hypothesis, he is sometimes obliged to differ from this first of antiquarians. —In the History o Manchester (vol. a. p. 168 octavo edit.) lv.r. Whitaker fays, " that Midacritus brought the first vessel of the Phœnicians to our coasts—that Midacntus opened the first commerce ol the Phenicians with our fathers. And this commerce began (lie continues) before the time of Herodotus, and about five centuries before the sera of Christ, At this time, the very first population of Lancashire was but just begun—the Belgæ were not yet landed in the island —and the original Britons possessed all the southern parts of it. The testimony of Herodotus (adds Mr. Whitaker in the notes) carries the Phenician arrival up to 440 or 450. And the progress of pop-

ulation in Britain and in Ireland, *as it has been already and will hereafter be described,* forbids it to be carried beyond the year 500." In answer to this, I must first observe, that Richard brings the Phenicians hither one thousand years before Christ, which makes the difference of five hundred years from Mr. Whitaker's account; and that the fame author describes the whole island as then inhabited and cultivated, though Mr. Whitaker fays, that Lancashire, five hundred years afterwards, was just beginning to be colonized. But I should almost suspect from Mr.Whitaker's manner, that he thinks the commerce might possibly have begun before; since he acknowledges, that his preconceived idea of the peopling of this island, " forbids his carrying the commencement of the Phenician trade above the year 500." This is, undoubtedly, true. To carry the commencement of the Phenician trade above the year 500, would be to shake his own theory of the peopling of the island. Yet I have scarcely a doubt but the Phenician commerce begun 'ong before the year 500. The testimony of Herodotus himself, as stated in the text, seems to prove the fact, beyond all contradiction—This trade was opened, Mr. Whitaker fays, with the natives of the Cassiterides, or the Scilly Islands. And he is decidedly of opinion, that the Scilly Islands were only ten in number (as Strabo asserts) at the time of the Phenician trade; and that Silura, the principal island, which reached almost to the shore of Cornwall, and which is now reduced to a number of insignificant ilts, was the very land and the only land where Midacritus first traded. The difference between the ancient and the present state of the Scilly Isles, may be accounted for (Mr. Whitaker thinks) by the incroachments of the sea.

That the sea has gained considerably upon the shore of Yorkshire, Norfolk, Suffolk, and Essex, the eastern coast of Kent, and that of Sussex, Hampshire, Dorsetshire, and Cornwall, we have sufficient prool from Camden and Borlase. (i) And it has visibly usurped upon the Scilly Islands, within the present century. The sea, also, has greatly plundered the coasts of North Devonshire. (2) These gradual and successive depredations, have reduced the Scilly Islands to their present condition—have widened the narrow strait of Solinus into an expanse of forty miles, have covered half the great island of Silura with the waters of the ocean, and left only its mountains and promontories rising like so many ilets above the face of the waves." There is a curious passage relating to the Scilly Isles in HaiTifon's Description of England, dated 1586. »«The violence of the sea (says Harrison) hath devoured the *greatest* part of Cornwall and Devonshire on *either* fide: And it doth appear yet by good record, that whereas now there is a great distance betweene the Syllan Isles and point of the Land's End, there was of late yeares, to speke of, scarcelie a brooke or draine *of one fadame of water* betweene them, if so much, as by these evidences appeareth, and are yet to be scene in the hands of the lord and chiefe owner of those lsles."(3) The distance here, betwixt Cornwall and the Scilly Isles (as Mr. Whitaker observes) is contracted too much. But the whole (fays Mr. Whitaker) serves strongly to shew the *original* distance between them to have continued *a,good while ie/ow the conquest.* If this be the case, the incroachments of the sea were not gradual, as before represented, but rapid beyond all credibility. A good while below the conquest, the sea had permitted the Scilly Isles and the continental island to approximate to each other, as they did in the days of Strabn or of Solinus. A good while below the conquest, therefore, those *forty miles* of land, which reached almost to our shore, and the place of which is now occupied by the sea, must have been overwhelmed and lost! Surely such an event could only have been occasioned by some *sudden* and *-violent* convulsion of nature! But if such an event had happened so lately and within our own times, in so instantaneous a manner, it would, doubtless, have been recorded. I would infer, then, from these circumstances, that the question relating to the original distance of the Scilly Isles irom this con inental island, is in-

volved in much doubt. That great incroachments of the sea have taken place in those parts, since the time of the ancient geographers, I readily admit: But, in my opinion, it would be a fruitless labor, to attempt to reconcile the present state of the Scilly Isles v«ith such descriptions of them as occur in Strabo or Solinus; since neither Strabo nor Solinus had any accurate idea of their situation or their form Borlase, however, seems to think otherwise: And his remarks on this subject are very ingenious. " These islands being so noted among the ancients, I expected to find among the inhabitants a conscious esteem of their own antiquity, and (1) Camden, c. 899, 467411, an, 237, 199, ac.$, 8tc. (a) Sec Camden. p, 47 and 757.

Vj) Prefixed to HoUngfhead's Chron. p. S36, 1586.

Shinar, they marched along the face of the targe continent of Asia, by movements, gradual and progreliive. Nothing was done, *per saltum.* In their migrations towards the.

west, and of the figure they had made in history before the other parts of Britain were at all known, or at leist regarded. I was not without some hopes of si.ding old towns, old castles, perhaps inscriptions, and works of grandeur; but there is nothing of this kind; the irhabitants are all new comers; not one old habitation, nor any remains of *Phentcian* anil *Grecian* art in the ports, castles, towns, te nples, or sepulchres. All the antiquities here to he seen, are of the rudest *Druid* times, and il borrowed in any measure from the oriental tnders (super sttion being very in ectious) were borrowed from their most ancient and fim, le rites. We are not to think however bui that Scilly was really inhabited, and as frequently relbrted to anciently, as the old historians relate. All the Islands, by the remains of hedges, w ills, ho ses contiguous to each other, and a number of sepulchral *bwrnfis* Ihew that they have been tully cultivated and inhabited. What the ancients fay of its name, custo.m, trade and inhabitants, I (hall not trouble you with, as affr rding us lew lights 5 you will find all this collect-

ed in the last edition of *Camden,* pag. 1510; but 1 should not excuse myself, if I did not lay before you the hints, which things themselves suggested, and which our own records supply us with all. That these islands were inhibited by *Britons* is past all doubt, not only from their ne. Thbourhood to *Britain,* but ftom the *Druid* monuments; the several *rude pillars, circlet* of *ftoncs-ereily kijivaens* without numbers, *rock-basins* and *zolmns,* all monumtnts common in *Corn wall* and *Wales,* equal evidences o. the antiuity, rel gion, and original of the old inhabitants; they have also many *British* names at present tor their little islands (1), tenerrients (2), karns:3), and creeks(a.), and more, doubtless, have been forgot-r jostled out hy modern ones. How came these ancient inhabitants then, ic ay be iiked, to vanish so, as th.it the present have no pretensions to any affinity, or connexion of any k.nd either in blood, language, or customs? How came th y to disappear and leave so few traces ot trade, plenty and ar s,.. nd no posterity that we c m hear 01 behind them? In answer to which, as this is the most remarkable crisis in the history cf these islands,you will excuse me if 1 enlarge, and if 1 make use of the feme argu ments which I h..d the honour l.itely to lay before the Royal society,5), it is because they have the fame weight with me new as they had befora, ana the course 01 the present subject will not surfer so momentous a part of natural history to be omitted. Two causes of the extinction of the old inhabitants, their habitations, and works of peace, war, and religion, occur to me; the gradual advances of the sea, and a sudden submersion of the land, she sea Is perpe ually preying upon these little islands, and leaves nothing where it can reach but the skeleton, the bared rock. It his before been mentioned that many hedges now under water, and flats whicn stretch h orn one island to another, are plain evidences of a former union subsisting between these now distinct istands. History speaks the fame truth. ' The isles of Cassit F Rides, fays *Straio(6),* are ten in number, close to one mother, one of them is desert and unpeopled, the rest are inhabited;" but see how the sea his multiplied these islands: they are now reckoned more than an hundred and forty, into so many fragment are they divided. The continual advances which the sea makes upon the'land at present, are plain to all people of observation, and within these last thirty years have been very considerable. I was shewn a passage which the sea has nv.de within these seven years through the sand bank that fences the *Abbey-po-.d,* by which breach, upon the first high tide and violent storm at east, or east-south-east, one may venture to prophesy that this still, and now beautiful pool of Iresli water, will become a branch of the se 1, and consequently exposed to all the rage 01 tide and storm. What we see happening every day may assuie us of what has happened in former times, and trom the banks of sand and,the low lands gi.ing way to the sea, and the breaches becoming still more open and irremediable, it appears that there has been a gradual declension and di imnition of the *solids,* and as gradually a progressive ascendancy o the *fluids* for many ages. B.t farther, ruins and hedges re freq icntly seen upon the shifting of the sands in the *fritbt* between the islands, jtid the low lands which were lormerly cultivated, (particularly those stretching; from Samson to Tr Iscaw) have now ten feet water above the foundations of their hedges, although at a reasonable *medium* we cannot suppose tliese foundations formerl/ to have bsen less than fix feet above high water level, when the lands were dry, arable or pasture grounds; this therefore will make sixteen feet difference at le.st betwei n their ancient and present level; there are several *phenomena* of the fame nature to be seen o these il.o es, as particularly a straight lin'd ridge like a causeway, running cross the *Old Ttrwn Creek* in St. Mary's, which is now never seen above-water. On the Isle of An Net, there are large stones now covered by every full tide, which have *Rock-bafois* cut into their surface, and which therefore must have been placed in a much higher situation when those basons, in other (1) Men-ar-warth,

Mm-ar-widen, Penbros, Gwynhill, GwynhiUveor, Enys-an-geon Bighal, Enys-withek, Car-reg-flcna Crihawethen, Cribanek, Rolvean, Rosvcor, Treamnen, Men-caer-low, Trescaw Guel, Henjak, Arwothel, &c. (2) Trenowith, Salakee, Trewarlelhen. Hablingy, Tolmen, &c. (3) Karn.morvai, Kam-givavel, Karn-leh, Pcn-envs, Mount-Todn, &c., (4) Porthmellyn, Porthloe, Por'hcrassou, Porthelik, &c. (5 In a letter to tlie Rev, Dr. birch, Secretary of the Royal Society, on the alterations which the lOandi of Scilly hare dergonc since the time of the ancients. (6,i Lib. iii. Geog. west, they would find themselves at length obstructed in their advance, by those waters that divide the continental ifle of Europe from Alia and Africa. This would check, the forward Other places generally so high, and probably of superstitious use for receiving the waters of heaven, were worked into thtm.(i) Again—Tin mines they certainly had in these islands two hundred years before Christ. What is become of these mines? for the mines at present to be seen (hew no marks of their being ancient. To account for these alterations, the gradual advances and flow depredatons of the sea will not suffice; we must therefore either allow that these lands, since they were cultivated and built upon, have funk so much lower than they were before, or else we must allow that since these lands were fenc'd and cultivated, and the houses and other works now under ater, the whole ocean has been rais'd as to it's surface, sixteen feet and more perpendicular j which latter supposition will" appear to the learned without doubt much the harder of the two. 1 conclude therefore that these islands have undergone some great catastrophe, and besides the apparent diminution of their islets by sea and tempest, must have suffered greatly by a subsidence of the land, (the common consequence of earthquakes) attended by a sudden inundation in those parts where the above-m ntioned ruins, fences, mines, and other things of which we have no vestiges no v remaining, forintrly stood. This inundation probably destroyed many of

the ancient inhabitants, and so terrified those who survived, and had wherewithal to support themselves elsewhere, that they forsook these islands, by which means the people who were the *Aborigines,* and corresponded so long with the *Pheniaans Greeks,* and *Romans* were reduced to the last gasp. The few poor remains of the desolation might soon lose fight of their ancient prosperity and eminence, by their necessary attention to food and rayment; no tasy acquisitions, when their low lands, ports, and towns were overwhelmed by the sea. Give me leave to observe in the next place, that this inundation may be traced in the traditions we have had for many ages among the *Cornifi,* and stands confirm'd by some *phanomena* on the shores of *Cornwall.* That there existed formerly such a country as the *LioneJJe,* stretching from the *Land's-End to* Solly Isles is much talked of in our parts. *Antoninus* places a little island called Lissia here, but whether he means the *Wolf* ledge of rocks, or any portion of the Scilly Isles is uncertain; however there are no appearances of any Island in this Channel at present. iV.r. *Cerew,* in hit Survey of *Cornwall,* (pag. 3.) argues from the plain and level surface of the bottom of the channel, that it must at one time have been a plain extended above the sea. In the family of *Trevilian,* now resident in *Somerset* but originally *Cornifi,* they have a story, that one of their ancestors saved himself by the help of his horse, at the time when this Lioness E was destroyed; and the arms of the family) were taken, as 'tis said, from this fortunate escape. Some fishermen also have insisted that in the Channel betwixt the *Land's-End* and Scilly, many fathoms under water, there are the tops of houses, and other remains of habitations; but I produce these arguments only as proofs of the tradition and strong persuasion amonglt the *Cornifi,* that such a country once existed and is no buried under the sea, not as proofs of the matter of fact, for of that I am very dubious, the Cassiterides, by the most ancient accounts of them, appearing always to have been islands. I rather guess that this tradition of the *Lione.J.Je,* and a great country between the *Land's-End* and Scitiy's being overwhelmed hy the sea, might have taken its rife from that subsidence and inundation which not only these islands have certainly undergone, but part of the shores of *Cornwall* also, for in *Mount's-Bay* we have several evidences of a like subsidence. The principal anchoring place is call'd a *Lake),* but is now an open harbour. *St. Michael's Mount,* from it's *Ctrnifi* namefd.), must have stood formerly in a wood, but at full tide is now half a mile in the sea, and no tree near it. *Leland,* (Itin. vol. iiw pag. 7.) talking of this *Mount,* fays that an « ould Legend of St. *Michael* speaks th of a tounelet in this part, now defaced and lying under the water;' in confirmation of which alterations I must observe, that on the *Beach* betwixt the *Mount* and the town of *Penxance,* when the sands have been dispersed and drawn out into the sea, I have seen the trunks of several large trees in their nitural position, (as well as I can recollect) worn smooth just aboie their roots, upon which at full tide there must be twelve feet of water; neither is what Mr. *Scawen* fays in his MS.(5) an inconsiderable confirmation that *Cornwall* has lost much land on the southern coast, that there was ' a valley between *Ramhead* and *Looe,* and that there is to be sesn in a clear day, in the bottom of the sea, a league from the shore, a wood of timber lying on its side uncorrupttd, as if formerly grown therein, when it was dry ground thrown down by the violence of the waves. Of this several persons have inform'd me (fays Mr. *Scawen)* who have, as they said, o ten seen the same.' So that the shores in Scilly, and the neighbouring shores in *Cornwall* (not forgetting the *Wolf* ledge of rocks midway between (1) " A person taking a survey of the Channel in the year 1742, took one of his stations at low water, as he told me, upon this rock, (vi2-the Gulph-rock, midway betwixt Penzance and Scilly) where he obferv'd a cavity like a brewer' copper, with rubbish at the bottom, without being able to assign a cause for it' coming thoie." Heath's Account of Scilly, p. 157. This

could be no other than a Rotk'bason, and consequently this rock is g eatly funfl by being now entirely cover's! wkh the sea, at least nine hours in twelve.

(2) Gules, from a Fesse Wavy Azure and Argent, a Horse issuing Ar. (3) Gwavas Lake-. (4) Carreg luz en K.uz, a hoary rock in a wood, (5) Pag, 9, xo, written in his own hsinrj. forward steps of colonization: And Egypt, by means of that little junction of land, which connects the continental IUe of Africa, was probably peopled before any part of Europe. Navigation, at first, must have consisted solely in occasional exertions for crossing small arms of the sea. A voyage from Asia to Britain, would have been a most miraculous effort of the human mind. It would have been as unnatural as miraculous.

" The land was all before them, where to chuse

Their place of rest, and providence their guide." Why, then, should they attempt long voyages, to go they knew not whither 5 and to seek unfruitful regions near the pole, when they had all the soft climes of Asia before them, equally uninhabited, and directly inviting txhem? Nor could they, if they would, have taken such voyages. The Phenician voyages are no proof to the contrary. They were in a much later age; whatever Kichai d has said (who makes the *Gratci Pbanicesque mercatores,* to have come hither about the original plantation of the island) as the Phœnicians came hither only a little before Herodotus—he mentioning the Caliiterides and their tin, but not knowing where thole islands lay; and as the Grecians came long afterwards. We deceive ouritlves on these points, by using the words *Grecians* and *Pbenkians* at large.

The bet veen both) are equal evidences that there has been a subsidence of the land in these parts, and the memory of t!ie inundation which followed upon that subsidence is preserved by tradition, though, like othtr traditions, greatly enlarg'd and obfcnr'd by fable. When this inundation happen'd we may be willing to know, but must be without hopes of knowing with any certainty, in

the time of *Strabc* and *Diod. Siculus,* the commerce of these islands seem to have been in full vigour; ' abundance of tin carried in carts,' fays the latter; « but ten islands in all, *faysStrabo,* and nine of these inhabited.' The destruction therefore of Sciily, must be plac'd after the time of these authors; that is, after the *Augustan* age, but at what time after, I find nothing as yet that can determine: *Plutarch* indeed (of the cessation of oracles) hints that the islands round *Britain* were generally unpeopled in his time; *if* he includes Scilly among them, and wajrigltly inform d, then this desolation must have happened betwixt the reign of *'Trajan* and that of *Augustus.* There was a great subsidence in the southern coasts ot *England* in the time of *Edward* the First, whereby *Wtnthilfta* near *Rye* in *Suffix* was swallowed up, and its ruins are now three miles within the high sea(1), and for the unhappy inhabitants who had lost their town, *Ed-ward* the First bought land and gave it them, and there stands the new *Witcbeljea.* But I must observe that if the subsidence at Scillv and *Mour.t's-Bay* were so late, we could not have been without some notice ot it, and in the tornplaints of the monks of Scilly to *Edward* the First, we must reeds have found so great a misfortune particularly mentien'd; whereas their petition was only for protection from pirates and foreign sailors. In the year 1014 happened a great inundation, of which the *Saxon* Chronicle gives this account: « *Hoc item anno in vigitts Sancti Michaelis contigit magna ista Maris Inundatio fir latam hanc terram qua longius expatiata, quam antea unquam, demersit multa oppida et bominum tmmerum inenarrabilem.* ' But I think the catastrophe ol these islands cannot be placed even so late as this; for the monks being placed here either by *Atbelstan,* in the year 938, or soon after, nothing of this kind could have happened but it would have appeared somewhere or other, in the papers or history of *Tavistock Abbey,* at least, if the monks of Scilly were united to that Abbey at it's first foundation in the year o6r. I therefore co jecture that this inundation must have happened before

Athelstan's time; and by the *Irijh* annals I find an inundation which might probably have affected the south of *Ireland,* and at the fame time reach'd Scilly and the coast *Cornwall,* which are not above fifty leagues distant from it to the east, nor much more than a degree to the south of it. 1 Ir, the end of March A. D. 830, *Hugh Dorndighe* being Monarch of *Ireland,* there happened such terrible shocks of thunder and lightning, that above a thousand persons were destroyed between *Corca-Bajcoin,* a part of the county of *Cork* then so called, and the sea side. At the same time the sea broke through it's banks in a violent manner, and overflowed a considerable tract of land. The island then called *Inn'nsadda,* on the west coast of this county, was forced asunder and divided into three parts. This island, says my author, lies contiguous to two others, *nix. Hare IJland* and *Castle IJland,* hich lying in a range, and being low ground, might have been very probably then rent by the ocean.'(2) As this inundation in the southern parts of *Ireland* seems well attested, and might not unlikely have reached *Cornwall* and Scilly, I should think it most suitable to history, that this was what reduced, divided and destroyed the Scilly Islands, and over-run the lands on *Mount's-Bay." Observations on the an.ient and the present state of the Istands of Scilly, and their importance to the present state of Great Britain.*

In a letter to the Rev. Charles Lyttelton, LL.D. Dean of Exeter, and F.R.S. p. 84 to 99. This book is scarce; as, indeed, are Borlase's Antiquities and Natural History of Cornwall. 1 have frequently made extracts, therefore, from these well-written volumes, for the gratification of my readers.

(1) Nordcn's Survey of Cornwall. jJ Smith's Natural and Civil History of Cork, vol.ii.pag.n, Keating, pag. 5a,———An old Irish MS.

The men, who came trading to our Cassiterides, were not proper Phenicians or proper Greeks. They did not come from Tyre and the Morea. The Greeks were the Phocæans of *Marseilles,* and the Phenicians were the Tyrians of

Carthage, settled at *Cadiz.* And thus considered as inhabitants of Marseilles and Cadiz, these bold voyagers can lend not a shadow of pretext to a voyage from Asia to Britain. But let me further observe concerning thele voyages; It is a common opinion, which I lee you have adopted, that these miscalled Phenicians came to the south-western pirts of this ve y island Britain. They came on!y to the Casliterides—to islands, which.itrabo (hews us, were ten in number. And the idea, that Cornwall, and perhaps Devonshire, were considered as islands, is all a dream of romantic antiquarianism. When Devonshire and Cornwall were as well known to the Romans as Kent or Somersetshire; they still distinguished the little islands of the Casliterides, from the great Isle of Britain." These observations of Mr. Whitaker, will suggest to us some retlexions on the *Phenician* trade, with respect both to *time* and *place.* Ixt us first appeal to *scripture,* and next to *profane* history. That the eastern people were acquainted with navigation and commerce, at a very early period, is plain from a passage in the Psalms: They that go down to the lea in ships (fays David) and occupy their bufineis in the great waters." This argues an established commerce familiar to his countrymen more than one thousand years before Christ. Let us look to another part of scripr ture:-' *Tarfiifi* (a) was thy merchant (exclaims the prophet Ezekiel) by reason of the multitude of all kinds of riches;' with silver, iron, tin, and lead they traded in thy fairs," the fairs of Tyre. This 7 *arshisb* was the city of *Tartejj'us,* situated near the pillars of Hercules, and poilest by the Carthaginians; who found it a very convenient situation for maintaining a commercial intercourse with their original countrymen of *Tyre,* on the one hand,, and with the *British Isles,* on the other. Hence they were enabled to supply the markets of Tyre with iron and tin; and the west of Britain, with the Tyrian purple; and both Tyre and Britain, with the commodities of Spain. Vessels, we find, built for longer voyages, and greater burthens, were named the *ships of Tar-*

jhijh, because they were built like the ships of Tarsliilh properly so called. Thus Solomon's navy (which traded to *t)* Lowth, in his notes on Isaiah, has thrown some light on this subject, and on the *Navigation of the ancients.* P. 26. Note on chap. xii. ver. 13 — 16. " Ships of Tarsliilh are in scripture frequently used by a metonymy for (hips in general, especially such as are employed in carrying on traffic between distant countries; as Tarshisli was the most celebrated mart of those times, frequented of old by the Phenicians, and the principal source of wealth to Judea and the neighbouring countries. The learned seem now to be perfectly well ageed, that Tarlhifh is Tartessus, a city of Spain, at the mouth of the river Bætis; whence the Phenicians, who first opened this trade, brought silver and gold, (jer. x. 9. Ezek. xxvii. 12.) in which that country then abounded; and pursuing their voyage still further to the Casliterides, (Bochart. Canaan, 1. cap. 39. Huet, Hist, de Commerce, p. 194.) they brought from thence lead and tin. Tarsliilh is celebrated in scripture (2 Chron. viii. *ij,* 18—, ix. 21.) for the trade, which Solomon carried on thither, in conjunction with the Tyrians. Jehofaphat (1 Kings, xxii. 48. 2 Chron. xx. 36.) attempted afterwards to renew that trade; and from the account given of his attempt, it appears, that his sleet was to fail from Eziongeber, on the Red Jea: they muf therefore have designed to sail round Africa, as Solomon's fleet probably had done before; (fee Huet, Histoiie de Commerce, p. 32.) for it was a three year's voyage; (2 Chron. ix. 21.) and they brought gold from Ophir, probably on the coast of Arabia, silver from Tartessus, and ivoryr apes, and peacocks, from Africa. It is certain, that under Pharaoh Necho, about two hundred years afterward, this voyage was made by the Egyptians, (Herodot. iv. 42.) they sailed from the Red Sea, and returned by the Mediterranean, and they performed it in three years; just the fame time that the voyage under Solomon had taken up. It appears likewise from Pliny, (Nat. Hist. 11.67.) that the passage round the Cape of Good

Hope, was kno n and frequently practised before his time, by Hanno the Carthaginian, when Carthage was in its glory; and by one Eudoxus, in the time cf Ptolemy Lathyrus, king of Egypt: and Cælius Antipater, an historian of good credit, somewhat earlier than Pliny, testifies, that he hid seen a merchant, who had made, the voyage from Gades to Æthiopia. The Portuguese under Vasco de Gama, near three hundred years ago, recovered this navigation, after it had been intermitted and lost for many centuries." P. 130. Note on Chap.

xxiii. r. Howl, O ye Ships of Tarsliilh. " This prophecy denounceth the dastruction of Tyre by Nebuchadnezzar. It opens with an address to the T"rian negotiators, and sailors at Tarsliilh, (1 artessus in Spain) a place which, in the course of their trade, they greatly frequented. 1 he news of the destruction of Tyre, by Nebuchadnezzar, is said to be brought to them from Chittim,"the islands and coasts of the Mediterranean: ' For the Tyrians, (fays Jerom on ver. 6.) when they saw they had no other means of escaping, fled in their (hips, and took refuge in Carthage, and in the islands of the Ionian and Egean sea.' From whence the news would spre d and reach Tarstlifll: so also Jarehi on the place. This seems to be the most probable interpretation of this verse." to Ophir, or the East Indies, for ivory, apes, and peacocks, more than one thousand years before Christ) was called a *naiy os Tar/hijh.* And thus Jehosaphat's 'navy, designed for a voyage to Ophir, but unfortunately broken at Eziongeber, were called *ships of Tarjbijb.* This city of Tarlhisli, so convenient for the British trade with its Tyrin colony, is mentioned by Polybius under the name of *Tarfeium* ; where the historian it reciting the words of a league between the Romans and Carthaginians.

To return to our *Britijh* commerce—I think we may plainly infer, that if the trading vessels from Tarlhiih were so famous in the time of Solomon, as to impart their name by way of distinction to the commercial navies of those days, the Tyrians or Carthaginians must have been long before exercised in the arts

_of navigation and commerce. Jesus, the son of Sirach, speaking of Solomon's glory, fays: " By the name of the Lord God, which is called the Lord God of Israel, thou didst gather gold as tin, and didst multiply silver as lead"—which shews, that tin in those days, was brought in great quantities to the holy land. And it is remarkable, that tin and lead, in this place, are *both* mentioned, and distinguished: Yet, characteristically different as they are, the ancients often mistook the one metal for the other. By the sliips Solomon lent out, he had a return, in one voyage, of no less than four hundred and twenty talents of gold. It is said in Kings: " money was in Jerusalem as *stones* for plenty." Tin, therefore, must have almost covered the streets of-Jerusalem, to be spoken of in the same figurative way. From these passages, we see that commercial voyages were of high antiquity; that the chief articles of commerce were silver, iron, tin, and lead; and that those articles were in great abundance in Judea, even in the reign of Solomon. The question is, whence those articles were imported: If tin, in its mineral state, were, at this time, unknown to all other countries but our own; there is ample realbn to assert, that we supplied all the markets of Europe and Asia with this commodity, in the earliest ages.

If we recur to heathen authors, we find Homer, who flourished more than nine hundred years before Christ, expressly noticing *tin,* by its Greek appellation *KuavAepos.* That the Greeks had *the use* of tin, and adopted the word *KototrAipos* to express it before the time of Homer, is evident from his mention of it, more than once, among the metals employed in the fabrication of the shield of Achilles; and also in the greaves for his hero's legs. But that the Greeks were unacquainted with the situation of the islands that produced this metal, five hundred years after the time of Homer, is as evident from Herodotus, who wrote more than four hundred years before the birth of our Saviour, and who confesses his ignorance of the islands called the Cassiterides, whence their tin came, but supposes that it was brought

to them (as he fays amber was) from the remotest parts of Europe.(æ) oJIo *no-as owx xao-o-skpio'txs cuo-as,* Ex *rait* o *xavo-Aipos ipoflac, i cs%x%s* S' *m xxo-o-ilipos tiij.ii $oslx, xai To* tExlpov. From which conjecture of Herodotus, concerning the Cassiterides, we may plainly infer, that they had been discovered by the Phenicians some time before he wrote; instead of concluding with Carte from this passage, that the Phenician trade with the Britons for tin, did not exist till the very period of Herodotus. Carte's is a most ridiculous supposition. For surely their tin-trade, the particulars of which the Phenicians were interested in concealing from other nations (so that we need not wonder at the ignorance of Herodotus) could never have been so far settled with the Britons, in the course of a few years, as to admit of a negotiation between the Phenicians and Greeks, and a regular interchange of commodities in consequence of this commercial establishment. Before the Phenicians discovered the Cassiterides, they must have taken several adventurous voyages, perhaps, to little purpose. On the dilcovery of those islands, we cannot suppose, that they in a very short time determined their business with the Bri. tons. And it is likely, that when this commerce was absolutely fixed, some little time elapsed before the Phenicians had recourse to the Greeks, for the disposal of their tin. Even when this intercourse was settled, the use of our tin was hardly adopted, throughout all Greece, in an instant: And it was *familiar* to the Greeks in the time of Herodotus. So that Carte's supposition is fall of absurdity. May we not imagine with much more reason, that the Phenicians were acquainted with the Cassiterides before the time of Homer; since we have Homer's own authority to fay, that tin was, in his days, well known to his countrymen? This corresponds with Richard, and carries us as far back as the age, when our (j) Herodotus. Thalia. III. p. 150, 253. (Edit. Glasg. 1761.) our island, according to Mr. Whitaker, was first peopled. (a) Those *Phenicians* then, who traded here, were by no means the modern

Phenicians, but Phenicians of a far more ancient race. How the Phenicians or Tyrians could have performed these long voyages from Asia to Britain, may be a question of difficulty: But from the passages I have already quoted, it is plain that they were (killed in navigation. That'their descendants, the Carthaginians, were skilful pilots, v e have abundant proof. And if, as Strabo tells us, the captain of a Carthaginian vessel, seeing himself followed by a Roman fleet, *chose to steer a false course,* and land upon another coast, rather than stiew the Romans the way to Britain; they certainly *had the use of the com/tass.* And the use of the compass must have been derived to them from their progenitors the Tyrians. If it be objected, however, that the Carthaginians, had they possessed the knowledge of the compass, could not easily have concealed jt from the Romans, and other nations with whom they were connected, I would hint to the objector, the *commercial secrecy* of the ancient nations. The precaution, indeed, of the Carthaginiaqs, to guard the compass from common observation, was, at length, the very means, perhaps, of their losing the use of it, themselves. The knowledge of it was intrusted to a few: From these few, it was imperfectly transmitted to others: And the; secret, thus feebly retained, funk gradually away with the possessors of it. But, whether the loss of the compass were owing to this or any other cause, we need not here enquire. No person, who is not ignorant of the history of the arts, will doubt the existence of an art in one period, because it hath disappeared in another. The ancient nations were acquainted with various arts, which have expired, and, after the lapse of ages, have revived. That the voyages of the Phenicians, were not mere *coasting* voyages, may be inferred, I think, from their *monopoly* of our trade for *se-veral centuries.* For a long space of time, they carried on a regular trade with this island, to the exclusion of all other nations. Even our neighbours the Gauls were unacquainted with them. But if the Phenicians had been unskilled voy-

agers, timidly pursuing the line of the coasts, it is impossible that they could have kept their secret, long. They would have frequently exposed themselves. to the observation of the maritime people. And curiosity, once awakened, never acquiesces in ignorance. Their periodical return would have been expected and. eagerly watched; and their whole scheme of navigation would have been unavoidably detected. Such a discovery would naturally have taken place; even if, by a singular good fortune, they had escaped the dangers of the sea for hundreds of years, nor ever suffered siiipwreck on the coasts, so as to expose their cargo to the eye of the jealous merchant or of the savage plunderer, and, in either case, lay open their destination. This much for the *time.(b)*

With respect to the *place* or *places,* whence our tin was ssiipped in the time of the Phœnicians, many fruitless enquiries have been made. Some fay it was ssiipped from the Cassiterides, without being able to determine, what the Cassiterides were: Others assert, that it was exported from Falmouth, or from St. Michael's Mount, or from the Land's. End, The Greek and Roman writers were so ignorant of geography, and their descriptions are consequently so perplexed, that this point must ever remain a matter of conjecture, as far as it depends on their uncertain testimony. As the ancients had such obscure notions of the situations of countries, they must have been necessarily indistinct in giving;iames to the places they discovered. Thus Mela mentions some isles of the northern ocean, which he fays, " *quia plumbo abundant, uno omnes Cassiterides app:U lant.,'c)* Why then might not the tin-districts of Devon and Cornwall be included, together with the Scilly Isles, under the name of Cassiterides? Strabo, it is true, fays, *i* . that *(a)* And, surely, the Britons were long in possession of the island before their connexion with the Phenicians: For, as I have already observed, it is impossible that the British isles could in a moment be discovered, peopled, and cultivated for the subsistence of their inhabitants, and explored for their mineral treasures,

and again found out by eastern adventurers, and frequented for their tin-manufacture!

/) According to some accounts, the Phenicians (after they had become acquainted with all the coasts of the Mediterranean, and had *p/anted colonies,* and *built cities* on several parts of these coasts, and had carried on an extensive trade with all the countries bordering upon that sea) passed the Straits of Gibraltar, more than Iioo years before the christian æra (Strabo fays, soon after the Trojan war) anH pushed their disooveries both to the right and left of those Straits. On their right hand, they built the city of Cadiz, on a small island near the coast of Spain, and thence prosecuted heir discoveries and their trade with great spirit and advantage, as far as the British islands. () Mela seems to have been almost as ignorant of these islands, as Herodotus. that the Cassiterides are ten in number: But this was, probably, a random assertion. It stands unconfirmed by the testimony of any other writer: And there are, at present, more than one hundred and forty islands that go by the name of the Scilly Isles. Nor mould it be forgotten, that Cæsar takes not the least notice of the Scilly Isles; which he certainly would have done, had they monopolized, for centuries, the tin-trade of the world.(a) That Richard of Cirencester understood Devonshire and Cornwall to have been included in the Casliterides, is plain from his description of Danmonium. He tells us, that the country of the Danmonii abounded in minerals, and was frequented in the *earliest ages,* first by the Phenicians and afterwards by the Greeks, on account of the tin which it produced in great abundance. As a proof of this *commerce,* the three chief promontories of the Danmonii, he lays, were called *Helenis, Ocrinum,* and *Kons .flunoti* which three names he adds, were partly of Greek, and partly of Phenician origin. Immediately afterwards, he notices the Cassiterides, without saying a word of their tin or their commerce. " *Ultra bracbium in oceano Jitx Cunt insuLe Sygdiles, qua etiam Oestrominides et* Cassiter-

rides *'vccabantur, dicla.'"(b)* In short, we have no foundation for asserting, what is commonly believed, that the Phenicians *first* traded with the inhabitants of the Scilly Isles. And if we place the original trade at Plymouth, or in the neighbourhood of the Tamar, we shall approach, I think, very near the truth. Among the Phenician exports, the most plentiful commodity was, evidently, our tin.

Lead t» " That the Phenicians accounted their trade to the Scilly Islands, for tin, of great advantage, and were very jealous of it, is plain from what Straho says(i), that a master of a Phenician vesse bound hither, perceiving that he was dodged by a Roman, ran his ship ashore, risking his life, ship and cargo (for which he was remunerated out of the public treasury of his country) rather than he would admit a partner in this traffick by shewing him the way to these islands. The Romans, however, persisting in their resolution to have a share in this trade, at last accomplished it. Now, plain it is, that the few workings upon Trefcaw, were not worthy of such a competition: Whence, then, had they their tin? I will answer this question as well as I can. Some tin might have been found in the low grounds, washed down from the hills, and gathered together by the floods and rain— some found pulverized among the sands of the sea-shore, washed out of veins covered by the sea, and thrown in upon the sand by the same restless agent. In Cornwall we often find tin in the like situation. There may be, also, tin-veins in those cliffs which we did not visits), although the inhabitants, upon enquiry, could not recollect that they contained any thing of that kind; as the *Guel-Hill* of Br Eh Ar, *Guel* Island, the name *Guel* (or *Huel*) in Comiso signifying a working for tin. Other tin they had from their mines; for though their mines at present extant are neither ancient nor numerous, yet the ancient natives had mines, and worked them as appears from *Dhd. Siculus(i)*, and from *Strabo()*, who tells us, that, ' after the *Romans* had discovered a passage to these islands, *Fublius Craffus* having sailed thither and seen

them work their mines, which were not very deep, and that the people loved peace, and at their leisure (5) navigation also, instructed them to carry on this trade to a better advantage than they had dene before; though the sea they had to cross was wider than betwixt it and *Britain;*' intimating (if I understand him rightly) that, before that tirfie, the *Pbtnic'ans* and *Greeks* had engrossed the sole benefit of buying and exporting their tin, and that *Fubliut Crajfus,* seeing their mines shallow, taught them how to pursue the ore to a greater depth; and, finding the inhabitants peaceably disposed with regard to their neighbours, and therefore the fitter for commerce, and very apt at navigation, and therefore able themselves to carry the product of their country to market, encouraged them to enter upon this gainful trade, and depend no longer on foreign merchants and shipping, although it was somewhat farther for them to sail to the ports of *Gauls Spain,* and *Italy,* than to the coasts of *Britain,* which had till that time been their longest voyage. Besides the tin therefore, which they found granulated and pulverized in valleys and on the sea-shore, they broke tin out of their mines, though those mines are not now to be found; and, in the last place, it must not be forgotten that the ancients had great part of their tin from the neighbouring coasts of *Corn-wall,* famous for their tiivtrade as anciently as the time of *Augustus Cajar*; and whoever fees the land of *Corn-wall* from these islands, must be convinced that the *Pbtnicians* and other traders did most probably include the western part of *Cornivall* among the islands called Cassiterides. *Ortelius* is plainly of this opinion, and makes *Corn-wall* a part of the Cassiterides: And *Dhdorus Sicu/us(6),* does as plainly confound and in his description mix the western parts of *Cornwall* and the Cassiterides indiscriminately one with the other." *Borlascs Observations,* &c. p. 72 to 76.

(b) Ricard. p. 20,11. (1) Geog. Lib. iii. (2 I have been lately informed, that, under one of the cliffs of Annet, there is a load, in which there is the appearance of tin, and that it looks as if it had been

work'd. (3) Lib. v. Ch. a. (4) Geogr, Lib. 111. (5) i.e. when they were not employed about their tin. (6) Lib. iv. pag. 30 Edit. Han-1604.

Vol. I, Qj»

Lead was, also, an article of exportation. And not the least valuable article was the lkins of wild and tame animals—under which was, probably, comprehended thefcvool of the British stieep-of great use to the Phenicians in their woollen manufactures. In return, the Britons received from the Phenicians, salt, brals-ware, and pottery, (a) Our earthenware was furnistied, we fee, by the Phenicians: and I have no doubt but that many of the earthen urns found in our barrows, were fabricated by that people; though, indeed, so easy (a) An ingenious correspondent says: " It is observable that the articles in which the Britons dealt with the Phenicians, imply a settlement of some standing. They were tin, which requires some skill and labor to bring it to a merchantable state; gold and silvers i J, pearls, and the curious dye from the *z)murex,* which was here in great abundance, and which, probably, was the boasted Tyrian dye. " , % (A) Musgrave, in his Belgæ (p. 160 to 166) speaks thus of the British commerce: " De Gemmis *Mela Britannicis* quid dicam, incertus sum, nisi eas e Rupe *Bristoliensi,* quæ nunc *Vmcentn* dicitur, captas statuam. Profert Adamantes ea perspicuos, pulchros, ab Indus advectorum æmulos, usque urm duritie secundos: Utrum *Mela* ætate reperti futrint, non exploratissimum est; quare in his dicundis non parum hæsito. Judicent eruditi, prout cujusque libido est. Margaritarum vim magnam fuisse, constat ex iis, quas hodie præbcnt Ostrea *Britannica.* Nescio an *Rutupina,* quæ *Romanis* erant delicio, præ cæteris scaterent Margaritis. *Julius Cæsar* Britanniam *petti/se dicitur spe Margaritarum, q'uarum amplitud'wem conferens-, intcrdum J'ua manu potidus exigent,"* Sed (3) w Britannia *parvos & decohres nasci certum est.* Et(4) *Ælianus* ait, *Margaritam* Britannicam *magis fulvi coloris effe, minusque splendidam.* D'rvus Julius *Thoratcm, quern Veneri Gcnetriei in Templo ejus dicavit, ex* Britannicis Margaritis *faflum-voluerit intcl/egi:* subjects, inquit *(c,)Solinus,* Inscriptions quæ id testaretur. Hæc omnia more suo exagitat *If. Vofcius,* & Gemmas, & boni coloris Margaritas veteri negat *Britannia?. £iuat:am,* (6jinquit, *sunt ilia; Gemma? F/umina ista Gemmifera, &f Margaritifera mera projc&o sunt commentay ad apparandum stulti Imperatorts triunipbum,* At pace tanti viri, non adeo viles sunt Adamantes supra dicti, quin *Julii* sæculo facile placerent. Hæ videntur esse Gemmæ prædictae, & *Satr'ma* nostra Flumen illud Gemmiferum, de quo dubitar vir egregie doctus. Margaritas cum *Tapiotaniticis* nostras nequaquam audeo comparare, præcipue sl magnitudinis habeatur ratio: at ex Foro iiostro *Exonienji* Piscatorio, & Margaritis liic repertis fi liceat judicare, facile potuit earum in hac Insula comparari, satis magnarum neque decolorum numerus, qui ad exornandum *Vcncr'n* Thoracem omnino sufficeret. Calx etiain inter *ixyuiyix* meiito putanda est; fed quæ Cretam & Margam comprehends: his enim tribus Agricolæ fæcundant agros. Testantur optimæ fidei Inscriptiones, Aitem Calcariam olim a *Britannis* exerceri, & ut Terra Figularis hodie ad Tubos Tabacarios e *Dunmonio,* sic Cretam, Margam, *k* ejusmodi alia ad stercorandos Agros hinc exportari. *Calcaria, Brigantum* oppidulo, i. e. *Tadcaster)* fuisse unam Inscriptionem opinatur Doctiss.(7) *Ga/aus,* sedob literas fugientes & propemodum exesas, vix legendam. Ad quod ad rem nostram maximopere facit, in Colle, cut *Soriiodunum (Old SarumJ* insldebat, Fodinæ Cretacæ præcipue frequentabantur, & ab iis Creta in exteras regiones cxportabatur. Unde Versificator *Anglus Eft ibi defcBus Lymf a, fed copia Creta.* Arti Calcariæ præfuit Dea *Nebalennia,* quæ a *Brigan'iius,* (opinante Clariss. *(%)Galao)* sorsan etiam a *Bclgis* nostris colebatur. Ei Negotiators *8c* Mercatores navicularii vota solvebant, ut ex Ara, quæ *(g)Domburgii* in *Zelandia* dudum effossa est, conjicimus. Est autem hujusmodi.

Deae Nehalenniae
Ob Merces Rite Conser

Vatas M. Secund Silvanus,
Negottor O Retarivs
Britannicianvs
V. S. L. M.

Npvam Lunam *Nebalennia* fignificari velunt nonnulli, quæ cme navigantibus benigna suit & propi tia, sic, ut ea de causa cultu digna videretur. De *Gagate Solini Britannico* aliquid dicendum: Ac' cipit ille nomen a *Gage* (tradente *(io)Ditscoride) Lycia* amne, ad cujus Ostium iste Lapis primum. inventus est, Aliquande dicitur Lapis *Gbjidianus;* fed *Anglice* a *jfeatstone.* Succinum nigrum esse contendit (1) The Muscle Pearl—Museuli, quibus inclusam sæpe margaritam, omnis quidem coloris optimam inveniunt. Ricard. p. 13.

(?) Sunt et Cocklcæ, satis iuperque abundantes, qnibus tinctura coccinii coloris conficitur, cujus rubor pulcherrimus, nullo unquarn solis ardors, nulla valet pluviorum injutia pallescere: fed quo vetustior est, eo solet else venustior. Ricard. p. 13. Tiic Murex of Devonshire, is noticed in my Sketches of the Natural History. (3) Vide Plinii, Lib. ix. Cap. XXXV. (4) *AoiLH (se TFaiS % £vCT(tlrnoTEC&' tlSeiV, HVZl TOLS* TE *CCvyxt ajjift'kvlzpxs' tywv,. KCtt tTy. 0TwS$Sfxs.* De Animalihus, Lib. xv Cap. viii. Ed. Tigurina, Kol. (5) Vide Solinum, Cap. liii; & in illud, Doctifs. Salmafti Plinianas exercitatrones.. (6) Vide ejus Observationcs ad Mclæ, Lib. iii. Cap. vi. vers. 36. (7) AU Antonini Itei, it, pag. 42. (8) pag. 43 (9) Rcincsii Syntagma, p. 190. (10) Lib.v. Cap. cxlvi. easy a workmanship was *Coon,* imitated by the Britons.(A) We are told, that the *Phcrdclans* considered their commerce with us of such consequence, that they erected *forts* and *caftles* on our coasts, for the protection and preservation of it. This was their usual custom in every country where they traded. And it is a certain fact, that they planted colonies along the coasts of the Mediterranean, for the further security of the trade which, they had established there. Nothing, therefore, is more probable, than that they colonized a part of Danmonium.

How long (a) the Phenicians enjoyed this trade exclusively, is not certainly known: They, doubtless, took every precaution to conceal the source of their mercantile wealth. Though the Greeks in the time of Herodotus, knew perfectly well, that all the tin which they used, and which they received from the Phenicians, came originally from the Caffiterides, or from Danmonium; yet they could scarcely guess, it seems, at our situation. The Phenician merchants could easily avoid instructing the Greeks in the course they steered-. But the Greeks were acquainted with the names of the tin-countries, in the time of Herodotus. And from their love of novelty, and the restlessness of their temper (the peculiar characteristic of the Greeks) it is very unlikely, that they mould indolently sit at home, indifferent about the commodities of Danmonium (though secondarily experiencing the blessings of those commodities) when once they were instructed in the art of navigation. That Pytheas, the Greek Philosopher of Marseilles, gave an account of the British, isles from his own inspection of them, three hundred and thirty years before Christ, is unquestionable. This geographer was an adventurous mariner, and " is laid to have sailed as far as the Arctic circle, where there is no night at the summer solstice." In this voyage, we are told, he found out Iceland. This spirit of adventure, so conspicuous in Pytheas, would be equally discoverable, I conceive, in his countrymen. And, when we consider the connexion of the Greeks with the Phenicians, we should not err, I think, in bringing the Greeks to this island half a century at least before Pytheas. In this cafe, the Greeks entered Britain about 380 years before Christ. The history of Herodotus containing an obscure hint about the Cassiterides, would, immediately on its publication, have excited the curiosity of so inquisitive a people. (A) As to the passage in Richard, where the Greek merchants are said to be introduced as coeval with the primitive Phenicians, I do not fee, that it is capable of such a construction. The passage (which was quoted before with another view) is as follows: " A. M. M. M.

M. *Circa bac temportt cultam et habitatam frimum Brittanniatn arbitrantur nonnulli,* cum illam salutarent Græci Phænicesque mercatores."(f) The meaning of which seems to be this: " About the year of the world three thousand, the Greek and Phenician commerce was first established in contendit *Aldrovattdus,* cui fuffragatur Doctiss: (1) *Anfelmus B. dc Boct.* Paleas enim attritu calefactus, Succini instar, trahit, & odorem habet Sulfureum. De eo *(2)Sc!hus* Gagates *hie* (in *Britar.ma) flurimus opt'mujque est Lapis; si decorem requiras, mgro gimmtus; si naturam, aqua aides; oltt resthgu'uur ;* Est in Museo (3) *Regia Soaetatis* hujusmodi Lapis insignis, & in *Clea-ve-land, on the top ofHuntly and Wbitby Clifts,* 8 puteis effodi solet in Agro(4) *Surreienji* qui cum *Rtgncrum* olim patria suit *Belg'w* proxime vicina, fortasse an a *Belgit* hinc exportaretur. Multiplex est *Gagatis* usus. In Medicina calidæ facultatis csse dicitur, *le* Mania, Morbo comitiali, sleut etiam Hysterico correptos Suffitn liberare. Diureticus est, & Hydropicis, urinam movendo, prod est. Oleum ejus destiltarunt maxime prædicatur ad Dæmoniacos, (id est, Epilepticos) Paralysin, Convulsionem, Tetanum, ad Podagram frigidam, omnesque frigidas Fluxiones, parti affectæ illitum: Unde Podagricis remediis & Acopis adrrumeratur. Pulvis ejus ad unius Drachmæ pondo, ex Vino liaustus ad tempus aliquod. Colicam integre sanare dicirur. Emollit, discutit, (5) *Diofcoride* teste j unde adversus scdis affectiones, quam levislime tritus, *6)Ætii* judicio valet j & ad Condylomata, eum *Scribemi Largi* Emplastrum habet. Ornabantur eo Galeæ, Scuta, Gladii: Mundum etiam muliebrem ingrediebatur; Fœminarum Aures, Colla, Pectoraque, colore contrario, commendabant. Hinc Aurium lobis etiam nunc appenditur ex eo Inauris; Collo Monile: in quibus Puellæ non parum gloriantur. Denique ad preces numerandas, in globulos formatus, & silo Irajectus, nonnullis est in usu." *a)* After the first ages of the Phenician commerce, the Tyrian colonies of Carthage and of Cadiz, carried on the Danmonian tin-trade, con-

junctively.

(4) Polybius, the Greek, wrote his large treatise on the tin-manufacture of Danmonium, about two hundred years before the christian æra. And Polybius was a very accurate historian. And he, probably, received his intelligence from the Grecian colony settled long before in Danmonium. (c) Ricard. p. 50. (1) De Lapidibus & Gemmis in Specie. Lib. 3. Cap. tlxiii. & seqq. (2) V.Solinum, Cap. xxii. & in illud Doct. Salmafii Plinianas Lxercitaliones. (3) V. Museum Reg. Societ. edente Nch dew, Partem. iii. Cap. iL (4) Vide Addiuaienta ad Camdcn.i Coujiutuiu Suiiy, Loco jam citato. (6) Lib., tctrabibli, Cap. 24. in Britain." Richard does not mean to fay, that the Greeks actually traded to this ifland about the year three thousand: Had he intended specifically to describe the merchants, and the exact time when they respectively traded with the British islanders, he would, doubtless, have placed *Phanices* before *Graeci;* for he must surely have known, that in point of time, the Phenicians were prior to the Greeks. This is plain, from his observing in another place, where he wishes to discriminate between the different merchants who traded here, that that country (Danmonium) " utpote metallis abundantem, *Phœnicibus, Gracis* et *Gallis* mercatoribus probe notam fuisse. "(«) Here the Phenician, Greek, and Gaulish merchants come successively, in the proper order of time: And to have inverted this order, would have been a glaring impropriety. Yet in the very next period, where Richard is pointing out to us the etymologies of places, we see the Greeks again put over the head of the Phenicians—*(b) Gracam Phœniciamque* originem. Nothing, therefore, can be clearer than that, in the passage first qujted, our author speaks in general terms, and that he simply intends to mark the first establishment of the ancient British trade in this ifland: And whether this trade were entitled, the *Greek* and *Phenician,* or the *Greek* only, would be little to the purpose. Who the first Greeks that came into this island, were, is uncertain. But, in process of time, the Greeks of Marseilles obtained

a considerable sliare of the Britisli trade: And tin, lead, and (kins, are laid to have been the commodities which the Greeks exported from Britain. And their imparts were, possibly, the fame as the Phenician. In the mean time, the Greeks of Marseilles endeavoured, like the Phenicians, to conceal their commerce with the British isles from other nations. Strabo tells us, from Polybius, that the Greeks pretended a total ignorance of the Britisli isles, when questioned by the famous Scipio, respecting their situation or productions. With respect to the *Roman trade* with Danmonium, before the time of Cæsar, there is very great uncertainty. Yet we are told, that the Romans, after they became acquainted with navigation (which was not till after the first Punic war, about two hundred and sixty years before Christ) lent out a vessel in pursuit of the Phenicians, in order to discover the place where they traded for tin. But the Phenician mariner, suspecting the design of the Romans, voluntarily ran his ship among (hallows, to decoy his pursuers into the fame perilous situation, from which their imperfect skill in navigation would not enable them to emerge; whilst he knew how to disengage himself and his ship, with some present lois indeed, but little or no danger. That he did not sink his ship, or go down to the bottom with his crew and all, as some writers have imagined, is sufficiently clear from Strabo; who tells us, that, preserving himself from stiipwreck, he was afterwards paid, out of the public treasury, an equivalent for the loss of his cargo. Notwithstanding every precaution of the Phenicians, the Romans, as Strabo assures us, at length discovered the situation of the tin-countries. In consequence of this, Publius Crassus came hither with the discoverers, and made observations on the tin-mines, then of no great depth, and the disposition of the people to peace, and their readiness to give directions to voyagers. Who Publius Crassus was, or when he made this expedition in quest of our tin, we are not informed: But his voyage was certainly posterior to the fi ril Punic war, when the Romans were little acquainted with the seas.

I have already remarked, that it is very uncertain from what places the primitive Phenicians exported our commodities: And there is the fame dubiousness in regard to the ports in Danmonium, which were frequented by th e subsequent merchants.

The channel through which the trade of Britain wa s at one time carried on, is obscurely marked by Diodorus Siculus. The passage to wh ich I allude, hath exercised much conjecture: It is as follows, together with the context. *Vm* Se *irspi rn xx 'xvkv* pi»/sti(C *xxtro-ilepu cid-i/Aty. Tms yxp ŒpilTxvixvs xxrx To xxp urn* fxov To *Xx'au/jlcvod* BsAspiov *01 xxloixuvles tyiXol-stoi* Te *Sixtpt-ponTus tiai, xxi* J/a *Tw* Tw» i;£»a'v *aftropm iirifimy tTifAipu/jLivoi rxs xyuyxs. tiToi Toy xxorsltpov xxtxaxevx-uot,* $iaote%vus *tpyxfyiJ.evoi T"w tytft-sax xvroy yviv. AvTTl* (Js TTETfi'UJ' *HITX, OIXVXS lyil ySxlli,* fv a/r *TOV iropot XXTipyXOflltOI XXl T/lXiTtS xxSxipaaiy. Avcorvituilis* S' *us xo-pxyxxv pvQ/jLiis, Xo/jli.* 'bow *Us rnix mcrov irpoxu/Atmt /Aty rris @fElTxvtxvist oyoiJ.xZpiJ.tmv* Oe Ixliv. ' Kara *yxp rxs a.unuTiis, xyx-tipxti/ofA.svH rs sixv TOITH, TxtS XfJ. XXiS US TXVT1JV* £0pti«o" *Sx'iav)* roy *xX:Tcriipoy* saov 06 *Ti (rvj.Qxtvtt ITtpt rxs itAtiTiov nans, rxs pt-rxl-v xtip-tyxs rvs* Te *Kvpuns x xi* T»f *@plrxyixr)S.* Kxrx *p.tv rxs* 7rm/ji./«.'fiiW T« *(/.slxv Tsopu* 7rA»f«/i£»B Jjijoi *tyxiyoylxi.* K. *clx* $e Tas *apitwltis xnoppzums* Ti)f , *Oxhxvaris, 7Siik%Q-cn)S,* xas *noKvt totsoy ayatrifxivuo-ris, 6exfu»lxi* tffont-ni. Ivijkoo/ S'oi *c/jiVofoi Umax, ran tyyufinn* witstlai, x«i Xi3nto//.;£«3-i» *its* T»v *YaXciUtxt.* To Si *rcXivlanoy* iren Sias T)jt *faXaltar iropwBtylts Vftefs us Tfutxoylot, xotTxyao-iy mt* T« *tirirmy* To *(pofita, its os rr,y tx.CoXrit T* PoSaeya *volaiJ.a.(a)* In this passage, our historian is generally conceived to inform us, among other particulars, that " the people who inhabited the *extreme parts of Cornwall,* after they have prepared their tin for exportation, carry it in waggons to *thelfte of Wight.*" According to the interpretation of others, Ix1« is supposed to mean, one of the *I/les of Scilly,* or the *Black-rock of Falmouth.*

Among those, who entertain the *common idea,* are Dr. Henry and Mr. VVhitaker: The advocates tor a *ne--w* constru£Hon, are Borlase, and Pryce. Before I venture to give my own opinion on this passage, I shall present my readers with the sentiments of these different writers. First, then, for the *common idea.* Dr. Henry writes thus: " Whether the Greeks of Marseilles were discouraged from continuing to trade directly with Britain, by the length and danger of the voyage, or by the wars between the Romans and Carthaginians, which rendered the navigation of the Mediterranean very unsafe, we.cannot be certain. But this we know from the best information, that the trade between Britain and Marseilles, after some time, began to be carried on in a different manner, and through a different channel. Of this we have the following plain account from Diodorus Siculus: ' These Britons who dwell near the promontory of Belerium (the Land's-end) live in a very hospitable and polite manner, which is owing to their great intercourse with foreign merchants. They prepare, with much dexterity, the tin which their country produceth. For though this metal is very precious, yet when it is first dug out of the mine it is mixed with earth, from which they separate it, by melting and refining. When it is refined, they cast it into ingots, in the shape of cubes or dies, and then carry it into an adjacent island, which is callect Ictis (Wight). For when it is low-water, the space between that island and the continent of Britain becomes dry land; and they carry great quantities of tin into it in their carts and waggons. Here the merchants buy it, and transport it to the coast of Gaul; from whence they convey it over land, on horses, in about thirty days, to the mouth of the Rhone.' As Marseilles is situated near the mouth of the river Rhone, we may be certain that it was the place to which the British tin was carried, and that from thence the merchants of Marseilles sent it into all parts of the world to which they traded. It is not so clear, from the above account of Diodorus Siculu:., who were the foreign merchants who purchased the tin

from the Britons in the Isle olf Wight, transported it to the coast of Gaul, and from thence over land to Marseilles. Some imagine that they were Greeks from Marseilles, who had factories established in,the Isle of Wight, and on the coast of Gaul, for the management of this trade; while others think that they were Gauls, and that the people of Marseilles remained quietly at home, and received the British tin, and other commodities, from the hands of these Gaulish merchants. There seems to be some truth in both these opinions; and it is most: probable that the merchants of Marseilles, finding the difficulties and dangers of trading directly to Britain by sea, contrived the scheme of carrying on that trade over the continent of Gaul; and sent agents of their own to begin the execution of this scheme. But they could not but soon discover that it was impossible to carry on a trade through so great an extent of country, without the consent and assistance os the inhabitants; and that it was necessary to employ them, first as their carriers, and afterwards as their agents. By this means, some of the Gauls becoming acquainted with the nature and profits of this trade, engaged in it on their own account. For it is certain that the Gauls were instructed in trade as well as in arts and learning, by the Greeks of Marseilles. It is evident that the Isle of Wight was the place from whence these foreign *a) Nune de stanno, quod Ulic effodilur, dicendi locus est. Qui* Bzlekium *Britannia promontorium accolunt, bospitales sunt apprime, et propter mercatorum Ulic commercia mansuetiore-vita cultu. Hi stanrtum, terra, qua Mud parturit, solerti opere subaila, conficiurt. ££ua cum petricosa Jit, venas qua/dam babet terrestres, e quibus erutum metalli proventum liquesaciunt et expurgant. Talorum deinde modo conformatum in* quandam Britannia? adjectam Insulam, *cut nomen* Ictis, *deportant. Dum entm per re ftuxus intervaUum locus in medio dejiccatur, plaustns interim largam stanni vim tranjvetlant. Insults bifes vic'tnis, qua Europam atque Britann'iam interjacent, pecultare quippiam accidit. Traflus enim Me, sub inundaticTjem*

aslus, aquis oppletus, Infulas ejfe often-
dit. decedente per reciprocationem
mari, ingens loci fpacium, aquis defe-
clum, peninfularum speciem reddit.
Inde stannum ab incolis emtum in Gal-
liam mercatores transferunt. Et xxx
dierum itinere per Galliam pedestri
farcing! equis impofitas, ad Rbodani
tandem ostia deportant. Died. Sicul.
Wejseling. tom I. p. 346, 347.

foreign merchants, whether Greeks or
Gauls, exported the British tin; but we
are not told at what port of Gaul it was
landed, (a) A modern writer, of great
learning, hath engaged in a long and
particular discussion of this point; and
after examining several different opinions, he concludes at last, that Vennes,
in Britanny, was the port at which the
goods exported from Britain were dis-
embarked. It is, however, probable that
the merchants ot Gaul landed their
goods from Britain at different ports,
as it suited best their own situation and
conveniency."(A) Dr. Henry is sufficiently accurate in his translation of this
passage from Diodorus. It is, therefore,
very extraordinary, that whilst he introduces the Britons of the *Land's-end* carrying their tin into an *adjacent island*
(mo-ov *trfox.siiJ.tvm)* he lhould at the
fame instant determine this island to be
the *J/le of Wight* lying off the coast of
Hamp/bire I According to this writer,
the Cornisli could pals with their waggons, from the Land's-end to the Isle of
Wight, whenever they thought proper. It
was but a step: And they could go over
drystiod with all imaginable ease r By
some strange magic, indeed, the Isle of
Wight, in Hampshire, used, in the days
of Diodorus, to be directly opposite and
almost adjoining to the Land's-end in
Cornwall. Thus, also, Mr. Whitaker: "
The Greeks of Marseilles first followed
the course of the Phenician voyagers j
and some time before the days of Polybius, and about two hundred years before the age of,Christ, began to stiare
with them in the trade of tin. The
Carthaginian commerce declined. The
Massylian increased. And, in the reign
of Augustus, the whole current of the
British traffick had been gradually di-
verted into this channel.' At that period

the trade of the island was very considerable. Two roads were laid across it,
and reached from Sandwich to Caernar-
von on one side and from Dorsetshire
into Suffolk on the other; and the commerce of the shores was carried along
them into the interiour parts of the country. The great staple of the tin was no
longer settled in a distant corner of the
island. It was removed from Scilly, and
fixed in the Isle of Wight, a central part
of the coast, lying equally betwixt the
two roads, and better adapted to the new
arrangements of the trade. Thither the
tin was brought by the Belgæ, and thither the foreign merchants resorted with
their wares. And the trade was no longer
carried onby vessels that coasted te-
diously along the shores of Spain and
Gaul. The tin was now transported over
the neighbouring channel, unshipped on
the opposite coast, and sent upon horses
across the land or by boats along the
rivers to Marseilles and Narbonne. And
the Veneti of Gaul were the merchants,
that resorted to the Isle of Wight with
their vessels, that bartered with the Britons for their metal, and transmitted it
across the continent afterwards. This
isle, which is now separated from the
remainder of Hampshire by a channel
little more than half a mile in breadth
about the point of Hurst-castle, was then
a part of the greater island, disjoined
from it only by the tide, and united to it
at the ebb. And, during the recess of the
waters, the Britons constantly passed
over the low isthmus of land with their
cart-loads of tin. *This ivas also-the ease*
with many other places on the southerly
/bore of Britain, which appeared as islands only on the tide of flood, and became peninsulas at th ebb." (r) Here all
is beautifully consistent with the general narrative and with itself. But, as Mr.
Whitaker informs us, that " *many oth-*
er places on the jtuthtrfy Jhore of Bri-
tain, appeared as i/lands only on the
tide of flood, and became peninsulas at
the ebb;" I think we may be warranted
in fixing on some other spot on the
south-coast of Danmonium, less liable
to objections than the Isle of Wight. It
was with this notion, that Borlase and
Pryce have attempted a *new construil-*

ion of the famous passage before os.
Borlase, in his Natural History of Cornwall, fays: " The short description
which we have of the tin-trade in
Diodorus Siculus, must not be omitted,
though it is too general for us to learn
many particulars from it. ' These men
(fays he, meaning the tinners) manufacture their tin by working the grounds
which produce it with great art. For
though the land is rocky, it has soft
veins of earth running through it in
which the tinners find the treasure, extract, melt, and purify it; then shaping it
(by moulds) into a kind of cubical figure, they carry it off to a certain island
lying near the Brkisli shore, which they
call lit is; for at the recess of the tide,
the space betwixt the island and thfc
main land being dry, the tinners embrace the opportunity, and carry their tin
in carts, as fast as may be, over to the Ictis (or port); for it must be observed, that
the islands which lie betwixt the continent and Britain, have this singularity, that when tide is full, they are real
islands; but when the sea retires, they
are but so many *peninsula:.* From this
(æ) *Set Memoires it V Accticm'te in In-*
scriptions, torn. 16, p. I eT8. *t)* Vol.
t. p. J8i, 381. () Manchester, vol. 2. p.
170 to 172. this island the merchants
biiy the tin of the natives, and export
it into Gaul; nd, finally, through Gaul,
by a journey ot" about thirty days, they
bring it down on horses to the mouth of
the Erydanus, meaning the Rhone(«).'
In this description it will naturally occur
to the inquisitive reader to ask, where
this Ictis was, to which the Cornilh carried their melted tin in carts, and there
sold it to the merchants. I really cannot
inform him i but by the Ictis here, it is
plain that the Historian could not mean
the Ictis or Vectis of thie ancients' (at
present called the Isle of Wight), for
he is speaking of she Britons of Cornwall, and, by the words, it should seelri,
those of the most western parts. TV *yaf*
Bfi)ae»x)f *xalet* To *axgajlngio* To t«X!;/
«»ov BeXsfion *01* MMtttMlhf, *i$c.* Oi/
ioi Tor *xxmligit* xatWxtwtfuo-i
$i'kokj(ias, that is, " those who live at
the extreme end of Britain, called
Belerium (/), find, dress, melt, carry,

and fell their tin." Now it would be absurd to think that these inhabitants mould carry in carts their tin near two hundred miles (for so far distant is the Isle of Wight from them) when they had at least as good orts and harbours on their own shores as they could meet with there: Besides, these inabitants are said, in the some paragraph, to have been more than ordinarily civilized by conversing with strangers and merchants. Those merchants then must have been very conversant in Cornwall, there trafficked for tin, that is, there bought, and thence exported the tin, or they could have no business there; their residence would have been in some of the ports of Hampshire; and Cornwall could scarce have felt the influence of their manners, much less have beert improved and civilized by them at that distance. Again: the Cornish, after the tin was melted, carried it at low-water over to the Ictis in carts. This will by no means suit the situation of the Isle ot Wight, which is at least two mile distant from the main land, and never (a far as we can learn) has been alternately an island and a *peninsula,* as the tide is in and out. The Ictis therefore here mentioned, must lie somewhere near the coast of Cornwall, and must either have been a general name for any *peninsula* on a creek, (Ik being a common Cornish word, denoting a Cove, Creek, or Port of traffick,) or the name of some particular *peninsula* and common *emporium* oh the same coast, which has now lost its iltmus, name, and perhaps wholly disappeared, by means of some great alterations on the sea-shore of this county, *(c)* In his ancient and present state of the Isles of Scilly, Borlafe ventures to give his opinion upon the point: Dlodorus Siculus (fays he) talking of the Promontory *Belerium,* alias *Bolerium,* the tin-commerce, and courteous behaviour of the inhabitants, fays, that they carried this tin to an adjoining *British* Isle called Ictis, to which at low tide they could have access. Now there was no such island as Ictis on the western coasts of *Cornwall* in the time of *Dioii. Siculus,* neither is there at present any one with the properties he mentions, unless it be St. *Michael's Mount;* and the separation between that and the Continent must have been made long since that time. By the first, therefore, *DM. Siculus* can mean nothing but the *Lands-end,* by the geographers called *Belerium;* but (confounding the tin-trade of those western parts of *Cornwall* with that Carried on in Scilly) by the second, he means one of the Scilly Isles, to which they conveyed their tin before exportation froul the Other smaller islands; for thus he goes on, ' There is one thing peculiar ta these Islands (meaning, that there was no such thing in the *Mediterranean,* where the sea stands nearly of one height) which lie between *Britain* and *Europe,* for at full sea they appear to be Islands, but at low water, for a long way, they look like so many *Peninsula's*a description exactly answering the appearance of the Scilly islands, which were at that time successively Islands and *Peninsula's,* and lie between *Europe* and *Britain,* as the old. authors all agree, but, through the inaccuracy in geography, were not able to point out the situation of these islands more distinctly. This Ictis of *Diod. Siculus* is probably the fame Island which *PRny,* from *Timceus,* calls " Mictis, about fix days fail from *Britain,* said to be fertile in tinWhere I must observe, that the distance here laid down is no objection to Mictis's being one of the Scilly Isles, for when the ancients reckoned this plate six days fail, they did not mean from the nearest part of *Britain,* but from the place most known, and frequented by them (i. e. by the *Romans* and *Gauls)* which was that part of *Britain* nearest to, and in sight of *Gaul,* from which to the Scilly Islands the distance was indeed, six days usual sail in the early times of navigation; therefore *(a)* Rhodamis, fays the Latin translation; to Marseilles, fays PofBdonlus, in Strabo, lib. iii. page '1+7, edit. Par. x6ao. *h)* Now called the LandVEnd, (c) p. 176, J77. fore I am apt to think, that by Mictis here, *PUxy* tneant the largest of the Scclly Isles(a), as I do not at all doubt but *Disdarus Siculus* also did, in the passage mentioned abore."(i) Dr. Pryce has gratified us with a conjecture on this topic, which is, at least, plausible. " It has been hitherto (lays the Doctor) an object of enquiry, from whence our Tin was shipped in the time of the Phenicians: some fay from the Cassiterides or Scilly Islands; Bolerium, or the Land's-end; others lay, from St. Michael's Mount; and others, from Ostium Kenionis Valnbia, or F-almouth. The ignorance of true geography and navigation in the times of Timæus, Strabo, Diodorus Siculus, Polybius, and all the ancient historians and geographers, was so great, and their descriptions so obscure and contradictory, that it may ever remain a matter of conjecture and controversy, whence our Tin was exported for Phenicia or Rome, by the records they have left behind them. It seems probable, that they included the promontory of Bolerium among the Cassiterides, and denominated all the south-western coast of Cornwall as part of them; which being the first land discovered by the navigators of those days, gave one general appellation to the whole. Without partiality to any particular opinion, we must own the harbour of Falmouth seems to us the most commodious, both for natives and foreigners, to have carried on the business for exportation of this grand monopoly, which supplied all the Mediterranean markets: and we are not singular in this thought, but are very plausibly supported by a learned collator of our own country, in whose MS. we find an ingenious etymology and topographical agreement in relation to the matter before us. ' This harbour of Falmouth has been famous over Europe and Asia ever since the island was first known, though but darkly distinguished by the Greeks and Romans under several appellations; for instance, by one (in Greek) « the Mouth of the Dunmonii Island;' for neither Greeks nor Romans knew whether this province of the Dunmonii was an island of Itself, or part of the insular continent of Britain, till the time of the Roman emperor Domitian, when he circumnavigated the whole island with his fleet. Besides, it was the custom of the Jews and Greeks, to call remote and strange lands, Islands, and the natives,.

Islanders-.. to which purpose we read, Ilaiah Ixvi. 19. Tubal, Javan, and the isles afar off,'" which were the continent of Greece and Spain." Also, Genesis x. 5. and elsewhere, by the name of the isles are meant the islands, and in general all the provinces of Europe. Arid it is observable, that where the prophet Isaiah foretels the calling of the Gentiles, he makes particular mention of the islands, (chap. xli. xlii. xlix. li. lx.) which many interpreters have looked upon as a 'plain intimation, that the Christian religion should take deepest root in those parts of the world, which were separated from the Jews by the lea, and peopled by the'posterity of Japhet, who settled themselves in the islands of the Gentiles, So that the islands, in the prophetical stile, seem particularly to denote the western part of the world, the west being often called the sea in scripture language. But to'proceed: Strabo calls this mouth of the Vale river, Ostium Kenionis, and more properly Valuba, or Valubia; that js, the wall, defence, point, or promontory, of the said vale, now St. Anthony's Point; or Val-Ubii from the colony of the Ubii, a people of Belgia,. who planted themselves on the Vale river before Cæsar's days. Further, Diodorus Siculus tells us, that all Tin was fetched out of Britain: as it is in some authors, after the Greek version, from *NUms lx.ra, Ki* Oxrsr, which seems to fay in British, first, the!Gbod Lake, or Haven Island, and the second (what we now call Bud-Ok) a Bay of Oak Island; and, indeed, the memory of such Ike seems yet preserved in the present names of Car-ike road, the chief part of Falmouth harbour, from whence, to this day, the_ major part of our Tin is still exported; and Arwynike, and Bud-ike lands", by which the said harbour is bounded. Now, this word Ike, I am informed, is derived from the fame Japhetical origin as the Greek *w,* venio, to come, arrive at, or enter into a place; and, therefore, as aforeiaid, in Cornifli. British, it means not only a haven of the sea for traffic, but a place where a river of water hath its current into the sea; from whence, perhaps, the Latins had their Ictus, to signify the course of

a river. And from this etymology, we may the better understand the words of Diodorus Siculus., The Island which he calls Ictam or Icta, adjoining with Britain, is certainly that which is now called the Black Rock Island in Car-ike road aforesaid; which, as he. said, was then an island at flood or full sea, though at low water passable from the main land. There is also a Cornish MS. of the Creation of the World, a Play, brought into Oxford in 1450, and which is still extant in the Bodleian library there; which will at the (*«*) As *Baxter,* Gloss, in roee Sigdeles.. (4) p. 76, 77, 7S. the feme time serve to evince, that the now Black rock of Falmomti was m old time the Island, the Ikta of Diodorus Siculus, from which Tin was transported into Gaul. Leland the elder, in his Itinerary, tells us, that this river was encompassed with the loftiest woods, oaks, and timber trees, that the kingdom afforded, in the time of Hen. VII, and was therefore, by the Britons, called Caili-tir, and Caffi-ter; that is to fay, Woodland. From which place and haven, the Greeks fetching Tin, called it and the Wand, so often here mentioned, in their language, Casliteros. In further praise of which famous port, may the reader accept the following lines: In the calm south Valubia's harbour stands, Where Vale with sea doth join its purer hands;
Twixt which, to ships commodious port is shown,
That makes the riches of the workl its own.
Ike-ta, and Vale, the Britons chiefest pride,
Glory of them, and all the world beside,
(In fending round the treasures of its tide.
Greeks and Phenicians here of old have been j
Fetching from hence, furs, hides, pure com, and Tin,
Before great Cæsar fought Cassibelyn. "(*«*)
Having f» Pryce's Mineral. IntroA p. ui. to vii. The above, we find, is borrowed from Hats or Hatse: It occurs in HaUvs Parochial History of Cornwall. As there is an entertaining singularity in

this writer's manner, and a small part only of his history hath been printed (and of this only a few copies) I shall here permit Mr. Halsc to speak at large for himself, though the substance of his theory appears in the text. " Falmouth, *alias* Vai-moitth, *alias* Vals-movth, a Rectory, is situate (fays Halse) in the hundred of *Kerryer,* and hath upon the north *Bud-ike,* east the haven or harbour of *Tthumb,* south the *Slack Rock* and *Pendcms* Castle, west part of *Bud-its* and the *Britijh Channel.* Foe the name, it's taken from th» *Vale* river's *month,* which here empties itself into the *Britijh* ocean. And the river itself takes its' name from the original fountain' in *Roach* under *Haynesturrougb,* called *Pea-ta-vale Ftutor.,* or *Ventan* j that is to fay, the *head* or chief *good* or consecrated *spring,* or well of water or river *Valley;* alias *Pen ta-uail fenten,* i. e. the *sacred* or consecrated *famoni bead veil* or spring of water: From thence called the Vaii river. This place in *Cornish* is called *Valgcmtxr,* or *Falgenne* ; in *Saxon Val-mun* ; in *English Va/t-moutb,* synonymous therewith. This harbour of VaiiMouth hath been famous *over Euros e* and *Asia* ever since this island was first known; though but darkly distinguished by the *Greeks* and *Romans* under several appellations; for instance by one (in *Greek*) signifying *the Mouth os the Danmonii Island t* For in former days neither *Greeti* nor *Romans* knew whether this province of the *Dannnuii* was an island of itself, or part of the insular continent of *Britain* ; no, not 'till the time of the *Roman* Emperor Domitian, when he circum-navigated the whole island with his fleet of (hips. Besides, twas the custom of the *Jetv,* and *Greeks* to call remote and strange lands *Islands,* and the natives *Islanders.*-To which purpose we read, *Isaiah* Ivi. 19.) *Tnhal, Jo-van, and the Isles afar off;* which were the Continent of *Greece* and *Spain.* Again; *Straho* calls this mouth ot the Vale river *Osfiunt Cevionis;* who also more plainly speaks of this place under the names of *Valuta* and *Voluba*: A corruption either of the *British* word *Vat-eta,* i. e. the *tlting,* flowing, budling, or flashing, os the Vale river; or *Val-*

ubia, that is, the point or promontory of the said Vau, now Sis. *Anthony's Point*; or *Val-Ubii*, from the colony of the *Ubii*, a people of *Beigia*, that planted themselves on the Vale river before Cæsaj's days. From which *Ubii* might come *Corn-ubi-ensis*. Again; *Dkdorus Sicutus* tells us that all tin was fetched out of *Britain* ; as it is in some authors, after the *Greek* version, from N«7or Ix-tss, *xi* Ox-rat, *Ness, li-t/t*, it *Oc-taJ* which seems to fay in *Britijh*, the first, the *Good Lake*, cove, or haven, *island*, and the second (what we now call *Bud-ek*) a *bay* of *Oak Island*. And indeed the memory of such *Ike* seems yet preserved in the present names of *Car-ike* road, the chief part of the harbour of *Falmouth* (from whence comparatively still all tin is transported) and *Ar-viyn-ike* and *Bud-ike* lands, by which the laid harbour is bounded. Now, this word *Ike*, I am inform'd, is derived from the fame *Japbetical* origin as the Gr. *vxui, eke vt-nio*, to arrive at, or enter into a place; and therefore, as aforesaid, in *Carnijh Britijh* it signifies not only a *haven*, harbour, or creek, of the sea for traffick, but a place where a river of water hath its current into the sea, or other places of water. From whence perhaps the *Latins* bad their *ISlus* to signify the course of a river. And from this exposition, or etymology, we may the better understand *Diodorus Siculus '%* words, as out of the *Greek* rendered into *Latin*, thus:—*Britani, qui j'uxta Valerium promontorium* a corruption of *Pet-ter-an Provtcntsrium*, i. e. the remote or far-off promontory of land; viz. the *£arf's End of Cornt-valJ—imolnnl, mercatoribus, out.-0 ftanni gratia navigant, humaniores reliquis erga bofpites habentur. Hi ex terra saxosa, cttjvs trenas Jcqnuti, effadiunt flannum; quod, per ignem edutlum, in quandam insulam fernnt Britannic at juxta, qitans Jctam meant. Marit jluxu videntur insular; cum vers result exsiccate, interjelio litlore atrrs&ut t fta»* VOfc. I. Rl «w

Having thus laid before my readers the *common* interpretation of the pastage in question, as well as what I have called the *new* theories concerning it, I proceed to state my objections *rum*

deferunl, &c. Ese bis insults mercatores ems turn stannum in Galliam porlant; inde diebus fere tr'f ginta cum equis ad fontem Eridani fluminis perdvcunt. h. e. ' The *Britons* who inhabit near the Promontory *Valerium* (or the *hand's End*) are by the merchants who thither fail for tin, accounted more courteous or civil to strangers than the rest are. These people, pursuing the course of its veins, out of the rocky earth dig tin; which commodity, being melted or run down by fire, they carry to a certain *British* island nigh, which they name *lila*. In time of highwater indeed they appear *islands;* but at ebb, the shore between them and the (insular) continent being dry, they thither in carriages convey the tin, &c. From which islands the merchants transported the tin they purchase into *Gaul, Sec'* The Island which he calls *Warn*, or *Ida*, adjoining thus with *Britain*, is certainly that which is now called the *Black Rock* Island, in Car-iif road aforesaid; which, as he said, was then an *Ijland*, at flood xr full sea, tho' at low water passable from the main land. Which was *then* a true description thereof; tho' since by the raging flux and reflux of the sea the said lands and rocks are so much wash'd away, that it is not now passable to the said *Black Rock Ijland* on foot at low water from *Arwinic* lands contiguous. From or by which place the tin then made was, and still is, by merchants transported into *France;* and from thence in those days it was carried thirty days journey on horseback; and so over (the *Alps* into *Italy*, even to the fountain *Eridanus*, now called the *Po*. This harbour of Falmouth, as mariners declare, is in all respects the largest and safest haven for ships which this island of jrifin affords. Its mouth or entrance from the *British ocean*, between the castles of St. *Maws* and *sjestdenis* (situate one in St. *Anthony*, the other in *Falmouth* parishes) is about a mile and half wide; die centre or middle thereof above a league from the said mouth or entrance up the Va L x river, by the very *Rock Ijland* aforesaid, to *Car-ike Road, King's Road*, and *Turner's Were*. South east, about two leagues from thence, still on the *Vale*

river, a navigable arm or Chanel of the said harbour extendeth itself up the country, by *Xregny;* to the bridge place of which formerly it was navigable. And it is overlooked on the south east side by St. *Anthony*, St. *Just*, *Pbilley*, *Ruan-haiony-Horne*, and *Cuby* parishes; Within the said parishes of St. *Jujl* and St. *Anthony* are also two navigable creeks *tx* channels. Here stands the castle and incorporate town of St. *Matves*, where formerly stood a monastery of black canons *Augustine*, dedicated to the Virgin Maky, called St. *Mary de Vale*, for that it was situate on the *Vale* harbour or river; as its superior monastery is from the *Plym* river in *Devony* called St. *Mary de Plym*, whereon it is situate. From the north west part of this harbour of Falmouth, between the parishes of *Budock*, *Gluvias*, and *Myler*, another navigable channel extendeth itself up the country to the incorporate town of *Penryn*. And towards the north another channel thereof higher up extendeth itself through the country from the centre about a league, and is navigable to *Peran Well* and *Carnun Bridge*. Further up north east another channel or arm of *Fa/mouth* harbour extends itself to the incorporate and coinage town of *Truro*, and the manor of *Marts*, aod is navigable there, about nine muts distant from the *Black Rock* or *Istand* aforementjon'd. Lastly, another branch of this harbour extends to *Trestlian* bridge, where it's navigable between the parishes of St. *ttermey Probus*, and *Mcrtber*, about ten miles from the mouth of the bjyen and the aforesaid island. AU which members or branches of this noble harbour, are overlook'd by pleasant hills and vales of land, and within the memory of man abounding with flouristiing woods and groves of timber; and before that time *Leland* the elder in his *Itinerary* tells us, that this river Vale was in his days encompassed about with the loftiest woods, oaks, and timber trees that this kingdom afforded, *temp.* Henry VII. and was therefore by the *Britons* caljed *CaJJi-tir*, and *Cajst-ter* that is,to fay, *Wood-hand-x* from which place and haven the *Greeks*, fetching tin, called It and the *Ijland* so often here mention'd in their language *CaJJiteros.* Thus in Bodman, *CaJJiter-street* formerly *a coinage* town. But now this commodity of TIN hath made such havock of woods and timber trees, in searching for and melting the same, that scarcely any of them are to be seen in those places. For the woodj arid trees being cut down arid grubb'd up, the hills and vales have submitted to agriculture, and are become arable and pasture lands, abounding with corn, iheep, and cattle. From the premises, I suppose, 'tis evident, what Mr. *Careiv* in his *Survey* faith, of this excellent harbour of *Falmouth,* that an hundred ships may lie at anchor within the fame, and none of them fee the others main-tops; the reason of which is, because of the steep hills and long windings of the several ehanneh or branches thereof." p. 123 to 125. And again: " Between the parishes of *Budock* and *Gluiiiiis,* on a promontory of land shooting into the sea creek of *Falmouth* harbour, between two valleys,and hills, where the tide daily makes its flux and reflux, (lands the ancient burrough of *PEN-RIN,* or *PEN-RTN;* i. e. the hill-head, promontory, or beak, of land; for *as.pen* is a *tcad* in *Corni/h,* so *rin,* or *ryn, is* derived from, and synonymous with, the *gaphetical Greek Jif,* i« *nasus,* a nose, nook, promontory, or beak of any matter: A name given and taken from the natural circumstances of the place, as aforesaid. And here are lofty lands, still called *the Rins,* above the town. By the name *Pen-rm* it was taxed, as the voke lands of a considerable manor, in *Dome's day* roll, 20. William I. 1087. This glace I apprehend to be the. Oxgw/4 *Obinum* of Ptolemy, the objections to both. With respect to the former, Dr. Borlase has, in a great measure, anticipated me; whilst he points out the absurdity of the supposition, that the inhabitants of the Land's-end should convey their tin in carts near two hundred miles, when they had as good ports on their own mores as on the Isle of Wight. Not that Diodorus meant to confine this business to the Danmonii of the Land's-end. But the remoteness of the Isle of Wight, eTen from the people

who lived on the banks of the Tamar, would be a sufficient objection to it. Dr. Boilase's remark, also, on the civilization of the Danmonii, from their intercourse with merchants, ieems to have some weight. For, surely, if the) Isle of Wight had been the common emporium, those merchants need not have mixed with the Danmonii. They would naturally have resided in the sea-ports of Hampshire, not of Devonshire or Cornwall. The last objection of the Doctor to the Isle of Wightits present distance from the main land—has no force. I am willing to allow, that the Iile of Wight was alternately an island and a peninsula, jn the days of Diodorus. Since those days, our coasts have undergone various changes. But, to carry on their tin-trade in this manner, must have been extremely inconvenient to the Danmonii. And it is improbable, that they stiould lay themselves under obligations to the people of Hampshire, without a motive—that they stiould prefer a restricted and uncertain commerce in a distant territory, to an unembarrassed and unprecarious trade at home j though, at the fame time, the ports of Devon and Cornwall were equal, if not superior, to those of Hampshire. But let us dismiss the Isle of Wight. One of the Scilly Isles, called *Miclis,* has the next claim to our attention. Yet it deserves a momentary attention only. At this advanced the *Greek* geographer of the *Danmonii, An. Pom.* 140. (by *Camden,* through his ignorance of the *British* tongue, placed at St. *Michael's Mount)* it being only a corruption of *Oc* or *Ok-rin-an* j as much as to fay the *Oak-h'ofi-HJl,* or Oak-Promontory-Hill; referring to the terminative particles of the compound words Bud-oc and Pen-W». To prove this conjecture, I find, in the manuscripts of the *Britifl)* and *Welch* bards and the *traidts. An. Dom.* 600, this place is distinguifh'd with two appellations, *Pen-rin-Gtad* (i. e. the Promontory Head Wood) and *Pen-r'm Hauf-ton* (that is to fay Penrin Summer-Town); it being even to this day suitably called in modern *Eng/ijh* the *Summer Court Town.* It being thus situate on the sea shore, it was heretofore walled and fortified for its defence

against enemies; near which two watch-towers are still in being. Moreover, to prove that this town was formerly situated in an *oak wood,* or at least some other wood, I call for evidence the *Cornij h* manuscript of the *Creation of the World,* a play, brought into *Oxford* in 1450, and which is still extant m the *Bodleian* library there; which will at the fame time serve to evince that the now *Black Rock* of *Falntcuth* was in old time the *Island* (viz. the *Ikta)* of Diodorus *Siculus,* by which tin was transported into *Ga.Tia.* A few words therefore of it here follow faithfully transcribed, with their translation; they being spoken as by *Solomon,* rewarding the builders of the universe: *Bannetb an Tas wor why; Why fyth «a £wyr Gobery. Why Goher eredye' Wurbartb gam ol Gweel* Bohellh, v *Hag* Good Penrin *entien, An* Ennis, *bag* Arwinick,

Tregimber, *bag* Kcgillack.
Anlbotko Gurry the why Chanter, h. e.
Blessing of the Father on You;
    You shall have your Reward.-,
    Your wages is prepared
    Together with all the Fields of *Bobellan,*
    And the *Wood* of *Penrin* entirely,
The *Island* and *Arwinick",* Tregember and *Kegyllack.*
Of them make you a Deed or Charter. Lastly; though at present *Penryn* hath no timber *wood* pertaining thereto, yet within the memory of the last age much *oak* timber trees were extant about it, and lately some antient trees were growing in the streets thereof; all pointed at and preserved in the name of *Bud-Ock,* a *cone,* creek, or bay of *oak.* And that the now *Black Rock* of *Faliisomb* is the NioOf *lurot, m Oxtx,* of the *Greeks,* i. e. *Nefos Ik-ta ki Okta* i. e. the island *Ike-ta* and OA-ta, signifying the cove, creek, or harbour good, and oak good, (now *Falmoutb)* I make no question. Of which see more under Falmouth. Other? wife, I comVss, *Bud-ike* may. be interpreted the bay, creek, cove, or bosom of waters, leading to the sea." p. 145, 146. advanced stage of the Danmonian tin-trade, to have recourse to the Scilly Isles wottH be ridiculous. Borlase allows that

Devonshire had a principal sliare in the trade. And would he bring down our Dartmoor-tin to one of the Scilly Isles, to be imported thence to the. Continent of Gaul? Besides, he rests his hypothesis upon an unwarrantable assumption; not scrupling to assert, that " Diodorus *confounds* the tin-trade of the Land'send with that of the Scilly Istes. As to the situation of the Scilly Istes, they lay, according1 to odd writers, between Europe and Britain." This, it seems, was all the ancients; knew. Here, then, it suits our author's purpose, to expose the geographical inaccuracy of the ancients, and, particularly, their indistinct notion of the Scilly Isles, Let us proceed. The Ictis of Diodorus is discovered to be the Mictis of Pliny: But, unfortunately, the Mictis of Pliny was fix days fail from Britain. Thus, at the moment of 'its, appearance, it vanilhes: And we have seen it, only to regret its loss! Vainly would the Doctor tell us, that " when the ancients reckoned this place six days fail, they did not mean from the nearest part of Britain, bus from that part of Britain nearest to Gaul, from which to the Scilly Islands the distance was, indeed, six days usual sail in the early times of navigation." If this be admitted as a solution of the difficulty, it brings an argument in favor of the accuracy of the ancients. Thus, at one time, the geography of the ancients is dark as Erebus, at another, as clear as the mn. But when we fay, that an island lyings eff the coast of Britain, is six days tail from it, are we not understood to mean, the part of Britain nearest to the island? Any other interpretation seems forced. Grant, however, ' for the fake of argument, that Mictis was fix days fail from that " part of Britain nearest to and in sight of Gaul." Does this concession bring us nearer to the point in question? Hath Mictis any new prefensions to our notice, as the Ictis of Diodorus By adopting Bortbse's ojjiiiion, we degroy at once the authority of Diodorus—we dash to atoms the very paflage which is the groundwork of a)l our theories. *If Wis* be *Mifiis,* it muss either be *the ijle to ivhich tin was conveyed from the surrounding islets of*

Scilly ; or it must be *the isle to wiiich tin--was conveyed from the Land's-end*—in both cafes *pre-vioujly to the exportation of this metal into Gaul.*—In the *first* cafe (which Borlase supposes to be true) Diodorus talks absolute nonsense. And Borlase obliges him to inform us, in the self-fame words, («) ' that the people of theLand's-end convey their tin in carts to an adjacent island, whence It is stiipped off for Gaul—and that the people of Scilly convey their tin in carts from all their islets, to one common island, whence it is stiipped off for Gaul." This is all in one breath L It is like the satyr blowing hot and cold! Thus is our poor historian pressed into the service of conjecturists. Thus cruelly is he tortured, and forced to mutter fallhood, as he writhes npon the wheel of the executioner. In the *second* cafe, Diodorus leads our nierchants to their journey's end, by a route most unconscionably circuitous. When the Cornish would go eastward, the Greek, in mere wantonness, turns their faces to the west. Not to insist on the expedition of the Devonshire miners from the hills of Dartmoor to the Scilly-Isles, to have their goods shipped off for France, let us look only to the hard lot of the inhabitants of the Bolerium. With the view of conveying their tin to Gaul, Diodorus orders them to set off—for the Isles of Scilly. The Scilly Isles lie about nine leagues west of the Land's-end: And over nine leagues were the Danmonii doomed to drive their waggons. Having accomplished, however, this more than Herculean labor, they had, I suppose, to felicitate themselves on the progress of their tin towards the Gallic coast. But a truce to badinage. Borlase was clearly misled by sounds, when he substituted *MiQis* for *isis.* In his Natural History of Cornwall, he fays s Where this Ictis was, I really cannot inform the reader." Yet, in his ancient and present State of the Isles of Scilly, he ' does not at all doubt but that by Ictis, Diodorus Siculus meant Mictis"—whence we might almost infer, that in the theory which I have been examining, he was occupied by the delirium of the moment. Next comes the *Black-rock* conjecture;

which, though it was thrown out at random by Halfe, who understood neither Greek nor Latin, and hath been supported by Pryce, who was confessedly ignorant of Greek, and whose knowledge of the Latin was equivocal, is yet specious, and I will venture to fay, ingenious. Such it appears, when we consider the periodical peninsularity of the Blaqk-rock in former times, the name of *Ickta* corresponding with Ixlr, and the situation of Falmouth harbour less objectionable than that of the Isle of Wight, or of the Scilly Istes. But several Islands on our coasts were temporary peninsulas: So that the case of the Black-rock is not singu aj « It is all the Came in the Greek"—to *literalixe* a vulgar proverb. lar..As to the name of *hkta* (or *Ick*) it is commonly applied to *creeks* in Comwall(a) i And, the situation of the Black-rock (though comparatively good) was not the most eligible for the Danmonii east of the Tamar. In short, as it is the casual name of Ickta which wings us to the harbour of Falmouth, I can by no means alight on the Black-Rock as the »»»7o» 7r$exttp. t»iv of Diodorus. Here, then,-we hover in vain: And, though we have loug fluttered over the world of waters, we have found no resting-place. To raise objections in this manner, against the theories of others, is easy: But to form a new theory, is difficult. Perhaps, in the present case, no conjecture can be thrown out, that may boldly claim tuiiveilal attethio. i. it is not, therefore, with an air of triumph that I propose my own opinions. With the view of exciting antiquarians to this enquiry, I liave only to intimate, that I have often looked tp the *Island of* St. Nicholas, as the Ictis of Diodorus. In this light, St. Nicholas seems to be entitled to a moment's consideration. It is situated in *Plymouth-Sound,* " the first promontory on the west side of which, (iays Carew) is *Rame-bead.* From thence trending *Penlee-Point,* you discover *Kings-sand* and *Causam-Bay.* In the mouth of the harbour, lyeth St. Nicholas Island; in fashion losengy, in quantity about 3. acres, strongly fortifyed,.carefully guarded, and subject ta the commaunder of *Plymmouth* fort.

From this island, a range of rocks reacheth over to the south'wefi /bore, discovered at the low ivate'r of /bring tides, & leaving onely a narroiu entrance iu the midst called the Yate, for Jhips to safe thorow,-whereto they are directed by certaine market at lavd." (i) From the correspondence of this description with that of Diodorus Siculus—from the appellation of *I3is*—from the scite of St. Nicholas at the mouth of the Tamar—from its central position in regard to Devon and Cornwall—from the actual conventions of the Devonshire and Cornish miners, in its vicinity—from the ancient mines both to the east and west of it, particularly the tinworks of Dartmoor—from its situation in reference to Gaul—and from the Grecian factory at the Ramhead, near which it lies, as connected with the Greeks of Marseilles, I confess, I have a strong suspicion that this little isle might have been the identical *lulu'. The correspondence of this description voith that of Diodorus Siculus,* must be evident at a glance. Diodorus describes a certain isle adjacent to the shores of Britain—*nn irfoxtiy.cnt.* Such is St. Nicholas. And this isle (he intimates) is situate between Britain and the continent: So is St. Nicholas. The name of this isle, lie lays, is *IBis.* And *Itlis,* we shall see (which is Cornubritisli) was probably the first name of St. Nicholas. The space between Ictis and the main-land (he adds) becomes an isthmus at the reflux of the tide. Such, even now, may almost be said of St. Nicholas; since " from this island, a range of rocks reacheth over to the south-west sliore, discovered at the low water of spring-tides." It is remarkable, that this range of rocks is called the *Bridge.* Nor have I a doubt but that in the time of our historian, this bridge was pasiable: And great quantities of tin, from the west, were, probably, carried over it, in Cornish waggons. Diodorus, also, informs us, that die isles in general, between Britain and the continent, were, in this manner, alternately, islands and peninsulas—the truth of which is abundantly proved by the British history, and tradition, and the observations of the naturalist. " But the Ic-

tis of Diodorus, may the objector fay, must have been a larger isle than that of St. Nicholas." Doubtless it was a larger isle than St. Nicholas appears at present. Let us recollect, however, the vast" changes that have taken place, on all the coasts of Britain and its neighbouring isles, since the time of Diodorus: Let us look only to the alterations in the Scilly Isles. That they have been greatly reduced from their original size, is evident. And, very possibly, St. Nicholas has been reduced in the fame proportion. All the south-west coasts and adjacent islands have suffered, more or less, by the *(a) " Ick—a* common termination of creeks in Cornwall; as Pordin/ci, Pradriici, Portyfs;V.' Borlafe's Vocabulary. 1 () Carew's Survey, p. 99. Rifdon's description of this harbour and of the island, is as follows:

" Between Tamer and Plym, is situate that town sometime called *Suttm,* of-its southerly scite. In the Saxons heptarchy, this harbour was called *I'amenvortb* (as is to be read in the life of St. Indrac tus) if St. Nicholas Island be not meant thereby. For *fPcortb,* in Saxon, is a river-island Just before the harbour's mouth, Heth St. Nicholas's island, for form lozengee, by estimation three acres of land, strengthened *by* art as well as nature, and is subject to the command of the captain of Plimouth fort." Leland says, that « *Walterus de ValU toria* gave to Plymtoun-Priorie the Isle of S.nicolas *cum cumculis,* conteyning a 2. acres of ground, or more, and lying at the mouthes of Tamar *tc* Plym ryvers." Itinerary, vol. i. p. 45. 1 »' ' the force of the elements, particularly by the depredations of the sea. Why, then, should we except St. Nicholas from the wreck? Those, however, who are acquainted with the present appearance of St. Nicholas, will make no such exception. From its shelving coasts towards the sea, there are rocks that run out to a great length. At low water, their surfaces are visible: And they are evidently very extensive. When we consider, then, the defalcation os the shore, from subsidences of earth and other causes, it seems reasonable to suppose, that these ledges of rock towards the sea, were

once covered with ftrata of gravel and sand and earth, forming a part of the Isle of St. Nicholas; but that these different layers were removed in a course of time from their foundation of rock, fretted away by the gradual fluctuation of the sea, disturbed and tumbled into the deep from the mining of subterraneous waters, divulsed and dashed to atoms amidst earthquakes and the violence of the tempest. In short, sailors have made precisely the fame observations on the rocks contiguous to St. Nicholas, as on those between the Scilly Hies and the Cornish coast. Excepting towards Mount-Edgecumbe and the sea, no rocks are discoverable adjoining to this island. The other parts of its coasts are washed by deep water. Towards the sea, however, the water is extremely shallow, and large beds ot rock are very apparent—whence I conclude, that a great part of the island hath disappeared: Nor is it unlikely, that in the age of our historian, St. Nicholas was even in point of size, as eligible an emporium as the Isle of Wight, (a) With respect to the; name of *lilis, Ick* is undoubtedly a Coi nisli word, signifying *a creek.* It is preserved in the names of various places in the neighbourhood of the Tamar, and the Plym: And all die land near the mouths of these rivers is full of *creeks.* In his description of the course of the Tamar, Borlafc tells us, *(t) "* that the Tamar receiving the Tavy on the east, and having made a creek into the parishes of Botsflemming and Landulph on the weft, becomes a spacious harbour; and wasliing the foot of the ancient borough of Saltam within half a mile, is joined by the Lynher creek and river; then passing straight forward forms the noble harbour of Hamoze, *(c)* called formerly Tamerworth; where making two large *creeks,* one called St. John's, the other' Millbrook, at the west, and Stonehouse *creek* at the east (after a course of about forty miles, nearly south) the Tamar passes into the sea, having Mount Edgcumbe for its western, and the lands of Stonehouse and St. Nicholas Island, in Plymouth Sound, for the eastern boundary." The *vwo* of Diodorus, then, had received a

Cornijb name,' in the days of the historian. On the coasts of Hampshire, we are acquainted with no such term as *Ick* or *Ickta,* or fitV, a synonymous with *creek.* And the Cornisli would naturally give this name to an island on their own shores, not to the Isle of Wight. was a Cornish island, on the

Cornish coast, known by a Cornish name, and so denominated by the people of Cornwall. In the mean time, the name of Ictis may, with as rrich reason, be appropriated to the Isle of St. Nicholas as to the Black-Rock: Yet it was chiefly the name, which ted Halse and Pryce to exalt their Black-Rock into the *no-ov* of the Greek historian. The present appellation of our Island, is evidently modern. In the Saxon Period, its name is supposed to have beeti *Taihernxjortb, an i/land at the mouth of the Tamar.* But Ixl« is a term more peculiarly descriptive of it—*the island of creeks,* or *the creek-island.*— From it's *situation at the mouth of such a fine navigable river as the Tamar,* St. Nicholas Was well calculated for the purposes of merchandize. And the Tamar was, undoubtedly, navigated by the Pheniciaris and Greeks. As it was entered, in a subsequent period, by the Danes, whence they committed their depredations both 011 the Devonshire and Cornish sides os' it, so was it frequented by the earliest inhabitants of Danmoniuiri, Who, with their freights of tin, failed down to the Isle of St. Nicholas.—*The Central situation of St. Nicholas, with regard both to Devonshire and Cornwall,* will afford us, also, just grounds for supposing it to have been the general depository of the tin raised both to the east and west. The Phenician navigators are thought to have come-up the

Tamar, () Let me repeat, that I do not here acquiesce in probabilities. Mr. Scawen tells ns,-in his MS. that " Thiii Was *A* Valiev BiTWEiN RAMHEAD Ani LOOE." And in a clew day, he lays, " there is te-be seea *at the bottom of the sea,* a league from the shore, *a sewd if timber."* b Nat. Hist. p. 37, $. —" Scant a mile lower lyith Liner *Crete,* goyng up onto S. Germsfter«. Then brekith a-ti-

tle *Creke,* out casllid John's or Antony. And at the mouth about S. NiCotAt brekitti in a *Creek* goying up to Milbrok a. miles up in land from the mayn haves. " Ldand's I tin. vol. z, p. 41. (0 Saxon name Ham-oze j that is, the wet eozy habitation,'urc«ittdr inclosure () Camden, page »6.

Tarriar, very soon after their acquaintance with Danmonium.(a) They mult have cfift 6overed, therefore, the Isle of St. Nicholas, before they had established any factories iri this county. But, in the present advanced state of the British commerce, St. Nicholas was surely familiar to the different settlers; who availed themselves, I doubt not, of its1 advantageous situation. Whilst the colonists of the north of Devon conveyed their tin to the banks of the Tamar, whence it might have been shipped off and brought down! the river to this island, and whilst the inhabitants of Dartmoor and all the country bordering upon the Tamar, freighted their vessels in the fame manner, and unloaded thenty also, at St. Nicholas; the. Cornish even from the Land's-end (as Diodorus intimates) were driving their waggons towards the lame common depository to which they might easily pass at low water.—That our idea of the convenience of such a central spot to thS tin-traders of Devon and Cornwall, is perfectly just, seems evinced in the strongest manner, *by the actual meetings of the Devonshire and Cornish miners on (b) Hengston-down, at no great distance from our (stand,* for the purpose of renewing the remembranBe of their unwritten laws (their traditional observances of high antiquity) and of fettling various points in which both parties were interested, either as tin-manufacturers or merchants Periodical associations of this kind were natural. And such periodical associations tbek place in the vicinity of St. Nicholas from time immemorial, many ages before the existence of any written stannary laws, arid probably in the British Period. If, then, the! Devonshire and Cornisti miners were in the habit of consulting their mutual convenience; by such meetings at a central spot, is it not fair to conclude,

that they had a regard, alibi to the common advantage, in the adtual exportation of their tin, and that they conveyed this metal to some port of traffick, equally commodious to both parties? This port was1 some island on their coasts: And where can an island be found more accessible to both parties, than that of St. Nicholas? If St. Nicholas were in those days sufficiently large fof such a general port of traffick (and I doubt not but it was) its situation more eligible than that of any other island on the south-west stiores, would instantly deternjine its pretensions to the rank I have given it in the commercial world. —Let us add to this, *the vestiges of ancient tin-nvoris tn its-vicinity.* We are informed, from *records,* that " all the old mines on Dartmoor, are on its western side towards the Tamar." This is a curious dr cumstance. And there is no doubt but the *traces* of old tin-works are chiefly on the west side of the forest. Here are strong marks both of fhode and stream works. The boldest vestiges, also, of our ancient Cornisti mines, are very near the Tamar. (r) It is natural therefore, to conjecture, that the greater abundance of tin on the banks of the Tamar would give a proportionate consequence to the adventurers of the neighbourhood; and that the weight of interest thus irresistibly acquired, would render their own district the! principal seat of commerce. Others, indeed, reasoning differently, may imagine, that thtf frequentation of the Tamar by our tin-merchants, or the establishment of an emporium on the Isle of St. Nicholas, was itself the occasion of multiplying the tin-works in the neighbouring country; since the expences of carriage or conveyance must have decreased in proportion to the nearness of the commodity to the place of exportation; not to mention other advantages which would accrue from raising and preparing the tin, amidst the confluence of merchants and the fervor of commerce.—In the mean time, *the situation of St. Nicholas in refpeB to Gaul,* is surely preferable either to that of the Seilly Isles or of the Blackrock. To the Isle of Wight I shall not recur; as the trade in question was not with Hampshire but with Devonshire and Cornwall. But on this point, as singly taken *(a)* Mr. Pinkerton Is certainly correct in his idea, that the Cassiterldes did not mean, exclusively, the Scilly Isles, but, also, Great Britain and Ireland.

(A) " From Plymouth Haven, passing farther into the countrie, *Hcngsten downe* presenteth his" Waste head and fides to our sight. This name it borroweth of *Hengst,* which in the Saxon fignifieth a *horse,* & to such least daintie beasts it yeeldeth fittest pasture. The countrie people have a by word that Hengsten-downe, well ywrought,
Is worth London towne, deare ybought.
Which grewe from the store of tynne, in former times, these digged Up i But that gainfull plentie is now fallen to a scant—saving scarcitie." Carew's Survey, p. 115.

(c) " By the ry ver of *Tamar* from the hedde north north est ysluyng owt towarde the sowthe, the eontery being hilly, ys fertile of corne & gresse with sum *tynne ivarkes* wrougth hy *violens of-water. Hengiston* beyng a hy hylle, and *nere Tamar,* yn the east part, baryn of his self, yet is fertile by *ycld ing of tynne* both *be water* & dry wsrlfes." Leland's Itin. vol, 4; p. 113. (Oxford edit. 1769.)

Von I. 3 taken, I lay Ho stress; though it may be adduced, with others, in favor of my hypothesis.—My last argument was drawn from *the Greek faSory at the Ramhead* (near which St. Nicholas lies) *as conneSed tvith the Greets of Marseilles.* The Greeks of the Ramhead had called this promontory K$I« //.tlanroi ; they had given the name of T/Mtfor(«) to the river, at the mouth of which our island is situated j and to the island itself they had probably affixed the appellation of Ix)«. And nothing is more likely, than that this Grecian factory supported a regular correspondence with their brethren at Marseilles. As the communication, therefore, of the Danmonii with foreign merchants through the port of Ictis, Was *indisputably* with the *Greeks of Marseilles* (for this is an historical fact, not an hypothetical position) I conceive it probable, that the port of Ictis

was ar the Isle of St. Nicholas adjoining *to our Grecian faBory of the Ramhead.* Diodorus notices our tin-trade with Marseilles from the port of Ictis, at this very conjuncture: And, at this very conjuncture, a Grecian factory corresponding with the Greeks of Marseilles, were establilhed at the nfis *pJluisat;* close to which lay the Isle of St. Nicholas.—On the whole, I think, these concurring circumstances give a plausible air, at least, to my hypothesis: And I have stated my ideas merely as theoretical. At all events, I conceive, my readers will agree with me in opinion, that St. Nicholas hath as fair a claim to the commercial preheminence of 1x1/?, as either the Isle of Wight, or one of the Scilly Isles, or the Black-rock of Falmouth.

At this advanced stage of the British commerce, there were, doubtless, other marts of trade on the south-coast of Danmonium. Such was the case, also, on the north shore; whilst commercial settlements were formed on the *Jugum Ocrinum,* communicating with the country on either side of it. Among other ports was the *Ostium Isca flwvii,* immediately connected with the capital: and at *Helenis Promontorium, Ocrinum Promontorium,* and *Promontorium Anti'vestaum,* inferior factories, possibly, were established.*hi)* And, in the north of Devon, the Phenicians, we doubt not. were carrying on a trade of some consequence at *Hertland-Point;* whilst *Okebampton,* on the *Ocrinum Jugum,* was the principal link in the great commercial chain.

Who these foreign merchants were, that purchased the tin from the Danmonians in this island, and transported it to the coast of Gaul, and thence overland to Marseilles, the historian hath not informed us. Probably, the Greeks of Marseilles, at first, sent agents of their own to Ictis, to negociate this business, but afterwards received the British tin, and other commodities, from the hands of the Gauls; since the conduct of such a trade over the continent of Gaul, required the assistance of its inhabitants. The Greeks *ot Marseilles,* after they had begun to trade in this manner, could not expect to confine the British commerce

to themselves. They had seen rivals in the Gauls, particularly the merchants of *Narbonne,* a rich and flourishing city, on the coast of the Mediterranean, not far from the mouth of the Rhone. After the division of the Britisli trade between Marseilles and Narbonne, the merchants of Gaul opened several new routs for conveying their goods from Britain over the continent of Gaul, to these two great cities. They brought their goods from Britain up the river Seine, as far as it was navigable, and thence conveyed them, on horses, overland, to the Rhone, on which they again embarked them; and, falling down that river to the Mediterranean, landed them either at Marseilles or Narbonne. On their return, they brought goods for the Danmonian market from these cities up the Rhone, as far as it was navigable, thence overland to the Seine, and down the river, and across the channel to Ictis, and other parts of Britain. But, because so long a navigation up so rapid a river as the Rhone, was attended with great difficulties, they-sometimes landed their goods at Vienne or Lyons, carried them overland to the

Loire, *(a) TaiA.tt.fos* from *trolaciMS. (b)* Dr. Stukeley seems to insinuate, that there was a Greek settlement or factory at Seaton. " Just by the present haven wall, at *Seaton* (says Stukeley) is a long pier or wall jutting out into the sea—made of great rocks piled together, to the breadth of fix yards. They told me, it was built 'many years ago by one Courd, once a poor sailor; who being somewhere in the Mediterranean, *was told by a certain Greek,* that much tre sure was hid upon Hogfdon-hils near here, and that *this memorial was transmitted to him by his ancestors.* Courd, upon his return, digging there, found the golden mine —and at his own expence built this wall, with an intention to restore the harbour. The people hereabouts firmly believe the story; and many have dug iivthe place with like hopes." This tradition reminds me of the old Greek pilot, who referred Mr. Anfon to the days of his ancestors—pointing with conscious pride to the isle of Tenedos, and exclaiming—" (here *our* fleets lay"—during the siege of Troy.

Loire, and down that river to Vennes, and other cities on the coast of Britanny, and thence embarked them for Britain. The trade, by this second route, was carried on by the Veneti, the best navigators of the ancient Gauls. A third route was from Britain to the mouth of the Garonne, up that river as far as it was navigable, and thence overland to Narbonne. The trade of Britain, however, was not long confined to Danmoniuna, after it came into the hands of the Gaulish merchants. It gradually extended to all the coasts opposite to Gaul: And the Belgæ and other nations, who possess these coasts, kept up a constant intercourse with the continent whence they came, *(a)* 1 In *(a)* The following is an extract from Chappie's long digression on the British commerce—a digression from which he frequently digresses; *u/uch oagatory deviations"* serving, in his opinion, to relieve the tedkrofnefs of " *invariably plodding in the same dull trasi I /.*'" u It may be proper to remark that although, in the course of our enquiries on this subject, we have supposed with Dr. *BorlaJ'e,* that the *Phænicians* took those parts of *Devon* and *Cornwall* which produced tin to be *islands,* and included them as such, with those now denominated the *Scitly* Islands; yet this was only meant of the notions they might have of them at the time when they first discovered them; when they could know no more os *Britain* or its isles than the situation of those parts of the coasts on which they landed, or had observ'd from their ships; and could no more guess at their extent or connection, than the modern *Europeans* could, 'till very lately, whether *New Holland* or New *Zealand* were islands or continent. But we cannot suppose, that such expert navigators, as the *Pbtenicians* undoubtedly were, could long remain ignorant that the eastern parts of the tin-countries, with which they must soon, have establilh'd a constant trade for that metal, were connected with, and parts of, a much larger tract of land than any of those little islands with which.th.ey had at first confounded them. And yet the

Creeks, who were by them supplied with it, but were wholly unacquainted with the situation or extent of the countries whence they had it, might still continue the name they had originally adopted to distinguish them, and which became the common appellation of all places productive of tin; which metal was by the ancients taken to be a species of *lead,* and frequently so call'd. Thus *Mela,* speaking of the isles of the northern ocean, mentions some *Celtic* ones which, because abounding in *lead,* were all call'd by one common name, *CaJJiterides(i)* : AndiVinjr says,(i) the *Ctjpteriies* were so call'd by the *Greets* from being fruitful in lead; meaning *that* white sort of *lead* (as they supposed it to be, tho' in reality a different metal) which *Cæjar* in his commentaries (speaking of the tin of the midland or interior parts of *Britain)* called *plumbum aliunt.* That the *Phænicians* themselves did not immediately know or distinguish the tin-country of the *Daxmonii* from the *Scitly* Isles, as they were afterwards call'd, cannot be wonder'd at; tho' for the reason above suggested, we can't doubt of their being soon apprized of their being distinct and separate from them, and that they could furnish them with tin in much greater abundance than those detach'd little islands could produce. Other nations however, for above 500 years after this, knew very little of ttie *British* Isles, or whether *'Britain* itself were really such or not r And tho' *'Julius Casar,* at his invasion oi *Britain,* appears to have been well inform'd of the extent of its *southern* coasts (for the account he gives of it differs but a very few miles from the truth, according to our modem maps, however incorrect in his other dimensions deduced from the random guesses of the inhabitants), and had been apprized of its having tin in its interior parts as above mention'd; yet be takes no particular notice of those islands which had long supplied the world tlierewith—And tho' *Strait,* who wrote 70 years after *Ctrjai'%* invasion, in his account of the bearing and situation os the *Cajjiteridcs* from *Cades,* plainly directs us, towards the Land's End in *Cornwall,* and the islands situate near it

5 and the number of the principal ones (of which, he tells us, all but one were inhabited) were not unknown to him (3); yet he appears ignorant of their real distance; of which he, in bis third book, only (1) In Celtki aliquot fans, quas, qnia phtmbo abundant, uno omnes Caflitfriiias appellant. Pomp. Met. lib 3. cap. at.

(2) Casliterides dicta; a Giæcis a fertititate plumbi. Plin. lib. 4. tup. 22, " stanni l'ctf. quod plumbi species habebatur. " Hilt. Comment. Dionys. p. 222. ed. 1679. (3) He reckon, ten of them lying close together: *At* §e Kixti/tejjsj *lxotfA£y tl(Tt, xeir-TXt tyyvs dhnAair, utgls aaxrat ann* Ttf *ran"AruBui itthocylxi. pia* o" *a.irm* Ef»i/iOi Is"', *rots* S` *oxKXtXS otxMCTlV OLV&putlsOt* WtsOi, &c. Strab. lib. 3. prope finein.— Caifitcrides inftilæ decem sum numero, vicinas invicem, ab Artabrotnm portu versus ieptentrionem in alto sitae mari. Una earum deferta eft, reliquæ ah homimbus incomntnr, fcc.Interp. Xylandr. And Camden, who doubts not but that these Caffiterides were those new call'd the Scilly Islands, observes, that there are really but ten of them of any note, viz. St. Mary's, Anneth,-Agnes, Sampson, Silly, Bicfer, Ruseo or Trcscaw, SL Helen's, St. Martin's, and Arthur. Indeed he reckons 145 ishnds that go bv the name of Scilly Islands, all clothed with grafs, and coveied with greenish moss; besides many hideous rocks and great stones above water." But, as he had before intimated, this number (tho' it exceeds that of ten, as reckon'd by Eustathius and Stfabo, by above ten times as many) affords no gooti argument against their being the fame with the Cafljterides of the ancients; since the fame would hold equally good against the numbere of the Kxbudes and Orcades as reckoned by Ptolemy. The truth on"t is (fays he, the ancient writers knew nothing certain of these remote parts and illands; no more titan we of the Islands iu the Stieigbts of Magellan, and

Vol. I. Sa « a what manner the commodities I have noticed, were conveyed from one district, or from one country to another, we may have casually oblerved: But it is a point, worthy a distinct pnly fays, they were to the northward of *Gades,* but out in the high seas, and here seems to have fuppos'd them somewhere off that coast of Old *Spain* which was then possess'd by the *Artabri* and *fejtici flerii* in the northern part of the ancient *Lufitania,* near the promontory of *Nerium,* now call'd *Cape-Finistcrre:* But elsewhere (lib. 7..) he had directed us to a much more northerly situation of them.(1) *Mela* also, — who wrote about 20 years after *Strata,* when the Emperor *Claudius* fiad just made his expedition into *Britain,* and was about to triumph for his success there,—declines giving any description of a country so little known to the *Romans* as *Britain* then was; but only ex presses his expectation of its being soon more certainly known, since the Emperor had, by his conquest of people before untamed, and of some 'till then unknown, open'd a way to further discover ries of what it was, and what it might produce.)—Yet it was not 'till 40 years after this, when *Agricola's* fleet sail'd round it, that the *Romans* certainly knew it to be an island. After the coalition of the *Phœnicians* of *Gades* with their brethren the *Carthaginians,* that powerful nation in conjunction with them, must have continued to carry on the tin-trade with the *Danmonii;* still carefully concealing it from all competitors. These they bad taken every precaution to exclude; and having Jong preserv'd to themselves the uninterrupted and unrivall'd enjoyment of this beneficial branch of (their' commerce under the protection of the *Tyrians,* would be (as we are assured they were) equally attentive to it in concert with their new colleagues and no, less powerful protectors; who could not but esteem the continuance of this monopoly a most important object of their national concern. And so sollicitous were they to secure it, that when the *Romans,* aster they became acquainted with navigation, (of which they were wholly ignorant 'till engaged in the first *Punic* war, about 260 years fcefore *Cbrift),)* sent out their doggers to watch and follow a *Phœnician* (hip, with a view to a discovery of the place where they trad-

ed for this valuable commodity; the *Phœnician* mariner perceiving their design, which it behoved him by al means to disappoint, would voluntarily run his ship on some shoal, to decoy the *Romans* into the like perilous situation; which from their as yet imperfect skill in navigation might prove fatal to *them,* but from which he himself well knew how to disengage himself and his ship, with some present loss indeed, but little or no danger. For that he did not fink his ship, and himself and crew in it)(4) as some hive groundless supposed, is sufficiently evident j %t whole tract of New Guiney.' See Gibs. Camd. 1112. ed. 1695. where he gives other reasons for supposing the Scilly jslands to be the Casliterides; but none inconsistent with our supposition, that the stannary tracts of Cornwall and Devon were included with them under the fame denomination. Chappie.

(1) Strabo, in his 2d book here seserr'd to, aster describing the course of the navigation along the western coast of Spain *yp* that *os* the Artabri, and then turning with an obtuse angle eastward, 'till off the Pyrenees; adds as follows: *Tovrots* Cje *Too icnVEgtcc Tns BgETtzvtxr.s avrtnEtvrxt tspos ocpxTov, opoluis* ce *xdt rot's Aglcc(3pots fiXifXCC t$gVA.htXlt* His occiduæ Britanniae partes pppofitae stint versus feptentrionem. Itemque ArtatbrU versus feptentrionem opponuntur insulæ Cattiterides, -quasi si stannarias dicas, in pelago, & Britannico propemodum sitac climate. (Interp. Xylandr) i. e. Opposite to these towards the north, are the western parts of Britain. Also over against the Artabri so the north lie those islands which they call Cafliterides (Attice Cattiterides), situate out in the main sea very nearly in the same climate with Britain.—This evidently points out to us the.Scilly Islands, as no other will so well answer this descrip? tion: And tho' Strabo might not suppose them so near that western part of Britain which he mentions, nor their being so.exactly in the same climate and latitude, as they really are; this is less to be wpnder'd at, than that, from the intelligence he could then have concerning those British Isles, he

should be enabled to give so true an account of them. Chappie. (2) Brittannia qualis sit, qualesque progeneret, mox certiora & magis explorata dicentur. Quippe tamdiu clausam aperit pece principum maximus: nec indomitarum modo ante se, verum ignotarum quoque gentium victor, propriarutn re mm fidem utbello affectavit, ita triumpho declaraturus portal." Pomp. Mel. lib. 3. cap. 8. (3) Ech. Rom. Hist. b. 2. ch, 9. (4) If it cpuld be so understood, it had been a more extraordinary instance of patriotic madness than that of Curtius him self; who for the supposed good of his country leapt alone into the pit of destruction, without involving his slaves or dependents in the fame perdition. This might be deemed heroic in a Roman knight, who might promise himself immortal fame as the fancied reward of so much merit; but it would have been condemnable as the height of folly and most-ridiculous knight-errantry in a Phœnician sliip-master, to devote himself and his crew to the devouring waves to prevent the discoyery pf a state secret; when, as none could escape to testify his patriotism, it would for ever remain doubtful whether his fate were owing,to accident of design, and consequently could not insure him even the empty applause of his countrymen as a tribute to his manes.—Could a Dutch trader to Ambqyna be prevail'd on by the warmth of his patriotism to hazard, his iDwn life at least, by a voluntary shipwreck, to secure the monopoly of the spicertrade? Jf not, we have as little reason to suppose the monopolizers of tin would take any such desperate methods to guard against and preclude interlopers from having any share in it. Foi the dispositions pf the modern Dutch and the ancient Phœnicians seem extremely similar, in respect to trade and commerce and the means of securing it; and tho neither might much scruple, on Urgent pecasipns, to offer human sacrifices to Plutus, yet to make themselves the victims, merely to promote the advantage ospthers, and in total exclusion of their own, would be quite out of character. Avarice and selfishness are inconsistent with public spirit; and tho they may accidentally contribute to promote the public welfare, this seldom or never happens but when they are stimulated to it by interested views. We have heard indeed of a miser who died to save charges; but this was to preserve his, owrj hpard undiminifh'd, not to increase the riches of the community. Chappie. a distinct examination. We have already seen, that the ancient Britons were not unacquainted with the most perfect method of land-carriage yet discovered, long before they were dent; fince *Strabo,* from whom we have this account, immediately adds, that " preserving himself from shipwreck, he was afterwards compensated out of the public treasury for the loss of his cargo(i)." Hence we learn that the custom of the *Phœnicians* in such cafes was, to run their ship aground in some (hallow place, with which and its soundings they were previously acquainted, and could guard against its danger; and from which, after having drawn their competitors into the snare, such expert navigators knew how to get free, by throwing overboard a sufficient quantity os the Jading to lighten the ship; and getting her afloat, to return with safety home; where they were sure to receive an adequate compensation, for the loss they had sustain'd by sacrificing the profits of such an interrupted voyage to the security of the trade. But notwithstanding these precautions, the fame author assures us, the *Romans,* by frequent attempts of the like kind, at length discovered the situation of the *Cafftterie*Jes; and having found their way to them, *Publius Craffus* afterwards came with the discoverers, and made observations on the tin mines here (then of no great depth) and the disposition of the people to peace; their attention to navigation as their leisure permitted, and their readiness to give directions to all who were inclinable to make this voyage(i). Who this *P. Craffus* was, whether some mariner of *Gallia Narbonenfis,* or of what other parts of the Empire, and at what time he made this expedition hither in quest of our tin, we are not inform'd. All we can with certainty affirm is, that it must have been after the first

Punic war; 'till which time the *Romans* traded in foreign bottoms, having no (hips of their own, and being 'till then (as has been already observ'd) wholly unskill'd in navigation: And if *Crajfus* was of *Gaul,* as it seems most probable he was, this discovery and examination of our mines by him and his co-adventurers, can't be fuppos'd to have been till after the third *Punic* war and the destruction of *Old Carthage* (in *anno ante Cbr.* 144); perhaps not 'till the conclusion of the *Allobrogit* war near 30 years after, viz. in the year before Christ 116, when *Narbonne Gaul* was reduced to a *Roman* provinces 3). And even this, was rather *before* than *after* any *Greeks* had sailed to *Britain,* if *Bochart* mistakes not, in supposing their first voyage to this island to have been in the time of *Ptolemy Lathyrus* King of *Ægyft;* who begun his reign (of 36 years) but the year after the commencement of the last-mentioned war, *viz. an. ante* CLr. *117,* (4) in which, or the following year, the *Allobroges* (5) (who had invaded their *Majfilian* neighbours then in alliance with the *Romans)* were totally subdued by *Fabius Maximus. Camden* however, (6) supposes the *Greeks* had visited *Britain* near 100 years before this, *vim.* in the 160th year before *Cæsar's* invasion, that is, in the year before Christ 215; and others have brought them hither still earlier. But perhaps he time referr'd to by *Bochart* was when they made the first trading voyage to this island for *tin:* And *this,* indeed, we can hardly suppose to have been much earlier. For, had any *Greeks* been acquainted with our *Cajjiterides,* and commenced any trade to them, at any time during the preceding century, it could not have been long concealed from the *Romans,* when they had once perfected themselves in navigation; to which they diligently applied themselves after the first *Punic* war, and quickly improved on what they had learnt of naval architecture from the construction of some lost *Phœnician* vessels accidentally driven ashore! After which, to what purpose would be the above mention'd precautions of the *Phœnicians,* to conceal from the *Ro-*

mans .what (on the above supposition) was no longer a secret to the *Greeks,* nor could long be so to any maritime people. That the *Greeks* really traded with the *Britons* some time before *Julius Cæsar,* no-one doubts: But *how long* before his invasion, and at what time their knowledge of, and trade to this island commenced, and for what commodities they first traded here, whether for *tin* or what else,—the disagreement of authors concerning them has left very uncertain; and among a variety of opinions on these subjects, we can only judge, from selecting and comparing such authentic testimonies as seem corroborated by collateral circumstances, which to prefer.—Dr. *Borlase* (7), from *Herodotus* and */irjjlotle,* supposes that the first passage the *Greeks* made into the Western or Atlantic ocean, was 550 years before Christ, when ' the people of *Samos* sending a colony into *Egypt,* were driven by the winds down the Mediterranean, and quite through the Straits of *Gibraltar';* about which Straits, he thinks, « they stuck and fettled for some ages, without making further progress': And that they ventur'd not into the northern seas, 'till *Pytheas,* an astronomer *o Marseilles* about the time of *Alexander* the Great, undertaking a northern voyage, is said to have sail'd as far as the Arctic circle, where there is no night at the summer solstice: A circumstance which, to the unastronomic *Greeks,* must have seem'd not less wonderful (tho' indeed more true) than many other strange things he pretended to have seen in those parts (1) Strabo's words are,. avros, ScrajS cWsle *xXVSty'lH,* xocl *otZJiXotl* o»/AOO"/(ZV *Triv Tl/.r,i* tfy *KTSsXoxpS QogTlOJV,* which Xylander thus renders: luse e nausragio servatus ex ærario publico pretiurr. auiiflaruni mercium recepit. lib 3. prope finem. (2) Strabo ubi supra. (3) Ech. Rom. Hist. b. 2. c. 13. (4) Prid. Connca. Part 2. b. 5. (5) The Allobroges were a people who dwelt at the foot of the Alps, to the southward of the lake of Geneva, in and about the countries now call'd Dauphine, Savoy, and Piedmont. Chappie. (6) On the name of Britain, p. xxjii. Cribs, ed.it, tooj. (7) Anticj. of Cornw. p. 32 and 33. were invaded by the Romans; since the Danmonians, after they had refined their tin, and cast it into square blocks, carried it to Ictis in *carts* or *'waggons*.

As parts in his history of *Tbule;* for I take him to be the fame *Pytbeas,* whom *Strain,* more than once stigmatizes as a propagator of known falfhoods. (i) Incited by *his* success, and conducted by *hit* observations, the Doctor tells us, the *Greeks* were afterwards bold enough to attempt frequent voyages of this kind: On which he remarks, ' It is very strange therefore, if true, that the *Greeks,* who made a voyage thro' the Straits as anciently as *Alexander's* time, should not sail to *Britain* before the tiroes above-mention'd to be fix'd for it by *Bocbart;* in which ' if he is right' it 'will shew how secret the *Phœnicians* kept this trade'—meaning, I presume, the ri/t-trade: For the Doctor seems to take for granted, that the *Greeks* could have made no. voyage to *Britain,* nor had any intercourse with its inhabitants, for any other purpose. But surely they might very early have had some knowfcdge of the situation of this detach'd part of *Europe,* from *Pytbeas't* accounts of it or otherwise, and might discover, and even trade to, some of the *British* ports (perhaps for skins, which was one article of the Phœnician trafiiek here), without knowing where the *Cajjiterides* were situated, or at what distance from *Britain,* or even suspecting them to be parts of, or appendages to it: These particulars feeing so carefully conceal'd by the *Phœnicians,* that the stannary regions,to which they traded, were antiently supposed, by all others, to be in some unknown and very distant part of that wide ocean which bounded the western extremities of *Europe* (2) Wherefore, although we should admit the northern vovage of *Pytbeas* to be in *Alexander's* time, and that some *Greeks* of *MaJJilia* (now *MarjeiUes),* for such it seems they were, encouraged by his example might soon after make the like attempts, and find their way to some port or ports on the *Briiijb* coasts; yet we cannot from thence conclude, that they so early discover'd from whence

the *Phœnicians* had their *tin.* Mr. *Carte,* inrfeeer,(j) takes for granted, that their hopes of a (hare with the *Phœnicians* in this trade, was the motive that induced them to fend their citizen, *Pytbeas,* to explore these northern coasts: as if any *Greeks* (whether *Phocsan* colonists at *MaJJilia, or* any other *Grecian* traders) had at that time certainly, known that their tin came from *Britain:* Which, tho' he supposes this voyage to the north, and the discovery of *Tbule,* to have been not above 250 years before *Christ,* above 70 years after the death of *Alexander,* there seems no good reason to believe they were assured of, or in what parts the tinmines were, 'till about the time the *Romans* discover'd the navigation to them; which was probably above 100 years after the time he fixes for this *MaJjiHan* enterprize. For would the *Phœnicians* have madly exposed themselves ' to the extremist dangers, and all the horrors of shipwreck,' as Mr. *Carte* acknowledges they did, to secrete from the *Romans* what they could not but know the *Greeks* had, *on his* supposition, discover'd before? Besides, it is improbable that the *MaJJilians,* who constantly c Itivated a firm friendship and alliance with the *Romans,* (4) had they discovered the situation of these mines from whence the *Carthaginians* derived so valuable a branch of their commerce, would or (1) Strabo (lib. 2.) informs us, that this Pythcas, tho' he hart traversed but a part of Britain, pretended accurately to compare its dimensions and extent with those of Thule;— represented these northern parts as having neither land, nor sea, nor air; but some spongy matter like pulmo marinus, in which the earth and sea, and all hang suspended: That this matter is. a it were the bond of the universe; inaccessible to travellers or sailors;—with other particulars equally strange and incratiible. But perhaps much of the seeming absurdity of these wonderful tales, mav be charged on the then-'ignorance ©r misapprehension of his readers; who would be not a little startled at his representing the night as being, in the most northerly climate he visited, turn'd into day by an unsetting sun: The

snow-topt mountains hiding their heads in trie clouds; front whence the deiinxions down their sides, alternately slowing, and again congeal'd into the like glassy substance of which the ancients imagin'd the heavens themselves were composed; and which, with tac multangular rocks and islands of ice surmounting the swelling waves of the surrounding seas, variously reflecting and refracting the solar rays, would from some diilant points of view, exhibit the appearance of gilded ciouds here and theretinterfpers'd with the cccrulean brightness of tthe firmament itself; And this seeming conjunction of heaven and earth, and tea, with the intermediate air frequently fill'd with flouting feathers of falling snows, if somewhat poetically described, or in that ænigmaticai style, by which the ancient Creeks were fond of disguising the most important truths in the garb of fiction and romance,— would induce the generality of his readers, who knew nothing of the effects of a northern perennial winter, to imagine he had confounded heaven and earth, air and water, and In short turn'd the world topsy-turvy: And then, no wonder i£-fome men of good sense and sound judgment, but unfkill'd in cosmography, should censure hit accounts of these inhospitable regions, as replete with incredible stories and palpable falfhoods. For the best writers, in those early times, knew so little of natural philosophy, geography, or astronomy, as to have but very imperfect notions of the apparent course" of the sun, as seen from different parts of the globe; or how and from what causes the different degrees of his heat, or the contrary effects of cold, in different climates, were variously modified. Hence Herodotus seems to have understood literally, and of course disbeliev'd, what some had ajfirm'd of a people cover'd with feathers that every where surrounded them, and fill'd the ajr about them. And the same Herodotus ridicules the report of the Phœnician navigators (which however was certainly true), that when (about ann. ante Chr. 603) they first doubled the most southerly Cape of Africa (viz. of Good Hope), they had sun-rising at their right-hand when facing the sun's place at noon; which being contrary to constant observation in northern latitudes, those sailors, who bad never before been south of the æquator, could not but imagine that he rose in the west and sat in the east. Nay Strabo himself, whose judgment and skill in geography is in general unquestionable, and who must be allow'd to have excell'd all that/preceded him in that branch of science, absolutely denies the truth of their testimony concerning so strange a pheenemenon, as he mistakenly took it to be: And to the like hasty and erroneous judgment in such matters, his censures of Pythcas may very probably be, at least partly, ascribed. Chappie.

(%) Herodotus in Thalia. (3) Hilt.cf England, vol. j. p. 38, (4) Vide Polyb. lib. 3, and Strabo, lib. 4.

As to their (hips, the Britons are commonly represented as using vessels or boats, made of the flexible branches of trees, interwoven as closely as possible, and lined with hides. And, according to Pliny, Thnæus described,those boats of the Britons (in a history which is now lost) as a kind of wattle-work, covered with skins: Nor are those boats unnoticed by Cæsar, and other ancient writers. That the Danmonians were in poslession of vessels of this description, I entertain not a doubt. The construction of these boats was oriental. And "a kind of boats, formed of slender rods joined together in the manaer of hurdles and covered with skins," are still used on the Red sea.(«) That the Danmonians, however, were unacquainted with the use of larger vessels, before Cæiar, is a position *to* which I can never assent. Their voyage from the east to this country, could scarcely have been performed in vessels of so slight a construction as those already described. (A)

But, or could have conceal'd it from those whom they justly esteem'd their best friends and most powerful protectors; and to whom they on all occasions readily gave all the-assistance in their power in their wars with the *Carthaginians* and others.—Now the *Remans,* as we have seen, had never plotgh'd the

ocean till after the first *Punic* war; and consequently could not excite the jealousy of the *Phœnician* tin-merchants by attempting a discovery of this kind, or induce them to hazard the safety of their ships and the lives of their sailors; the more effectually to'guard against it, 'till *an. ante Cljr.* 140 at soonest: When, being more sollicitous to cope with the *Carthaginian* power at sea" by a numerous fleet, than attentive to the construction of trading vessels, it is not at all likely they would attempt any-thing of this nature, till the conclusion of the second *Punic* war had put them in possession of *Spain* and the islands in *the Mediterranean.* And even then, the revolt of *the Gauls,* and the continuance of the first *Macedonian* war 'till *an. ante Cbr.* 194; with the very short interval between that and the second; and the like between this and the third *Punic* war; and those intervals moreover employ'd in other wars of less note, *nix.* with the *Ligurians, Spaniards, Corjicans,* and others; must have too much engrofs'd the attention of the senate and the consuls, to admit of their advertence to commercial concerns. During these transactions, the *Roman* state, now growing up to the height of its glory and greatness, chiefly sollicitous to have brave and well-regulated armies, and paying little or no regard to mercantile concents, very little encouragement of even their domestic traffic could in such times be expected; much less the commencement of a foreign trade to a distant and undifeover'd country. That great body was as yet unanimated by the spirit of commerce. To eheck and restrain troublesome neighbours, and at length command and protect them; to humble the pride, and weaken the strength of dangerous rivals; to dethrone kings, and dispose of kingdoms, as best suited their own political or interested viejvs; to subdue, and to polish, the most savage and barbarous nations; to enlarge the boundaries and advance the grandeur of the empire; and to silt the public treasuryv and enrich individuals with the plunder of captur'd cities and conquer'd provinces;—were the principal objects of their care and con-

cern. Not that they were stimulated to great actions by a greediness of gain, but by a thirst after glory and honour: And though not ignorant that riches and power are mutually productive of each other, their aim was not so much an accumulation of wealth, as an extension of their power and dominion. Such immense riches as their rival state had derived from its extensive trade and commerce, and which rendered it so powerful as to dispute with the *Romans* themselves for the empire of the world, was to *them* merely adventitious; as being not the object they had in view, but accidentally resulting from that power and authority, which they had previously obtained." *Chappie's General Defcript. of Devon,* p. 106 to 114. *(a)* See Harmer's Observations on the Bible.

(4) " The poet Dionyfius, having described all the nations of the known world, concludes with the Indotscythæ; of whom he gives a more ample, and a more particular account, than of any, who have preceded. He dwells long upon their habits and manners; their rites and customs; their *merchandize,* industry, and knowledge: and has transmitted some excellent specimens of their ancient history. *ltov iroTa/o» Not/o TxvOxi vininnn,* &C. &C. Dion. Perieg. v. 1088.

Upon the banks of the great river Ind
The *Southern. Scuthte* dwell; which river pays
Its wat'ry tribute to that mighty sea
Stiled Erythrean. Far remov'd its source,
Amid the stormy cliffs of Caucasus:
Descending hence through many a winding vale,
It separates vast nations. To the west
TV Oritæ live and Aribes: and then
The Ara-cotii fam'd for *limn geer, Sec.* &c.
To 'num'rate all, who rove this wide domain
Surpasses human pow'r: the Cods can tell,
But (to drop this idea) their connexion with the Phenicians for many successive ageV before Cæsar, must render the above position at least improbable. The Phenicians, I need not repeat, were,

of all the ancient nations, the most skil-ful navigators: They were famed both for the structure and for the manage-ment of their vessels. *(a)* Is it at all like-ly, therefore, that the Danmonians, so long conversant with the Phenicians, should have indolently rested in their little osier boats, whilst the lofty ships of the Phenicians were continually at anchor in their harbours? Is it possible, that they should have acquiesced from generation to generation, in a rude fish-ing vessel, when they might have as-cended, whenever they pleased, the Phenician ship, and have thoroughly ex-amined its construction? Can we con-ceive, that, exposed as the Danmonians were, in their frail barks, to the dangers of the sea, they could have been satis-fied with such vehicles, even if none of a better construction had been ever pre-sented to their observation? Gratified, however, as they were, with a full view of ships, both safe and commodious, do we imagine them so senseless as to stare only, with stiipid wonder, at tliose ships? Had they wondered, their wonder would soon cease: Astonishment is a transitory passion: It does not last for ages. When the novelty, therefore, of the object was over, would not the Dan-monians naturally begin to consider the Phenician ships as excellent models for imitation? And would they not proceed to construct vessels for themselves, af-ter these models?

That

The Gods alone; for nothing's hid from Heavenj

Let it suffice, if I their worth declare. These were the first great founders in the world,

/Founders of cities and of mighty states: *Who shetv'd a path through seas,* before unknown:

And when doubt reign'd and dark un-certainty,

Who render'd life more certain. They first view'd

The starry lights, and *formed them in-to schemes.*

In the first ages, when the sons of men

Knew not which way to turn them, they aslign'd

To each his just department: they be-stow'd

Of land a portion and of sea a lot;

And sent each wand'ring tribe far off, to (hare

A diff'rent soil and climate. Hence arose

The great diversity, so plainly seen

Mid nations widely severed. Such is the character given by the poet Diony-fius of the Indian Scuthæ, under their various denominations. They were sometimes called *Pboinices:* and those of that name in Syria were of Cuthire extraction. In consequence of this, the poet in speaking of them, gives the fame precise character, as he has exhibited above, and specifies plainly their origi-nal.

'0 S' *aXos cyyvs* E3vT£r, *inun'jji.im pomy.!S.* Upon the Syrian sea the people live

Who stile themselves *Phœnicians.* These are sprung

From the true ancient Erythrean stock;

From *that sage race,-.vho first es-jay'd the dees,*

And *wasted merchandize to coasts unknown.*

These too *digested first the starry choir;*

Their motions mark'd and call'd them by their names."—Cok Vallancey. *(a)* According to Sammes, the Pheni-cians had built great (hips in the time of Solomon, and wereaccustomed to long and tedious voyages. " Now it is (fays this author) that we hear of *Danaur,* and his great (hip *Pentenconteros,* or fifty oars, in which he arrived out of *Ægypt* into *Greece,* which voyage may be gath-ered out of an Inscription upon an old marble, part of which by time is worneut. It is thus.

'ApS *Ioiv.... ut ut* t Aiyuwls.. *is rm* 'EAAaJas *tirtovcrt zoci uvoiJ.a.cr$ri Tttvlvixovt£g©'.koci X* Aatvtxa *hvy-acriis*

... *turn xcci ..../3as....* a *f uu xxi* 'EXixn xai As

aTTOKtoauSsTcrxi Xoinwi oevr. KOtt iSvcrcw itri Tvis «x%y i/jLtFctaat.. ot Trts PoS/jtf *trvt* XHHAAAAnil. By the learned *Se/den* rendered to this fence.

Since the Ship.... came from Ægypt *into* Greece, *and tvas called* Pentenconteros, *and the Daughters* osDanaus *and* Helice, *and* Archedice *chosen from the rest and sacrificed upon the Jhmr in*

Fan.... de *in* Lindus, a *City of* Rhodes. MCCXLVII."—Brit. Antiqu. Illust. p. is.

That they were not unskilled in the mechanical arts, their chariot is a suf-ficient proof: *On* this point, we cannot hesitate. The application, therefore, of their talents to ship-building, was easy, and, I will add, unavoidable. Cæsar, it is true, has noticed the osier-boats only, of the Britons: And Cæsar's authority, as far as it goes, is valid. But Cælar was not acquainted with Danmonium. The vellels he saw, he described: What he had no opportunity of observing, or of having satisfactorily attested, he left un-noticed. And so distant was Danmoni-um from the scene of his vi6tories, that he probably met with no Creditable peo-ple, who could answer his enquiries re-lating to the genius or customs of the western Britons. In short, I think, the silence of Cæsar as to this point, and the silence, indeed, of history in gener-al, will furnish no argument against my opinion, that the Danmonians were in possession of vessels superior to fish-ing-boats, long before Cæsar's time. That the British boats should have been so much noticed by ancient writers, was/ probably, owing to the singularity and novelty of their form: They were Asiatic; and, therefore, uncommon in the eyes of Europeans.*(a)* In the mean time, the British vessels of a better form, were more, perhaps, like the ships of other countrie's; and were, therefore, seldom mentioned. Though the larger ships of the Danmonians be not de-scribed, we have historical evidence, enough, I think, to prove that such ves-sels must have existed. To fay nothing of the *(b)"* Loncis Navibus Haud It A Multis," in which the colonial voyage from S. Scythia was performed, it is a certain fact, that many of the Danmo-nians embarked for Ireland at the time of the Belgic invasion, that such a body of people crossed the seas as to form a colony on the Irish coast, and that this emigration was made with the greatest dispatch, whilst the Belgæ were over-running the country. Not to notice the embarkation of troops from Danmonium on other occasions, this single expedition, I think (more than three centuries before Cæsar) should leave on our minds no mean impression of the Danmonian navy. That great numbers of people, furnished not only with voyaging stores, but with every thing necessary for an establishment in another country, ssiould set sail from Danmonium, on the alarm of a hostile invasion, and Consequently without time for much preparation, and that they should be conveyed in safety across the seas, and actually form a new colony on a foreign coast, is scarcely possible, unless we give them credit for having been good ship-builders as well as skilful navigators. They must have had capacious vessels in their docks: A colony, with all its provisions, in little osier boats—is ridiculous. With respect to the ship-building and navigation of the Greeks, who successively followed the Phenicians in trading to this part of the island, and probably in planting colonies here, there are certain facts on record, which cannot be disputed. We have it on the authority of Athenæus, that about two hundred years before Cæsar, the Greeks had made a rapid progress in ship-building and navigation. That famous sliip which was built at Syracuse under the direction of Archimedes, is at once a proof of the proficiency of the Greeks in the maritime arts and of their connexion with Britain. According to Athenæus, this ssiip had three masts, of which the second and third were easily procured; but it was long before a tree for the mainmast could be found. At length a proper tree was discovered in the *mountains of Britain;* and brought down to the sea-coast by machines invented by a famous mechanic Phileas Tauromenites. This is a curious fact. And the mountains of Britain, I conceive, were the mountains of Danmonium. In other parts of the island, the Greeks had very flight connexions. It was with Danmonium that they traded: It was here, they had established their factory: It was here, they had fixed

a colony. But, whether the timber for the mainmast of this Grecian hip were discovered in Danmonium or any («)
Primum cana salix, madefacto vlmine, parvam
Texitur in puppim, cœsoque inducta juvenco
Victoris patiens, tumidum circumnatat amnem.
Sic Venetus stagnante Pado, fusoque Britannu9
    Navigat Oceano Luc. Pharsal. *1*.4.
    '. rei ad miraculum
Navigia junctis semper aptant pellibus,
Corioque vastum sæpe percurrunt salumi Fest, Avienus in Oris Marit» flee, also, Cæsar, p. 240. and Pliny, 1.4. c. 16.
(i) Saxon Chronicle, p. 1. They were but *few* ships: yet they contained a sufficient number of people to form a new colony in a very distant country—a proof that, these *few* ships roust have, been *capacious.*
Vol. I. T any other part of the island, it is probable from this circumstance, that the art of ship building had been communicated to the Britons. As we advance in the argument, the ?roofs become more convincing. We fliall find them, indeed, irresistible. That the Iritons were acquainted with ship-building and navigation before the time of Cæsar, appears, I think, from the following circumstances. Though the Veneti of Britany confessedly excelled all the continental nations in their knowledge of maritime affairs, and in the number and strength of their hips, yet, when they were preparing to fight a'decisive battle against the Romans by sea, they asked and obtained auxiliaries from Britain. And this they certainly would not have done, if the Britons could have assisted them only with a few wicker-boats. The Britons, therefore, had, probably, /hips nearly of the fame form and construction with those of their friends and allies the Veneti. And the ships of the Veneti are described by Cæsar, as large, lofty, and strong, built entirely of thick planks of oak, and so solid, that the beaks of the Roman ships could make no impression

on them. In that famous sea-fight off the coasts of Armorica, the combined fleets of the Veneti and the Britons consisted of two hundred and twenty of these large and strong ships, (a) T close the whole, let us recur to Ossian: There are passages, I think, in his poems, which must determine the controversy. The very name of the British prince who was believed to be the inventor of ships, and the first who conducted a colony out Of Britain into Ireland, is preserved in these poems. ' Larthon, the first of Bolga's race, who travelled on the winds—who first sent the black ship through ocean, like a whale through the bursting of foam. He mounts the wave on his own dark oak in Cluba's ridgy bay—that oak which he cut from Lumon, to bound along the sea. The maids turn their eyes away, lest the king should be lowly laid. For never had they seen a ship, dark rider of the waves!' This expedition of Larthon must have happened two or three centuries before the first Roman invasion; from which period the intercourse between Caledonia and Ireland was frequent: Hence the people of both countries must have gradually improved in ship-building and navigation. These arts were so far advanced in the days of Fingal, that this illustrious hero made several expeditions, accompanied by some hundreds of his warriors, not only into Ireland, but into Scandinavia, and the islands of the Baltic. We learn from the poems of Ossian, that the ancient Britons of Caledonia steered their course by certain stars, in their' voyages to Ireland and Scandinavia. " I bade my white fails (fays Fingal) rise before the roar of Cona's wind—When the night came down, I looked on high for fiery-haired Ul-crim. Nor wanting was the star of heaven: it travelled red between the clouds: I pursued the lovely beam on the faint-gleaming deep." In another passage of these poems, no less than seven of these stars which were particularly observed by the British sailors, are named and described, as they were embossed on the shield of Cathmor, chief of Atha. " Seven bosses rose on the shield—On each boss is placed a star of night; Can-mathon with beams un-shorn;'Colderna rising from a cloud; Uloicho robed in mist; Cathlin glittering on a rock. Reldurath half sinks its west-ern light—Berthen looks through a grove—Tonthena, that star which looked, by night, on the course of the sea-tossed Larthon.". When a fleet of the ancient Britons failed under the command of one leader, the comman-der's ssiip was known by his shield li-ung high on the mast: And the several signals were givenjjjy striking the dif-ferent bosses of that shield, which were commonly seven; each.,yielding a dif-ferent and well-known found. " Three hundred youths looked from their waves on Fingal's bossy shield. High on the mast it hung, and marked the dark blue sea.—But when the night came down, I struck at times the warning boss—Seven bosses rose on the shield; the seven voices of the king, which his warriors received from the wind, and marked over all their tribes."

After this deduction of the British commerce, from the earliest times down to the Roman Period, it is natural to en-quire, whether this commerce was car-ried on by way of barter (the exchange of one commodity for another) or whether certain metals, as gold, silver, and brass, the great medium of commer-ce in almost every age, were adopted as die representatives of different com-modities. The primitive mode of com-merce was the exchanging of one com-modity for another: But the great incon-veniencies experienced by those who carried on their trade in the way of barter, soon occasioned the invention *of money*. It should seem from a few scat-tered passages in ancient authors, that the Britons were unacquainted with money, or with its mercantile uses. Vet that the I"'-

' () *Cahr,* Ub. 3. c.8, 9. c. 13, 14, 15, *it.* had the knowledge of (a) money, and that they used brass-money, is evident from this passage in Cæsar: *Uttttitur out area aut taleis ferreis ad cerium pendus examinatis pr« mtmmo.(b)* But Caesar is here speaking of the Britons on the sea-coasts, particularly those of Kent, who imported their brass from the Continent.

With the Danmonians, Cæsar had, at this time, little or no acquaintance. I on-ly quote, therefore, his authority, to prove one simple fact, that the Britons knew the uie of money before the time of Cæsar. For it is not probable, that the money in circulation among the peo-ple of Kent, mould' be confined to their own district. The principal trading towns in the island, were, doubtless, ac-quainted with money. Nor could the merchants of Exeter, in particular, be ig-norant of its use. That money coined at British mints had been long circulated through the island, is plain from the Ro-man edict suppressing all such coins, and prohibiting the use of any money in Britain, but what was stamped with the image of a Cælar. In the mean time, we are not to imagine, that the Britons used brass and iron money only; to the exclusion of those metals which were so obviously preferable for the mint. In our Danmonian mines were produced no small quantities of gold and silver. And that the Danmonians had gold coins, is plain from those of Karnbre, which Borlase has exhibited in his An-tiquities of Cornwall, plate XIX, and which he has properly attributed to the Britons. Iu his Natural History of Corn-wall, Borlase has also exhibited (a« sup-plemental) several coins of the fame kind, in plate XXIX. Of all these coins, I mall here insert my leirned country-man's description, as I think they are particularly curious, and then offer both Borlaie's and my own conjectures on the subject. " In the month of June 1749, in the middle of the ridge os Karnbre-hill, were sound such a number of coins of pure gold, as being sold for weight, brought the finder about 16 pounds, sterling. Near the fame quantity was found by another person near the fame spot, a few days after; all which were soon sold and dispers'd: some were much worn and smoothed, not by age, or lying in the earth, but by use, they having no allay to harden, and secure them from wearing. Seventeen I exhibit in plate XIX. of different impressions, size, or weights; several others found at th» fame time and place, I have seen, but being of the lame sort as these ex-

amples, I think it needless to lay them before the public. I range the rudest, and those which have figures most unknown first, (as others engag'd in the fame sub-ject have done) being, in all probabili-ty, the most ancient; the others follow according as their criterions seem to be-come more and more perfect, and mod-ern. I mention their weight also, as a material circumstance, (tho' omitted by other authors) for classing them, and discovering what are, and what are not the same sort of coin. The first has some figures upon it which I do not under-stand; its weight is twenty-two grains. No. II. has some figures on one iide, which I do not lo much as guess at; on the other side it has the limb, or trunk of a tree, with little branches springing from it in one part; and what I take also for the body of a tree, with two round holes, or marks, where the limbs have been lopt off, and roots at the bottom on the other part . it weighs only 23 grains. No.

III. has a figure, which, in the coin at-tributed to Cassibelan, (by Speed pag. 30) is more plain, and resembles two dolphins turning their crooked backs to each other; on the other side it has a plain large stump of a tree, with two branches breaking out on each side;' it rises out of the ground, and stands be-tween two smaller trees: it weighs 13 grains. No. IV. is quite defac'd on one side; but on the other, it has some parts of a horse, and some little round studs, or button-like embossments, both which marks will be particularly diseours'd (a) As to the antiquity, of money, it was certainly In use in Arabia, when the book of Job was written, of which Mos-es is supposed to have been the trans-lator; for in Job, mention is made of a species of money, called *Kcjitab*. The feminine termination of this word in Hebrew, according to Bochart, implies a female lamb; but he clearly (hews it as a piece of money so called. In the time of R. Akiba, the Africans preserved this name for a coin. Cum per Africam pere-grinarer, Obolurnvocabant *kefitam*. (i) " The Hiberno Scythian or Irish name for money is *kee(b, keejda,* or *kttjhtat* in Persic *keefeb* (fays Vallancey). The Irish word, I think, is derived from *etas* or *keas,* ore, refined! ore, or metal: whence *Cn-Keas,* or the mountain Caucasus, remarkable for its mines. The.famom iron mines in Armenia, are called *el-KuJes* by the Arabs at this day. The Chaldee *kefita* in Job, was undoubtedly the Scythian name for refined ore, i. *e.* money, and, as Bochart observes, had no rose rences to lamb or kid." b. Casfar, 1. 5. c. iz. discours'd of when we come to explain the several uncommon figures which these coins afford us: weighs 26 grains. No. V. has one fide etfac'd; the reverse is a horse, betwixt the legs of which there is a wheel, and from it's back rises the stem of a spear, or javelin: weight 26 grains. No. VI. has the stem of a tree, with its collateral branches very dis. tjnct; in the middle, it is croft'd slopewise by a bar like the lhaft of a spear; the reverie has the horse, the wheel, and spear, but somewhat differently p'ac'd on the gold. The weight is twenty-five grains and a half, by which I conclude, that the side which is defaced in No. V. was the fame as in this coin, for the reveries are the. fame, and their weight corresponds to half a train, which may be allowed for the greater use that has been made of this, than of the former. No. VII. has on one side some appearance of a human head, which side of the coins we shall henceforth call the *head,* as medallists generally do, to avoid a multiplicity of words; on the reverie the remains are so mutilated, that it can be only said, that this reverse was much ornamented, but what the ornaments were, is not to be discover'd. It weighs 23 grains. No. VIII. has the lines of a garland, or diadem on the *head.* The reverie has the *exergue* at bottom, supported by jagg'd lines interspers'd with dots, above which are some barbarous figures, which are to be explain'd as well as we can, and their orderly placing here, and in some of the other coins, accounted for in their proper place. It weighs four penny weights, three grains, No. IX. has a head much defac'd, but visible, as is also the outline of the neck, and the ear 5 behind the forehead, and nose, it has three semicircular protuberances; the reverie has

the fame figure as the reverse of No. VIII. but has more little round studs on it, (the die which gave the impression, being placed farther back in this, than in the former) and discovers therefore a circular figure, No. 7. with three pointed javelins No. fi. underneath it, which the other impression has not; but by the run of the die the former has one of the figures which is not in this. It weighs four penny weights three grains, which weight, and she reverse charg'd with like figures (though differently plac'd) lhews that these two coins were struck at one time, by the lame die, and are of the fame value, No. X. has a laureated diadem, across which, at right angles, is a fillet, or rather clasp, and a faint appearance of a hook at the end of it, the rest defac'd. The reverse has a very distinct *exergue* at bottom; the fame figures partly as No. VIII. IX. but the die was plac'd still farther back on the gold, therefore not altogether the fame, the javelins, or spears (or whatever those pointed stakes signify) being in this coin cut off by a descending line, intimating that but part only of those instruments were to be exhibited, Jt weighs four penny weights two grains, by which it is probable, that it is the fame sort of coin with the two foregoing, allowing one grain out of fifty for the wear. No. XI. has the laureated diadem and clasp, aboye which the hair turns off in bold curls; the reverse has the fame charge as the three foregoing, but better plac'd, and it should be a coin of the same sort, but it weighs four penny weights and seven grains, so that it must have been much less us'd, than the others, if of the fame time and value. No. XII. has on the head *several parallel lines fashioned into squares, looking like the plan of a town, of tvabicb the streets cross nearly at right angles, and the whole cut by one straight and nvider street than tie rest.* On the reverse are the remains of a horse with a collar or garland round his neck, and behind, something like a charioteer driving forward: underneath the horse is a wheel, and a few studs scatter'd near the extremities of the coin. One penny weight three grains. No. XIII. just shews the faint profile of a human

face; the reverse a horse, a spear hanging forward towards the horse's neck, some appearance of a charioteer above the horse: it weighs only twenty three grains. No. XIV. has a laureated diadem round the temples, above which the hair turns back n large curls: the diadem has the clasp, or ribbon, which has a hook at the bottom of it, and on the shoulder. is a *fibida* or button which tuck'd up the loose garment. The reverse has a horse with a wheel below it, and many small, and large studs above it, It weigh'd 25 grains. No. XV. exhibits a distin6t human face in profile; the head is laureated, cjalp'd, and cirrated as the others, which plainly shews, thatwhere there is only a simple laureated d.'adem now to be seen, as in Nos. X. XI. XIV. there the human face also was, though now worn out. The reverse has a horse, with a wheel below it, and crescents, studs, and balls above it. Weight 26 grains. No. XVI. is the best prefery'd coin as well as largest and most distinct, which I have seen of the gold coins found in Cornwall. The profile is well proportion', and neither destitute of spirit nor expression: and it is somewhat surprizing that an artist who could design the human face so well, should draw the horse so very indifferently on the other side. This head has two rows of curls above the laureated diadem, and the folds of the garment! rife up round the neck close to the Sr. The reverse, a horse, a wheel, balls and crescents, as in the rest. Weighs four ! UCLLC1 His ii Vi ll.iu.......j, *A* pole, which reaches the ground; whether a reclining spear, or what their scythes might be fasten'd to, or any other part cf the chariot is uncertain, but the charioteer is plain. I perceive no letters on any of them; some are plain, or flat j some a little concave on one side and convcK on the other, but not remarkably so. Eight coins are here lubjoin'd, from the cabinets of the curious, not yet publistVd, which may tend to illustrate the foregoing. The five following are copied from the collection of the Rev. Mr. Gistbrd, of Queen square, Ormond-street, London, and were in his posl'eslion before the gold coins above describ'd were found at

Karn-bre, but in what part of Britain they were found is uncertain. No. XVIII. on one side a head embols'd; the reverie a very uncouth ancient horie with its head to the right hand; the other ornaments as in the rest: the use we sliall make cf this, (hall be to explain the marks of those which go before, where, though the lame, they are not 1b distinct, nor treated of by any author I have yet seen. Weighs four penny weight, one grain; a little concave on the reverse. No. XIX. bars, stakes, or fragments of spears, or javelins crossing irregularly; reverse a horse, with a spear leaning forth over it's neck, the spear held (as it were) by an arm reaching forward; splinters or pieces of spears in other parts of the coin; a garland round the horses's neck, the mane made of a line of studs; a little convex on the reverse. Weight 29 grains. No. XX. a noble coin; the head is ornamented in the lam? manner as No. XVI. but has the clasp over the diadem much plainer; the hook at the bottom of the clasp also very plain, and stiews the ihape of this member, in Nos. X. XI. XIV. XV. where they are defective. It has more curls below the diadem, and the hair of the hinder part of the head seems traced in ribbons studded with pearl: it (hews also more of the habit than No. XVI. but it has either lost or never had the profile, in which particular it falls greatly ssiort of the other. The reverse is a horse in the same style, and surrounded with the same ornaments as No. XVI. the weight is four penny weight, nineteen grains, which is five grains more than the above coin, and if that difference may be imputed to the different use made of these coins, a) they are of one age, were originally of one weight and value, and very likely of one and the fame prince. No. XXI. the *head* defae'd. The reverse a horse well Ihap'd, and of neat design: underneath, is a star of five rays, form'd very artificially by the intersection of three equal triangles, (i) Both the horse and this geometrical figure, stiew this coin to be much more modern than any of our JCarn-bre coins; it is a little concave on the reverse, and weighs twenty grains and a half. No. XXII. a well pre-

serv'd face, and of elegant workmanlhip. In the reverse the horse is well proportion'd, has a charioteer behind it, pointing forward the spear, a wheel of dots under it supported by an *exergue,* and the chariot-wheel also close at the horse's heels: the mane of the horse is a line of beads or pearls. This coin is still more modern than the rest, and is of the fame sort in all appearance, as that publissi'd in the last edition of Camden, vol. I. tab. ii. No. XXX; though for want of the weight being specified, it can't certainly be affirm'd. It weighs 29 grains and a half. No. XXIII. is a coin from the cabinet of Smart Eetheullier, Esq. of Aldersbrook in Essex. In the *head,* it has the laureated diadem with some curl'd hair above it, over which comes the clasp. Under the diadem seems the collarornament of No. XX. but out of its place; underneath are two large crescents, so that this fide of the coin seems to be a collection of the ornaments of the *head* inserted too-ether, and the face never intended. I find this coin very near the fame as Dr. Plot's coin, (pag. 335. No. 21. Oxfordshire) who takes it to contain two faces of *Prasutacus* and Boadicea, but I see nothing tending that way. (r) In the reverse is a horse of the fame (a) There are four grains difference betwixt No. IX. and XI. which however are certainly coins f the fame sort. (b) I find the fame figure in one of the Britisli coins publistVd in Dr. Battery's Antiq. Rhutupianæ. page 03. *Borlase.* (c) The learned Mr. Walker (from whom Dr. Plot had this coin, which is also publistVd in Camden, Tab. I. No. 29.) I find of the same opinion, that it does not contain two faces: " I see UP resemblance (says he, Camden page CXVI.) of one or more faces, I rather imagine it to be some fortification;" which latter supposition, I can't but observe, is as far wide of the tiuth as Dr, Plot's j as by comparing this coin with the others here produe'd, will readily appear. *Btrbfi.* feme style as No. XVII. but the wheel is larger, and the ears and tail of the horse' more1 apparent, though of very clumsy design; the whole favouring of great antiquity, and? shewing the low pitch of the art of coin-

ing, at this time, in the nation to which this coirs belongs. But the greatest curiosity of this coin, and the reason, indeed, for which it is1 here introduc'd, is, that it is neither gold, nor wholly electrum, or any imitation of gold, but (eems to be copper plated over with a mix'd metal in imitation of gold. No. XXIV. Smd XXV. are silver coins of the fame kind, from the cabinet of the Rev. Mr. Wise, Radcliff Librarian, Oxford, and inserted here for confirming the descriptions that goi before, as will be more particularly explain'd hereafter; they were found in the parishes Swacliffe near Madmarston Castle, Oxfordsliire, 174.6." (a) " There are many parts of our British coins, which, tho' faithfully enough copied by engravers, are yet wrongly plac'd in the plates, because, indeed, they did not know what they had copy'd. This is the reason that we find the diadem, sometimes horizontal,(£) at other times perpendicular; *(c)* whereas we all know, that this mould life sloping from the ear to the forehead. In Montfaucon's plate No. 16. the horse is laid on his back with his legs uppermost; and in No. 36. the horse's body is perpem-icular, and so is the line of the *exergue;* which fame fault is committed in placing the reverse of Plot's No. 21. pages plain evidences, that the engraver did not understand the figure, tho' he drew the; size and shape, not knowing what animal it was, or whether an animal or not: and, whoever copy'd the fine gold coin in Camden's last edit. pag. 833, No. 21. (of the fame age with some of thole at Karnbre) most certainly did not know what figure he had before him, and therefore 'tis no wonder that the learned editor, depending on his engraver, should place the horse upon his back. There is one thing more necessary to be observ'd, in order to place these coins with propriety, Which is, that several of our Karn-bre coin have not the horse on the reverie, (as No. VIII. IX. X. XI.) but instead thereof, have certain members; and symbols adjusted together in such a manner as to imitate the shape ©fa horse, and become, when joyn'd together, the emblem, rather than the figure, of that creature, which the engraver knew no better how to design. These several symbols are not to be explain'd, but by the coins iri which we find the fame parts inserted in the composition os the entire figure in some, which in others are detach'd, and unconnected. The latter must derive their light from the former. For example. Iri No. VIH. you find three of the figures mark'd in the table of symbols *(d)* No. 1. In No. IX. there are four of the fame symbols; in No. X. two, No. XI. four. What should be the intent' ©f placing such figures, in such numbers on these reverses? Wily, in No. XVIII. and XIX. we find the legs of the horse made in this unnatural fashion; and it is observable, that where the horse Is not, there these legs (the most useful parts of this useful creature) are plac'd. They are sour in number, in Nos. IX. and XI. and would have been also ia the fame number arid place, in No. VIII. and X. (for by tile weight, and symbols,, these four must have been coins of the fame fort, time and value); but that the "mould in striking these latter, was miiplac'd. (r) They are plac'd two and two, with a ball, or wheel between them, as in the coins which have horses entire. Between them the halfmoon dips his convex part, something in the manner of the horses barrel), above which another crescent-like bunch forms the back; a round ball turns to shape the buttock, and on the forepart, a thick handle of a javelin slopes upwards from the breast to form the neck and crest of the horse. In coin XI. we find these symbols in full number, (i. e. four) very distinct, and as justly plac'd as the engraver's skill could direct. When these are plac'd double, as in coin XVII, they seem intended to denote there being two horses a-breast, a» was-the ancient custom of drawing the fighting chariots. Two little figures of this shape are also plac'd in the later coins. When, therefore, such figures occur in British coins we need but refer to these of Karn-bre; and we find immediately, that they vvere intended for some parts of a horse. Round the horse's neck of No. XII. there is a garland, or bracelet, which in No. XIX. is also plainly to be discover'd. There is

usually a circukrf fissure under the belly of the horse, which in some, is a distinct wheel, as in coins V, VI, XII, XIX, XX, XXII, XXIII. and therefore in the rest where this figure is less distinct it must be deem'd an aim at, or rude imitation of the fame thing. The wheel is to denotethe chariot *h)* "ffertaTeV Antiquities, p. 242 to 247. (i) Plot Oxf; No. 21, pag. 335. (0 Wife No. t. (0 plate XIX.. (f) Theft parts of the horse, (III.) are but very little better plac'd in coins XVII. and XXI& wbert the *UKft* is entire; these list mention'd coins, therefore, are next iri antiquity to No. XI. chiript Jo which the horse belong'd. The learned Walker says, *f* that the wheel under the horse amongst the Romans, intimated the making ot an high way for carts, so many of which, being in the Roman times made in this country, well deserved such a memorials)." What she wheel signified among the Romans I shall not dispute, but it could not be inserted in the British cojns (as he seems to imply) for that purpose; for there were no Roman ways made in Britain till after Claudius's conquest, and we find the wheel common in Cunobelin's coins, (4) and in Cassibelan's No. II. ib. in No. XVI, XVII, XVIII. and in Plot's 21; and also in the Cornish coins, which from all their characters appear to be older than the rest. The wheel is usually plac'd under the belly of the horse, but is sometimes found in two places on the fame coin, (as in No. 9, and j», of tab. II. in Camden) one above, and one below the horse, to denote (as I imagine) the two wheels of the *ejfeda.* One of these wheels (the upper one in No. 9. ibid.) Walker takes to be the fun". There are many balls, or globules, dispers'd in all the Cornilh coins, which are of two sizes; those of the.least kind are, or seem, merely ornamental, being strung in rows like beads or pearls, and serve now and then in a regular figure to fona the mane of a horse, (as in No. V, XVI, XVII, XX, XXII.); the circumference, or out line of the wheel, (No. XXII. and Mr. Wise's Bodlean No. 2.) or a kind of bracelet, or garland, (two of which may be seen in one reverse of the Bodlean No. 11.) round the neck, or body of the

horse. There is another round figure in these coins, which i» of the middle size, and is a ring, or *discus,* either pierc'd, or emboss'd. They are larger in No. IX, X, XI, than the wheel itself, a disproportion owing to the rudenefe of the art when first practis'd. When these are embose'd, as I find them in a well preserv'd coin in the Bodlean cabinet, I imagine they are to represent either the shield, or rather the *lamina,* and may soew that they had iron plates, as well as rings that serv'd instead of money. In No. XX. some of these balls are plainly pierc'd; in No. 11. of the Bodlean they are plain, and plac'd where the roundness of the horse's body, shoulder, and buttock, made 'em fall in with the sliape of the creature j there are others in the Bodlean collection, and in the reverse of Speed's Cassibelan, but no where more plain than in Dr. Plot's No. xi. (pag. 335. Oxfordshire) where there are five near the edge of the coin, and more, tho' of a smaller size, dii'pers'd in the *field* of the coin, not only of the reverse, but of the *bead.* I am persuaded that (lie little annular figures will make the lea ned reader easily recollect the *annuliferret* of Cæsar, and as easily assent to their being inserted on purpose to represent the ancient money which the Britans had before they coin'd after the Roman and Grecian manner; and, perhaps, afterwards too, for a while, when the gold, stiver, and brass currency fell sliort of answering the exigencies ol the state. These rings are taken notice of by Cæsar, as made of iron, adjusted to a certain weight, and standard, and us'd instead of money, and the figures of them on these coins, where this symbol is pierc'd may confirm the reading of that passage, to be as in Plantin's edit. (lib. v. pag, 87.) ' *annulii ferreis;*' as the emboss'd ones may in some measure assure us, that they us'd also *taleis,* or *laminis,* as we read it in others. Where there are many of these symbols, they mould signify the plenty of money in the little kingdoms where they Ijpere struck. In many of these Karnbre coins, viz. VIII, IX, X, XI, XVI. and in No. XXII, we find a crescent, or some such figure, (No. 3.) and in the *bead* of Dr. Plot' sNo. 11.) there are three; what intended to signify, is uncertain. We know the crescent was among the most honourable badges of the Druid order, and from the moon at fix days old, they regulated the beginning of their months, years, and ages, every thirtieth year; so that the moon was of constant and especial note among the ancient Britanst but whether it be really a crescent, or not, I do not pretend to decide. It might possibly be intended to represent the golden hook with which their priests with so much solemnity cut their divine milletoe, or to record the hooks or scythes fastened to the axis of their chariots of war, for such they had,(c) and on these coins we find several allusions to thi manner of fighting. Which of these suppositions is most likely, let the reader determine «s he thinks best. There is a remarkable rectilineal figure which leans obliquely in a line ifearly parallel to the crest of the horse, with which, or it's emblem, it is always comoin'd; It is seen in No. V. VI. more uncouth still in No. VIII, IX, XI. but very distinct in Camden, pag. CX, and in CXV. On No. a, and 3, be has an ohCervMion of the fame kind.

U See Speed No. VIII, and XHI. fc) « piniicant (scil. Britanni) non equitatu modo am pedite, veium et feigls et curribus Gallic Wnuti. CoYuios vecant, quorum falcaus axibus utuntur.' Pomp, M«k lib. iii. viil. in XHIi This I take to ltpresent the spear, with which the Britans were so dexterous in fighting, from their chariots. In No. VI. it is plac'd cross the tree, out of which the shaft was made, and in gratitude perhaps to the tree, for affording the best shafts foif these useful arms. In these coins then, the principal figure is the horse; the wheel, (emblem of the chariot,) constantly attends the horse; the spear is visible in fen of these coins produc'd, and in No. XXII. the human figure is plain, pointing forward the spear, dr javelin, as if advancing to attack the enemy. In No. XIII. there are some traces of the lame kind, and more rude attempts to delineate the fame in No. VtlI. IX, X, XI. for the spear has the fame direction in all. In No. XVII. the chario-

teer is very apparent in some winged like a victory—the bridle—and something like_a trapping—a pendant or trailed spear, or scythe. To what other purpose then are these warlike thing collected and inserted in their coins, but to signify, that the chief glory of the Britans was their skill in fighting from their chariots? The Britans (soys Cæsar, lib. iy.) have this manner of fighting 'from their chariots; « first they advance through all parts of their army, and throw their javelins, and having wound themselves in among the troops of horse, they alight and fight on foot; the charioteers retiring a little with their chariots, but posting themselves in such a manner, that if they fee their masters prefs'd, they may be able to bring them oft: by this means the Britans have the agility of horse, and the firmness of foot, and by daily exercise have attain'd to such (kill and management, that in a declivity they can govern the horses, though at full speed, check and turn them short about, run forward upon the pole, stand firm upon the yoke, and then Withdraw themselves nimbly into their chariots.' The Britans being train'd to, and excelling all others in this peculiar manner of fighting, (Cassor himself, more than once acknowledging the disorder, into which these *effedarii* had thrown the Roman soldiers) (a) liad slothing more glorious to record in their coins than this artful and efficacious manner of combat; and no coins with such symbols, so likely to be of any nation as of Britain. Thence come the horse, the wheel, the spear or javelin, and the charioteer, and perhaps the hook with which their chariot was arm'd. In the first six Karn-bre coins here exhibited, there is no appearance of the human *head*. In No. VII. and VIII. there are some faint traits of a diadem. In No. IX. the profile of the face, the ear and clasp, and outline of the neck is plain, but the diadem, which was certainly there (as must be inferr'd from No. X. and XI.) is effac'd, and the coin has lost four grains more than No. XI. which shews that it has been so much more us'd. In No. X, XI, XIV, XV, XVI, the diadem is plaia and strong. It is fbrm'd of leaves which have

this peculiarity, that they point downwards, whereas, in the ancient Roman and Grecian coins the leaves point upwards. There is another difference between the diadem in the Karnbre coins, and inthe Greek and Roman; for, whereas, in the last mention'd, the fillet or ribband on which the diadem is grounded (or by which tis bound together) makes a very elegant knot behind *the head*, the British coins have no such thing, but have a straight bandage, or rather clasp which crosses the diadem at right angles, and was doubtless design'd (like the fillet of the ancients) to keep the diadem firm in its place, and close to the *head*. This is the meaning of that straight figure crossing the diadem in No. X, XI. and XIV. and XVI. of the Karnbre coins; but is most plainly visible" in No. XX, XXIV, and XXV. with a hook or scroll at the end of it, and but for these well preserv'd coins, would have still remain'd uncertain and unknown. Above the diadem, the hair turns off in bold curls, sometimes in one tire or row, as in No. X, XI, XIV, XV, but in the larger coins in two rows, as No. XVI, and XX.(i) Round the neck, in No. XIV. the habit of the prince just appears; in No. XVI. a kind of scollop'd lace or ornament of embroidery; more of which is still to be seen in No. XX. In No. I, II, III, VI. trees are plac'd in the *head* part, (as was before observ'd in the description) but there are few if any rings or balls: the reason seems to be this; the riches of the country where these were coin'3, consisted in woods, (not in money) and therefore they took the tree for their symbol, as the countries abounding in corn took the *sfica,* and those which had plenty of pearls took the *ghbulut a)* " Ordinss plerumque perturbant." (lib. iv. pag. 83.) « Perturbatls nostris novltate pugnæ." ibid. lib. v. pag. 93. " Equites Hostjum Effedarlique acriter.prælio cum Equitatu nostro in itinert eonflixerunt."—« Novo genere pugnæ perterritis Nostris." ibid. () The Gaols were call'd Comati, ftom their long hair. The Britans had probably the fame custom, for all uncultivated nations wore long hair, except the Alani, (Lucian Tox.) It was an fu«

stance of their wildnefs. *Berlttse.* glob-ules resembling pearl, and those which had plenty of gold and money, took the ringlets, or *lamina* into their coins, (?) The figure in the *bead* of No. XII. has beert before obscrv'd to resemble the ichnograpiiy of a city, and was probably inserted in the coin by the founder, to record the erection of some city: for that the Britans had such cities, is very plain from the noble ruins (containing in cir-cuit about three or four miles) near Wrottefley in the county of Stafford, where (as Dr. Plot thinks) (A) ' the par-allel partitions, within the outwall, whose foundations ate still visible, and reprelent street running different ways, put it out of doubt that it must have been a city, and that of the Britans."(f) In the Natural History, plate XXIX. " Fig. v. and Vi. are two'goldeiins found at Karn-bre in the year 1749, with those published in the Antiquities os' Corn-wall. They seem both of the same die and value; but the impression different-ly corroded by time and use, may, by being exhibited in both, tend to their ex-planation. I cart say nothing decisive as to the symbols; but I conjecture, that on the convex side there is the rude figure of a (hip with two masts, and the fails spread; on the conv x seems as repre-sentation of the terraqueous globe, ei-icompa'ssed in the middle with a zone *iva'vjj* which divides the upper from the under hemisphere. In the upper hemi-iphefe are placed the sun aud moon, in the under the lesser luminaries. Fig. vn. and vm. are two different heads from any already pubiissied in.plate xix. of the Antiquities of Cornwall: the faces are bold, and not inexpressive, turned. different ways; the reverses are Charged with horses and wheels in the fame style as most of those already published. Pig. ix. is not an ill fancied head; the diadem and its clasp very distinct and uniformly set, aud the robing Of the shoulder plain and indisputable. In the reverse, the body of the horse is remarkably slender; the engraver, as I apprehend, being more intent to express the expeditions ana swiftness, than the natural fliape and proportion of the creature. The coins are of their real size and sliape. I

have only to observe, that Bouteroue's coins of the ancient Gauls have neither the weight nor true sliape expressed, ' because either worn with usei or cov-ered or eaten with rust,' as he tells us. Almost all, publissied by him of this kind, have plain legends. They can give little aid therefore towards explaining this treasure of British antiquity found in Cornwall; but if One can make any certain conclusion froni coins printed in such a manner, it must be that they were struck by a people well acquainted with the Greeks or Romans 5 they savour nothing of the antiquity, rudeness, and! simplicity of those of Karnbre."(/) Such is Bbrlase's description of ourDanmon-ian coins. " Having now described (says our author) the Karn-bre coins, and pro-due'd some others which may in some measure explain them, let us consider to what nation these coins are' to be aserib'd. As soon as the Gold coins, above def'crib'd, were found at Karn-bfe,and got into the hands of the curi-ous, it was by many imagin'd that they were foreign coins, and fbnle thought that they were Phenician. To this opin-ion the reverse, having generally a horse upon them, gave at first some counte-nance, some of the Phenician colonies having chosen that creature for their symbol. The place where they were found seem'd to confirm this suspicion, Cornwall having bee"n (from the first appearance of Britain hi history) cele-brated for its tin, which the Phenicians for many ages engross'd to themselves by their fuperiour skill in navigation. The only thing, then, that remains to be done in order to determine them to be Phenician, or not, is to confront the coins found! in Cornwall with those confessedly of Phenician original, and consider Whether coins of the fame style have not been found in other parts of this our isle where the Phemc'ian never traded. Now the Phenician leg-ends will always be known by their let-ters, when? they exceed the Roman con-quest of Syria (for after that conquest they used either Greek or Roman char-acters on their coins); but there is not one'character to be found in these our Cornish coins. The ancient symbol of

the Syrophenicians was the palm-tree, sometimes the *murex,* and of their west-ern colony, Hercules's pillars; but there is no such thing on our coins. The Ly-biphenicians about Cyrene took, indeed, the horse for their' symbol; but this horse had either the whole palm-tree, or it's stalk standing by it, allu . ding' *(a)* Camden thinks, that tribute for woods was paid in such coin, and thartribute-monies had thei impression from that destination. The reader may chuse whieh opinion he thinks most probabfe, (A) Stafford, p. 394. () Borlafe's Antiq-uities, p. 258 to 2.63. *(d)* Borlafe's Nat, Hist, of Cernwall, p. 3M, 323. ding at once to their descent from the Syrians, and to the horse for which their, own country, Africa, was always so famous, and for the taming of which they were indebted to their principal god, rleptune. With respect to the Phenicians of Carthage, they had the head and neck of a horse for their symbol, alluding to the fable of their being commanded by Juno to build their city where a horse's head was dug *up.(a)* Cadiz had her Hercules, his temple, and his pillars; but all these were modem and well executed, and of them nothing is to be seen in the coins now before us, which are neither well executed, nor have any reference, or re-lation, to the palm-tree, *murex,* bust of the horse, Hercules, or his pillars. But one argument, which will still weigh more than the above, is this, that coining money, came lb surprisingly late into use among the Phenicians, that filch skilful artists as they, and their colonies were, could not coin such artless money as ours is. Of the Phenician coins, (cer-tainly known to be such) there are none extant more ancient than the time of Alexander the Great;(A) so modern are they that the Phenicians were many ages celebrated for their ingenuity and (kill in other arts, before ever they coin'd money; and, besides, having borrow'd likely this art from the Grecians,(r) they cannot with any probability be sup-posed to coin money of so rude, and mean design as those of Karn-bre; arts among the Greeks being arrived, as we all know, to their summit in the time of Alexander the Great: history forbids us, therefore, to attribute such coins as what are now under consideration, to" so polite and cultivated a nationas the' Phenicians. Lastly, that they were not brought hither by the trading Phenicians, seems to be plain, because they are found, not only in Cornwall, but in Wales, and most parts *(d)* of Britain where the Phenicians never came, their trade being confin'd to Cornwall, *(e)* and their business, tin. As these coins cannot be ascribed to the Phenicians, so neither tp the Greeks npr Romans. That they are not of Roman workmanship, the first sight of them plainly fliews, much less can we attribute them to the Greeks, whose medals are still superiour to the Roman in force and delicacy, *(f)* They must be cither Gaulishtherefore, or British; for people must be very fanciful indeed (and extremely unwilling, or rather determin'd not to let their own country rights be impartially weigh'd) who will look out for a foreign father of these coins among the Spaniards, or Germans.Qf) That they do in a few particulars resemble the Gaulish coins must be allow'd; and for this, very good reasons can be given, without admitting them to be Gaulish. In the mean time, I must observe, that Cæsar's seeming to assert, that the Britans had no money in his time, having made several learned men think that we had no coin'd money in Britain before the Roman invasion, *(h)* and others being of a different opinion, (:) I will take all the care I can that the veneration which I have for the latter, may neither lead me blindly into their opinion, nor the respect which I have for some of the others, make me suppress what I think to be right. The reasons must be weigh'd, the passage of Cæsar set in it's proper light, and the reader must determine, *Utuntur aut areo, aut ialeis ferrets ad certum pondus examinatis pro nummo.1 (i)* The Britans, fays he, use either brass money, or iron tallies instead of money. This is the plain grammatical fense of Cæsar's words, and in Plantin's edition, the words run thus, ' *Utuntur autem nummo areo, aut annulTs ferreis, &c. pro nummo;*' by which it is plain, that according to Cæsar, the Britans had the knowledge

of money, and that in the place he is there speaking of, they had brass money; from whence it may be inferr'd, that the reason why they had not gold, and silver money there, as well as brass, was not because they were ignorant of the use of it (for the use of gold and silver money is much greater and more obvious, and convenient for exchange or purchase, than that os brass) but because doubtless they had none of these metals, and therefore could not coin money of them, but («) Æn. i. ver. 445. *(b)* Wife, pag-217. (c) Ibid, pag. 218. *(d)* « Several gold coins of the fame kind, and also a rough ruby were found not long ago in the Isle of Shepey.' Letter from S. L. . (f) " By Corn all here, as oftentimes elsewhere, I mean all that anciently went by that name,— the south and w estern parts of Devonshire, as well as what is west of the Tamar." *Borlaje. (f)* Mr. Jobert, pag. 3. translated by Gale. *(g)* N. Salmon, Nov Angliœ Lustratio, Lond. 1728, pag. 387, who thinks them coins belonging to the ancient Saxons. *(i)* See Moreton's Northamptonshire, pag. 500. Walker in Camden, pag. CXIV. See Mr. Wise's learned account of the Bodleian cabinet.
(/) Camden. Plot's Oxfordshire, chap. 10. The learned editor of Camden. Notes ibid. pag. 774.The late Mr. Ed. Lhuyd. ibid. () Cæf. Comm. lib. v. Jans. edit. pag. 52. but were oblig'd to be contented with coining the little brass they had, and endeavour to remedy the scarceness of their brass coin, by iron tallies, or rings of a certain weight. Cæsar is evidently here speaking of the maritime parts,(«) in which they might well use iron instead of money; for iron was found, fays he, ' *in maritimis,* ' on the sea coasts: in the fame place they had brass money, but their brass was imported, ' *are utuntur importato;'(b)* which argues, that the maritime coasts jiad no brass out of their own lands. Neither had they gold or silver in these parts, which is, doubtless, the reason that they did not coin any; for of the four kings, whom Cæsar mentions in Kent,—Cingetorix, Carnilius, Taximagulus, and Segonax, we find not one coin

which has any part of their name upon it; but this will by no means infer, but that the other petty kingdoms of the island, where these metals were, might have had gold and silver coins among them, altho' the other states, who had no such native treasures, might be without them; and that the other parts of this kingdom really had gold and silver coins, we shall soon find feme very strong arguments to believe. It is plain, therefore, that what Cæsar says, related pnly to that tittle part of Britain, in which he pafs'd the short time he stay'd in this island; all his whole account shews, that he pretended not to give any description of thole inland parts which were at a distance from the feat of action; let us add to this, that if the Kentish men had any gold coin or treasure, they certainly took all the care imaginable to conceal it from Cæsar. But supposing that Cæsar had positively said that the Britans had no gold coins, or money among them;-if by evidences, unknown to him, and since his time dit'cover'd, it should appear extremely probable at least, (if not as certain as things at this distance can be made) that they really had such coins; his authority must give way, he must be acknowledged to have been mis-inform'd, and the greater degree of probability must determine our judgment. There are several coins preserv'd and publilh'd in Camden, and Speed, which have been thought to bear the names of British princes; and I may add, that they have other evidences of their belonging to this island. Let us examine them. The first coin produc'd by Speed (pag. 29.) is that of Com. the reverse inscrib'd, Rex; and is supposed by him, with great probability, to be the coin of Comius, king of the Atrebatii in Britain, companion to Julius Cæsar in his invasion. I will only make one remark upon the reverse, which is, that the horse here is of much too good a design to be among the first essays of the Britisli coining, consequently the Britans must have had coins, before this, or they could never have made this horse and rider so bold and shapely. The next coin in Speed, is that'of Casfibelan, which he read CAS; but Moreton in his Northamptonshire (pag. 500.) reads it SCOV; the occasion of which difference, is this: Moreton began with the S, goes on to the C, mistakes the wheel (one of the British symbols) over the horse's head for an O, and takes the A without its croi's-stroke, (as it was anciently written) for a V; so that MoretonV objection to Speed's reading proceeds from ills own mistakes, and he concludes too hastily, ' That the Br'.tans had not the art of coining till they learn'd it of the Romans, and that they did not mark their coins with the names of princes till the time of Cunobelin." Speed's reading, then, remaining unimpeach'd, we have here a coin of Casfibelan, who was general of the whole war against Julius Cæsar, and cannot be suppos'd to have learnt any art from the Romans, having been engag'd continually in all the alarms of war from the time that they landed to their departure. In the *head,c)* (or the inscrib'd side) the horse is much better turn d than in our Karnbre coins, and therefore later; for arts and sciences must have time to ripen in such retir'd and uncultivated places as Britain; their beginnings will be rude, and the progress of every art towards perfection will be slow and gradual, especially, where no sister arts have been practis'd, and therefore, can't lend their helping hand to forward and cherisli that which is newly introduc'd. *l* he reverse of this coin confirms the foregoing observation, the ornaments of it being a kind of scroll-work, intermix'd with balls more uniformly dispos'd, and the whole better digested than our coins, and therefore later. Cunobelin's coin is later still than that of

Cassibelan, *(a)* As appears by the whole passage. " Britannia; pars Interior ab iis incolitur quos natos in in'ula Spse memoria proditum dicunt; maritima pars, ab iis, *Sec."* And then he goes on with the account of the maritime parts, till he comes down to *tmmmo;* then he passes on to the inland parts. " Nafcitur ibi plumbum album in mediterraneis regionibus, *Sec."* (h) Ibid.

(r) It must be remember'd, that one fide of a medal is call'd the head, whether it has a face 08 it, or not, and the other fide

is caU'd the reverse.

Vol. I;. *V-,*

£assibelan, a«d more elegant, the horse has stiape and spirit; and there is something Roman in the turn of the head *;a)* but there is great difference in the countenance of this king's coins; some are rude, and of coarse design, as Nos. "4, 5, 6, 7, 11. which may therefore be safely pronounc'd to be coin'd in his first years, either before his intimacy jvith the Romans, or before he could get the artists into the ready and masterly way of (designing; so that it may be inferr'd from the coins of Cunobelin, that he did not learn, or first bring the art of coining from the Romans, but that having acquir'd some knowledge that way, he greatly improv'd this art. Even this king's coins have been disputed, and by some insinuated not to belong to the British king of this name, tho' his name be at full length upon four coins in Camd. tab. I. and upon three of the fame in Speed j so that these scruples are apparently without foundation. The gold coin attributed to Csractacus by Camdep and Speed, has the *pica* well plac'd 011 the reverse, and in thp *bead* the horse in full speed, as well design'd as possible, and therefore seems a close imitation of the Roman manner. That of Venufius has nothing British in it, but that the curls of the hair are form'd of many contiguous circular rings studded with balls, which is indeed in the British style.(A) Tho' the coins of Cunobelin were at last so greatly imgrov'd by approaching to the Roman manner; yet these improvements seem to have been confin'd to his own dominions, for the coin of Boadjcea, queen of Verolamium, (if it be of her) has nothing Roman in it, but the letters BUDUO in the *head;* the reverse is of the fame style as those found at Karn-bre.(c) The silver coin ascrib'd to Arviragus,(i/) has the Britilh wheel form'd by eight detach'd studs,(e) but the horse is too good to be ancient. Tne next coin attributed by Speed to Galgacus, *(f)* but by Mr. Walker *(g)* to Cartismandua, has nothing of our coins, but the wheel form'd like a large ring under the horse.(A) As to the word Tascia found on many of the coins

above-mention'd, whether i,t signifies the taxation, or tribute-money as Mr. Camden believ'd, or whether such coins of tribute were ever us'd, coins being the ensigns of liberty and power, not of slavery, as other learned men think, I do not here enquire, there bejng no such word on our Corn fh coins. Let it suffice that here are several sorts of coins prodoe'd; we must ijext fee whether we have not sufficient grounds to think them British, apd yet, not the oldest of our Britilh coins, and so trace up the art of coining among the Britans to its first simplicity, where we may possibly find reasons to place our coins of Karnbre. Now, all these coins from Camden and Speed are found in Britain in several places, many in number, and the very fame in no other country. (;') Their inscriptions, and several others which might here be mentioned, have either the first, or more syllables of the names of Britilh princes, cities, or people, nay Cunobelin the whole name; why then should they not be British? *(k) t* If there be honey enough in our own hive, what neecl have we to fly abroad, and range into the names of neighbouring countries and kings to find out resemblances in sound, which are not near so exact as what we find at home? Before we deprive our own country of the honour of coining the money found here, one vould think it but reasonable that there should be produe'd from foreign countries, samT pies of the very coins we find in Britain, and in greater number, as being doubtless more plSnty where they were struck, than any where else; but there is not one instance of any, number of coins found abroad, which are of the fame kind as what we find here; altho in Roman coins, (which were not coin'd by little particular states, as the British must Jiave been) there is nothing more common. It is very wonderful that all the Gaulish coins, (for instance) correspondent to ours in metal and workmanship, should be destroy'd, pnd not one appeur, or be dug up in Gaul, whereas in Britain they are numerous, which makes the learned Mr. Wile, though dubious at other times, conclude very justly, that no *(a)*

See No. S, 9, ic, in Speed, and 12, 13, p. 32.

(A) See the mane of the horse in No. XVIII. XVI. XIX. XXI. VenutiuS in Camden xiv. tab. J. in Speed xv.' pag. 34. *(c)* Camd. tab. 1. No. 8. Speed No. 16, p. 34. *(d)* Speed No. 17. Camd. ib. No. 25. (f) As in No. XX. and XXII. *(f)* pag. 35, No. 18. *(g)* Camden pag. cxy. *h)* Other Brit, coins may be seen in Camden, and Speed, but these may be sufficient for our purpose. (i) See Camden, pag. 110. (i) It is held by some that there were no gold coins coin'd in England till Edward III. but this if probably a mistake, for'in the Saxon and first Norman times vast sums were paid in gold. The annual tribute to be paid by the Welsh apd Cornish to Athelstan, was ol. of gold, and 300I. in sliver, besides, other things. And in domesday, particularly, we find gold in irgots, contradistinguistYd! from gold coin, viz. Libras auri ad pen sum.—Libras ad numerum.— Must we suppose that all this coin was of Bizants, or other foreign coin?

»o country has a better title to the coining of them than Britain.*(a)* But, I don't know how it comes to pass, it is the unhappy fashion of our age to derive every thing curious ' and valuable, whether the works of art or nature, from foreign countries; as if providence had denied us both the genius and materials of art, and sent us every thing that was precious, comfortable, and convenient, at second hand only, and, as it were, by accident, from the charity of our neighbours. That the Britans had both gold and silver in their own country, is plain from Strabo and Tacitus;(A) and it is obscrv'd, Jo lately as Camderfs time, that Cornwall produc'd both these precious metals; () and this u confirm i by the reversation of both thole metals to the Duke of Cornwall in his grant to the tinners. Gold discover'd here I have seen, found among tin grains in the parish of Creed, near Granpont, in the year 1753; arid both that, and native silver, the produce of a Cornish mine in the parish of St. Just, I have now in my keeping; aad it mutt be allow d, that people, who have materials ready at hand, will take the first hint of an-

swering their neceslities therewith. That the inhabitants of Kent, and the adjoining.countries, had brass money, Cæsar plainly asserts, as we have seen before, and when one part of the island had 'experienc'd the ule of brass money, and knew the art of coining it, the neighbouring states must have had very little communication with one the other, or been veiy void of understanding, if they did not perceive the equal and superior convenience of gold and silver money, and for their own fakes procure it to be coin'd where£ver they enjoy'd the happiness of proper materials. And that the Britans had and us'd money coin'd at their own mint is really plain, because the Roman Emperours publifli'd a severe edict to suppress all such coins, and to forbid the use of any money in Britain, but what was stamped with the image of a *Cæfar.(d)* If it be insinuated that the Gauls brought over this money to traffick withal, this is a circumstance which wants to be.prov'd, nay wants probability, for it could not have elcap'd Cæsar, and the gold coins must have been in greater plenty on the maritime coasts where he was, than in the inland parts, the merchants from Gaul coming to the sea-ports andoasts of Britain, and having nothing to do with the other parts of the island; (?) but Cæsar says, they us'd *area nummo,* and takes no notice of any gold coin in these parts, which I think may make us reasonably infer, that the Gauls did not bring over any gold coins for merchandize; much less still can it be imagin'd, that if the Gauls did bring over such coins, we should find them infcrib'd with names so like at least to the names of our princes and cities. If any of the fame impression and legend with ours, found in many parts of Gaul can be produc'd, (which at present is far from the case) then let it be disputed whether the Gauls had these coins from us, or we from them, both sides standing upon even ground; but "till then it is a great piece of partiality to foreigners, to deny the origin of these coins to coir own country, and I am lurpriz'd to find my countrymen so fluctuating, and indifferent, not to fay carelels, which way the beam

may fall, in a point which concerns so much the history of medals in general, and affects the honour of their own country in particular." " To settle the age of our Karn-bre coins is perhaps impossible, but that the Britans had and us'd coins of their own making, and that the Romans forbad the use of British money, has been observ'd before; for which prohibition there could be no reason if the Britans did not coin in a different manner from the Romans; therefore, this different manner of stamping their money, 'tis not so likely they should learn of the Romans, as that they had it before the Romans came; for after the conquest, the Romans, we find, insisted upon the head of CæCar's being upon all their coins; therefore, that these Karnbre coins are prior to the Roman invasion is extremely probable. Further; both the Gauls and Britans being invaded nearly at the fame time, and by the lame general; the first conquer'd, the other frighten'd; both of them would either have had some symbol $f their subjection in their coins, if they had been struck under the direction of their conquerours, #) Maximo fane numero in hac insiila eruuntur, adeo ut nulla regio posseslionis jure magis cot (nummos) sibi vindicet." pag. 228.

it) " Aurum et argentum fert Britannia. " Strabo lib. iv « Fert Britannia aurum et argentum et alia metalla, pretium victorlæ.'.' Tacit, vit. Agric. chap. 12. (c) " Nec stannum vero hie solum reperitur fed una etiam aurum & argentum " Camd. in Cornw. *(d)* " Cautum suit Edicto Romanorum Imperatorum scvero ne quis in Britannia nummis uteretur sfiff fignatis imaginibus Cæsarum." *e)* Neque enim temere præter mercatores illo adit quifquam, neque iis ipfis quidqiiam prater ram maritimam atque eas regiones quæ sunt contra Galliam notum est." Cæs. lib. iv. p. 76. *(s)* Borlase's Antiquities, p. 247 to 254. conquerours, or would have borrow'd at least somewhat more of the Roman elegante than what we find in the Cornish coins. The inscrib'd coins produc'd by Camden, and fipeed, about the Julian age, confirm this conjecture, there being something of the Roman air, and regularity in all of them, but in ours nothing at all of that kind. There iit one other use which I shall now make of the inscrib'd coins beforemention'd, and may contribute to settle some particulars relating to the age of these Cornish coins; which is, that these inscrib'd coins could not be the first coins of the British mint, and consequently, that the rude uninscrib'd money found in all parts of England are older tlian the inscrib'd, as savouring more of the beginning, and infancy of the art. The series in which money was first introduc d, and arriv'd by degrees, to the Grecian and Roman perfection, seems to be this: first they weigh'd pieces of metal, then found out the way of impressing them differently, according to their weights, and the quantity and sort of cattle they would be taken tor in exchange; so as to save them the trouble of weighing;(«) then they impress'd symbols of religion, war, arts, and philosophy, peculiar to their country; then came in the heads of demi-gods, and princes; and then inscriptions, more certainly to determine, the age, works, and persons, iignify'd by the coins. As soon as the Gauls, or any other barbarous nations saw the great use of money, as it was manag'd among the more polish'd parts of mankind, 'tis natural to imagine, that people off authority would endeavour to introduce the fame convenient way of exchange among their own people; but being hasty, and impetuous, to have the thing done, were not over nice in the choice of artists for doing it. What first and principally struck them, was the use of money; to have the money coin'd with beauty and impression, was what hat! no place in their first conceptions, nor enter'd at all into their design; hence came the first coins so rude and inexpressive; because the art, tho' at full maturity among the Greeks and Romans, was sore d to pass thro' a second infancy among the Gauls, and like the gold that was cast into the fire, could not come out a better molten calf than the hands, which were employ'd, were able to mould and fashion it. The money, therefore, coin'd at first among the Gauls and Britans, could not but partake

of the barbarity and ignorance of the times, in which it first came into use, and the figures must have been miuch ruder, and more uncouth than those of the inscrib'd coins. Those coins then, which are not inscrib'd, are most probably older than those of the same nation which are inscrib'd; inscriptions, or legends, being a part of elegance, which at first was riot at alt attended to; but which, after-ages constantly practis'd, consulting at once the conveniency of their commerce, and the glory of their country. If this inference is right, our coins at Karn-bre, and the like fort in Plot, and Camden's English edition, are older than the inscrib'd ones produc'd by Camden and Speed, and consequently older than the Roman invasion."(&) Now, it is really surprizing, that after having so minutely examined these coins, and so clearly determined their antiquity, Dr. Borlase stiould have ftopt short in this place; without the slightest suspicion of a probability which their appearance hath very strongly suggested to me. That these very curious coins were British, and that they existed before the Roman invasion, hath been proved beyond a doubt. But we have as good reason to suspect that such coins were also prior to any voyage of the Pheniciins to this istand, whether trading or colonial. And having looked ib far into antiquity, another glance will easily carry us to the period of the first peopling of the island. That the Danmonians were a people from the east, I have mentioned as a very probable opinion: And that these coins were, also, of eastern origin, may be concluded from several circumstances. In the first place, they were found in the country of the Danmonians, who were confessedly more like the eastern nations than any other race of people in this island. In the next place, they were found on Karnbre, in the middle of the ridge of *Karnbre-hill*—the consecrated mountain of the Druids. Karnbre, indeed, was the most remarkable place of the Druid worship in all Danmonium. It is possible, then, that these coins have some relation to the Druids. That they resemble the coins of the east, is evident from the very face

of them. Many of the coins of India, at this present day, particularly the rupee, are nearly of the same size and figure: And, what is indeed a very striking resemblance, their symbols are exactly similar to those with which our British specimens (a) The first money us'd in Rome was of plain copper, without any impression till the time of Servius Tullus, who caus'd them first to be ftampM with the image of an ox, a lheep, a hog, whence. it began to be call'd *pecuma a pecudt.* Pliny.—Jobert's Medals, Engh p. 35. *by* Borlasc's Antiquities, p. 256 to Z58. specimens are charged: In the mean time, we are assured, that these figures on the Indian coins are of great antiquity-The little round ltuds, or button-like embossments, which I have described, are the lame on the rupee. Nor mould I forget to mention, that the convexity of these coins is another point of similarity. And as to their quality, both the British and the Indian are of *pure gold,* with little or no allay. Several of the ornamental figures are of a military cast—others of a religious. The trees are, probably, the oaks of the Druids: And the globular appearances are, possibly, repre entations of the fun and other luminaries—the great objects of worship among the people of the east, *(a)* That Phenician and Greek coins have been found in Devonshire, I have been often informed; though I have not been fortunate enough to meet with such specimens.(A)

Thus have I presented my readers with a deicnption of the Danmonian commerce, (hipping, and coins, from the very earliest times to the period of Cæsar's invasion, in some instances, perhaps, I have entered too much into di tail; in others, have been ton much on the wing. But whilst I have endeavoured, in every instance, to exhibit clear views, I have seldom detained my readers long, except where the points were curious; or rapidly led them from one topic to another, except where there was little matter for entertainment.

S E C T I O N ix.

VIEW of the LANGUAGE and LEARNING of the DANMONIANS, during the BRITISH PERIOD.

I. *The Danmonian or British Tongue, in its first stage—its affinity to the Irish and the Erse —Words, Compositions—The British, the Irijh, and the Erse, immediately derived from thi East—The Danmonian Language, in its second stage ; or the Britijh-Phenician—Words, Compositions—The Danmonian Language, in its third stage, as enriched by the Greek—. The Danmonian Language in its fourth stage, as corrupted by the Belgic—Under theft modifications, the Danmonian Tongue entitled Cornubritijb.—II. The Sciences and the Artt of the Danmonians.—III. Seminaries of Learning in Danmonium—Conclusion.* THE general state of knowledge, at this obscure period, is a subject rather hypothetical than historical: The language, and, the learning, however, of Danmonium. may "afford-room for curious investigation. The Danmonhns have been represented by some authors, as a very rude peopie, yet possessing minds, like other savages, lively and vigorous, and capable of cultivation. But, whilst we are assured that a very large body of men were maintained at the public expence, in considerable splendor, for the purpose of disseminating knowledge, we shall not, perhaps, be disposed to credit all the account of Danmonian ignorance and barbarity. That the Druids were skilled, in various learning, is evident from the attestation of the Greeks and Romans. And the learning of thi venerable priesthood, must, undoubtedly, have influenced the great mass of the people.

The *language* of Danmonium seems to be the first object for consideration. It hath been commonly believed, that the original *language* of the Britons, was the fame as that of the Gauls; though few have proper y discriminated between the south-western Britons, and the other inhabitants of the island. The ancient names of persons and places in

Britain *(a)* It mould seem from the obscure notices of ancient writers, relating to the Brltisli exports and Imports, that the first trade of the island was carried on without the assistance of money, and in the course of a regular exchange. But the gold coins of Karnbre (to throw

nothing else into the scale) are sufficient to outweigh this *opinion* an opinion so light, that it must fly up, and kick the beam!

(h) Several Phenician coins, I understand, were dug up, some years since, at leignmouth; whence the inhabitants conclude, that this place was frequented by Phenician merchants. One of these coins was casually inspected by the Rev. Jems) Templer, cf *Lindridge,* who regrets that he has now lost every trace of it. Had Mr. Tempier been able to procure the coin, I should, doubtless, have been gratified with a fight of it; since there is no gentleman in the county more sanguine than himself in wishing success to a History of Devon. To his various knowledge, indeed, J, am obliged for most essential information: And, whilst I am pleased with his politeness, I cannot but admire his ingenuity.—I have heard, also, a vague report, that Phenician or British coins were found, at Sxater, a few years ago my enquiries for these coin have been, hitherto, fruitless,

Britain and Gaul, we are told, have an exact resemblance. This, however, is a mistakes notion. Not even the *name* of the aboriginal Britons was known in Europe. The numerous tribes or nations on the continent, who extended themselves gradually into this island, from various causes, carried with them, as was molt natural, the *names* of their nations or tribes—such as were known afterwards to the Romans in Gaul and in Germany, by the Armorici, Belgæ, Brigantes, Allobroges, Iceni, and Morini: But among all the nations lettled on the continent, or afterwards fixing themselves in Britain, there never was once heard of such a name as the *Danmonti,* or the *people of Datimon.* Nor" was-such a name as *Caernou* ever known in Europe: And no one can point out, I believe, in what part of the continent of Europe, any tribes of that name have lettled, or we're' settled in thole times, when the Phenicians first traded with the Aborigines of our island.(«) The few who give credit to the Saxon Chronicle, with respect to the settlement of the first colonists in the South-Hams, are of

opinion, that one district there retains to this day some traces of their origin; and, consequently, may throw light on their language: It is the district of *Armine,* the very *name* of the country whence the Saxon Chronicle derives them. If we pass from the name of the nation (4) to that of their priesthood, from what European root can we satisfactorily derive the word Druid *t* It clearly comes from Darui or Drvi, still current in the east,-and signifying *spriest* or *magician.* Sir William Jones describing the great empire of Iran, tells us, that the origin of the language of this Empire was Chaldaic; (r) as proved_ by the words *Shemia,* heaven; *Meya,* water; *Fira,* fire; *Matra,* rain; *Werta,* a rose: And the word Drui, a magician, is also of Chaldaic origin.

But, in order to prove that the aboriginal language of Danmonium was derived from the east, let us recur to Ireland and Scotland. That the *British,* the *lrijk,* and the *Erse,* are to be traced to one fountain, is universally allowed. In truth, they are known to be dialects of the fame language. This is a fact which has never been disputed. If, then, we can clearly deduce, either the *lrijh* or the *Erse* from the east, we snail establish the Oriental Origin of the Britisli or *Danmonian* language, *(d)* That there was an eastern colony in *Ireland,* is evinced by the great affinity of the old *Jriji* with the language of Hindostan, which is derived from the Chaldaic. Sir William Jones, and Col. Vallancey, have presented us with long lists of corresponding words, from the Hmdostanic and the Irish languages. Sir William, as I have observed, describes an eastern empire by the name of Iran: And EiRiN'is the ancient name of Ireland. And " unlels (fays CoL Vallancey) there had been the closest connexion between the original inhabitants of *Eirin* or Ireland, and those of ancient *Iran,* it would have been impossible, that so great an affinity *a)* A learned correspondent observes: " The *AvroySovts* of the island settled chiefly in the west,` and southwest, with whom the Greeks, and, before the Greeks, the Phœnicians, maintained, at least, a commercial intercourse: And of both these people, some tokens yet remain in and about here, such as xf'o'J /xeziwov, or the *Ramb-cad; Tofotria-ri,* now *Totnes,* from the Greeks; and the Promontory of *Ajlarte,* now the *Start Point,* from the Phenicians. But who these *Aborigines* were, with whorrt the Greeks and Phenicians thus traded, is the question: They certainly did not come from the continent of Europe; and, probably, came from the east: They were known by the name of the people of (i)dm «»», and afterwards called *Druids;* though this was rather an appellation given to their priests; and the word signifies, in the *eastern* language, a soothsayer or wiseman. Who they were, would take a volume to explain—what they were, is very concisely described by *Julius Cæsar,* in hi» account of Britain, and by *Strabo.* They, probably, came to Britain not long after the dispersion, when the Scoti came to Ireland and Scotland. The Irish were certainly *Baelim,* as all their customr and language evince. I mould think the Aborigines of Britain were also of the *Cutbite* race, though not of the tribe of *Baal." (b)* The name of one of our rivers, *Columb* or *Columba,* is synonymous with the *Chaldaic* Ioka. And in Columb-john or Columb-ion (so denominated from the river) we have the Chaldaic word itself.

(s) Rowlands, in his *Mona Antiqua Restaurata,* is of opinion, that the people at first spread over Great Britain and Ireland, and the adjacent ifla»ds, were not more than five descents from Noah. With this view, he endeavours to (hew, that our language is one of the primary vocal modes produced among the builders of Babel. (/) And consequently prove the Oriental Origin of the *Danmoi &ans. m* (i) Why did Dan remain in ships? Judges v. 17. " The spirit moved him in the eamp os Dan." Judges itiii. "The snorting of horses was heard from Ban." Jer.viii, 16. « 0an and avaa occupied in thy fairv&c." Bisk. «.vi. i». affinity could exist between the languages of the old Irish and the *Sanscrit.* In the my thology of the Bramins, *Syon* is the goddess of sleep—her festival is kept on the nth day of the new moon

in June—she is fabled to sleep for four months; to signify that the rainy season setting in for four months, the care of *Biftnoo,* the preserver, is suspended as immaterial, the rain securing their crops of grain. All this is an equivocation on the twd Irish words *Suan* and *Soinion,* or *mor-soinion:* the first signifies *sound sleep,* the second *great rain and tempest:* and this again reverts to the Chaldean *Marbason,* a season so called, because of the great rains, i. e. *Otlober.* Again, *Lukee* is their goddess of all kinds of grain: her festival is kept in the month of August. *Unnunto* the unknown (god)—is in Irish, *anaibinte.* *Kartik,* the consecrated—Irish, *Creatath.—Sieb,* the destroyer (death)— Irish, *Sab* and *Saib.* And *Ogham* (as it will loon appear) is equally a Sanscrit and ari Irish word. («) With respect to the word *logan* (in use, at this moment, in Devonshire; as well as Ireland) Vallancey makes these remarks. " Ilad Dr. Borlase been acquainted witH *Sanscrit.* fa) Budh-dha

Crishna

Gapia

Syon

Suria

Baroon

Kesee

Burt

  Supreme

  Apollo

Muses

  God of Sleep

Phœbus

Neptune

Evil Spirit

A sacrifice

Budh, the world and its efeatof

  Buaidh, supreme, virtue, divine attribute

Crimean, the sun

Gube

Suan

Soire

Braine

Kise-al

  Beart &c. &c. &c.

Col. Vallancey refers us, also, to the ancient Language of Ægypt, which is strikingly similar so the Irish. " If an affinity of language (says he) be admit-

ted as a criterion of the truth of the Irish his-; tory, and of the ancient Irish being descended from those Scythians whp had conquered Egypt, and thither carried their language, arts and sciences; there cannot be a stronger proof than the following list of words common to both. The Egyptian language is certainly one of the most ancient in the/ world, and in all probability an original or mother tongue, formed at the confusion of Babel—It is in a great measure preserved to our times in the present Coptic: Its structure and constitution, differ so widely from all the Oriental and European languages, that it is impossible to conceive it derived! from any of them. (1) These words are taken from the Nomenclature Egypto-Arabica, pn-bKshed by Kircher, and from the Coptic Lexicon of the learned Dr. Woide.

  Egyptiace. Lat.

ath, panic, neg.

aiai, *adauclio*

a), *lapis*

amoi, *utinam*

amre, *princepi*

amre, *pijlor*

an, panic, neg.

ant, *pulcbritudo*

anoni, *luxuria*

aoon, *res smlejtd*

aouon, *aperire*

areh, *servus*

areghj, *terminus*

aghjan, *fine*

aYiki, *querela*

aso, *indulgentia*

as ebol, *indulgere*

ad, præpos. neg.

bcl, *sjutio*

bol ebol, *mitigari*

ban, *seedus*

bots, *bellum*

orjoi, *persona*

bann buathas, *vicJoria*

aoi

with the Irish MSS. He would hare found that the *kgan-stone,* which yet retains its name in the west of England, and as he confesses, is not to be explained in that or the

  Welsh

  Hib.

ar doi aisll, *punitio* cis ais bocan, *domus* boctain, *adificium*

baris

bois-ceil, i/acfa *fylvcjlris,* ceile, jfj'/ira bes, *pecunia ceraria*

bial buas

barr, bearra, beart bach, long-bach, long, *navis*

beac, buacal beac-arna gallun, *pajfer* ar abol

. ail

eamh, eamhainfi eamanmaca, *fcbola, collegium*

dod

ar, *respondit* dom-lac, i.e. baine claba, *lac coagulatum*

aifrion

ortog, *pollux, parvus cubitus*

earasaid

eas, eaflabra, *verba fuperba* mionn, *Jignum, litera* tiomna, *tefiamentum* tiomana, *tradere* iod, au-iod, an, panic. feilios naoi, *navis* uas, *os* ar tria uige, uigh-inge, *clajfis* taihfi, taibh real, *laurus viSor'ut* tul teal-mac, *paricldus* tais

tuidme, *turba, conjiratio* tua, *boreas,* doi, *ventus* teide, *congregation nundina mercatorum* toide, *aqua vita, aqua mixtay j4nglice* toddy, torf doid, *pradiolium cemmixtum,* a joint farm tos

teim, *mors*

ith

ibh, *potus* eag. ith, *triticum* pocan *unde Cadmus* keildei, ceildei *fanBm* cama Welsh dialect, is the Irish *Logh-onn* or stone, into which the *logh,* or divine essence, was laid to descend, when the Druids consulted it as an oracle." But it was pretended, that the

Hib.

keacht, *intelligentia*

keol, keolin

leiS .

mai, mai dhuin,

mith muinke muc

I naoib, Km/i'j naobh, naomh muhan, ut deas-muhan, real's *auslralis.* Desmond; tua muhan, *regio birealis.* Thomond. oir muhan, *regio orientalis.* Ormond. iar muhan, *regit occidentals* lis caichne, caine eag keo

Luimneach, *vel Limerick, portus marit'mus* In Hibernia, f. e. Laimri-oike, *juxta aquam (urbs) vil regio juxta*

aquam.i) tuam reagh, *nox*

Sob-sgeul *bistoria Jantla,* sgeul *bistor'm*

neid, *ventus*

neamh. *Tibetanici,* neam nath, *scitntia* os aos nodh, *supremus, nobilij/inuts* aire *frinceps,* Arab, har aine

uatat, uathath aoi, *grex,* aoire, *pastor* racam, *scribere* roinim troid reis, *spathalma* reim oilerap, *indigent* reimnacht ' reis, *septentrio* re, *Luna* rad, horizon, rad a dearglus, Aurora, *i. c. friens!u mjnis rubicundi*

re, *saSJus*

reit

rab, *remits*

rog, *pyrus*

soib sai

she divinity communicated motion to this stone; whence the people of Devon use *log(in* as synonymous with *tjio'vingj* -In

Julius Firmicus, Sacrarum literarum periti. i. e. /Vixciv.)——Hibernice *Reach-nab.*

Hib. ". t see, *libellus,* see na geug, &«r« *ramorum*

fe

seanam, *medicare*

seol

deag, wori oide, *praceptor,* dam-oide, *magijler* saoth, *iomo gcnerojus, validus, literatus.* Sethis sethreach, *homo validus.* Sith-be, *dux*

AeA

pocaire feite

fuar, *frigidvs* , forai na grian, *ortus fills* bual soir fairke soda 6g. *panis*

upta

sai-run, *nafus,* run, *fades* saoire, *la J'anire, dies fcstivitatis,* seire, *festum,* pran dium sadolr sae, *lignum,* saor, *carpentarius, i. e.* fabricator ligni sliuibhal fhar, *stlius,* mean sliior, *stilus natu maximus,* sheareach, *stilus equi*

sleigh

slli, *unde jhinim, facere extcnfionem* salach siol sllen, sen soc, *culter*

Iheod, *adamantbus*

famh, *fil,* samra, *astas*

lamh fuinn, *stnis astatis, autumuus,* ear an samh, *ver, initium astatis*

figheach, unde fighim, *texare,* fighedoir, *textor*

fos

putog, *reel urn* cailleach calladh cead, *judex,*

caban, *domus* (anglice *cabin)*

coga, *bellum* .

seim-loir, *conciliarius*

eol-air, *aedpiter,* ealan, *cygnus,* eit-ile, *vdatui* seibti, *qui judicat, judex* ceasam eile coib, *dot*

cru

obar i cot, *barca navif*

cait-fe t,

geall, *pignut*

gho,

In the mean time, the *Erse* tongue differs so little from the *Irijb,* that their common origin is plain: They are both equally derived from the east. That the *British* language, therefore, from itsallowed affinity to both, is, also, oriental, seems to be a fair induction.

But we have, hitherto, examined the British, the Irish, and the Erse as *oral* only: They should be considered, also, as *written.* Let us enquire in what characters these island dialects of the great Asiatic language were exprest, and whether any vestiges of such characters are traceable, at present, in Danmonium, in Ireland, or in Scotland.

With respect to the Danmonian *charatlers,* I have already had occasion to remark, that the Druids were not averse from committing their thoughts to writing; as is generally supposed. Not that in matters of religious or political concern, they used a character which was intelligible to the vulgar. Like the priests of India, they had, doubtless, their secret letters, which the common people regarded as mysterious. Cæsar tells us (in a passage on which I have already commented) that the Druids " *publUis pri'vatisque rationibus* græcis Literis *utantur."(a)* Here the word *Græcis,* in the opinion of the commentators in general, is supposititious. A learned antiquary makes the following remark on this passage. " We have said just now that the order of the *Druids* was prior to the existence of the *Greek* word Aft; and yet some persons will be apt to infer, from this last sentence of *Cæsar,* that they both spoke and wrote the language. But we must not conclude from this place, (see *Camden's Britannia,* p.

xiv.) that they had any knowledge of the *Greek* tongue. For *Cæsar* himself, when he wrote to *Stuintus Cicero,* (besieged at that time somewhere among the *Nervians)* penned his letter in *Grezk, lest it should be intercepted,* and so give intelligence to the enemy—which had been but a poor project, if the *Druids* (who were the great ministers of state, as well as of religion) had been masters of the language. The learned *Selden* is of opinion, that the word *Græcis* has crept into the copies, and is no part of the original. *Hottoman* and *D. Vofflws* also reject it. And it was natural enough for *Cæsar,* in his observations on the difference between the management of their discipline and their other affairs, to fay in general, that in one they made use of *letters,* and not in the other, without specifying any particulars. But if any plan is of opinion that a word sliould be retained in this place, tie emendation of *Sam, Petit* is very ingenious, that we sliould read Crassis instead of *græcis*—though not for the reason which he gives, because he conceived them to be rudely formed, and not equal to the elegance of the *Greek* and *Roman* characters; but because they were the *thick square letters* which themselves had introduced from the east." I have already noticed some monumental pillars in Danmonium, which, possibly, may be relics of Druidism, inscribed with these oriental letters. That such existed in Danmonium, there can be little doubt. And the characters which Sir William Jones mentions as discovered on the walls of the ruined

Egyp. *Lat.* Mb. gho, *annunciare* goch-aire, *magijlcr ceremonalivm* ghaph, *bycms* gamh-ra ghin, *aCtio* ghnim, *agert* ghinnau, *mjys* gnl ghoi, *navis* uige gliiphe, *pojpdere* gahh ghro, *victoria* cro flak, *supplicium* fleacht, *adoratio* x gratia, *re/igio* garait,*JanCtui*

The Nomenclator in Egyptian and Arabic, whence most of these words are taken, is often quoted by the learned Cr. Woide, in his Coptic Dictionary. It was found by Petrus a Valle, in the year 615, near Grand Cairo, in the hands of some peasants, who knew not its value. Peter transmitted it to Rome, where Kircher

found it, and published it with a Latin translation. It contains, by Peter's account, many old Egyptian woids, sacred and profane, now grown obsolete to the Egyptians themselves: But he can form no idea when it was compiled. It is a most valuable monument of antiquity. For, we know as little of the Egyptian dialect, as we do of their literary characters, as Count Caylus observes.(i) Before the beginning of this century, we were acquainted only with the Hieroglyphic. Since that period, many inscriptions have been found on the bandages of very ancient mummies, written in a *running hand,* or common character. One of considerable length has been engraved by the Count. The original is in the library of St. Geneveue at Paris, where 1 was indulged with the perusal of it." " (a) lib. vi. sect. 13.

(1) Antiquities, v. 1. p. 69. ruined palace of Jemschid, correspond with the *crastis literis* of Cæsar.—But let us return to Ireland.

The *Ogham* writing of the ancient Irish, was, probably, the fame as that of the Danmonian Druids. Colonel Vallancey has illustrated this point with his wonted learning and ingenuity. " The word *Ogham* in Irish, taken in a general sense, says Vallancey, signifies whatever is sacred, mysterious and sublime; purity of diction, eloquence; but is particularly applied to *sacred and mysterious writings.* Toland fays, the word originally meant, the *secret of letters,* and from signifying the *secret of meriting,* it came to signify *secret writing.* But *Ogham* or *Oghma* certainly signified learning, eloquence, sublimity of stile in composition. Hence it became a proper name, in Irish, as *Ogma Grianan,* who was one of the first of the Chaldæan race. As a character, it was never used but in sacred writings, unless in an epitaph for the deceased, by permission of the Magi or Druids. From its uniform combination of straight ljnes, many have thought it was the fame as the unknown characters of *Persefolis.* And the Perfepolitan characters, in the opinion of the learned *Millius,* were sacred and mysterious. ' Cum Zoroastres placita sua coriis mandata, Perfarum re-

gi Guflitasp tradidisset, ilia certo loco inclusit, eique sacerdotes præfecit, prohibens, ne hæc sacra vulgo manifestarent: quare etiam sacerdotum Perfarum cultui divino vacantium labia, linteo velata erant. Qui, de hodierno statu Persiæ atque religione, scripserunt, idem referunt. Quid, quod inscriptiones Perscpolitanæ, quæ adeo erudites excruciaverunt, notæ quaedam Hieroglyphicæ esse videntur, quibus Zoroastres, qui prope Persepolin cultum symbolicum condiderar, aliique Magi, præcipua cultus fui capita, profanum vulgus celare studebant.' *(a)* That learned Orientalist Sir William Jones (who, from his knowledge in the *Sanscrit,* has been admitted into the order of she *Bramins)* in a late discourse to the Academy of *Calcutta,* adverts to the word *Ogham.* He proves it to be a pure *Sanscrit* word, meaning the *sacred or. mysterious writings or language,* and used in that signification, in the books of the *Sanscrit* : He also observes, that the *Sanscrit* language, older than the *Hindu,* was the language of *Iran,* and of pure *Chaldaic* origin, He applies the use of this word *Ogham,* and the *ancient traditions of the* Irish, together with the authority of the *Saxon Chronicle,* to prove that these islands were first peopled by colonies from *Iran,* and that *their language, their customs, and their religion, were the fame both in these islands, in Iran, and in Hindostan*—but—all originating in Chaldea.(A)"

After this examination of the primitive language osDanmoniiim, both as an *oral* and 3 *written* language, we might naturally enquire, in what points it resembles its eastern original. There are some authors who inform us, that like the Chaldaic, it is energetic «md sonorous. Its phraseology is pompous: Its style metaphorical, *c)*

Of *(a)* Oratio de fabulis Orientalium, p. 77.

(i) " Iran and Iouran, the country of the Persians, and of the Turks. Persia and Oriental Turkey.—applied by eastern historians to signify *all upper Asia,* India and China excepted.'' (Herbelot)—But the ancient Iran, I believe, was of greater extent. Sir William Jones, in the

discourse above mentioned, proves from the books of the *Bramins,* the existence of a first great empire (before the Assyrian) which he calls by the name of the kingdom of *Iran;* whence, he fays, a colony emigrated to *Hindosian.* (c) The several proverbs in the Cornish language, that have been transmitted to us, all savour of truth—some of pointed wit—some of deep wisdom. Take the following as specimens of the eastern manner: *Neb 11a garey gwayn coll reftona* ; He that heeds not gain, must expect loss. *Net na gare y gy, an gwra deveeder;* He that regards not his dog, will make him a choak sheep. *Guel yi» gnetba vel goofcn j* It is better to keep than to beg. *Gurada, rag la bonan te yti gura;* Do good, for thyself thou dost it. *Tau tanas;* Be silent, tongue. *Cows nebas, co-ws da, ha da vetb cowjas arta;* Speak little, speak well, and well will be spoken again. *Cows nebas, cows da, nebas an ycvrn ytv an gwella;* Speak little, speak well, little of public matters is hest. *Nyn ges gun heb lagas, na kei bcb (ttvern;* There is no downs without eye, nor hedge without ears.(;)
Der taklow minniz ew brez teez gonvethes, *By jmall things are the minds of men discovered,* avelen taklow broaz: dreffen en tacklow broaz, *as well as by great matters: because in great things,* ma an gymennow hetha go honnen; bus en tack-*they will stretch themselves; but in small matters,* low minis, ema an gye suyah haz go honnen. *they follow their own natnre.*

Gwra,

Of compositions in the Danmonian language, at this early stage of it, we might vainly search for any extensive relic, at this hour: Nor will the Irish or Erse present us with a single literary Work of such high antiquity. There are, however, some Druidical verses extant. The Druids, after the manner of the Chaldeans and Ægyptians, delivered their instructions in verse. And the oldest kind of British verse has been called by the Welsh grammarians Englyn Milur—of which the following is a specimen;

An lavar koth yu lavar guir,
Bedh durn rever, dhan tavaz re hir;

Mez den heb davaz a gallaz i dlr.
What's said of old, will always stand
5
Too long a tongue, too short a hand;
But he that had no tongue lost his land,
(a)
We *Do, 0 King, these tbmgs which, with the best strength, may be thought the wonders of their time* j *and those things will gain glory to thee for ever. When tbou contest into the-world, length of sorrow follows; when thou beginnest the ivay, ytis not known _ which side, East, West, to the North, or South.* An beys yu cales kylden; *Thr world is an hard cara-vaifera.* Deu 1 uth ros flour hy hynse j *God made a rose-flower of thy sex.* (a) " The *Druids* couched their morality in triambics of rhyme, the better to imprint them upon the memory. They wgre above all things careful to inculcate taciturnity or secresy into their disciples, that their doctrines might not become vulgar, and to secure to themselves, as much as might be, the credit of learning and wisdom. Their verses were filled with strong images of nature, after the Oriental manner; always concluding with some wife sentence founded upon long experience. And to these, in all probability, we are indebted for most of the proverbial expressions now in use. The following were collected and committed to writing by *Lbowarch Hen,* a Prince of *Cumberland,* who lived in the year 590, and are purely *Vencdotian,* or the *Brit'ijh* of *North Wales.* For tho' the *Druids* wrote nothing of this fort, yet the ancient Christians who succeeded them, did, and were careful of preserving what was good and laudable. They are inserted by Mr. *Rowlands,* in his truly valuable work of the *Mona Antiqua,* but without any translation; nor does it appear by his remarks that they were sufficiently understood by than (otherwise) very learned author. Two very worthy gentlemen, well versed in the language, have been consulted concerning the meaning of them j whose literal sense of them is given belo.v. But we cannot be of opinion, with those gentlemen, ' that the first two lines of each triambic were never designed to have any connection

with the third, but were intended merely to furnish rh)me to it:' Because, supposing the three first triambics to allude to the corrective discipline of the *Druids,* which cannot well be doubted, the connection is easy j and there Is as much of it in these and the three last, as the oriental poets generally furnish.

Literal Sense.

-1.
Strong rods of green birch
Will draw my foot out of the hold:,
Reveal not thy secret to a youth.

II.
Strong rods of oak in a grove
Will draw my foot out of the chain:
Reveal no secret to a maid.

III.
Strong rods of leafy oak
Will draw my foot out of prison:
Reveal not thy secret to a blab.

IV.
Mountain snow, swift deer,
Scarce any in the world cares for me:
Warning to the unlucky saveth not.

V.
Mountain snow, fish in a ford,
The lean stag seeks the warm vale:
A lonp'og for death saveth not.

We have also some Druidical verses concerning the " *Tatal-Jione,* call'd so, as suppos'd' to contain the fate of the Irish Royal Family. On this the supreme Kings of Ireland used to be inaugurated on the hill of Tarah, and the ancient Irish had a persuasion, that in what country soever this stone remain'd, there one of their blood was to reign.(a)" The fatal-stone was enclosed in a wooden chair, and thought to emit a sound under the rightful king, but to be mute under one of a bad title. The Druid Oracle concerning it i» in these words

Cioniodh scuit saor an fine Man ha breag an Fais dine Mar a bh fuighid an Lia fail Dlighid flaitheas do ghabhail.

Except old saws do feign,
And wizard wits be blind,
The Scots in place must reign,
Where they this stone (hall find.(A)"

In the Erse language, the poems of Osllan, though the product of a much later age, are deeply tinctured,with the oriental genins. The following passages will give us a fine relish of the eastern manner. This address to the moon has an uncommon obscurity of allusion: " Whither dost thou retire from thy course, when the darkness of thy countenance grows? Hast thou thy hall, like Ossian? Dwellcst thou in the shadow of grief?'

Haves

Literal Sense.

VI.

Mountain snow the wind will disperse,

Broad the splendent moon, the dock is greeri:

Scarce a knave will want a pretext.

Druidicat Verses.

VJ.

Eyri mynydd, gwint ae tawl,

Llydan Iloergari, glass tavawl,

Odyd dyn dined dihawl.

Descrip. of Stoneheng &c. p. 64, 65, 66.

(

(a) " This stone was sent into Scotland, where it continued as the coronation feat of the Scottish kings; till in the year 1300, Edward the First of England, brought it from Scone, placing it under the coronation chair at Westminster. The Irish pretend to have memoirs concerning it for above 2000 years." Tol. p. 103.

(A) " After the example of the antients, (the Chaldeans, Egyptians, and Assyrians) the Druids eompriz'd all the particulars of their religion, and morality in hymns, the number of which, as Mr Martine(i) fays, was so great that the verses which composed them amounted to 20,000. In justification of this part of their disciplines it must be observ'd that the subject matter of verses is easier learnt by means of the metre, and more easily retain'd, than what is express'd in prose. Of the particular sorts of verses which the bards us'd, there is an account in the ingenious Dr. John David Rhys's Rudiments, &c. of the British language; (2) and Mr. E. Lhuwyd is there of opinion, ' that the oldest kind of Britisli verse is that call'd by Rhys's Grammar Englyn Milur, and that 'twas ia this fort of metre the Druids taught their disciples, of wliich there are some traditional remains to this day in Wales,(3) Cornwall, and Scotland,' and

a farther testimony.the verses themselves bear to this truths in that they generally contain some divine or moral doctrine. (4) As the bards (an inferiour class of Druids) were remarkable for an extraordinary talent of memory; (5) this teaching memoriter, and by verse, was likely their office, whilst the superiours of the order were employ d in higher speculations, or the more secret and solemn parts of duty." *Bcr/ase's Antiquities,* p. 83, 84. « The sort of verse I find most common among our oldest remains, is that called Englyn Milur in Jo. Dav. Rhys's Grammar, p. 184. And as I have (tlio' but rarely) heard the fame in the shire of Argyle in Scotland, and also in Cornwall, I am apt to conclude it one of the most ancient, if not the very oldest sort of verse we ever had; and that it was in this sort of metre the Druids taught their disciples; of whom Cæsar fays: *Ad bos magnus adolcfcentium numerus Disciplines causa concurriu—li certo anni tempore in jinibus Carnutum, qua regio totius Galiiœ media habetur, conjldunt, in loco consecrateHue omnes undique eonveniunt; eorutnque judieiis decrctijdque parent. Disciplina in Britannia reperta atque inde in Galliam translata, ejse existimatur. Et nuvx qui diligcntius earn rsm cognoscere-volunt, pierumque illo discendi caujfa projiciscuntur. Druides a bello abesj'e consue'verunt, neque tributa una cum reliquh pendunt militia wacationem omniumque rerum babent immunitatem. Tantis excitati prœmiis & sud fponte multi in Disciplinam conveniunt, & a propinquis parentibusque mittuntur.* Magnum ibi numerunv versuum ediscere dicuntur. *Itaque nonnulli annot vicenos in disciplina permanent,* fifV. Cæs. de Bello Gall. 1. vi. That this *it* ancient enough to have been the verse used by the Druids, is manifest from there being some traditional remains ef it at this day, in Wales, Cornwall, and Scotland; though it be immemorial when any such were last made. And that it really was used by them seems also highly probable, as a great number of the WeHh Engfyns of this sort have always some doctrine, divine (1) La Reliqh. de Gaul. Hi. pag. 50, (2) See

Archæol. Brit. pag. a$o. (3) A. *t.* 1743. At Bala in Merionethshire an annual meeting and festival of the Bards is celebrated, There assemble together 60 or 70 harpers. In all this company of musical poets scarce six of them can read, and yet some of them, have sucha, poetic genius that their compositions have both spirit and invention. (4) Ihuyd. 251. ($) Gallruchius's Hist. Pocticuc. lib. in, chap, iv.

Have *thy sisters fallen from heaven?* Are they who rejoiced with thee at night no more? Yes,, they have fallen, fair light! And thou dost often retire to mourn 1"—Are we not instantly reminded of that grand apostrophe—" *Hoiu art thou fallen from heaven, O* Lucifer, son of the morning?" The heavenly bodies appear to have been the common objects of veneration both in Scotland and in the east. The hospitality of an Arabian princess, is thus praised by a poet of Arabia: " The stranger and the pilgrim well know, when the iky is dark and the north wind rages, that thou art a fun to them by day, and a moon in the cloudy night."(«) In the lame manner, Ossian: " He was like the strong-beaming fun."(A) The following image seems more in the style of an Arabian, amidst his thirsty deserts, than of a poet of the Highlands: " Before them rejoiced the king, as the traveller, in the day of the fun; when he hears, far rolling around, the murmur of mossy streams; streams, that burst, in the desart, from the rock of roes."(s) The traveller and the hospitable chieftain, were equally the theme of the Highland and the Arabian poet. And the warrior was described by both, in the same figurative terms. The Arabian warnor advancing at the head of his army, is " compared (fays Sir W. Jones) to an *eagle* sailing through the air, and piercing the clouds with his wings." Thus the leader of Ossian, " comes like an *eagle,* from the skirt ot his squally wind! In his hand are the spoils of foes!"(rf) This allusion is frequent in Oflian. " From thy vales come forth a race, fearless as thy strong-winged eagles; the race of Colgorm of iron shields, dwellers of loda's hall."(f) " Erin *(f)* rose around him 5 like the sound of eagle-wing."(f) But love was the most prolific subject. The poets of Arabia compare the foreheads of their mistresses to' the morning, their locks to the night, their faces to the *fun,* or *moon,* their cheeks to *roses,* their teeth to pearls, hail-stones, or snow-drops» their eyes to the flowers of the narciifus, their *dark* coloured hair to hyacinths, their lips to rubies, the color of their breasts to *snow,* their shape to the *pine-tree,* their stature to the javelin.*(h)* And the *blue eyes* of an Arabian woman bathed in tears, are compared to violets dropping with dew.(;) And thus, Ossian: ' His *white-bosomed* daughter, fair as a *fun-beam* '"(?) " No more I see thee, bright as the *moon* on the western wave!"(/) " That fun-beam! that mild light of love! It soon approached. We saw the fair. Her *white* breast heaved with sighs. The wind was in her loose *dark* hair! Her *rosy* cheek had tears. "(»») " Her breast was whiter than the down of Cana—her eyes were two stars of light! Her face was heaven's bow in showers—her dark hair flowed round it like the streaming clouds!"(») " Daughter of strangers (he said) *young f ine* of Inifliuna!"(o) And Malvina, lamenting over Olcar, says: " I was a *lovely tree* in thy presence, Oscar, with all my branches round me I" " Hunters, from the mossy rock, saw ye the *blue eyed* fair? Are her steps on grassy Lumon, near the bed of roes?"(/) " The daughter of Starno came with her voice of love—her *blue eyes* rolling *in iears.*q) " She left the hall of her secret sign! lhe came in all her beauty, like the *moon* from the cloud of the east. Loveliness was around her, as light. Her steps were the music of songs. She saw the youth and loved him! Her *blue eye* rolled on him in secret!"(0 When we consider the vine or moral, In the conclusion; the rest being often insignificant, and.serving only as metre thereunto. And of this kind are those very ancient Epigrams called *Englynytn vr eiry:* as,

Eiry mynydh, guyn pob ty;
Kynnevjn bian a xanv!
Ni dbtriu da 0 dra %ysgy-(1)
Eiry mynydh, guynt ae taul,
Lhydan lhoergan, glas tavaul; *Odid*

dyn diried, dibaul (2-)
Eiry mynydh hydh ym mrdn;
Gojjuiban guynt yujj blaen on i *Try-dydb treed y ben y son.* (3) '
Dr. Pryce's Archaeol. p. 54.

(a) See Poems by Sir William Jones. (i) Ossian, vol. 1, p. 13. (c) Ossian, vol.2, p. t£it (rf) Ossian, vol. 1, p. 17. (f) p. 23. *(f) Eiriti, Iran,* Ireland.. *(g)* Ossian, vol. 2, p. 92. (A) See Jones's Poems, Essay 1, p. 16?. (i) ibid. (i) Ossian, vol. 1, p. 23. (/) p. 56. (m) p. 276. (») p. 24. (t) vol. 2, p. 146. (f) Ossian, vol. 2, p. 136. See Solomon's Song. ij) Ossian, vol. 1, p. 266. (r) ibid. the difference of objects which nature presented to the view, in Arabia and in the Highlands, and when we reflect that the poets of both countries were alike remarkable for simply describing what they saw and felt, we must necessarily make allowances for much Arabian imagery not occurring in the Highland poetry. But, after these allowances, we cannot but admire the similarity of Ossian, to the eastern poets, in various illustrations of his subject, and see every where a strong likeness in their style and manner. The Arabs and the Highlanders not only resembled each other in their poetry, but in their attachment to the persons of their poets, *(a)* " The fondness of the Arabians for poetry (fays Sir William Jones) and the respect which they shew to poets, would be scarce believed, is we were not assured of it by writers of great authority. The principal occasions of. rejoicing among them, were formerly, and very probably are to this day, the birth of a boy, the foaling of a mare, the arrival of a guest, and the rise of a poet in their tribe. When a young Arabian has composed a good poem, all the neighbours pay their compliments to his family, and congratulate them upon having a relation capable of recording their actions, and of recommending theif virtues to posterity." And thus, the Highlanders, fond of militaiy fame, and attached to the memory of their ancestors, delighted in traditions and songs concerning the exploits of their nation, and especially of their own particular families. In every Highland clan or tribe, therefore, those who were quali-

fied to transmit to posterity the actions of heroes, were as highly respected as among the Arabs. Ossian compares the " music of bards to the dews of the morning on the hill of roes."

Thus, in so late an age as that of Ossian, the Asiatic muse(4) illuminated the Highlands: yet Danmonium was fated to enjoy but a short/ time the pure splendor of eastern poetry. In the recesses of the Highlands, it was long preserved. But, Danmonium lost much of her primitive orientalism, as (he became the mart of commerce, or the seat of war. Her connexion with the Phenicians, was not favourable to literature.

The Phenicians, it is true, spoke nearly the same language as the people of Devonshire astd Cornwall. The British, the Irish, the Erse, and the Phenicinn, were branches of the fame oriental tree: They were dialects of the fame Asiatic language. But the Phenicians, from their mercantile connexions and various intercourse with half the nations of the world, soon permitted their dialect to be corrupted by foreign words and phrases: In this adulterated state they introduced it into Danmonium.

About the time of the settlement, therefore, os the Phenicians in this western part of the ifland, we may fix the *second* stage of the British language, as spoken in Devon and Cornwall. There are many who represent the ancient language of Danmonium as no other («) Poems, p. 173.

(i) Dr. Knox (the most sensible, spirited, and elegant of all our English essayist) informs us, that ' a resemblance has been pointed out by some ingenious critics between the Gothic and Oriental poetry, in the wild enthusiasm of an irregular imagination. And they have accounted for it, by supposing, with great probability, that in an emigration of the Asiatics into Scandinavia, the Eastern people brought with them their national spirit of poetry, and communicated it to the tribes with whom they united." There is no other way, indeed, of accounting for this resembtance. For, the Arabian or the Persian, " who is placed in a climate where the serenity of the weather constantly presents him with blue skies, luxuriant plantations, and funny prospects, will find his imagination the strongest of his faculties; and, in the expression of his sentiments, will abound in allusions ta natural objects, in similies, and the most lively metaphors. His imagination will be his distinguishing excellence, because it will be more exercised than any other of his faculties; and all the powers both of body and mind are known to acquire vigour by habitual exertion. He, on the other hand, whose lot it is to exist in a less favoured part of the globe, who is driven by the inclemency of his climate to warm roofs, and, instead of basking in the sunshine amidst all the combined beauties of nature, flies for refuge from the cold to the blazing hearth of a smoky cottage, will seek, in the exercise of his reason, those resources which he cannot find in the actual employment of his imagination. Good fense and just reasoning will therefore predominate in his productions. Even in the wildest of his flights, a methodical plan, the result of thought and reflection, will appear, on examination, to restrain the irregularities of licentious fancy." (1) Yet, the Scandinavian, the Highland, and tl Danmonian bards, have all the flightiness and fire of the oriental gœius. other than *Phenician.(a)* On this idea, they proceed to derive from the Phenitians the name of the island itself, of this western tract in particular, of its rivers, its mountains, its vallies, and its towns, together with its natural and artificial productions.(£) Sammes, in his description of Britain, intimates, that the name(r) of Britain was given to it by the Phenician navigators, signifying the *Land or Island of 'fin;* which they called *Bratanac,* or *Baratanac*; and that this was agreeable to the custom of those merchants, who gave names to many places on the sea-coasts, in Ægypt, Africa, Gaul, and Spain.—all the ancient names of which are of Phenician extract or origin; though many of them were afterwards perverted by the Greeks to their own idiom. (/)Thus (according to Sammes) *Corniyall* is so named from *cern* or *kern,* or *cheran;* a Phenician word for a headland, promon-

tory, or point of land like a *horn.* Cornwall has two such points of land—the promontory called *Bel ir* or *promontorium Belerium;* the other, *Meneg,* from the Phenician word *Meneog,* a peninsula. And thus Danmonium, including Cornwall and Devonshire, comes from *dan* or *dun,* a Phenician word for *a bill,* and *moina* signifying *mines,* in Phenician, or minerals, that is to fay, the *country of mines.'e)* It is to the *Phenician* age, that molt *(a)* Dr. Pryce Intimates, in his Archæologia Cornu-britannica, that the Cornish language was immediately introduced by the Phenicians. This idea seems to be derived from Scawen's MS. to which the Doctor had access. It is there observed that the West-British tongue was most like the Phenician—manly, lhort, and expressive. " The Passion, a poem, written in Cornu-Britifh, is no» easily understood by the Wellh, from the intermixture of those idiomatic expressions, originally borrowed from the *Phenicians."* Scawen's MS. as referred to by Borlase. Nat. Hist. p. 314. (A) We should remember, however, that the Phenician is derived from the *Chaldaic,* as well as the purs Britisli—the language of the Aborigines of Danmonium. *(c)* " Some have thought (fays Borlase) that the Phenicians—others, that the Grecians planted some of the sea-coasts; leaving colonies behind them: But the great uniformity to be observed among the ancient Britons, proves them to be of one original." That there was, however, a very striking distinction between the inland inhabitants and those of the maritime parts, Cæsar asserts upon the best grounds. And this position will be abundantly proved in the course of our disquisitions. With respect to the Phenicians, Dr. Borlase asserts, in opposition to Sammes, that the discovery and colonization of the west by this people, has no other foundation than the names of places derived from Phenician words. *(d)* " *Britain,* the most renowned island of the whole world, was called by the ancient *Greeks* ΛΛBlslN, afterwards it took the name of *Britannia,* but more truly, *Bretanica,* from the adjacent islands called, *Barat-anac,* or *Bratanac*

by the *Phoenicians,* from the abundance of tynn, and leadmines, found in them. It was ahvaies esteemed a very considerable part of the world, even in the height of the *Roman* Empire, and much celebrated in the writings and monuments of the *Grecians*; and, as if the genius of this nation did prompt the inhabitants, and insensibly lead them to trade and traffick, we find that besides that, the island received its name from it, insomuch, that, in the first; ages, it was frequented by the ablest merchants, and ikilfullest marriners, the *Phœnicians;* who carefully, and studiously concealed this treasure from the world, being exceeding jealous, least the source and head of their trade being discovered, the busie *Grecians* might put in for stiarers: And least the fruitfulness of the soyl, the pleasant and delightful scituation of the country, might tempt those of their own nation to neglect their barren soyl, and betake themselves to this more temperate and blessed clymate; we read, that, by a publick edict of those states, care was taken to prevent it, yea, all possible means used too, to stop the current which was visibly turning that way. " *Sammes,* p. 1, 2.—" The reason thawabsolutely confirms me in the opinion, the *Stilly* Islands gave name at last to this great Island, that now alone keeps the name of *Britannia,* is, because *Pliny* writes, that this island was called *Albion,* when as all the islands adjacent were called *Britain:* so that we fee the name of *Bratanac* first took place in the adjacent islands, before it came on the main land of *Albion,* but in succession of time the name gaining footing in *Cormval* and *Devon/hire,* it prevailed at last over all the island, and the greater part swallowed up at last the name of the whole, although corrupted and distorted by the several dialects it ran through." *Sammes,* p. 43. (f) " As *the Siluret* derived their name from the *Phœnicians,* so likewise did the *Danmonii,* the inhabitants of *Carnival* and *Devonshire,* in which two counties the *Phœnicians* were very conversant, by reason of their abounding in *tynn.* Upon this account some have derived them from *moina,* in the *Britijh* tongue signifying *mines*, but the question is, whence the *dan* or *dun* proceeds? for *Solinut* calls them *D unmonii* 3 *Ptolemy*, *Damnonzi*, and'in other copies (as *Cawden* faith j trulier *Danmonii*, although I think the transposition is very easie and usual, and hides not at all the original *dan* or *dun*. In the ancient *Britijh* language, as also in the *Phœnician*, *dun* signifies a *hill*, and *dan* of the *British*, *down* of the *Phœnicians* and *Englijh*, slgnifie *lorn*. Now whether we derive them from *dan*, from their low habitations in valleys, or, which 15 righter, from *dun moina*, signifying *bills of tynn;* I find Vol. I. ` Vi ` both both wales that they are of a *Phœnician* derivation. Besides, this word *dun*, being a frequenter word in derivation, and extending to the language of the *Gauls*, who called an hill *dun*, I think more proper to derive *Dunmonii* from it, for from *dun*, a hill, many cities ot' high scituation bpth in *Gaul* and *Britain* take their name, as *Augustodunum*, *Axellodunum*, *Juliodunum*, *Laudanum*, *Meloduiium*, *Noviodunum*, *Sedunum*, *Vellannodun.m*. *Clitopbon* exprefly, *Lugdunum*, *Corvi Collem*, because it was placed on a *bill;* likewise *Andomatunum*, with a *T*, in *Ptolemy*, the metropolis of the *Lingones*. The first country of the *Danmonii* westward is *Cprmval*, shooting into the sea, and running into a point of *Bi 'M 'mm*, the name of which country, if we examine the original of it, and what at this day it is called by the inhabitants, and the similitude it bears with other places, exactly agreeing in name and nature with it, we shall find it could be called so by none but the *Phœnicians*. To prove this, let 11s consider it is agreed upon by all hands, that it received its name from being like a *horn*, running smaller and smaller, with little promontories, as if they were horned on either fide: And this is brought from *Korn*, plur. *Kern*, signifying *hornj* in the *Britijh* language. Now as this *Kern* Or *Korn* is derived from the *Phœnician Keren*, signifying the *fame*, so the manner of calling places after that fort came from them also, a thing so frequent in the eastern countries, to call any corner or angle made, by the name of *horn*; as for ex-

ample, *Cyprus* called *Cerastis*, and Kf lu/jLiranra. in *Taurica Cherfoncfo;* that we are not to doubt but *Ccnrwat*, called *Kernaw* by the inhabitants, proceeded from the *Phœnician* here. To give an instance, the city *Carnon*, as *Pliny* calls it, *Canta*, as Ptolemy, meerly upon the account of its standing upon an angle, cut out by two high-waies that met there in a point on which *Carna* was built, one of which roads from *Mecca* leads to *Tafpb*, the other to *Sanaa*. But this way of the *Phœnicians* was frequently in promontories whose *Phœnicians Karnatha*, afterwards mollified by the *Greets* into *Kiftictris*, Kt£®, Kilfv©-, and all this, from its having so many promontories, which by the *Phœnicians* were called *Kern*. That *Comical* was called *Kernaw* by them rather than the inhabitants, will appear: First, because there is no other promontory in this island so called, notwithstanding the *Bntijh* language was in use through the whole. There are other places that run into the sea as much like a horn as this, which, in my judgment, is an evident sign of the *Phœnicians* in this part of *England* above others. Secondly, because it is more natural to imagine, that sailors (tp whom the shapes of countries appear at a distance, liiore than to the inhabitants) should give the name, than those that only ply'd us on the shears in small *caro-.us*, or *leather* and *-wider* boats, as the *Br 'ttains* did. It is to be observed that *Meneg*, a part of *Com-wal*, which of the south sea dpes make another direct horn, is also of a *Phœnician* derivation, agreeing to that description Mr. *Camden* gives of it, viz. that it is u*Demy-Jstand*, *Meneog* pf the *Phœnician* signifying *kept in by the Jea*, and which he proves in the *Meana* which *Jornandus* describes out of *Cornelius* a writer of antiquities; so that to sailors afar off, *Cornival* appears with two horns, striking itself into the sea, which part of *England*, I believe, was first: discovered by the *Phœnicians*, who, without question, finding a world of tynn in them, secured them for themselves. And altho' *jHeneg* is now destitute of all mettals, as long ago exhausted, yet that there were such mines in it, hear the

fame author: It has great store of Mettal Mines, very full of grafs and herbs, bringing forth more plentifully all those things which serve for pastorage of beasts, and nourishment of man. I will only mention one thing in this *peninsula*, which seems to me exactly to preserve its *Phœnicia/!* name, and that is a fortification of *stones* only without any cement or mortar, lying as upon thg lake *Leopcle*, a fortification after the manner of the *Britains*, as *Tacitus* describes them, *rides & 'nformis Jaxorum compagts*, which was the way of the eastern nations, as the scriptures themselyes inform us. This rude heap of *stones* the inhabitants call to this day *Ertb*, without giving any reason for so ancient a rampier, and of so great a compass as it is, so that none can induce me to believe but that it took its name from the lake on which it lies, for the *Phœnicians* call'd all *lakes*, *Aritb*, so that this military fence called, as I have said, *Er.h*, I believe from thence received its name. There are many places in these two counties, *Con.vsoal* and *Dnonjhire*, which retain exact spot-steps of the *Phœnicians*, that cannot be found any where else, which I lhall omit as nothing easier than to fancy similitudes, especially wtjere, perhaps, they will nos be allowed of. The truth of *Phœnician* trafficks in these parts cjo not depend upon such conjectures, but evidenced by authentick histories, so that I will not mention *Godolcan*, a hill famous for the plenty of the mines of tynn, as Mr. *Camden* witnesseth, which plenty of that mettal is included in the very word it self, only here let me observe, that in the w est and south parts of *England*, even where the *Britijh* language prevails not, we find many places begin with *Pen*, namely, such as are of a high scituation, which, without dispute, is an argument, tha(*fen*, a *bill* in fie *Britijh* language, came from the *Phœnician Pinnah*, signifying the *fame* thing, because we find it most used in those part$ of *England* the *Phœnicians* frequented most; nay through all this island ve shall scarce meet with any northward, when on the west and south coasts, we cannot go six or eight miles but w e find them.

-To instance in the south-side of *Cortrwal* only: *Penrojc, Petjans, Pengcst.k, Pen/ofe* again, *Pcnn/arron, Pendcnnis, Penkehvel, Penivyn, Pentuan, Penreck,* to which may be added that infinite number of towns beginning with *Ti e,* as *Treeioofe, Trenoivth, Tregtnno, Trcwarvencth, Trevafcus, Trenona, Trewarjdretb, Treivorgan, Tregernin, Trelifick, Trefujis, Tregamian, Trcmadart, Tregonoc,* which those very fame parts can have no other account given of them, if they proceed not from the *Phœnician lira,* and by contraction *Tra,* signifying a *castle,* so , that that they were forts built by them to secure their trade. Now give me leave to instance here in some *British* words that agree exactly with the *Pbccnhian,* which I shall put down in *Englijb* charac» ters, leaving the examination of the words, and the roots of them to the learned.

Brit. Phœnician. English.

Crag, or *Careg,* Carac, Crac, A *till.* *Corn,* plur. *Kern,* Coran, plur. Kern, A *born. Caer,* from whence came *Caerlyle,* Caer, from whence Carthago, A *city. Get,* Gwith, A *breach. Catursa,* Kat-erva, A *troop. Penn,* Pinnah, The *cliff* of a *bill. Cum,* Cum, *Low. Dan,* Douna, *Down. Pel,* furthest off, whence Mr. 7 p i-*est remove away Camden* brings *Bellrium,* 5 *Meatb,* Mawath, A *plain* or *valley. Ara,* Ahari, *Slow. Garw,* or *Gar aw, S* Garaph, *Swift. Dun,* Dun, A *bill. Bro,* Baro, A *country* or *region. Givitb,* Guet, A *separation."*

Sammes, p. 58, 59, 60,

« The name of Danmon, the country or province of Devonshere now by a syneresis or contraction named Denefheere was sometimes one and the fame province with Corncwall, and so by afl the old and ancient cronographers were reputed, and both by the name of Danmonia were called which is to fay the country of valleys, whith the old Britons, and now the Welsh (which be the remaynents of the Britons) foe name it, which fignifyeth deepe and narrow valleys, ffor the country is ffull of hills and mountaines. and where be many hills there consequently be also many valleys." *Hooker,* p. 1.

" And notwithstanding that the river of Tamer is the boundes and limitts betweene Devon and Cornewall saving that in some particular places the one borroweth of the other yet they both doe retain their old and and ancient name in the Latine tongue with this difference the one being called the East Danmonia and the other the West Danmonia, but when these two were joyned in one it was much greater.and did reach in length ffrom the ffarthest parte and pointe of the Ifle of Sillye in the west unto the confines and marches of Durotines and the Belgianes in the east which is Dorsetsheere and Somersetsheere. ffor in times past some writers doe hold that Sillye was continent land with Cornewall, but by the violence of raging seas in processe of time the land betweene them hath bin wasted and devoured., and whereof some instances be given, because in a ffaire summer and a sun shining clay the seafayring men doe see and discerne sundry monuments of houses and churches vnder and in the water. And yet notwithstanding the open space and partition betweene them, they be both in one and in the same province, of Cornewall, and both it and the province of Devon be in one diocesse and vnder one and the same Bishop of Excester, these two provinces when they were both one they were also called Corinia and so named (as it is thought) by Corineus cofen vnto Brutus and a special! man off accompt and of service vnder him, whom Brutus rewarded with this country at their ffirst arrivall and landing in the fame, And albeit some doe not allow this nor the history of Brutus to be true, yet fforafmuch as antiquity hath left it vnto us ffor a matter of truth, it were against all humanity to denyethe fame and to derogate that creditt which hath ffor ever hitherto bin received." *Hooter,* p. 3.

" It is obvious to vs in most authors, I mean Geographers and Historiographers, that either describe kingdomes or write their histories, that they are more troubled to search *tc* finde their primitive names & whence they are derived, & the reason why they were first imposed then in any other matter although of far greater worth and consequence:

This caused Plutark the great dictator of knowledge to complain in his preface to the life of Romulus, that the historiographers before him did, much varye in their writings, by whome or for what cause the great name of the great citye, Rome (in its time the glory of the whole world) was first imposed on it. Of such like we need not make search among other foreigne writers, in regard it is foe apparently scene in this our owne Country, whither you name it Albion, Brittaine or England, whose fame is now farder spred then Romes in her greatness, about each of these 3 severall names, and the first plantation thereof many worthy wife & learned men haue long busied wearied yea clean tyred themselues, & yet in fine left it but vpon fuppofalls & vncertaine conjecture. Let vs but seriously consider the alterations of names of such countries in the histories whereof wee are most conversant; And for our more assurance leaue poets & vncertain reporters, & such as come onely by tradition & folye observe how the countries tityes and" mountaines in the land of promise had their names altered from the time of Abraham; or when Moses wrote to the birth of Our Saviour (some 1500 of yeares) & from that age to this our time 1631 somewhat longer, & their with all the qualitie of the soyle, it wee shall finde much matter worthy our serious consideration *k* observation in the vicissitude & interchangeable course of places both in name *Si* nature, which diuerse haue both with eyes & minde rightly considered in their late traucllsj trasiells; when they saw & endured the penurie & barrenness of that region, they could hardly her Induced to belieue that that was the land that Jehova the great God of heauen had promised to his chosen servant Abraham should flow with milk and honey for

That pleasant soyle that did euen shame erewhile The plenteous beauties of the bankes of Nile Void now of force or vital vegitiue Vpon whose brest nothing can line or thriue. As the diuine poet srngeth: then who (if this world should continue yet the like time to come) will bee able to yield a reason why the ports, havens, ilands and kingdbmes in America liaue their now denominations imposed by their late discoverers or latest conquerors (the antient being rejected & irrecouerably lost) as Peru, Fflorida, Virginia, and especially the land of ffamine and desolation which two may long within that supposed time bee made as habitable & fruitfull, or some way found as benefitiall as any the other. Why then should there bee a certain reason expected of the names & original of countries foe long since inhabited, & foe often changed and counterchanged by the vicissitude of inhabitants, as the Poet excellently faith,

Sith it befalls, not alwayes that his feed Who built the towne doth in the fame succeed. And to say more, since vnder heauen noe race Perpetually possesseth any place, Ffor when as wind the angry ocean moves Waue hunteth waue, & billow billow shoues. Soe doe all nations iustle each the other And soe one people doth pursue an other. And scarce the second hath the first vnhowsed Before the third him thence again haue roused. And what hath beene lest vs written worthy our vndoubting beleise (the sacred scriptures onely excepted) before the watrs of Thebes or destruction of Troy (which is supposed neer the time that Jeptha judged Israel), both which are deliuered vnto vs rather poetically, than historically j which doth embolden mee to demand this question with the poet Lucretius

Cur supra bellum Thebanum et funera Trojæ, Non alias quondam veteres cecinere Poetæ? You cannot faile of a probable answere, that few languages had then characters; and few men were fearned, and fewer writers in that age, and those few treated of matters of greater worth, and more needfull to bee knowne & perpetuated to posteritie and what was by them written (being in neither of the strong& durable substance of Seth his pillars to resist the two contrarie elements of fire & water) ijerislied together in the great libraries. If the original of kingdomes, their primitive names, & the reason of those imposed denominations bee soe laborious to bee inquired after'and foe difficult to bee

found; much more industry will bee required, *Sc* much more obscure will it bee to find the same of subjected provinces within them. Of one of which (Devon I mean my native soyle) I intend by Cod's assistance (after my poor ljtill, & reading) to shew you a slight superficial veiw.

—TM-Dij cæptis ——
Aspirate meis —

Wherein if I shall endeavour to follow the poets good advice when hee faith—Omne tullt punctom qui miscuit vtile dulci; I hope that shall not discontent. And in such a confused chaos of varieties to intermix some inveterate traditions, somewhat differing but not disagreeing from the matter in band together with a slrang & pleasant tale, when I cannot shun it; with antient names, epitaphrs or armories well neer buried in oblivion, matters non supervacual or vnworthy to bee revived & kept, living, (vnless wee would haue our owne name & remembrance to perish with our bodies) or some etymologies seeming strange 5: far fetcht, old or new, serious tryvial or curious, with plain descriptions of places: for these and such like matters may (without peradventure) more ease and recreat the wearied mind of the reader (that reades for recreation) with more delightfull content, for varietye; then dislike the severe critick for fimplicitie, vulgarityе or doubt of veritie: Some sew things will occur in reading but much more varietie is to be added by search, collection and indusrious labour, wherein some suppositions are to bee pardoned if they err, (for hee that divineth in tilings of this qualitie vpon bare conjectures may as well shut short as overfhut the markes hee, aimetli at) if they bee not serious, but alleaged onely to furnish & beautifie the edifices as pictures and mapps in a gallery. Here you may converse with the dead (whose reliques long since dissolved to dust, will neither flatter nor accept thereof) see their obeliskes & monuments read their epitaphes (which shew vs either what they were and what wee shall bee, or sometimes what wee should bee) & see their actions registred or worthy to bee, to encourage their

posteritie to imitation. But herein if any mans expectation bee vnsatisfied, sciant presentes et futuri; that this poor cote was erected with brick burnt with stubble gathered with my owne handes in such barren sieildes as I haue traveld over wherein those of whome I haue had any assistance (be it neuer soe slender) shall not be forgotten, but somewhere remembered, & their mite made a beazant. And if such (as vpoja request) have refused to yield rnee any assistar. ee shall (as I am assured they will first of all) taxe mee os negligence in forgetting them as I passed by, such I could wish to baue more courtHye *Sc* affabilitie & not to presume to thinke they know others when they are ignorant of themselves, whom when they well know, not to chest vp that knowledge nor seornefully to refuse to participate it to other, *it* to remember the old verse, - Scire tuum nihil est, nisi te scire hoc sciat alter But it is high time to follow Diogenes councell to shutt the gate lest the towne run out, yet I shall desire if any thing sound or seem to your vnderstanding contrarie to my intendment, that my vnskifulness in regard of my willingness may haue a mild *le* favourable interpretation: And in all serious matters of anuquitie those authors I haue followed (hall plead for my integritie. It is dull doubtfuB and vncertaine travelling in an vnknown way without a guide, yet hee is driven to a far greater extremitie that at every crosleway of his journey is taught several! wayes by several guides, yet howsoeuer if you please to travle thither haue with you about Denshire.

Whence Devonshire tooke denomination *Sc* what diuers names it hath had. Deavonia, Devonshire, now by synæresis or abbreviation Denshire, a province of this little world of Brittaine as Claudian said. Nostro deducta Britannia mndo. It was sometime one and the same province with Cornwall & foe by all ancient chorographers reputed *Sc* both included vnder the Latins name Danmonia; by Soli mis Polyhistor, Dunmonia; by Ptolomeus, Damnonia, as derived front Monia, Mines, or from their habitation in low & deep vallies. These antient writers liued far remote, & could hardly haue a true relation of travelors that onely touched at our havens; or traveylinj through our country, vnderstood not the language, & perchance conversed with those which knew little of the etymoligie of the name. I should rather therefore (in regard it is a worke of assistance & that I shall bee hardly able to master it by my owne strength) craue ayd os the Brittaines thernselues which named it (& foe doe the Welsh which descended from them) Diffinint, Duffeneyn, or Dinnan, all which in one sense signifie deep *Sc* narrow valleyes; and doth in some sort expresse the nature & qualitie of the soyle; which is mountanous *Sc* hilly, & where the one is there must needes be the other, for there were neuer scene two hills without a valley, some in their private opinions may bee severally pleased with some one of these, others will derive it from the Danes & call it Dane's-shyre. but therefore as yet I could neuer find any probabilitie, onely a sympathy of letters or a synonima ia sound, but not in signification; for it had this name long before the Danes arrival (not above one thousand yeares since) and they had little time of command here (much less of qniet occupation) to giue names to stirps or townes much lesse to countries. But all these (which serve to noe better purpose then to shew the vncertentie thereof) I will leave, & every man to his particular choice of them, I will bee free from all; nullius addictus jurare in verba magistri; and I hope I may be excused if I differ from others in this particular *Sc* offer my opinion or conjecture among this multitude; Soe I would call it Avonlhyr De-Avonshyre by abbreviation Denshir. Avon in the most antient speech of this land is a riuer and (taken generally as it signifies) is a name for all running wells, brookes, riverets, rivers and fleeting streames & waters, and this countrie abounding more in water springs *Sc* rivers that (as the prophet faith) cleeve the earth, then any that I have heard or read offj I am induced to think it may with good reason take name from them as from mynes, valleyes, or Danes, for Here many

brookes as through the groves they travle

Doe sport for joy vpon the silver gravle. Deavon or Devon the country of riuers or waters, which is sooner granted with less alteration of letters by farr, then any of the other, & agreeth more fitly with the nature of our soyle *Sc* propertie of language, and as the poet faith,, conveniunt rebus nomina fepe su-is. And the light of reverend antiquitie & knowledge Mr. Cambden, proveth that the Gawlifh and Bryttish speech was all one. Being foe, Diu in the Brittish speech fignifieth with vs God, & Avon a spring or riuer, as Ausonius writing of a ffountain neer Burdeaux, faith,

Diuona Celtanim Lingua, sons addita Divis. Diuona in the Celtifli words A well sacred to God affouards. Or a diuine riuer. there are alsoe diuers riuers in this kingdome, which haue noe other name at this present (nor euer had) then Avon, the riuer. one of good note in Wiltshyre, that falls from Dorset into the ocean, another of that name which breaketh out of the earth at Avon Well in Leycestershire by Malmesburye called Avon the Lesse, passeth through Northamptonshire, *Sc* cleeveth Warwick, Worcester, & Somersetshire, running many miles ere it visit Bath & Bristoll and there increaseth Severne. In Glamorganshire you haue a to vne bearing the name of Aber-Avon; as if wee said the mouth of the riuer; and in Monmouth *Sc* Merioneth in each of them one of that name. And that work of admirable magnificence built by Cardinal Wolsey, in ostentation (as it was said) of his abundant riches, Hampton Court, now a royal palace of our Soveraigne, was fust called Avon in that it stood on the river as Leland avoucheth—

Nomine ab antique iam tempore dictus Avona.

Hampton Court is the fame

In elder time that Avon had to name. And as if it had not hyn soe onely in the Bryttish speech, wee find it also in the sherifdome os Srer-f.ting, in Scott-Uud, that Hadrianus the Emperour or his adopted Titus Ælius Hadrianus Antonius

Pius, most of our antiquaries recur, in settling the etymology of British words. But the name of our rivers, («) were certainly prior to the Phenicians—names, which they preserve!
to

Plus, or his Lieutenant Lolllus Vrbi-uS did for the defence of the country erect a wall of turfe which began as the Scots write at Avon (or the ryver Avon) that falleth into Edenborrow Frith. And that it was foe in more languages, which haue little concurrence now with our speech (perchance antiently all one) in the kingdome of Ireland, in the counties of Corke & Waterford, ther runneth the ryver (now lately of vs called Broad-water but in passed times) Avon-more the great or broad ryver, on the banckes whereof standeth Ardmons, of which place & ryver Necham long since ver-fifieth thu Et vrbem Lyfmore pertranfit flumen Avon-more Ardmore cernitvbi concitus æquor adit. And as we fay commonly in our vulgar phrase, «vhen go you to the towne, not giving it any name, tehither!t bee London, Yorke, or Exeter, but meanmg the nearest: foe wee alsoe say shall wee goe to the ryver (to Avon) whether it bee Thames, Ousc, or Exe. but to conclude all by the sentence' of the dictator of knowledge, whose words I will onely exemplifie. Avon in the Bryttish speech (sayth Mr. Cambden) importeth a ryver, whereof Aventowne takes denomination, which is ho more strange then in the fame signification (to omit many other) Water-towne, Ryvertowne, & Bourne: and as the Latines haue, Aquinum *et* Ftuentum. I am not so apelike affected to this my conjecture as to applaud it j neither haue I reason to feare opposition, for this aetiologie Can neither seeme harsh or absurd, in regard the words are foe consonant, & the name alsoe as a true picture doth plainly represent the things which in etimologies is chiefly required & sought after. Others haue alleaged the like of other countries, authors of great credit. Jvo Carntensis affirmeth that Aquitania (a great dukedome in Ffrance, well neer a third part thereof) tooke name de Aquis of waters. Junius main' taines that Denmark tooke denomination from Denne, firr-trees. Verstegan allegeth out of Engelhiljius (hat the Saxons tooke appellation from their swords or knives, which the Seaxen or Seaxes (it was with such they made the massacre of the nobilitie vpon the plaines neer Amefbury). Another would haue foe named of Satfum, a stone, as stony-hearted. My conjecture may seeme as probable as either of these: but I can neither persuade nor intreat, but leaue it to your favourable opinion hoping it shall seeme noe marvell or strange to see my blindness grope, fiith those that fee perfectly and are sharpest sighted cannot find a right way. It is alsoe written of the Bryttaines by Gyldas that they yielded divine worship to waters & riuers; as in cold water or ordial tryall (as they termed it) for discouerie of witchcraft; wheiein their opinion was, that the element of water was foe pure, that it would not suffer itselfe to bee contaminated by receiving the bodies of any such vile & reprobate person, though cast thereinto bound hand and foot; but that the witch would swim; for if hee sanck they were held guiltless & presently drawn on land. It is not for christians to make such vse of ryvers, or to trust them foe farr; yet are wee to take it as a great blessing of the Almightie that wee haue such store, to inrich our grounds & as the kingly prophet saythf Hee sendeth springs into the brookes That runn among the hills Wherewith wild asses quench their thirst And ail beasts drink their fills. But yet it was not the Bryttaines alone that had their ryvers in this estimation, for the Germaines did the like of the river Rhyne, making it a judge in question of defiled wedlock: and those of Thessaly had the like of Pa:neus for his pleasures profitts & vertues. Julius Solinus ascribeth the like propertie to a spring in Sardinia for the tryall of theft, for whosoeuer by oath denyed the fact & washed his eyes with the water thereof, if hee swore truly his fight became the clearer, but forswearing himselfe, the culp was presently discouered by his blindness, & the delinquent was forc't to confess the fact in darkness with lost of his fight. But in this ordeal triall (though the way bee

spatious and pleasant) I will lead you noe farder. But leaving the better explanation of the name of Devon to him that can with Nauius Cotem novacula scindere; and tell you how & when Deuon & Cornwall were diuided &fundred." *Westcote*, p. I, to p. 7.

(a) The late Rev. Richard Lewis, of Honiton, in a letter to Dean Milles, dated June 20th, 1757, makes the following remarks on the names of our *riven, mountains, tonvnt,* and *castles,* « Mr. Baxter, m his most valuable glossary, would willingly btlieve, that *all* places of *note* in Devon and Cornwall, derive their origin from British fountains; and I can't help flunking that he is for the most part in the right j though in order to support his favourite system, it may be suspected that he sometimes impresses, as it were, words into his service. But though an unprejudiced reader cannot always subscribe to his opinion, yet he cannot chuse but admire his sagacity in languages, and his singular ingenuity in the derivation of words and account of places. This judicious author makes the knowledge of the British language so necessary an ingredient in the composition of an antiquarian, that without it, he thinks it impossible to investigate the meaning either of the antient or even the modern names of places. In his Epistola Dedicatoria, he observes, ' Vix opus esse videtur ut moneam Antiquarlo Britannico *frorsus ejfe necejfariam* Britannicae Linguæ peritiam; ob hujus tamen insoitiam *muhi oee parvi nominis* viri non raro in errores incidere.' The rules which Mr. Baxter has collected from to the present hour; " still as they flow, referring us to that remarkable era in our history, when the British stag took shelter in their streams from the chace, or the British warriors' from his friend Mr. Llhuyd, for the derivation of words, are almost an unerring guide for arriving at fheir true meaning. Now *places* take their names from *things* or *circumstances* coeval with the places' themselves; seldom from any *modern improvements* in arts and sciences; seldom from things or circumstances of a *precarious* nature. They are generally derived from-the

names of the rivers near which they are situated. Sometimes, indeed, they are named agreeably to their situation, foil, &c; as Church Staunton or Stoneton, and Clayheydon, in Devon; whefe the name of the one parish is derived from the *clay* or dirty foil for which it is remarkable; and the name of the other from the number of *stones* or *rocks,* which are found in almost every part of it. But most places of any note in the kingdom are named from the *rivers* which run near them; is Exeter, Taanton, Dorchester, and many others. Exeter being the Castrum, Arx, or Civitas upon the Exe orlfc: Tauritbn the town! hpon Tone, or the British word Tai's: Dorchester the Castrum upon the Dur. All which words, Exe, lie, Tone, Tawj DSr,(1) and a great many more in the British tongue signify water or a river. Of the Names of Rivers.

I. In the time of the old Britons, Ifc, Asc, Esc, Osc, and Use (all which words signify water) were names of several rivers. The English or Saxons partly retained the fame names, especially in the north," and partly changed them into Ax, as in Axmouth, Axley, Axholm; into Ex, as in Exmouth, Exeter j into Ox, as in Oxford, or Ouscford; and into Ux, as in Uxbride. These alterations were probably owing to the pronunciation of the Britons. The Saxons might fancy the British pronunciation to be: too rough and guttural, ahd for the better sounds f.ike they very likely changed Asc, Esc, Jsc, Uysc,l &c. into Ax, Ex, Ux, &C. This is certain, that the Saxons, for want of understanding the British tongues took the British *appellatives* for the *proper* names of rivers. Whereas the words abovementioned signify nettling but water, and retain the fame signification, to this day, m Ireland and the Highlands of Scotland. 2. There are several rivers called Taw, Tav, Tivi, or as they were anciently Written, Tarn and Ti'm (from whence Thames and the Tamar in Devon). Now Taw, Tav, &c. signify only water or a river: Tarn is certainly the fame with Tailor in the word *norafios. i.* Others are called Guy, Uy, Uys, Ey, Y, and 1, i. e. the" water in such a place; and they are as often the *final* syllables of our rivers as Tav, Tis, Tam, &c. are the *initial* ones. 4. Others are named Llhyr?' which word also signifies water. 5. Clet, Cluyd, Clyd, &c. are likewise proper names of rivers in Scotland and Wales; whereas they signify nothing more than a river or biOok in general. 6. Mar and Mor signify a large brook or river, as well as the sea, and give names to several rivers in Wales: Lastly, some rivers take their denominations from the *colour* of their sand or gravel. Others are; metaphorically denominated from the *nature of their current,* with regard to their rapidity, slowness, straitness, or windings. Others from some remarkable *trees* or *plants* growing oh their banks. Anc? others have no other name than that of the *village* they pass by.

Of the Names of Mountains or Hiils.

The most common way of naming hills was by metaphors, drawn from the several parts of the human body. Thus some were called, Y Voel, bald-pate— Y Benglog, a skull—Tal, the forehead— Cern, one side of the face—Ael, an eye-lid—Lfygad, an eye—Rhyn, a nose—-Genaw, a mouth—Pen',' the head—Munugl, the neck—Guar, the nape of the neck—Braich, an arm— Bron, the breast—Kest, she belly— Clun, the hip—Cevan, the back— Ystlys, the side—Bontin, the buttock— Efgair, a leg— and Troed, a foot.

Of the Names of Cities, Towns, Castles, and Villages.

i. Tin or Din, was, according to the Guydhelian BritHn, Tun or Dun, and is ft used 6y th Highlanders and Irish. The Romans, in their orthography of the word, agreed with them rather than us. For they wrote Uxellodunum, Ncodunum, and not Uxelsodinum, Ncodinum, &c. *i.* Maes (a field or plain) was called Magh. This the Romans wrote Magus. 3. Caer is a town, which the Old English turned into *Ceaster,* and afterwards into *Cester, Cistsr,* and *Chester;* and is the fame witlr the Romans Castrum. 4. Tre, though at first it signified only *a family,* denotes a *town.* 5. Lilian 6r Lan, figrtifieth a *church,* though it originally denoted an *inclfure.* Lastly,

the most general way of naming towns among the Britons was, as before hinted,,from the *rivers* on which they were situated; as we find by the Roman towns in Wales, Ifca Legionum, Gobanniiim, Nidum, LeuCarum,' Conovium, ahd Segontium, which were all made out of the British names Uysc, Keni, Nedh, Llychur, Conui, and Seiont.

These things being premised, I propose to mention some places from the head of the river *Ottet* to *Otterton,* where it empties itself into the sea. And then beginning at *Exeter, to* pursue the sea coast (1) Asc, Esc, Ifc, Osc, Use, which the Saxons pronounced" Ax, Ex, Ox, t'x. As also Avon, Alain, Dur, Dwr, Treau, Trome. Coy, *VJ,* Uyl, By, Y, J. Tain, Thame, Taw, Tav, Tiv, Tauy, Tivy, T«Wn. Ta»n,Tone. All vrhk words signify water.

tei, *lj %* warriors were mustered on their banks for fight." But, as the aboriginal Britons and Phœnicians had one common origin, it is difficult to discriminate between the language of coast as far as *Lytfe.* The river Otter (as it is now called) rises in a parish called *Otterford,* in thecounty of Somerset, which is no more, in common signification, than the spring or fountain head of the river Otter. Now I would suppose the old British name to be *y Dtvyr,* the water, which the Anglo-Saxons afterwards softened into Otter. Camden, indeed, derives the name of the river from the number of water dogs, called *Otters,* which are found in it. But I cannot find that it is more peculiarly remarkable for this kind of animals than other rivers in this county are. The first parish upon this river is *Up-Ottcry,* which according to the English name denotes its situation up the river. *Mobuns-Ottery* is the next remarkable place on the river. From thence the river descends to *Honiton,* which, if there is any thing in the etymology of Mr. Camden, of the river, may be derived from the British words, Cwn y Tun, i.e. Oppidum Caninæ Aquae: Cwn signifying dogs and the water. The only difficulty is about the C's beihg changed into B. And to solve this, it is to be observed, that such a change was very frequent from the Bri-

tish language into the Anglo-Saxon. See the word *bide* in Ley's edition of Franciscus Juniua, which is deduced from the Welch word *Cydbio,* according to Mr. Llhuyd, K or C in H mutato, quam mutationem, fays the editor, non infreqnentem pluribus docet exemplisi Qualia sunt Kellyn Holly—Korn, Horn, *Sec.* Below Honiton lies *Warrinston,* in the parish of Bokerel. I presume it may be derived from the British words *liar Rbyti Tutu,* Oppidum ad nasum fluminis, it being very remarkable that the ridge of hills running through Bokerel parish terminates above this village in the shape of a man's nose. Upon the river *Wolf,* which falls into the Otter at Warrinston, lies the parish of *Aulijcomb,* surrounded by Henbury fort, and the ridge adjoining, to the north and east, and the ridge in Bokerel, to the west and bv south. I would fetch the original of this place from *Ael,* is, *Cum,* i. e. Supercilium vallis aquosæ; which answers extremely well to its situation. Below Warrinston, the river Otter v alhrjs the parish of *Bokerel* to the south thereof; which word may be dsduced from the words *Beau,*or *Bo* Pecuaria Vaccarum, *Kor* cervus and *ael* supercilium, and signifies supercilium montis juxta quod Pecuaria Vaccarum est vel cervorum Grex. There being a lidge of hills running through the middle of the parish exactly resembling an eye lid. (See the word Bovium in Baxter's Glossary). Whatiavours this conjecture, is, that the greatest part of the parish is peculiarly fitted for a dairy; and that there was a noted park there in former times; and that Deer Park, is supposed to be the ancient lodge of this park. Add to this, that the deeds of Matthew de Backington, were sealed with a deer's head, as his proper arms. Opposite to Bokerel, and the other side of the Otter lies *Gittijham,* through which is the road from Honiton to Exeter, where are evident remains of a Roman road. This word may be derived from the British words, *Gu'tdb* Silva, *ys* Aqua, and *Ham* vicus, i. e. a town on a woody rivuletr which is very apposite to its situation. The chief objection which will lie against the British etymology of the above places is, that they cannot be supposed to be of sufficient antiquity to be entitled to such an extraction. The answer I would give to it, is, that there are so many marks of Roman antiquities in and near *the* said parishes, that as it is certain they were known to the Romans, so it must be probable, that the names had their existence in the time of the Britons. It is a thing not to be controverted, that the Romans left the British names of places as they found them: except that in places of note, they added a Latin termination to the old British word, and in other respects *latinixed* the fame. Below Buckerel, at the head of a little rivulet, which falls into the Otte.-, is *Fenitott*, which is certainly nothing else but a composition of *Pen, y, Tun*, i. e. Villa ad caput aqua?. I own I cannot give a satisfactory etymology of *Ottery;* which, however, was anciently written, *Autre*, as I find it in old maps. On supposition that this was its old name, it may come from *Aii Tre*, i. e. Oppidum ad aquam. I would willingly believe this town to be known to the Romans, on account of its vicinity to Woodbury and Belbury castles, of which hereafter. The river Otter leaving the last town, not far from which it runs, descends to *Harford*, which I would make So fcg Uar, fordh, i. e. Traiectus Aquæ. This is undoubtedly the place where the river is crossed in Antonine's Iter, from iica to Moridunum. Opposite to Harfotd, on the other fide os the river, is *Fcn-Otteiy*, which lies under Woodbury-hill, above the Otter, which may not unnaturally be deduced from *Pen y Bur*, i. e. ad caput Aquæ. The river then passing through *Ouertcn*, empties itself into the sea. This place may probably be fetched from *y Dvr Tun*, i.e. Oppidum aquæ vel ad aquam. I finrf this place in some authors is called *Articumba*, which may signify in the British tongue Domus vel Villula aquofe vallis, from *uar, ti, cum.*, 1 would now beg leave to visit you at *Exeter*, and the favour of your company as far as *Lyme*, upon the sea coast, near which place you must necessarily travel in your own performance, if not in my route. This famous city is, as is agreed on alt hands, the Isca Danmoniorum,

though some have injudiciously confounded it with the Isca Silnrum, which is *Caer Leon*, in f. onmouthshire, in Wales. It is now called by the Welsh *Caer Ifc*, i. e. Oppidum aquæ. And the county of Devon, *Duvntint* (or else *Duffneint*, which signifies deep vallies) from whence *Dumnonii*. The next town, which is *Topfiam*, and which Mr. Baxter erroneously supposes to be the *Moridunum* of Antonine, is, as the fame author would have it, derived from *Koppay Sea, Ham*, i. e. Oppidum ad caput marls—the word *Koppa* signifying in the British tongue, tongue Caput vel vertex. Possit etiam, faith he, *Topejbam* correpte die! pro *Topjeabant*. Not far l'rom Toplham, on the river Exe, is *Limpfione*, which may easily be deduced from *Lim, ui, tun*, i, e. the town on a rapid stream. Below Limpltone is *Exmoutb* (the *Uxelis* in Ravennas) i. e. lscje Ostium. The word Uxelis being nothing else but *Ucb, ael, Jsc*, Sive Super Supercilium Aquæ. Over against Exmouth, but something lower is *Kenton*, the Vercenia of the antients—the word Vercenia being as it were *uar Kend, ui*, Sive super caput undæ, quod est prope amnem. De Ibrida voce, faith Baxter, ICenton; et Fluviolus hodie dicitur K.cn, ritu sequioris ævi. Crossing the river Exe again, we come to *Sidnautb*, above which is *Hidford*, and higher up *Sidbury*, called by the anonymous writer Tidertis, forsan Britannis, faith Mr. Baxter, dicebatur *7ud, ar life*, five populus vel curia ad Tiscam, ut et Sidbury and Sidmouth ibrida dicantur compositione. Notissimum estDumnoniorum veteri Dialecto dici potest Sid pro Tid, Sicuti et Coes pro Coet. More to the east from hence is *Branfcanb*, where three vales center near the churchj through each of which very rapid streams run and unite there. So that according to Mr. Baxter's eighth rule, concerning proper names of rivers, it may be denominated vallis citæ aquæ, from *Bran*, a crow. He observes, that there is a brook of this name by Lan Gollen, in Denbighshire, whence the name of Dinas Bran: There are two or three more Brans in Brecknockshire and Carmarthenshire, so called from their

swift current. Not far from hence is *Been*, for which I can find no antient name. But I think it may consistently be supposed to be of antient note, and may be derived from *Ber, Rbui*, ac si dicatur, faith Baxter, crus Rivi. About a mile from Beere is *Seaton*, which was, undoubtedly, the Moridunum in Antonines iter a Calleva ad Ifcam. It is so called fram *Mor, y. Dun*, i. e. Oppidum magnæ undæ sive maris; to which the present name Seaton exactly corresponds. Opposite to Seaton, on the other side of the Tiver, is *Axmouth*, which is one of those places in which the Saxons changed the old British w ord Isc into Ax, and calk:d it Axmouth, itfceing situated near the mouth of the river, i. e. near the point where the river discharges itself into the sea. If this place w as a town in the time of the Romans (which is much to be doubted) its old name was probably *Uxelis*, which they made out as at Exmouth, from *Ucb, Ael, is*, that is, a town upon the brink of the water. A little to the north of Axmouth, on the *Colly*, which falls into the Ax, stands *Colliton*, which signifies a town upon the Hazle Brook, from *Co/lyb, y, Tun*. Below it is *Col/yford*, i, e. Corylorum amnis trajectii6. In the British tongue it would have been *Collh, y, f'ordb*, a passage over an hazle brook or river. And now *ire are* arrived at *Lyme*, which though it is in Dorsetshire, is yet so very near the limits of Devon, that I thought it no improper stage to rest at. This place is thought by Mr. Camden to be of no great antiquity. And yet from the great antiquary Mr. Llhuyd, we learned that the Britons called it *Llbtrng Pardb*, i. e. according to Mr. Baxter, a port for the reception of ships. And though the town has been reduced more than once to a low ebb with regard 4o trade, yet it was probably inhabited in the time of the Romans. It took its name from the river *Ljm* or *Lym y*, which runs through it: and accordingly the name whicli the Romans gave to it (if credit may be given to one of their corrupt i tin era judiciously corrected) was JLoria, which with the addition of a Latin termination, is no mor-e than the British words *Lym y*, i. e. a rapid stream. Camden, indeed, as I observed, informs us, that we scarce meet with the name of Lyme in antient books; which is very true; and from thence it may be concluded that it was not a port of any conseqnencc till some time after the Romans left our island. However, Camden himself tells us, that R. Kinwlf, in the year 774, gave in the following words, ' the land of one mansion to the church of Scireburn, near the western banks of the river Lym, and not far from the pl.ice where it falls into the sea, so long as for the said church, salt should be boiled there for the supplying of various wants.' From this old record it appears, first, that at *Lyme,* salt was made in the eighth century, and consequently that there, must liave been inhabitants to attend upon the business. Secondly, that the river was known by the name of *Lym,* which is British, and signifies rapid; that consequently this was a place, not only known to the old Britons, fcnt probably inhabited by them, till the Romans drove them into Wales, Cornwall, and the northern parts of the kingdom. And thus, Sir, I have presumed, being confessedly a blind guide, to conduct you as far as *Lyme,* if your patience has held out to bear me company. A dry-dissertation upon words is certainly of the opiate kind, unless it be to gentlemen who have a relish for antiquity. And from the little smattering I have in this respect, 1 have learned how necessary a virtue patience is, to make any proficiency in researches of this nature. If ypu have a mind to sleep, said a friend, get into a quiet room, Uke an ounce of Tom Hearne's soporific mixture, add to it a small quantity of Welch etymology, from the learned Banter's Glossary, and work with it a night draught of scholastic nonsense upon absolute predestination, measured by an hour glass, and divided into ten equal parts; if you have not a comfortable rest before you come to tenthly and lastly, I am much mistaken. However, / am not displeased with the little pains I have tiken in enquiries into antiquities; much less, I imagine, can you be, who have collected materials sufficient to execute so general a plan as your queries bespeak your intended ac-

count of Devon to be. Nor indeed does the pleasure which attends this sort of study, arise wholly from the little knowledge which a man acquires of the geography of his own country, of the antient names of places, of their situation, &c. but from the light which such knowledge throws upon the luftory, the customs, and exploits of our ancestors; from the insight which it gives us into the great and surprizing alteration made on the face of things during a period of about 1700 years. The antiquities of Britain considered in this light, display a scene Vol.. I. Z 2, whicli which Is worthy the notice of every thinking creature. In this light we observe not only the names pf phces altered, but the most magnificent works of power, the strength and pride of architecture humbled and reduced into rubbilh and ruins. In this light we observe providence visibly interposing in the administration and revolution of affairs. In this light we pbsorve the supreme Being either punishing or rewarding our ancestors, in proportion to their virtue or immorality j and leaving mor numents of the divine mercy or vengeance in almost every age to this very day."

Mr. Chappie (who was furnished, soon after *his* undertaking was announced, with a transcript of fhis MS.) deserves, also, some attention as an etymologist. His etymologies are drawn from various sources. " We have some words (fays he) of *Britijb* extraction, from which language most of the; names of the *rivers,* in this as well as other counties, are derived j so that, as Mi. *TVhitakcr* observes i) most of them retain to the present hour the names which were imposed upon them 2ooq years ago. But in the derivations of many of our names, both of *riven* and *places,* we must frequently conten' ourselves with probable guesses, rather than conclusive deductions from any certain rinciples: And the best etymologists have been accused (the learned *Baxter* particularly, and peraps not unjustly) of being sometimes tpo fond of scr-fetch'd and improbable derivations; of pressing words into their service, and deriving from them whatever might be agreeable to a favourite

opinion; and in shori, of substituting meer imagination or conjecture for regular analogy. It must however be allowed that etymologies have their use, and are far from being always frivplpus apd impertinent; and however uncertain and precarious when unsupported by collateral evidence, they frequently prompt us to further enquiries by which we are led to more certain truths, which either confirm the etymology by concurrent circumstances, or tend to detect oqr former mistakes concerning it. Again, the apparent mistake of any one person in the etymology of the name os a place, may induce another to attempt a correction of that mistake; in consequence of which he may hit upon the«true meaning of the name, or at least a more satisfactory guess at it, than had resulted from the,unsuccessful search pf the former: And this may also be a sufficient apology for any attempts of this kind in the present 'work, and for this addition to the text of our author, who seldom meddled with etymologies. But as some who have been but little conveisant in enquiries of this sort, may imagine, that such supposed derivations of tbe names of our rivers, whereih we occasionally have recourse not only to the *Wefi* and *Cornijh,* but also to the *Iris),* *Erse,* arid *Armoric,* and in some instances even the *Greek* language,— are rather too far fetch'd; and tho' they may acknowledge some of them to be appellations receiv'd from the *Britons* whilst in possession of this county, and before their expulsion by K. *Athel? pan,* y«t may be apt to ask, with what propriety we ramble into *Ireland* or *Scotland* in quest of explications of *Devon/hire* names; or consult the sages of ancient *Greece* on the denominations of places they never possess'd? It may be proper to observe, in answer to such objectors,—that the affinity pf the *Irish* and *Britifi* languages is taken notice of by *Cantden,* who makes no doubt but that the first inhabitants of *Ireland* came from *Britain;* (2) and among other evidences of it, mentions the) many *Brits/h* words in the *Irish* tongue, as also their ancient names which shew themselves to be of *British* extraction: In short, as

Mr. *Bcfwell* observes, (3) we are entirely obliged to the 7ri Ian-, gunge for the meaning of many words which are every-where found amongst us; from whence he concludes with *Camdcn*, that the *Irish* were probably once inhabitants of this island, and went from hence to *Ire/and*. But I presume, the agreement of *British* and *Irish* words and names, no more proves *Ireland* to be peopled from *Britain*, than *Britain* to be peopled from *Ireland* j especially if the *Irish* have preserv'd (as they certainly have) the use and signification of many words which the *Britons* have lost." For the following etymologies, Mr. *Chappie* was chiefly indebted to Mr. *Lewis* pf Honiton, and Mr. *Bosvjell of* Taunton, in a letter of his to *Walter Oke*, Esq. then of *Wbit/ands*, n Axmouth, *Devon*; which lettter being in the possession of the Rev. Mr. *Mallock* of *Colyton*, he very obligingly favour'd me (says *Chappie*) with the loan of it, at the request; of my worthy friend Mr. *Thomas Wbttty* of *Axminjler*, to whom I am moreover obliged for many interesting observations relative to divers places in that neighbourhood, and the procurement of others from his friends, which will be duly attended to in the particular desciiptions of those places; the *present* subject of our enquiry being the origin of the names of our *r'rvcrs*. The old *British* names of rivers, *Asc, Is,* or *Esc, Osc, Use,* and *Uysc,* (in Irish *Uisge,* Comifh *Isge,* Armoric *Vijge,*) which all signify -*water*, were partly rewin d by the *English Saxons;* but for better sound's sajte, and perhaps from a dislike to the rough and guttural pronunciation of the *Britons*, changed into *Ax, Ex, Ox,* or *Otise, Vx* and *Vsk.* Besides the rivers which thus derive their names from *British* words which figii'y *water* or a *river* appellatiyely, there are others of a *second* class, whose names are compounded f *Britifi* words expressive of some *qualities* of their water, the velocity or direction of the current, colour of their sand or gravel, &c The names of those of a *third* class are either wholly of *Saxon* origin, or partly *Britifi* and partly *Saxon* A *fourth* class of rivers are metaphorically denominated from the

nature of the current bnly; of which we have also a few instances in Devon:— And lastly, others have no other names but those of the villages situated near them. Etymologists have mentioned other circumstances from which rivers take their names; but as these five ciasses include most, if not all those ill this county, and which may on that acepunt claim pur notice, I shall here '"' particularize (1; See his Manchester, p. 118. (2) Gibson's Camd. p. 966, 967. (3) Boswell's Method of Study, vol. 1. p. 48. particularize such of our *Devon/hire* rivers Belonging to each, as have hitherto occurred to me, in alphabetical order; adding some observations, conjectures, and queries, relative to the etymologies of their names respectively. But that such of them as are of *British* derivation may be the better compared with their supposed originals, it may perhaps be acceptable to some of our readers (however unnecessary for others) to be inform'd, in what respects the *Weljh* pronunciation of the vowels differs from ours Their A, as we learn from the Rev. Mr. *Richards* and other *JVelJh* grammarians, is pronounced as A *Englijh* in the word *man;* but is lengthen'd, by a circumflex, to the sound of our *a* in *ale, pale,* &c. Their E, if acuted, as E *Englijh* in *men, ten, Sec.* in some instances as *e* in *er;-, aver, Sec.* and in others as *ee* in *check;* but if circumflex'd, as *ea* in the word *league,* or as *e* in *Jane,* and sometimes as *ea* in *fear, dear,* &c. Their I, as our *ee* in *tree,* or as *i* in *thtng:* Their O, as ours in the word *gone;* if circumfiex'd, as *o* in *bone:* Their U, as our I in *this, blijs, Sec.* and if circumfiex'd, as our *ee* in *queen, green, Sec.* Their W being also a vowel, and agreeing in sound as well as shape with the Greek *Omega,* is pronoune'd as *o* in the *English* pronoun *who;* but if circumflex'd, as *oo* in *root, loot, Sec.* And their Y (which is likewise one of their vowels), in the Penultima, Antepenultima, &c. is sounded as *u* in the *Englijh* words *furs, burn, Sec.* but in the ultima, or in monosyllables (with a very few exceptions), as in the English *tin, Jiin, Sec.* and if circumflex'd, as *ee* in the English *meci,*

feet, Sec.—To these rules for pronouncing their *vowels*, we may add,.that among the *consonants* their Dd has the sound of a hard *Theta,* or as *th* in the English *thou* and *that;* also that their F (being the *Æolic Digamma*) has the sound of our V consonant, but when doubled (Ff) is soften'd into the sound of our *Jingle* F. These extracts from the above-quoted author, and other writers on the *British* pronunciation, may suffice for our present purpose, without enlarging here on the various substitutions of one mutable consonant for another in that flexible language; tho' some instances of these may occur in our intended inquiries into the etymologies of the names of our rivers respectively, to which we now proceed.

I. Os the *frfl* class, *viz.* of names of rivers derived from *British* words signifying merely *water* or a *river,* this county affords us the following: *Arme* or *Erme.* Qif lar a river, (or perhaps only the prepositive article *TrJ* prefix d to *am,* water? m in the *Latin* aud ancient *Celtic,* according to *Baxtcr,* i) making *v* in the *Britijh* (or rather their *f* used instead of our *v);* so *Am %* the same as *av, Vnda* vel *Amnis. Ot Ar me* may possibly come from the Cornish *Ara,* slow, and *am,* water; but Qif this derivation can be justified by any lemarkahle tardity of its current? If so, this river beJongs to the *A* class. Note, *Ara* in *Gothic* signifies *water,* and *Armor* in *Cornijh* a *wave;* but neither of these seems applicable here, unless we might suppose the former join'd with the British *am,* when it has the fame signification.—*Atrey,* possibly *Awy-ter-y* the *river of clear water,* or *clearnvater river* (see *Otter)*—*Avon, Aven,* or *Awn; Avon* or *Afon* in *Britijh,* signifies a *river,* as already ohserv'd; as do also *Avon* and *Avar,* or *Awan* in *Cornijh,* and *Avan* or *Abhan* in *hip.*—*Awtre,* see *Otter.*—*Ax,* from the old British *Ajc,* which has been already shewn to signify « ater.—*Deer* probably from the Cornish *Deura,* a *Dwr,* Br.) *water;* unless we suppose the *Saxons* call'd it *Deer,* from the swiftness of its current; and as such to be rank'd in the 3d or 4th class; but the former seems preferable. — *Dtwrijh* or *Dowrich-Brooi,* possibly from *Dwr*, and the old t'.ritish *IJc*, or Irish *TJifge*. But if *Dwr-ifc* be deem'd an unnecessary junction of two *Britijh* words, *both* signifying *water*, (tho' there may be some instances of the like in other name1; of rivers,) we may suppose it a compound of *Britijh* and *Saxon*, and refer it to our 3d class: If so, *Dwr* might have the addition of *Ricg*, a *ridge*, which not only signified the ridge of a *hill*, but frequently (as we may have occasicr. elsewhere to observe) a *raised military way;* and this if *Kicg* be allowed a place here, is most likely to be its meaning, and that the brook having imparted its name with this addition, to *Dowrich* barton, which is water'd by it, might at length be imagined to have borrow'd that name from it; in like manner as will be hereafter observ'd concerning *Sturcombe* brook. What is here said of *Dowrich* brook, is equally applicable to the *Terridge* or *Tawridge*, changing *Dwr* for *Tav* or *Tau*, or else the *V* in the former into T; these being occaf ohally commutable letters in the British or Welsh orthography *Exe;* from the old British *Ijc*, Irilh *VJge*, signifying *water* as before observ'd.(2)—*Forda* (or as sometimes called *Forder);* doubtless from the Br. *Ffordd*, a ay or passage, with the addition of *da,* good; or else of *av* water, or the Irish *Aha* a ford; denoting a shallow water, that admits of an easy passage through or over it; a fordable brook.—*Letver;* from the Br. *Llyr* or *Lkyr,* water; for so it signified anciently, as well as the sea.(3)—*Ludbrock* and *I.yd* or *Lid;* perhaps from *Clyd,* a river or brook 5(4) but if derived from *Llid* fury, or *Lhuyd, Turbidus,(\$)* or the Irish *Luath,* swift, or from the Saxon *hlydan,* tumultuous or noisy, they belong to the *26* or 3d class.—*Lyff* or *Lif*; probably from *Llif,* (Cornish *Lyv,* Armoric *Lifat* or *Linfat,)* a flux, flood or inundation, an overflowing of waters.— *Lyn; Llyn,* a lake, a *pool* in a *river,* and perhaps also a *current.* Note, *rivulets* are in *Devon* commonly call d *lakes.* —*O/dye;* if from *WeMgi* or *Gweilgi,* which in *Britijh* signifies a *torrent* as well as *the'sea f* Its modern name, *Shobbrock* or *Stobbrook-Laic,* being of *Saxon* derivation, falls under fl) See Bax-

ter's Glossary, p. 222. Also Llnvd in Baxter, p 222.
(2) There are some, who derive ifca or Iscau from kalian, an elder tree—as the banks of the liver Exc are said to have been orice covered with ciders. (aj Sec Lluyd. in Baxter, p, 266. (-1) Ibid. (5) Ibid. p. 974. under our 3d class, which fee further on.—*Otter,* or (as eall'd in some old maps, *Sec.) Avjtre; Camden's* supposition that'it took its name from the number of Water-Dogs eall'd *Otters* found in it (which supposes it *Saxon),* has been objected to, because *this* river is no more remarkable for these animals than any *other;* wherefore we may rather suppose (with the Rev. Mr. *Lewis)* its old name to be *TDur,* i.e. *the water,* which the old English Saxons, with little variation in the found, afterwards eall'd *Otter:* Or if its name should rather be spelt *Awtre,* Qif it might not come from the British *A-wedd-wr,* which signifies *running mater,* or *frefb-water f* or else from *A-wy,* an old British word fora *river,* and *Ter, clean, sure, clear;* and so mean *(A-wy ter)* the *clear rivers* Or if the Britons gave it a name expressive of that rapidity of its current which is observable in some places, it might possibly be some old *Celtic* word derived from the Greek 'OrfWfor *celer, mpiger;* on which, as well as on the two former suppositions, it (hould belong to our 2d class; and according to the last its name spelt *Otrer,* tho' the first *r* would be lost in pronunciation. *Baxter* (1) takes it to be *Godre* or *OJre,* a *boundary,* and fays, *Ottery* was formerly the limits of the *Dunmonii* or *Danmonii;* but others (as Dr. *Borlase, Sec.)* think the river *Exe* was their boundary 'till *K. Athelstans* time.— *Stour* or *Stourcombe* Brook; the *C-wmm* or valley through which it runs, probably had its original name from it j the brock itself being caH'd *Star or Stour,* a name given to several other rivers, from *Es dur* faith Mr. *Baxter,i.)* which answers to the Cornilh *Es dour, the-water :* The valley being thus denominated *Stour-Combe,* and the origin of that compound being afterwards forgotten, it was used to distinguish the brook running through it. Instances of the like

might be given in other rivers and places. See *Dvwrich.—Tamar* and *Tame* already accounted for; supposing the former to be a compound of *Tarn* (which *Baxters)* tells us signified in the old *Celtic* the fame as *a-v),* and *Mar, Mer* or *Mor,* which, tho' when taken singly they generally mean the *sea,* yet, in the compound names of rivers, signify only *water :* But if, with Dr. *Bor/ aje* (4) and Mr. *Le-wis,* we suppose it to be rather *Tamma-wr, tM* great *river,* as being the laigest that pastes thro' any part of *Corn-wall,* to which it is for the most part a boundary), it then belongs to our 2d class *Tavy;* it has been before obscrv'd that *Tauy, Ye'rvi, Sec* signify - *water* or a *rimer.—Ta-w;* from *Tav,* of the fame signification with *Tauy, Sec. ut Jupra.—Teign* (or as commonly pronoune'd *Ting);* may be the fame as *Tain,* an old *Briti/b* word for a *r'rvir;* or rather perhaps derived from *Teg, fair clear, pretty, Sec.* and *Afon,* a *river,* contracted *into Aun; (oTeg aun* (since fhorten'd into *Tigan* or *Teign)* denotes a *fair* or *clear river,* and so claims place in our 2d class. Either of these seems preferable to *Baxter's Jsc tene,* or *Teniscat* i.e. *Tenuis aqua;* (5) for the *Teign* is far from being a *small fender* stream *Tenny* or *Tinny;* perhaps from *Tain,* a *river,* or rather from *Tenau, fender,* with the addition of *y,-water;* it being but a small and inconsiderable brook, at least 'till it unites with the *Tbrufhel:* But if this last be right, this also should be rank'd in the 2d class.—*Wane* (more commonly eall'd *Wondford Brook);* from *Afon ot Avon,* Cornisli *Avjan* or *Auan,* a river; contracted into *Wan,* or *Wone.—Yeo, Yeau,* or *Yea-w,* (the name of several rivers or brooks in this county and elsewhere, and frequently of farms which adjoin them,) signifies -*water;* agreeable to the French *Eau* which the *Normans* (if they introduced it here at the conquest instead of *Saxon Ea)* seem to have pronounced *E-au* or *Yeau;* to which the old Britifli *av, uy, eu,* (and we may add the Cornilh *Ave,* and *a-wy,)* seem to answer; all which as well as the Gothic *Ara,* the *Ifiandic* and modern Swedish *Aa,* (6) and the Saxon *Ea* above mentioned, signify -*water* or a *river.* We also learn that Mr. *0 Halleran's* Antiquities of *Ireland* that *Aba* in Irish is a *ford;* and indeed it is chiefly to snch small brooks as are *fordable* that the name *Yet* (in *Dcvonfiirt* at least) is generally given. II. We come now to the *Devonshire* rivers of the *second* class, *viz.* such whose *Briiijh* names express feme *quality* of their waters, or circumstances relative to them; and among these (besides the *Ar mt, Lud, Lyd, Otter, Tamar, Teign,* and *Tcnny,* above taken notice of as of the *former* class, bus some of them, as there hinted, perhaps more properly belonging to *this;)* the following may here claim our examination.—*Beera* or *Beera-brooi;* perhaps from the Cornish and Armoric *Bera,* to *glide* or *ftvw;* unless it may be rather derived from the Saxon Beora a *grove* or *plantation of trees,* and so mean a brook passing by or through some remarkable wood or grove; which supposition, if justified by its situation, would intitle it to a place in our 3d or 5th class—*Cary;* possibly from *Garr,* the *bam,* the bending or bowing of the knee, and *uy* or *y* water; so *Garr-y,* in pronunciation soften'd into *Cary,* might mean the *knee-bent-water* or *bending stream;* and such a bending this river really has, after its arrival at *Ajhvoatcr* in its course from *Beaviortby;* near which last, the old maps, as well as our author, place the head of its stream: But if its derivation from *Varog* (in Cornish *Karrog*) (ignifying a *brook* or *river,* be thought preferable, it should have place among those of the former class. *Cater-brttk ot Katcrbrook,* more commonly called *Cate-brook,* and by some *Katber'aie* brook j perhaps its true derivation may be from the Br. *Caeth,* narrow; and *(oCaeth* or *Cate-*brook may mean the *narrow* brook. — *Crecdy;* or perhaps antiently *Cridian,* since the Saxons eall'd *Crediton,* which had its name from it, *Cridiantune;* Oj if derived from *Grydian* or *Crydian, murmuring f* So *Crydian-y* might denote the *murmuring-ftream,* and be afterwards contracted to *Crydny* and *Creedy.* Or it might come from *Cryd-y,* the *trembling* or *dimpling* water; or from *Cr-wydr,-wandering;* but the former seems most I probable.

(t) Sec hi Glossary, *f.* 187. (2) ibid. p. 110. (3) ibid. p. 28 it lJ1. (4) Cor. voc. in Antig. of Corow. p. 456. ($ BdxC Clos. p. *22v-*(6") Vid. Dict. Islandicum Hickesii. probable.—*Claw;* possibly from the Br. *Clau, fast* or *swift;* or the Saxon *Chugh* a *Cleft.—Clyst* we find mis-spelt *Cliffe* by *Speed* and otheis, and in most of our old maps. But its true spelling is Certainly *Cl'ist* or *Clyst,* agreeably to its constant pronunciation. I take it to be derived from the *Irish* or *Guydbelian* British *Leasg, slothful, sluggish;* which was aMb the ancient signification of the Welsh *Llesg,* now used to signify *feeble, negligent, Sx.* and with *cil* prefix'd, denotes a *feeble fight,* a*stow retreat, tec.* Hence the dull sluggish current of this river *Clyst* might well take its name; its flux being very slow, and almost stagnating in some places.— *Cberry-Brook* in *Dartmoor;* (from the Br, *Sirian,* a *cherry* ;) doubtless so call'd from the *cberry-colour* with which the reddifls gravel and soil of its bed (visible enough in a sunshining day) seems to tinge its transparent stream.—*Cole* or *C.oly* Qjjf not derived from *Chwyl* a rolling or revolving1-? *Culm;* probably so called from the Cornislj *Cylm, swift, rapid;* which is agreeable to the general rapidity of its current.—*Doric;* perhaps from *Dior,* water, and *ial,* pleasant; the *pleasant* or *agreeable* water: Or if, instead of *ial,* the Cornish *bel,* a *river,* be thought more eligible, it becomes *Dwr-bcl,* the *river of water,* and belongs to the former class *Glaze* in the British and Armoric *Glas* signifies *blue, pale, green* and *gray;* and this river was probably so denominated from the colour reflected from its waters; whether from the azure tinge of its smooth stream in a calm clear day, or the obscurer gray of its ruffled waves in windy and cloudy weather.—*Goutsford;* perhaps from the Br. *Cbwydd,* swelling, and *Fford,* a way or passage; and so may mean a *ford* or *passable brook,* but liable to swell and overflow, as most small ones quickly do after great rains.—*Grind/e;* possibly a compound of the Br. *Craiun,* a *stoppage* or *obstruction,* and *Dal* which also signifies to *hinder* or *flop:* Hence perhaps the Saxon *Grind/e,* which likewise sig-

nifies an *obstruction* or *hindrance;* and the brook scsms to have had this name from its being frequently render'd unpassable, by its own inundations as well as those of the river *Clyst* into which it discharges itself, which often obstruct travellers in the road from *Si/hop's Clyst* to *Clyst St. George, tec.* even since the erection of the bridge called *Grind/e* bridge; and to prevent accidents, they are now warned of their danger in time of floods, by graduated posts fixt at proper places to shew the depth, puisuant to the late Highway Acts. This seems to justify our supposed etymology of the name of this brook; otherwise we might rather derive it from the Irish *Gbrinnioll,* the *channel* of a river.— *Ken;* probably from the Br. *Cain,* which not only signifies *white, fair,* or *beautiful,* hut also, according to *hlhuyd,* (z) *Limpidus, clarui, illimis;* and so this river might take its name from its *clear limfkl* stream; at least this scems more likely than any derivation from the British *Cefn,* or the Irish *Ceann* or *Keann,* signifying the *bead* or upper part of a thing; which Mr. *Baxter* (think wrongly) applies to *Kenton,* whose Roman name he takes to be *Vercenia,* deducing it from *uar tend iu,* i. e. *super capite under;* and then supposes this river to take its name from it, whereas the river doubtless gave name to it, as well as to the parish of *Ken,* which being nearest its head might be more truly said to be *super capite undo;;* than *Kenton;* tho' this be indeed, as he explains it, *prupe amnem.—Lemmon;* Qif from *Llymn* or *Llyfn* (Br.) a lake or meer, a stagnant water, and *etfon, avian* or *awn,* a river, and so denoting the *fi"ggijh* or *stagnant river t* Or perhaps rather from *L/am* (or its plural *Llammau) as on,* a stone or stones in a river to step over; for such this shallow and fordable brook has, in one or more places (if I am rightly inform'd) and this not far above its bridge; particularly where it is cross'd by a foot-path between that part of *Newton* call'd *Newton-Abbot* and the other part call'd *Newton-Bushel,* the former being in the parish of *Wolborough* and the latter in *Highweek,* to which two parishes this stream is for the most part a common boundary.—*Loman* or *Lumman*. This name of the river which discharges itself into the *Exe* at *Tiverton*, is, according to our author, comparatively modern; for he tells us its ancient name was *Suning:* But whether *Suning* or *Lumman* were its most ancient name, they having much the fame signification, it might be known at different times, or by different people, by both or either of those names; *Lumman* being probably derived from *Llymn* and *avon* or *awn,* meaning a *flow* or *sluggish river;* anc) *Suning* perhaps a compound of *Syn,* dull, *uy,* water, and *ing* or *yng,* narrow: So *Synnuy-ing* might mean the narrow, dull, or slow water; which is agreeable to the tardity of its current, it being (if I am rightly inform'd) no-where rapid, but its flux in general remarkably slow— *Maries;* perhaps as *Marias,* a river in *Caermartbenshire,* from *Mar,* water, (3) and *Allwys* or *urlloet,* poured out, cleansed or purified: Or *aMorlas,* which according *toLluyd* (4) signifies *Aqua cœrulca,* the sky-coloured water. —*Matford-brook,* which separates *Alphington* from *Exeter; Mat,* as well as *Med* or *Mad,* according to Mr. *Whitaker* (5) (tho' he mentions not in what dialect of the British) signifies *fair ;* and if so, this with the addition of *Ffordd* (denoting the way or passage through it, where now a stone bridge is also made) may signify the *fair ford. Mad* also in the eld British signified *good, benefic.al,* &c. and *Baxter* fays, (6) *Mat* in the Armoric signifies *Bona* atque *Divit'ue,* goods and riches.—*Meavy* or *Mevy;* possibly from *Mwy,* enlarged or augmented, and *uy,* water. This brook, after it leaves *Dartmoor,* is increased by another rill from thence, which comes down from (hat part of the sorest where *Siward's* cross stood; with which being united, it is call'd . *Meaty* (1) The Clyst signifies properly in the British language, the ear: And the curve which this river forms in its course, much resembles the human ear. The British word Leasg, dull, slothful, has little resemblance to Clyst in soundj though Xtft meaning answeis to the sluggish current of the river.

«) Lluyd in Baxt. p. 274. (3 ibid.p.266. (4) ibid. p. B74. fo) Manchester, p. 219.

Baxt. Gl. p. i6e.
() But, Cl. p. 171. *Meavy water,* at least 'till It also joins that stream which comes down from *Eylisburrow,* arid whicri has its confluence therewith not far from *Mevy Cburcb,* if it be not also so call'd lower down, before it takes the name of *Plym;* of which last Mr. *Dorm's* map makes it a principal branch, tho' omitting its name, and taking no notice of the rill from *Siward's* cross above-mentioned.—*Moutc* or *Mole:* As this river has no subterraneous passage, like the river *Mole* in *Surry,* to justify its taking its name from the animal so call'd, Q;_ whether it might not be some old *Briti/b* or *Celtic* word derived from MtAX©", i.e. *curvus, tortuofus;* and so have its name from the crookedness or turnings and windings of its channel? Or if the British *Miol,* or Saxon Mul, a *Mule,* be rather preferr'd, (since *rapid* rivers, such as this is, sometimes have their names from swift-footed animals,) it then more properly belongs to our 4th *zteSs.—Nadder-Water;* probably so call'd from its abounding with *water-snakes;* for *Neidr* irt *Weljh,* and *Naddyr* or *Nadar* in *Cornish,* signify an *adder* or *snake,* and *Neidr y dwr* a *water-snake.—Ock,* may possibly be from *Osc* (water) as has been already observ'd, the *s* being lost in a rapid pronunciation, which would rank it in the 1st class; but more probably from *Aivcb,* signifying *vigour, liveliness, vthemency;* which is very applicable to that river *Ock* which gives name to *Okebatrpttm;* but whether it be equally so to a river of the fame name near *Aiingdon* in *Berkshire,* I know not. But here are two separate streams, the *Ocks* or *Ockment* (the plural of *Ock).* Is it not remarkable that *Oczakow,* remote as it is, corresponds with *Ockbampton* in its situation on the *Ocks f Ot-brcok;* Qif from the Irish *At* or *bat,* agreeing with the British *buedb,* a *swelling* (and this perhaps derived from *Oise.v tumeo)* If so, it means the *swelling* brook; and this may possibly be preferable to its derivation from *od,* excellent.—*Plym; Baxter* (1) derives it from *Pilitn,* which in the *Erse* or old *Scotobrigantine Irish,* he fays, still signifies *volvere* to roll; and thinks the *Pi/*

ais of the anonymous *Ravennas* should be writ *Pilmis,* or *Pilim isc,* i. c. *convolvens aqua,* the rolling waterj denoting the impetuosity of its current. But QJ— *Rakern-brook* rises-in the forest of *Dartmoor* and falls into the *Tavy,* not far above *Mary-Tavy:* Another such brook runs by, and gives name to, the parish of *Rackenford* in this county, 'anciently spelt *Rakerneford,* and in Domesday Book *Raeheneforde* : Being both but small ones, the nirne may possibly be derived from *Rhegain,* to *murmur, mutter;* or *'whisper,* and so mean the *murmuring* brook.—*Redsord* or *Reddasord;* perhaps from the British and Armoric *Rbudd* (whence' the English-Saxon *red),* red or *ruddy;* this brook being remarkable for the reddish colour with which its waters are tirjed by the stones and gravel in its bed (as before observ'd in *Cherry-brook J,* and *Fsordd, the ford* or *pass?ge* through it. Note also, *Rbydj* both in Welsh and Cornish, signifies a *ford—Redlaie;* possibly the first syllable of this may have the fame meaning as in the last, and so want no further explanation; for *lake,* in *Devonshire* language (as has been already hinted) commonly means a small brook or rivulet. Or if its colour should not justify its borrowing this name from thence, it may be from tire Br. *Rhedeg,* to *run* or *flow ;* (thus *Dwr rhedegog* is *running water:)* Or else from *Rh:/ad,* roaring, if this torrent be really remarkable for its noise and rapidity; but *query* as to this?— *Tale;* Qif from *Tav-ial,* the pleasant stream. —*Tbrushel;* Qif from *Dwr;* water, and *Osgle* a branch? Or rather *Dwr-is-tyle,* the Water belovf the steep ascent of a hill?—*1Valdon;* perhaps from *Gwaiol, light, clear;* and either *Dwfn* (or *Dounj* Armoric) *deep;* or else *Davon,* or as shorten'd *Daun,* which, as *Baxter* (2) informs us, signified m the old British, *Amnis,* a r'tver or *brook,* and if so, *Gtvawl-daun* or *Waldon* means the *clear river* or *limpid stream.—Wever;* in *British* probably *Uy-aber,* compounded of *Vy,* water, and *aber* Which properly signifies the fall of a lesser water into a greater, as that of the *JVever* intd the *Culm;* but as we learn from Mr. *Ricbards,(y) Aber* is in *North-Wales* used for any *brock* or *stream* whatever, and if so, this river belongs rather to our 1st class: In the old *Cornish* also, it signified the meet'ngof two rivers; but sometimes a *ford*, and also the mouth of a river. See Dr. *Borlase's Corn'fh* Vocabulary. *Wotes-brook;* possibly from the Cornish *Huedbyx*, swoln; or rather *Huedb*, a swelling, with the addition of *isc* water; the swelling water. (See *Ot-brook.)*—But as this rivulet rises in *Dartmoor*, (at the boundary of which forest it falls into the *Teign)* and might be supposed to be form'd by melted snow from the hills there, if its derivation from *od* which signifies *falling snow*, with the addition of *isc*, water, may not be preferable to the former? — *Tail*, or *Taall* brook; perhaps from *ial*, pleasant, and so means the *pleasant* brook; but if it be (rom the Cornisli *Hail, Hal, Hel*, or *lltyie*, river or brook, it more properly belongs to our 1st class.—*Yalm* or *Tealm;* Qif from *Teau* or *Eu*, water, and *Llimp*, smooth? the *smooth* water.—*Tamer;* perhaps from *Ial*, pleasant, and *Mor* or *Mer* water; if so, it should rather be spelt *Talmer*, but the /.melts away in pronunciation *Tarty;* Qif from the old British *lar* or *Iear*, a river, and *teg*, fair, clear, pretty? So *lar teg*, shorten'd into *Tarty*, denotes the fair and clear river. III. Having thus particularized those *Devonshire* rivers whose names belong to our 1st and *zA* classes respectively, we come now to those of the *third, mix.* those which are either wholly of *Saxon* origin, Or partly *British* and partly *Saxon;* with which we may also rank such as have *Roman* names with *Saxon* terminations, or the contrary: Of this class (besides those already reserr'd to it), thiv County affords us the following.—*Bathcrm*, perhaps a compound of the Saxon Bath, *Balneum*, and the Latin word for *hot* baths, *Thermo: (a* ©sffi©-*calidus);* and possibly, as the Romans seem to have (Us (.1) Baxt. Cl. p.: 96. (a) ibid. p. 99. (3) Sec his W. Dict. in AW. had a station at or near *Bams ten*, which is situated on, and takes Us name from this river, they might also have artificial hot baths near it, and supplied with water from it *Bourn* or *Burn;* Sax. *Burn*, signifying a

torrent, brook, or *river;* also a *-watery ditch.*—*Cran-brook;* probably from the old British *Cretin*, to *fall down, roll, tumble*, and the Saxon *Bro:a* a brook or torrent. This rivulet give name to a farm in *Moretonbampjlead*, near which it rises, and falls precipitately into the *Tcign*,- *Dalcb* or *Dalk;* Sax. *Dale, recula*, a small matter or thing; so *Da/c-broca* may signify a small or inconsiderable brook, as this really is.—*Dean-burn;* Sax. *Dane-burn*, the *torrent* in the *valley.*—*Long brook* ; Sax. *Lange-broct*, needs no explanation.—*httmburh;* perhaps from the Br. *Llynh* or *Lymnt*, ft lake or pool in a river, and the Sax. *burn*, a brook, or watery ditch; and so may mean a brook that has such pools or stagnant waters in it.—*Pullabrook;* from the Sax. *Pul*, or Br. *Ptvll*, a pool, pit or ditch, and *Broca* a brook. It receives a small rill called *Reddiford.*—*Sbeb-brook;* possibly *Shotbrook*, and so called either from the swiftness of its current, or from its abounding with a sort of trouts, in some parts of this county called *Jbots:* which derivation seems preferable to either *Shot" brook* or *Short-brook*. This brook doubtless gave name to the parish of *Sbobbrook* thro' which it runs but being afterwards supposed to take its name from it, is now commonly ctll'd *Sbobbrook Lake.* See its other name, *Oldyt*, explain'd among tbose of the 2d class.—*Silver* Brook; so call'd from the colour or reflection of its water.—*Small-brook;* Sax. *Smal-broca;* the propriety of this name is not less evident than its meaning, it being indeed a very small brook *Tedboun* Brook; Qif from the

Br. *Tyivod*, sand, and the Sax. *Burn*, a brook or river? So *Tywodburn* shorten'd into *Tedburn* may mean the *Sand-brock:* Or it may be compounded of *Tutb*, a trotting or jogging pace, if agreeable tc the motion of its current, and *Burn* as before. It runs into the *Culverley*, and is more likely to have given its name to the parish of *Tedburn St. Mary*, which is water'd by it, than to have derived its name from it *Torridge, Touridge, Tawridge*, or *Turridge;* possibly frpm the British *Diur*, water, and the British *isc* or Irish *ui/ge*, which also signify -

water.—*Vg-brook;* probably from the Saxon Wog, *curvus;* so Wog-broca may mean the *crooked, bending*, or serpentine brook. This rivulet runs by, and fives name to, the feat of Lord *Clifford*, in the parish of *Chudleigb.*—*Walbrook* or *Wallabrook* and *Wellabrook;* from the Sax. Weal, *vertex ajuarum*, or else from Waella, *sons:* Brooks coming immediately fiom their fountain, and not yet joined with any other; and such those in *Dartmoor* so called, really are, but lose their names at their influx into the *Dart* and *Avon* respectively. *Wajh burne*either the old British *Uyjc* or Irish *Uifge*, water; or else, *Bail* or *fait* (the B and V being comroutable letters), a *ford Ot shallow place* cipable of a foot passage; with the addition of the Sax. *Burn*, a river.—*Wijhford;* the "first syllable of this, may have the fame derivation as the last, with the addition *of ford*, a ford or passable brook. The fame may be applied to that part of *Dalk* brooK which gives name to the parish of *IVajhford Pyne*, it being there indeed *Uyfc-Ffordd*, a ford or passable water.—*Womburn* ; perhaps from the Saxon and old English *TVedlm*, to *tvalm* or break forth a3 from a fountain; *and Burn*, a river; If so, it should be spelt *Waimburn.*—*Wrixel;* possibly from the Saxon *Wrixle*, vicissitude, an alternate change or mutation; perhaps from its swelling after every shower, and in the intervals reduced to a small rivulet: But Q?

IV. It now remains to take notice of those few rivers in this county which belong to our 4th and 5th classes, and have not been already specified. Of the 4th, *viz.* such as are metaphorically denominated from the nature of their currents only, I know of none but have their names either from some bird or swift-footed animal, or else from some missile weapon, to denote their velocity; of which we have the following instances—*Chackerel;* if not derived from the Br. *Ch-wai*, swift, speedy, quick; and *Ciryll*, a sparrow-hawk?-*Culverly;* probably from *Culfre*, a *dove* or *pidgeon* (for which the country-people in *Devon* still retain the Saxon appellation *Culver)*, with the addition of *bel* (Cornish) a river, and *uy*, water: So *Culverly* might

be originally *Culfre-bel uy,* the dove-like river of water; and be so call'd (as is the *Dove* in *Staffordshire)* from a comparison of the swiftness of its stream to that of the flight of a *dove.—Dart;* this in the *JVelp* and *Armork* has the fame signification as the *English,* a *dart,* and sometimes an *arrow;* and this river (as well as the *Arroio* which runs thro' part of *JVorcefterJbire* and *Warwickjhire)* was doubtless so call'd from the swiftness of its current. The chief river (for there are two or three others) of this name in *Devon/hire,* rises in and gives name to *Dart-Moor;* and, in its course, to *Darlington,* and *Dartmouth,* where it discharges itself into the ocean. Probably its Roman name was *Darium* ; and the *Durio Amr.e,* in the itinerary of *Ricardus Corinenjis,* (as Dr. *Borlafe* supposes,) should be *Dario amne,* and meant the passage over the *Dart* near *AJhburton.—Harburn;* probably *Hareburn,* the *Hare-brook;* the swiftness of its current being compared to that of a *bare.—Harford* Brook; Sax. *Hare-ford,* a rivulet that runs into *Tedburn* brock: This *ford* doubtless derives its name from the fame origin as the last. *Sidde,* or *Syd;* probably from the British *Saetb,* an *arrow* ; and if so, we cannnot doubt but it had this name for the reason above given for that of *Dart.—Wolf;* Sax. *Wulf.* This little river, the velocity of whose current claims a name from that swift footed animal, passes by *Awlijcombe* and *Buckere.%* and falls into the *Otter.*
V. Lastly, although It may be taken for a general rule, that where *riven* and *places* take their name from each other, the derivations of the latter from the former are, for the most part, to be preferr'd to those of the former from the latter; since the *rivers* existed, and perhaps had distinctive appellations, before any *towns* were built on or near them; yet there are some instances of rivers

Vot. I. A which of the one and the other. From the Phenicians are deduced, also, the names of our owns, by many who reject the idea of a Phenician colony, (a) Sammes, (A) and others, derive *Caerijk (c)* and other names of Exeter from the Peniciaa. *Hartama* or *Hertland,* doubtless comes from the

Phenician Hercules, *(d)* In trade, the Phenicians were the first which having lost their ancient names (If they ever had any), have borrow'd their modern ones from the towns or villages by which they flow: Among these, which are here distinguished as a *Fifth* class, we have in this county, the *Hayne, Holwell-Brook, Priatott-Brctk,* and perhaps some few others." *Chappie.* (a) A *colonial* rather than a *mercantile* connexion seems to be implied in the following paragraph: *u* Tria promuntoria, *Hesenit scilicet, Ocrmum,* et Kf *tu fAtiumn,* ut et nomina civitatum (such as *Termolut* and *Arta-via)* Græcam Peniciamqve *originem* redolentia." Richard, p. 21.
(A) " When I considered, fays *Sammes* in the preface to his Britannia, what *Leland* writeh of the British or Welch language, namely, that the main body of it consisteth of Hebrew and Greek words, I began to reflect with myself, how it should come to pass that the ancient Britains could have any commerce with the Jews, who were never known to fend out colonies, and of all people in the world were most fond of their own country; certainly I concluded, tills could proceed from no other root but the commerce of the Phœnicians with this nation, who using the fame language with the children of Israel in Canaan, even in those primitives were great traders and skilful mariners, and sent out their colonies through the world; and this Mr. *Cambden* himself touches on, where he gives the derivation of the British Caer Eske, now Exeter. For Caer, to tell you once for all (says he), with our Britains is as much as to fay, a city, whereupon they used to name Jerusalem, Caer Salem, Lutetia or Paris, Caer Paris, Rome, Caer Ruffaine. Thus Cartilage in the Punick tongue was called, as *So/inus* witnesseth, Cartheia, that is, the new city. I have heard likewise that Caer in the Syriack tongue signified a city. Now seeing that the Syrians, as all men confess, peopled the whole world with their colonies, it may seem probable that they left their tongue also to their posterity, as the mother of all future languages.—What can be more plain than this; and yet this is but

one example of ten thousand; but I hope that in the following discourse I have plainly made out, that not only the name of Britain itself, but of most places therein of ancient denomination are purely derived from the Phœnician tongue, and that the language it seise for the most part, as well as the customes, religions, idols, offices, dignities, of the ancient Britains are all clearly Phœnician, as likewise their instruments of war, as slings, and other weapons, their slthed chariots, and their different names, and several distinctions. Out of the fame tongue I have illustrated several monuments of antiquity found out and still remaining in Britain, which can no other waies be interpreted, than in the Phœnician tongue, where they have a plain, easie, and undeniable signification. And as to that concordance which was between the ancient Britains and Gauls in point of language and some other customes, I have shewn that it proceeded not from hence, that they were the feme people, but from joynt commerce withhe Phœnicians." (r) The Britons called Exeter, among other names, *Kaerpcnbuelgoit,* or " the *chief city in the wood;* as appears by Geoffry of Monmouth. It was also called *P enneheltecaire* or the *chief city cn the hill.* The Cornish very lately caHed Exeter by the ancient names of *Pennecaire, Caireruth,* and *Cairijke. Pennecaire* signifies the chief city; *Caireruth* the red city, from the red foil on which it is situated, and *Cairijke* the *city of iJke,* or the river Exe, in British Iske " This citty now the object of your sight, and the emporium of these western partes is very pleasantly seated on a hill (gently arising among hills with an easy ascent.) and therefore called Penchayr the head cyttie, Penhaltcayr the principall or chiefe citie on a hill. It declines towardea the south west parte after such a manner that be the streets never so ffoule, yet with one shower of raine they are presently clean? fed and made sv eet, as is fung of Hierufalem,
For one fayte ffloud doth send abroad
His pleasant streames apace,
To fresh the citty of our God
And wash his holy place.

That it hath bin antjently called Corinia or Corinea is very apparent; but that it had its denomination from Corineus who vpon his arrivall with Brutus into this land was first created Duke of these two provinces, I cannot averr; for 1 haue it not vpon such warrant as I dare trust;—for Circefter was also of Ptolomye called Corinium yet not from Corineus." *Wcftcote,* p. 73.

(d) " Not much distant from Hertye Poynt, or Hercules Promontory; which to derive down from Hercules that renowned tyrant-queller, would require more time and labour then I can well affoard, yet for that diuers will haue it foe: I willdeliuer the opinion of a much better man, even the dictator of knowledge Reverend Mr. Cambden, who I hope will yield them satisfaction to contentment, if not I confess I cannot. Ffrom Cornwall the first fhoate in this shire (faith hee) that stretcheth out it seise in length towards the Severn sea is by Ptolomye called the Promontorie of Hercules, & retayneth still some littie smack of the name being at this day called Hertye Poynt: and hath in it twe prettie towns Herton *tc* Hejtland famous in elder times, *for* the reliques of that holy first to give names. Observing our *tin* in its native bed, they called it *(a)stean* or the *mud.* And it is asserted, that the British manner of fighting, the names of their warchariots, and of their weapons of war, were all of Phenician origin—such as *Covin, Ejfeda, Rhedd.* *(b)* This much for the *Britijh-Phenician* of Danmomum.

The man St. Nectan: in honour of whome was here erected a little Monasterye, by Gltha wife of Earle Goodwine, who had this St. Nectan in especiall reverence: for that shee was persuaded, that for his meritts her husband had escaped the danger of shipwreck, in a most violent & dangerous tempest: howbeit afterwards the Dynants (now Dynhams) that came out of Bryttaine in Ffrance (whose demesnes in fee it was) were accounted the founders thereof. The name of the Promontorie hath gruen credit to a very formal tale, that Hercules forsooth came hither into Brytaine & here vanquished I wot not what gyants: but if it bee true that Mythologers (or expounders of moral tales) tell vs & affirme that there was «euer any Hercules; but that by him the power of human wisdome is vnderflood; whereby wee overcome pride, lust, envye, theft, & other such like monsters: Or if according to the divinitie of the Gentiles, by Hercules they mean the sunn, & by those 12 labours endured and performed by Hercules, the 12 signs in the Zodiack, which the fun in his yearly course passeth through: what it is they fay let them look to it themselues: but for my owne part I willingly believe there was an Hercules; nay 1 could bee content to grant with Varro, that there were of them 43, all whose acts-were ascribed to that Hercules who was the son of Alkmena: yet can I not persuade myselfe that ever an Hercules came hither; vnlefs happily hee came sayling here over the ocean in that cup that god Nereus gaue him whereof Athenius maketh mention. But you will fay that Ffranciscus Philelphus in his epistles & Lullius Gireldus in his Hercules aver noe less: I pray you pardon me, these late writers may moue but not remove mee; considering that Diodorus Siculus who went on with the Greekish Historye in order, euen from the most remote & first records of all antiquitye, in playn ternu affirmeth, that neither Hercules nor father Bacchus went ever into Brytaine. I am therefore veryly persuaded, that the name of Hercules came to this place, either through the vanity of the Greekes; or from the superstitious religion of the Brytaines: for as these being most warlike nations themselves, had valiant men in marveilous estimation & admiration, and highly wonderd at such as conquerd monsters; foe the Greekes againe, whatsoever was any where stately & magnificent, that they referred to the glory of Hercules. And because hee had been a great traveller, such as travelled were wont to offer sacrifices to him, and to him likewise did consecrate the places of their arrivalls: hereof came Hercules Rock in Campania; Hercules Haven in Lyguria; Hercules Grove in Germanie; hence likewise the Promontories of Hercules in Mauritania, Galacia, & Brytaine. Well, what Hercules soever hee bee, wee are escap't his ringers and clubb, and are cleer of him." *Wtsttote,* p. 160, 161.

(a) Whence the Cornu-hritish *Jletm,* of the same meaning. *Pryce.* (i) But these are *Cbaldaic* words: and they were used in Danmonium before the existence of our Phenician colony. The *Pbcnicicm,* indeed, was derived from the *Chaldee,* in common with the *aboriginal British,* the *Irish,* and the *Erse.* The affinity of the *Phtnician* with the *Irijh* is provjd, beyond all controversy, by Vallancey, who hath given us a specimen of the Punic,(i) curiously collaud with the Irish. A part of this collection is as follows:

Punic.

" Nyth al o nim ua lonath ficorathissi me com syth.

Irish.

Tsaith all o nimh uath lonnaithe! socruidhse me com fith.

O mighty Deity of this cpuntry, powerful, terrible! quiet me with rest.

Punic

Chim lach chunyth mum ys tyal mycthi barii im schi.

Irish.

Chimi lach chuinigh! muini is toil, miocht beiridh iar mo scith.

A support of weak captives; be thy will to instruct me to obtain my children.

Punic.

Lipho can ethyth by mithii ad ardan binuthii.

hip.

Liomhtha can ati bi mitche ad eadan beannaithe.

Let it come to pass that my earnest prayers be blessed before thee.

Punic.

Byr nar ob syllo homal o nim! ubymis isyrthoho.

Irish.

Bior nar ob siladh umhal; 0 nimh! ibhim a frotha.

A fountain denied not to drop to the humble; O Deity, that I may drink of its streams." In this manner several other Punic lines are collated with the Irish j and bear the same resemblanceto it.

(1) From the Pxnulus %i Plautus. *Vol.* I. A u

The *third stage* of the Danmonian language, may be said to commence with the *Greek* colony. As the Greeks extremely plumed themselves on their language, and were ltudious to disseminate the knowledge of it, there are many who think, that, even as a.mercantile people, they lest the more cultivated Danmonians in possession at 4east of the rudiments of their tongue. That a great number of Greek words were incorporated with the language of Danmonium, may be clearly shewn.(a) The names of *(b) Britain* itself; cf the (c) *Castiterides;* of several (J) promontories and () rivers in Danmoniurn; as well a,s towns and villages, are attributed to the Greeks. But the *numerous (f)* Greek words in *(a)* " Mr. *Bostuell* asserts, that the *British* language bears a greater resemblance to the *Greek,* than any other whatsoever; and that there are more *Greek* words incorporated with it than there are *Latins from* which, and other circumstances, he thinks it evident that a colony of *Greeks* were once here, and lived some time amongst us. *Camden* seems also to favour the opinion that the *Greeks* landed in and had some knowledge of this island; being supposed to have had colonies and plantations along the sea coast in most parts of *Europe, Britain* not excepted; or, according to Sir *Thomas Smyth's* supposition as quoted by him, that a great number of them fled hither for safety, when all *Europe* was embroil'd in war: However, he seems elsewhere partly to retract this, and gives it as his opj nion that it was late before the name of the *Britons* was heard of, either by the *Greeks* or *Romans.* But whether we had any *Greeks* here or not, the mixture of *Greek* words in the *Britip* language, is a fact whioh *Camden* admits, and will hardly be denied." *Chappie. (h)* See derivation of the names of Britain. Borlasc's Antiqu. p. 3, 4, 5.

() The Greeks called the Scilly Isles Cassiterides. Sammes, p. 73. *(d)* There were promontories in the Taurica Chersoncsus, and in the island of Crete, which the Greeks called *Iov /j.tlojirx.* In the fame manner we have the promontory of *Kgiov ttlumof,* ipvhich I take to be

the *Ram-Head* Point. *Helenis Promontorium* was also a *Greek* promontory. (?) The *ClyH,* for instance, derived, perhaps, from *.icra-os,* it being a gently-flowing stream—or from *xtpot* only because it overflows the marshes every spring-tide to a large extent, but also because (the country lying much upon a flat) the land floods, even in summer, frequently deluge the meadows for many miles together. *C/J* " The footsteps of the *Greek* language are evidently seen not only in particular *British* words, which agree in found and fence, but in the very nature and idiom of the two languages. Some are of opiiiipn, that the Greek characters were used in *Britain.,* and that they were changed ly the *Roman* conquerors, who alwaies were very careful to obtrude their language upon them whom they overcame, as a certain sign pf dominion over them, and a surer union with such provinces; and his I am spf to credit, because *Cæsar,* after the conquest os the *Hc'netii,* found their public, records written in Greek characters. The ancient *Greeks* had but two and twenty letters, tin more had the *Britains,* and as afterwards the Greeks, for conveniency, did receive two more into t!r»ir alphabet, so haye the *Britains.* Moreover, it is to be observed, that the *British* letters agree exactly in sound with the *Greek,* as is most remarkable in *c* and *g* (not to instance in *d* and *u)* which *c* and *g* are alwaies pronounced by the *Britains,* as x, and *y,* and not as now they are before *i* and *e,* w here *c* is pronounced like an J, and *g* like an *j* consonant. Of *newels,* the *Britains* had anciently six, now they have added a seventh, *vint,* a *iu,* but this relishes of the *Tcutonitl.* Their *consonants,* after the man-er of the *Greeks,* are divided into *semvyeceln* and *mutas,* and these again into *temies medias* and *aspiratas,* which, in the flexion of nouns and verbs, pass one into another exactly after the Greek manner. *R,* in the beginning of words, is alwaies with an *'aspirate,* as it is in the *Greek* tongue; out of which observations in the *British* and *Greek* language, I would note these things. *First,* that the *Druids* of *Britain* and *Gaul,* by the number of letters hav-

ing only twenty two, as may rationally be supposed, after the manner of the ancienter *Greeks,* came into *Britain* very early, when the *Greeks* had not as yet learnt the use of their other letters, or if they had, notwithstanding they were not frequently known among them. *Secondly, the Druids,* using the fame characters which were common in *Greece,* in the time of *Julius Cæsar,* it appears, that neither were they of so ancient a standing in this iflanH and *Gaul,* as the first and primitive times of *Greece,* when the *Greeks* learnt their letters from the *Phœnicians,* and without doubt something nigh their character. Besides, *Pliny* observes, out of an ancient inscription in the *Greek* tongue, that formerly the *Gracians* had very nigh the fame characters with the *Latins;* and if I be not mistaken, did write an *H* instead of their *aspiration,* after the manner of the *Phœnician:* and if the *Phœnicians* did not themselves bring the use pf letters, and the number of them into *Britain,* but contented themselves with trading only hither, yet I am sure the *Gracians* had not only the first number of their letters from them, but characters also, and as may be very rationally conjectured, might bring them into this island, after they had new modelled them, and before they had added any new ones to them. The-true attaining to the just circumstances of time, as to the navigations pf the *Phœnicians* and *Gracians,* makes much to the stating gf she antiquities of *Britain.* But care must be had, that as we bring pot the *Greeks* too early into in the Danmonian language, very *little altered* by their transplantation into it, would be iufficient to throw an air of probability over the supposition of a Greek settlement at: circumstance? Should we not suppose in. thb case, that the *few* Greek expressions; accidentally adopted from the conversation of merchants, would have been soon soft amidst the these islands, as by the more modern characters they used, do appear, so we must not assign the time, too late, of their discovering them, which their long settled customes in *Britain,* the great esteem they had gained with the islanders, the very idiom of the *Greek* language introduced, and their religious ceremonies and rites, though never fo cruel, allowed and approved by the whole state, argues ' them of a very ancient standing in these parts, and that not suddenly, but by long use, and against/ much opposition, they vvjere at last admitted and entertained. Seeing we have here spoken of the', concordance of the *British* tongue with the *Greek* idiom, it will not be much out of the way, if we take notice, that as the number of their letters agree exactly with the *Phœnicians*, though we will not suppose them to have received them immediately from the *Phœnician:* but the *Gracians,* so there are a world of words in the *Brit'sh* language, which agree exactly with the *Syrian* or *Phœnician* tongue; for, I verily believe, that the extream number of *aspirations,* and guttural pronunciations, were peculiar to no western nation, but only the *Britain!* of *Armorica,* and *Wales,* and the *lrilh* (which may well be supposed to be peopled out of *Britain,* or else to have been traded unto by the *Phœnicians* themselves) is an evident sign of the *Phœnicians* once conversing in these islands; for it is to be observed that the eastern languages, and that they as well as the *Greeks,* contributed much to the making up of that language which was used here in *Cæsars* daies, and since, the mixture of the *Saxon, Roman,* and *Norman* tongues, only excepted. But to returu to the *Greeks,* besides the peculiar conformity of idiom, which the *Britains* have of their language in general with the *Crucians,* it is to be observed, that the *numerals* of both nations are most the fame, where sometimes our *Britains,* sometimes they of *Gaul,* have the greatest resemblance. As for example, I will set down in order. Ekcbtot, A Hundred.

XiX/fi, In the Latin *Mille,* a Thousand.

Mvgidst A Million.
Most of these may be easily supposed to come from the *Greek;* if we consider how variously that language alters the letters of foreign words it receives. And if any think, that some of these may better be referred to the *Remans* than *Gracians,* as Jlffl. «35ato, Cfl, £ant and

Hist, I shall answer them in Mr. *Sherirgham's* words, *That hejtdcs these so like the* Greek *numerals, the* Britains *have no other to express themselves by. But if these ivords lucre lately introduced, it behoved that the old terms jhould have remained in their tori ir. gs, as the Old* Saxon *and* Latin *ivords, though out of use, re main still in the writings of the ancients;* But l fear by his words lately introduced, he supposes the objection made, as if they were brought in later than *Casar's* daies, perhaps by the clergy of *Rome,* otherwise it is not improbable but they had seme of these from the *Romans,* although there be no mention of any ancienter words of the fame signification in their old poets, because they have no writings of such antiquity, and *numerals* are (of all other words) used according to the acceptation of the present time. But the greatest argument, in my opinion, that the *Britains* had not any of them from the *Romans, is,* because that the *Armorican* Britains in *Gaul,* who fled over (not long after the coming of the *Romans)* into this island, cannot be supposed (in fo sliort a time) to change so considerable a part of their language, do notwithstanding keep the same *numerals* as our Britains of *Wales* do, setting aside some small variation, as ©OtD for ©9ul, which is rather to be attributed jto a difference in dialect, than that they had them from the *Greeks.* But, besides the names of *numbers,* the *Britains* have in their language a whole lexicon of words, whose original is undoubtedly Greek xfs pnlvnpt, had we no other testimony to support the fact. It does not appear, that hall" so many words in our language are derived from the Latin as from the Greek. Yet the *Greet:* I will put down some examples ont of Mr. *Sheringham,* which he collected, most of which, as he writeth, hath no synonymous words to express them.
Britjfi. Creek, English. "*Ayyos,,* A neighbour, or that which is near at hand. "AXX©-, Another.
'Afc&l, Round about, of all sides, or of all parts. *yAnivu,* To defend, or afford aid or assistance. *An,* is a Particle privative, »it i3 among the *Greeks.*

" A bear.
A stammerer.
   More cruel, hasty, or uniuly.
Strong, or valiant.
To purge, or clear.
   An ornament, garnishing, or decking of any thing.
Grewel, or pottage.
A shell, or cabinet.
Warm.
A rafter.
   Praise, or commendation.
To strike.
To bite, or gnaw.
A petition, or request.
Manifest.
Water.
   An oak, or grove of trees.
Proper, or particular ones own.
A cubit.

The Particle *Er* increascth his signification, as "Ei doth among the *Greeks.* the Romans traversed almost every part of Danmonium, and settled here king after the Greeks. If, then, the Greeks were trading voyagers only, is not this a very singular circumstance?

A friend of Carew, « one Master Thomas Williams," was of opinion, " that the Cornish tongue was derived from the Greeke: And, besides divers reasons whish hee produced to prove the fame, he vouched many words of one fence in both; as for example:

This language is stored with sufficient plenty to expresse the conceits of a good wit, both in prose and rime: yet can they no more gipe a *Cornish* word for *tye,* then the Greekes for *ineptus,* the French for *stand,* the English for *emulus,* or the Irish for *knaue.* Others they haue not, past two or three naturall, but are fayne to borrow of the English: mary, this want is releeued with a flood of most bitter curses, and fpitefull nicknames. They place the adjective after the fubstantiue, like the Grecians, &c." See Carew's Survey of Cornwall, p. 55 If the reader cursorily inspect the following list, he will see many words that speak *a fettled people—a colonial,* not a mere *commercial* establish ment.

Ebron,
Echrys,
Fflur,

Plananth,
Skez, (1)
Scod,
Taran,
Aha,
Alston,
Antron,
Ik,
Porth,
Ryn,
Rhyn,
Rynen,
Tarn,
Dour,
Kren,
Caul,
Dryst,
Neonin,
Arth,
Garan,
Kei,
Murrian,
Ren,
Carat "
Karadow, *beloveds*
Karenza, *love,*

(1) From Ikez, a fliadow, comes skezy, (h.tdowy, or fleeting like shadows. Jtople chafing one another, or patting in quirk succession, arc sleesmg.

£aj Hence Tamar, or TalB'inawr, the great rTvsr, tke Urgeil in Corautfit.
the
Dzoules,
Forrior,
Crene,
Crenna,
Dacron,
Flaw, (1)
Geylelsio,
Klowo,
Methow,
Mufac,
Mousegy,
Poan,
Renki,
Ronkye,
Rhedec,
Ate,
Carthu,
Dathisky,
Deyfif,
Diliis,
Eiddio,
Faellu,

Hezuek,
Hyrch,
Moccio,
Ny,
Tin,
Theu,
Choarion,
Ancar,
Bochim, (2)
Airos,
Skath,
Elin,
Fer,

hate, to clear, to teach, a petition, manifest, proper, to err, ease, to command, to mock, 1VC, US, terrible, # # God, # sports, an hermitage,
the house of oxen,
» »
stern of a stip,
a boat,
» a cubit, dn angle, plena. damage, loss. hence falladou, *falfocstl. recedt, to unmoor, to set to sea. a stiff.* s *$ipu, to carry,* whence *feran, a fairing* , J and *popos, tribute, taxes, a market.*

Ferna, (1) Hence " Flaws of winds"— a common expression in Cornwall.
(a) The Bochim of scripture is well known: And it is remarkable that there is a Bochim in Britany as well at Cornwall (3) Hence the Furry-day of Heliton, commonly deduced fromfciiac.; But fense comes from the fame root. the Roman conquests and settlements? And should we not expect to meet with a much greater number of Latin than of Greek, words? Even if the Greeks had been posterior to the Romans, merely as traders to Danmonium, we should have looked for more of the Latin than of the Greek, in our language; whilst we considered the provinciating spirit cf the Romans, and their establishment in this island for centuries. Admitting the reality of a Grecian colony in Danmonium, we are almost surprised at the predominance of the Greek over the Roman: For the Greeks in this island were for ages, prior to the Romans. But without admitting the reality of a Grecian colony, this predominance can never be accounted for: A Grecian colony, therefore, must have existed in Danmonium. My argument, however, does not depend merely

on the *number* of Greek words: The *little alteration* they have undergone, in general, in consequence of their insertion into our language, seems a striking fact in favor of my theory. I need not insist on this point: P'rom the list of Greek words given below, my readers will judge for themselves. Many of these words are pure Greek, retaining their original founds, without the slightest variation. There is another argument in favor of this colony, from the *quality* of the Greek words. Had the Grecians been only *traders* to this island, the words they might have scattered here, would have been chiefly of a mercantile complexion. But examine the list6 below: There such words occur, as could not have been casually dropt into the language by a few merchants: They relate to the *ordinary affairs* of lite. They carry conviction of a familiar intercourse between the Greeks arid Danmonians: They, evidently, imply a settled people. In the mean time, the Danmonian language resembles the Greek in many particulars. It is a circumstance worthy notice, that many Danmonian words which are not obviously deducible from the Greek, have yet *a Greek termination:* And many, though neither deducible from the Greek, nor having a Gsreek termination, are but *mere echoes to this sonorous tongue*— which seems to intimate, that the Danmonians, imitating the Greeks *ore roiuudo,* were ambitious of forming their words after the Greek model. And this must argue the closest intimacy between the Greeks and the Danmonians.
(a) It is to be observed, also, that like the Greek, there are numerous *(J) compound* words in our language, equally as expressive as the Greek. And our language, *a wife't portion. to join. talidus.*
(1) (a) With respect to Cornubritisli words of *Greek found,* such as the following, are profusely scattered through the Vocabularies of Borlase and Pryce: Gockorion, *foolish people;* Guarimon, *theatres;* Guirion, *a man of-veracity;* Nenpynion, *the brain;* Dorossen, *a mole-bill;* Fellores, *a woman-fiper*j Palores, *a chough;* Eiriafdan, *a binfire;* Splan, *splendor,* b) Such as Bartine, or

tbe bill of f res —the Cornilh for *fire* being *tan;* Boscawen-rose, *tbe bouse in tbe elder tree-valley;* Boleit, the *dairy-cot;* Carminow, *tbe little city,* from *car* and *minow* or *minys,* small—hence *minows,* the small fish that abound in our streams j Caer-edrls, *tbe learned city;* Cuttayle (in Calftock) *tbe wood near tbe river;* Crugfellick, *the barrow in open view,* Colhlwyn, *a gro-ue of hazel;* Delabol (in St. Teth) *the house in tbe clayey soil;* Dinemour (from din and mor) *a fort at tbe sea*—whence Moridunum; Dinsul, *a sunny bill,* or *a hill dedicated to tbe sun;* Gundron, *tbe down's-bill;* Keneggy, *the mossy hedge by tbe water;* Kuzkarnnahuilan, *the lapwing's rock by a wood;* Leskard, *tbe castle court,* from its castle, *one of tbe ancient seats of the Dukes of Cornwall;* Misguerdiu, *the month of black storms,* i.e. *December;* Nanfladron, *the valley of thieves* j Pendarvis, *bead f* (i) Hence tinder. " Tine the slant lightning." Milton's Paradise Loft, B.x.1.1075.

Vol. I. B b language, like the Greek, abounds with *expletives-.* Like the Greek, it has many *redundancies-.* And in its (a) *idioms,* it is often similar to the Greek. On viewing the intermixture, therefore, of the Greek language with the Danmonian, we are struck by the *number* of Greek words, by their *undisguised* appearance, and by their *quality;* whilst, in our language, the *terminations* and *sounds, compounds* and *expletives, redundancies* and *idioms,* which relemble the Greek, are no less remarkable.

Whether, at this stage of the Danmonian language, the Greek characters were adopted or not, in *writing,* is a point which I (hall not, at present, discuss. The " *Grtecis litteris"* of Cæsar, is a dubious passage. *Gracis* is dismissed by many of the commentators as ah interpolation: And, if there were any epithet, I think *Crafsis* was the word.,

The *fourth* and last *stage* of the Danmonian language, must be fixed at the time of the Belgic and other European settlements on our island. But on this topic I shall not enlarge, *(b)* The different tribes from the neighbouring continent, brought with them, undoubtedly,

a barbarous tongue, which greatly corrupted the languages of Danmonium.

The language of Danmonium, then, From its first existence in the island to the time, of Caesar, Teems to have undergone various modifications. Originating in the east, a daughter of the Chaldee, it was nearly coeval in these islands with the *Irish* and the *Erse,* of which it was a sister dialtct. And we termed it the *British* tongue; as spoken in South-Britain, But in South-Britain, it was adulterated with various mixtures. In the western parts of South-Britain, Devon and Cornwall, we have seen it corrupted by the *Phenician,* the *Greek,* and the *Belgic* and other *European* tongues. In the mean time, 3t had spread from the west over the remaining part of South-Britain. In the interior parts, it was comparatively pure: On the coasts, particularly the Kentish, it had lost its primitive color and its original flavor. At this crisis, *three* several dialects seem to have prevailed in South-Britain—the dialect of those *aboriginal Britons,* who, at the invasion of the Belgae, had fled from Danmonium into the centre of the island; the dialect or jargon of the *Gauls* on a great part of the *coasts* of South-Britain; and the dialect of the *£anmonians,* or of *the people of Devon and Cornwall.*

The *dialeil* of Danmonium, then, (derived from the Chaldee, and blended with the Phenician, the Greek, and the Gaulish) may be termed in contradistinction with the *Pwo other dialeds* of South Britain, the Cornu-british or the Cornish tongue, *(c)*

I have *tf the oak field;* Penmennor, *the principal mountain;* Polwhele, *the pool-work;* Poughill (Pouguil) *the country frequented by gulls;* Roseorla, *the valley of the peep-fold;* Rosevallen, *the apple-valley;* Sulleh, *tie rocks of tie fun;* Trehane, *the old town*—in Probus, the feat of one of the most respectable families in Cornwall; Trevagheon, *giant'stown;* Tre'r-druw, *the Druid's-toiun;* Tremadah, *the toivn of extafy;* Trembleath, *the wolf's-town,* (a) " The *Cornish* and *Devonshire* tongue seems to retain the footsteps of the most *ancient British language,* and has in it the

very Idioms of the Phenician and Creek nations." Sammes' Britan. p. 4.

(4) " The greatest argument produced to make this island peopled from *Gaul,* is the confinity of language between the ancient *Britain!* and *Gauls.* The confinity of language between the ancient *Britains* and *Gauls* proceeds not from their being one nation, but from the *Grecians* and *Phœnicians* vvho traded to both, and the words produced by Mr. *Cambden* for that purpose, I shall shew to be most of them *Phœnician,* some *Greek,* and as for the rest they have little analogy one with another, and that which is, may proceed from the invaslon of *Britain* by the *Gauls,* and the intercourse of Druids in both nations." Sammes, p. 11.

" If we take away the words which, were introduced into *Britain* and *Gaul,* either by the *Phœnicians* or *Greeks,* or last of all by the *Romans,* possibly no two languages may be judged more remote than theirs was, and then Mr. *Cartbden's* large catalogue of words will be reduced to a small number indeed." Sammes, p. 90. " That *Britain* could not have been peopled from *Gaul* (fays Sammes) Cæsar methinks makes it evident—where he fays, that the inlanders reported themselves to be Aborigines—which they could not have done, had they agreed *in language* with the maritime *Gauls,* It would be vanity in any country, to pretend a different original, and not to speak a different language, the chief criterion." Sammes, p. 10.

(c) " The most material singularities in this tongue are, that the substantive is placed generally before the adjective; the preposition comes sometimes after the cafe governed; the nominative, and governed case, and pronouns, are oftentimes incorporated with the verb; letters are changed in the beginning, middle, or end of a word, or syllable; some omitted, some inserted; and (much to the commendation of this tongue) of several words one is compounded (as in the Greek) for the fake, of brevity, found, and expression. (1)" Borlase's Nat. Hist. p. 314.

I have now sufficiently descanted on the language of the DanmonianS.

How far the *sciences* and the *arts* were cultivated at this period, in Devonshire, cart only be learnt from our observation of the Druids. That the Druids applied themselves to *(a)* astronomy and geography, Cælkr and Mela assure us: But what proficiency they made in these studies, is a subject of dispute. Mr. Chappie (as we have seen in his account of the Cromlech) represents the Druids as deep astronomers. Their mode of computing time was certainly remarkable. *Spalia omnis (&) temporis* (fays Cæsar) *nort numero dierum, fed noBium finiunt: et dies natales, et menfium et annorum imtia Jic observant, ut noilem dies subsequatur.* This is one of the most extraordinary of the Dmidical Usages. It evidently speaks the high antiquity of the Druids; whilst it discovers a tenet of this venerable priesthood, that in the beginning of the world, the night was anterior' to the day. The Druids believed, that before the creation, one universal darkness prevailed, and that the day sprung out of night; and, therefore, computed by nights and not by days. This agrees with the Mosaic history; and thus the Hebrews computed time. When " in the beginning God created the heaven and the earth, *darkness vjas upon the face of the deep* :" And " when God divided the light from the darkness, *the evening and the morning mere the first day. (c)* Does not this strongly savour of the oriental? Was there any such custom among the continentals of Europe? Was there any such custom even in Italy, the peculiar feat of superstition? The Druids (and British Princes) were also acquainted with the virtue of simples, and skilled in the application of them to the body. Thus we fee a Caledonian chief, in the poems of Ossian, " who had searched for the herbs of the mountains, and gathered them on the secret banks of their streams, and whose hand had closed the wound of the valiant." And of another, it is declared, " that to close the wound was his—he had known the herbs of the hills, and had seized their fair heads on high as they waved b/their secret streams." Medicinal Botany, indeed, was engrafted on the stock of the British

religion: And the Druids were at once our physicians and our priests. The*samol,* probably the*seamar,* or wild trefoil (what the Irish Britons wear at present in their hats on St. Patrick's day)—the *vervain*—the*selago,* a kind of savin—and the *mijletoe* of the oak—were the favourite plants of the Druids in medicine as well as in religion. Anatomy was another science with which the Druids are said to have been acquainted; though I can scarcely conceive, that they applied their anatomical knowledge to medical uses. Yet the Druids of Danmonium were famous *in* medicine—not less so than the physicians of Persia. In the mean time, the Druids attended greatly to physiology. They searched into the secrets of nature. They speculated on the essence of God, the origin of all things, the dissolution of the world. Their doctrines relating to the immortality and transmigration of the soul, which were taught by the Brachmans, and are still maintained by the priests of India, are manifest proofs of their religious learning. With respect to the *imitative arts,* it appeal's that the Druids were versed both in *painting* and *poetry.*' Their picture of Hercules Ogmius, as described by Lucian, displays their delicate refinement in emblematical representation; whilst it marks the affinity of their genius to the Asiatic: And their attachment to the fublimer poetry, seems to prove their superiority to every European people. But some engravings on the British coins are unequivocal testimonies of the taste of the Britons for engraving. The war-chariot I have mentioned, was *designed* by a Briton—it was *sketched* out by a British hand, and *engraved* upon a British coin. This is a proof of some degree of proficiency made in the *elegant* as well as *mechanical* arts.

For the instruction of the Danmonians, in those parts of their knowledge which they thought proper to communicate, the Druids instituted seminaries of learning, and were themselves *(a)* That the Brachmans are well acquainted with astronomy, appears from M. Le Gentil's account of a Voyage to India. The Indians on the coast of Coromandel, ex-

press their knowledge, we find, *in verses or allegorical symbols;* and the explication of the characters is often difficult and doubtful, on account of the incapacity of the interpreters. The curiosity of M. Le Gentil was excited by the accounts he had heard at Pondicherry, of the astronomy of the Tamoult Indians; and nothing could equal his surprize, when he saw the facility with which one of these Indians calculated, in his presence, an eclipse of the moon (which he had proposed to him) with all the preliminary elements of that phenomenon, in three quarters of an hour. (i) lib. 6. *(c)* Genesis, c. 1. This circumstance escaped not the observation of Richard. See p. 9.

Voi. I. gb themselves the teachers of the British youth. And some solitary cavern, or kam, or saci ed wood, was commonly the place of instruction. That our Danmonian leaders were not illiterate, must follow from the necessity of their attention to learning; since no person, we are told, who had not been educated under a Druid, was qualified for public employments. It has appeared, that theDruids instructed their disciples in verse; which, the latter were not allowed to commit to writing, lest they should render the Druidical wisdom familiar to the public eye, or trusting too much to what they had written, suifeir their memories to be impaired for want of exertion. Such are Cæsar's, and such are, doubtless, the true reasons which induced the Druids to lay this injunction on their scholars. Yet there are several antiquaries, who assert, that the Druids prohibited all kinds of writing. The Druids were accustomed also to convey their instructions to their di'ciples through the medium of allegorical picture; and this with the true oriental spirit. Such, then, was the learning of the Druids, diffused in a certain degree among the superior ranks of the Danmonians. To enquire into the personal history of any learned men among the Danmonians, during this obscure period, would be idle and absurd. It is satisfadlory enough, at this early stage of literature, to shew, that the language of the Danmonians, in general, was relpectable; and that their knowledge (a) was by. no means contemptible.

SECTION a) Not contemptible, Meed! Let us close our view, with some remarks of Col. VALLANCEY on the Learned and Intelligent people, whence they sprung; and with an extract fYom ShWILLIAM JONES'S *Asuuc Researches.* " The S. Scythians of the Saxon chronicle (fays Vallancey) were originally seated in Mesopotamia, Shinar and Armenia, and had settled in Egypt, Palestine, and Phœnicia, whence they emigrated to Spain, and lastly to the *Britannic I.JJes."* " The true *Scntbai* (fays Bryant) (i) Were Un Wubtidly A Vxr Y Learned And Intelligent PeoPle; but their origin is not to be looked for in the north of Asia; or the deserts of Tartsry. There was a country named Scythia, *far in the east,* of which little notice has been hitherto taken. It was situated in the great *Indie Ocean:* and consisted of a widely-extended region, called Scythia LYMvncA.(i) Though the inhabitants of this country were unknown for ages, there was a time when they rendered themselves very respectable. For they carried on an extensive commerce, and WERE SUPERIOR IN SCIENCE TO ALL THE NATIONS IN THEIR NEIGHBOUR-HOOD; *and thit wds long before the dawn of learning in Greece ; even before the constitution of many principalities, into which the Hellenic slate tvas divided.* As they are represented of the highest antiquity, and of great power, and as they are said to have subdued mighty kingdoms, and to have claimed precedency even of the Egyptians, it is worth while to enquire into the history of this wonderful people. To me then, it appears very manifest, that what was termed by the Greeks *Ixvdot IzvQix Tkvoixx.* was originally Cutha, Cuthai, Cuthica, and related to the family of *Chus.* He was called by the Eabylonians and Chaldeans *Cutl,* and his posterity Cuthtes and Cutheans. The countries where thsy at times settled, were uniformly denominated from them; but what was properly stiled Cutha, the Greeks expressed with a Sigma prefixed. Epiphanius has transmitted ta us a curious epitome of the whole Scythic

history. Those nations, fays he, which reach'southward from that part of the world, where the two great continents of Europe and Afia incline to each other, and are connected, were universally stiled Scythæ, according to an appellation of long standing. These were of that family, who erected the great fewer called Babel. They woe the Cuthite Shepherds, who came into Egypt, and many of them settled in Ar M E N I A. " In another place, Bryant fays: «' We may, Ithink, be assured, that by the term *Scntbai,* are to be understood *Cuthai.* They were the descendants of Chus, who seized upon the region of Babylonia and Chabdea; and constituted the first kingdom upon the earth. Among themselves their general patronymic was *Cuth,* and their country *Cutha.* They were an ingenious and knowing people, as I have before observed; and at the fame time very prolific. A targe body invaded Egypt, when as yet it was in its infant state, made up 6f little independent districts, artless and uninformed', without any rule or polity. They seized the whole country, and held it for some ages in subjection: and from their arrival, the history of Egypt will be found to commence. The region between the Tigris and Esphrates, where they origirtally resided, was stiled the country of the *Chafd'm* j but by the western nations Chaldea. It lay towards the lower part of the Tigris to the west, and below the plain of *Shinar.* This country is said to have been also called *Scutha*; and the author of the Chronicon Paschale mentions *Scuthæ* in these parts, who were so called In his days. "(4) " If i mistake not (fays Vallancey) the *Scutha* were so turned *iota* their being the first navigators—this is the character given of the *southern Scutha* by Dionyfius." (i) Mythology, *voU* g, p. 135, le. (2) ftolern. Ceogr. I.. 4, p. lei. (3) Mythology, Vol.g. p. 175. (4) Bcrosiu lays, that Noah Left Che Scythian Armenians bis ritual hooks, which only prieils, and that only among priest night read. SECTION X. *VIEW of the PERSONS and POPULATION of the DANMO-NIANS, during the BRITISH PERIOD.*
I. *View of the Persons of the Danmo-*

nians—Cæsar's difthiBion between the maritime Britons stem Gaul, arid the Aborigines—the Aborigines of Danmonium, resembling the Iri/b and the Highlanders, in stature, bodily strength, fair complexion, and red hair—in these points more like the oriental nations, than the Gaulish tribes.—II. Phenicians, Greeks, and Gaulish tribes.—III. Popidoufnefs of the Island, at the close of this Period.* IT seems to have been the opinion of Tacitus, that, among the great variety of contingencies, which act both upon the body and the mind of man, the climate hath not the slightest influence. Agreeably to this notion, an analogy hath frequently been formed' between the air and soil of a country, and the bodily and mental constitution of its inhabitants. The Britons, in particular, have been represented wild as the winds that howled around them—and rough as their native hills. But this is, for the most part, a picture from Dionysius."-Let us now turn onr attention to Sir WILLIAM JONES. At the opening of the sixth discouife, (5) on the Persians, delivered 19th February, 1789; the president, Sir WILLIAM JONES informs his audience that he turns with deJight from the vast mountains and barren defert9 ef *Turan,* over which he had travelled last year with no perfect knowledge of his course, to pursue his journey through one of the most celebrated and most beautiful countries in the world; a country, the history and languages of which he had long attentively studied, and on which he might, without arrogance, promise more positive information, than he could possibly procure on a nation si» disunited and so unlettered as the *Tartars.* He proceeds to describe the situation of *Persia,* as it is improperly called by Europeans; the name of a single province being applied to the whole empire of *Iran.* "Having finished his preliminary remarks, he adverts to a variety of topics, among which the *ancient languages,* and the *primeval religion* and *cbaratlers of Iran,* have a considerable share os his attention. He concludes bis discourse, by recapitulating the principal positions, which he has endeavoured to establish:

" Thus has it been proved by clear evidence and plain reasoning, tli3t a powerful monarchy was established in Iran long before the Assyrian, or Pishdadi, government; that it was in truth a Hindu monarchy, though, if any chuse to call it Cusian, Casdean, or Scythian, we shall not enter into a debate on mere names; that it subsisted many centuries, and that its history has been ingrafted on that of the Hindus, who founded the monarchies of Ayodhyi and Indraprestha; that the language of the first Persian empire was the mother of the Sanscrit, and consequently of the Zend, and Parsi, as well as of Greek, Latin, and Gothick; that the language of the Assyrians was the parent of Chaldaick and Pahlavi, and that the primary Tartarian language also had been current in the same empire; although, as the Tartars had no books or even letters, we cannot with certainty trace their unpoliflied and variable idioms. We discover, therefore, in Persia, at the earliest dawn of history, the *three* distinct races of men, whom we described on former occasions as possessors of India, Arabia, ar.d Tartary; and, whether they were collected in Iran from distant regions, or diverged from it, as from a common centre, we shall easily determine by the following considerations. Let us observe, in the first place, the central position of Iran, which is bounded by Arabia, by Tartary, and by India; whilst Arabia lies contiguous to Iran only, but is remote from Tartary, and divided even from the skirts of India by a considerable gulf: no country, therefore, but Persia, seems likely to have sent forth its colonies to all the kingdoms of Asia: the Brahmans could never have migrated from India to Iran, because they are expressly forbidden by their oldest existing laws to leave the region, which they inhabit at this day; the Arabs have not even a tradition of an emigration into Persia before Mohammed, nor had they indeed any inducement to quit their beautiful and extensive domains; and, as to the Tartars, we have no trace in history of their departure from their plains and forests, till the invasion of the Medes, who, according to etymologists, were the sons of Madai; and even they were conducted by princes of an Assyrian family. The *three* races, therefore, whom we have already mentioned, (and more than three we have not yet found,) migrated from Iran, as £fom their common country; and thus the Saxon chronicle, I presume, from good authority, brings the first inhabitants of Britain from Armenia; while a late very learned writer concludes, after all his laborious researches, that the Goths or Scythians came from Persia; and another contends, with great force, that both the Irish and old Britons proceeded severally from the borders of the Caspian $ a coincidence of conclusions from different media by persons wholly unconnected, which could scarce have happened, if they were not grounded on solid principles!"

' (1) Asiatic Researches,.vol, 2. _from fancy.(a) Whether, however, this connexion between the climate of Britain and its inhabitants be admitted or rejected, we would wish to be acquainted with the real character of both. Yet, here, ancient authors are again at variance. Whilst Diodorus intimates, that the air of this island is cold.O) Caesar talks of the milder temperature of Britain as compared with Gaul, and Tacitus particularly noiiees the softness of our climate.(s) With respect to the first Britons, Diodorus calls them *cciloyrbotx yen;* and Tacitus fays: " Britanniam Qui Mortales Initio Coluerint, *indigenœ advefti*, sit inter barbaros, parum compertum." *(d)* For the persons of the Britons, Cæsar s report is, that " thole who lived nearest Gaul, were very like the Gauls; probably owing to their being descended from the *fame original siock,* and their dwelling almost in the same climate."() Here Cæsar establishes a clear distinction between the maritime Britons and the Aborigines. He attributes the likeness of the maritime Britons to the Gauls, to their having sprung from the same stock: Whence we may infer his opinion, that the inland Britons or Aborigines, not resembling the Gauls, points out a very different origin. Though not decided as to their real origin, yet Caelar clearly saw, that the Aborigines could never have come from Gaul. And this was evidently the fense of all his contemporaries. The cafe was so plain, that to assert expressly, that the Aborigines were not derived from Gaul, would have struck Cæsar as an absurdity. The direct affirmation of an obvious truth, which has never been doubted, is always ridiculous.

The Aborigines were a different race of beings from the Gaulish coasters. They were remarkably *large* and *tall.* " The Britons (lays Strabo) exceed the Gauls in stature; of which I had ocular demonstration. For I saw some young Britons at Rome, who were half a foot taller than the tallest men."*(f)* If, as we have frequently done, we turn our views to-Ireland and the Highlands, we shall discover a striking likeness in the inhabitants of both, to the first Danmonians, or the original race of South-Britain. The Irish and the North Britoins were remarkable for their Targe limbs and high stature: And in other particulars, we shall see, they resembled the unmixt, undegenerated people of Danmonium.

(j) One of our writers, drawing the character of the Danmonians, fays: " The ancient inhabitants of this county are represented as intrepid, prodigal of life, constant in affection, courteous to strangers, and extremely fond of popular applause. For the barbarity of these times, the Danmonii were a civil and courteous people; They were stout and puissant; *taking heart even of the soil itself, and emboldened by the roughness of their country."* Richards, in his " Aboriginal Briton S," often starts this idea—in my opinion, not happily. And his portrait of the ancient Briton, may be poetical enough: It is, certainly, not a just one— *Rude* as the *-wilds* around his sylvan home,

In savage grandeur see the Briton roam:

Bare were his limbs, and strung with toil and cold,

By untam'd nature cast in giant mould.

O'er his broad brawny shoulders, loosely flung,

Shaggy and long, his yellow ringlets hung.

His waist an iron-belted falchion bore,

Massy, and purpled deep with human gore.

His fcarr'd and rudely painted limbs around,

Fantastic horror-striking figures frown'd,

Which, monster-like, ev'n to the confines ran

Of nature's work, and left him hardly man.

His knitted brows and rolling eyes impart

A direful image of his ruthless heart;

Where War and human Bloodshed, brooding, lie,

Like thunders, lowering in a gloomy sky. h) *Eioior. Sicul.* Wess. Tom. I. p. 347-" *atts Siaflto-iv n-xZltXus y.x%vyjj. tm.*" c) *Casar*—Bell. Gall. 12. " Loca sum temperatiora, quam in Gallia, remissioribus frigoribus." *Tacit.* Vit. Agric. c. 12. " Afperitas frigerum abest. " *(d)* Jul. Agric. c. ii.

(c) Cæsar, 1. 5, c. 12. Caesar's knowledge of the Britons, was in some points superficial: But it was enough to enable him to draw a just outline of them. The particulars Cæsar learnt relating to the Danmonians, were from the Gaulish merchants and from the people of Kent, who knew little of Devonshire.

Danmonium. The Danmonians were no less celebrated for their *bodily strength* («) than for their gigantic size. And the Irish and the Highlanders were wonderfully vigorous. Wrestling is an exercise well calculated for the display of bodily strength: And the Danmonians, the Irish, and the Highlanders, excelled all the Europeans in wrestling. Ossiaa thus describes Fingal and Swaran, wrestling. " Their sinewy arms bend round each other: they turn from side to side and strain and stretch their large spreading limbs below. But, when the pride of their strength arose, they sliook the hill with their heels: Rocks tumble from their places on high: the green-headed bullies are overturned." (A) It appears, that the sirst Danmonians had, in general,(s) *fair complexions, cLtid yelloiv, or red hair:* Such was the cafe with the Caledonians. The hair of

the Danmonians was, also, ioft and curling: So was that of the Highlanders. " Was he white as the snow of Ardven—blooming as the bow of the stiower? Was his hair like the mist of the hill, soft and curling in the day of the fun? Was he like the thunder of heaven in battle? Fleet as the roe of the desart?" *(d)* With respect to the females of Danmonium, they were distinguished for their beauty—if they resembled the Caledonians, in the blue radiance of their eyes, and in fairness, and the softness of their persons. The bosom of one of the Caledonian ladies is compared by Ossian, to the down of the swan, " when slow slie sails the lake, and sidelong winds are blowing." *(e)*

That the eastern nations (particularly the Arabians and the Persians) approached much nearer in their persons, to the inhabitants of Danmonium, Scotland, and Ireland, than any of the Gaulisli tribes, might easily be proved. The blue eyes of the eastern female, in particular, have been already remarked, *(f)*

By the intermixture of the Phenicians, Greeks, and Gallic tribes, with the Danmonians, great alterations in their original stature, strength and beauty, must have gradually taken place: But to discriminate thele changes, would be impossible. From their swarthy complexions and curled hair, Tacitus conjectured, that the inhabitants of the south-west coast had come from Spain. And the Phenicians, undoubtedly, formed settlements in Spain; and, probably, in Danmonium. To enquire further into these particulars, would be fruitless.

To what age the Danmonians commonly lived, is a question to which an answer cannot be reasonably expected: Yet the longevity of the Britons is memorized by Plutarch, who fays, that they lived to the age of one hundred and twenty. And Plutarch's intelligence (with that of the ancients in general) seems to have been derived from merchants trading to Danmonium.

With respect to *population*, Diodorus and Cæsar agree in their reports, that the island was well stored with inhabi-

tants. The number of towns, indeed, on the south-west shore, which, according to Suetonius, were subdued by the Romans, sufficiently prove the populousness of this part of the island, about the close of the British Period.

(a) See Carew's Survey of Cornwall, p. 56, 57, 58. *(b)* Ossian, v. i, p. 6i, 63. *(c)* Strabo, 1. 5, p. 200. (/) Ossian, v. 1, p. go. (e) Ossian, v. 1, p. 58. *(f)* For an illustration of this topic, I would refer my readers to the Arabian Nights' Entertainments, and Sir W. Jones's various descriptions of the oriental nations. SECTION SECTION XI. *VIEW of the CHARACTER, MANNERS, and USAGES os the DANMONIANS, during the BRITISH PERIOD.*

I. *The Courage of the Danmonians—their restless Activity—their Simplicity—their Fidelity and Attachment to their respective Tribes—their Frugality—their Hospitality—their Cbaracier from Diodorus—their resentful Temper—their Cruelty—their intemperate Curiosity, a Grecian feature—their Superstition.*—II. *The modes of Address among the Danmonians*

—their matrimonial Connexions—their Dress—their domestic Accommodations and Usages their Diet—their principal Sports—their Customs in War, and military Apparatus, partirularly the scythed Chariot—Examination of the question, ivbether the scythed Chariot was Oriental or Gaulish—the Rites of Sepulture in Danmonium.—III. *Character, Manners, tend Usages of the Danmonians, highly favourable to the Eastern Hypothesis—this Hypothesis founded on strong circumstantial Evidence; ivhich, on a revieiv of the whole Chapter, seems irresistible.* HISTORY presents us with few subjects more curious or pleasing, than the manners of nations. But the æra of the Danmonians is much too remote, to furnish us with any satisfactory views in this line of speculation. The perlons of the ancient inhabitants of the west have been already described. We are now to examine their mental character, their *virtues* and their *vices*—and their more remar kable *habitudes* and *customs.*

Among the virtues of a people not highly polished, courage or personal intrepidity is generally the most prominent. And *courage* was a virtue of the Danmonians. After having enumerated the different tribes, from the continent, that gradually established themselves in Various parts of the island, Richard mentions the Danmonii, as a race of people the strongest and most courageous of all: He describes them, as *gens omnium validifsima.* But another part of their original character, seems to have been a *restless activity*—an ardent desire of change, and a fondness for discoveries, which prompted them to range over the earth, and to invade the most distant territories. If we recur to the eastern countries (whence we have derived the Danmonians) we shall find that the Chaldæans, mentioned by Xenophon as a warlike nation of Armenia, poffest the fame fierce and wandering spirit j in allusion to which the prophet («) Habakkuk exclaims: " I raise up the Chaldæans, that bitter and hasty nation, *ivbo shall go over the breadth ef the earth,* to possess the dwelling-places which are not theirs." The *simplicity* of the Danmonians is, alto, worthy notice, *(b)* Diodorus intimates, that they were sincere and honest. " They are simple in their manners (fays the Historian) very different characters from the men of our times: The obliquity and improbity of the present day, are far removed out of their sight. " This openness of disposition, this abhorrence of all diffimulation, was a striking characteristic of those countries, whence the Danmonians probably emigrated. The eastern nations and the Danmonians were alike distinguished for their love of truth, *(c) Fidelity* and *attachment to their respective tribes,* were traits of character no less remarkable in the Danmonians. And there is no passion by which a Highlander or a native Arab is more distinguished than by an attachment to his clan or tribe, and jealousy for its honor. *Frugality* was another virtue of the Danmonians: This, too, marks the Highlanders and the Arabs, who adhere to their old plain diet, nor wish to provoke appetite by luxuries. Yet the frugality of the Danmonians, was connected with the most generous *hospitality.* The natives of Scotland and Arabia still preserve this social spirit; and in the frankness of their domestic attentions, exhibit the ancient Danmonian character. Their kindness to strangers, in particular, brings back to view the generations that flourished in Devonshire and Cornwall j when the halls of the *(a)* Chap. i. v. 6. *(i)* " As Tacitus hath preferred the genius of the Britons to that of the Cauls; so hath Diodorus, their integrity to that of the Romans." *Magna Brit.* p. 12.

(c) An ingenious man of this county used often to say—" that the people of Devonshire and Cornwall were certainly derived from the orientals, for these three reasons; Their skill in the bow—their Aill in horsemanship—and *thtir knit of truth."*

Hjftory thus enables us to touch, lightly, on the Danmonian virtues and vices: And we cajt do ao Eaore—unless we contemplate this people as tinctured by *superstition,* which, gives a strong color to the human mind j particularly in the ruder æras of" society. Superstition, indeed,-mil be seen to influence the Danraonians, in almost every situation: And, though we have already marked it under the form of religion, yet often shall we *dot* it flirting tip, in various fashions, usages, and customs.

With respect to the customs or fashions of the Danmonians, in common life, we can sey very little with certainty. Of their *modes ef address,* for instance, we have scarce any account; unless the homage they paid to persons of distinction, by walking three times round them Unani east so west, be numbered among the ceremonials of fashion.

Id regard to *matrimonial cosmexians,* it appears, that the Danmonian mode of courtship was entirely in the oriental style. The lover addressed himself first to the father of the maid, and requested his daughter in marriage. And the father, if he agreed to the overture, " opened the hall of the *(a)* maid," the apartment in which me generally fat *retired from tit ma* of the family—and introducM the suitor to his daughter, *b)* The period of this courtfmp was very short—resembling that described (c) in Genesis: It was, in every respect indeed, patriarchal. Though a man married but one woman, whom he regarded at Me wiie; yet a certain society of brethren or friends were accustomed to com. ræœairsie tlieir wives to one anotluer, for their reciprocal enjoyment.*(d)* This *community sf naves* was no way similar to the marriages of the Gauls, or any other western nation. The ceremony of binding girdles, imprest with several mystical figures, about the waists of women in labor (when a birth was attended with any difficulty) was, doubtless, of icastern origin. The words and gestures that accompanied this ceremony marked ks high antiquity. In the lame manner, the wise of the Highlander, when advanced in her pregnancy, was bound with the sanctified girdle, to alleviate the pains and expedite the birth, A hundred of thole girdles are promised by a chief, " to bind highbosoiaed women *V(f)*

Of the *dress* of the Danraonians, we have had a momentary glimpse in the survey os their manufactures. The £y) skins of beasts have been too commonly mistaken for the cleathing of the Britons. Loose woollen garments, however, not kss artificial than the maatles of the Scotch or the Irish, were certainly worn by the Danmonians. And this was an oriental dress: It was in fashion, not long after the dispersion, *(i)* But the Danraonians were Armenians, PhenicLuiB, Greeks, and Gauls: Their dress, therefore, must have varied according to the faflrions of the countries whence they came. And, in each race, the different ranks and ordere of people must have been distinguished by different mode of diyjfe. Strabo deseribes the dress of the Danmonians, as of a flowing robe down *to* their seer, and long sleeves made fast at the wrists. And the historian terms this robe *p£jtjjjxti-/*— which is descriptive of the color, as well as the materials of which it was composed.

rd) The British virgin was marriageable at fourteen. *Ho.vel Dwa* L. *ii, e.* I. (£ OctSæi, vet i. p. 50, and 155. (r) *Genesis, c* 14.

» yi) » The Batons framed themselves (fays Mr. Wbitaker) into a strange set of matrimonial clubs, which generally comprehended ten or twenty families, and each husband had free access to each wife in *it?* ' Carfssr, p. 3 9.

%e) The Britons had one remarkable enstom peculiar to themselves, and not to be *mit* with, as far as we know, an the wactice of any other nation. We mean *a fort 0/ community of unmet,* which acoarfirng to *Cxfar,* was after this manner. Ten or twelve of them, especially brethren with each ttther, and pareets with their children, had wives together in common; yet so, as that, when a woman brought forth, the child was accounted his only, who first married her. *Die* and *Eufeiius* fce£ much the fame story; and *fe* strange it appeared to the *Romans,* that *yutia Vomna, Stwrus's* Empress, reproached a *British* lady with it, as a way of living infamous in the women, and barbarous in «jss men. The lady having observed what passed at court, brifkiy reply d-. *We ds that publicity toitb the best of cur men, mbicb you do privately with the worfi of yours.* *Selden* mentions another odd cu&oo!, with which we will conclude this article about matrimony. Upon the death of aay great man, his friends made diligent enquiry concerning it. If any of the friends of his wife were found accessary to it, Shey proceeded against them with *fire* and other torments. To this custom *it* is, that *Coke* refers; the original of our *Exgiifi* law, that orders a woman who has killed her fcirfhand to *be burned."* *Mn£tia Brie.* p. 13. (fj Qffian, vet 1 p. 115. (j) Ctefac, p. 89. £ Genesis, xlv. 23, &c &c. composed, (a) Trawlers were equally worn by the Danraonians and the Persian. The vesture of the Druids seems to correspond with that of the priests of Iran, or the present Sufi of India, who are clad in woollen garments or mantles.(t) The Danmonian soldiers appeared naked in battle: They painted, also, their bodies for the fight, and wort a ring round their middles.(r)

I shall make one observation only on this topic—which is—that we are too apt to draw our notions of the dress of the Britons from Cselar. But Cæsar's is a very superficial notice of the Britons, in this particular: It is an outline so faint, as to be scarce discern, able. Cæsar could not possibly have been so well acquainted with the Britons as Strzbo, and other Greek writers, who derived the most authentic information from their countrymen, the Greek'merchants and settlers on the coasts of Danmonium. Britain, or rather Danmonium, was known to the Greeks, long before the invasion of Cæsar. 'Strabo has more particularly described the Cafliterides, or Devonshire and Cornwall and the Scillyisles—a part of Britain, of which Cæsar was ignorant.

Of their *domestic* accommodation, we may bave conceived some idea, from the houses of the Danmonians already described. (/) The seats of our chiefs (like those of the Highlanders) were surrounded with hills and hanging woods, and thus sheltered from the inclemency of the weather. Near them generally ran a large stream, abounding wish fish. The woods were stocked with wild-fowl; and the downs and mountains behind them were the natural seat of the red deer. Nor were the fides of the hills or the vallies unproductive in com or herbage. In his great hall fat *(e)* the British chief, with his children and guests around him, listening to the song and the harp of his bards or daughters, and drinkiDg from cups of shell. *(f)* The hearth of the Britons seems to have been fixed in the centre of their great halls—as in some parts of Scotland to this day. That the Britons were acquainted with *coal,* is evident, among other proofs, from its British appellation, which subsists among the Irish in their *Gual,* and among the Cornish in their *Kolan* to this day. And peat, the most inflammable of all fuel, was certainly in use among the Dannionii. The venison of the Britons was thus.prepared.. It was laid.upon a bed of flaming fern, and covered with a layer of smooth flat stones, and another of fern above it. *(g)* The fame mode of cookery was practised in Ireland, and is still in some measure *(a)* See Sammes, p. 117, 11.8. &) We are told, that the Britons suffered their beards to grow to a considerable length, but confined (as among the Irish) to the upper lip. The Druids had, doubtless, venerable beards. (c) Even so late as the battle of Killicranky, the Highlanders threw off their plaids and short coats, and sought in their shirts.. , (d) « Their cottages were very small, and thatched with straw. What then? So are they still in several places of *Britain.* But.can we thence conclude with a late learned writeri that *Cafar,* at his landing, *found not so much as tnt jlont ufm amibrr.* The direct contrary to this assertion seems to be probable from some passages in *Cafar* himself, who gives us an account of large cities and long sieges. We think it past doubt, that some of these cities, at least the walls of them, were of stone. Why should *Britain* therefore, which exceeded *Caul* in almost all other respects, be thought to come *So* very short of it in this? It cannot easily be imagined that all the cities in *Caul,* mentioned by *Car/ar,* were built by the *Ramans.* We will therefore, at present, suppose theie anciently were upon the coasts of *Britain* some good towns, to which strangers had recourse to buy and (ell, and exchange wares with those of the island." Mag. Brit. p. 13. (e) Their manner of sitting at meat, not on scats or benches, but upon the ground, was evidently oriental. " When they fat at meat, it was not upon seats or benches, but upon the ground; whereon, instead of carpets, they spread the skins of wolves, or dogs. The guests all of them fat round about, and the food was placed before them, and every one took his part; they were waited upon by the younger people of both sexes. Such as had not skins were content with a little hay or straw, which was laid under them." *Strutt.* vol. 1, p. 188. *(f)* Ossian, vol. 1. p. 72, 240, 16, and 27, and Pegge's Coins of Cunobeline, 4—1 and 3. The custom of pledging each other amidst their cups, and the order observed in drinking, were similar in Danmonium and Arabia. In the " Arabian Nights," " Amine silled out wine, and drank *firfi herself,* according to the custom of the Arabians, then she silled it to her guests."(i) *(g)* See Ossian, vol. 1. p. 15. , (1) See AiabUn Mights, vol. 1. p.

134. ThH is die present mode of thinking in Devonshire, among the lower oiderj 'if the people.

Vol, I. C c measure retained by the present Highlanders in their hunting parties, (a) Of our indi *goosander)* was esteemed a dainty: As such the Romans prized it. Mr. Whitaker thinks, that the domestic pigeon was introduced into Britain by the Romans. But, I conceive, it was prior to the Romans, for the very reason he has given in support of his idea. *(/)* The cock of the wood was known in the forest of Dartmoor; but, as our woods diminished, it retreated from the south-west, and gradually from South Britain, into the Highlands of Scotland, and into Ireland—where it is now rare, and, probably, will be soon extinct, (c) In their abstinence from particular meats, the Danmonians certainly resembled the Hebrews and many of the eastern nations. It does not appear, that the Romans or any other European people, had ever any exception of this fort to certain animals. The hare, as Cæsar and other authors inform us, was one animal from which the Britons («/) abstained: And the hare was prohibited to the Hebrews, *(e)* The Romans, in the mean time, esteemed the hare a great delicacy; and, in this island, secured the luxury to themselves. The eating of geese and of hens was, also, prohibited by the Druids; since these birds were consecrated to religion, *(f)* Even now the common people, both in Devonshire and Cornwall (but particularly in this county) have an aversion to the hare, and to most kinds of poultry—which they reject under the general appellation of *holloio fowl.* The abstinence of the Danmonians from fish, must have originated in the, same principle of religion; since the very rivers and the sea were deified. The scaly inhabitants, therefore, of the rivers and the sea, would naturally be considered as the little naids of both, and as sharing a part of their divinity. ' In the interior parts of the Highlands, the *fijh* of their brooks and lakes are seldom eaten by the natives, to this day.(£) These prohibitions, with respect to meats, have been often mentioned: But the abstinence of the British

sailors, recorded by Solinus, seems to have been overlooked. *Sluantocunque (a)* As to the diet of the Highlanders, there is qpe very remarkable particular, that occurs in Bin's Letters, (vol. 2. p. 121.) In the interior parts of the Highlands, it seems, thf lower ranks of people subsist on a little oatmeal, milk, and *blood drawn from their living cattle.* The Abyslinians, then, are not singular in *drawing Hood from their living cattle!* The Cornish (and the Devonians in some parts of Devon) *bake* the *blood* of animals.

(b) " The domestic pigeon was once equally a stranger to Asia and Britain, and bespeaks its introducers into the latter, by the name of *khmmen,* which it bears in the Welsh; of *kylobman* and *iclom* in the Cornish, and *kulm* or *holm* in the Irish and Armorick." Thus Mr. Whitaker. But *tolumba* was derived from the British words. (f) Our original island birds (according to Mr. Whitaker) were the duck, teal, widgeon, swan, crane, stork, bustard, *(1)* capercalze, co:k of the wood, woodcock, quail, snipe, (2) heathcock, lark, itockdove Several of these are extinct in the island, and others not existing in Devonshire. (/) The Danmonians kept hares about the courts of their chiefs. (c) " They looked upon it as a crime to eat either hare, hen or goose, which however, *Crfar* assures us, they kept for their pleasure. Nay *Pliny* affirms, that the *chenerotes,* which are of the fame species with *geese,* were looked upon as the choicest meat in *Britain.* They were very sparing in their diet, according to *Diodorus,* which both he and *Car/ar* affirm to have been usually either venison, or fruits or milk. *Strabo* fays, they knew not how to make cheese; but that cannot be altogether true, for it will not easily be allowed that all of them, especially those that dealt with the *Phœnicians,* were ignorant of so common a piece of lkill. *Dion* assures us they tilled no ground: But he too must be understood with restriction; for *Pliny* assures us, they manur'd their ground with marl instead of dung, which argues no such ignorance in husbandry as *Strabo* and *Dion* charge upon them. Their drink

was usually made of barley, as *Solinus* hath informed ns. We shall only farther observe, that this distinction of meats, their making some lawful, others unlawful, in Mr. *Selden's* opinion, relish'd somewhat of the *Jews,* and was rarely practised by any but eastern nations, such as *Phœnicia, Egypt, Syria,* &c. who had conversed with the *Jews.* So *Dion* tells us, the antient *Britains* symbolized with the *Syrians* in refusing to eat fish." Magn. Brit. p. 12. *(f)* The Danmonians had their domestic cock; though not for the purpose of food. *See Richard,* p. 5— and *Sammes,* p. 109. ' *(g)* Birt's Letters, vol. *2,* p. 121. (i) Rieard, p. j. (1) The capercalze was common to all the island; but from its feeding on the tender tops of fir-branches, and loving high and solitary mountains and woods, it has now for ages been peculiar to the Highlands. (2) " The heathcock's head is beneath his wing. The hind sleeps with the hart of the desart. They shall rife w;th morning's light, and feed by the mossy stream —but my tears return with the fun, My sighs come en with the night 1 — O&an, vol. 1. p. 378,... *terns ore cur/us tenebant, ut auti* me of the abstinence of the sailors noticed in St. Paul's voyage to Rome.(«) The providing *(b)* of bread for every family among the Danmonians, was the province of the women: And the bread was *baked upon Jlones,(c)* which the Welsh denominate *Greidiols,* and we *Gredles.* In the fame manner, we find in scripture mention of bread baked among the ashes. Sarah made cakes upon the hearth, when the three men came to see Abraham, *(d)* This custom is retained by the Arabs. Dr. Leonhart RanwolfFs informs us, that " in the tent where he was entertained, the Arabs made a paste of flour and water, and wrought it into broad cakes, about the thickness of a finger, and put them in a hot place on the ground, heated on purpose by lire, and covered it with ashes and coals, and turned it several times until it was enough. Some of the Arabians have in their tents (fays he) stones or copperplates made on purpose to bake their bread."-The (f) luxury of cheeses is said to have been unknown to the Danmonians. But the Danmonians made curds and butter of their milk from the earliest times—*densantes in acorem jucundum et pingue butyrum,* fays Pliny, *(f)* And, indeed, the art of making curds and butter was not a European art: The Romans, we (hall fee, were ignorant of it. As Pliny describes the *Danmonians, so* Herodotus *(g)* describes the *Scythians* as famous for their curds and butter: And it is remarkable, that the *four-curd* (or the *acor jucundus)* is familiar only at the present day, to the *Tartars* and the *(.ornijh* and a few of the *Deuonians.* *(b)* Water, milk, or metheglin, were the common liquors of the Danmonians. But on festal days, their drink was *curmi,* (;') the *curiv* of the Welsh, and the *ale* of the English. This liquor was made in Ægypt immediately after the dispersion, as a substitute for the juice of the grape, to which that country was unfavourable. And, the Aborigines of Danmonium, rinding the fame defect in this country, supplied it in the same manner. There are some, indeed, of opinion, that the Danmonians planted vineyards and orchards in very early times j and that they used, as their principal liquors, the fermented juice both of the grape and of the apple: But, though perhaps the vallies of Danmonium were sufficiently sunny for the grape, yet our climate must have been always too variable for the regular produce of it. Cyder, possibly, was drank by the first Danmonians; since the orchards of Devonshire were very ancient. *(k)* The Danmonians, whatever might have been their usual liquors, seem to have possessed the secret of quenching their thirst in a very singular manner: But the ingredients of the composition to which I allude, we should vainly attempt to discover. (/) The Arabs use gums for this purpose, in their passage over their sultry desarts. And this expedient of the Danmonians to quench thirst, seems to have originated amidst the burning sands of the waste,. where they might look around them with wisliful eyes, for refresliment from the fountain stream*s* (a) Acts, c. 27, v. 33. (£) The Britons were well acquainted with

the use of *batid-mills* before their submission to the Romans; and these mills were distinguished by the name of *querns, camcs* or stones. Whitaker. (r) Is the custom of *baking bread* upon the hearth, *under a kettle,* known any where but in Devon and Cornwall? Is not this a relic of the ancient mode of baking? (/) Genesis, c. 18. («) The crook was probably of very ancient date in Devonshire. It consists of two long poles, generally, I believe, ashen, which, affixed to a pack-saddle, and branching off on each side to some distance, are then bent upwards; so that by means of the curvature, they become (when flung on the backs of horses) the receptacle of various articles in husbandry, longitudinally placed on them. Thus bundles of hay and faggots, or sheaves of corn, are heaped up, within the curvature, to a considerable height. For corn-carrying, these crooks are particularly convenient. They are very common in this county, but occur no where besides in England. But what inclines me to think them of great antiquity, is, that they are still to be seen in the Highlands of Scotland 1 And the Highland crooks are constructed in the fame manner as the Devonian. *(f)* lib. xi. c.41. *(g)* lib. iv. *(b)* The use of butter was certainly *aboriginal* in this ifland: The Romans were unacquainted with it. See Musgrave's *Avtiqu. Brit. Bclg.* vol. I. p. 47, 48. (i) The South-Britons had long used the spume which arose on the surface of their *curmi* in fermentation, for rendering their bread light. This the Welsh and the Cornish denominate *bum,* evidently derived from *curmi.* And the common people of Devon call yeast by the name of *barm* to (his day. See Sammes, p. 108, 109., (i) See Wolridge's Vinetum Britannicum, p. 18. (Lond. edit. 1676.) (/) H But I cannot imagine, what meat that should be which *Dio* saies they preserved on all occasions, whereof, if they eat but the quantity of a bean, it satisfied their hunger and thirst." Sammes, 1(9.
I stream: It is an expedient, which by no means accorded with the situation of tie western Britons, amidst innumerable springs and rivers.(a)
For their accommodation by night,

the Danmonians had a dormitory common to the whole family, both males and females.(fr)

If we pursue the Danmonians from their habitations to the field, we (hall fee them chiefly occupied by manly exercises. Their principal *sports* seem to have been hunting, fowling, the baiting of wild beasts, and wrestling and hurling. Hunting and fowling, at ft-st necessary to the subsistence of our colonists, were afterwards continued as mere diversions. And our woods were sufficiently stocked with bears and (f) boars and wolves, for the chaee: The wild bull was, also, roaming at large, *(d)* Nor was the red deer less frequent; whilst the segh, now lost in Britain and in Europe, but subsisting in the moose of America, was often hunted in the forests of Devonshire, *(e)* The dogs which the Britons employed in the chace, are well described by Mr. Whitaker. According to this gentleman, theie'were five original Britisti dogs; the great houshold dog, the greyhound, the bull dog, the terrier, and the large slow hound. The last mentioned breed is, at present, almost peculiar to Manchester. But near the close of the last century it was frequent in the south-west. It is called at Manchester the southern hound. This hound, large and slow as it is, was once considerably larger and slower. Tlie boar, the wolf, and the stag, were all too fleet for its motions. Its genuine object, therefore, must have been ibme animal as heavy and slow as itself. And that could have been only the Britisti segh or moose. When, therefore, the segh inhabited the forests of Devon, the fegh-dog employed in the pursuit of this enormous animal, was the favorite companion of the Dnnmonian hunter. (/

Of the birds that furnislied amusement to the Danmonian sportsman, perhaps the eagle was not unfrequently pursued from height to height. Whilst our woods were deep and extensive enough to afford covert to the eagle, this bird was, undoubtedly, an inhabitant of Devonshire and Cornwall. It hath left its name, indeed, in *Killigreiu,* the *grcve if eagles:* Whence we may presume, that it was once an inmate of the place. The eagle was (hot, I suppose, with arrows. But the Danmonians were principally fond of hawking or falconry. Every British chieftain maintained a number of birds for the sport. Oman mentions " a hundred hawks with fluttering wing, that fly across the fity." There is a curious passage in Pliny, where this diversion is described. " *In Thracix parte super Ampbipolim, bomines atque accipitres societate quadam aucupantur; ii ex Jylvis et barundinetis excitant aves; Mi, supermolantes, depriviunt; rursus capias aucupes dinjidunt cum us. Traditum eft, mi/fas in sublime Jibi excipere eos ; et, cum tempus Jit captura, clangore e(vclatus genere invitare ad occastouem." (g)* The Thracians and the *(a)* Whether any of these springs or flyers were converted *by* the Aborigines, to the purposes of *letting,* or not, is a question which I have examined in the next chapter; where the Roman baths, fo famous in this island, cannot be left unnoticed.

(b) See Genesis, c. xKx. and Beda, 1.3. c. 27. and Giraldus, p. S38. for the common Welch having their bids upon the ground, and for the Welch and Highlanders lying all in one apaitment. *(c)* The boar remained in our woods, several centuries after the wolf.. *(d)* Our woods bred a number of wild bulls. The wild bulls and cows were all milk white; 8 furnished with thick hanging manes like lions, and almost as savage as they. Boetii Scot. Reg. Peso, fel. 6. and Leslæi Hist, p. 18.—The bulls of Augias, in the 25th Idyllium of Theocritus, answer very well to this description: three hundred white-legg'd bulls were fed, (Curl'd their smooth horns) two hundred glossy-red 5
While, silver as the swan, in gambols run
Twelve, chief of all, and sacred to the sun!
These, in the flowery pastures kept apart,
Rush on the mountain beasts that, frequent, dart
From their deep thickets on the herd below;
Bellowing glance death, and gore the shaggy foe! (f) Branching horns of a

most enormous size, have been found in Devonshire (and other parts ef England, and in Ireland, also) the reEcs of this enormous race of deer. See *Nat. Hist. 0/ Devon/hire. (f)* See Hist, of Manchester, vol. » p. 72. Shakspeare's description of the southern hound, must readily occur to my readers. *(jr)* Pliny, *I* x. c. 8.
th: Britons, according to Mr. Whitaker's account, *were the only follo-wers of the Jheri.* Among the former, it was pursued merely in a particular district of the country: But, witii the latter, it seems to have s een universal among the barons, (a) And hawking remained the favorite recreation of our gentlemen for many ages. It exists, at present, only in the Highlands. In the mean time, the Gauls, from whom Mr. Whitaker deduces our origin, knew nothing of hawking: They had, probably, never heard of it. Nor was It a sport of the European nations. The Asiatics, however, from whom I have deduced our origin, were universally fond of this diversion. In Pilpay, and other eastern writers, hawking is often described. " It happened (says Pilpay) one day, that Humaiun Fal went out a hunting. The towering hawk, like the arrow discharged from the bow of the archer, directs his flight to the height of heaven. And the falcon, bountiful to the hungry, with bloody talons tears the veins from the throats of the birds."(4) The Arabians, to this day, hunt the rockgoat with the falcon, *(c)* Falconry, then, of which the Europeans, in general, had no idea, was familiar to the Asiatics : And it was the favorite amusement of the Danmonians. That, " it was imported, therefore, into this country from the east," is a necessary conclusion. And, granting this, who dares pronounce our theory improbable? " An eastern colonization, independent of Europe," Items forcibly prest upon us, from every quarter. And, for the present topic, I cannot but remark, that our love of hawking, notwithstanding the inconveniencies of innumerable hills and vallies ill adapted for the sport, strongly speaks our descent from the eastern nations, whose sine campaign countries may be ranged *by* the falconer without interruption and with little danger. Among the sports of

Danmonium, I have mentioned the baitings of wild animals—a diversion that well accords with the temper of a people just emerged from barbarism: And the amphitheatres of Danmonium, seem to have been occafionally used for this purpose. But wrestling and hurling were the sports, that more peculiarly characterized the Danmonians. " Among the general customs (fays (/)Borlase) we must not forget the manly exercises of wrestling and hurling; the former more generally practised in this county than in any part of England, the latter peculiar to it. *a)* In the establishment of the British court, we fee the *bead of the* Falconers ranked. among the great officers of state. Howel Dha. . i. *c.* i. and Florence of Worcester, p. 623, Frankfort edit.—At this day, the Dukes of St. Alban's and Ancaster, are hereditary Chamberlain and *Falconer to* the King of England. (A) See the introductory chapter to the *An-var* e Soheili, or Fables of Pilpay—translated from the Persian by R. Llewellyn. And see *Pilfay's Fables',* 4th edit. London printed for J. Rivineton, a766, p. 32, 152, 153, 154
Xs) See Dr. Hasselquist s travels.
(d) Nat. Hist. p. zc/9, 300. *Carew* is more minute in his description of these manly exercises. See *period of Henry the %tb,* where I have adverted to Carew's description. In his remarks on the-story of Corineus, we perceive his notion of the Danmonian wrestling. " I am not ignorant (fays Carew) how sorely the whole storie of *Brute,* is shaken by some of our late writers, and how stiffely supported by other some: as also that this Wrestling Pull between *Corineus* and *CogMagog,* is reported to have befallen at Dover. For mine owne part, though I reverence antiquitie, andreckon it a kind of wrong, to exact an ever-strict reason for all that which upon credite shee delivereth; yet I rather incline to their side, who would warrant her authentic by apparent veritie. Notwithstanding, in this question, I will not take on me the person of either judge, or stickler . And, therefore, if there bee any plunged in the common floud, as they will still gripe fast, what

they have once-caught hold on, let them sport themselves with these conjectures, upon which mine averment in behalf of *Plymmouth* is grounded. The place where *Brute* is said to have first landed, was *totnes* in *Cornwall,* and therefore this wrastling likely to have chaunced there sooner than elsewhere. The province bestowed upon *Corineus* for this exploit, was *Cornwall.* It may then be presumed, that he received in reward the place where hee made proof of his worth, and whose prince (for si» with others stake*Gegmagog* to have beene) hee had conquered, even as *Cyrus* recompenced *Zopirut* with the citie *Babylon,* which his policie had recovered. Againe, the activitie of Devon and CorBifhmen, hi this faoultie of wrastling, beyond those of other shires, doth seeme to derive them 1 speciall pedigree, from their graund wrastler *Corineus.* Moreover, upon the *Ha we,* at *Plymmouth,* there is Cut out in the ground, the pourtrayture of two men, the one bigger, the other lesser, with clubbes In their hands, whom they terme *Gogmagog:* And (as I have learned) it is renewed by order of the townesmen, when cause requireth— which should inferre the same to bee a monument of£ some moment. And lastly, the place having a steepe cliff adjoyning, affordetli an opportunitie to the fact.". Survey of Cornwall, p. 2. *h.(a)* The Cornilh have been remarkable for their expertness in athletary contentions for many ages, as if they inherited the skill and strength of the first Duke Corinæua, whose fame consists chiefly in the reputation he won by wrestling with, and overcoming the giant Gogmagog— a fable perhaps founded five hundred years since upon the then acknowledged and universal reputation of the people of this county for wrestling. But to leave fables; what should have implanted this custom in such a corner of Britain, and preserved it hitherto in its full vigour, when either never affected at all, or with indifference in other parts of the island, we cannot lay: Certain it is the Grecians, who traded hither for tin, and hither only, had the highest esteem for this exercise. The' arts of the *Palæstra*

were chiefly cultivated by the Lacedemonians: And yet Plato himself among the-Athenians was so far from disapproving the exercise, that he recommends it to the practice of old as well as young women, and thinks it proper for them oftentimes to wrestle with men, that thereby they might become more patient of labor, and learn to struggle with the difficulties incident to a warlike state. The ardor for this exercise ib prevailed at last, that all Greece devoted their time and inclinations to the *Gymnasia* and *PaLestra,* and chose rather to be accounted the most expert wrestlers, than to be celebrated as the most knowing and valiant commanders.*(b)* Whether the Cornish borrowed this custom from the Grecians, or whatever else was the cause, you mall hardly any where meet with a party of boys who will not readily entertain you with a specimen of their skill in this profession. Hurling is a trial of skill and activity between two parties of twenty, forty, or any intermediate number; sometimes betwixt two or more parishes, but more usually, and indeed practised in a more friendly manner, betwixt those of the same parish; for the better understanding which distinction, it must be premised, that betwixt those of the same parish there is a natural connexion supposed, from which *(cateris paribus)* no one member can depart without forfeiting all esteem. As this unites the inhabitants of a parish, each parish looks upon itself as obliged to contend for its own fame, and oppose the pretensions, and superiority of its neighbours. It is 1b termed from throwing or *hurling* a ball, which is a round piece of timber, (about three inches diameter) covered with plated silver, sometimes gilt. It has usually a motto in the Cornish tongue alluding to the pastime, as *Guare nuheag, yiv Guare teag,* that is, *fair flay is goad flay.* Upon catching this ball dexterously when it is *dealt,* and carrying it off expeditiously, notwithstanding all the opposition of the adverse party, success depends. This exercile requires force and nimbleness of hand, a quick eye, swiftness of foot, skill in wrestling, strength and breath to preserve in run-

ning, address to deceive and evade the enemy, and judgment to deliver the ball into proper hands, as occasion shall offer: in ' short, a pastime that kindles emulation in the youngest breast, and like this requires so general an exertion of all the faculties of the body, cannot but be of great use to stipple, strengthen, and particularly tend to prepare it for all the exercises of the camp."

From those vigorous exercises of the Danmonians, the transition is easy to their more serious contests on the field of battle; where we may cursorily survey their warlike apparatus. The Danmonian foot are represented as remarkably swift -t and never encumbered with armour, from which they could not easily disengage themselves, (r) The Danmonian chief was accustomed to communicate his instructions to his soldiers, by the striking of a spear against his shield. Cathmor's shield had seven principal boffes, the sound of each of which, when struck with a spear, conveyed a particular order from the king to his tribes. " He struck that *'warning boss,* wherein dwelt the voice of war." On their cavalry the Danmonians prided themselves: And the Britons, in general, were famous for their skill in horsemanship. Julius Cæsar found the Britons plentifully provided with *horses:* And these horses were so well disciplined as to excite both the terror and the admiration (a) Borlase, speaking in this manner of Cornwall, means Danmonium, or *Devonshire* and Cornwall. The old topographers generally include the both counties under the appellation of Cornwall. With respect to -*wrestling* and hurling, they were, undoubtedly, as common in former times, on the east as on the west side of the Tamar.

(b) Alex, ab Alexandra, lib. ii. vol. I. page 494.. (r) ""The *Britaim* were very swift, neither did they encumber themselves with any armour, which they could not at pleasure fling away. They had a shield and a short spear, in the nether part whereof hung a bell, by the shaking of which they thought to affright and amaze their enemies. They used daggers also, and girded their swords to their sides by an iron chain."

Mag. Brit. p. I4t admiration of the Romans. The necks of the Danmonian garrons were frequently' ornamented with collars, and their manes decorated with strings of British pearls, (a) Several of the eastern nations were fond of displaying the spirit of their high-mettled steeds s And the dexterous management of the horse, seems to have characterized, in an equal degree, both Persia and Danmonium. Of the war-chariot, I have already given a description: We have here to consider chiefly the Danmonian mode of fighting from the war-chariot. The British chariots had their wheels frequently furnished with scythes; were always drawn by two horles, and carried sometimes two persons, the driver and the warrior, and sometimes only one. And the British manner of fighting (as we have seen) was totally different from that of the continent; and so new to the Romans, as to terrify Cæsar's army, and occasion his defeat. Herodotus tells us, that in the army of Ninus, there were two hundred thousand horles, and of *scythed chariots* above ten thousand. Sa that the scythed chariots of war were used in the first ages after the flood: And they were introduced into Danmonium by our first Asiatic colonies, (b) And the *Pbenicians* mult have been acquainted with the chariot of war, before they discovered our illand. " The combined nations that came and pitched together at the waters of Merom, to fight against Israel, were even as the *sand that is upon the sea-shore in multitude,* with *horses and* Chariots." " Now Joshua was old and stricken in years; and the Lord laid unto him: There remaineth yet very much land to be poslest—from the south all the land of the *Canaanites*—and all the *Sidonians*—them will I drive out from before the children of Israel. And the children of Israel said: The hill is not enough for us: And all the *Canaanites* that dwell in the land of the valley, have ChaRiots Of Iron; both they who are of Bethfliean and her towns, and they who are of the valley of Jezreel. And Joshua spake unto the children of Israel: The mountain shall be thine; and the outgoings of it shall be thine: For thou shalt drive out

the *Canaanites,* though they have Iron Chariots; and though they be *strong.* And the children of Judah went down to fight against the Canaanites (after the death of Joshua) that were in the mountain, and in the south, and in the valley. And the Lord was with Judah; and he drove out the inhabitants of the mountain, but could not drive out the inhabitants of the valley, because they had *chariots of iron.'"* Such were the multitude of war-chaiiots in the hosts of the Canaanites and the Sidonians: And to the descendants of these people the same kind of vehicles must have been familiar, when they reached the shores of Danmonium. (c) That the Greeks used the war-chariot, very anciently, is plain from Diodorus; who tells us, that the Britons lived after the manner of the *old ivorld;* and that they used *chariots* in fight, like the *ancient Creeks* at the *Trojan ivar.(d)*

With *(a)* Borlase's Coins, No. 12, 19, 20, and 22. and Ossian, vol. 1. p. 11. *(6)* Of the island of Panchaia, lying off the coast of Arabia, Diodorus calls the inhabitants *ftuloyions*, and notices their war-chariot, also, similar to that of the Danmonians. *TZnai Se me emtigas* n-oXifi/xBf, *x.aii axcri x$yo-Qcti xnilaras ixocyrcts.* asf*ya.ix.us.* Diod. *Wiff.* torn. 1. p. 367. *(c)* The vast number of these *chariots* in the armies both of the Canaanites and Britons, is a striking circumstance. " Sifera gathered together all his chariots—even nine hundred chariots of 1 *Ægypt.* In scripture, when *Joseph* was prime minister there, we find chariots frequently mentioned, both for civil and military uses. In *Josjua's* time, the *Canaanites, Repbaim* or giants, and *Perizzites* had them: So the *Phitifiines.* Our ancestors, the *Britons,* coming both from *Ægypt* and *Canaan,* brought hither the use of chariots: And they remained, in a manner, singular and proper to our island, to the time that the Romans peopled it. And it was fashionable for the *Romans* at *Rome,* in the height of theft luxury, to have *British chariots,* as we now *Berlins, Landaus,* and the like.
Esseda cælatis fiste Britanne, jugis."
Cellinfin's Beauties of British Antiqii. p.

18, 29.
(a) Richard thus describes the British mode of fighting . " Genus hoc erat ex essedls pognæ, ut Cæsar in IV. narrat. primo per omnes partes perequitant, & tela conjiciunt, ac ipso terrore equorum, & strepitu rotarum, ordines plerumque perturbant: & quum se inter equitum turmas insinuavere, ex essedis defiliunt & pedibus dispari prœlio contendunt. Aurigæ interim paululum e prœlio excedunt, atque ita.se collocant, ut, si illi a multitudine hostium premantur, expeditum ad suos receptum habeant. ita mobilitatem equitum, stabilitatem peditum in preeliis prajstantj ac tantum usu quotir diano,
Vol. I. Dd

With respect to our *Belgic* colonists, if they really used the military car, they clearly borrowed it from the Aborigines. " The celt and the *military chariot,* fays Mr. Whitaker, were introduced into the island with the first inhabiters of it. At the arrival of Cæsar, the use of the chariot was *universal in Britain,* and formed one of the discriminating marks in the national character ot the natives." " At the arrival of Cæsar, also (Mr. Whitaker confesses) a *Jew Gaulish tribes only* used the military car." This is a curious point; which is worth examining for a few moments. From Mr. Whitaker's statement of the case, then, which is exactly agreeable to the truth of history, are we to conclude that the celt and the car were derived from the Gauls to the Britons, or from the Britons to the Gauls? Mr. Whitaker asserts the first; intimating, " that the *use* of them in Gaul *was gradually worn out."a)* But, if the celt and the car had been originally used by all the inhabitants of Gaul, why should they have almost disappeared on the continent, in Cæsar's time, and have remained common in this country? The celt was frequent long after Cæsar, in Danmonium, in Scotland, and in Ireland: And I need not remind my readers of Cuthullin's car. Mr. Whitaker brings the first colony from Gaul into Britain, about one thousand years before Cæsar. At this juncture, the continental Gauls must have used the war-chariot universally: Otherwise, Mr. Whitaker's colony, the island Gauls, who are supposed to have emigrated from different parts of the continent, could not have been all alike acquainted with the car, and have introduced it where-ever they settled, whether in Danmonium, or Ireland or the Highlands. Notwithstanding, however, this universality of the car in Gaul, this vehicle was almost unknown there, after the lapse of a thousand years. But, at the end of the some period, it was as common in Britain as at first. How can we satisfactorily account for this great difference? Surely the car was introduced from this island into Gaul: (4) and not long before the time of Cæsar. The following observations, I think, may form a clue, to guide us through the intricacies of the question. Where *declining* customs have prevailed *universally,* the *remains* of them will as *universally* appear. We shall detect them in various places and situations. Wherever we go, their evanescent colors will momentarily catch the eye: And these colors will be *scattered* and *feeble.* This is the case with every declining custom that has once been general. But, where customs or fashions are *just beginning* to be imitated by one people from another, the imitators, betrayed into extravagance by their fondness for novelties, instead of faintly copying the original, represent it strongly, though not perhaps justly. If this idea may be illustrated by a familiar example, I should instance the conduct of a little country town—which invariably exhibits a new fashion just introduced from the metropolis, in all the glare of tawdriness of which it is capable; and rather than suffer it to fall short of its fancied splendor, caricatures it in colors the most ridiculous. Let us apply these observations to the point of the military car. If the Gauls, as Mr. Whitaker supposes, at first " used the warchariot *universally,*" and if the " use of this vehicle were *beginning to wear out*" we should, doubtless, find, where-ever the usage existed, the *relics* of it *scattered* and *saint.* But, if the chariot *were just introduced into Gaul,* we should discover it among a *jew tribes,* who had recently imported it from our

island, and we should detect it, perhaps, on the continent in *situations absolutely new,* whilst other uses would be super-added to its original design.

Now, dlano, *tc* exercitatione efficiunt, ut!n declivi, ac præcipiti loco incitatos equos sustinere, & brevi moderari, ac flectere, & per temonem percurrere, & in jugo insistere, & inde fe in currus citiflime recipere consueverint. Equestris autem prœlii ratio, & cedentibus & insequentibus par atque idem periculurp inferebat. accedebat hue, ut nunquam conferti, fed rari, magnisque intervallis prœliarentur, stationesque dispofitas haberent, atque alios alii deinceps exciperent, integrique *le* recentes defatigatis succederent. utebantur & telis." p. 6, 7. This contains the substance of the descriptions to which we are commonly referred in Cæsar, and Tacitus and Mela. The description of Cuthullin's car has been already quoted from Macpherson's Ossian. In a poem, entitled " Oflian departing to his fathers," an allusion to it is thus introduced:

J saw Cuthullin's car, the flame of death,

As Swaran darken'd, like a roaring flood:

I saw his high-maned coursers spurn the heath,

Snort o'er the slain, and bathe their hoofs in blood. See " Poems by Gentlemen of Devon and Cornwall," vol. 1. p. 150.

(a) Thus, also, he states the cafe of the British religion. Yet the Gauls repaired to t!u» islands when the stream of their religion failed, as to the fountain-head, whence it sprung. *(b)* It was probably introduced, soon after the opening of our trade with the continent

Now, we find, from several ancient writers, that a few *Gaulish tribes only,* used the car. It was not casually observed, here and there, in different and distant parts of Gaul: The use of it was not scattered or promiscuous; but a *fetv tribes* of Gaul used the war-chariot, in contradistinction to the other numerous tribes, who did not use it at all. Neither Cæsar nor his soldiers, though they had traversed a very large part of Gaul, had

ever seen in Gaul a military car. They were startled at the appearance of the British car. If they had seen one car only in Gaul, they could not have been struck with terror or astonishment at the reappearance of the same kind of vehicle, in Britain. As to the few Gaulish tribes who uled the car, let me add another circumstance, which coincides most happily with the general position: " those tribes (we are told) used the car *equally for the journey* and the fight." They were not content with the original use of this car. The Britons, from whom they had borrowed it, still appropriated it to military purposes. But this was not enough for the imitators. Captivated by its novelty, they applied it to other purposes: They used it, in peace as well as in war—on the road, as travellers, as well as in the field, as soldiers, *(a)* These are facts; to the truth of which Mr. Whitaker assents. Have we not here, then, a decisive proof that the use of the car in Gaul, was a fashion just imported? If it had ever been universal, and was now beginning to be dropt, is there not reason to wonder, that thole tribes, who are supposed to retain the custom, should retain it with an obstinacy so strong, the very moment when their countrymen had totally abandoned it r In what manner shall we account for this strange—this singular contrast? State it as a new fashion—and all difficulties will be done away—all doubts will instantly vanish: It was looked on, as an innovation by the Gaulish tribes in general: It was regarded as yet, with a jealous eye. But state it as an antiquated custom; and I again ask, is there a circumstance in the whole volume of history, more extraordinary—is there any thing in fable more incredible, than that the *greater part* of the Gauls, should have *lost* every vestige, evjen the *faintest trace,* of a usage transmitted immemorially, from age to age; whilst the *remaining part* should have grasped it, with a tenaciousness so persevering? Can we believe, that mouldered as it was all around them into atoms, those few tribes could have displayed it fresh and vigorous J—But, enough: abruptness is better than tedioufness.

The last particular which, I shall notice, is the mode of burying the dead, or the rites of sepulture in Danmonium. The primitive mode of burial was that of consigning the body entire to the ground. In this manner were the heroes of Oman buried. But, to reduce the body to aflies, and then interr it, seems to have been, very soon, the practice in Danmonium. Under both forms, the body was either deposited in a cavity, or laid upon the surface of the ground; when a barrow was constructed over it. The ashes, however, of burnt bodies, and the bones in particular, were usually collected and put into urns. And, in various parts of Devonshire, both the barrow and the urn still detain for a moment the curious eye. It was usual to bury with the body what the deceased in his. life-time most regarded. Hence their bow and their sword, the horn of their hunting, and a boss of their shield, are so often laid with the warriors of Ossian, " in the dark and narrow house of the grave." And the broken remains of swords, some half-melted by the funeral fire, have frequently been found in the barrows of the British warriors, in Danmonium. The celt, also, which (A) w»s an aboriginal instrument, introduced from the east, hath been often discovered in the sepulchres of the Britons. In the sacred writings, there is a striking passage, which proves that this custom was oriental. Ezekiel, prophetically exulting over the fallen armies of the Persians and other neighbouring nations, cries out: " They sliall not lie with the mighty, that are fallen of the uncircumciscd, which are gone down to hell with their weapons of war; and they have laid their swords under their heads!" It may be worthy of remark, that so early as the British period, a suicide was buried at the intersection of two highways: And the passengers threw stones upon his grave, till they had raised a considerable heap over it. Thus Hactor wishes Paris to have a cairn over him; or to be clad in a coat of stone—-(f) *Aounv trro yfima,.* A proverbial sort of curse, to the fame purpose, prevails at this day in Ireland and (a) See Strabo, p. 306. Frontinus's

Stratagem. 1. 1. c. 33. and Diodorus, p. 342, *tfeJeTnig. b)* Borlase, p. 138 and 239, () Iliad, 1. 3.

Vol. *h* D d a and Wales: (a) And in Scotland, the custom of throwing stones on the corpse of the person who dies suddenly in the field or on the road, is still religiously observed. (A)

Thus have I inspected a few leading traits in the character ctf the Danmonians, chiefly as illustrated by their manners and customs.

And, on this view, also, it appears, that the aboriginal Danmonians came not from the continent of Europe; since far different manners and customs characterized the other inhabitants of Britain, who emigrated long afterwards from Gaul. We may, therefore, conclude, that the first inhabitants of the Southaras, instead of being a colony from Gaul, made their settlements there, independent on the neighbouring continent. From their retaining so lively an impression of the Asiatic fashions and usages, we may also infer, that they advanced hither with the greatest expedition, and, probably, reached this island very soon after the dispersion. For had they migrated by slow degrees, and settled here after the lapse, of many ages, they would have brought with them very few of their original manners or customs. ()

But

I *(a)* Ware, Harris p. *147..* and Mona, p. 2J4.

(h) In the four parishes of *Jtedrutb,* Gwennap, Kenwyn, and St. Agnes, where the four western hundreds of Cornwall unite in a point, there is a barren heathy spot, called *Kyvur an Kcu,* or *the flace of death.* Here all self-murderers, belonging to the adjacent parishes, are deposited. And this has been, from time immemorial, the spot appropriated for suicides. Perhaps there is not so remarkable a place of this kind in any other part of the island. (c) To this argument, Mr. Whitaker replies, in a letter to the author: " If the Britons came, in the course of progressive migrations, from east to west, from Asia jnto Europe, and from Gaul into Britain; you think they would have loft the *charaBer* of their

original country in the long interval of successive movements: And yet they did not-you apprehend j as their *manners* and *usages* bere a very near resemblance to those of the Asiaticks." 1 know ot no such resemblance. There is only a resemblance that was sure to arise where the origin was common, and that exists between all the nations of the globe, in consequence of their common origin—*$ualem decet esfe sororum.* The most striking part of this resemblance between the Asiaticks and the Britons, is the use of military cars. Vet the use of them was equally common to the (i)Ægyptians and the Britons. And in these arguments from resemblance, we deceive ourselves, I think, by taking general similarities for particular, by considering human characters (if I may so express myself) as national character!sticks, and by so proving an origin to be analogically true, which is historically false." *(1)* Common, undoubtedly, to the.-Egyptians and the Bntons; a fact that favours my hypothesis. For who were the Egyptians? The following curious analysis will shew us who the Ægyptians were.'' It was found among Badcock's MSS. and, it is in the handwriting of Dr. White, It is the very outline, indeed, of the projected Egyptian history, in the composition of which Mr. Badrock had engaged to "Hill Dr. White. And, to give Mx. B. au idea of tlie plan, Dr. W. had hastily thrown together the following hints.—hints, which discover so per fe £1 au acquaintance with the subject, and which are exprest with so much perspicuity that I (hall hope to he excused the liberty I take irrprinting them. The language, indeed, of the analysis, is stowing and elegant; nor can 1 help adding, thi't it brings to my mind the best part of White's BamptonIrctures, » There is no doubt of the great antiquity of Egypt, as a regular Empire; and every thing conspires to shew that it was the first country of the world, which was improved. It *h* to be considered, then, as the mother of civilization; as the scene in which the powers of the human mind first began to display themselves, in the foundation of government, the acquisition of knowledge, and the investigation of truth. It is therefore a curious and important enquiry, what are the causes which have given to Egypt this singular distinction, and given it the lead in the history of human improvements. These causes may perhaps be found in the natuie of the country itself. However doubtful it may be, where the remnant pf the human race settled after the deluge, it seeins in general to be admitted, that it was some where in Arabia. Description of *the* soil and climate of Arabia. Particularly adapted to pasturage. Not so to agriculture; from the want of water. The same want naturally rendered the inhabitants migratory, for the supply of their flocks, &c. In such a situation men could not increase fast. Immense territories were necessary for the subsistence of small hordes, and not communities of S.iy extent. From these causes theif improvement must have been st»w, and their progress short. The knowledge which their slate demanded was soon acquired. Their cares were confined to the charge of their flocks: anpas their foil and climate offered them no other manner of subsidence, their invention was naturally confined within that narrow sphere. No divisions of rank, or great inequalities of fortune could take place. The science of government therefore, must have remained unknown, and the form of it naturally continued in that patriarchal state, in which it is at first found. Illustration of this from the modern state of the Arabians: the description of their ancestois *in* the books of Moses, is still applicable to them; and after the lapse of so many ages, they seem to have advanced little from that state of nature, in which we first find them. While men therefore remained in this climate, and under these circumstances, impossible that they should make any material advances in civilization. It is now, also, impossible to trace, what were the causes which led them from Arabia into Egypt—-#hether war, or conquest, or what is most probable, their natural disposition to migration, Whatever it was, great difference in the nature of the country, from that which they had formerly inhabited.-—De-

scription of the foil and climate, &c. of Egypt. Of the Nile, and its phenomena..—This country ill suited to the pastoral state, from the overflowing of the river; but favourable peculiarly to agriculture. Impossible, that they should not perceive the fruiti fulness of the foil, and the supply it afforded for the wants of men. Agriculture rendered them stationary j introduced the idea,

Bat I do not rest my *argument* on the resemblance of the Aborigines to the eastern nations, in this particular only: Review the whole chapter; and mark the *circumstantial evidence* on which it is founded..That the settlers in this ifland, were not a colony from Gaul, has been proved, on every view of the subject. And the vulgar theory of the original European plantations, would be abandoned, I think, on all hands, after a candid and liberal investigation of it. To such an investigation I mould be happy to excite the learned. From the dubiousness of the common theory, I had a right to form a new hypothesis. And I have imagined a rapid emigration to these islands, for. the most part by lea, from Armenia or one of the neighbouring countries. I have not grounded my supposition on the sole authority of the Saxon Chronicle. The Saxon Chronicle is one of its weakest supports. The evidence of Cæsar himself, is strong in my favor: And the voice of the Greek historians and geographers is still more decisive. But the character of the orientals, so strikingly contrasted with that of the Europeans, and yet according with that of the aboriginal Danmonii, seems almost to determine the controversy. The orientals, at the *time of their first emigration* into different countries, were imprest with various traits of character; such as we have discovered in their modes of settlement, their civil government, their religion, their commercial communications, their language and learning, their genius and their customs. The wandering spirit and *(a)* patriarchal policy of

Armenia (u) According to Monsieur D' Ancarville, this mode of government was *Cutbite.* " The Scythians (fays he) were a wife and politic people: Having

conquered Asia, they imposed a tribute so light, that it was rather an acknowledgment of their conquest, than an impost. Asia was then a fief depending on Scythia: It was the first state governed by this kind of constitution: and here may be discovered the origin of the *feudal system,* brought into Europe, by the descendants of these vers Scythians. The law terms, used by the ancient Irish, *(ot feud,* and every other word appertaining thereto, are Arabic, or Chaldæan; but chiefly the first." idea of property in land; afforded the means of subsistence to an infinitely greater number of men, than the fame portion of territory in pasturage. The increase of population led to the division of employments, and opened a wide field for invention in the arts. Hence the foundation of cities, the division of ranks (introduced by the inequalities of property) the beginning of commerce, and the great outlines of regular government. While the rest of the inhabitants of the globe, ia this early perod, were wandering in hordes through Arabia, the citizens of Egypt were led by the nature or theit foil anat climate, to establish themselves in a fixed territory; to cultivate the ground instead of living by their flocks j and in consequence of this difference of situation and employment, were gradually advancing in improvement, in population, in subordination, and in laving the foundations of future greatness. Egypt was therefore naturally the mother country of improvement: because it was the country which first led men to settle; in which agriculture was first practised; in which the number and the diversities of property among men, first called for the establishment of regular government; and in which: the extent of population fist gave rise to the various arts, which an extensive population requires. The nature of the climate and foil of Egypt, may therefore be considered as the cause os its being the mother of civilization, and of ics taking the lead in the history of human improvements. Tho'we can thus, perhaps, with some probability assign the cause os the earh/ civilization of Egypt, yet we are altogether at a loss, when we enquire into the period, when this improvement began. The first ages of the history of this country, covered with impenetrable darkness: and so far from being able to trace the progress of improvement in it, the sirst credible accounts which are come down to us commence with the period of its greatest refinement: We fay, the first credible accounts, because there arc not wanting writers, who ascribe to Egypt an antiquity utterly incredible—Account of the Ægyptian claims to antiquity. Insufficiency of these claims demonstrable.—-lit, from their total want of coincidence with the universal history of mankind; there being no appearance that the earth wag inhabited previous to the time assigned by Moses. 2dly, From their want of correspondence with our uniform experience of the manner in which population is extended—men being always found to encreafe in propoi tion to the means of subsistence; and to spread themselves in an infinitely smaller space of time than the Egyptian chronology arrogates, round the common centre from which they sprung. Is the Egyptian claims therefore were true, the whole earth ought to have beesi fully peopled, many thousand years before the first æra of history commences. The real history of the population of the earth, on the contrary, accords perfectly well with the period of the deluge, and affords a strong proof, that more distant sen cannot be true. $&y, From the history of arts, sciences, fkc. which upon the Egyptian supposition, ought to have made great progress, and to have been generally diffused among mankind long before we know that they were. 4thly, From the progress pf the Egyptians themselves in the sciences and arts; which, however great, is no more than might naturally have taken place in the long period that intervenes between the æra of the deluge, and the first certain accounts we have from other nations of their police and institutions. These arguments may be thought sufficiently conclusive against the Egyptian pretensions in particular. It may still however be urged in their favor, that other nations have made the

fame pretensions; and that therefore there is a general concurrence of opinion, which, as it hath prevailed in different ages and in different countries, may be thought to militate against the Mosaic system. It is therefore necessary to subjoin a brief confutation os these opinions; which may perhaps be classed under these three heads. First, the opinion of those who rest their arguments on ancient records, such as Sanconiatho, Berosus, the Chinese, and Indians. Secondly, of those who argue from the advanced state of the arts in particular countries, as in Peru. And thirdly, of those who argue from the appearances of nature, as Brydone. The confutation of these pretensions, and particularly of the Egyptian, supplies a proper basis, on which wt may establish the truth of the Mosaic history: and in the prosecution of this enquiry, we shall find, that as the former betray evident marks of fallhood and imposture, whether we consider their internal or external evidence, so the latter is-recommended by every argument, of which the subject is capable. Suiwaary view'of the ajgujueaU in favor of the Mosaic fcr of the creation and of the deluge." '

Armenia and Arabia, and the religious peculiarities of Persia and of India, were originally fixed to one spot. And, at the time of their first colonial separation, these characteristic lines were equally discernible in the Armenians, the Arabs, the Persians, and the Indians. At this crisis was kindled the flame of adventurous colonization: At this crisis the orientals emigrated to Danmonium: And, whilst the Armenians and the Arabs were nationally distinguished by one pjrt of the primitive eastern character, and the Persians and Indians by another, the Danmonians seem to have retained the leading features of the whole, *(a) (try* Whilst I was revising the proof of this very sheet, the two following letters were communicated to me. They (i) were addressed to the Editor of the Gentleman's Magazine, in answer to a query which I had proposed, (2) in that excellent miscellany, on the topic of the Armenian emigration. And, I think, they may, with propriety, appear

at the close of this chapter, as in some measure a recapitulation of it. The first letter signed T. E. is written in support of the old theory:

Si»» Exeter, January 9th, 1791.

I trouble you with an answer to R. P's question concerning the signification of that passage of the Saxon Chronicle, which fays that the Britons came from Armenia. I shall attempt to prove, in the first place, that it is a mistake in the Chronicle; and secondly, to show whence they really came. Cæsar says, in the 5th book of his war in Gaul, " Brittanniæ pars interior ab iit tncolitur, (3) quos *natos in irtfula ipj'a,* memoria proditum dicunt; maritima pars ab iis qui prædar ac belli mferendl *causa ex Belgis tranjierant,"* Thus we fee that the inhabitants of the maritime parts were descended from the Belgæ. *Tbe natives of the tnteriour country therefore must be meant by tb Chronicle.* Now the Armenians were beyond doubt a Gothic or Scythian nation, and consequently *their* (4) *language must have been widely different from the Belgic,* because the latter was Celtic. We have never heard that *there tvas at that time more* (5) *than one tongue used in Britain,* whereas if the inward parts had been peopled from a Gothic, and the maritime from a Celtic nation, there must have been two. Reason will inform us, that people who come from countries far distant one from the other, must have different languages: now as this was not the cafe with the Britons, who had only one,(6t *uie must conclude that they tvere but one natkn.* And that this nation came from Armenia, is hardly credible. If they did migrate from thence, it must have been in very (7) ancient times, when they were *at least as* (8) *rude and uncivilised* as they were in the days of Cæsar; and from the description he gives of them, we can scarcely believe that a people so (9) *destitute of almost every art,* could have undertaken and performed so very long and hazardous a journey. This is, 1 hope, sufficient to prove a mistake in the Saxon Chronicle. Secondly, the place from whence they came, must be Gaul. Now for this we have the *authority* of both (10) *Cæsar* and Bede, though they differ about the precise place; the first making them come (11) *from the Belgæ, the latter from the Armoricans.* Bede appears to be the *more refpcSable authority,*(12) and to have had the *greatest opportunities of coming at the truth,* whereas we all know,(i3.) that *Cæsar had little or no acquaintance* with the inhabitants of this island. Now Cæsar, when he mentions the " maritima pars,'' must mean the southern, as that was the only part he was acquainted with 5 and the Chronicle (14) *expressly speakt of the southern coast.* This coast being the nearest to Gaul, appears to have been peopled from Armorica, allowing Bede to be (15) *better authority than Cæsar,* arid because the language of Brittany as at this very time a dialect of the Welch, though it may be (16) *objected that the Britons carried their language there with them,* when they fled from the Saxons in the fifth century. But as the Britons did. not immediately settle in Armorica, but roamed up and down in various parts, it is very *probable, nay almost certain,* (17) *that the reason of their settling* there, was because they found the customs and language of the country similar to their own; otherwise they would not have chosen it, for they could have found far more fertile tracts in any of the other provinces on that coast. *AU histories.* 0) But not printed. f) See queries in the Gentleman's Magazine, for December, 179a, p. 1120. (3) Our ifland fathers are thus strongly contradistinguished—two races of beings, as different in every respect, as tht English and the Otahcitans, at the present moment. (4) So it unquestionably was. *Isi* Often have we heard, that there was more than one tongue used at that time in Britain. Bede declares that the Sivinity was worshipped among us in the languages of five different people, the Angles, the Britons, the Pists, the Scots, and she Latins; which perfectly agrees with the Saxon Chronicle, where five nations are said to inhabit Britain. .the Angles, she Britons, the Pict-i, the Scots, and the Bocledene, or the Romans. See Bede's Hist. c. 1. 1. 1. and Saxon Chronicle. (6) But the premises

are false. (7) True. (8) The Britons were not rude and uncivilized in the days of Cæsar. so.) The contrary os this would approach nearer to the truth. See Whitaker's Manchester, and Genuine History of tbt Britons asserted. (10) Cæsar's authority: Where? quos natos in insula ipfa Is this Caesar's authority? (si) Here the two racesof Britons are jumbled together. (re) More respectable than Caesar? (13) I confess I. scarcely understand this. Cæsar conversed with the Britons whom he describes. He was at least acquainted with one race of the Britons. Had Bede any " such opportunities of coming at the truth?" Does T. £. imagine that Bede was a contemporary of Julius Cæsar? (14) Yet T. E. just before observed, that11 the natives of the tnteriour country must be meant by the Chronicle."

£13) Ko.not far a meusent, (16) And the objection 16 unsarrnounublc. ('7) would be impossible to prove oV *tyiaris of credit agree* (18) that they were originally of Gaul, excepting the Saxon Chronicle, tlie beginning of which seems to be taken from Bede; for which reason I am inclined to think it the fault of the transcriber. What has been said, is, I believe, enough to prove, that the original country of the Britons was not Armenia, but Armorica. I am sorry to have troubled you, Sir, with *(a* long a letter, and hope you will excuse it, as the subject is of consequence towards illustrating the history of Devon. I am yours, *tx.* T. E.

The second letter, signed T. Y. L. contains several arguments in favor of my hypothesis.

Mr. Urban, Exeter, 17th January, 1791.

In answer to Mr. Polwhele's question concerning the Saxon Chronicle, which speaks of the settlement of the Armenians in the south part of this istand, I must beg leave to observe, that the history of the original inhabitants of this island is so very obscure, that after the strictest and most remote searches, we are obliged to rely for the far greater part of our information on probability and conjecture. Although, therefore, the facts on which the following observa-

tions are founded may be considered as wanting historic proof, yet it is hoped they will be allowed in some measure to answer the question before us, and tend to elucidate a passage somewhat obscure in a very ancient and venerable register of our nation. Armenia, I apprehend, was a large district, comprehending the moHern Turcomania and part of Persia: It is a country famous for being the first inhabited of the world: And in this region the great Babylon is thought to have stood; for we are certain that this was the residence of Noah and his descendants, for a considerable time after the flood, and that from hence it was they migrated, on the confusion of tongues, and subsequent dispersion of mankind. But the descendants of Japhet, from whom the western nations are considered as derived, although they sent out colonies, yet still retained possession of this their former residence, and Asia minor, which perhaps was all included by them under the name of Armenia. If this be admitted, there cannot remain a doubt of their being the founders of Troy. Thns then we fee the Trojans might fairly deduce their origin from Armenia. Now there is a well known tradition concerning; the first inhabitants of this island, that Brutus, a Trojan, great grandson of Æneas, having by chance killed his father in hunting, was obliged to fly into Greece, and having sojourned there for some time, and being admonished by an oracle, he with other Trojan fugitives, travelled fiom thence into Britain. That this was a generally received opinion amongst our ancestors, we may gather from the number of authors who have adopted it. Others, it is true, have regarded it as a fiction of Geoffry of Monmouth; but that he was not the inventor, is plain from its being mentioned by Nennius, who flourished upwards of three hundred years before: and Sigebertus GemWasensis, who preceded Geossry by one hundred years, particularly describes the passing of the Trojans through Gaul, in their way into Britain, and the city which Brutus there built. It is to this circumstance of their passing through Gaul, that we are to attribute what Bede fays, concerning the Britains coming from Armorica. Armorica was the ancient name of that part of France which is now called Bretagne, and probably was considered as the country from which Brutus took his departure for Britain. Noc have there been wanting poets to celebrate this expedition; amongst whom, our countryman Josephus Iscanus makes no inconsiderable figure.

— His Brutus avito

Sanguine Trojanus patriis egressus ab oris

Post cafus varios consedit finibus, orbem

Fatalem nactus, debellatorque gigantum

Et terræ victor nomen dedit. I do not recollect in any other history besides the Saxon Chronicle, mention being made of the Briton as coming immediately from Armenia, but we fee it was by no means uncommon to derive them from a country bordering on and originally peopled from Armenia. I am well aware of the many objections that are brought against this account. It may appear to be somewhat improbable. It was not mentioned here with a view to establish its authenticity: But considering it altogether as a fiction, still it affords us grounds sufficient to authorize a conjecture, that this tradition concerning the Aborigines of our island having prevailed among the natives, and been received by many authors into their histories, the passage in the Saxon Chronicle under consideration, refers to it aral is grounded thereon. The Britons, if we regard them as a colony of the Cimbri or Cimmerii, descendants of Comer, may possibly appear to have a more immediate connection with Armenia; but I do not believe this idea to have been general previous to the reign of Elizabeth, when Mr. Camden published it in his Britannia, and consequently the writer of the Saxon Chronicle could not allude to it. As to their settling first in the southern parts of this island, there can be hut little doubt 5 for even to this day it is the custom for people whenever they land on a country unexplored, although they fend out parties continually for the fake of making discoveries, yet

to establish their colony in those parts where they first landed. The southern part of Britain is the nearest of any to the continent, and of course first attracted the notice of those who possessed the opposite shore, whether Armenians or Armoricans: And there is great reason to suppose that Cornwall was looked upon as the place of their first settlement. An antient author ha; from hence derived the appellation of Britannia prima, (it) No such tbinj.

by which the south of Britain was fc merly distinguished; and I am inclined to think, riotwiffiftanding what Mr. Camden and others have said, that Cornwall owes its name in great measure to this tradition: for we find the western parts (by which we must understand the south western) assigned to *Corineus,* a companion of Brutus, and Brutus himself proceeding eastward into Kent, where he is supposed to have erected his kingdom: Prima dicta est pa/s occidentals insular; quia primum in ilia Britones Bruto & Corineo ducihus applicuerunt, eaque primo a Corineo et suis & occupata est & habitata. Britannia secunda Cantia quia secundo a Bruto *Sc* suis inhabitata suit. In the time of Julius Cæsar, we are told that the stacoasts of Britain were inhabited by a set of Belgic freebooters, who had passed from the continent over hither, for the fake of plunder, and dispossessed the Aborigines, whom they had driven to the innermost parts of the island. This has been made *vt(e* of by some as an argument to prove that the first inhabitants of Britain were of Gallic extraction: but considering the time in which Cæsar wrote, and that he speaks of a more ancient race inhabiting the Inner country, I think that it only tends to shew that the custom of pirating (afterwards carried to such length by the Danes and others) even then existed, and in those parts was attended with considerable success. Iam, Sir, yours, &c. T. Y. L. (i)

As I take leave of these speculations, I cannot but remind my readers of Sir WILLIAM JONES; referring them to the second volume of his Asiatic Researches; where is *one idea* in particular, sug-

gested by the learned president, which I have already noticed, and which must have left, I think, an impression in favor of our oriental hypothesis. I cannot but repeat it. " The *Saxon Chronicle* (fays Sir William) brings the first inhabitants of Britain from Armenia; while a late *very learned writer* concludes, after all his laborious researches, that the Goths or Scythians came from Persia; and *another contends,-with great force,* that both the Irish and old Britons proceeded, severally, from the borders of the Caspian; a Coincidence of Conclusions, from different media, *by persons vibolly unconneBed,* Which Could Scarce Have Happene D, IF THEY WERE NOT GROUNDED »N Solid Principles." And Sir *William Jones's conclusions,* from a still different medium, fall in with the rest, to establish the point. Nor should it be dissembled, that *Dr. Borlaje's parallel between the Persians and the Aborigines* of this island, had long excited in my mind the strongest suspicion of their affinity; though the Doctor was tracing their features of resemblance with very different sentiments. That the religion of the Druids, in particular, almost the fame as that of the Magi, had its origin in Britain, I always considered as a very absurd supposition, notwithstanding the specious arguments of Dr. Borlasc: I could not but conceive, that, to the most incurious observer, it must wear the appearance of orientalism. Who, indeed, on a fair view of the subject, can imagine the Danmonians to have been originally Gaulish, and the Druids a priesthood formed in Britain out of those Gaulish emigrators? Who, with such a dejected idea of the Druids,

Could haunt, in rapture, Cornwall's wizard caves,

Or wander thro' the faery-peopled vales

Of Devon, where posterity retains

Some vein of that old minstrelsy, which breath'd

Thro' each time-honsr'd grove of British oak.

There, where the spreading consecrated boughs

Fed the sage misletoe, the holy Druids

Lay wrapt in moral musings; while the bards

Call'd from their solemn harps such lofty airs,

As drew down fancy from the realms of light,

To paint some radiant vision on their minds,.

Of high mysterious import. Itt short, that the Danmonians were an eastern race, appeared to me more than probable, before X kad read a syllable of the *Saxon Chronicle,* or knew that a passage existed there, relating to Armenia er South Scythia; before I had the slightest acquaintance with either *Bryant*` or *Vallancey;* before *Pinkerton* had pnblished his admirable book, or *Sir William Jones* had formed his literary society in India. Thus prepossest, it was with real satisfaction, that I received notices from SIR GEORGE YONGE, relating to an eastern colony, soon after I had turned my attention to the History of Devonshire. And my *right honourable correspondent* had settled *his* theory, unconnected with the opinions and independent on the disquisitions of others—formed from his comprehensive view of men and manners—original in his own enlightened mind I / f i) I know nothing of the letter-writes): Nor can I guess who they arc.

END OF VOL, I.

CPSIA information can be obtained at www.ICGtesting.com
Printed in the USA
BVOW07s1951260514

354513BV00009B/599/P